Machine Woodworking

Machine Woodworking

John R. Clayton, Mim Wood T., A.M.I.W.T., A.B.I.C.C.

London
Northwood Publications Limited

First published in November 1974 by Building Trades Journal for Northwood Publications Limited,
49-50 Hatton Garden, London, EC1N 8XS.

Text set by Quickset Limited, 89-97 St. John Street, London EC1M 4AS
Screened positive litho bromides and film by Rumph & Waite Ltd., London, WC1. and printed by Tinlings Limited, Warrington Road, Prescot, Lancashire L34 2TJ

ISBN 7198 2620 9

Preface

This book has been based upon a collection of articles which have been published in the Building Trades Journal over a period of time. It has to some extent been compiled to meet the request of enquiries of readers who have at some time in the past read an article, and found it necessary to write to the Editor to obtain information at the time of requirement. Some chapters will be found to include examples of enquiries which are in Imperial measurement, as they were received. The remainder of the book is in metric (S.I. units).

Several excellent books are available on machine woodworking, but this collection of work covers a wider field than most, and it is presented at a level that I hope will either satisfy or stimulate readers who desire to obtain more detailed knowledge.

The book will be found to be useful to those engaged in the many fields of woodworking, from those designing a machine to carry out a particular type of work, to production supervisors, and machine operators. It will without a doubt be of great use to students in their courses of study, particularly in the preparation of project and assignment work.

Illustrations of machines and operations being carried out have been included as far as space will permit.

The author J. R. Clayton

Thanks are expressed to other publishers, which have permitted articles of mine to be included which have previously appeared from their establishments. Namely: The Times Educational Supplement, The Timber Trades Journal, The Journal of The Institute of Certified Carpenters, The Woodworker and Her Majesty's Stationery Office for allowing reproduction of "The Woodworking Machines Regulations 1974".

Many manufacturers of machines and processing equipment have kindly supplied photographs and offers of assistance during the publication of the articles, and I would like to make mention of these: Cuprinol, Frome; Dominion, Halifax; Fell, Windermere; Brookman, Leicester; Interwood, London; J.K.O., High Wycombe; Micor, Sheffield; Multico, Redhill; Pye Thermal Bonders, Cambridge; Pickles Ransome, Hebden Bridge; Stanley Tools, Sheffield; Trend Elu, London; Robinson, Rochdale; Wadkin, Leicester; White, Paisley; Stenner, Tiverton; Rentokil, London; Armstrong, U.S.A.; Weinig, West Germany; also Princes Risborough Laboratory, and The Institute of Machine Woodworking Technology.

I would like to express my appreciation to Leslie Black and Robert Kiernan of the Building Trades Journal who have worked in close co-operation with me at various stages of the publication.

The enduring support of my dear wife Thea, has made the book possible.

J.R.C.

Machine Woodworking

Contents

Machine Woodworking

Section 1 Economics and method planning

The Economics of Joinery Production

Waste ellimination. Use of sheet material. Moisture content. Waney edged timber. Machining sequences. Construction methods. Sub-assembly. Moulding in multiple. Number of product lines. Machine running time. Group working. Productivity. Incentive schemes. Management labour relations.

Production Planning in the Machine Shop

Work planning. Delegating responsibility. Presentation of instructions. The prototype. Advantages of sub-assembly. Machining minor operations. Roll of the setter out.

Trying To Cope With Small Orders

The problem of "one offs". Planning to cope. Limitation of order acceptance. Stock sections. Selection of operatives. Secondary production line. Cost aspects. Use of medium weight machines. Educating the customer. Colour range.

The Technician in Industry

Recognition of skill. Technical management. Training required. Knowledge of timber. Plant utilization. Metrication. Planning work flow. Jig design. Work study. Use of machine setting aids. Requirements of other branches of industry. Research and development.

Planning Maximum Production

Machines as aid or producer. Comparison of unit requirements. Cramping methods. Radio frequency and low voltage strip heating. Use of jigs. Limiting joint formations. Planning timber requirement. Machine layout. Work movement. Batch production. Adherence to work plan. Noise ellimination. Planning area.

Layout for a Woodworking Machine Shop. Reply to a problem

Type of work. Direction of work flow. Stacking area. Coping with sheet material. Positioning of machines. Reference to pneumatic extraction, and tool room.

Planning a Woodworking Machine Shop. Reply to a problem

Area required for various fields of work. Line of feed involving safety. Planning gangways. Stacking components. Fire exit. Admittance to public. Provision for portable tools.

The Advantages of Power Feed

Basic facts. Various machines involved. New developments.

The economics of joinery production

The mass demand for goods made from wood, will probably only continue as long as the cost of the product compares favourably with other suitable materials. People like wood, it is pleasant to the touch, and where the grain is visible it can be decorative without the pattern repeating itself.

Many other characteristics are also in its favour; it is difficult to imagine a world without wood.

When goods are constructed from such materials as metal or plastic, the consistency of the material remains the same throughout. This is not the case in timber. This variation does of course provide a feature in the design of the finished product, in some cases. In others it simply adds additional labour, in handling, cutting out defects, and the creation of waste. In this way it is not as easy to plan economic production working in wood as in some other materials.

The utilisation of plywood, blockboard, chipboard, etc., can bring timber into use in a comparative way to some of the other materials, in as much that when a manufacturer buys a sheet of panel board he knows just what he will get out of it. He can also plan his machine, and working space, as he is working with a consistent material. Success in the bulk use of panel boards depends on the initial planning of a product.

Sizes should be such, so as to create a minimum of waste. Advance ordering of materials is important to enable the required grade and size of panels to be obtained. Failure to carry out this advance planning could result in a direct loss due to waste.

A large amount of costly equipment is involved in the production of panel boards to enable them to be marketed at their acceptable cost, and this standard of efficiency should be aimed at in their utilisation.

When solid timber has to be used for joinery construction, various points have to be considered. The grade of timber used must be matched to the item for which it is to be utilised. Selection in its use should also ensure that the best of the material in a batch should be used where it is most visible in a product, and the lower grade used in the more concealed locations. Similar rules can also apply to the use of kiln dried timber.

Where wide boards are required, and shrinkage is liable to take place, then kiln dried timber may be necessary. Other items requiring only narrow stock may be from unkilned material, providing the moisture content is not excessive. Some manufacturers producing building joinery mainly in softwood, manage to produce a large proportion of their goods without kiln drying equipment. Material is stacked in skid, in open sheds for a period of time to allow the air to circulate.

Moisture content can be reduced to about 16

Fig. 1. A suggested specimen for the checking of productivity on a fourcutter. An eight hour working day has been chosen. Pre-set blocks enable the setting up to be completed in 45min. Two 10min. breaks during the day, and two 5min. periods for the hygiene of the operators. After lunch 30min. was required for minor servicing, and changing two cutter heads. This left an actual running time of 6¼hrs. The rate of material feed per hour could be applied to this, and the expected number of metres linear determined.

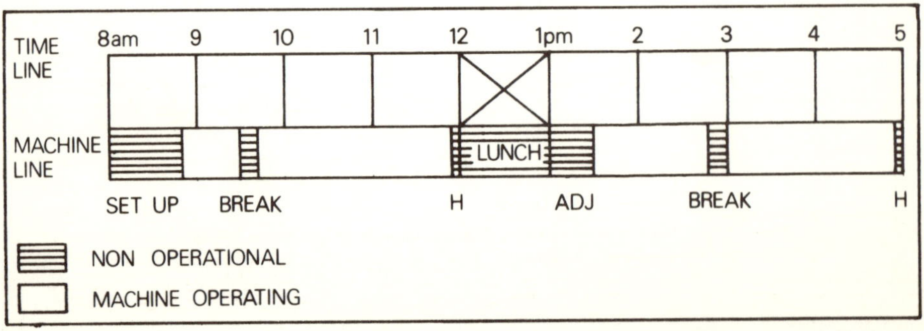

per cent in this way, under suitable locations, and a further drop of about 3 per cent is anticipated during handling in the factory.

Hardwoods are more costly than softwoods per cubic metre, and also the waste factor may increase due to the way in which they are marketed. Hardwood timber with waney edges can produce a considerable amount of waste, plus additional labour. The purchase price should be less than square edged.

Also hardwoods, although consistent in thickness, invariably come in a variety of widths. Due to these factors, hardwood sills affixed to softwood window frames can cost more than the actual difference in price of the timber per cubic metre.

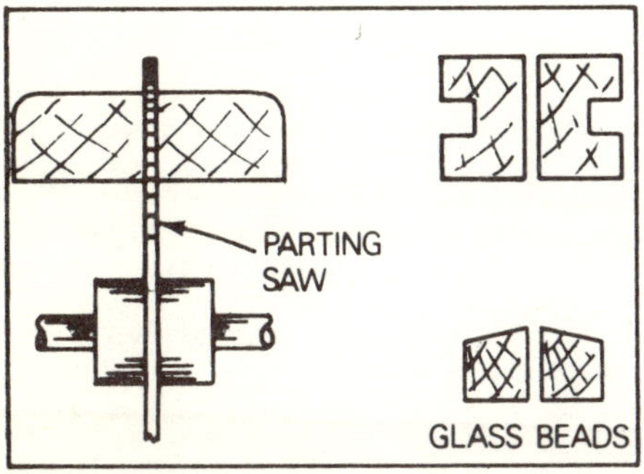

Fig. 2. By using a parting or splitting saw, on a fourcutter, output can be doubled for the given amount of running time. It also enables small sections such as glass beads to be fed through without danger of breaking. This method of working has caused many a bonus clerk a sleepless night.

Fig. 3. Suggested additional equipment required by the joinery manufacturer to produce veneered work in quantity. Sanding machines will also be required, but these will probably be already installed. Machines available from: Interwood, 326, Old Street, London, and others.

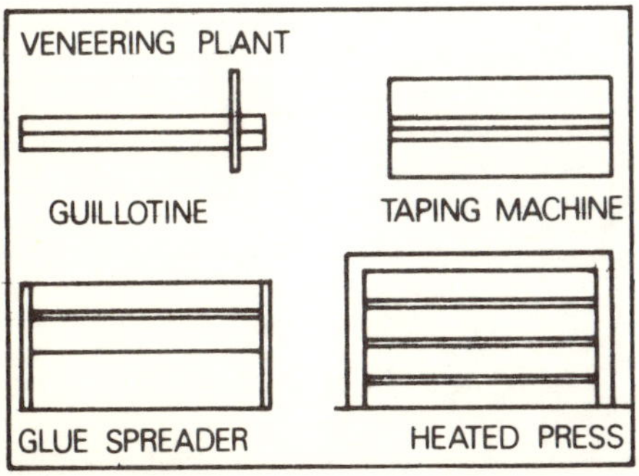

Where timber can be machined in the length rather than crosscut first, into the approximate final sizes, a saving of time may be achieved. However, this method has its disadvantages as stacking during machine operations can be difficult, unless a lot of space is available.

With such items as door stiles, which need to be planed out of twist, it is advisable to cross-cut such members before fourcutting. A finger feed surfacing machine is ideal for planing the stiles out of twist.

In large-scale production, a careful check should be taken on the number of times timber is being handled. A batch of timber delivered to the factory and put into production at the one handling, is much more economical than one which is, say, dropped in the yard, skidded, pushed into a kiln or drying shed broken down again, from skid, and taken into the production unit.

The method of unloading timber at the factory should always be made clear to the merchant also. There would be no point in delivering a load of timber stacked in 4 ton lifts on the wagon, if only a 2 ton capacity crane was available for unloading.

Many of the joints used in woodworking have been in use for hundreds of years. The development of modern adhesives, coupled with present-day design, is eliminating a large amount of jointing operations. Modern flush door production units no longer use mortise and tenon joints. Either a small tongue located in a continuous groove is used, or butt joints held with metal fasteners. These joints are adequate providing the outer skins are securely bonded to the centre core.

For board jointing as in table tops, butt joints may be progressively used when radio frequency, or low voltage strip heating is utilised for setting the glue lines. A die-pressed compression joint is also being developed for the jointing of window frames instead of mortise and tenon joints. This involves mitreing the corners as in a picture frame, die-pressing to form teeth, then cramping together after coating with adhesive.

Timber connectors are being used extensively in the construction of framed roofing units for domestic buildings. These are normally factory produced saving time on the building site.

In the planning of a product, constructional methods should not be overdone. The minimum amount of machined joints should be aimed at.

Sub-assembly into a series of frames as soon as possible after machining is recommended to prevent wastage, where this can be applied. Hot pressing of plywood to frames is superior to gluing and pinning. Fewer joints are required this way, and timber section can be reduced. Interchangeability of parts whenever possible can cut down setting up time.

A scientific approach to the use of timber can be the means of its continuity of use in the years to come. The aim with timber for the future should be to demonstrate how simple it is to use with modern techniques, rather than showing how difficult it has been in the outdated methods of the past which we can no longer afford.

Experience has shown that a factory producing only one item of joinery can have the highest productivity, and so can very often offer goods at the lowest figure. It must be prepared to have a wide area of distribution, and marketing is an important factor with an organisation of this type. A change in national policy can also have a sharp effect.

In building work, the wooden door is still with us, the hardboard faced type of flush door being the most economical. Efficient methods of production must be maintained if this item is to continue to be classed as an item of joinery in domestic building work. How long before it will be pressed out in a mould?

There was a period several years ago, when metal appeared to be taking over for window frames and kitchen cabinets. In domestic building, wooden framed windows are now very much the order of the day. I would say that the metal furniture failed on corrosion, insulation and noise.

A new field to look to for batch production by the joinery manufacturer is in built-in furniture units. Providing these units are built into houses during the construction stage, they can be paid for by the purchaser as an all-in cost of the home. Very often on mortgage.

Kitchen furniture is being marketed in this way, other rooms such as bedrooms could be fitted with louvre-fronted robes, pine or hardwood. Furniture manufacturers are already aware of this method of selling, through the builder, but I think that joinery manufacturers with their knowledge of building could carry out the scheme to a greater degree. It may require a study of design, and also the installation of modern veneering equipment.

Polished built-in units are also in demand in schools, and halls of residence in colleges. These requirements lend themselves well to a joinery production line which is furniture inclined. The gap between furniture and joinery is closing as our standard of living increases.

Quite a number of woodworking establishments although specialising in a current line of production also operate a secondary unit producing a quite different type of product. Availability of plant and labour makes this an economic venture.

Caravan building is one craft that is being developed along with building joinery in some factories, and finding a ready market. Laminated beams is another item. Probably boat building will be finding its place too with the increasing development of inland waterways for pleasure use.

With the ever-increasing cost of labour, and shortening working days, it is essential that the operatives' time is used to the best advatage. Incentive schemes are intended to encourage workers to be productive.

They are usually based on the principle that a given quantity of work is to be completed within a given agreed time. Time saved is converted into cash value for the workers involved. The big factor concerning incentive schemes is that it does make a worker, time or cost conscious.

It has, in the majority of establishments, replaced the man with the loud voice and the bowler hat.

From an economics point of view, absenteeism, and time-keeping generally should be an integral part of an incentive scheme. If an operator, takes a day off, during his agreed five day week, an employer has probably still to cover the same

Fig. 4. Experimenting with number of operatives in a working group. Don't be fooled by the results. A drop in productivity may not always be the fault of the workers. This is explained in this article under Labour utilisation.

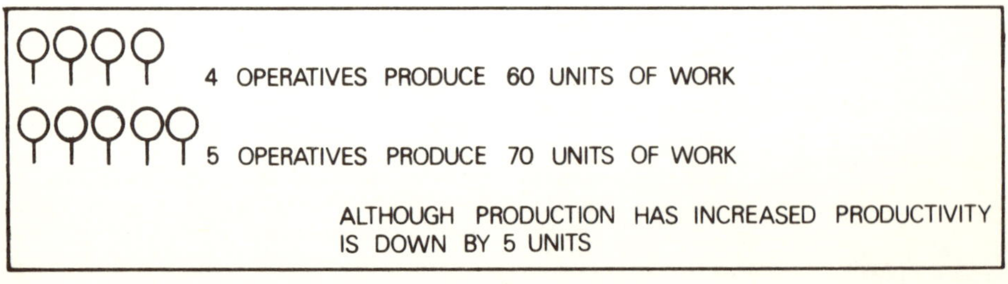

amount of overheads as if he had worked the full five days. In other words the financial aspect of the working week for that operative requires to be amended. This point is becoming more important as statutory payments for employees increase.

In some factories operators work in groups for productivity payments. This cuts down administrative work, and gives an air of team spirit among the workers. Increasing the numbers in a group should in general increase production but not necessarily productivity per operative.

A loss may not be the fault of the workers, it could be flow of supplies, working space, or a work pile up at the output end. Experiments with numbers of workers in a group can be worth considering.

Machines which are mechanically fed are in general more productive than those in which the timber is fed through manually. In addition a less skilled worker can feed timber through the machine. This widens the field of labour recruitment, and enables employment to be offered to those with a lesser amount of skill.

In our present age, a man may be classed as a craftsman, but he may be only familiar with a small section of a production unit. In this, of course, he will be a specialist.

Selection of woodworking machinery, particularly if it is to be used for line production, should be given careful consideration. Working heights are important where components in the course of processing are being transferred from one machine to another. Relative feed speeds of the various machines have to be considered.

A machine on the line having a comparatively low feed speed, may have to be duplicated. A high standard of cutter finish should be aimed at for planed surfaces. This can eliminate sanding operations in a large amount of building joinery work.

Not only is sanding time consuming, but it can in some cases reduce the efficiency of the workmanship in the previous operations.

When considering the selection of a new machine, it is important to define if the machine is to be used principally for one operation only, or if it has to be versatile. Some machines are designed with versatility in view, and very often they are more expensive. It is quite common to see costly attachments belonging to a machine, permanently laid to rest underneath a work bench.

This kind of occurrence should be kept to a minimum. Pre-setting of cutters on machine blocks should be confined to the tool room, and prepared in advance. This reduces non-operational time of the machine as much as possible. Efficiency checks on major machines should be made from time to time, to ascertain the percentage of "down" time, to running time.

These can help when fixing production times for future work. Light cutting on square sections can be machined on a fourcutter at a much higher rate of feed than heavily moulded sections such as sills for window frames.

A financial point, worthy of note, which is operating at the present time, is the Government Investment Grant. Factories which are being built and equipped in Development Areas benefit mostly from the scheme. It is a scheme to encourage expansion in parts of the country where new industries are required.

In some industries, their economy has been made unstable by strikes and general unrest. I am happy to relate that no major dispute has taken place during my 40 years in the woodworking industry. The trade unions concerned must be very proud of this fact, but it is also due to the close relations which exist between employers and workers in the various branches of the building industry. This close association must have proved its worth during the recent years.

Recreation facilities do operate in the larger work units, and these establishments usually welcome operatives from the smaller firms in competitive activities. In this way no firm is really too small to encourage sport among its young people.

The team spirit is an all-important factor to the new entrant to industry. Once he realises that his employment can also be a means to his recreational activities, his job will become more important to him.

The future of the building industry depends on the young people who require to be craft trained. New Training methods are being recommended by training boards.

If statements quoted in the press are anything like correct, the economy of the building industry cannot accept any costly changes at the present time.

Production planning in the machine shop

The Prototype. A sample of an article to be produced in quantity. It provides a means of production planning, and conveys information to operatives. It could also prove an ideal aid in the change to the metric system of measurement.

Successful large-scale production of woodwork depends very much in the planning of the machine operations. It is usually the duty of the machine department manager, or his close associates, to decide on the procedures to be followed in the production of a given unit of work.

Establishments producing only one type of article, say doors, are in the minority, more often than not a variety of goods are in the course of processing at the same time.

In these circumstances, strain at supervisory level can be considerable. Production planning can be an aid to reducing this strain. Planning can devise methods of passing on responsibility in a successful manner, to a number of people—so reducing the load on oneself.

Information regarding the requirement of an article to be produced in quantity, may be presented to machine management in a variety of ways. Some of these are quoted below, and all require their respective treatment to put the items into production.

1 **Scale drawings.**
2 **Drawings and specification.**
3 **Written specification only.**
4 **Repeat order of a standard line.**
5 **Word of mouth.**

Standard lines should produce no difficulty as operatives are educated in the procedures to follow from previous experience. When new lines are introduced production planning must be introduced to convey the requirements to the operatives concerned.

Very often in a factory, many of the operatives are not technically inclined, although they are quite capable of carrying out first-class work providing it is presented to them in a way they can understand.

One method, not confined to the woodworking trade, is to construct a prototype. This is a sample, or part sample, of the item to be produced in quantity. It serves as an ideal means of transferring responsibility to the machine operator. He can visually see what is required, and check his own work as it proceeds. The prototype will also be available for inspection by the customer or his representative, and any doubtful points can be cleared up before the main production begins.

Cutting lists can be prepared from the prototype, and materials can be ordered with a fine degree of accuracy. Some timber may be delayed due to the requirement of kiln drying, but such materials as plywood, and chipboard can be cut at any stage as definite dimensions can be taken from the prototype.

Present-day production requires more attention to be paid to the moisture content of timber being used. Cupboards are becoming more an item of furniture, in particular in kitchens. Centrally heated buildings require timbers to be dried out in keeping with their final location. An electrically operated moisture meter is seen being operated above.

Working with a prototype could be an ideal method of introducing metric measurement to a department.

Very often the production of drawers is left until carcases have been completed. Under the prototype method of working, work may proceed in any order. This gives better plant utilisation, and keeps the work moving.

In the manufacture of woodwork, in particular building joinery, the question of handing is always with us. On inspection of the prototype much help can be derived on this subject, and components machined in pairs where required.

Where a range of similar items are being produced such as kitchen cabinets, interchangeability of parts should be noted for group production, and so reduce setting up time.

Most factories operate incentive production bonus schemes. Provisional times can be taken from the prototype regarding the number of operations, and standard of finish required. The interior of cupboards, and some drawers, may not require machine sanding, if the standard of planing is of a high standard.

Where articles in production are of a large cubic capacity, it is advisable to plan so that the sub-assembly system can be employed. This enables work to be assembled in a series of frames which can be stacked to economise in storage space until near delivery date.

In this system of working, sometimes a few extra rails may be required to make a frameable unit, as in the case of drawer runner frames. The back tie members need only be of small sectional dimension.

An alternative method to making a complete

If the complete prototype is not constructed, a front frame may serve a very useful purpose when dimensioning drawer fronts. See-through drawer fronts are being tried in the drawer openings.

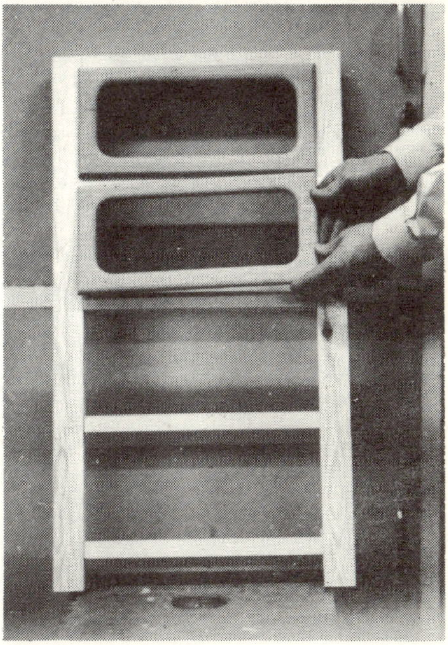

prototype is to make only a part of it, where particular accuracy is required. This could be the front frame of a multi-drawer unit. It will help the drawer-producing section to get ahead with the minimum of supervision. Flush-fitting drawers need a high standard of accuracy, rebated front drawers, not quite as high a standard.
A study of the prototype, can also determine how many of an article to put through in one batch. Machines require to be evenly loaded, and a customer buying for a housing scheme will not want a large quantity of one item, and none of another. Often the storage of completed goods decides the batch quantity.
The fewer number of lines being produced in a department the higher the productivity. On the other hand, there is a greater danger of redundancy. Specials, or "one-offs," as they are often

more efficient approach, more complete utilisation of plant, and economy in materials.
Not forgetting the easing of mental strain at supervisory level, where a large variation of goods are in production at the one time.
called, can hinder production, but these do unavoidably occur from time to time.
The setter out is still required to some extent, when the prototype system is used, in particular where angular, or shaped work is involved. Many setters out prefer to work on rolls of drawing paper, these can be easily stored, in a cupboard or such, unlike long wooden boards.
The only point that can be raised against the making of a prototype, is of course the time involved.
The materials will most likely be utilised at some later date. The reward should come with the

All operations should be carried out on drawer fronts, and cross rails before they are passed for assembly. The top rail has been pocketed for the lock bolt. The inside of the drawer front has been recessed to take the lock. The keyhole, and the handle fixing holes have been machine prepared.

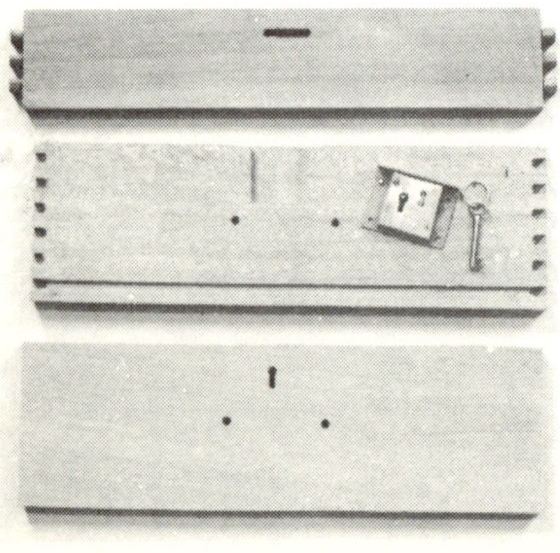

Drawer dividing rail and runners, framed together with the aid of a light dimension back rail. This enables this unit of work to be sub-assembled.

Sub-assembled frames can be easily stacked, and are ready for quick final assembly to the remainder of the carcase when delivery is required.

Trying to cope with small orders

In a busy machine shop, working in batch production, the question of "one-offs," or small quantities of a special item, can create difficulties. It is very easy to say to a customer, "No we don't do specials," but there is always the danger that larger orders may be lost due to unwillingness to co-operate.

It is better to lay down some kind of policy as to what extent a production unit is prepared to go in the manufacture of specials, if at all, and to plan with this in mind. All operations relating to industry, benefit from beforehand planning, even the non-productive ones such as tea breaks, medical care, or recreational activities. Planning can decide where an activity can start, and where it shall end. Strong management can ensure that policy is enforced in an acceptable manner.

Most production units operate on some specialised section of the woodworking industry, such as general joinery, contract furniture, kitchen fitments, etc. It would be unreasonable for a customer to expect a special item to be manufactured in a production unit not producing goods in that particular category. Very often, machined parts are available, if the special is one that is in current production, and only a modification of size is required. In this way, some of the special requirements may be met with only a minimum of inconvenience.

Some designers plan an item to be produced, with specials in mind. Fitted kitchens, for instance, often require wall to wall accommodation, and making out pieces, or small units should be planned as stock lines, so preventing specials having to be made. Cabinets also having screw-off plinth units, can easily be adjusted in height. A standard box plinth can be conveniently reduced by running the circular saw low in the bench and passing the unit through it. If the requirement was for a taller plinth, this would have to be manufactured, but it is much easier to construct a plinth than a whole cabinet.

Where specials involve only a modification of sizes of a standard unit, the average operative will probably be able to deal with this. However, where a more complicated type of special is required, a more technically inclined craftsman may have to be called in. In this way, we find ourselves with the higher skilled operative involved in the least productive type of work. He will probably also be one that is being paid an additional rate of wages, and rightly so if he has spent time and effort improving his knowledge. If situations of this type are likely to arise, some beforehand planning must be made to reduce the highly skilled operative's time to a minimum.

In the construction of the average article, it has been noted that about half the machinist's total time is taken up in the preparation of the material from the timber stack to the completion of the planed section. A considerable amount of walking about may be involved here, plus sorting, planing, rejecting, and replacing. It is at this point the higher skilled man's time can be saved, if a system of prepared stock sections can be arranged. These timber sections would be common to the ones in general use in the department, and would be suitable for the line of

A plinth base being reduced in height by cutting on a circular saw. Cabinet heights can easily be reduced in this way, providing the bases are removable. The minimum amount of saw blade should project above the bench, on no account should the cut be made with the saw fully exposed.

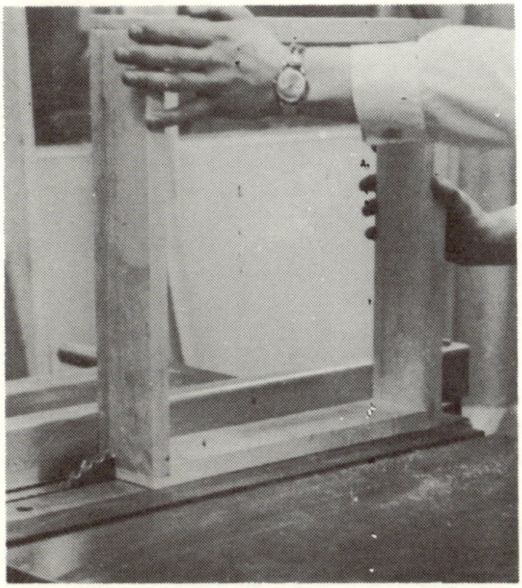

Providing stock sections are prepared in advance, windows can be produced to special sizes with the minimum of interference to the main production line. With the simple example above, the preparation of the timber sections would take much longer than the framing joints, if processed entirely as a one-off job.

Prepared sections are here being worked on a medium weight machine. These machines have been developed by the manufacturers to meet the demand for a secondary production line with minimum overheads. The advantage of this system, from a work study point of view, is that it permits an uninterrupted flow on the heavy duty line.

specials planned to be undertaken.

Where such things as window construction for domestic buildings is concerned, this system should provide no difficulty. For cupboard units, a stock of ex 50 mm by 25 mm is always very useful for present-day type of construction. A stock of prepared drawer section material can save a lot of preparation time at the point of requirement, and also, plant-on beading for accommodating drawer bottoms, is a very useful stock section.

When the specials' operator knows what prepared material is available, he can also plan accordingly. Specials which do not come within the general range of the department, and the prepared stock sections, should, in principal, be refused, as no beforehand preparation has been made for these.

The stock sections generally required pass through only three machining operations. Cross-cut saw, rip saw, and moulding machine (four-cutter, etc.). It will be necessary to record the machine cost of these operations, in bulk. The footage of each must be recorded and a cost worked out for the quantity required for each special order. The saving in labour will be considerable this way and better than individually handling each job.

Machining operations

The machining operations to the prepared timber such as rebating, moulding, mortise and tenon joints etc., may not run in a continuous flow due to the availability of machines on bulk production. For this reason the operator involved with the specials should also have other work available to him. Sometimes an operator may be fortunate enough to catch a machine carrying out the process which he requires. An alert worker will always be on the lookout for this kind of situation.

Hand operations

It may, in the case of single items, be more convenient for some of the operations to be carried out by hand tools. Hand work should be kept to a minimum at all times. When an establishment is geared to machine production, and overheads costed as such, mechanisation should be maintained. The availability of skilled hand workers must often be considered also.

Where additional machines can be provided to cope with specials these could be limited to say, a mortise machine, single end tenoner, spindle moulder, and a dimension saw bench. Some manufacturers use a medium weight type of machine for this secondary line, such as the Wadkin Bursgreen range. This leaves fewer operations to be carried out on the main production line.

What causes specials

Specials seem to occur in woodworking more than in any other type of industry. Every individual appears to be his own designer. I have, in fact, seen customers' specials adapted for the production line, and successfully marketed. The introduction of large-sized corn flake packets (often only half-full) has, of recent years, been the cause of many housewives asking for an unusual form of shelf-spacing in cupboards.

Standards do exist relating to the general dimensions of timber products, and many manufacturers also publish literature relating to the standards, as they apply to their particular designs. This literature must have played a major part in the elimination of many specials. It has educated the customer.

The introduction of decorative laminated plastic surfaces has also created a problem for manufacturers engaged on advance production. No establishment could stock goods faced with every brand and every colour. The quantity would be astronomical. This is being overcome by offering a given range of surfaces, and others become specials to order, at an understandably increased rate of cost.

We must not forget that many large production units, started by making "one offs" and it is probably some form of sentiment that makes them still accept the special request. Planning can help, if the request is not unreasonable.

The technician in industry

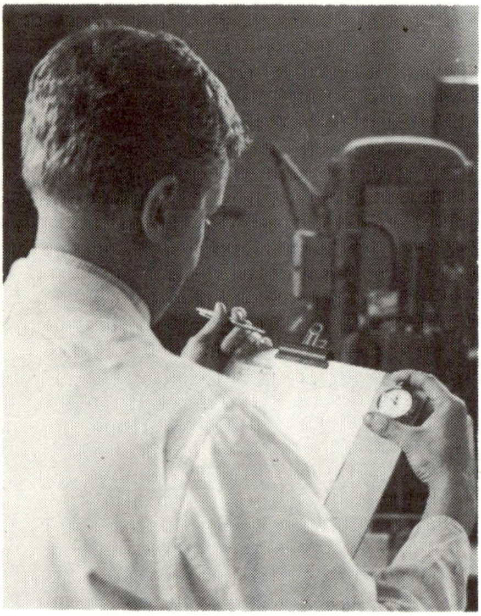

Time is an all-important factor in production—not only to direct cost, but also in the planning of flow of work where several operations are involved. Components awaiting the availability of a machine take up space, and deterioration and wastage often takes place.

Practically all industrial units producing goods by modern methods require the services of technicians—and the woodworking industry is no exception.

Quite often, in the smaller or even medium-sized woodworking establishment, the technician gets little or no recognition as such, unless the individual himself presses the issue.

Once an employee has been recognised, due to the fact that he has something to offer, it is customary to expect staff grading. This may not always be possible unless he is fully employed on technicalities and so contributing to the managerial side of production.

Technical management is an important part of works management, and could be defined as the "how to do" rather than the "what to do".

General management can give an order for a batch of goods to be manufactured, but it is technical management that decides on the most acceptable method of producing.

In the majority of cases, technical management takes place on the shop floor, whether it be recognised or not, but some office space should be available to cope with the paper work involved.

The requirements of a technician, or technical manager (as some are fortunate to be termed), can vary considerably according to the type of goods being manufactured, and the size of the establishment. Very often the technician's job is several posts of responsibility rolled into one, and can be pretty hectic.

The technician, as opposed to a departmental foreman, should be capable of following work through from the timber yard to the completed article.

His training should not be confined to one section of the industry, or his field could be very limited. He will find himself involved with many of the personnel in a factory, and not all will appreciate the results of his efforts.

Ability to convey instructions to those operating under him is an all-important factor. It is also necessary to be able to handle decisions made by those superior to himself. The aim to get flexibility in decisions whenever possible is a good point. This can save going back to consult again when a small modification becomes necessary.

Some of the basic requirements of a technician serving the average woodworking production unit are:

Knowledge of the various types of timber in general use, and their characteristics. Ability to advise on the bulk storage, and kiln drying. He must be familiar with methods of checking moisture content. He must also be able to advise on a suitable moisture content for the job in hand. This can be very important in some types of work. It is also necessary to be able to plan material requirements in advance.

Without a sound basic training in the operation and maintenance of woodworking machinery, he would have to depend very much on others, in a large production unit. To understand only how to feed timber into a machine is not sufficient, as ability to plan full utilization of the plant is important. Success in machining techniques over other competitors can play a major part both in production, and marketing potential of completed goods.

The technician should be familiar with mechanical methods of repetition assembly, such as the use of compressed air. The design of durable jigs for simple operation. The planning of work flow at this point can also be important.

A knowledge of geometry and mathematics are essential for planning and setting out problems on the drawing board. An appreciation of design is important in many branches of the industry. Present-day trends should be noted and introduced. Operators on the factory line will also probably look to the technician for guidance into the introduction of the metric system of measurement.

In the larger production units, the method of putting out work to operatives differs considerably than in the smaller works. Cutting lists require to be broken down, and individual items or groups of items directed to those responsible. Large orders have to be divided into workable quantities, and it is very often the technician who decides plant capacity at any particular time. Planned production should be practised at all times, and suggestions of diversion from the plan resisted. The technician has to plan the most economical use of labour and machines.

In woodworking the jig designer is seldom labelled as such, and the technician usually gets involved in this job. Construction of jigs can be planned to take place in the same section of the works as prototypes, as similar skills are required. It is not unusual for the technician to have to spend some of his time on this work as it is classed as non-productive, and has to be limited to a defined section of the staff.

A technician should be capable of making use of modern aids to efficient production.
A cutter shape is being developed with the aid of an attachment manufactured by Thomas Robinson and Son Ltd., Rochdale.

An appreciation of working methods, and just when to apply them, is essential to the technician. The aim of his job is very much concerned with efficiency. Operations should be planned so as to be progressive. Machining aids should be introduced wherever possible to increase productivity and reduce fatigue. The layout of the various departments should be checked from time to time, as the nature of the work changes. The technician should be able to advise on replanning. This involves factory planning generally.

Where products being manufactured in the woodworking unit are to be utilised by another branch of industry, such as general building, engineering, etc., it would be beneficial to have a member of the staff who has made himself familiar with the industries concerned. This is usually the job of the technician, who should have a broad training and not solely confined to woodworking.

Visits to various types of industries during training, and afterwards with technical associations, can be educational in this respect. For this reason it is advisable that he should be a member of a technical organisation. The Technician in a factory is bound to become involved in cost although he will probably not handle any money beyond that of his salary. If a method he has devised is not being productive, he will soon be reminded that it is losing money. The duty may also come his way to deal with job cards recording the time worked by operatives. He is very often the link between the shop floor and the administrative unit.

The technician may also become involved in incentive bonus schemes which benefit the operators on the shop floor, but not himself directly. In this way he is bound to meet up with the trade union mechanism, now an accepted part of industrial procedure.

In the medium-sized factory a technician may, at times, be in direct contact with marketing, in as much as he may have to meet buyers for the approval of prototypes, or completed goods. He must be able to discuss a product with a customer, and appreciate his requirements.

Research should be a continuous process with the technician. He should always be on the lookout for new ideas. The trade journals provide a good medium for keeping up-to-date, and visits to trade exhibitions can be most helpful.

If more recognition could be made of technically trained men in the woodworking industry, probably a higher grade of entrant would present themselves for training. Fron this, industry would benefit.

The Furniture and Timber Industry Training Board are at present planning a course of training in conjunction with The City and Guilds, to provide a qualification which is to be called the Furniture Management Technician Certificate.

It covers all the aspects of furniture manufacture, in which the machine production of wood components plays quite a large part. It could raise the status of the woodworking technician —and the industry as a whole.

A similar recognised certificate will probably evolve in the section of the woodworking industry relating to building work.

Planning maximum production

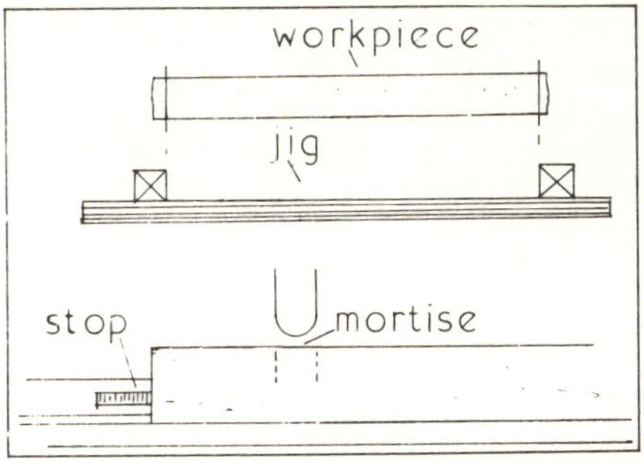

In repetition work it is customary to cut all prepared timbers to a constant linear dimension for the purpose of fitting the workpieces into jigs or positioning to stops on machines.

The approach to machine woodworking can be looked at in two different ways. The machine can be taken as an aid to the hand worker, or in a very more advanced aspect as a complete producer.

An operator can be largely influenced during his period of training as to which group his mind will be orientated. Also it may be necessary for a machinist to re-adjust his aims on moving from one type of production unit to another. A machinist working on one-offs or small batches may leave some small detail operations for the hand worker to complete.

In large scale repetition production, this just would not be acceptable. Additional hand operation time would reduce the efficiency rating, and also perhaps produce work of an inconsistent standard. Also facilities may not be available in the process flow to carry out hand operations, or the suitable type of skill located at that point.

In progressive units the aim is to transfer machined parts directly to assembly jigs. Factors governing the economics of a line of this type, are the complexity of the product and the continuity of the quantity flow. This has to be related to market demand.

It is essential that mechanised aids should go further than the machine processing components. The use of pneumatic cramping, RF and LV adhesive curing units can assist this. Jigs should be designed to cramp units square without the need for individual checking. Metal fixing pins can be gun injected much quicker and with less fatigue than by hand percussion application. The application of adhesives and suitability of the various types are points which require consideration. The economic loading of RF units or heated presses can be governed by the time it takes to apply the adhesive to the components.

If the time relationship between the availability of prepared components and the adhesive curing process can be matched, full utilisation of labour can become involved. An ego incentive can be created in this way.

Most production units are built up with the manufacture of a particular line of items in mind. When it comes to the introduction of additional lines it may be necessary to consider the design

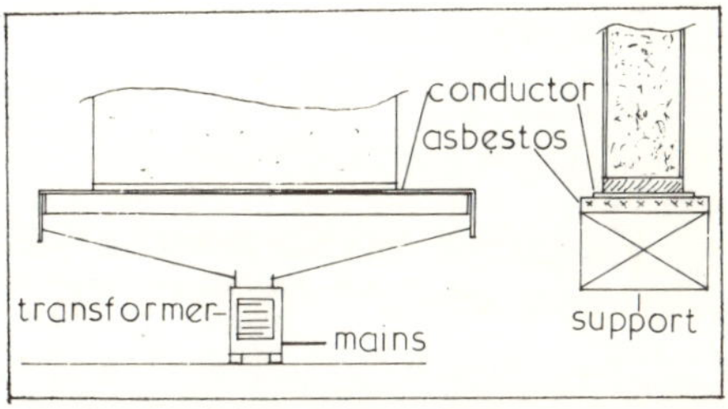

Line diagram of low voltage strip heating system. The transformer output is usually between one and 10v and capable of high amperage.

Section of a cramping head which is operated with compressed air. These heads are usually designed so that they can be dismantled for servicing. This consists of renewing leather cup washer, replacing weak or broken spring, cleaning away rust caused by moisture in the air system.

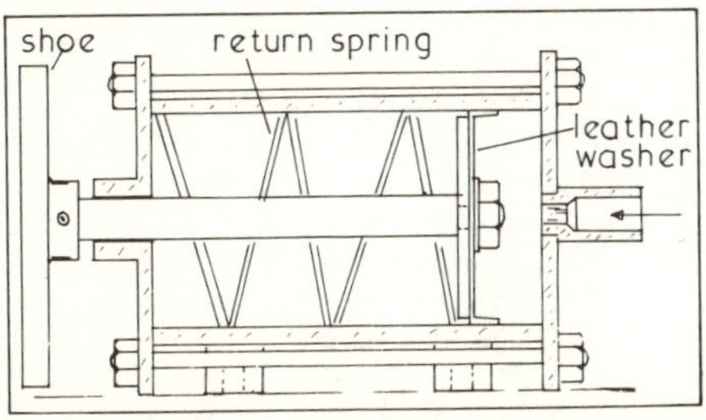

factors of the anticipated product if the existing plant is to be used.

A joinery unit planned for the manufacture of window frames would not accommodate very readily to stair production as a fill in line, but it could do cupboard framing, roof trussing, and door casings.

Many establishments have secondary production lines which work in smaller quantities than the main flow line. This line is often forced on to the manufacturer in order to supply his customers with special requirements to accompany larger orders from the main production flow.

Where an establishment has a large range of machinery, it is desirable to plan the work to spread the operations over as much of the plant as possible. Failure to observe this can result in build-ups behind some machines, while others may be standing idle.

Some specifications for contract items, detail construction methods, which have in the main to be adhered to. Others are more flexible and give the planner some scope of adapting construction methods to suit the factory at the particular time of operation.

Some planners in large production establishments base their advance planning on the money value of the goods turned out per given period of time on the calendar. On this system the greater number of machines that can become involved will ensure the target can be met. If only a small section of the plant is involved, shift or overtime working may have to be resorted to which will be detrimental to the costing method.

Basic methods of applying electrodes to create heat in the glue line using radio frequency equipment. A: Direct application through the glue line. B: Through the timber method of application. C: Stray field system.

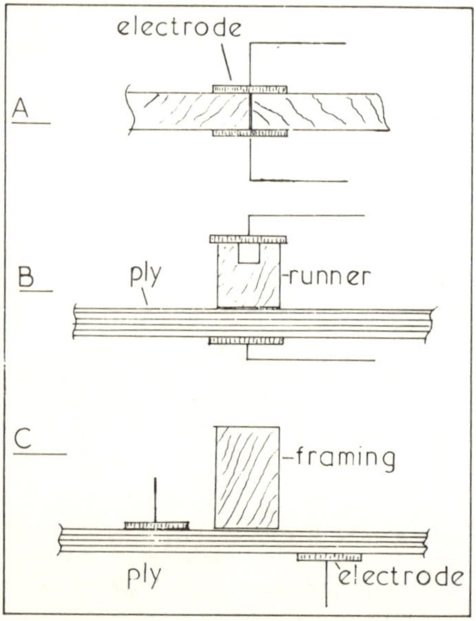

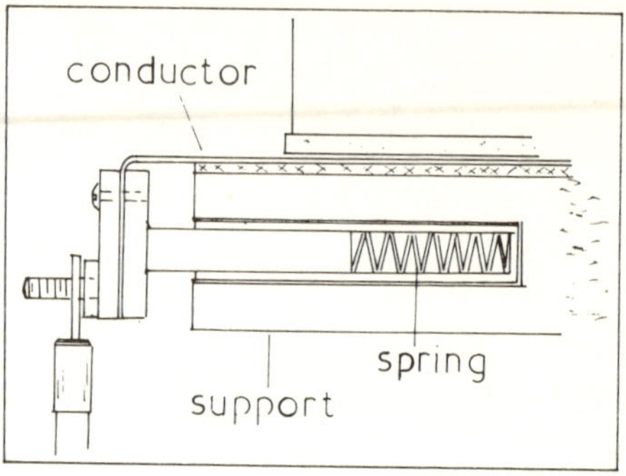

Section of unit applied to heating strip on low voltage strip heating. The conductor strip expands when heated and this can cause an uneven surface if the metal is fixed. The straining unit ensures a taut strip at all temperatures.

Practically all fabricated units can have alternative methods of construction. Sometimes a non-traditional method may be used because it suits the machine loading in certain sections of the plant. Present day gluing techniques have made new forms of construction possible, with a tendency of reducing some of the more intricate joint formations used in the past.

Plywood panels which are glued to skeleton framing in a heated press, require only the minimum of joint formation at the corners. Panels which are simply glued and pinned require a substantial jointing method. Here we use the term 'framed', where as today's method is more of a 'fabrication'.

Where a factory is producing a large number of different items, the full utilisation of machines becomes more possible. Too many lines can make an establishment uneconomic due to intermittent flow, but it has one particular safeguard. That is if the demand for a particular product suddenly drops it has others to concentrate on.

Many successful production units are run mainly on certain items, and labour is taken from or directed to the secondary line according to requirements.

In a woodworking establishment it very often falls upon the machine department to plan ahead for timber requirements. The size of the unit will govern how the demands are to be met. If timber is to be kiln dried within the unit, time must be allowed for this, bearing in mind the capacity of the drying chamber. If a fourcutter is set, for instance, to run a batch of material, it can be very frustrating to find that the load is not complete due to the shortage of kilned timber.

Marketed hardwoods of 25 mm in thickness frequently require three to five days in the drying kiln for average use in the furniture field. Considerable delays can be caused unless some thought is given in advance.

In the smaller works unit, cutting lists are very often prepared and handed to the machinist to get all the material for the job. In the larger unit this method is not acceptable, as several machinists will be involved, some on solid timber, others on plywood and other sheet material.

Experience has shown that operatives tend to ponder, and perhaps get unduly worried at overcomplicated listing, so this should be kept as simple as possible. Only the items concerned with the particular operator should be on his list.

A method which is in operation where large batch production is being carried out is what is known as "the piece parts system". Under this method one component of a unit is dealt with at a time. Instructions, and a detailed drawing are passed around with the work as the batch of items is progressed from one machine to another.

This system lends itself well to costing, and incentive payment schemes as so much time is allowed at each machine per given quantity of parts. Accuracy of the initial marking out is important under this system, and the work must be methodically imspected at all stages.

The introduction of steel checking gauges is usual to maintain the standard of accuracy required. Where piece parts are being manufactured with a number of machines involved, the operatives may work as a group in preference to individual effort for costing purposes. This does produce a team effort which can help considerably with accuracy standards, and checking between processes.

The deployment of labour in a woodworking machine shop can either be in favour of specialisation or versatility of the operatives.

In the smaller unit versatility is usually essential, as one machinist may be called upon to carry out a large number of operations. In the larger units a choice can be made as to policy but not spontaneously. Many operators spend long periods of work time on one type of machine. Some prefer this and it is as well to leave them this way if the work programme permits.

Other like to move around and welcome a change. These types can be very useful when absenteeism occurs and a standing machine has to be got into operation. Care must be taken when transferring operatives to another machine as to their personal safety. An operative that may be classed as a specialist on his own machine may be in a high accident potential group when transferred to a machine of which he has no experience. A short period of supervision may rectify this.

The layout of machines is always a point of criticism. Machines suitably positioned for one type of work-flow in a factory, can often be found no be in error for another type of work. This seems to have led to machines not being bolted to the floor in many establishments, so

A radio frequency unit attached to a pneumatic-operated cramping table designed for board jointing. Curing time for the adhesive in units of this type is usually under two minutes. The preparation tables adjoining the machine help to speed the work flow. (Pye Thermal Bonders, Cambridge).

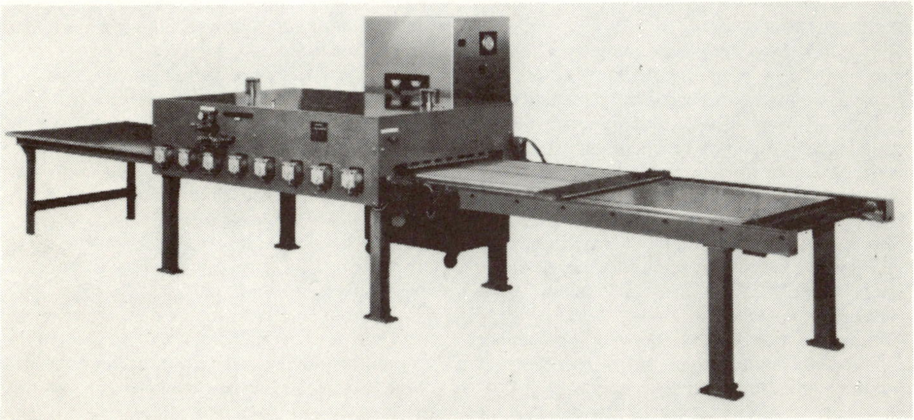

Machine shop engaged on batch production. Note that all the components are stacked on raised trays (pallets) for ease of movement to the various machines.

that they can be moved at short notice. Machines firmly secured to a level bed absorb vibration better, and this is particularly important if they are of light construction, as many present day ones are. Firm anchorage can also play a part in noise reduction.

The marking out of work for machining differs considerably from that of the basic hand worker. This also can apply to the sequence of processing operations. In machine setting out, techniques are based on methods that eliminates marking out after the initial setting up. The term face mark, as used by the hand worker is better described as the work face or datum in machining, since it is not always the best face, but the one that is in contact with the locating portion of the machine.

For repetition work it is customary to cut all the members to a constant length before joint formation takes place. This is not generally done in hand working. The importance of this linear dimensioning may not be understood by those who have not had experience of repetition machine working, but it is carried out for two basic reasons.

Firstly, very often the components have to fit into jigs for processing. One millimetre over or under correct dimension may slow down working procedures.

The second reason is that the work is positioned in the machine against stops to eliminate marking out. When stops are operative at both ends of the member, accuracy standards of the linear dimension are very important.

To enable work components to be moved from one machining process to another they should never be stacked directly on to the floor. Trays or pallets should be used, perhaps boxes for the smaller type of item. Forklift trucks are also in use for the transfer of large or accumulated items.

Machines are also in some flow production units linked by what is termed transfer systems, this cuts out stacking after each operation, so saving operative time. When work has to be transferred over a number of floor levels the system has to be planned according to the type of work involved. If roller shoots can be used instead of a hoist much operative time may be saved.

A man can spend his whole time operating a lift, and one direction may be completely non-productive. Carrying work manually up and down stairs which can be seen in some establishments, should be avoided.

Medium-sized factories usually operate on batch production. That is, a quantity of items is put out for manufacture at one time.

The number can depend on storage room available, and consideration must also be given to the amount of finance tied up within the establishment. Machined batches standing for too long awaiting assembly can deteriorate.

An RF unit in use for curing the adhesive on the edge lipping of doors. This method ensures that the joint is under pressure throughout the whole setting process, giving close bonding.

It is customary to number the individual batches to ensure the various components match up. It is not always possible to interchange components between batches unless the work is of a simple nature or the machining of a very high standard. Design here again can have an effect on whether or not components can be interchanged between batches.

Large units specializing in one product, such as doors, can have continuous flow production. This does not necessarily mean that all the machines are in full operation at all times.

Planned variations of dimension and design can occur withing the flow, and an over-productive machine may also have rest periods when the operators transfer to another area of the process.

Units of output are very often also measured on this flow system, and when a target has been reached towards the end of a work period a halt may take place to carry out the necessary main-

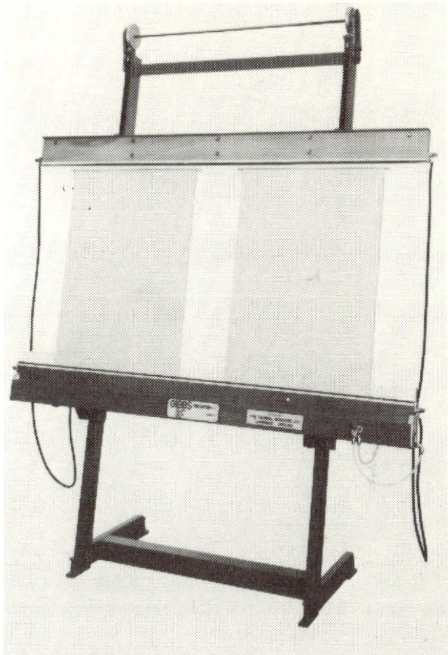

A unit designed for the edge veneering of panel boards. Thermosetting adhesives are used, and a low voltage transformer is required to heat the metal strip which is in contact with the veneered edge. (Pye Thermal Bonders, Cambridge.)

tenance, and housekeeping of the work area.

Medium-sized production units, involved in a large variation of types of goods can put a heavy load on a supervisor. His job can often be a combination of many responsibilities rolled into one. In a busy establishment of this kind, batches of items can be mislaid unless a completion area is arranged. The term "bonded stock", is often given to a supervised area for holding completed parts.

Difficulty also can be experienced in the allocation of job times in a busy establishment where a number of items are in production. If an

A precision balance for comparing the weight of cutters used on high-speed rotating heads. By working to a methodical procedure, a pair of cutters can be dynamically balanced by the use of this type of equipment.

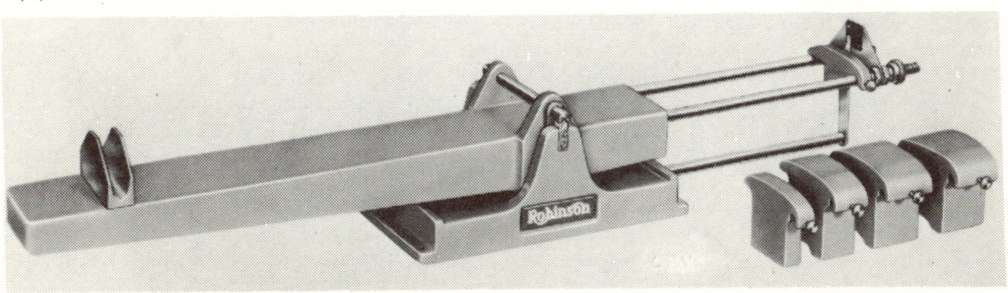

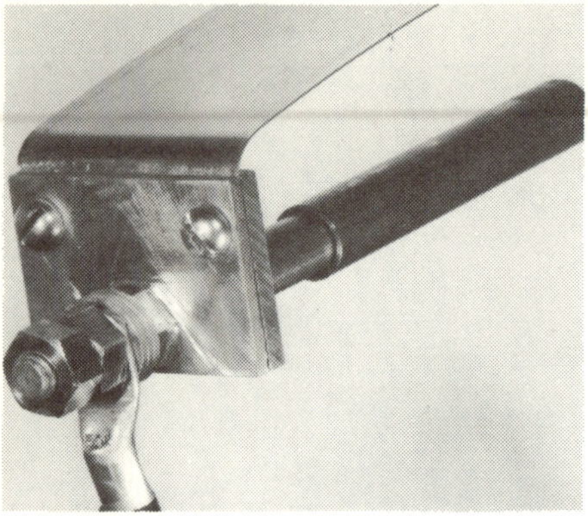

A tensioning unit designed to keep the heating strip taut on low voltage strip heating units.

incentive system is to operate, working must be planned in advance to permit a concentration period on each particular job rather than just let jobs be taken at random. Interference with planned working arrangements should be resisted, but these will occur at times very often to meet delivery requirements.

The problem of noise in the operation of woodworking machinery is now gradually receiving consideration. Noise can be reduced by the selection of suitable cutter heads in addition to paying attention to the accurate balancing of cutters. Circular blocks for straight planing always run quieter than square blocks even if the square block cutters are paired and balanced. The increased noise is very much due to the displacement of air during the high speed rotation.

Solid profile cutter heads run reasonably quietly, and do not require extra high speed rotation if serviced so that all the cutting points are operative.

Most waste collection hoods fitted to machines are made from light gauge sheet metal. This can in many circumstances amplify the noise created by the cutters. Forms of lagging the portion of the extraction system adjoining the machine can

Efforts require to be made to reduce noise to a minimum when machines are positioned close to each other in a busy production shop.

help to muddle the sound to some extent. Glass fibre hoods are being used for guards on machines and this material can also be used for portions of the waste extraction system.

Screening of noisy machines into work bays benefit those outside the area, but probably intensify the sound within the bay. Methods are also being experimented with where the machine, such as a fourcutter, is encased in a box lined with sound-absorbing material, the only access points being at each end during operation. Doors are provided at the necessary points for setting up the machine.

Precision working machines which are manually operated should not be located in the heavy duty cutting area. Noise affects concentration, and if excessive can introduce a danger aspect. Work requiring the use of the ring fence on a spindle moulder comes into this precision category.

The noise from some types of machines is not objectionable, and some workers do in fact prefer to be engaged in an industrial atmosphere which mechanisation often produces. Most circular saw blades when free running produce very little noise except for one type. This is very often a cross-cut blade which has a large number of teeth and produces a high-pitched note.

The frequency of this note can be changed to a more acceptable tone by cutting slots in the blade at intervals around the rim. This should not, however, be done at random without consulting the manufacturers of the blade.

Many blades of this type are supplied ready prepared for service with the slots inserted. Another method of changing the frequency note is to divide the teeth into a number of groups by forming deeper gullets at intervals around the periphery. This method may, however, upset the mechanical sharpening operations in the tool room if not done with some consideration.

In the case of the spindle moulder the first thing an operator does on starting the machine is to listen to hear how it sounds. From this he can judge how well the cutters are in balance, and also decide whether or not he can change to a higher number of revolutions. This does indicate that noise has an advantageous part to play in the operation of machines, and to eliminate it altogether, if it were possible, would be unsatisfactory.

The planning and marking out area in a production unit is very often in the vicinity of the machine shop, and should be located in an area that is reasonably comfortable regarding noise, dust, and light. In a small or medium sized unit, this point may be the control centre of the factory where many decisions are made, and details worked out for incoming requirements.

In the larger factory this point will be linked with the higher administrative unit, but this shop floor location is very often the point where the final decision is taken on how to do the job.

Information is then passed to the machinist in a way that he can understand. If he is a specialist in a large unit, his responsibilities will be limited to his particular machine operation on batch work.

If he is a machinist in a small works unit, his approach will be very different, and also the nature of his responsibilities.

A circular cutter block being checked for static balance on a setting and balancing stand.

Layout for woodworking machine shop

PROBLEM

Woodworking machines are to be installed in an existing store and I wish to place the machines in the most suitable layout to obtain the best work flow.

A proposed joiner's shop adjoins and there is a separate timber store. The only storage space required in the machine shop would be for timber being machined.

The machine shop will contain: 762mm (30in.) push circular sawbench; 508mm (20in.) push circular sawbench; pull cross-cut saw (610mm [24in.] table); 762mm (30in.) bandsaw; 508mm (20in.) under and over planer; spindle moulder; single ended tenoner; chain and chisel mortiser; hollow chisel mortiser; 2.13m (7ft.) belt sander; Interwood router.

T. B.

SOLUTION

In planning the positioning of machines it is necessary to consider the type of work to be generally carried out. This can affect the spacing of the machines to the best advantage. In this query, building joinery would appear to be the principal item.

I suggest the layout shown in the accompanying drawing.

For domestic work, room height is a general guide to the length of members after they have passed the cross-cut saw. Space requires to be fairly generous at the input end of the shop where the material is in the most bulky state. Some built up storage is always required at this point.

As saw benches are right-handed they need to be positioned on the right for ease of access, so with a shop of this width the cross-cut is best on the left. Some incoming timber will be taken to the cross-cut, others may go first to the main rip saw.

Panel boards such as plywood and blockboard will most likely be cut on the smaller saw bench. Room to cut at least 2.44m by 1.22m (8ft. by 4ft.) sheets must be allowed for.

Long members, such as stair strings or handrails can be accommodated quite easily in a shop of this size providing the machines are positioned slightly out of line of each other. It is advisable to have room on all sides of the spindle moulder if possible to enable attachments to be used. The bandsaw does not require space on the left so can stand near to the left-hand wall.

The chisel mortiser could be positioned inside

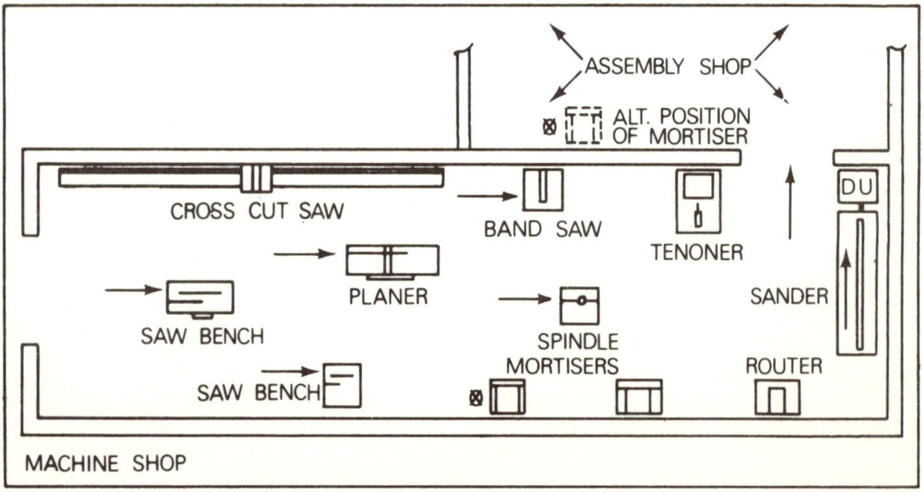

the joinery assembly shop if desired for use where items have to be mortised after a first assembly, to cut down movement. A small multi-cutter dovetailer could take its position to advantage in the machine shop.

Space is not generally required to the left of a tenoning machine if it is of the pillar type. It can be useful with the swan neck type on trenching work. The sander plus a dust collecting unit could be positioned along the end wall. A collecting unit must be installed or conditions will be very bad.

I appreciate very much the Querist's statement that the building is to be used as a machine shop and not a stacking area. I hope he manages to keep it that way. I have been trying for years. No mention is made of pneumatic waste extraction or tool servicing area. These two points must be kept in mind.

Planning a woodworking machine shop

PROBLEM

Please let me have your suggestions for arranging woodworking machines in the premises described in my sketch. Machines required will probably include a mortising machine, cross-cut saw, circular saw, vertical spindle moulder, over and under planer, and a table sandpapering machine.

It is proposed to use the ground floor as machine shop and the upstairs as joiners' shop. A partition would be required to stop draughts from existing gates. Stairs could be re-arranged and windows enlarged and re-positioned.

A small office would also be needed, the position of artificial lighting points and power points. P.K.

SOLUTION

When planning the layout of machines in a workshop for machine woodworking it is helpful if the type of goods to be manufactured can be defined. If this is possible a more economic arrangement can be made and every part of the floor area utilised for the most suitable purpose.

Generally, machines operating on cabinet work, can be closer together than for joinery work. For the manufacture of domestic furniture, 3 to 4 metres at the back, and front of each machine could probably be accepted as a minimum.

This would not apply to general joinery where double the amount could be required for such items as stair strings and handrails. Shopfitting work can demand the processing of very long members.

In the smaller workshops, and even in the larger ones, it is advisable to plan the line of feed to be offset with the machine immediately in front. Greater length capacity can then be obtained. There is also a safety factor involved here. Workers have been trapped at the outfeed end of mechanically fed machines due to the lack of working space. Also machines do at times eject timber if being carelessly used, and this offsetting can prevent an operator of another machine becoming involved.

The off line positioning of machines should not be excessive as this can reduce the planning of gangways, which is most important when working on batch production. Components should be stacked on trays or trollies for easy movement, never on the floor.

Safety regulations regarding woodworking machinery, recommend that where natural lighting can be improved by additional windows this should be done. The querist appears to be in a position to do this, and I think it would be well worth while.

The size of the workshop seems reasonable for the number of machines mentioned. If the floor is substantial in the upstairs room the sanding machine may be installed there to advantage.

This would allow space on the ground floor for another machine, say a tenoner or bandsaw, and may save goods being carried back downstairs for sanding after assembly.

The partition mentioned to be erected at the entrance I do not altogether agree with unless it must be, as it will hinder the entry of long timber. It would be better if the gates could be replaced by doors, if this is a workable proposition, to keep out the draught.

A door of some kind at the other end of the building could provide some scope, and act as a fire exit, a point which should not be overlooked, in particular as no pneumatic waste system is mentioned. Portable extraction units are now available for individual machines, to assist in housekeeping.

I like very much the proportion of the machine shop. There is no doubt as to which direction the work should flow. The location of the shop floor office depends on the nature of the trade. If many callers are anticipated for such as the do-it-yourself trade, the office must be near the entrance doors.

Inexperienced persons must not walk through a machine shop which is in operation.

On the other hand, an office and setting-out bench could be comfortably arranged at the far end of the shop, away from the unprepared timber for which it has no immediate concern.

When determining the position of the circular saw, it is important that sufficient space is allowed for the cutting of panel boards, such as

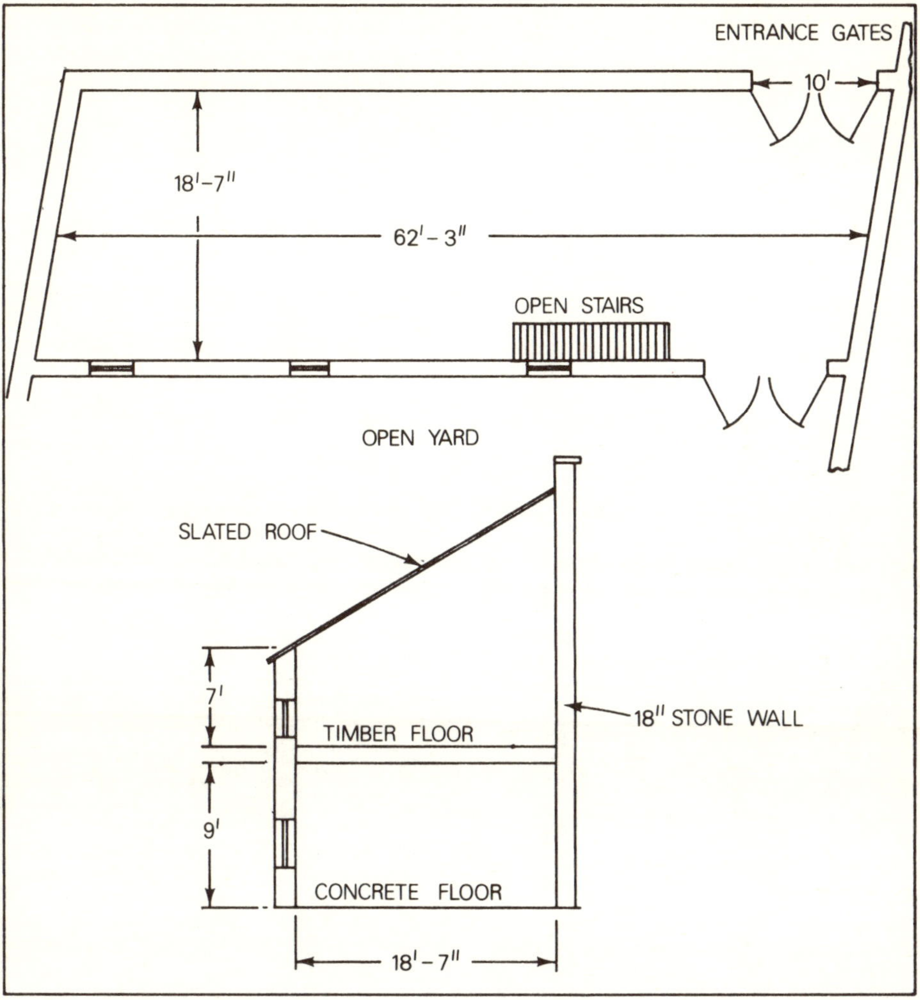

plywood and blockboard. This is a point often overlooked, and the use of sheet material is increasing in an effort to save labour costs.

I suggest that provision should be made for the cutting of up to 8 ft. by 4 ft. sheets which are a standard at the present time for this size of machine shop.

I can see no immediate reason for moving the position of the stairs. The well may benefit from being widened to facilitate the passing up of materials, and a lift-off handrail unit would help to increase the clear way, when required.

A trap door in the upper floor between the two entrance gates could be useful for loading completed goods, and will help in the unloading of the machinery, a point well worth noting.

General points regarding the position of the various machines are as follows: The most length will be required by the crosscut saw to handle the incoming timber. Rip-sawing, planing, and spindle moulding, all require a minimum of 5 metres at each end of the machine.

This should be obtainable without any difficulty by offsetting the machines.

For mortising cupboard stiles, room height, 3 metres left and right of the machine would accommodate. Precision operations require the location giving the most natural light. Spindle

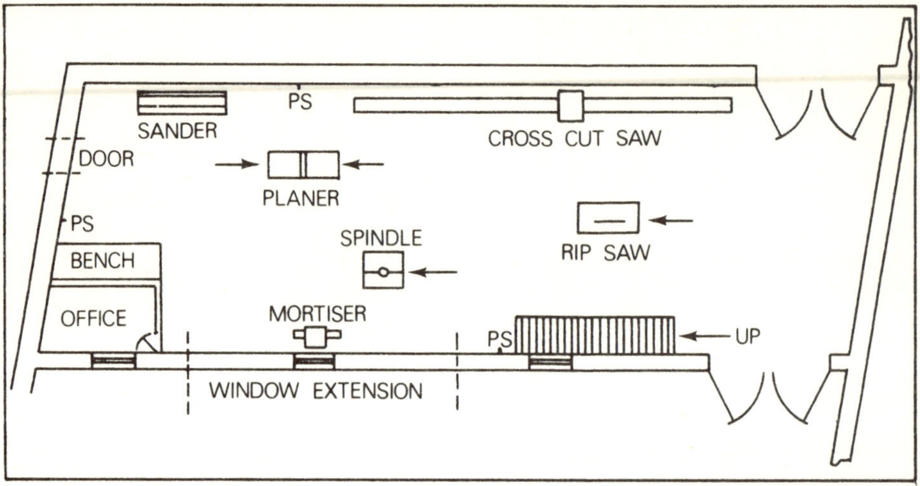

moulding, mortising, and planing, come into this category. Natural lighting at the setting-out bench, would also be to advantage.

The power supply would be best located near the entrance doors for quick access in case of fire to isolate the building. Individual lightinɑ for each machine is the general rule with this type of workshop. The lights should be positioned high enough to prevent dazzle to the operator.

Three-pin plugs 240 volt power points can be very useful in a machine shop for using portable tools for operations which do not come within the range of the installed machines. The main call for these will be in the room upstairs.

The drawing shows a suggested layout of the machines mentioned. The extension of the windows would be most beneficial in the centre of the building to get the light where it is mostly required. Other windows may also be constructed as required. A position for a fire escape door is shown, and this could be also opened if very long timber had to be planed. Power sockets for portable tools are indicated P.S.

The advantages of power feed

The Wadkin Bursgreen power fed multi-rip saw is a machine designed to give maximum production for an economical outlay. It can be used for either single- or multi-sawing. The speed at which the timber is power fed into the machine can be varied to suit the circumstances.

In expanding woodworking establishments two factors which very often govern increased output are: (a) Difficulty in obtaining sufficient skilled operatives, and (b) Shortage of floor space to accommodate additional machinery.

In a machine shop where the majority of the machines are fed by hand, meaning that the timber is pushed manually past the cutting unit, factors (a) and (b) above can very often be eliminated to some extent by the introduction of power feeding.

Outlay in capital will understandably be involved, but this may be confined to the installation of machinery (power fed) rather than adding more hand-fed machines which will require additional floor accommodation.

Let us examine the advantages of power fed machines generally.

1. Very much increased output.
2. Less fatiguing for the operator.
3. It encourages the operator to work.
4. The "taker off" can be kept fully occupied; in some cases more than one may be required to cope with the high output.
5. Continuous feeding gives a more efficient finish to the work, and puts an even strain on the cutting unit.
6. One power-fed machine may have the output of several hand fed, so saving space and labour.
7. Mechanically fed machines are often safer to operate, as hands are at a considerable distance from the point of cut.
8. Once a power fed machine has been set by an experienced operator, a less experienced one may feed the machine.

One method of providing power feed to an existing machine is by fitting a powered attachment. This method is proving very successful, as the reasonable cost of these attachments is soon recovered by the increased output. A spindle moulder fitted with such a unit can increase its daily output by 500 per cent on continuous work, without requiring any additional floor space for the machine itself. This statement may well apply to the attachment fitted to a surface planer or a rip saw, on some operations, but I quote from personal experience in the case of the spindle moulder.

Where a large amount of repetition shaping work has to be undertaken on the spindle moulder, shaping machines are available with mechanical feed, the type required being determined by the size and shape of the components. These machines provide a high standard of safety to the operator, they will produce a variety of work, and are capable of large output of a high standard.

Power fed rip sawing often becomes necessary when a fourcutter planing and moulding machine is installed. One hand fed rip saw, or push bench as they are sometimes called, cannot produce sufficient output to feed a high-speed fourcutter. This is a point not always realised when contemplating the installation of a first or additional fourcutter, which is a high powered machine.

For power fed rip sawing, a variety of machines are available.

1. The radial arm circular saw: Will cope with heavy or medium work.
2. The straight line edger saw: Deals with waney-edged timbers, etc.

3. The bandsaw, power fed resaw: Produces a minimum of saw kerf waste.

There are, of course, many variations of the above machines, multi-rip saws being one in the case of the straight line edger, where several strips of timber may be produced at one pass of the board through the machine.

Mortising

A hydraulic electric mortising machine occupies no more floor space than the standard chain and chisel machine, but due to the fact that the clamping of the material and the operation of the cutting head are done by hydraulic pressure, output is greatly increased. Control is by foot pedal, which leaves the operator's hands free to deal with the placing of the work.

Tenoning

A change over from a single ended tenoning machine to a double ended machine is quite a big step to obtain power feed, and additional floor space will be required also. The introduction of this machine, however, may eliminate other less efficient machines in the plant, as it will carry out many operations in addition to tenoning. All work done on the double ended tenoner will be power fed, and in a busy factory it is a machine that is seldom idle.

Sanding

Machine sanding can very often determine the acceptability of the finished product. For high class work which has to be polished power fed sanding may not meet the required standard. With the older type of drum sanders snake lines do from time to time appear on the finished surface, and these need to be removed by a hand operated machine. Modern drum sanders, combined with the increasing efficiency of sanding paper manufacture, do provide a high standard of finish, providing the machine operator endeavours to obtain this.

A recent development in the power feed sanding field is a machine known as the Speed Sander, or Time Saver. It is a less costly machine than the three drum sander, and gives a high standard of finish to even veneered panels. A really good addition to power feed machining. This machine is manufactured in a variety of widths which makes it ideal for installation in a production line for a specific purpose without wastage. As with most power fed woodworking machines, a pneumatic waste extraction system is necessary, but this can be an individual unit if so desired requiring only a small amount of installation.

The Speedsander, although a comparatively recent development in power feed sanding, is already in use in many parts of the world. Its use contains all the advantages mentioned in this article. (Photo: Thos. White and Sons, Paisley, Scotland.)

Section 2 Basic machines and their uses

The use of circular saws

The circular saw bench is probably the most widely used machine in woodworking, and it is not surprising that it is to be found in many different forms. It would not be a practical or economic proposition to design one machine which would carry out all the sawing work found within woodworking to the quality standard required. However some machines can carry out a greater variety of operations than others.

The requirement of a versatile circular saw bench has changed over recent years due to the increased use of prepared wide panel boards instead of solid material. Sheet material was confined to interior uses prior to the introduction of synthetic resin adhesives and laminated plastics. The large sheets call for a greater cutting width capacity on machines, and due to the material content of the boards tungsten carbide tipped saws are often required, in particular for quantity work. Tipped saws are a high precision tool, and the standard of the bench in which they are used must be in keeping with this.

A joinery unit serving a builder has very often in the past been equipped with a heavy duty type saw bench. This type of machine is described by sawyers as a push-bench or resaw. This machine is ideal for the purpose for which it is designed, but it does not give the standard of precision required on some operations.

Fig. 1. Heavy duty circular bench of the resaw type. Points of note on this particular machine are, guard and adjustments, accessability of switch gear, screw adjustment to fence, encased raising and lowering gear to table.

Fig. 3. Dimension saw bench of the heavy duty type. Many joinery units use this type of machine in preference to the resaw bench (Fig. 1). A dimension saw reduces the number of operations to be carried out by hand, in addition to introducing efficient construction techniques of a geometrical nature. The saw blade in the machine illustrated can be tilted to 45 degrees, and raised and lowered.

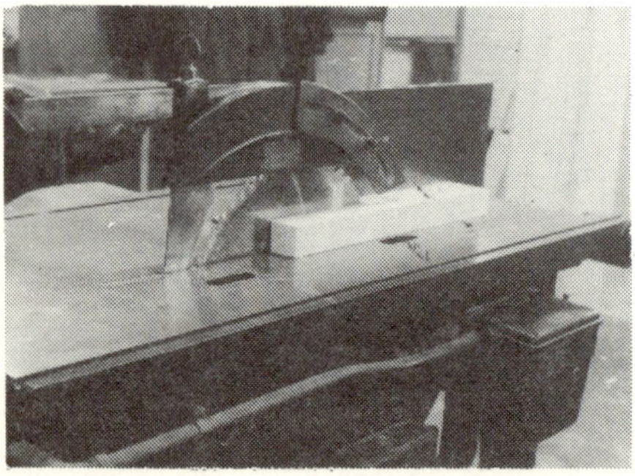

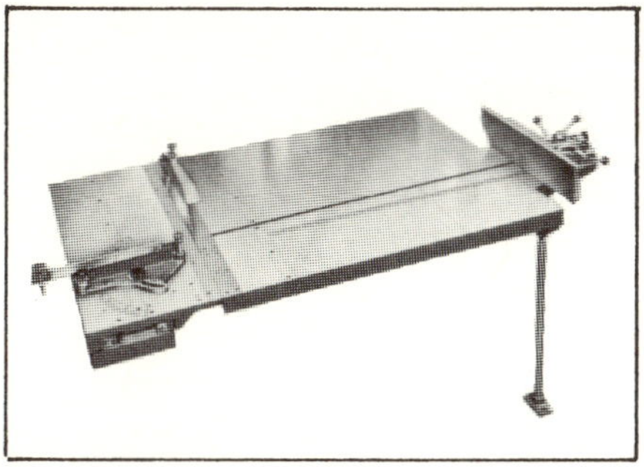

Fig. 4. An extended table suitable for the machine in Fig. 3. The increased use of prepared panel boards has created a demand for larger cutting capacities.

Fig. 5. A dimension saw bench of medium weight design. Machines of this range have many of the operational facilities of the heavy and more costly models. They are designed with the smaller work unit in mind. Note extended dimensioning facilities.

It is regrettable to hear of persons meeting up with trouble from using this basic type of machine in ways it was never designed for.

This type of saw bench in semi-portable form is often to be found on building sites and estate workings. It is of great value here as in the joiners shop for re-sawing timber to the required dimensions. Scraps of timber need never go to waste even on an outdoor location if a push bench is at hand to convert it to usable sizes.

Suitable sized machines can be used for deep-cutting operations, this is something that the more precision type of machine cannot cope with.

Saw benches capable of taking blades of 750 mm in dia. (approximately 30 inches) are usually fitted with motors from 12 to 15 horse power, according to the type of work on which they are

Fig. 6. A multi-pupose saw bench with a power feed unit incorporated in the design. Feed is transmitted through a toothed wheel within the table. Grip marks on the timber are eliminated in the saw kerf.

Fig. 7. A straight line edger saw. Machines of this type produce straight sawn timber irrespective of the edge profile when fed in. Timber cut in this way is ideal for feeding through a fourcutter or moulder.

to be generally used. It is also advisable that a choice of the spindle revolution speed should be available.

It is generally accepted that the rim speed, (the speed at which the saw tooth is travelling) should be 10,000 ft. per min., or S.I. approximate equivalent 50 metres per sec.

Therefore the diameter of the saw plate has a relation to the speed of rotation of the driving

spindle. The smaller diameter saws require the higher speeds of rotation.
When using saw blades of large diameter, say over 500 mm, it is necessary to provide some side support during rotation. The most common method of attaining this is with the use of packings which fit into a recessed portion of the machine table.
These packings are very often fitted by the sawyer, suitable material can be obtained from machine manufacturers. They can be made from felt, soft leather or textile material. Packings should be an easy push in fit.
Tight packings will generate heat in the saw blade, so causing expansion of the metal.
Expansion near the rim of the blade causes instability, which can produce a snaking effect when sawing.
Tightening of the packings on the inner part of the blade can be beneficial under some circumstances to prolong the life of the saw a little longer before servicing.

Points relating to a resaw type bench

A strongly built machine will give many years of service with practically no replacements other than saw blades and packings.
The main body should preferably be of heavy construction, although scientific advancement of materials and design is reducing the metal content which reduces cost.
Lighter machines have the advantage of easier movement when planning production layouts, but heavy machines absorb vibration and are more pleasant to use.
Providing that the portion of the saw blade below the bench in fully encased with the metal frame of the machine it will conform to the factory acts without further protection at this point.
The spindle must run in ball bearing assemblies.
If the machine is to be fitted to a pneumatic waste extraction system, a suitable collecting point will be required. This may be a compulsory factor on all woodworking machines in the near future.
A rapid setting scale, engraved within the machine table can probably be to more advantage on this type of saw bench than any other as most settings are not of a high precision nature, and slight inaccuracies do occur with these scales.
In addition to an adjustment locking handle for the fence, a screw fine adjustment should also be fitted to the machine. The screw adjustment should not have an excessive amount of backlash.
The fence on a push bench can usually be canted to an angle of 45 degrees.

It is essential that the fence should be adjusted to line with the root of the gullet of the saw teeth. On the larger type of saw blades packings are required to give support. The hardwood insert prevents the packings from coming into contact with the saw teeth.

The crown guard should not be raised any higher than that shown in the drawing. The extension guard should be lowered to within 6 mm of the timber being cut. Experienced sawyers prefer to "feel" the timber through the saw, rather than just push it. A small amount of "lead" is given to the fence line.

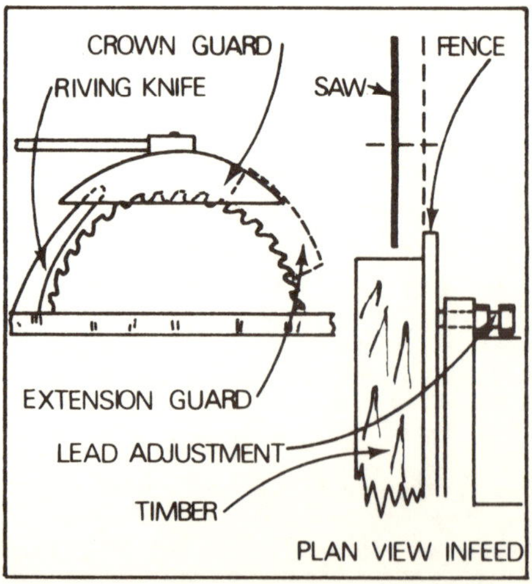

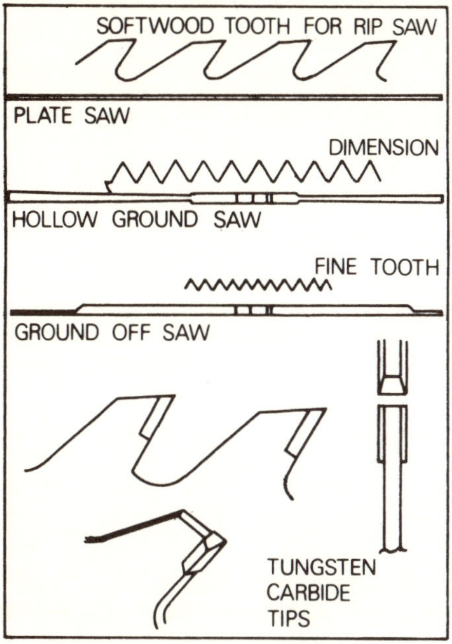

Typical section of saw blades, and types of saw teeth. Many others are also in use. The design and maintenance of saws requires a considerable amount of experience.

Saws running in and out of vertical position must be in first class condition regarding plate rigidity. Slackness within the plate will encourage sag due to gravitational pull.

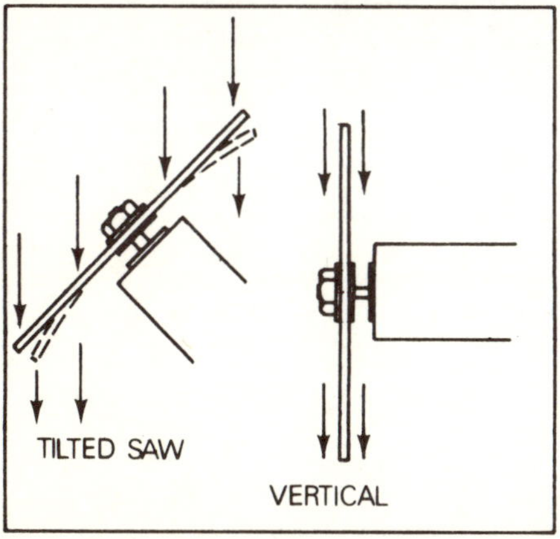

This is useful in the joiners shop for easing the spindle moulder cut on production work, or on site machines it is often used for forming bevels on roof purlins and wall plates.

The line of fence should in theory be parallel to the line of the saw plate. Some experienced sawyers prefer to give the fence a slight amount of what they call "lead in." This means the front points slightly towards the saw blade.

Under this method of working the timber can be allowed to be held slightly off the fence at the operator's end. A considerable amount of experience is required to operate and maintain a push bench in continuous production.

Many saw benches of this type are equipped with a raising and lowering action for the table. This is intended for adjustment for cutting rebates, and grooving when a more suitable machine is not available.

Only a small amount of saw blade usually projects above the bench for these operations, and if the operation has to be done in this way, suitable non standard guards must be arranged.

The gears and threads involved in the table raising device, should not be located in such a position that they become clogged with sawdust immediately the machine is used. A point to note when selecting a machine.

If a device for squaring timber to length on the machine is to be used, the table edges must be machined parallel or grooves must be provided in the table face to accommodate guides. With the older type of push bench, which were flat belt driven, it was not uncommon to find the driving pulley projecting above the table line.

This is a feature to avoid when purchasing a machine of this type if squaring timber to length is anticipated.

Two main types of riving arrangements are in use. The knife is either suspended from the saw guard assembly, or fixed within the bench, projecting upwards.

One important point regarding the knife, it must always penetrate the machine table.

This is a point very much in favour of the knife being fixed within the table, but unless they are made from very durable steel they have a habit of being bent by careless operators.

Under no circumstances should the machine be used without a riving knife. The purpose of the knife is to grip the timber after cutting in preference to the saw plate, and to keep it in line.

The knife should therefore be slightly thicker than the kerf made by the saw. The distance between the teeth of the saw and the riving knife should not exceed 12 mm.

The curvature of the knife should follow that of the saw for maximum efficiency. The guard over the saw should be easily adjustable, preferably without the use of spanners.
The bottom of the guard should not be raised higher than the root of the gullets of the top-most point of the saw.

In other words, it should not be possible to pass an object over the top of the saw teeth and underneath the guard.
Some operators are in the habit of removing the guard assembly to cut wide panel boards. If this involves the removal of the riving knife also, the operator, and those around him, are in grave danger. Procedures of this type should not be undertaken, as the risk is considerable, and it is also a defiance of the Factory Acts.
Many points relating to the push bench also apply to other types of saw benches. This applies particularly to safety procedure, although the mode of safety differs from one machine to another. With a push bench engaged in ripping timber, the purpose for which this machine is mainly designed, the operator can in most instances work at some considerable distance from the cutting unit.
With the finer more precise type of machine, namely the dimension saw bench, the machinist has to work at much closer quarters to the cutting blade.
An increased sense of safety procedure is therefore necessary. This is a point which must be considered by supervisors when changing operators from one machine to another at short notice. Changing an operative from a large machine to a smaller type does not necessarily mean an increase in the safety factor.
It is more likely to mean a change of the safety procedures involved.

The dimension saw
This machine is designed to carry out a large number of machining operations, and is suitable for use in joinery production in addition to many other branches of woodworking.
The machine is available in various ranges, from table mounting models, then medium range machines, followed by heavy duty production stock.
This range brings the dimension saw even into the smallest workshop.
Many of the larger production units use heavy duty machines on the main production line, and medium range models on the secondary less demanding flow.
A small joinery unit serving a builder could probably meet the majority of its demands with a medium range machine, in particular if a sample form of push bench is also available.
Present day dimension saws are designed with the cutting of sheet material in mind. Large size tables are also available, substantial riving knife and guard units are positioned within the tables to give unlimited cutting area.
Extension units are also available to support material for squaring off purposes. Also due to the fact that the saw blade can be lowered in the bench, more splinter-free cutting can be obtained on the fine veneered sheet materials.
Dimension saws are usually designed to take saws up to about 450 mm in diameter on the production type machines.
Using the correct type of saws, the machine can be used for both ripping and cross-cutting operations.
A high standard of accuracy can be obtained. Hence the name of dimension saw is given to this machine. A wide range of types of saw blades can be used, and some examples are briefly explained below.

Plate saw
A saw with parallel faces, requiring set on the teeth to give clearance. Used for ripping, tooth design should be in keeping with type of material being cut.

Hollow ground saw
This saw is full thickness at the outer rim, and ground away on both faces to the point where it meets the mounting collars. No set is required on a saw which is in first class condition, but an ageing saw may require a very slight amount if burn marks appear on the work.
An ideal saw for squaring components to nett length. Good for cutting mitres, and ripping fine beading.

Ground off saw
This is a plate saw of robust gauge which is ground off to a much thinner gauge on one face only for a distance of say 50 mm from the outer rim. This saw may be lowered in the bench leaving only the ground off section exposed.
Saws of this type are capable of working with delicate material with a minimum of waste.
Tungsten carbide tipped blades can also be used in dimension saw benches for cutting such materials as chipboard, and laminated plastics.
These saws are usually of the plate type, no set, clearance being provided by the carbide tips projecting and diminishing beyond the face of the saw.
Saws of this type can be used continuously for several weeks without attention.
If servicing cannot be done within the unit, the

saw makers readily accept this operation with quick return.

Most heavy duty dimension saw benches are equipped with a sliding table, and squaring fence. This enables work to beüheld firmly on a moving unit instead of having to slide the work along on a fixed surface as in the case of lighter machines.

Angular cutting for mitres can be carried out with either a hollow ground saw or a sharp tungsten carbide tipped saw.

The squaring fence design on these machines permits both left, and right hand mitres to be made on moulded work without alteration of fence position.

The saw unit also be tilted in addition to the lowering and raising movement. This is usually described as a saw with a tilting arbor. The amount of tilt is limited to 45 degrees, in one direction only.

For mitring it is preferable to work with the saw in the vertical position, and cut the angle with the aid of the squaring fence set as required. The reason for this is, unless the saw plate is in ideal condition it may not run evenly in an out of vertical position. Gravitational pull has an effect which may cause a wobble, particularly on a saw that requires tension treatment.

When mitring the wider type of item such as 150 mm plinth material, the saw will have to be used in the tilted position. The tilting arbor is particularly useful when used in conjunction with the canting fence, for angular ripping.

The fence can be set to the approximate angle required, and the fine adjustment carried out by tilting the saw with the screw wheel.

Due to the fact that the squaring fence can be set to make angular cuts with the saw in the tilted position, very often two operations can be carried out at the one pass. An end cut for instance, on a table leg which is splayed in both direction, can be cut in this way.

This compound cutting facility could probably be used more if joinery designers were more aware of its capabilities. Period designs which are creeping into domestic building could create a demand for geometric skills which this machine can cope with.

Saw spindles on dimension benches usually rotate at about 2,800 rpm. This makes some moulding operations possible using suitable large diameter cutter heads.

Trenching as used for shelving, or angular trenching as in the case of louvres can be accommodated using cutter units known as dado heads. These cutter heads are very often adjustable within a given range, for width of cut.

An important point relating to the dimension saw bench, is that it should be regularly serviced. Unless all the adjustments are in free working order, the machine can be very difficult to use.

Failure to provide lubrication on sliding parts causes wear which in turn reduces the precision qualities of the machine.

Circular saws with power feed

These are machines used mainly in the larger production units or timber mills. They are much more productive than hand fed machines, but the number of operations which they can cope with is very limited. The timber which they cut is usually unplaned, although there may be exceptions in some establishments.

The straight line edger saw

This power fed circular saw produces straight timber irrespective of the shape of the edge adjoining the guide fence. The timber is gripped between pressure rollers and a travelling chain located within the machine table.

Two distinct types are in use regarding the location of the saw blade within the machine.

On some machines the saw will be found operating above the bench, on others it is positioned below.

These machines, being power fed, at all times, are not usually fitted with riving knives. A safety device is fitted in front of the machine to stop timber being thrown back in event of it being released from grip.

The table of the machine should always be kept

Line diagram of a straight line edger saw with the cutting unit above the table. The parts are: A. Waste extraction pipe. B. Saw blade. C. Raising wheel for stock feed. D. Safety fingers. E. Raising wheel for saw plate. F. Chain track. G. Access door to saw. H. Guide Fence. J. Driven feed roller.

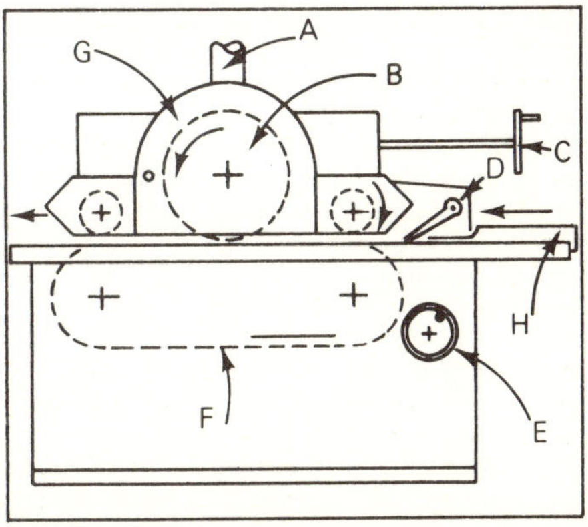

clear of chippings and saw dust, as the efficiency of the finger guards depends upon them being able to rest on the table surface.
Rates of feed can be varied on the straight line edger. The slower speeds are for use when cutting short material to enable the feed unit to be kept full, or backed up as it is often called.
With modern machines glued butt joints can be made straight from the saw without planing the finish being particularly suitable RF heating processes.
Work produced by the straight line edger is particularly suitable also for feeding through the fourcutter or moulder. This is due to the fact that it is straight and constant in width.
In establishments handling waney-edged timber, that is timber that still has the uneven shape of the extremity of the tree, the straight line edger saw is the correct machine to use for dressing. No marking out is necessary to cut a straight edge.
Although the machine has a fence, it takes no part in the guiding of the timber other than positioning for cutting.
Lubrication and an efficient pneumatic waste extraction are important. The chain will very soon become clogged unless the dust is constantly removed.

The operation and design of planing machines

The operation of planing timber can be for a variety of reasons, not just to produce a smooth surface, but often as a preparatory step for future machining. The term 'thicknessing' is generally a planing operation, its main consideration being to produce uniformity in sectional dimension.

The desired quality of the planed finish will be governed by the purpose for which the timber is to be used. In repetition work involving the use of jigs, and locating stops on machines, unless the timber is of uniform dimension, errors, or difficulty in progression will be experienced.

In addition to planed sectional dimension being required, constant linear measurement is usually called for also. These factors can be a new experience to an operator or planer, changing from making single articles to batch production.

It is generally more advantageous to shed the linear waste at the commencement of processing, than to leave it to the final stages and lose the privileges of linear uniformity.

Planing is very often the follow-on operation after rip sawing. The waste factor in planing can be governed by the way in which the timber has been sawn. A wide board being cut into a number of strips on a push bench may require to have the guiding edge straightened first on a surface planer. In this way the waste factor is reduced, as only one heavy straightening operation per board is required, instead of, perhaps, say three or more. The straight line edger saw method of ripping, as explained in my previous article, would be used if available, so contributing to economy.

A surface planing machine can be designed solely fo this purpose or can be part of a combined surface planer and thicknesser. The combined machine calls for greater skills in engineering design, than to produce separate machines for planing and thicknessing.

Design is very often governed by the cost of producing so it is not unusual to find that a two-in-one machine has not got all the refinements of

An operator at work on a surface planer. Note the positioning of the bridge guard. This model of machine is a post war development, designed to meet the needs of the smaller woodworking units, and training establishments.

Surface planer equipped with overhead pressure springs for heavy cutting work such as moulding operations. The bridge guard is of the telescopic design. Note the convenient positioning of the infeed table adjustment handle.

separate machines. Neither has it the operational capabilities.
A machine designed for surfacing only is often referred to as a jointer. This describes its ability to prepare timber for precision working.
With hand fed surface planers, the cutter block must be of the circular type. The use of square blocks is prohibited by the Woodworking Machine Regulations. A bridge guard must also be a permanent feature of the machine.
The guard must cover the cutter on the working side of the fence, and in addition, the part of the cutter behind the fence should also be protected. The circular block, often described as the safety type cutter block, has many points in its favour over the square type.
Due to this it is often preferred on other machines where its use is not compulsory. It does run quieter than other types of block as it is less disturbing to the surrounding atmosphere.
Cutters used in circular blocks are of light construction and are easily re-ground.
Cutter balance is to some extent obtainable visably by comparing cutters. The weight ratio between the small amount of metal in the cutters compared to that of the block helps to maintain smooth running.
Many circular blocks on surface planers have cutter setting devices which locate the cutters with the correct projection beyond the surface of the block. If this projection is exceeded, some of the safety characteristics are lost.
In the event of a loose knot in the timber being worked, the body of the circular block will give it support during the cutting operation.
When using a square block, or a circular one with excess cutter projection, the knot could be pulled out, causing an acute disturbance to an unwary operator.
Some circular blocks are designed to accommodate moulding cutters without disturbing the planing cutters. Leaf springs should be used for holding the timber down firmly on to the machine table. The operation should always be planned so that the cutters have a minimum of projection.
The canted fence is helpful for this purpose. The work can be tilted, and in addition to the increased safety factor, better work is obtained, due to the approach angle being more constant.
With cutters correctly set, rebating can be carried out on the surface planer, but it has its limitations.
For some operations the bridge guard cannot be set in an effective manner. Work of this type should be transferred to the spindle moulder where it can be carried out with correct procedure.
Machine design also limits the depth to which a rebate may be cut on a surface planer. This is usually about 12 mm, which will, in fact, be sufficient for a large variety of requirements.
Excellent bevels and chamfers can be produced on the surface planer. This is due to the fact that the work is canted to produce the angle required with the aid of the fence, and the cutters operate at right angles to the line of the material being fed through.
This set-up is not generally achieved when bevelling operations are carried out on the spindle moulder. Cutters have to be ground to produce the required angle.
Very often hogbacked bevels are produced, bevels which are not flat across their width, due

Bevelling a pipe box casing on a surfacing table. The guard is set as close up to the work as possible. Excellent flat faced bevels can be obtained by this method of working.

Rebating door casing material. Guards should not be removed to carry out rebating operations. Well designed machines provide for a wide scope of operations to be carried out within the Woodworking Machinery Regulations.

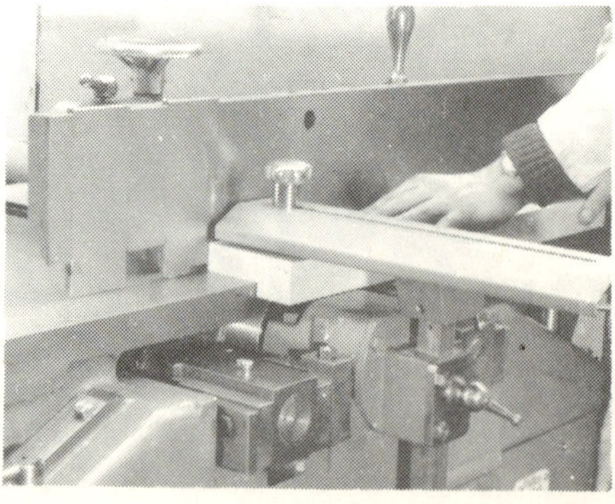

A thicknessing machine. This machine is fitted with a sectional infeed roller and pressures. This enables the full width of the machine to be utilised irrespective of variations in timber depths. Note the comfortable stance of the operator using the thicknesser, and compare this with a person feeding shorts into a combined machine. Cutter jointing device, and grinder, are in a retracted position, in front of the operator.

to incorrect shaping of the cutters. So if a surface planer can be used for a bevelling operation economically, by all means use it.

For dropping on to the cutters as in the case of stopped chamfers, the amount of kickback will be governed by how much timber is being removed, and the sharpness of the cutters. It is most definitely advisable to fix locating stops to prevent the timber from being thrown back at the commencement of the cut.

Also, if the outgoing table has been lowered below the cutting circle line a stop is important at the finishing point as the work will drop suddenly on to the cutting unit if the work is progressed too far.

The tables on a surface planer play a major role as to whether the timber is straight after surfacing.

The table at the infeed end of the machine is known as the front table. The outgoing table is the back table. The longer the tables are on a machine the higher the accuracy range becomes. The ideal situation is that the member being planed should be capable of being accommodated on the infeed table without any overhang.

Cost or floor area does not usually permit machines to be of such magnitude for, say, surfacing 2,000 mm door stiles, although large production units specialising do have machines designed in this way.

An example of this is the pre-straightening unit on a four-cutter or moulding machine. An experienced user of a surface planer can produce good results on a machine having tables of only

Details of the construction of a sectional feed roller kindly supplied by Messrs. Wadkin Leicester. This roller is an advancement of the solid type. It is used only at the infeed of the machine. A greater feed capacity is obtained by its use. Safer working is also experienced.

a small span, but additional time is required to do the operation in a satisfactory manner.

The outfeed table should be set with the cutter block stationary. The topmost point of the cutting circle should be in line with the surface of the table. When setting, the table should be wound down, then brought up to the setting line.

This method takes up any backlash in the screw adjustment, and prevents drop when the machine is set into motion.' Machines which have had long service must be set in this way.

Some machinists prefer to make the final adjustment with the cutter rotating.

There is no objection to this, providing the table is raised, up to line, not lowered. The infeed table for normal working should be set about 1.5 mm below the cutting circle line. The adjustment arrangements for this table should be in keeping with the general nature of the work being carried out.

A machinist working for long periods on an operation which requires many changes on the amount of cut, requires the adjustment facilities to be easily accessible. These facilities are more important on the front table than the back one. The adjustments should be in free working order.

Setting cutters inn a surface planer depends on the attachments provided, if any. Some machines have automatic setting devices which fit on to the block, the cutter positioning being done by spring loading behind the seat of the cutter. This, in theory, should be good if correctly applied.

Other methods depend on the cutters being set to line with the outfeed tables. A straight lath of hardwood can be used for this method, checks being made at various points along the cutter.

If a coating of chalk is applied to the contact section of the lath, a more accurate set can be obtained. An advance on the previous method is to use a specially designed magnified scale gauge. This records the amount of error, perhaps 10 times or more, the final accuracy depending on the ability of the machinist to position the cutters.

Securing bolts should have their final tightening, working from the centre outwards in a balanced procedure. Failure to carry out this pattern could cause a build up of slack in the centre of the cutter which will accumulate wood chips, and could be a source of danger.

Overstraining of the bolts should be avoided.

Cutter setting should always be an uninterrupted procedure. Machinists have been known to

A combined surface planer and thicknesser. The operator is surfacing the material to obtain a flat race to put into contact with the bed of the machine for the thicknessing operation. This procedure should always be followed.

Finger feed surface planer. This machine has an overall length of approximately three metres. The long tables ensure flat straight results. The makers claim it can carry out the work of at least four hand fed machines. (John Pickles and Son, Hebden Bridge, Yorkshire.) Considering the reduction in operator fatigue this is a very modest figure.

tighten the one cutter twice, leaving the second cutter only finger tight.

On the hand fed surface planer, cutters should not be jointed (trimmed) with an abrasive stone during rotation. This operation is done on thicknessing machines to ensure all the cutters have the same projection.

The slight heels formed on the cutters would force the timber off the back table and it would be impossible to plane a level surface.

The thicknessing machine comes into a different category of planing from that of the surfacer as it is a mechanically fed operation. For this reason the finish on the timber is a constant one. It is immediately variable inasmuch that several rates of feed are usually available which has an effect on the finished surface.

A machine designed specifically for thicknessing can have advantages over a combined planer and thicknesser. Larger diameter feed rollers are possible. Sectional feed rollers and pressure units can be incorporated in the design.

Better accessibility can be made for cutter setting and general servicing. The waste collecting hood can be of a more permanent nature than that of a combined machine. The length of the bed table of the thicknesser is not important, as it only reproduces a parallel cut to the face of the prepared surface.

The machine, therefore, can be more compact than a combined planer.

It is important in precision machine utilisation that a working face must be prepared first on a surfacing machine before the timber is passed through the thicknesser. If this point is ignored, imperfections on the underside of the timber will be reproduced on the planed face to some degree.

The timber will also retain most of the twist and curvature that it had before going through the machine. Unsurfaced timber will not feed as freely as that which has had preparation.

Most timber as supplied from the merchant has been converted from the log with wide bandsaws or gang saws. This leaves ridges across the timber face which tend to locate themselves over the bed rollers of the thicknessing machine.

Bed rollers, or antifriction rollers as they are called, are not usually power driven on the standard type of thicknessers.

However, if unsurfaced timber is to be thicknessed constantly for a particular reason, it is preferable that the bed rollers should be power driven to assist the feed.

Machine woodworking covers a very wide range of work, and a great number of differing situations arise.

Built up laminated beams, for instance, are frequently dressed level by passing them through a large size thicknessing machine prior to the final sanding stage.

The face in contact with the machine bed at the first pass through has to be reasonably free from ejected adhesive, or the planed upper surface will not be constant.

Infeed rollers of the sectional type are designed to give more efficient feeding and to enable the full width of the machine to be utilised under variance conditions in timber dimension.

They also provide for safer operation of the machine as there is less likelihood of timber being ejected due to failure of contact with the infeed roller.

Both circular and square type cutter blocks are used on thicknessing machines. Some operators prefer square blocks, claiming that they permit a faster rate of feed. There is a greater area of clearance for the waste material to free itself.

Circular blocks may tend to produce a braking effect under heavy loading, if the cutters have insufficient projection.

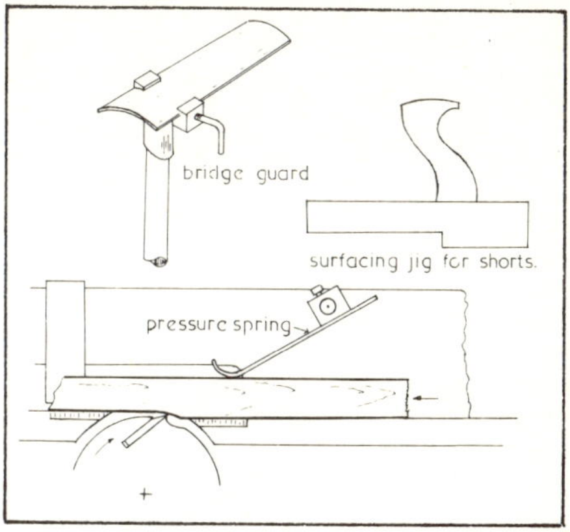

Three aids to safety on surface planers. Recent reports on woodworking machinery say that 25 per cent of all accidents occur on planing machines. (40 per cent. on circular saws.) For an operator to use safety aids, he must first be aware that they do exist.

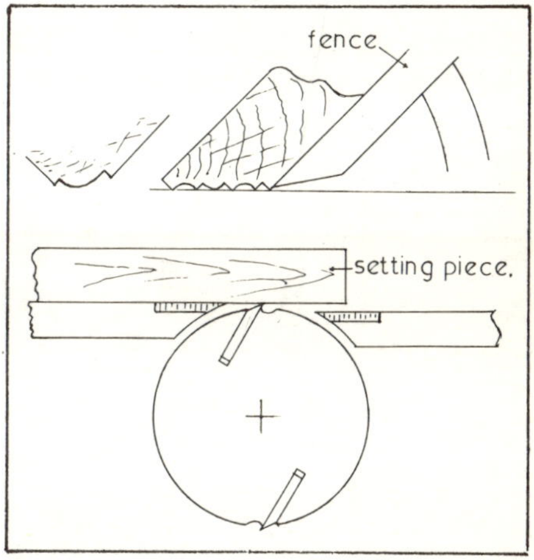

Moulding operations on the surface planer can be accomplished with a reducer cutter projection by canting the work with the aid of the adjustable fence. Setting the outgoing table (back table) with the aid of a straight edge.

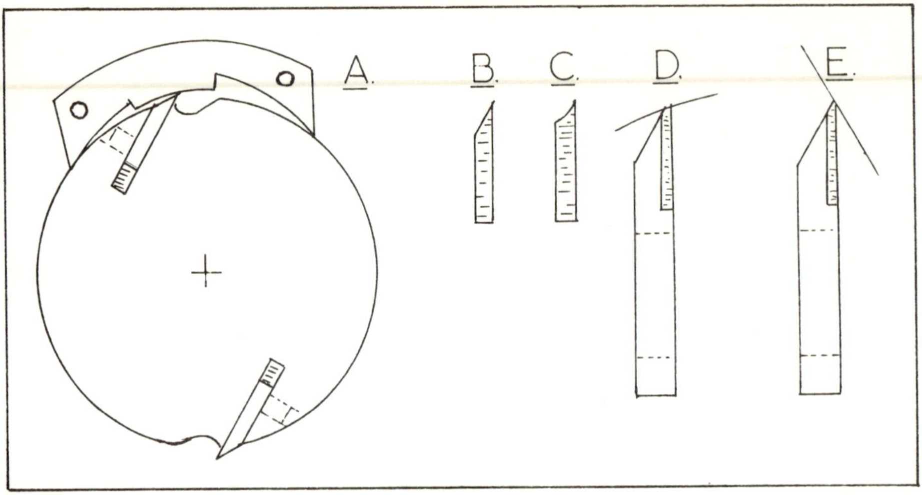

(A) Setting the cutter to correct projection with the aid of a manufacturers' gauge. A spring behind the seat of the cutter forces the edge against the machined surface of the gauge. The cutter is then clamped tight. (B) Straight ground cutter giving a strong edge. (C) Hollow ground cutter, giving a very sharp edge which is easily honed. (D) Effect of jointing cutters during rotation. The abrasive stone wears a heel on the cutter which should not be excessive. (E) A front bevel on the cutter decreases the approach angle, and gives a scraping action to the cut.

If the cut chips are taken around with the rotating block, a chip printing effect can occur on the surface of the planed timber.

Providing that the waste extraction system is in order, a slower feed speed may be required, or additional projection on the cutters will have an increased airflow effect which can clear the situation.

Most thicknessing machines have now setting aids for the cutters built into the structure. The alternative to this is to set the cutters to a prepared piece of timber positioned on the machine bed. The adjustable bed should be set to give a reading on the measurement scale to correspond to the thickness of the setting piece.

No further adjustment of the setting scale will then be necessary on the completion of the setting. For convenience, two setting pieces are often used, one at either end of the cutter.

On completion of the cutter setting, planed test pieces should be produced from various locations along the machine bed, and checked for uniformity of thickness.

Where a jointing attachment is fitted to a thicknesser it must not be regarded as a tool which permits careless setting of the cutters. If the jointing operation creates excessive heels on the cutters it limits the types of timber which can be planed.

Heat is generated with the denser types of material, and additional load is put on the machine bearings.

With correctly jointed cutters the feed speed of the timber can be increased. With a high standard of planed finish, sanding operations can on some types of work be eliminated.

Some thicknessing machines are fitted with blocks which have four cutters.

Unless these cutters are jointed, or ground on the block, it is unlikely that all four cutters will play a part in the finishing cut. A small amount of front bevel applied to the cutters when planing abrasive or erratic grained timbers really does help the process.

A stronger edge is formed to deal with the abrasive work, and a scraping action is created to deal with the erratic grained material.

General neglect of the machine is usually the cause of bad feeding. The bed rollers must be clean, the bearings lubricated, and the rollers must line with the table surface.

The feed rollers and pressure bars should line approximately with the circle described by the periphery of the cutters. The outgoing roller can be slightly below the cutting line to give grip, but if the adjacent pressure bar is also set down, this may cause an interruption in the feed flow.

On modern thicknessers, the feed rollers and pressure bars are easily accessible for adjustment purposes.

Frequent lubrication is advisable, and the bed table must be kept free from gum.

The amount of lubrication applied to the table surface may be governed by the type of work being processed. Some machinists apply tallow instead of oil for lubrication when the work must be kept as clean as possible.

The combined planer and thicknesser

The combined machine is very often preferred in the smaller type of woodworking units, or where floor area is limited.

The cutter block on a combination machine must be of the circular safety type as the material is hand-fed for surfacing operations. Due to the fact that many operations in addition to planing, such as rebating, bevelling, and limited moulding, can be done on the machine, it is in extensive use.

The feed rollers are usually of the solid type, not sectional, due to the limited space in which they have to be accommodated.

Cutters have usually to be set in relation to the surfacing tables due to accessibility. This means that the thicknessing scale may require to be adjusted after cutter setting. This is usually provided for. Bridge guard arrangements for the cutter block are similar to that of a surface planer. For thicknessing it is necessary to fit a hood over the cutter to convey the waste material.

Thicknessing machines turn out large quantities of waste in a very short time, and a collecting system of some kind is very necessary. Regulations sensibly state that the infeed roller must be suitably guarded, to prevent the operator coming into contact with it.

The thicknessing of short material is a point which requires some consideration. The two feed rollers are usually about 300 mm apart, from centre to centre. This means that if material shorter than this is fed into the machine, it will be propelled past the infeed roller and stop, having not reached the outfeed roller.

In a situation like this, more likely than not, the timber will be thrown out of the machine violently. The length of timbers being thicknessed should always be well in excess of the centre to centre measurement of the feed rollers.

Short material which has not been trued on a surface planer, should not be offered to the thicknessing machine. The danger is that it may spin out of line during feeding, with not very pleasant results.

If a quantity of shorts has to be thicknessed, of acceptable length, it is advisable to make a channel on the machine bed by fixing guide laths to prevent the timber from spinning out of line. En-

Comparative sketches of a thicknesser and a combined machine. The thicknesser has uninterrupted space above the bed table for the inclusion of large feed rollers, and jointing and grinding attachments. The combined machine involves more complication in design. Either square cutter blocks or circular can be used on thicknessing machines. The combined machine must have a circular block.

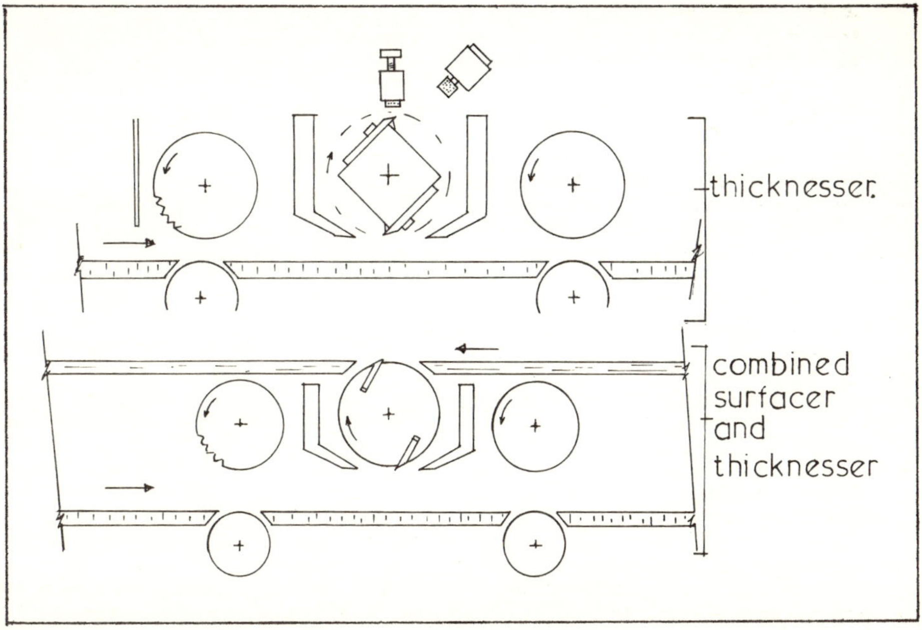

couraging results can be achieved in this way, providing the flow is continuous.

The finger feed surface planer

This machine is a surface planer which is automatically fed. It is capable of handling large quantities of preparatory work to pass on to machines such as the fourcutter, with a prepared face. Large tables are usually a feature of this machine, to enable accurate work to be obtained.

The overhead finger feed unit, which has almost a human touch, is power driven. The raising and lowering action of this unit is also power operated.

It is customary to have operators at both ends of the machine. Should a second pass be required on a workpiece, the timber is simply deposited on top of the finger unit, and it is conveyed back to the infeed operator.

Circular cutter blocks seem to be preferrred on the finger feed machine, although the general outline of the regulations suggest that other types could be used as it is not a hand-fed machine. A selection of feed speeds are usually available, to give the quality of finish required for either a preparatory surface, or a final one.

Planning work for mortising machines

The two principle methods of machine mortising are by the use of the hollow square chisel with rotating auger, and the cutting chain. Slot mortising is also used in some branches of the industry, in particular in conjunction with jig work on the high speed router. Machines using a reciprocating, and oscillating action on a cutting tool, are also favoured for some operations.
The most familiar type of mortising machine is the hollow chisel mortiser. The size of the chisels used start at ¼in. (6.4 mm) and go up to 1in. (25.4 mm) for general work.

Chisels with complete millimetres of dimension will not be any different in performance when they arrive, but they will assist the setter out and work planner using timber planed to metric dimensions.

Drive to the auger within the chisel can be directed from the motor shaft, the speed being about 2,800 rpm. Most mortising machines are fitted with an isolating switch plus an automatic contact which closes the circuit when the cutting unit is lowered towards the workpiece.

This ensures that the cutter is stationary when the components are being positioned in the machine.

Cramping of the work in the machine has in the past year been mainly by a hand operated screw. With the rapid development of pneumatics and their simplicity of application, many machines are being converted to use compressed air for the cramping operation.

Not all establishments favour pneumatic cramping on a mortising machine.

This is be cause they look upon a mortiser as a

Typical chain and chisel mortising machine driven by two individual motors. This type of machine is often described as the side by side model. Note the raising and lowering refinement to the cramping table, and the tool sharpening unit to the right of the machine.

An economical type of chain and chisel mortising machine found particularly in use in the smaller works unit. Drive is from one motor only, tool mounting heads being changeable.

basic training machine, and they are reluctant to involve an additional mechanically operated device. Pneumatic cramping is less fatiguing to the operator on long production runs, but it must be in charge of a person of some responsibility.

More advanced machines incorporate a system of hydraulic clamping of the work by oil under pressure.

The oil pressure is created within the machine, whereas compressed air is usually taken from an outside source.

The pressure face of the cramping shoe should be free from any sharp projections which will mark the timber. Such things as a fixing screw for the wood facing piece left in an unsatisfactory manner, could cause additional finishing work to be done on a large batch of work.

Some operators face the cramping shoe with rib-

Sharpening of hollow square mortise chisels can be done either by grinding on a revolving cone shaped stone, or with a sharpening tool fitted in a joiner's brace.

Mortise chain unit fitted to machine. Drive spindle runs anticlockwise. Chip breaker positioned for use.

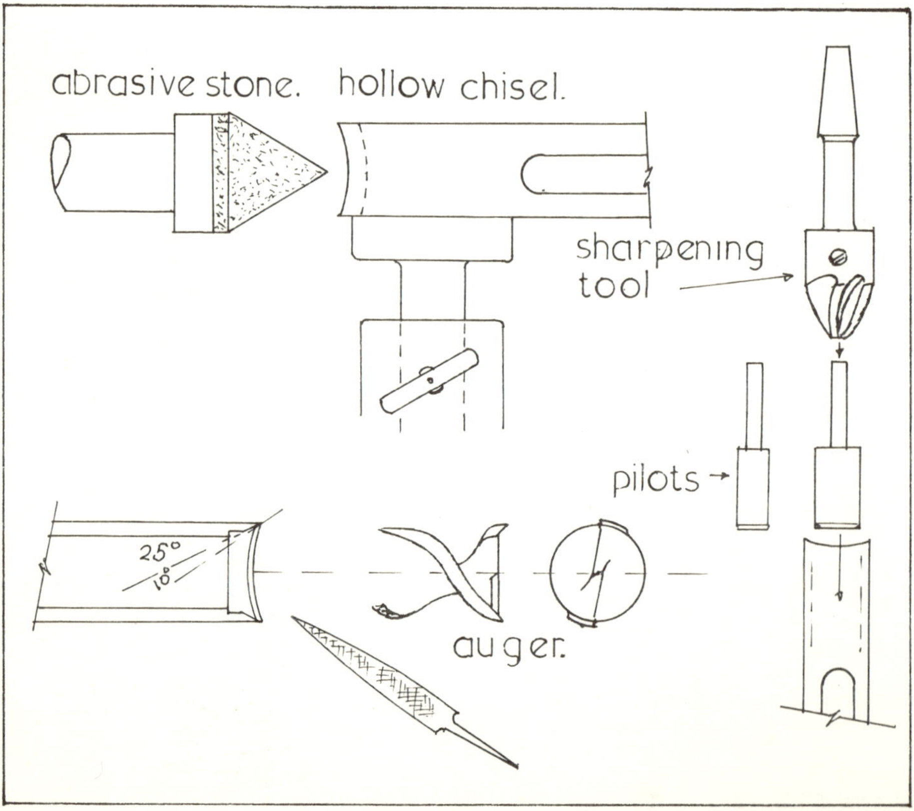

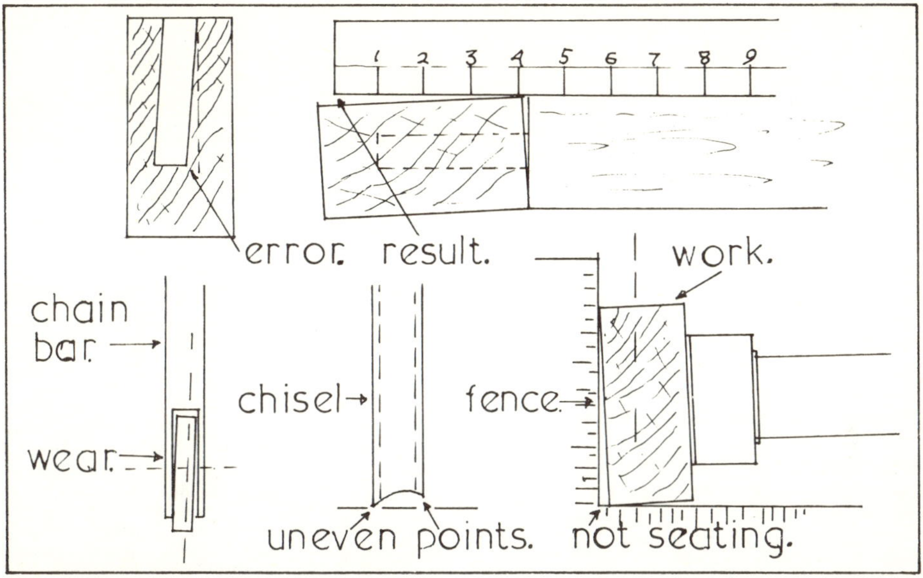

bed rubber; this gives additional grip and prevents damage. The upstand of fence and of the cramping table should also be kept clean and free from gum. A build-up of gum is not uncommon when chain mortising.

Whenever possible the workpiece should be in direct contact with the metal fence. If a wood packing is inserted this can be compressed by continuous cramping causing variations in the line of mortise.

Overnight shrinkage has also been noticed to cause variations when packings are used on machining operations.

Work cramped in the machine should always have an identifiable working face which must be in contact with the fence. The identification may not necessarily be a pencil mark. It could be a rebate of mould.

In some instances the mortise may be visibly out of centre, so deciding the working face for future operations. Marking should only be used as a last resort in repetition work, as opposed to one offs.

Wooden bed boards in the cramping table require to be renewed from time to time. A secondary board is usually applied if through chain mortising is to be carried out.

It is permissible to cut through in one operation using a chain, but not so a chisel and auger.

This is because a chain actually does cut its way through with a minimum of down pressure.

An auger in good condition will also cut its way

Mortise out of vertical is a common fault. Sketch shows the result on assembled framework, and some of the causes to check for.

Chisel unit fitted to machine. Cutting auger rotates clockwise. The chip breaker is raised clear as it is not required for square chisel working.

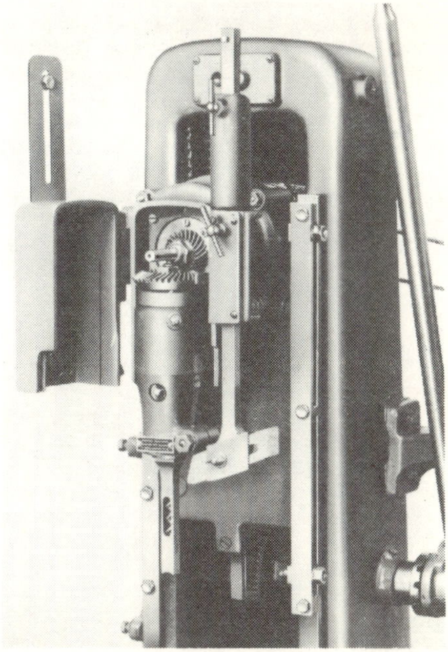

through, but the chisel is a pressure action. It is this pressure action and the varying degrees of sharpness of the cutting edge, that prevent chisel mortising to be carried through in one operation.

The work must be mortised to just over half the depth, then turned vertically over, not around, then completed.

Depth of cut can be controlled in two ways on some machines, on others only one method is available. All machines have an adjustable stop to control the vertical movement of the cutter head.

Some machines have a multiple device which permits a range of depths to be set, and bgought into operation quickly at the time of requirement. This is useful for mortising and applying the haunch depth.

The secondary adjustment for controlling depth is by the lowering of the cramping carriage by a screw action. Not all machines are fitted with this refinement. It is a useful asset as it can usually be adjusted without the aid of spanners, and set to a very fine degree.

The slides of the cramping table should be cleaned and adjusted periodically. Fluctuating accuracy standards in mortising can often be traced to undue slackness in the carriage slides. Lubrication should not be overlooked.

The hollow square chisel and auger

This cutting tool, when maintained in good condition, can produce a high standard of accuracy. Correct fitting in the machine is an important feature. The auger should always have advanced clearance from the chisel for two reasons.

It is important that the auger should cut before the chisel enters the timber. When working hardwoods it will be found that a little extra advancement of the auger will ease the force required to pull the chisel into the timber.

Projection clearance to the auger is also required to prevent the cutting section coming into contact with the chisel during rotation.

Hollow chisel manufacturers are concerned about this point, and suggest that the thrust bearing on the machine should be checked to see if there is any vertical play under load.

This vertical play can, in fact, go unnoticed, and may account for the short life of mortising gear on a particular machine.

Some types of timber put a heavy strain on mortise chisel gear, not so much the hardness of the material but due to the clogging action. Beech at some stages of moisture content is reluctant to rise up the rotating auger and be expelled.

When this occurs. chisels of the smaller sizes may split after only a short life. The development of a variety of twist patterns on augers gives some help to the problem, but a transfer to chain cutting is better if this is possible.

Mortising machine with oscillating cutting tool. Can produce very thin mortise slots if required.

Damage or bluntness to augers is confined to the cutting faces and side wings.

If these are not maintained in sharp condition the waste is torn from the timber instead of being cut, and this can encourage clogging within the chisel. The operation life of a chisel and auger is governed very much by the person in charge of it. The servicing of both the chisel and the auger is quite a simple operation once it has been practiced.

Chains are built up from links and are available in three sizes of pitch, 0.54in. (13.7 mm), 0.62in. (15.7 mm), 0.89in. (22.66 mm). These three sizes cater for the various grades of work required.

It is advisable to use the largest pitch which can be used for the operation, as durability is increased with the larger sizes. The finer chains are used for light joinery operations or cabinet work.

The minimum size of mortise obtainable with

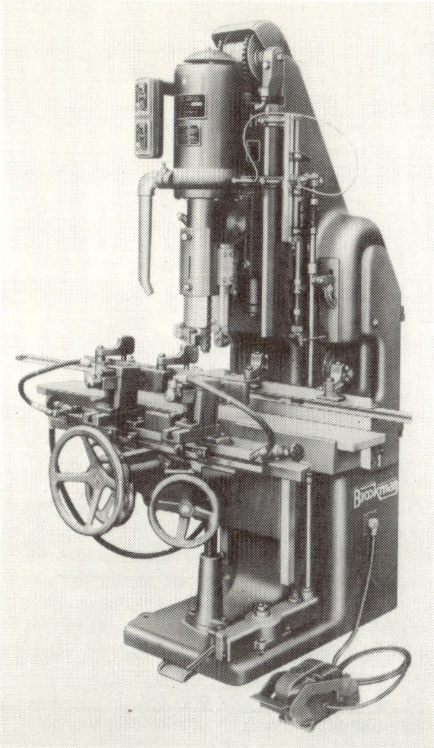

The Hydraulectric mortiser. Chain or chisel working can be done on this machine. The cutting head movement and cramps are hydraulically operated with an electronic device.

The Hydraulectric triple chain head mortiser. Cutting heads can be adjusted to suit mortise locations, and additional heads added if required.

standard equipment is $\frac{3}{16}$in. × $\frac{3}{4}$in., using the fine link chain. The medium pitch, and large pitch chains are used in various grades of joinery work. The length of the mortise determines which pitch to use for a particular operation.

The length of mortise cut obtainable can be varied within limits by the use of a selection of guide bars. When marking out for chain mortising in quantity, the width obtainable by a given bar and chain should be kept in mind.

If a cut can be made with only one insertion of the chain, a considerable amount of machining time may be saved by this planning. The increased cutting capacity is where a chain gains over the square chisel, and this should be exploited to the full.

The cramping carriage should not be traversed when the chain is within the cut to increase the length of the mortise. This puts an undue strain on the links due to clogging on the down stroke and if practised on the up stroke splitting on the surface will occur.

The chip breaker is an important unit in the chain mortising operation.

This prevents splintering as the cutting edges leave the work on the up stroke. The chip breaker shoe is usually made from hardwood, beech being very suitable. Some machinists laminate the shoe to improve the durability.

Care must be taken not to set the chip breaker too close, particularly when using the fine pitch chain, as it can cause link breakage if it has too great a surface of contact with the chain.

It is essential that a chain mortiser must be fitted with an efficient guard. It is also very important that the isolator switch should be in the off position when any fitting or adjustments are being made to the chain.

It is also good safety procedure to remove chains from mortising machines when they are not in constant use.

Sharpening facilities for mortise chains are usually in the form of attachments located at the side of the machine. Some woodworking units prefer the sharpening operation to be done within the tool room.

Only a very small amount of metal should be removed when sharpening with a rotating fine grit stone. The stone used is of the dished type and No. A60 MV usually 100 mm in diameter. Points to consider when sharpening. The angle of the tooth pitch must not be altered without good reason.

Some experienced machinists do experiment in this field when operating on large batches of a given species of timber. The grinding cut must not be taken down towards the pivot pins as this will weaken the linkage. The stone should be dressed to produce a ridge-free gullet on the chain, this will prevent the clogging of cut waste.

Driving sprockets require little attention, beyond the fact that the correct one must be used for the size of chain.

The roller bearing on the guide bar should be lubricated every 15 minutes during use. Wear in this bearing can cause the chain to tilt slightly under load and cut a mortise out of vertical. These bearings are replaceable by the manufacturers, who will also straighten the guide bars if so required.

It is customary to immerse chains in an oil bath when not in use. The bottom portion of the guide bars can also benefit from this treatment.

Breakages to mortise chains do occur during use. Repair procedure has been simplified to some extent by the use of purpose made kits supplied by machine manufacturers. These kits consist of an anvil and punches of various types, and a breaking fork.

A set is required for each of the three pitch sizes of chain to operate correctly. When ordering mortise chains it is customary to state the width required, the length of mortise to be made, and the machine make and model.

The suppliers stock chains in pitch sizes, and a given number of pitches in a particular chain. If the given number of pitches can be stated when ordering the goods stand a much better chance of being correct.

Spare links are available for repairing or extending chains, and it is good policy to obtain these along with a repair kit as they will be required. New links added to a used chain must be ground down to the same point of wear after insertion, or an immediate breakage may occur when the chain is put into use.

The hydraulectric morticer

This machine has been designed to increase operator output by the reduction of fatigue. Work is held by hydraulically operated clamps and the same pressure method operates the stroke of the cutting head. The hydraulic system which uses oil as a medium of transmission is built into the machine. The oil used under standard conditions is Mobil DTE Light.

No external services to the machine are required other than the electricity supply.

This simplifies installation and future locating, in addition to giving an all around clear working area.

The chains and chisels used are of the standard type, and can very often be interchanged with other types of mortising machines whithin the production unit. My personal experience on this

Alternative method used to prevent chip breaking of the workpiece on a machine which is fitted with vertical holding clamps, when chain mortising. (As fitted to the Hydraulectric mortiser.)

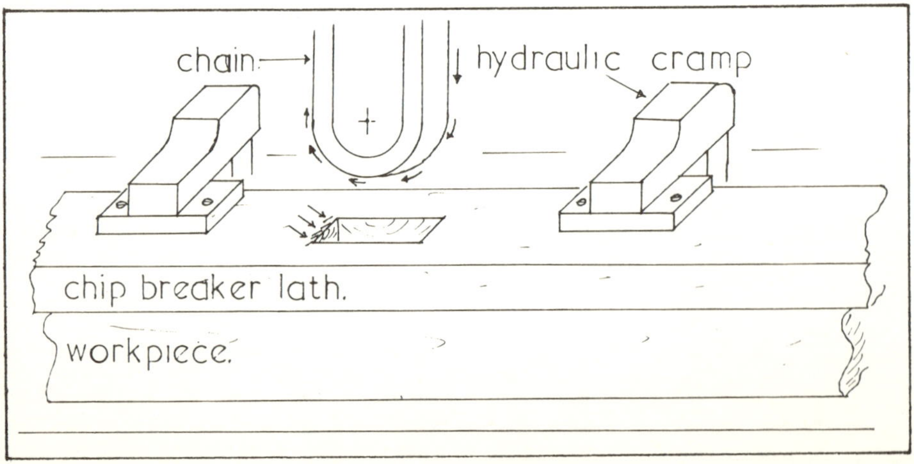

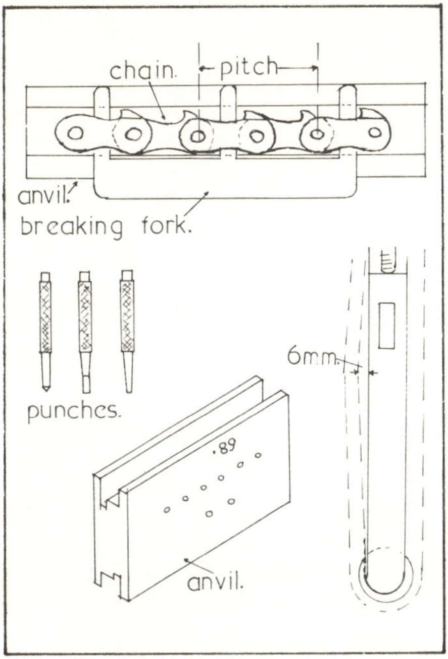

Mortise chain repair kits consist of an anvil, a breaking fork, and a set of three punches. A separate kit is required for each pitch of chain, three in all. Right: The chain should have 6 mm of slack when fitted ready for use.

Typical example where slot mortising can be done on a high speed router while the workpiece is positioned in a jig for a shaping operation.

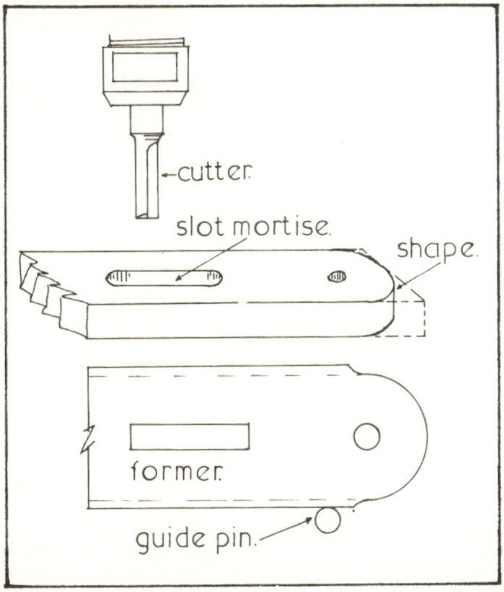

point whas that an additional bush had to be made for a square chisel to enable it to be interchangeable with a particular machine involved. A very small detail.

A variety of machines are available in this Brookman Hydraulectric range. They are, briefly, Chisel only, Chain and Chisel, and Multi-Head Machines.

The machine is foot controlled, which enables the operator to have his hands free for loading the work, and traversing the table movement. The depth of the cut can be regulated by the head stroke, and also the speed of penetration in relation to the work loading.

The clamping table can be raised and lowered, and this is particularly useful for the setter up. After provisionally setting the machine which is highly automatic, the clamping table can be lowered while a mock run is made.

Once the operator is satisfied, the table is raised to the required level and operated with confidence.

In addition to the holding cramps on the face of the work, overhead cramps are also provided. This method of overhead particularly useful due to items pressure is at the present time being made from wide sheet material which can be suitably held on in this manner.

Improvised cramping is usually resorted to when this refinement is not available, or the work transferred to router slotting. A much more fatiguing operation.

Sub-assembled items can also be mortised using the overhead clamps only. It is at times to advantage to assemble frames and apply further mortise work at the time of carcasing. This method cuts down handing, very often in the early stages of machining, and enables a more progressive flow.

The overhead cramps also permit an exclusive method of chip breaking to be used on chain mortising. A continuous clamp lath is screwed to the underside of the clamp heads, and the cutting chain completely penetrates this when making a cut.

In addition to chip breaking, chain whip is taken up within the depth of the lath instead of in the workpiece, and any excess lubrication is deposited on the upper surface of the lath leaving the work clean.

On the hydraulectric mortiser the cutting chain sprocket rotates clockwise. This can be considered natural, but it is opposite to the majority of other types of mortising machines. Mortising machine rotation has always been governed by the design of boring augers which require right hand rotation (clockwise). In a single motor

drive mortiser (not hydraulectric) the chisel requires the necessary gear train to convert the horizontal motor drive to vertical.

This decides, then, that the motor must run anti-clockwise.

The chain sprocket is directly attached to the motor spindle. It has one advantage over right hand rotation, that is, that the sprocket securing nut runs tight during use.

The hydraulectric machine, however, has a securing nut with a left handed thread to achieve the same object.

Although the hydraulectric mortiser is a sophisticated machine it is not bogged down with cupboards full of attachments which are very often more subject todeterioration in inefficient storage than in use. It is virtually complete within itself.

Comparative output over a hand cramp pull machine must be experienced to be appreciated. Productivity figures of three to five times the amount for full day working on a single head machine are not unrealistic.

When highly efficient mortising capacity is available production planning must be designed with this in mind. Mortising can be required as an essential part of framing construction.

It can also serve the purpose of component location on some assemblies. In modern flow production establishments the conventional joiners bench is almost now a museum piece as assemblies become mechanised. These assemblies can be speeded up with efficient preparation of components.

Mortises, as opposed to through grooves, reduce the complexity of framing assembly jigs.

Also, a slight alteration to positioning of a rail can be done at the machining stage without having to further educate the assembler.

To install a machine with increased output efficiency and have no all-round scheme for productivity gain could be a folly. The full use of a high production machine could be the incentive required to motivate the very often less productive assembly operations.

Well machined components also require a less highly trained type of operator on assembly making labour recruitment less selective.

Increased mortising capacity can also provide a service to other woodworking establishments in

View of hydraulic cramping table. Horizontal cramps can be removed and "parked" on the end of the work table without disconnecting pipes. This enables wide panel work to be mortised using the overhead cramps only.

the vicinity. This plant availability system which is used in other industries, can have attractive potentials both to the user and the supplier.
The user can work in larger batches than his establishment would otherwise permit. The supplier can exploit his overheads to the full by keeping his plant in operation, and may in some areas justify a grant or tax reduction for plant purchase.
Components for mortising in large quantities require to be accurately cut to a uniform length. This is so they can be positioned in the machine with the use of stops, usually affixed to the fence. It is only necessary to mark out one item, set to this, and keep it for periodical checking.
Having positioned the component in the traversing carriage the length of the mortise can be controlled by the carriage movement stops.
Several mortise lengths can usually be catered for within the set-up.
This, in many instances, enables all the mortising to be done on a component at the one handling. Mortise planing on large batches is important, relating to economic handling.
Repetitive mortising in the smaller establishment can also be carried out by positioning the components are cut to fit accurately in the jig.
Hand of items must always be kept in mind. of the mortises. Methods of this type are useful for short runs, a minimum of setting up time being required.
Re-occurring oddments can be mortised in this way without any marking out providing the components are cut to fit accurate in the jig.
Hands of items must always b kept in mind. Where pairs are required the machine stops have to be set for left and right hand working. This is most important where flush fitting surfaces are involved.
The involvement of the tenoning and scribing operation also requires a high standard of accuracy at the mortising stage.
Slot mortising is used in a variety of circumstances. It could be that it is the only mechanical means available in an establishment where woodworking is a fringe operation.
A component mounted in a jig for a shaping operation may also require a mortise. If this can be slot mortised while the component is already in the jig the operation may be well worth while.
Slot mortising can also be carried out on the router with the workpiece held against a wooden fence fitted with hinged stops to give location.
This method can be highly progressive, and very versatile but it is fatiguing if prolonged. Cutting can be done by left to right movement of the timber only, this pulls the work towards the fence.

Tenoning... single and double end machines

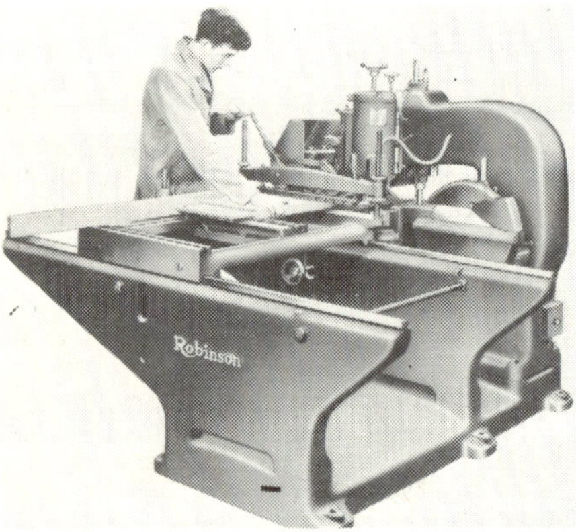

A swan neck pattern of tenoning machine. Work projecting beyond the width capacity of the cutters can be accommodated. Pneumatic clamping and table traversing can be fitted to this machine by the manufacturers. Capacity of the machine 600 mm x 150 mm.

A pillar type tenoning machine. In addition to the tenoning heads the machine has top and bottom scriber units and a crosscut saw. Can process timber up to 380 mm x 155 mm.

Although there are various layouts in tenoning machine design, the principles involved in the cutting operation, setting up, and general maintenance do not vary to any great extent.

There are exceptions to this statement where alternative approaches to the cutting operation have been made in an effort to produce a more economical form of machine suitable for the occasional or less demanding user.

Single end machines, those which process only one end of the timber at a pass through the cutting unit, are the most common type in use.

The call for double end tenoning machines has, however, increased due to closer standardisation of products relating to building joinery permitting longer runs of the component unit. Double end machines have many advantages over single enders other than increased productivity. Accuracy standards, versatility of operations, and adaptability to transfer line systems are some of these factors.

In constructional layout, single end machines are of two main types. These can be described as the pillar machine, and the swan neck pattern.

The pillar type is limited to the selection of operations it can carry out in addition to tenoning. These additional operations, however, may not be called for in some branches of the industry.

The swan neck machine allows work to pass which projects beyond the cutter units, such as shelf trenching operations or louvre slotting. This machine provides more scope for persons in training, and is favoured in establishments which have this in mind.

These increased uses within a production unit help with machine load planning, and can at times prevent build-ups of components awaiting processing.

The two essential cutter heads are those which form the tenon, although other cutting units are also to be found on modern production machines. Methods of vertical adjustment vary on the tenoning heads with different manufacturers, and this is a point an operator needs to make himself familiar with when encountering a machine new to him.

On some tenoners the vertical adjustment of the top and bottom heads are entirely independent of each other. The snag here is that a tenon of the correct thickness can be set for, but it may be positioned the wrong distance from the face of the timber. This means that both the heads have to be moved independently and the correct tenon thickness will most likely be lost in the process.

An advancement on the above arrangement is by means of introducing a link action between the head units. Under this system once the tenon thickness has been obtained, the link connection is made by the simple action of a lever, and both heads can be adjusted without losing the thickness set.

A third method of adjustment is to have a hand wheel to control the movement of the top head only, and another which controls the top and bottom heads permanently linked. Under this system the bottom head is usually set first to the approximate position. Tenon thickness is then obtained by adjusting the independent top head. Slight adjustment for face line can be made finally with the linked control which will not alter the thickness setting.

Most tenoning machines have locking screws or friction devices to prevent movement due to vibration which must be used, particularly on quantity working.

The action of gravity encourages the heads to creep downwards, particularly under conditions of ill balance or cutters which require their cutting edges servicing.

Material being tenoned should always be positioned with its working face down to the machine table, just as mortising is carried out with the working face to the cramping table fence. Mortising should always precede tenoning, as the tenon thickness can be varied, not so the mortise opening.

In addition to vertical adjustment on the tenoning heads, lateral (left to right) adjustment is also available. This enables shoulders of unequal length to be obtained to give complete intersection when framing rebated stock. The amount of offset must be checked to suit any preformed rebate, just as the cutter heads must be checked for line when long and short shoulders are not required.

Tenoning heads usually run at a speed of about 2,800 rpm. Due to the fact that they describe a circle of relatively large diameter, compared to planing machines they can produce an ideal gluing surface at this speed of rotation to the surfaces of the tenon.

Slightly hollow ground cutters are preferable to minimise impact, particularly on tenons of the thinner dimension which are subject to vibration. The cutter mounting blocks are designed to produce a shearing cut on the timber. Cutter seatings will be found to be nearer the axis of rotation at one end of the block than at the other.

For this reason the cutter edge is not straight, it has convex curvature. Present-day machines in general tend to have less curvature than those of the past. This is probably due to experimentation which has, indeed, taken place of recent years in block design and cutter positioning relating to the approach angle of cut. A grinding template should be kept at hand regarding the edge profile of the cutters, this is usually available from the machine manufacturers, or it can be obtained geometrically if relative data can be taken from the block.

A set of cutters consists of two left hand, and

A double end tenoning and scribing machine.

two right hand, as the heads run in opposite directions. Some machines which are designed for producing long tenons have the cutters built up in length in two parts. This spreads the impact load, as their positioning is staggered around the cutting circle.

This method has also the advantage that on occasions, only the outer cutters may need regrinding if short tenon work has been continuously produced.

The shoulder cutters or spurrs, as they are often called, are mounted on the outside face of the tenoning blocks. Their purpose is to cut slightly in advance of the tenoning cutters. They should not project more than 0.5 mm in excess of the circle described by the tenoning cutters. The amount of projection can be governed by two factors. The rate of the stock feed, and the thickness of the tenons being produced.

If a machine has been set for the production of tenons, say, 20 mm in thickness, and a change over to 6 mm is required, it may well be necessary to check and reset the shoulder cutters for projection to obtain maximum strength adjoining the shoulder.

If the tenoning cutters project beyond the face of the shoulder cutters, ragged shoulders will result. It is also important that the shoulder cutters have the necessary tilt to minimise friction. Burn marks on the tenon shoulders will indicate that either grinding or setting of the shoulder cutters is at fault. The shoulder cutters have a considerable amount of work to do, and as much of the cutting edge of the spurr as possible should be involved.

The Multico tenoner. Designed with economy of floor space, and cost in mind. Adjustments on the machine provide for all the standard tenoning operations. Shoulder scribing is possible with suitably shaped cutters. With a preset range of cutter heads in the tool room, a machine of this design could carry out a variety of operations with a minimum of setting time.

Sash corner lock joint. Produced by using the tenoning heads, scribing cutters, and combing saws.

The setting of cutters on the tenoning blocks has usually to be in relation to the shoulder cutters. If the tenoning cutters are set with unreasonable projection, either over or under, it will be found that the shoulder cutters will not locate just as they should. It is good policy to note and record the radius of the cutting circle described by the shoulder irons or cutters to aid future setting. Some machinists keep a setting piece which resembles a tenoned workpiece of generous dimension for positioning the cutters to with a minimum of frustration.

It must always be kept in mind that very often a machinist on the shop floor is under pressure to get his production unit into operation.

Any rapid setting aid he can devise is a welcome asset. Tool room setting of tenoning heads as in the larger works unit is to advantage if a replacement set is available for pre-setting. This is a point worth considering by management.

Scribing heads on a tenoning machine not only increase its potential of operation scope, but very often are an aid to produce a joint superior to that done by other methods. Through scribes, as machine formations are termed, have better weathering qualities than mitres or chopped-in scribes. It must, however, be pointed out that moulded sections must be suitably designed to enable through scribing to be possible without coming into contact with the tenon line.

Various types of tenons used in framing which machines are called upon to produce.

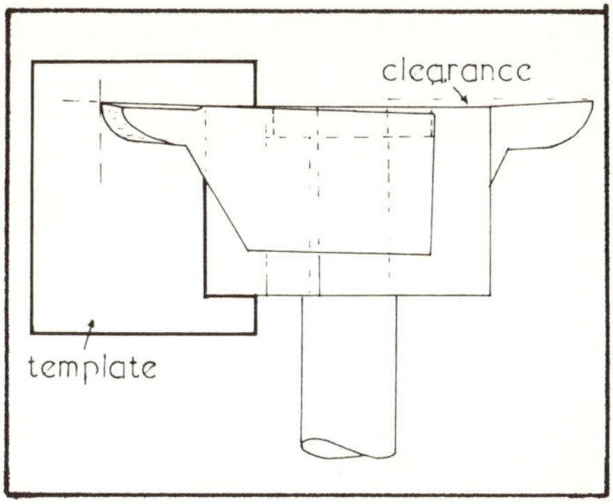

Positioning cutters on the scribing head. Note the template as a setting aid.

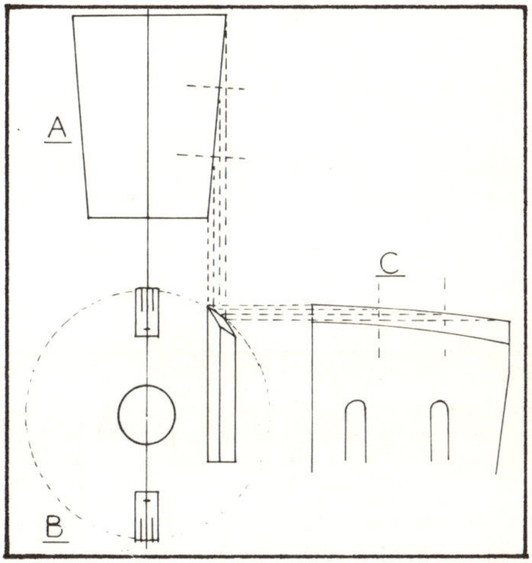

Basic procedure for developing the tenoning cutter shape. 'A': Cutter head seatings. 'B': Cutting circle. 'C': Cutter shape required.

Instances do occur in some branches of the industry where dowels are used in preference to a mortise and tenon, but the rail ends are scribed on the tenoning machine. This method permits a wider scope of mould formation, but still makes through scribing possible.

When rails are to be scribed on a tenoning machine, it is preferable that the tenoning and scribing is done before the rails have any moulding profile applied. In this way the material can be backed up with a flat piece of timber to prevent spelching as the scribing cutters leave the timber. Very often, however, when working in quantity using stock prepared moulded sections, profiles have been already applied. The most efficient method possible in these circumstances is to prepare a shaped backing piece which acts as a saddle to prevent the spelching. This backing piece can, in fact, be moulded on the tenoning machine using the scribing cutters which will produce the profile required.

It is preferable that the shaped backing piece should be made from hardwood to increase its lasting qualities and give firm support. It will be found that if the following points are considered, spelching will be reduced when the use of packing pieces is not economically possible as in the case of double end machines on large production runs of moulded stock.

Vibration on the machine must be reduced to a minimum, this means all cutters in balance. Scribing cutters must be hollow ground, kept

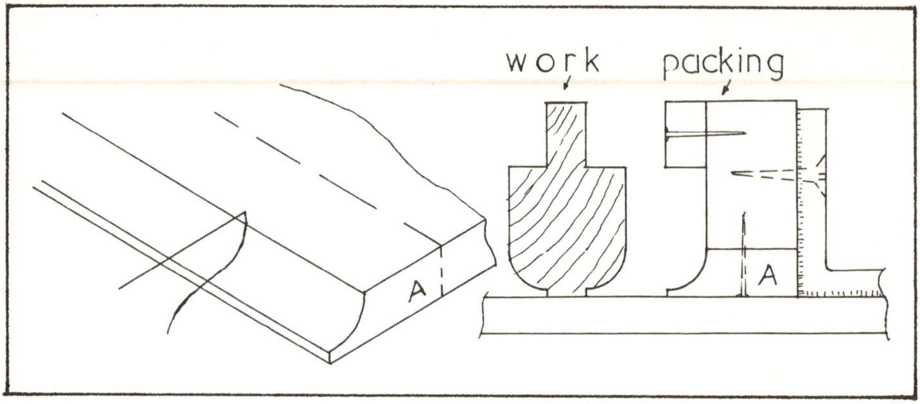

The application of a built up packing, or backing piece, which is used to prevent spelching when tenoning and scribing moulded stock. Part 'A' can be prepared on the scribing head, using a wide piece of material and cutting to width afterwards.

sharp, and free from heels. Large diameter of cutting circle, 125 mm square block will give better results than a 75 mm block due to the fact that the peripheral speed is increased, and the cutters leave the workpiece in a more gradual manner due to the increased radius. A constant feed speed of the timber past the scribing cutters will also help to reduce spelching if the other factors are all considered.

Scribing heads are usually fitted to both the top and bottom tenoning assemblies. This means that they have opposite directions of rotation requiring cutters of suitable hand. The cutters are mounted on the blocks with a slight tilt for the scribing operation to prevent friction between the surface of the block and the faces of the tenon.

The profile of the scribing cutter is, generally speaking, the opposite to that of the moulding machine cutter. A small difference is created due to the necessary tilt and the diameter of the respective cutting circles involved.

Due to this close relationship between the moulding cutters and the scribers, it is not generally considered necessary at shop floor level to plot scribing cutter shapes as probably a more accurate result can be obtained by matching.

A setting template for positioning the scribing cutters on the block is essential, and if it includes a projection scale it can be used to advantage. Let us assume that the cutters have been mounted on the block, a trial run has been made and it is found necessary to remove the cutters to correct an error. If the positioning is marked on the setting template, the cutters can be refitted in a similar position, and no major adjustments will be necessary to the machine.

The scribing head assemblies also play an important part in the forming of combed joints used particularly in window sashes of the storm-proof type which do not lend themselves well to mortise and tenon joints. Much of the timber is cut away by the external rebate on this type of sash and a combed joint secured with a moisture resisting adhesive is standard practice.

Prepared cutter heads in the form of insert tooth plate saws are available for this operation which requires no hand work, all formations being done on the machine. Scribing heads could also be used to a limited extent for the cutting of finger joints, a method developed during recent years for jointing timber in a linear manner. This method eliminates waste, and is also used for the building up of laminates for beam construction where a more powerful cutting unit is introduced.

On single end tenoners the cut off saw is usually situated at the rear of the machine. The safety aspect is good with the saw so located, but a saw positioned at the front of the machine will probably be utilised more for square cutting operations. The saw mounting has usually lateral movement only, this enables prepared tenons to be cut off at the required length while still positioned in the machine.

The saw can be used for square or angle cutting of material. Saws used are of the plate type, although hollow ground can be used for fine squaring operations providing the carriage line and the saw mounting are in relation to one another.

The table on the tenoning machine as an adjustable fence and stop devices for positioning the timber. The fence can usually be adjusted out of square in one direction only. This is not very helpful when splay shoulders are required at both ends of a door rail, and face down working has to be maintained.

The problem is overcome by preparing a splayed packing piece to insert between the fence in its square position and the workpiece. Reversing of the packing, end for end, will give the necessary splayed location in an identical left and right hand manner.

The table on a tenoning machine is usually hand operated, including the cramping of the work. Compressed air adaptions are favoured by some both for the cramping and propulsion of the table. These adaptions could be described as an aid to bridge the gap between a single end machine and a double ender.

Their aim is to reduce fatigue of the operator, which can be considerable on long production runs.

On a purely hand operated single end tenoning machine, a hard working operator may actually be cutting tenons for only 25 per cent. of his working time due to loading, feeding, returning, and stacking. A look at operational efficiency, and labour utilisation may be the means of justifying the introduction of a double end machine into an establishment.

Many of the technicalities of a single end machine apply to the double end tenoner. One of the attractive factors of the double ender is that it is power fed. The stock travels in one direction only. It is continuously progressive. Both ends of the workpiece can be processed at the one pass through the machine.

The cut off saws on this type of machine are at the front, and these can be used simply for squaring material to length only if desired. In addition to vertical and lateral movement the saws can be tilted to an angle, usually up to 45 deg. This can be used for cutting mitres, and some machines have reverse rotation of the saws to enable a cleaner cut to be made for this particular operation.

A type of saw known as a hogging saw is commonly used on this machine which breaks up the offcut waste on such items as wide chipboard panels in the process of squaring to length. Failure to get rid of such waste at this stage can cause clogging in the machine or interruption of the feed altogether.

The tenoning heads can be tilted to about 15 deg. on standard type of machines which per-

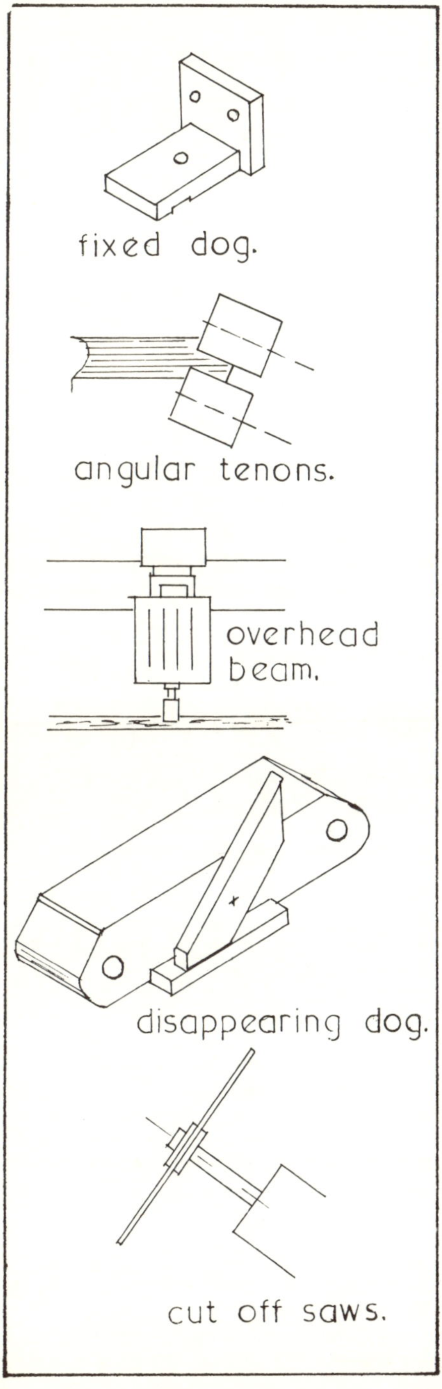

Sketch details relating to the double end tenoner.

mits the formation of angular tenons which are particularly applicable to rails in chair construction, and other operations of this nature. Other adjustments on the tenoning heads are much the same as on the single end machine regarding movement, and the top and bottom head linkage.

The scribing heads on a double end machine can be put to a much greater variety of operations than those of a single end machine. Framed work can be rebated and moulded with the scribing heads, and taken to a constant overall width. The term 'cope heads', is often quoted when referring to these cutting units when they are to be used for purposes other than scribing. Although it is customary for these heads to run at about 3,000 rpm, some manufacturers introduce a frequency changer and increase the rotation to 6,000 rpm if the machine is to be used for a considerable amount of moulded work.

Scribing heads can usually be canted; this increases their use and makes it possible to apply, say, a slight bevel to a door edge using a block set for square work.

With planning, a double end tenoner need hardly ever be standing waiting for work in a busy establishment as it can be put to a large variety of uses in addition to the traditional tenoning operation. Many machinists carry out the haunching operation on tenoned rails on this machine when their sectional dimension is such as that they can be fed through the chain track stood on edge, perhaps several in a bunch. It is advisable to haunch first, then tenon on the secondary run through. In this way splintering is less likely on the tenon.

Work laid on the travelling chain is propelled forward by projecting arms known as dogs. These dogs can be of various types according to the nature of the work being processed. An important point is that the work must be fed squarely into the machine. The dogs must locate the work at right angles to the line of flow.

Facilities are usually provided for checking and adjusting to obtain the square infeed. Some types of dogs include an adjustment arrangement for this purpose as an alternative to slipping the chain. Dogs may also be of the disappearing type which permit wide material to be fed without disrupting the set up of the chain for general work.

The work is held down on to the chain by a rubber faced caterpillar-type track. This track is not power driven, and requires to be adjusted to obtain holding pressure on the work. Failure to apply this pressure can put an operator in danger from a throw back, but experience has shown that the cut-off saws usually give an early warning before the cutters are reached in cases where insufficient pressure has been applied.

A positioning fence is located at the infeed of the machine, usually on the left of the operator. Work is positioned with its end against the fence as the dogs take up drive. The use of this fence is extremely important when work has to make more than one pass through the machine as in the case of a haunching then tenoning, which requires identical location at the second pass.

The taker-off at the outgoing end must also stack his components methodically so that they can be fed through the second run correctly positioned.

Side pressure units are available which assist the operator to ensure that the work is held to the fence at the infeed to the machine.

An advance on the basic double end tenoning machine is the introduction of the overhead beam. This permits the mounting of additional cutter heads to form mainly trenching or recessing details, as the work passes through the machine. The heads usually take the form of a high speed router unit which can be permanently in contact with the flowing stock or controlled mechanically to make cuts as required.

With the availability of such an addition as the overhead beam in an establishment, constructional planning of repetition production must take into consideration its capabilities and design around it. In this way maximum efficiency can be obtained.

On a double end tenoner the right hand pillar unit is usually fixed to the main bed of the machine and the left hand pillar is adjustable to shoulder or component width. The movement of the left hand unit is power operated, and an indicator setting scale is usually provided to assist in the positioning. Final trimming is by hand wheel, and in this way a high degree of accuracy can be obtained.

Hand and automatic woodworking lathes

A compact lathe with a range of speeds from 425 to 2,300 rpm. Designed to meet the requirement of schools and other training establishments.

One of the smaller type of lathe made by this manufacturer, but it has most of the features of the larger machines. The travelling tool holder has compound movement. The range of speeds are from 400 to 2,400 rpm. Distance from the centre point to the bed is 152 mm. (Dominion Machinery, Hipperholme, Halifax.) Designed with the educational field in mind.

On wood turning lathes where the cutting tool is controlled by hand a considerable amount of skill is required to become an efficient operator.

Trained persons of this type are few in number compared to operators on other woodworking machines, but there are many who are involved in a small way, and are capable of producing work to their requirement standard.

As the wood revolves and the tool remains stationary, just the opposite to other woodworking machines, it is comparatively a safe machine to use.

For this reason many people have used a lathe either in a course of training, or as an exercise in the development of general skills.

Working on a lathe does give a person the opportunity to express himself in a creative way, under suitable circumstances. Results produced too, reflect back some of the capabilities of the operator regarding his artistic abilities and methodical neatness.

Some knowledge of the characteristics, and use of timber is required before an operator can become all round efficient. Some timbers lend themselves better to turning than others.

Moisture content of the material can play an important part. The application and suitability of adhesives in the use of built up work.

Cutting methods relating to working on the face of the wood grain, as compared to working on the side or the end. An understanding of these facts and others are necessary to obtain safe and successful working, and produce finished articles with a minimum of wastage.

Many of the older lathes were driven from overhead line shafts, complete with stepped pulleys, very much in evidence. Some of these older machines can still be seen in country areas where bygones are a feature of the commerical set up.

Stepped pulleys are still retained in most present-day lathes, but the drive is from an electric motor usually situated in the base of the machine. The pulley system provides a selection of rotation speeds to the stock drive.

This selection is necessary due to the work being of varying diameters.

Also when work is first mounted in the machine it may be considerably out of balance, large diameter items being the most critical. Speeds available on woodturning lathes generally are from 200 rpm up to 3,000 rpm. Work of large diameter is run at the lower rpm and small diameter at the higher speeds.

Under this arrangement the chisel is in contact with a periphery which is travelling at the most

Heavy duty lathe which is available with a selection of lengths of bed. Well equipped to carry out unlimited types of work. A section of the bed can be removed to increase the diameter capacity of face plate working.

A work steady. An alternative to fitting a wooden back stay to support slender work. The top half of the steady is hinged to permit admittance of the work. (Wadkin).

A tailstock unit with screw controlled adjustment for offsetting to produce tapered work in conjunction with a travelling tool holder. (Wadkin).

suitable speed, i.e. in metres per second, irrespective of the work diameter.

Too great a speed on some items can create a danger of the work breaking up, and also the cutting tool may become overheated shortening its life.

Care should be taken in the action of changing speed if this is done with the work rotating. An

An automatic lathe for producing turned work in quantity by rotary cutting action. Work up to 36in. in length can be accommodated in this type of machine, making it suitable for most domestic furniture and joinery requirements. (W. A. Fell, Windermere).

An automatic lathe designed for boring turned items. The stock is rotated at high speed, and the boring bit is fed into the timber by pneumatic pressure. (W. A. Fell, Windermere).

increase in speed will tighten up a screwed on face plate, a sudden decrease will tend to do the opposite. Some lathes are designed to change rotation the introduction of keying should be considered in many cases.

The change here is almost instantaneous on the drive shaft, but a heavily laden face plate will endeavour to maintain its original speed for a period, and a rotor decrease can cause the plate to screw off.

This rule applies to all threaded shafts carrying loads. If speeds are to be changed during

A copying lathe for producing articles of irregular shape. Four items can be in the process of shaping at the same time with this model. Profile is obtained from a master item. (W. A. Fell, Winderemere).

rotation the introduction of kehing should be considered in many cases.

The main parts of the lathe on the smaller type of machine are mounted on the machine bed. On the larger machines the headstock or drive unit is usually connected to the bed which in turn supports the movable tailstock unit.

A section of the bed adjoining the headstock is on some machines removable to provide a gap which permits face plate work of greater diameter to be carried out than otherwise would be.

Larger work still can be processed on a face plate fixed on the outside of the headstock. The face plate thread on the outside of the machine is left handed, as opposed to right hand on the inside face plates.

The tool support for general work is secured by cam action to the lathe bed. Various lengths of support bars are available, and these can be adjusted for height to permit either a cutting or scraping action to be obtained by the tool.

An alternative to the fixed tool support is the travelling slide carriage.

This permits a tool to be gripped within the unit at the required angle, and traversed between the head and tailstock by screw action. In addition to the traversing movement the tool can be control fed into the work.

With the slide carriage, such items as tapered legs can be quickly produced with a minimum of skill. This is made possible by an adjustment on the tailstock which provides movement to put the tailstock centre out of line with that of the headstock.

For a leg to be tapered from 45 mm to 25 mm, the tailstock would be offset 10 mm.

Tailstock are usually designed to take Morse taper centres, and the centres can very often be automatically ejected with the adjustment wheel in its fully wound in position.

The centres or poppets as they are known can simply be plain, or with rotating supports which eliminate friction between the support and the workpiece. Plain centres require lubrication and constant observation.

Rotation of the work can either be with the aid of chucks or the face plate method according to the type of operation. The chucks can be of various types the four pronged type being the one in general use.

The size of the drive chucks must be less than that of the cross section of the work to prevent any contact with the cutting tools during operation.

Three jaw self centring scroll chucks can be

Working on the face plate. A wooden bowl in the final stages of turning.

Turning a tapered leg using the slide carriage, and the tail stock positioned off centre.

Work mounted between centres. Lamp standard stem in the process of turning.

Mouldings with a small radius of curvature can be prepared on the lathe by face plate working.

used on a woodturning lathe, this is the pattern adopted from metal turning machines.

These chucks are very versatile, being capable of inside or outside gripping of the work by using the appropriate jaws. Twist drills can also be mounted in this type of chuck as an aid to a boring set up.

Face plates are used for the mounting of block type work which can be of a substantial area. The size of the face plate selected should be as large as possible without projecting outside the work. The plates are bored for wood screws to secure the work at several distances from the centre.

The holes towards the outside are the most effective, and these should be used where possible, considering the thickness of material for screwing in the finished article.

If a piece of work is removed from a face plate in a near finished state and it is to be returned, it is advisable to mark the positioning on that particular plate so that rotation about the same centre will be maintained.

Heavy gauge wood screws should be used in keeping with the size of the workpiece, and they should be checked periodically for grip.

This checking particularly applies to occasions when the work has been subjected to a sudden jar, such as a chisel being incorrectly applied or other form of additional stress.

Mouldings having a small diameter of curvature can be produced by face plate working on the lathe. An additional wooden face piece must be prepared for fixing to the metal face plate.

The workpiece for moulding is screwed to this, from behind, then the whole lot screwed to the face plate.

Turning of the circular moulding can then commence, and it is not a long operation once the preparation has been done.

Tools used are either of the long handled variety

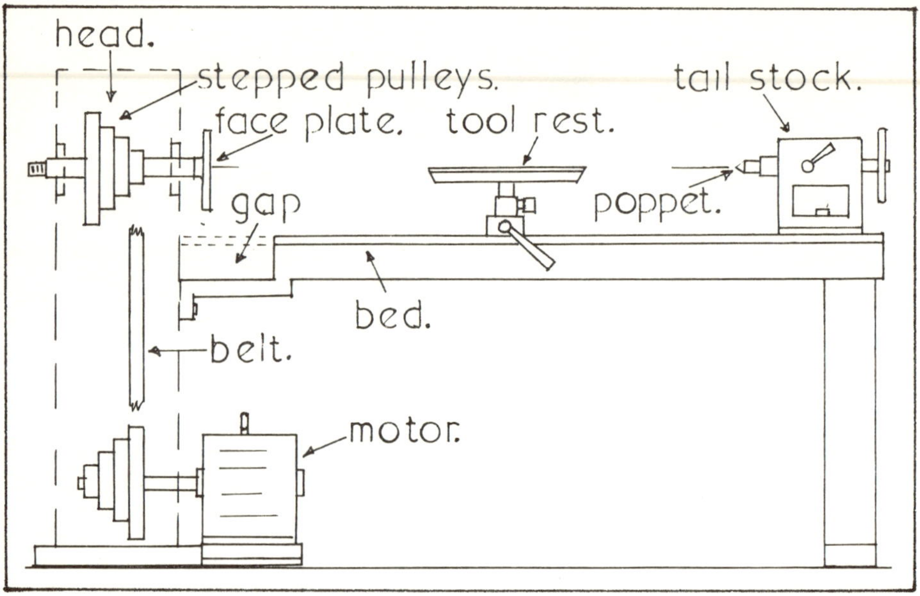

Line drawing naming the various parts of a wood-turning lathe. Pulleys and driving belt are usually fully enclosed on modern machines. These may be either flat or of the Vee type.

which provide a good grip, or of all metal stubbs for mounting in the travelling carriage. The shape of the tools depends upon the nature of the work in hand. Strong gouges are used for roughing the material into shape prior to the finer operations.

Round end chisels are favoured for hollowing out work on the face plate as they are less likely to catch in than others. The widest chisel possible should be used for this operation to give rigidity and prevent chatter.

Straight and skew chisels are used for levelling and shaping convex curves. Concave shapes should be formed with tools preferably slightly less in radius of curvature than the finish required.

This enables movement of the tool to provide down grain cutting.

Parting tools are used for cutting away or dividing finished work. When working between centres a cutting action should be aimed at rather than a scraping one.

This is both kinder to the tool and the work, giving a superior finish. Scraping tends to cut away the softer grain and leave the hard out-standing. Chisels are bevelled on both faces to aid the cutting action when offered to the work at a suitable angle.

When turning slender material between centres, it is good policy to do the light detail work first to maintain as much strength for as long as possible. Instances do occur when the work requires to be supported to reduce vibration.

The support generally termed, a back stay, can either be a wood arrangement made by the machinist, or an engineering metal one available from machine manufacturers.

Additional skill is required to carry out work of this nature and produce results, but the work can be speeded up with the aid of a support in the hands of an experienced user.

Callipers are a tool required for checking diameters during the turning operation. Inside and outside callipers are part of the standard kit required. Screw controlled types are capable of finer adjustment than the purely friction type. More than one pair is recommended. One can be set slightly over size, and another to finished dimension.

Marking out methods can depend on whether the turning is a one off, or it has to be repeated. One of the skills in turning is to be able to produce a quantity of items as near identical as possible.

It may however be able to group completed turnings into sets of, say, twos or fours, in accordance to how they are to be used. Grain and colour has often in any case to be considered in the final matching for polished work.

When working betweeh centres it is

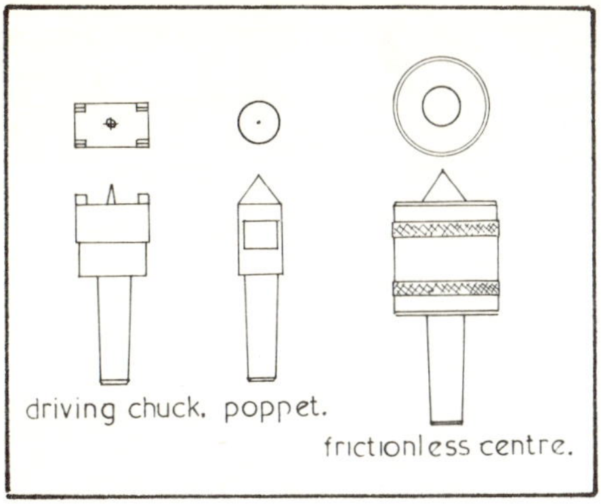

Mounting devices used when working between centres. Driving chucks require prongs to rotate the work. These are available in a variety of sizes. Poppets, and frictionless centres are used in the tailstock.

necessary to draw diagonal lines across the ends of the stock to determine the positioning of the centre.

It is preferable that the centre is found before any corner waste is cut away or the true positioning may be lost and an undersized article produced. Once the stock has been turned into a true cylinder of acceptable dimension it can be marked out for further working.

For repetition working the marking can be done by scoring with nail points positioned in a setting out stick. It may then be convenient to turn in a series of steps first to obtain correct diameters at various points, then apply shaping as required.

Following a set sequence is one of the key points of speedy repetition. If sandpaper is used in the finishing, care must be taken not to destroy the sharp corners, the changes in profile should be definite.

When gluing timber for built up turning in the lathe, the following points could be of interest. The timber should be reasonably free from moisture, not higher than 12 per cent for many operations. Heat is generated while working, particularly in the sanding operation, and this can cause fractures due to local shrinkage.

Surfaces prepared for fabrication should be flat, not depending on a great amount of pressure to close the joint.

Components coated with hot animal glue will bond together for the smaller type of work without clamp pressure. Synthetic resin adhesives in the main require pressure to bond the joint.

For timbers used in multi-colour build ups, adhesive setting hardeners must be kept away from contact with metal to prevent staining of the decorative woods.

Glass or plastic containers should be used for mixing the adhesive.

Examine fabricated work on mounting in the late, and run at low speed initially. It is also advisable to make a habit of standing clear of the line of destruction when switching on the machine.

Hardwood items can be polished in the lathe during rotation by the use of carnauba wax, or other manufactured preparations. A thin coat of light french polish should be applied first to seal the grain, with the machine stopped.

The wax is then applied by moving the block over the work while rotating. Buffing is then done with a soft duster until a high gloss is obtained.

A good surface must be prepared on the work before the wax is applied, as the coating must be very thin or chipping may occur during future service.

A specially prepared friction polisy for use in the lathe is Speedaneez, obtainable from the maker, Thomas Pavitt and Sons, Old Street, London. It is applied in much the same way as carnauba wax.

Turned items can be produced on the lathe, and later fluted on the spindle moulder with the aid of a jig. This produces a highly decorative type of item.

Competition within the woodworking industry may eventually create a turn towards increased use of the lathe in conjunction with other machines. Domestic joinery is now running very close to furniture in design which offers scope to the introduction of turned work suitably applied.

The subject of cost in high repetition work could probably be catered for with greater use of automatic types of lathes.

These machines are operated by only a small fraction of woodworking establishments who supply furniture makers, tool manufacturers, and industrial requirements. A sudden demand for this type of machine could take place if turned goods became a requirement on entry to the Common Market.

Many of the turned items in use today are the products of automatic lathes. These machines can turn out the work in a fraction of the time of that of a hand tool machine.

They have also the advantage of being able to produce identical profiles in quantity without any additional effort.

Machines of this type are designed with the production of a defined range of items in mind. Efforts are then concentrated in the design to be able to produce the work quickly and of an acceptable standard.

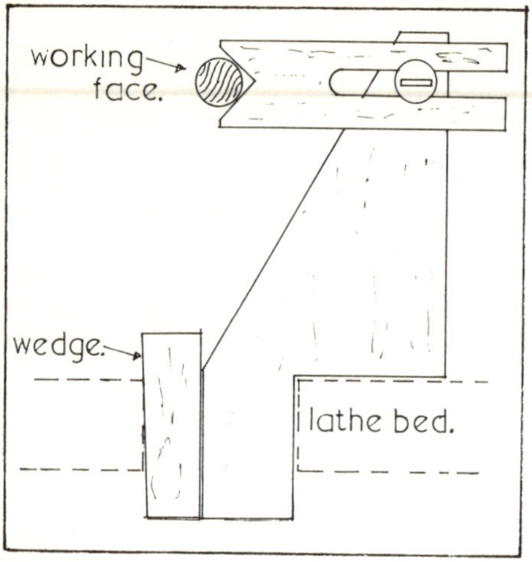

A wooden stay for giving back support to slender work. Metal versions of support stays known as steadys are also available.

The century old firm of W. A. Fell, situated in the Lake District, produce a large range of automatic lathes and equipment for which they are known throughout the world.
The basic principal as used in automatic lathes for rapid production, is that the work is fed into rotating cutters which have been prepared to produce the required shape.
While the work is in contact with the cutting unit it is rotated, either in a circular movement, or as the finished profile requires. Some items require to be oval in shape as in the case of hammer handles and other tools, to produce grip to the user.
The cutter units are built up with cutter mounting sleeves and mounting plates, the latter sometimes having to be considerable in diameter to cope with the variations in dimensions involved in a product.
Cutter plates are catalogued with diameters up to 14 inches. The manufacturers produce cutter sets for making the required items, these have to be balanced in keeping with the speed of rotation.
To set up the cutters in a tool room a setting stand is required in order to get balanced projections, and relation between the various cutters involved to produce the profile.
Shear cutting is favoured for this type of work to lessen the impact load and produce a high standard of finish.
This means that the cutter profile is an elongaged version which may in some circumstances have to be geometrically developed.
Rotation of the work in contact with the cutters is controlled, some machines making provision for rotation in either direction.
A considerable amount of work goes into the preparation and setting up of cutters for a component, but modern machines are designed for quick change overs to different lines.
It is, of course, understandable for a turnery supplier to quote the minimum number of an item he is prepared to set up for if it is not one of his standard lines. The writer has personal knowledge of an instance where a prototype had been manufactured of a furniture item including turnery as a main feature.
Due to the fact that the requirement number was too large for hand turning within the works unit, yet too small for an outside supplier with an automatic lathe, the design had to be abandoned.
Availability of an automatic lathe within the works unit would probably have solved the problem and increased the design potentials generally.
The rotating cutters on an automatic lathe require to be fitted with a guard to a fixed standard of requirement. The guard is arranged so that the cutting unit is entirely enclosed while the work is being loaded.
As the work is fed to the cutters the guard opens to permit contact, closing again on completition.
The problem of boring turned objects for wires or fixing rods can be done with an automatic lathe designed specially for this purpose. The component is rotated in the machine at speeds up to 3,000 rpm and the boring bit is forced in by pneumatic pressure.
A stream of compressed air is forced into the hole as it is being bored and this clears the waste so that the bit need not be withdrawn until completion.
A beech block 600 mm in length can be bored with an 13mm bit in as little as 20 seconds on a machine of this type. Cutting is done all on the face of the bit, the waste being ejected by way of a hole through the centre.
Copying lathes are another form of automatic lathe. These are designed mainly to produce items which have no regular geometrical shape.
Under this classification there are such things as, Queen Anne Legs, Rifle Stocks, Sports Items such as Golf Club Heads, etc.
The cutting profile is governed by the guidance of a master item, which can be of wood or a more durable material if it has to be in continuous use.
To increase productivity these machines are

designed in such a way that more than one component may be in the course of formation at one time.

Batches of four are standard practice with some machines. As much waste as possible should be removed from items before they are positioned in the machine. It is customary for roughing cuts to be made, and then a finishing cut. Feed speeds, and cutter rotation speeds are adjusted accordingly.

Use of attachments on the spindle moulder

Dovetailing attachment set up for use on a spindle moulder. Suggestions are made in this article on procedure for quick setting up for dealing with small batches.

Experience has shown that the spindle moulder can be used for a very large number of operations in machine woodworking. The scope of the machine is increased considerably by the use of attachments and work-holding jigs.

The design of jigs is very often the responsibility of the operator, which means that new approaches are continuously being developed.

Machine manufacturers' attachments are designed with the smaller works unit in mind. They enable operations to be carried out on the spindle moulder when a specialised machine is not available. It is desirable that an attachment should be capable of being set up in a reasonable amount of time, considering the fact that it may be required in circumstances where the number of components to be processed is small.

A trained operator who is familiar with a full range of attachments is a useful asset to a machine shop. The use of attachments in the course of training of machine operators is something that can prove very worth while.

Typical heavy duty spindle moulder. This machine has rotation speeds of 5,000 and 8,000 rpm as standard. It is driven by a 4 hp. motor.

Probably the most efficient operation of attachments in a production unit can be obtained by having one machinist specialising in their use. In these circumstances he usually puts the attachments away after use in a partly set condition so that they can be brought into service again requiring only the minimum amount of adjustment.

Dovetailing attachments can, for instance, be kept set for standard drawer work. Setting up time is then mainly confined to fitting the required cutter-head unit to the machine.

It can be to advantage to have more than one attachment of a similar type. These machining aids do last through many years of service, their cost being spread over a considerable period of time.

When working in small batches of material, timber dimensions should be kept in mind relating to the suitability in the use of machine attachments.

In preparing drawer material it is customary to make the sides to fit the carcase opening and the backs narrower to admit the bottom.

In small quantity working the sides and backs will most likely be cut from the same width of board. It is preferable for dovetailing purposes to

Spindle moulder shaping jig showing the lead out section at the completion of the cut. In this way the operation is well under control.

Corner locking attachment fitted to a spindle moulder. It is suitable for the construction of trays, and also for drawers where false fronts are applied. Hints on the setting up are included in this article.

keep all the components the same width until after the dovetailing operation, to reduce setting time on the attachment.

The excess material can then be cut away, perhaps with some end spelching also. Some machinists favour the use of inserting packing pieces instead of moving positioning stops, but this method tends to call for an extra pair of hands.

The cutters used on corner locking sets are usually numbered and located on a keyed shaft so that cutting is distributed throughout 360 degrees. Boards up to 150 mm in width can be accommodated in standard attachments.

Various thicknesses of cutters are available, and spacing collars are required to make up the unit. Penetration of the cutters into the material should be preferably up to 22 mm.

This allows for framing material to be worked in addition to drawer and tray components.

Components are processed in batches, a backing piece being inserted to prevent spelching at the completion of the cut.

On setting up the machine for a quantity run it is important that the joint fit is not over tight at the start. It will be found that as the cutters lose their sharpness the joint will increase in tightness.

To slacken the joint a few thin pieces of paper may have to be inserted at one side of the collars only. Say every other at a first trial.

This creates a slight wobble, making the cutters work over size. Over slackness in a joint may be corrected by stripping the cutters from the head and cleaning the contact surfaces with paraffin. Sandpaper should not be used on the machined faces.

Thin paper washers can then be added to increase the thickness of the pins. Varying degrees of tightness on the clamping nut can control the final fitting of the joint. Well fitting joints require only light pressure on assembly, so preventing damage to the components.

Here again, the preparation of material width can contribute towards a well-designed joint. Thin members which break away on assembly should be avoided. Face edge working to the machine bed is advisable, particularly if variations in widths of material is suspected.

When purchasing a corner-locking cutter-head assembly, it should include the threaded collar which secures the head unit to the driving spin-

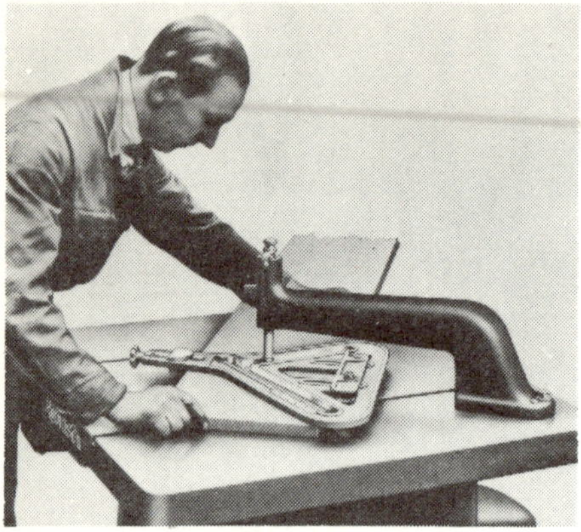

Stair trenching attachment in operation on the spindle moulder. Very little marking out is required after the initial setting.

Tenoning attachment. Particularly useful in the smaller works unit or as a secondary line in a busy production shop.

Adzemod Experimental Unit attachment for the spindle moulder. (Patend No. 1289619). Rollers with varying amounts of eccentricity may be used to produce the finish desired.

dle.. The reason for this is so that the head may be taken out of the machine complete with the cutters ready set for future use.

If it were necessary to take off the threaded collar, all the cutters would have to be removed, then reset at the time of requirement.

Careful storage of the cutter head is necessary in its built up state, the cutting edges should not be allowed to carry the weight. In the larger production units the head would most likely be stripped down after use when long runs are involved, but some thought should be given concerning this in the smaller works unit.

For trenching stair construction members it is essential that the material is planed square and flat. It is good policy to trench the material as soon as possible after the planing operation to give the most comfortable working.

The trenching attachment is designed to accommodate the tread and rise dimensions within the range generally required. Marking out of the timber is limited to that of the preparatory setting after which the advance movement of the template becomes constant.

The one attachment is capable of producing the left and right hand members required. Various types of cutters are available for the trenching operation, their main aim being to produce the sinking with a minimum of applied pressure.

This ensures the minimum of material splintering at intersections.

This can also be reduced by the order of working which is gained by experience. The width of the trench produced is governed by the diameter of the cutter in relation to the guide pin in the template slot.

When the diameter of the cutter and the guide pin are the same, the trench width will be as the template. The higher rotation speeds should be used for trenching operations due to the small diameter of the cutters involved.

The guide pin should be positioned directly over

Adzemod Unit positioned on the infeed fence on a spindle moulder.

the cutter when setting up.

Stair strings are very often one of the longest members dealt with in a joinery shop. Consideration must be given when positioning machines which are involved in the planing and trenching operations.

Although three metres is sufficient for floor to ceiling members in domestic cupboard units, it is not enough for stair members where five metres may be involved.

Fortunately, during the trenching operation on the spindle moulder, the work need not be kept in line with the machine positioning, so this makes the accommodation a little more convenient.

Machines designed solely for stair trenching usually process a pair of strings at the one operation, having a cutter above and below the timber. Although the spindle moulder attachment cannot compete with the output of a specialised machine it is acceptably progressive.

Example of finish obtained in a simulated Adzing operation.

Fireplace mantel surround from stained softwood. (Ex 100 mm by 25 mm plus white plastic grooved in slips.) Surfaces prepared with the Adzemod unit.

Early tenoning attachments for the spindle moulder entailed the work to be stood on end and fed across a tenoning machine-type cutter head.

The cradle in which the stock was held had then to be swung over and the return stroke cut the other cheek. Present-day users of attachments favour the work to be clamped in a slide, operating horizontally.

This requires the cutters to be mounted on arms to enable lengths of tenons up to 125 mm to be produced. Many establishments require tenons much shorter than the attachment's full capacity, and it is to these that it is particularly attractive.

In a busy machine shop, tenoning capacity can at times be very much in demand. A secondary method such as the spindle moulder attachment can deal particularly with the lighter cuts.

Whitehill-type cutter heads working in tandem will produce tenons working through a face board, but the length of the tenon is limited.

With the horizontal cutting action, scribing of the tenoned shoulders is also possible with the attachment. Half lap corner joints and forked joints can also be produced. The moulding of small items such as newel post caps can be processed, using the slide instead of mounting the work in jigs.

Due to the larger diameter of the cutting circle described by the cutters the lower rotation speeds should be used.

Probably one of the most productive units used on the spindle moulder is the automatic feed attachment. This type of unit takes most of the fatigue out of feeding large batches of stock through the machine.

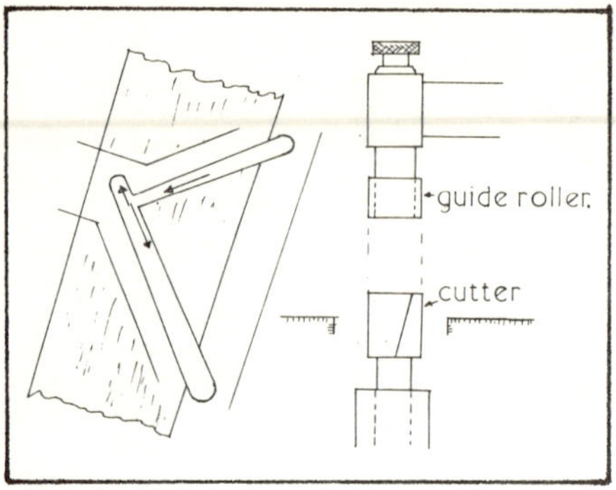

Planning order of cut can reduce the risk of splintering at corner intersections when stair trenching. The guide roller is positioned directly over the cutter when setting up the attachment.

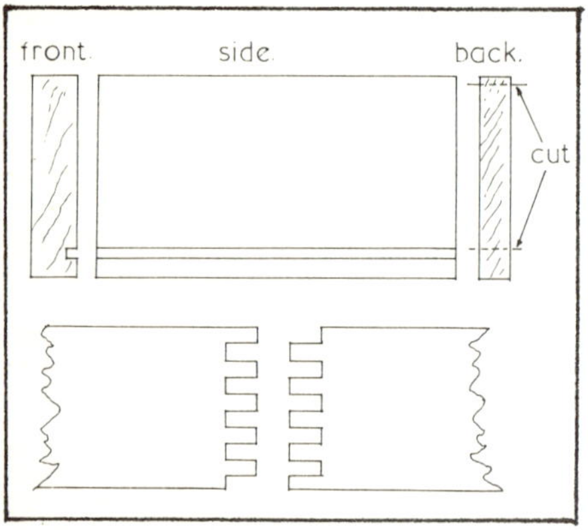

By keeping drawer components at the same width until after the dovetailing operation setting up time can be reduced. A useful suggestion for small quantity work. Plan component widths to suit corner locking unit to give balanced construction without weak outer pins.

Output can be greatly increased, and the quality of the resultant work is constant due to the continuous flow. Safer working is also experienced as the operator is always at a distance from the point of cut.

Lubrication of the machine table is important when using the feed unit, this enables less pressure to be used to obtain drive. The feed unit should be positioned to give a small amount of lead to push the work towards the fence.

Too much lead will put undue strain on the feed rollers and creates wear. The unit can be used for back fencing operations such as widthing doors, and other wide items.

The use of jigs and other holding appliances are a form of attachment for a machine, but they are usually constructed within the works unit. They increase the number of operations possible and are a means of obtaining precise repetition.

They also contribute towards safer working, particularly on small or shaped work.

A shaped component that may require a highly experienced operator to process on the spindle moulder could probably be done by a less experienced person with the aid of a well-designed jig.

A point of danger can arise when the less experienced worker attempts a job using a working aid only suitable for the more experienced. A study of jig design and operation has shown that the grade of operator on some tasks must be considered.

Likelihood of a jig being in communal use must also be considered. For working small items, the jig should be designed to add to the dimension and increase the weight.

Sometimes a batch of components can be accommodated in a jig, so gaining the increased mass. Provision for a lead-in must be made when working on a ring fence so that the jig is supported firmly before the cutting operating starts. This is a point very often overlooked where marking out templates are used as a shaping former without any other additions.

In the larger works units, more time can be spent in the planning and construction of jigs due to the quantities of components involved. Smaller units very often have to modify existing jigs to meet demands.

For this reason, screws should be used in their construction and small dabs of adhesive, to prevent slip, and yet permit removal. Consultation between the jig maker and the person who has to use it can be recommended.

The completed aid is more readily accepted in this way. The spindle moulder, and the high-speed router lend themselves to the use of jigs more than any other of the woodworking machines.

A choice has often to be made whether to carry out a particular operation either on the spindle or the router. Generally speaking, the cleaning up of shapes, rebating and moulding is better done on the spindle moulder if it can be accommodated.

Trenching operations and pierced work are usually applicable to the high-speed router.

The sharpness life of cutters is much greater on the spindle and their servicing is less complicated. The development of the high-speed router has taken over much of the small curvature work done by the French head on the spindle moulder. A few points in favour of the

use of the French head are quoted below:
The French head operates with a scraping action which makes it particularly suitable for working hardwoods. With a high speed of rotation, say, 9,000 rpm, a finish can be obtained which requires very little sandpapering before being polished.
The quality of the finish depends upon a burr being created on the cutter during the sharpening process. This action, known as burnishing, must be repeated when the finish begins to deteriorate.
Long runs between servicing are not usually possible unless only a small amount of material is being cut away. The steel used for the cutters

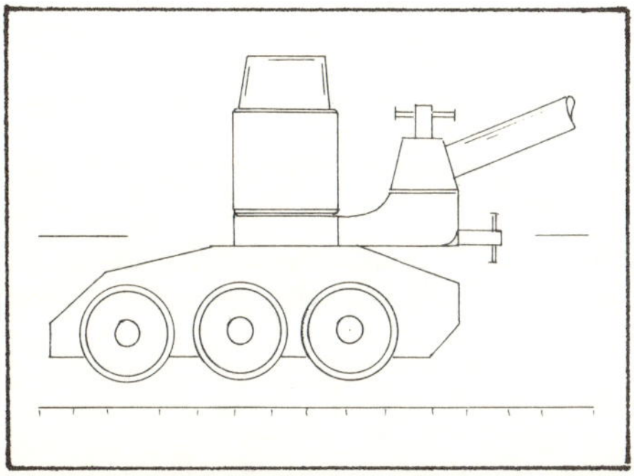

Outline of an automatic feed unit as used on a spindle moulder. Various rates of feed are available in both forward and reverse direction. The attachment can be mounted vertically as shown, or horizontally to apply pressure in the direction of the fence.

A lead in and out is important in the design of shaping aids on the spindle moulder. A highly experienced operator is required to carry out a shaping operation using only a work template.

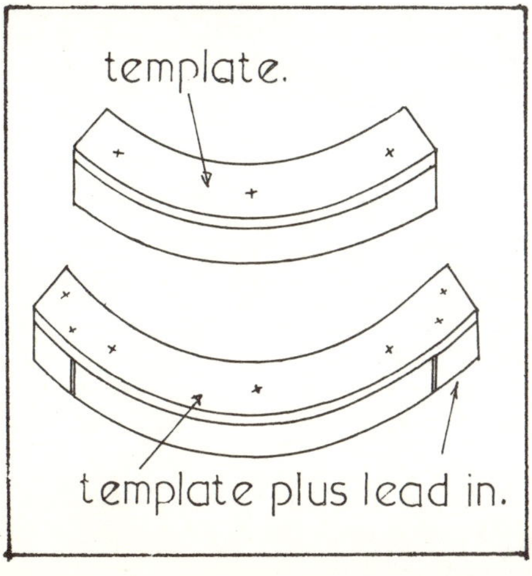

must be of a suitable type to enable the burr to be formed.
Hardened steels are not suitable. As the cutting face is almost on the central rotating line of the spindle, cutter shapes are accepted as identically opposite to that of the mould required.
For this reason some very attractive moulding profiles can be found on old furniture produced by comparatively primitive machines using this method. As lavish mouldings are not in demand at the present age, the convenient aspects of French head working have been put aside by most.
One of the most versatile cutter heads used on the spindle moulder is the Whitehill pattern. It is economical in the use of cutter steel, and the cutters can be quickly ground to shape due to the light thickness of material involved.
More than one profile can be formed on each piece of steel, and cutters can be set in the head at any angle. Tungsten cardide tipped cutters can be used in the Whitehill head for processing materials such as plastics and chipboard.
Cutters can be mounted in the head either on a setting stand in the tool room, or with the head already positioned in the machine.
In the latter case a setting template should be used. The head should be located between spacing collars, not slotted collars, as the diameter of these prevents the operation of the vice-grip action which is so necessary for securing the cutters.

The use of slotted collars as a means of mounting cutters is favoured by machinists who have to set up frequent repeat runs of the smaller type of cutting action. The cutters are usually approx. 6 mm in thickness, but thicker cutters are also available with stepped edges to fit in standard slots.
The security of the cutters in the machine depends upon the clamping action of the spindle nut. Both cutters must be of identical width, although some collar sets provide for a limited amount of variation.
The cutters should be a sliding fit in the slots, not tight, or this may prevent the clamping action. If the machine is to be run in reverse, two spindle nuts should be used.
Slotted collars are generally run at speeds up to 6,000 rpm, but higher speed collars are available which have deepened slots to accommodate safety pins or lugs on the cutters.
Although slotted collars are capable of long service without attention, they are an item which should be considered for renewal when considering safety aspects.
Solid profile cutter heads have the advantage of

simplification of setting up. Economical forms of these heads are now available for such items as T and G formations and mouldings in popular use. Wadkin Bursgreen offer a range of these for their spindle moulders.

These have only two cutter faces compared with the usual six on the more elaborated type of solid profile cutters. They are particularly suitable for the smaller establishment, and safe in use as they are secure in the machine at all times. The original profile is maintained during sharpening.

The use of square-cutter blocks on the spindle moulder is still permitted, due to necessity, although other forms are often preferable from a safety and noise point of view.

The continued use of the square block is due to the fact that a large variety of cutting operations can be carried out with profiles prepared within the unit.

Several pairs of cutters can be mounted on a block to carry out a series of shaping operations at the one pass through the machine. Balance is an important factor in the setting up of these blocks. Pairs of cutters must be identical, and set to the same projection.

They should also be positioned directly opposite to each other to obtain perfect balance within the set. Attention should also be paid to the uniformity of the securing bolts and washers.

Any deviation from these points will result in additional strain to the machine bearings, excessive noise, and a possible danger due to vibration. Noise from a correctly set up block should be limited to a purr which is caused by the movement of the atmosphere by the rotation.

Good rates of feed can be obtained using an automatic feed attachment, say, moulding and rebating window sections. The fan effect of the cutters throws the waste clear as it is produced.

Spindle moulder attachment: new development

A recent development of a spindle moulder attachment is the Adzemod Experimental Unit, patented by the writer of this article, J. R. Clayton.

It was originated from an effort to produce an adzed finish by adapting a machine in general use. In addition to producing a simulated adzed surface to timber it can produce an unlimited variety of finishes by the use of different profiles of cutters. In this way it lends itself to experimentation by the user.

In operation, the timber is fed in contact with an eccentric roller which creates an oscillating motion to and from the spindle moulder cutter. More than one feed through can be made if desired.

Timber can be fed ideally with an automatic feed attachment, or by hand, using standard pressure springs to keep the timber in contact with the roller.

Finishes produced enables the less costly types of material to be made suitable for decorative purposes as a light and shade effect is created by the undulated surface. Material processed could be suitable for exterior surface cladding, panel framing, beam facings, fireplace surrounds, architrave linings, etc.

In some instances, softwood, suitably stained, can have the appearance of oak due to the cuts made into the surface grain by the oscillating motion during the forward feed.

Simplified form of solid profile cutter heads having only two working faces. A selection of this economical form of head could probably fulfil all the requirements of a small works unit. The sketches are based on a few of the large Wadkin Bursgreen range.

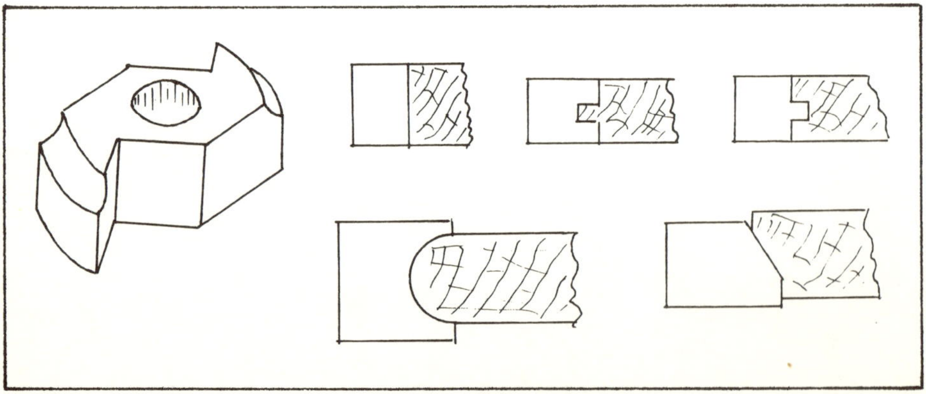

Sanding machines

The operation of machine sanding plays an important part in the production of timber items. In a highly mechanised unit it is very often the last operation on the work before the application of surface coatings which can govern the quality range in which the goods can be placed on the market.

Sanding should not be over exploited by producing work of low accuracy standards, and expecting the operation to rectify deficiencies. Two of the principal reasons for sanding are (a) to level off intersecting members and (b) to improve the standard of the planed surface. High accuracy standards can reduce the (a) group to almost elimination point before sanding, (b) group is concerned with cutter mark pitch as produced by rotating cutters. Grain structure of the timber concerned also often decides the amount of sanding required to produce an acceptable finish.

Such items as mouldings, which are difficult to sand mechanically without special equipment, should have a high efficiency rating during profile formation. The cutter mark pitch should not be in excess of 0.75 mm, to quote a debatable figure.

For high accuracy standards in machining

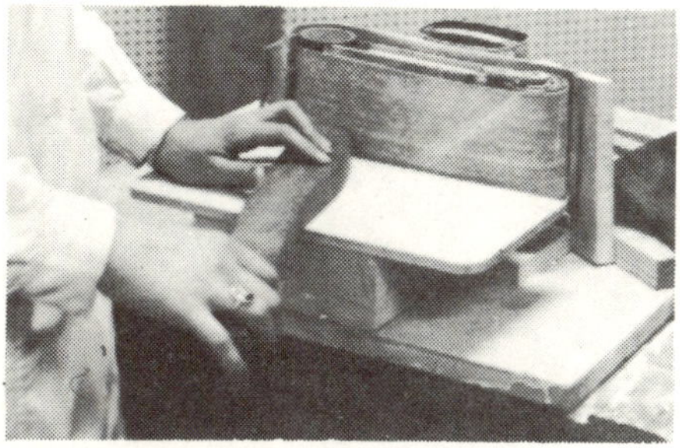

A portable belt sander mounted in a holding jig. A useful asset for the occasional user.

A popular four-in-one machine, manufactured by Dominion of Halifax, fitted with an additional pressure strip which prevents drag on the pad during use. The deep throat on the right hand support allows for extended work to be accommodated.

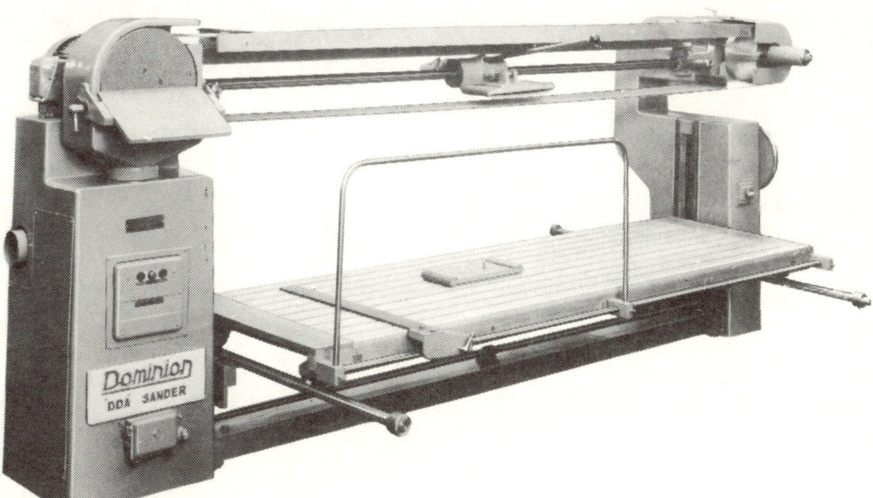

generally, sanding during the processing stages should be kept to a minimum. Polished cabinet interiors may be acceptable straight from a planing machine using trimmed cutters and a carefully planned feed speed. The sanding of inernal surfaces can cause inconsistency in a batch of items, and upset shoulder working lengths.

Sanding in some forms of construction require to be carried out prior to joint formations. A typical example of this is in dovetailed drawers.

If the inner surfaces of the backs and fronts are machine sanded after dovetailing, ill fitting joints will result.

In large scale production, goods very often have to be designed with sanding in mind for economic reasons. Window frames can be more conveniently sanded if projecting sills and drip bars can be applied at a later stage.

Efforts have been made in some automatically fed sanding machines to accommodate projecting sills by providing a well at the side of the feed bed, and so encouraging the production of a high standard item.

Also in shaped work the radius of concave curves should be in keeping with the bobbin sanding equipment readily available to cut down work to a minimum.

Machines for sanding can either be mechanically fed, or with the components manually applied to the abrasive surface, where additional skill may be required. The use of hand controlled pads is also involved. At the bottom of the scale a portable belt sander may be mounted in supporting jig to give it the characteristics of a fixed machine.

With a minimum of skill and a high safety factor this mini method can be particularly useful. Also in this adaption field, a sandpaper faced disc can be mounted in the wood turning lathe and used for shaping operations.

Belt sanders are probably the most common type of machine as they can carry out a large variety of operations and are particularly useful to the smaller works unit. The present day design of machine provide for the sanding of large surfaces such as doors, also disc and bobbin work.

Where tension to the abrasive belt is applied by spring action instead of a jockey pulley, and over table is usually provided for edge sanding.

The main work table on these machines can also be lowered to admit assembled carcases to allow sanding operations to be carried out at the final stage.

Belt sanders require dust extraction equipment, but this is partially provided for within the

A compact sanding machine of the Wadkin Bursgreen range. The table may be lowered to accommodate assembled units.

Sanding an assembled drawer on the overhead belt on a Wadkin Bursgreen machine. A cover has been applied over the disc unit.

machine itself in the form of a fan driven by the main motor. This fan has to be designed to rotate in either direction and be effective, as reverse rotation is advisable when using the over table. A dust collecting unit located adjacent to the machine will give acceptable results without an additional fan in many circumstances.

If a fan is fitted to the collecting source it is customary to remove the fan from the sanding machine. The advantage of a fan on the collecting source is that it always rotates in the same direction irrespective of that of the sanding machine.

When working on the machine table, two methods can be used for applying the belt to the

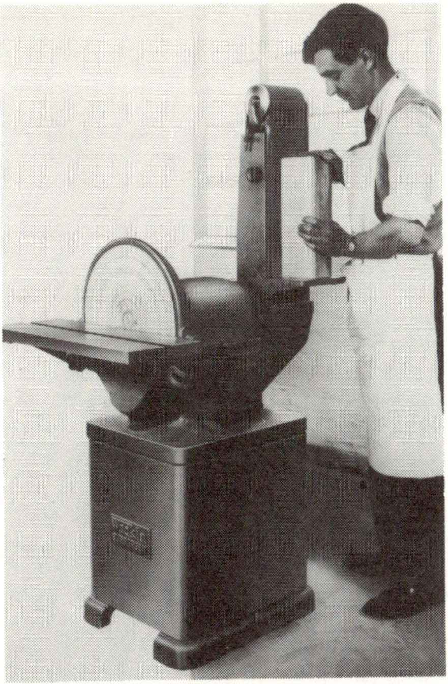

A useful machine for precision working. Ideal for jig making, and taking up only a small amount of floor area.

work. This is either by the use of a hand pad or the lever controlled pad.

The hand pad is used mainly for delicate work such as fine veneers, or open work such as sash frames. There is a danger of belt breakage when sanding open frames by the inexperienced when using the lever controlled pad. A considerable amount of pressure can be applied by the lever and care must be taken not to create ridges in the work.

When operating, in addition to keeping the pad moving, the table must also have back to front movement. The height of work table should be such as to allow a clearance of about 12 mm between the belt and the work when no pad pressure is being applied.

The most comfortable working position (when sanding short items) is in the centre of the belt run, where the least pressure need be applied. The application of a small amount of tallow to the back of the belt will reduce friction and ease the working procedure.

Most users of belt sanders buy the belts ready made up to length, and the problem of jointing does not occur. Jointing equipment can be useful if broken belts accumulate which are in a serviceable condition. It also gives the sander operator some sense of responsibility of keeping his house in order.

The most suitable method of jointing within the works unit is to cut the ends of the belt to an interlocking pattern with the aid of a purpose-made tool. Linen backing is then secured across the joint with adhesive. Pressure should be applied, irrespective of the type of adhesive used usually with the aid of layers of paper, battens and cramps.

Care must be taken to trim the ends square when preparing the joint, or it will be impossible to track the belt when applied to the machine.

Belts should be examined periodically during service, or if any clicking noise is heard when running.

If small tears or fractures at the edge of the belt can be bridged with adhesive strip, a breakage can very often be delayed considerably.

From the point of view of safety, and dust collection purposes, the appertures at the infeed end of the belt should be as close as possible, when working on the over table.

Careless operators can get work, or even fingers, trapped at this point. Also small work

A bobbin sander designed specifically for this purpose. The bobbin can be raised and lowered to distribute wear, and has oscillating action during rotation. The machine table can be tilted.

components can be taken through, very often resulting in a broken belt.

Pressure pads require to be faced with felt which plays an important part in the efficiency of machine sanding. The introduction of felt between the pressure medium and the work creates additional amounts of oscillation.

Experienced sander operators working on such items as veneered panels, pay much attention to the condition of the felt on the pad. They must be taken off and cleaned free from internal dust and grit to maintain results.

When working on any form of disc sander it is important that the gap between the work supporting table and the face of the disc is as small as possible, for safety reasons. On a machine which is reversible care must be taken when offering work to the disc to ensure that the downgoing section is being used. An error here could throw the work up in the air.

An indicator light could be very welcome at this point on machines in communal use. Abrasive paper is usually fixed to the disc with adhesive on the smaller type of machine. On large discs it is secured with a metal ring fitting into a recessed portion of the rim.

Special adhesives can be obtained for this purpose but I find that many that are in everyday use seem to serve the purpose.

The operation of disc sanding is particularly useful to the machinist making jigs for precision work.

The main purpose of bobbin sanding is to clean up internal curves that are a product of the bandsaw or high-speed router.

Bobbins in general use are approximately 75 mm in diameter which serve a variety of purposes.

Other diameters are available, and their construction can depend upon the purpose for which they are intended. Wooden bobbins are in use, which are split and hinged to allow the paper and felt to be gripped. The clamping is done by metal collars at each end, the internal hole being cone shaped to match that of the bobbin.

As pressure is applied with the aid of a nut the two sections of the bobbin are pulled together so securing the paper. All metal bobbins are also available with a variety of paper securing methods. Pneumatic bobbins, which are blown up like a car tyre are fitted with **endless** abrasive papers. This is a point in their favour providing a stock of these is at hand at the time of requirement.

In sanding, the most popular type of automatic machine has been the three drum sander. Development over the last decade have introduced other types of automatic machines which can be more advantageously used on many operations.

A dust collecting unit suitable for a belt sander which is already fitted with a fan. Note that the unit is positioned close to the machine.

Availability of machine sanding facilities can increase the scope of non-vocational students in training establishments. Edge profiles on this table end have been designed to enable them to be sanded on a 75 mm diam. bobbin, so reducing hand work.

A three drum sander as found in many production establishments. Note the current flow meters at the left of the machine.

The Speedsander as supplied by White of Paisley. This machine is designed to carry out two abrasive units, one of which may be a finishing set.

There are however a large number of drum sanders still in use in the many aspects of woodworking.
The basic aim in the use of three drums is to have various grades of paper fitted, working from coarse to fine so as to carry out a series of operations at the one pass through the machine. The amount of sandpaper involved is limited to the circumference of the drum concerned, and this has a tendency to imprint a repetition shadow pattern on the workpiece.
To reduce this the drums require to oscillate from left to right during rotation. For painted work, a drum sander finish can be acceptable,

Interior view of a Speedsander having two units and a finishing set. Belts can be conveniently changed by this access means.

but for high standard furniture finish completion may have to be done on a belt sander after drumming.
Changing the papers on a drum sander can take a considerable amount of time as dust extraction hoods require to be removed, the felt covers inspected and brushed, and the new papers cut and fixed.

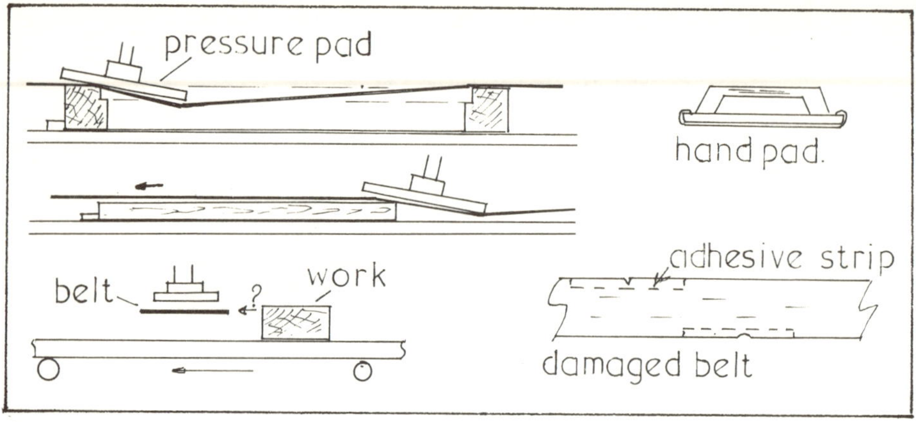

Common reasons for sander belts being broken or damaged due to ill use. When sanding open frames a sudden tilt of the pressure pad can cause a fracture. It is preferable to use a hand pad. Care must be taken not to run off the end of the work at the ingoing end when sanding panels. The table should always be lowered to allow 12 mm of clearance of the belt above the work. Work pushed into the edge of the belt will cause damage. Slightly damaged belts can be repaired with adhesive strip.

View of the machine showing abrasive wheels and cleaning brush. (Weinig).

It is not a task that can be carried out single handed.

The nature of the work decides upon the paper grades and how long they can be used before renewal. Worn papers often contribute to the appearance of snake patterns on the work, but this may not be important for such operations as levelling lipings on chipboard prior to a veneering operation.

An operator generally plans his sequence of work to suit the life stages of his papers. Im-

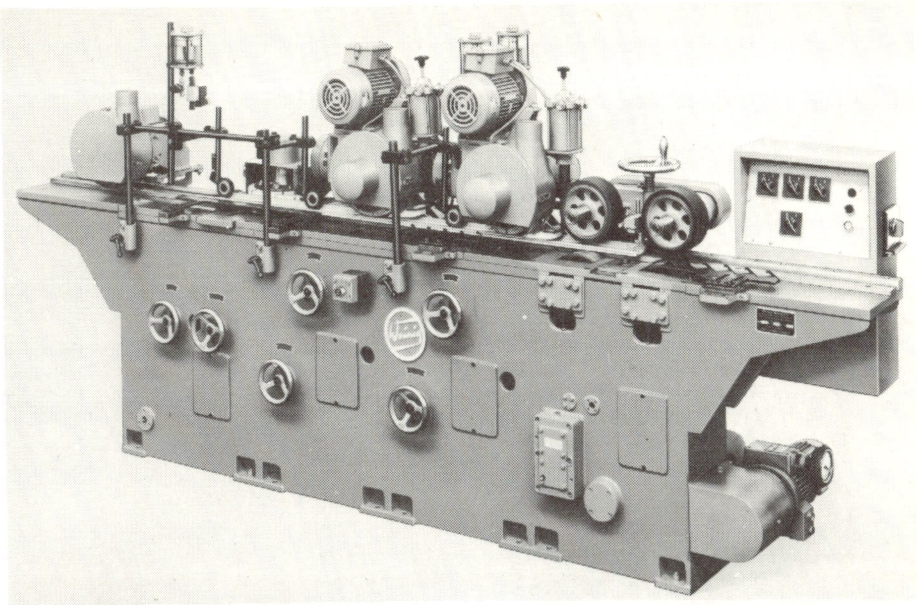

A power feed moulding sanding machine by Weinig of West Germany.

Building up an abrasive unit from segments. (Weinig).

portant work is done while the papers are at their best, and the less demanding jobs are laid aside for later.

Drum sanders have seen considerable use on such jobs as levelling off the faces of painted doors for flushing with plywood skins. Papers abused in this way would no longer be suitable for high standard finish work.

On the older models of drum sander the operator had to determine more or less by ear whether the machine was being overloaded due to excess pressure being applied.

More modern machines are fitted with meters to indicate the current flow at all times. Papers can

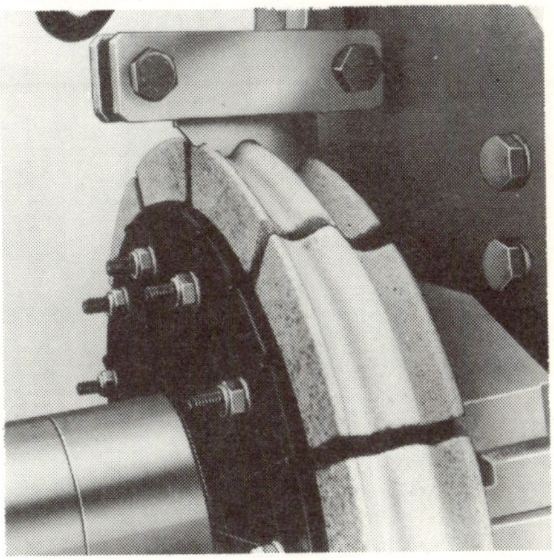

fracture during use, and in some instances the covering felt on the drum concerned can also become damaged.

Due to the large number of moving parts on a three drum sander, pressure lubrication is often used. This must be carefully controlled since too much oil is liable to come into contact with the work in its final stages. Rubber endless tracks for feeding the work into the machine have become more favoured than metal slatted ones which required an abundance of lubrication on their frictional surfaces.

A development of power feed sanding which to my experience is now in its second decade is that of the Speedsander. Messrs. White and Sons of Paisley have largely pioneered the successful development, and they claim that this pattern of machine has practically superseded the three drum sander.

The machine had originally one sander belt and the feed was confined to rollers, having no travelling bed.

The Speedsander now has a travelling bed and up to three abrasive belts, the last one which is generally a finishing unit. The model most popular in joinery establishments is the Twin Sander, which is fitted with one contact roll unit and a finishing unit. Two contact rolls, or two finishing units can be fitted if desired for specialised types of work.

The advantages over the traditional drum sander are that the surface area of the abrasive material is greatly increased, so providing a much longer life and eliminating pattern printing.

The changing of a belt can be done by one person in about three minutes if necessary, so reducing down time to a minimum.

The feed table can be firmly locked for thicknessing operations when the machine is used as an abrasive planer. For purely finishing

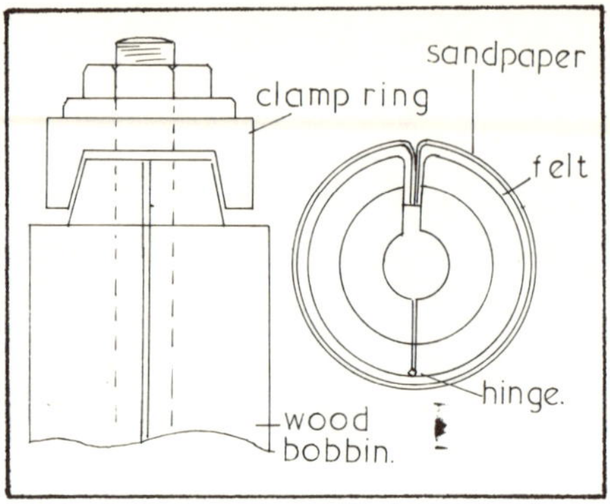

Build up of a wooden type sander bobbin. The bobbin is tapered at both ends, and drawn together with a tapered metal ring so holding the felt and abrasive paper.

Line diagram of a three drum sander layout. Figures and proportional diagram show the comparison between the amount of abrasive belt involved in a drum compared to that of the modern Speedsander.

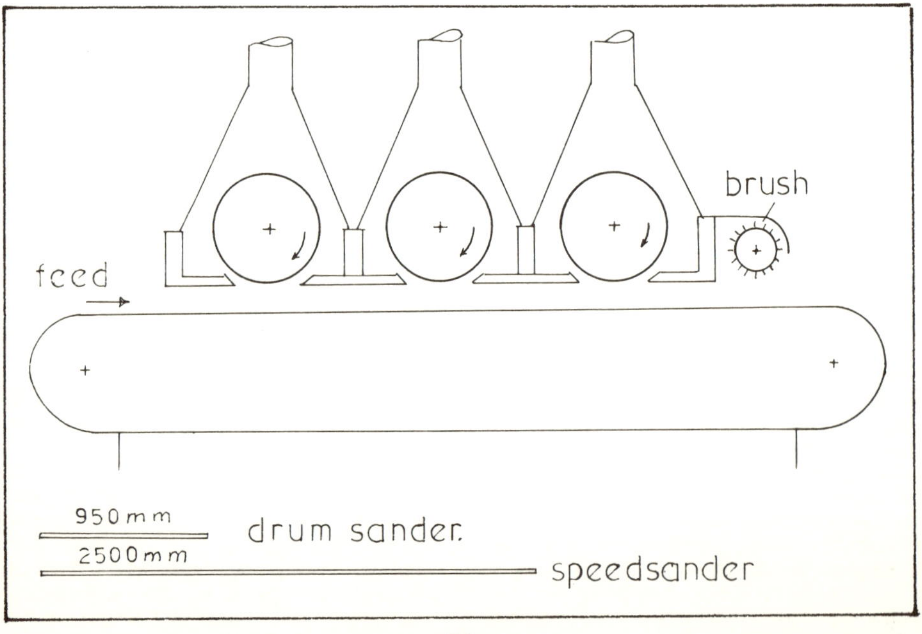

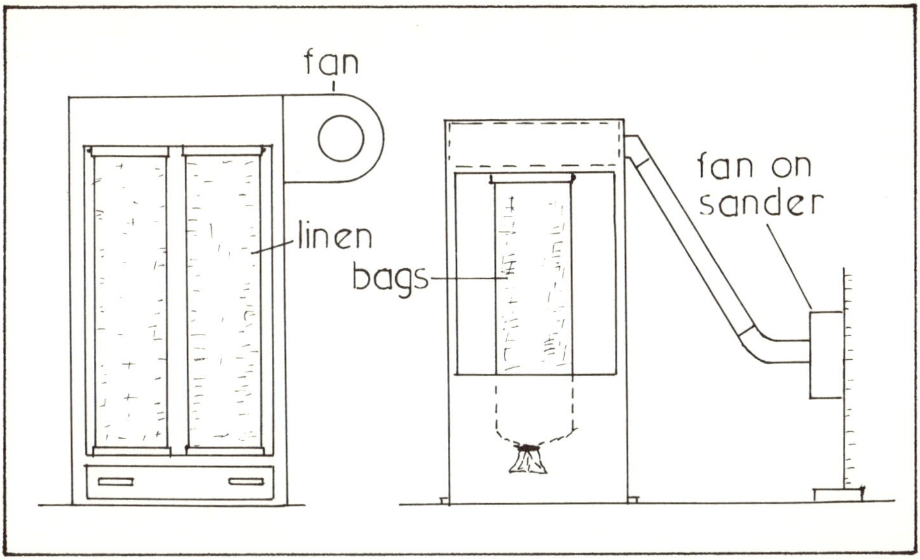

Two arrangements of collecting sander dust from the machine.

sanding the table may be allowed to float to follow the surface profile. Feed speed is infinitely variable from 10 m to 30 m per minute.

Dust collection

Dust collection is required on all sanding machines, but on some it must be efficient to produce high standard finishes. Most automatic machines work with the operational surface facing upwards.

As much of the dust as possible should be extracted at each of the various grades of sanding to ensure a satisfactory finish. Dust ground in, can have a burnishing effect which gives rise to absorbency problems in finishing coatings. The dust removal efficiency is a point worth investigating if finish standards depreciate.

It is advisable at times for a sanding machine operator to wear a face mask. Softwoods generally have little or no irritant effect, but some hardwoods can be like pepper. When removing paints or varnishes, masks should always be used, and if quantities of this type of work is to be encountered some preparation should be gone into before commencing the work.

Dust collection units can either be for an individual machine, or on a larger scale serving a number of sources.

Its collection differs from that of wood chips as produced by planing machines.

The most common method is to pass the dust through a fan and deposit it in a linen bag. The conveying air is released through the pores in the linen leaving the dust behind. The collection bags should not be allowed to fill to any great extent, as back pressure may be set up if insufficient area of linen is available to disperse the air flow.

The collection bags should be shook from time to time to clear the pores, but the practice of washing them is debatable as any shrinkage could have a closing effect on the outfeed.

Grits used on sander belts depend on the nature of the work generally undertaken. Suppliers are always ready to advise on this and welcome criticisms on new developments. Grit used can either be of a natural material or very often of a manufactured one.

In addition to the difference in grit types and grade, it can be deposited on the backing as either a close coat, or an open coat. Open coats can generally be faster cutting due to less clogging. Close coats give a finer finish but may soon burn on some materials.

A recent addition to the aids for sanding moulded sections is a machine manufactured by the firm of Michael Weinig, of Tauberbischofschein, West Germany.

A first glimpse at the machine denotes that the layout very much resembles that of a fourcutter. The feed method is similar to a fourcutter, but the working heads are sanding units. The Type SM. 12 machine has two horizontal and one vertical sanding disc. A power driver brush is located at the outgoing end of the machine to remove dust on completion.

The sanding discs are made up from square faced abrasive segments, and these are shaped to the required profile with a prepared metal template.

The width capacity of the machine can be extended up to 120 mm by using two 70 mm discs offset to each other. The heads can be tilted, 15 degrees in one direction, and 45 degrees in the other. Due to the fact that the profile blocks can be prepared within the works unit, no hold-ups waiting for machine components need be experienced.

The abrasive material is available in a range of grit sizes to produce the required finish.

The high-speed router

Success in the use of the high-speed router can depend on the preparation of the material being worked. It is essential that the workpiece lies flat on the bed of the machine or holding device or the resultant efforts will be inconsistent. Overhead working, as applied to the high speed router, cuts excess material away if the work is raised off the table surface.
This is one of the reasons why overhead working

A familiar model of Wadkin router but fitted by the manufacturer with pneumatic head control movement. This reduces fatigue of the operator, and so increases output, particularly on long runs.

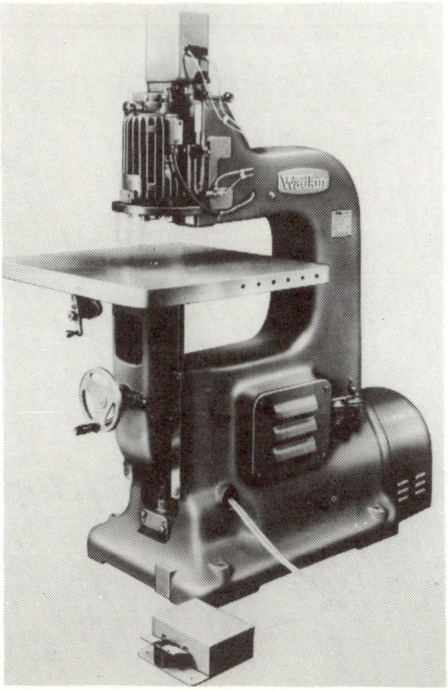

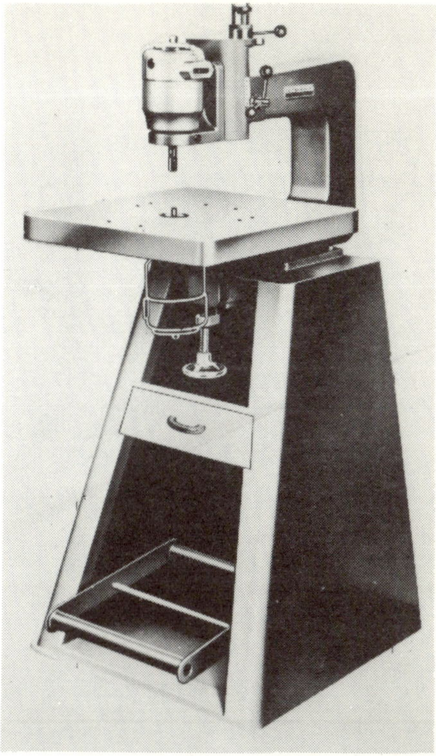

The Elu High-Speed Router Model 11/30. The motor head on this machine can also be mounted below the table and used similar to a spindle moulder. Particularly suitable for some types of work. Elu Trend Machinery, Stirling Corner, Boreham Wood, Herts. Machine listed at £298.

is avoided on the spindle moulder where cutting is done on the underside when ever possible. Working on the underside has also an increased safety factor from that of cutting overhead.
This points out clearly that the use of guards is most essential at all times when working on the high-speed router.
The methods of working on the router can be divided into various groups:

(a) The use of jigs, where a former is used on the underside of the work holder which is in contact with a guide pin located in the machine table.
(b) A sliding table can be fitted to the machine, giving back to front movement. Tenons and lap joints can be formed by this method.
(c) A guide fence may be used and operations carried out much in the same way as on a spindle moulder.
(d) Machines fitted with a compound table

One of the 14 different types of high-speed router manufactured by Interwood. This is the Model OFL, which has a particularly large throat capacity. A 50-page operational manual is supplied with their machines which leaves the operator in no doubt as to the correct procedures.
Interwood Ltd., 326 Old Street, London EC1V.

which can both be traversed and have cross motion, make provision for additional methods of working.

(e) On some routers the cutting head may be canted, which provides for additional scope.

(f) Shaping work related to the periphery of a circle can be conveniently carried out to radial perfection by pivoting about its centre. Circles can be cut from material in this way with a minimum of setting up time.

The high-speed router probably offers itself to jig working more than any other woodworking machine. This makes it highly suitable for repetition work. The standard of work produced by the machine is governed by the quality of the jig construction and the condition of the cutting unit.

Additional effort in jig design can reduce the amount of hand work required in finishing operations. The planning of successful jigs requires some thought and experience. Such factors as wear in use, work holding and multiple purpose, should be considered. Loading and unloading jigs takes time, if more than one operation can be carried out at the one mounting, so much the better.

Jigs should be constructed in such a way that guards can still be effectively used on the machine. Approach to the work should always be to meet the rotating cutting edge, not to travel with it. Work should be kept in motion while in cut to prevent the generation of heat which can quickly dull a cutting edge and also cause burn marks. No component is actually too

The Wadkin router Type UR in use in Sweden on the production of builders spirit level stocks. Machine set for fence working. The head may be canted on this machine.

small to be worked on the router providing it is suitably supported in a work holder.

The habit of attempting to hold small items with the finger tips should not be practised. Well designed jigs and work holders can be gripped in the hand.

The fence on a high-speed router can either be a metal attachment supplied by the machine manufacturer, or made from wood secured to the table with G cramps. Wooden fences, which can also be added to the metal ones, have the advantage that the cutter can run in close contact with them, so supporting the cutting action on the stock being worked.

On a fixed table machine (not compound), the fence does not generally require to be positioned square off the table edge. Where the table has compound movement and it is to be used along with a fence to position the timber, the fence must, in this case, be fitted square to the edge of the work table. Failure to recognise this may cause trenching cuts, etc., to be in error.

Hinged stops, or bars to accommodate disappearing stops can be applied to router fences much in the same way as mortising machines. This eliminates a multitude of marking out on repetition work.

Many operators of fixed table machines construct their own sliding table from blockboard and guide battens, which fit snugly against the machine edges of the table. The smaller type of tenon, in particular, can be produced by this working method, and also many forms of trenching can be readily carried out without the preparation of a specialised jig.

Machines that are fitted with movement in both directions have increased scope over fixed table machines. Work can very often be clamped to the table and worked without the aid of jigs. Movement of the table can be controlled by the setting of stops which are fitted with repetition work in mind.

Machines are continually developing and the introduction of the tilting head to highspeed routers has increased the potential of the cutting tools which have previously been limited. Bevels and vee grooves can be formed with standard panel cutters.

Jigs are usually constructed within the works unit. They are prepared on the assumption that the guide pin in the machine table is directly central with the cutter mounted in the cutting head. This point must be checked when setting up, particularly on tables which have compound movement. The vertical contact surface on a jig former should not be less than 9 mm. This allows the guide pin to project a generous amount above the surface of the table and so prevent overriding.

Multiply is mainly used for the construction of jig

The Elu router being used with the motor below the table. Inset: Cutter with guide roller which engages on the former template.

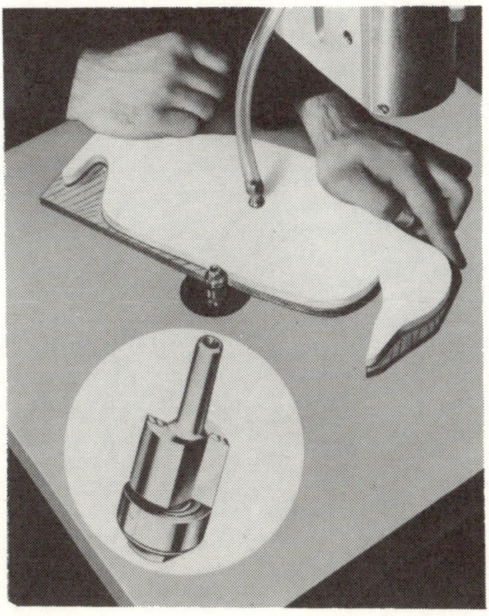

Canting head, which increases the range of operations possible, and very often eliminates the use of saddles to support the workpiece at an angle.

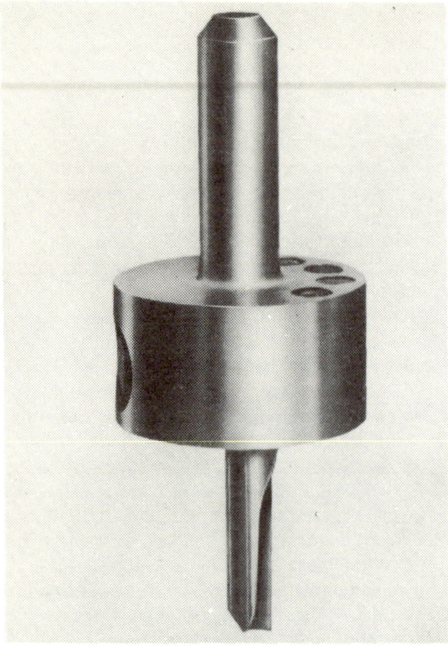

Eccentric chuck on balancing table. The table is first set level with the aid of the roller only. The chuck is then inserted and brought to balance by adjusting the weights, adding or taking away.

The eccentric chuck are used on the high speed router. Balancing weights consist of grub screws inserted into the top of the rim.

When working plastic laminate or quantities of multi-ply, tungsten carbide tipped cutters must be used. Although their cost is higher than high-speed steel, with considerate use they can have a long period of service.

When sharpening tipped cutters, only a very small amount should be dressed away using a diamong dust coated wheel. Hand lapping tools are available which can be used to advantage between services. Care should be taken in the storage of tipped cutters to prevent chipping, formers, but this is subject to wear on long term use, and metal or tufnol facings are very often applied. When operating, the machine table must always be kept free from wood chips to give the jig a constant seating.

In jig design, cut waste must not be able to drop through between the former and the guide pin. Generally, a jig should consist of a former, a dust collecting or mounting board and holding devices. If a former is attached directly to the work piece, omitting the dust board, waste will drop and come into contact with the guide pin.

Experienced router operators working on batch production prefer to take as heavy a cut as possible when engaged on shaping work. The reason for this is that if a cut is first worked on an item at half depth, and then a repeat run taken to complete the cut to full depth, only the bottom portion of the cutter is being used.

Cutter life can be extended if an increased amount of the cutting edge is utilised. Load on the cutter must at times be considered, particularly when its diameter is less than 12 mm, when breakages are most likely to occur.

also in their fitting and removing from the machine.
For cutting out shapes, the router has several advantages over the band saw, or jig saw. Items cut with saws require to be marked out first. This can take a considerable amount of time when working in quantity. Jig working on the router requires no marking.
The router also produces a clean planed edge if correctly operated for a fair percentage of its work. Bandsawn edges require quite a lot of effort to bring them to the standard of those produced by routing.
If breaking away is being experienced at points of short grain during routing operations, this can be reduced by punching through with the cutter at these points before the commencement of the main cut. Cutters of around 12 mm in diameter are favoured for general shaping work on the router. They stand up to the stress of average working speed for most operations, and create a not objectionable amount of dust.
The dust produced from the high-speed rotation in routing can be unpleasant when the larger type of cutters are used over long periods. Face masks at times can be welcome when working some types of materials. Siting of a machine should be considered with relation to the dust aspect. A batch of these machines would be preferable in line rather than back to back, as an instance.
A case history showed a few years ago when wooden lavatory seats were being produced in very large quantities from timber, that these could be shaped and moulded on the router with a high standard of finish, and a good working safety factor. The alternative method was to shape on the router using a ½in. cutter then applying the mould profile on a spindle moulder.

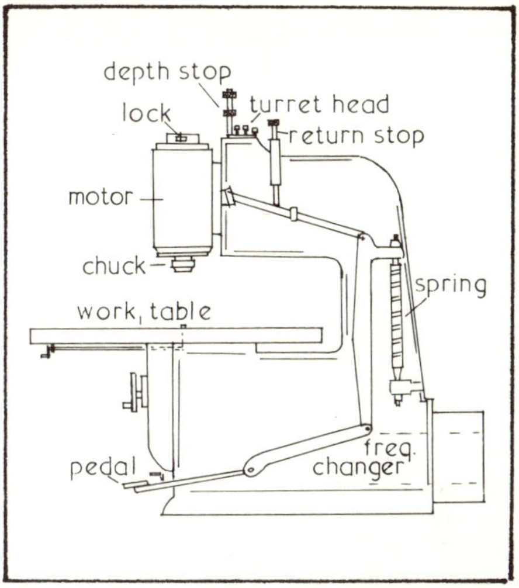

General view of a high-speed router to show operational points. The turret head enables a series of working depths to be preset. The locking device is necessary to enable pressure to be applied to the chuck when securing cutters. The work head is controlled with the foot pedal, and can be secured in any height position.

Two working methods. The sliding table is an attachment that can be made within the works unit. The use of a stop, and the usual guard, is important. Fence working with a hardwood fence, secured with G cramps. This is useful for slot mortising, rebating, etc.

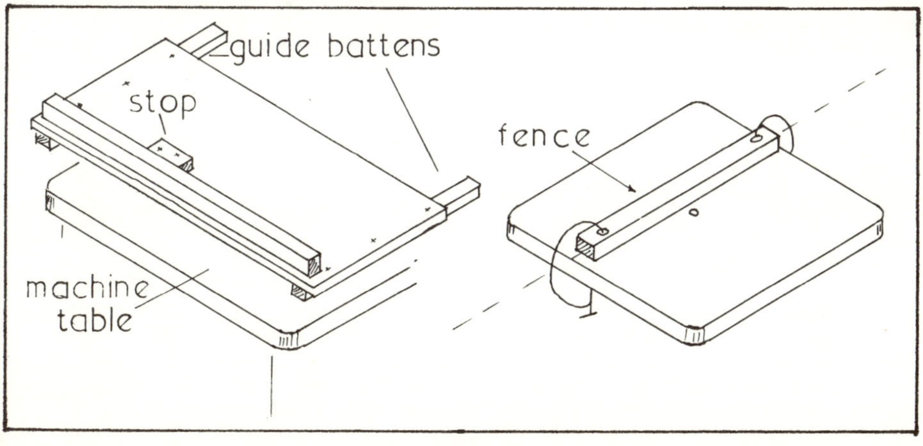

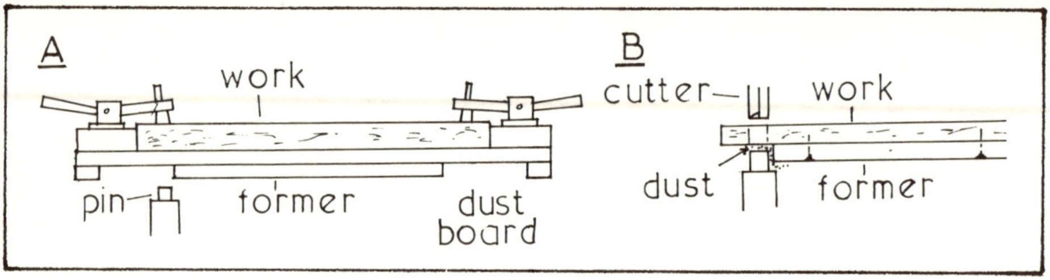

A. shows the essential requirements of a routing jig. Holding devices must be set well clear of the working area. The dust collecting board forms the main body of the jig.

B. If a former is nailed directly on to the workpiece, dust will accumulate between the guide pin and the former, so producing a substandard finish.

The latter method was often preferred, due only to the reduction of the dust, the spindle moulder producing chip waste. The safety factor to the operator was greater on the router, as a considerable amount of skill was required to drop on for the inner cut on the spindle moulder.

Router cutters which have backing clearance as used in standard chucks, lose working diameter due to sharpening. Two methods are in operation to overcome this when continuous precision is required. When working with jigs with formers, the size of the cut is governed by the diameter of the cutter in relation to that of the guide pin.

After a cutter has been subject to sharpening, the diameter of the guide requires to be slightly reduced. This can be coped with, when necessary, by using a tapered guide pin. Lowering the pin reduces its effective size. When working with a tapered pin, the jig must be held firmly down on to the table or the cut will be over size.

The alternative method of maintaining size is with the use of an eccentric chuck. Cutters can be adjusted to give increased eccentricity to produce the amount of cut required, within their range. The cutters used are of the single edge type, and do not require to be backed off as the method of mounting provides the clearance. They are not suitable for use in the standard concentric type of chuck mounting.

Eccentric chuck working is favoured in many branches of machine routing where burn free and high precision is required. It is important that a procedure of balancing is followed when mounting a cutter in the eccentric chuck. This is provided for by the use of a balancing table, and screwed weighting devices on the chuck.

The cutter is first set to produce the dimension required, then the balancing procedure before the machine is set into operation. Excess strain will be put on the machine bearings if the chuck is not in balance, and objectionable noise will be experienced.

High speed routers usually have a selection of rotation speeds, the principal ones being in the region of 18,000 and 24,000 rpm. These high revolutions, compared to other forms of woodworking machines, are necessary in order to produce a suitable peripheral speed of travel on the cutting edge.

The speed at which the cutting edge travels is related to the rpm of the spindle, and the diameter of the cutter. Therefore, a small diameter cutter requires a higher number of rpm than a larger one.

The speed of the cutting edge can be calculated as follows . . . Diameter of cutter x 3.142 x rpm. This will give a solution in distance per min., depending on what unit of measurement is used for the diameter of the cutter. If metric is used it may be desirable to present the answer in m/sec.

From an operational point of view it is customary to use the lower rotation speed if satisfactory results are being achieved. Higher speeds may well shorten the life of the motor bearings and should only be used for the purpose for which they are intended.

Nothing will be gained by changing to a higher speed if a cutter requires servicing, except perhaps a cloud of blue smoke and burnt patches on the work.

Although reverse rotation is not usually readily provided for on the high-speed router, there are instances when it can be used to advantage. Left-hand cutters are, of course, required for the operation. The work concerned mainly applies to slotting, either straight, or dovetailed. While slots can be run in from the left hand side of the machine, using a guide fence, they cannot be paired off by running in from the right.

Right-hand rotation would throw the work away from the fence. Reverse rotation will cope with this situation which can arise, and it can be very useful for quantity work for an operation known as slip dovetailing. Left-handed dovetail cutters are generally available from stock.

The high-speed bearings on the machine are foremost important on the subject of lubrication. The machine manufactured by **Wadkin** is fitted with a patented form of mist lubrication. The correct grade, and type, of oil must be used to obtain the planned results, and also the frequency of application. Details on point are usually displayed on the machine.

The head raising and lowering movement which is foot operated must be kept in free working condition. Dust must be washed out of the slides from time to time with paraffin followed by lubrication with a thin oil. Other adjustments relating to the table movements must also receive attention.

Fine wood dust, as produced on the router, quickly soaks up lubrication, and daily attention may be required on machines in continual use. Most high-speed routers of the heavy duty type contain a frequency changer. This is a rotary unit which will run for long periods with little attention, although its presence should not be forgotten.

Router cutter grinding may either be done with an attachment on the machine itself, or within the tool servicing room. Freehand grinding of solid cutters should not be encouraged, or working efficiency of the machine will be reduced, and tools quickly destroyed. Cutters for flat knife chucks can be ground freehand, also other flat cutters for head mounting.

Where pairs of cutters are involved in a mounting head, the question of balance will arise which calls for precision in the preparation and setting. Heads of this type do widen the scope of the machine considerably.

Trend Elu Machinery market a high-speed router that can also be used in the form of a spindle moulder. The motor head can be mounted either above or below the work table.

In this way the normal routing procedures can be followed and also the advantages of underneath working. As explained earlier in this article, the latter working method has points in its favour. A large range of attachments and cutters are available for the Elu routers, also wall charts explaining their uses.

A recent new development to their range is a basically portable model which has a range of rotor speeds from 8,000 to 22,000 rpm. The lower speeds are for working nonferrous metals and some forms of plastics where the generation of accumulated heat must be avoided. It has a power consumption of 1600W producing 2.2 hp. Cost £120.

The use of compressed air has been introduced into the operation of high-speed routers, both in new models and conversions to the ones in service. The action is related to the feed movement of the working head which is normally operated with a foot pedal. Foot pedal operation is still favoured for pneumatics, which leaves the hands free for guiding the work.

The method of head control could well be

Method of producing gouged work on the high-speed router. The sliding inclined table is made within the works unit. The method is highly productive compared to a hand process, and skill is mainly confined to the setting up of the operation.

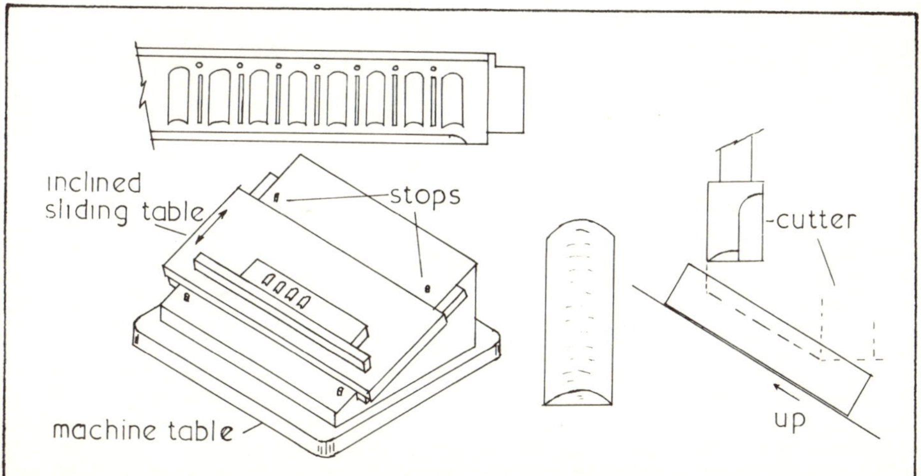

followed with pneumatic movement of the work-piece, say for slot mortising or other forms of recessing in quantity production. Set ups of this type should provide only minor difficulties, but provide a good step towards automation.
Router heads can be used as additional detailing units on such machines as the double end tenoner.
Portable high-speed routers are favoured in the smaller works units, and also for conversion work in situ. They are particularly useful as an aid to mechanise site operations.
A planned survey of repetition work being carried out by hand methods on a project may well merit the use of a mechanical aid. Recessing for hinges and door furniture may come in this field.
Also additional rebates to window members to accommodate double glazing, has created a demand on the services of portable routers for economical forms of conversion. Edge trimming to plastic laminate can probably be carried out in the greatest variety of work by the portable router type of appliance.
Tungsten carbide tipped cutters must be used for this work.

Elu portable router levelling off solid timber edging to a chip board panel on a site location.

The bandsaw

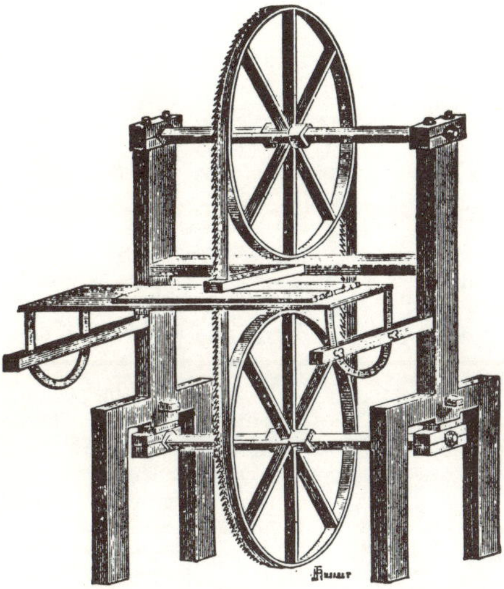

The first bandsaw, invented and patented by William Newberry in 1808. Illustration by permission of Crosby Lockwood Staples Ltd.

The bandsaw is claimed to have been invented and first patented by an Englishman, **William Newberry** in 1808. Other patents are said to have followed by other inventors relating to additions to the basic machine regarding saw guides and straining devices.

The chief problem which retarded progression was the development of the ribbon blades. Suitable steel which would flex to go around the wheels was not available, and there were jointing difficulties. The French produced blades of acceptable standard by about 1850 which were used on Newberry type machines.

Other machines had been designed and constructed by this time, but the original is the work of Newberry. The French have in the past been noted for the manufacture and use of fine saws in furniture making, and they must have appreciated the introduction of the narrow bandsaw.

Also Wheelwrights, and those engaged in the manufacture of shaped joinery which was so popular at the turn of the century must have made much use of the development. The machine replaced the hand bow saw and adze methods, although these tools can still be found in some present day catalogues.

As far back as 1856 two inventors filed provisional patents for a double type of bandsaw which cut both the inner and outer curve of a wheel rim, (the felloe) at one pass through. Similar operations are developing today in the use of band resaws for ripping.

Present day machines have advanced considerably since Newberry's original, but we still require to treat the blades with every respect to obtain lasting results. Most users obtain their blades from the machine manufacturer simply by quoting the machine number and the width of the blade required.

An alternative to this, where suitable equipment is available, is to purchase the saw strip preferably from the manufacturing source and make up the blades. The correct gauge of saw strip must be used in relation to the diameter of the wheels on the machine. Small wheels require a lighter gauge to enable the saw to flex.

Band saw users do from time to time have a spate of breakages not usually at the point of jointing, which is at once understandable if it does occur. Some of the causes, based on experience, are listed below: —

1. The wrong type of file may have been used for sharpening. Files should have slightly rounded corners so as to prevent a sharp corner at the bottom of the tooth which will encourage cracking.
2. A build up of resin on the rims of the wheels causing vibration and sudden strains. The rims should also be inspected for uneven wear.
3. The straining unit must have free movement, it must not be locked solid by over adjustment.
4. The top wheel must be free running without any tightness. Its rotation depends entirely on the energy transmitted by the blade. Any tightness, say due to lack of lubrication, will put unnecessary load on the blade.
5. Bandsaw teeth require to be set, in particular for cutting work involving curvature. The set should be confined to the upper half of the tooth, not fully down to the root.
6. The selection of width of blade for a particular

operation should be considered. Narrow blades for small curvature only, the wider blades for straight cutting.

7. A bandsaw must always be mounted on a firm floor, a springy wooden foundation is not suitable. This particularly applies where the strain on the saw is applied by weights. Vertical vibration will put continuous variation on the strain creating an unsatisfactory situation.

8. Over-pressure by the workpiece on the saw blade due to bluntness, can cause the back edge to be in heavy contact with the thrust wheel. This can upset the temper structure of the blade and cause failure in due course.

The saw guides and thrust wheel unit can be looked upon in two ways when it comes to criticism of design. The purpose of the guides is to maintain the saw steady so the work can be fed accurately into the cut. Very little demand is put upon the guides or thrust wheel by a trained operator using the correct width of blade in a well serviced condition.

On the other hand, when careless or inexperienced persons put undue demands on a machine which is also in need of servicing, the saw control unit may be put to unreasonable tests.

Most narrow bandsaws are now fitted with metal guide surfaces. A guide to be effective requires to be as near to the tooth line as possible without making contact. The thrust wheel should only come into contact with the back edge of the saw when material is being cut. An operator should always bear in mind that force is being exerted at this point depending on the condition of the saw and the rate of infeed of the material. The examination of a thrust wheel on a bandsaw can very often tell a story about the type of person that has been using the machine.

Guide and thrust wheel unit on a narrow bandsaw machine. The guides are brass and are adjustable for positioning to fine limits in relation to the saw blade. Guards have been removed for the purpose of this photograph.

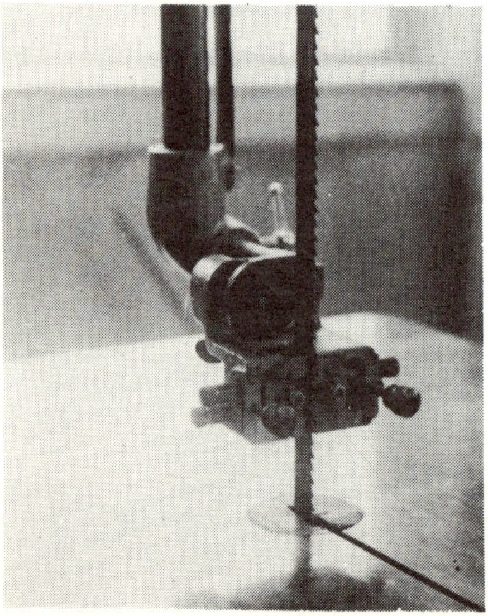

A bandsaw fitted with hardwood guides. Note the positioning of the guide unit to give maximum support and safety.

Some operators prefer hardwood guides instead of metal, and they do have points in their favour, depending very much on the type of operative or operatives that are using the machine. Metal guides give high precision working for those who require it, but for the less demanding, wood can be more suitable as adjustment is not as critical.

Set and the cutting edge can soon be taken off a blade by a careless operator with metal guides. Not so much with wooden guides.

On the more efficient machines, guides are provided both above and immediately below the work table. This gives the fullest control possible of the portion of the saw engaged in the cutting operation. A brush is also very often fitted to operate on the lower wheel to prevent sawdust building up on the running surface.

The method of keeping the saw taut, or applying strain as it is usually termed can be done in two ways. Simply to spread the two wheels apart is not enough as a certain amount of movement must be provided for to meet fluctuations in strain due to cutting load, or breakages would be very frequent.

The methods used are either by spring loading, or gravity acting on weights. Spring loading is

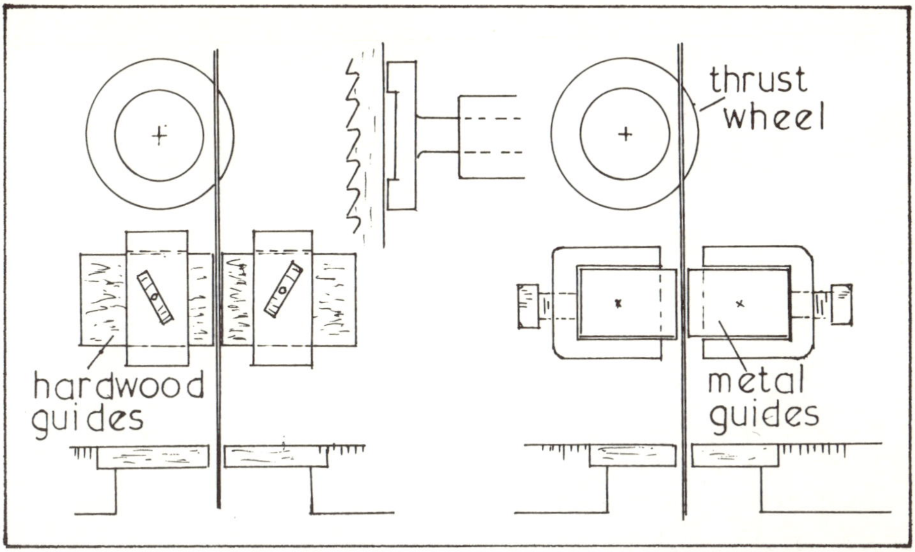

more compact and is less affected by any localised vibration. Measuring devices can also be conveniently fitted to give indication as to suitable pressures to be used with various widths of saw.

Under the weight system, a series of weights would be required to meet this service, or an extended bar to increase the effective load. An advancement on the setting guide of **Bursgreen** machines is an electrical device which prevents the machine from being started until the correct tension has been put on the saw. A red indicator light is also fitted.

The top wheel on a bandsaw has also an adjustment for tracking the blade to run in the centre of the rim. This adjustment should not require very much attention once it has been set, but it should be checked each time a new blade is fitted.

Blades that have several joints may have peculiarities when it comes to tracking, if the back edges have been out of line in the jointing operations.

Most narrow bandsaws are fitted with canting tables. This refinement can be useful for easing cuts on shaped moulded work. Most of the waste can be cut away before the spindle moulding operation. This ensures a better finish and safer working.

Many operators use the bandsaw for ripping along with a fence and a wider type of blade. With the canting table, bevelled stock can be produced.

The bandsaw is not a machine that makes use of

Guides on narrow bandsaws can either be of hardwood or metal, such as brass. On some machines the guide unit is repeated below the worktable to give the maximum support to the saw blade.

The Stenner Band Resaw VHM 36. This machine has 36 in. (914mm) dia. pulleys. It can take blades up to 75 mm in width. Feed speeds range from 7.62 to 30.48 metres per min. Machine being used for dressing edgings.

Interior view of a narrow bandsaw machine showing many of the features mentioned in this article. This machine is manufactured by Thomas Robinson and Son Ltd., Rochdale. Model Type EY.

A simple example of a set up for repetition working on the bandsaw. The shape template is lightly secured to the work by spikes, and guided by the pin fitted to the machine. This eliminates marking out the work.

an assortment of jigs like the router and spindle moulder. Shaping templates can be fixed to simple items, and the template edge may be guided by an extension pin fixed to the saw guide unit. This eliminates marking out, so saving time in quantity work.

Jig methods of cutting wedges have also been illustrated in my previous articles. Radial cutting can also be carried out, by pivoting an arm, and mounting items at the extreme end of the arm to come into contact with the saw. When these guided jig methods are used on the machine, the saw must be in first class condition or the cut will not follow the intended path.

I always consider that a bandsaw blade is at its best when it has been used for a short while after fitting. A newly fitted blade tends to be giddy and oversharp. After some use it runs more steadily, and the small amount of pressure required on the workpiece after blunting a little, ensures control of the cut. A supply of sharp blades should always be readily available, to get the best from the machine.

The length of the saw blade for a machine can be calculated by taking the circumference of one wheel, and adding to this, twice the distance between the wheel centres. The positioning of the top wheel should be in the centre of its adjustment run when the measurement is taken. This will allow an error margin in the making up of the blade.

Narrow bandsaw machines are usually right handed, as standard. That is, the working part of the blade is on the right of the machine. The

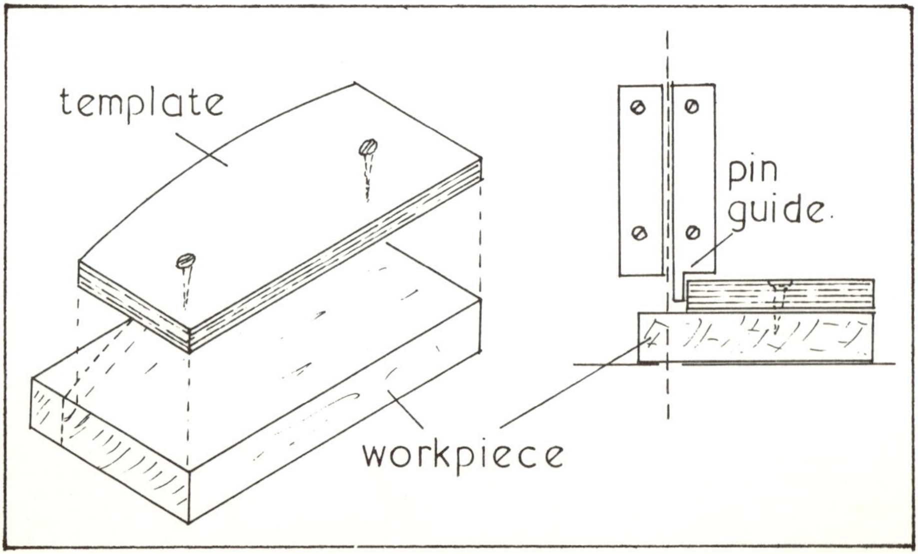

Double Bandsaw unit for log conversion and re-sawing operations. Width adjustment can be from 76 mm up to 508 mm on this machine. Photo by Mr. F. Shaw, Stenners, Tiverton, Devon.

machine can therefore usually be positioned with a wall at reasonably close distance on the left. Ample space should be provided on the other three sides to allow for curved work to be fed into the saw.

Most bandsaws are now marketed fully guarded to meet the present regulations. One adjustment does fall on the operator to carry out. This is the positioning of the guide unit to clear the thickness of the work being cut. When the material is constant in thickness there is no reason why the clearance should exceed 6 mm. This not only gives safer working, but also firmer control of the saw blade.

A push stick can also be very useful on the bandsaw table, in particular for clearing away small pieces of waste from the vicinity of the blade. A bandsaw is a comparatively quiet machine in a busy machine shop, and if a brake is available it should be used by the person after switching off. Machines should not be left rotating unattended, particularly in some circumstances.

Brake systems very often only operate on the lower wheel of the machine. In the event of a saw breakage, no attempt to remove the broken blade should be made until the top wheel has come to rest also.

The term, band resaw, refers to a band saw machine which cuts timber that has already been converted from the round log. It is designed to accommodate material of uniform dimensions.

The width of the blades used in this type of machine usually start at about 75 mm. although narrower blades are in use. Blades also loose width in the process of sharpening. Minimum wheel diameters could be said to be 914 mm. (36 in.).

Machines of this type are described as "wide bandsaws", which refers to the width of the saw blade. Narrow bandsaws as previously described in this article are principally designed for cutting shaped work. Wide bandsaws cut in a straight line only.

Band resaws also require to be a much more robust machine than a narrow bandsaw to carry heavy loading. Round logs can be converted on a band resaw providing that they come within the capacity of the machine. Larger machines than the band resaw are termed "band mills"

It is customary for band resaws to be fitted with

Band resaw operating in a timber mill. Note the supporting bench at the output end which also acts as a guard when high speed sawing.

A band resaw of the smaller type which takes blades up to 76 mm in width. It can be accommodated in an area a little larger than two metres by one metre. This could be ideal for training establishments or production units where space is limited. Model E.F.T.

power feeding equipment. This is usually transmitted through serrated rollers, with a range of feed speeds. Other methods of feed are in use with the larger machines in this range, such as roller feed beds and chain drag equipment.

Band resaws, and more so band mills, are very often designed to suit a particular location, much more so than the average woodworking machine. It could be said that band resaws can be bought off the shelf, but band mills require specialisation at their early stages of construction.

Although band resaws have been looked upon in the past as a timber mill machine, they are now being used within the woodworking manufacturing unit.

They have advantages over the circular saw, the chief one being the saving in timber due to the width of the saw kerf. A kerf line on a band resaw deep-cut may be 1.5 mm. compared with say 3.5 mm. with a circular saw blade. This can make a lot of difference when dividing material up in a busy production establishment.

Such items as boards 50 mm. in thickness can be cut into two making an acceptable pair of 25 mm. boards. This would just not be a proposition with a circular saw, due to kerf loss. The bandsaw also requires much less effort to make a cut, resulting in a saving in power, and strain on the cutting unit.

High rates of feed are possible with the band resaw depending on the machine capacity and loading. As the operator can control the machine at a considerable distance from the cutting point, it is a safe machine to use.

A one time disadvantage to some was the servicing of the saw blades. This requires more working space and equipment than that of circular saws. However in many areas now, specialists are available who service saws at reasonably short notice when this cannot be done within the works unit.

The requirement of first class servicing to blades cannot be over stressed. This may well be left to the highly experienced person. Tooth design relating to the type of material being cut must be noted, also the moisture content when dealing with extreme situations.

Sharpening is usually confined to machine grinding in the main, and this permits hardening processes to be practised on the saw teeth. Stellite tipping, a process of applying hard metal with the aid of a welding torch is favoured for dealing with abrasive hardwoods. Experience with the use of welding equipment is required for the stellite process, along with the preparation and pre-heating of the saw teeth.

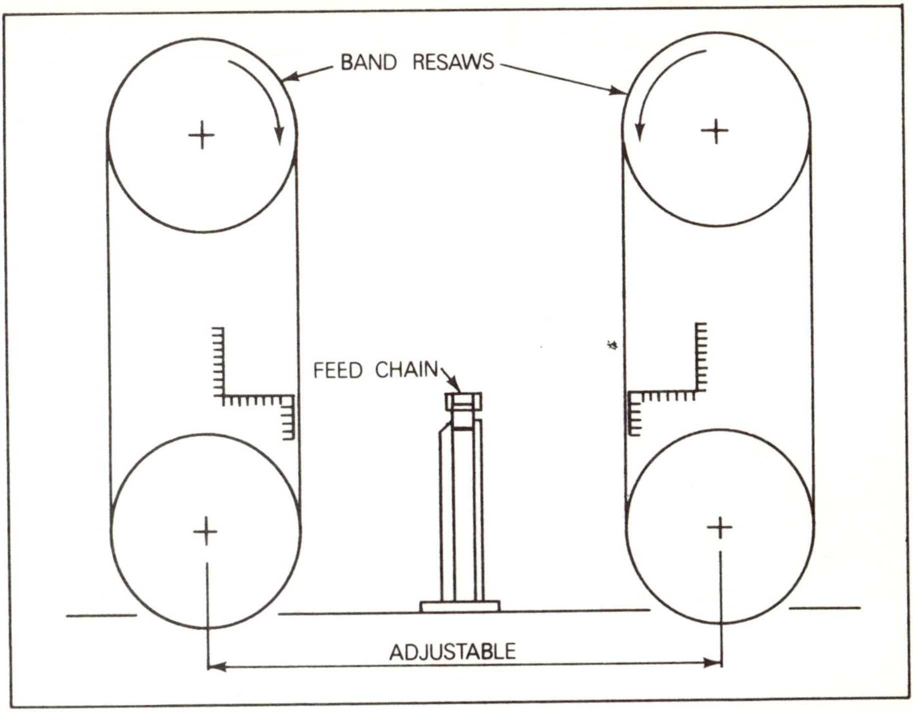

An example of how two wide bandsaws of the resaw type can be mounted to make parallel cuts at the one pass through the machine. The adjustment is power operated. Sketch based on a machine produced by Messrs. Stenner of Tiverton, Devon.

Twin line set up for resawing timber. This method is now favoured over reciprocating multi sawing due to the reduction of waste in the saw kerf.

Tungsten carbide tipping of wide bandsaw blades is not in general use at the present time of development. This is mainly due to the flexible nature of the blades and the narrow adhesion surface. It must be accepted also, that some vibration due to hammering will take place in the servicing of a wide band saw.

Set, on the saw teeth can either be by spring setting in which the cutting points are levered in alternate directions to provide clearance, or swage setting which is carried out with the aid of special tools.

With swage setting the front of every tooth is spread and dressed uniform. Each tooth, therefore, cuts the full width of the saw kerf. The strain on the saw blade is more centralised than with spring set which is a favourable point when working with strip blades.

The amount of set required on a band resaw blade is very small. A 20 gauge blade measures 0.89 mm. in thickness. With average set a saw

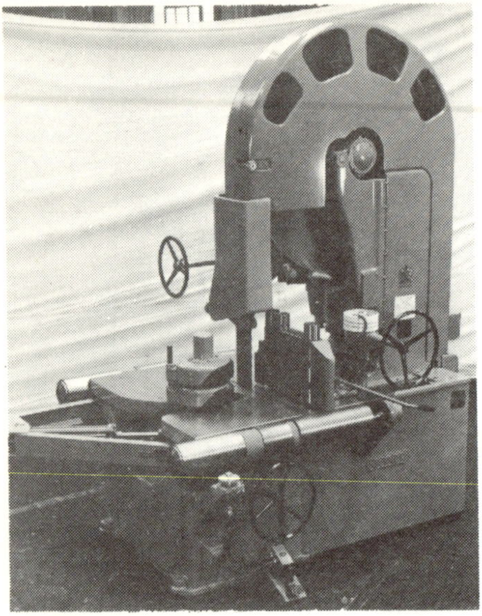

Stenner band re-saw looking from the in-feed end

kerf of 1.65 mm. will be produced. Over-setting puts a greater load on the machine and also increases the waste factor.

Wide bandsaw blades, unlike narrow bandsaws run directly metal to metal on the wheel rims. The teeth overhang the edge to prevent the set from being removed.

Guides are provided in loose contact with the blade, immediately above the line of cut, but no thrust wheel is necessary. The guides are often faced with lignum vitae blocks, or specially prepared synthetic material with self lubricating properties.

Recent developments of the roller feed units fitted to band resaws have increased their efficiency and simplicity in use. Under the advanced systems now being used, operations such as deep cutting timber into two equal slabs is easily accomplished, the saw equally dividing the timber at all points irrespective of variations in thickness.

Fixed distance from the leading roll can also be set for, with the offcut bearing any variation.

The installation of a band resaw to a timber unit, to be an economic proposition, must have the recognition of supporting factors. It is a highly productive machine, capable of handling large quantities of material. Man handling of material should be kept to a minimum.

Systems of roller conveyance and transfer units should be considered. A larger capacity machine than is actually required could put an added strain to costs both initially and in operation. Two band resaws working as a unit can increase productivity by reducing labour costs and step up quantity output also.

Not many training establishments have band resaws available, as their original use was mainly confined to saw-milling. With the introduction of a wider range of these machines they are finding a place within woodworking fabricating units of all types. This calls for the technical training operatives in this field and suitable machines to meet the demand.

Space is very often limited in training establishments, so this, and the consideration of finance may well command the smaller type of machine.

Both **Robinsons** of **Rochdale**, and **Stenners** of **Tiverton**, manufacture band resaw machines, and have wide experience in their operation and design.

The use of this type of machine is increasing considerably as more timber users are becoming aware of its capabilities.

As with all automatically fed machines, particular attention must be made to the outfeed end to ensure ample space is available to prevent the taker off from being trapped. In a production shop using a band resaw for general work occasions have been known when the feed unit has been taken out of service and the work fed by hand. This very often concerns the cutting of short material.

Care must be taken under these circumstances that the cutting unit is efficiently guarded. The guarding arrangements for power feeding may well not be suitable for hand feeding. The use of a push stick should also not be overlooked.

The fourcutter or moulding machine

The machine is usually described by the manufacturers as a moulder, since it very often has cutter heads in excess of the basic four. The term four-cutter does however prevent the machine from being confused with the spindle moulder when discussing woodworking machines generally.

Some operators describe their machine according to the number of cutter heads with which it is equipped. It is not unusual to hear the term six cutter used in the mill. This description does convey more information as to the machine's capabilities than the term moulder, and it may define it from a lesser machine in the mill which may only have, say, four cutter heads.

The question may arise, "If four cutter heads are provided, one for each face of the timber, why do we need any more?" There are a number of reasons for this which are very evident to the experienced operator.

Although the layout of the positioning of cutter heads vary in machines designed with particular operations in mind, the first head is most commonly located to work on the underside of the timber.

Its purpose is to straighten the surface to ensure a balanced passage through the machine. Unless the timber is very flat and straight before

Glazing bars can be planed and rebated at the first pass through the machine. They are next tenoned and scribed A second pass through adds the mould and final dimension. This is a suggested method of working favoured by some operators.

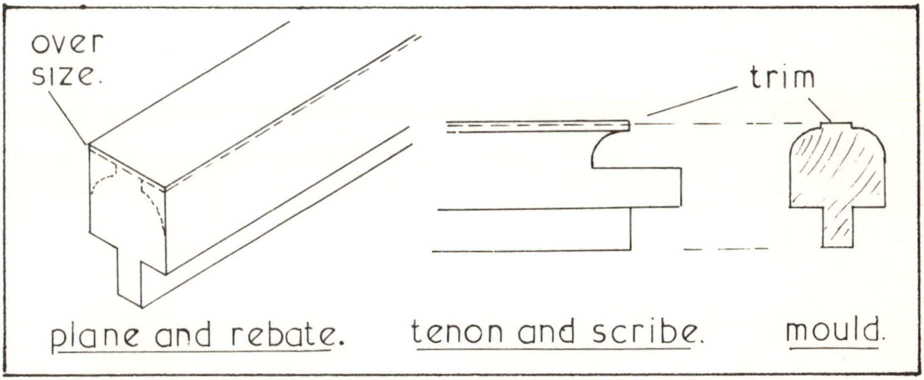

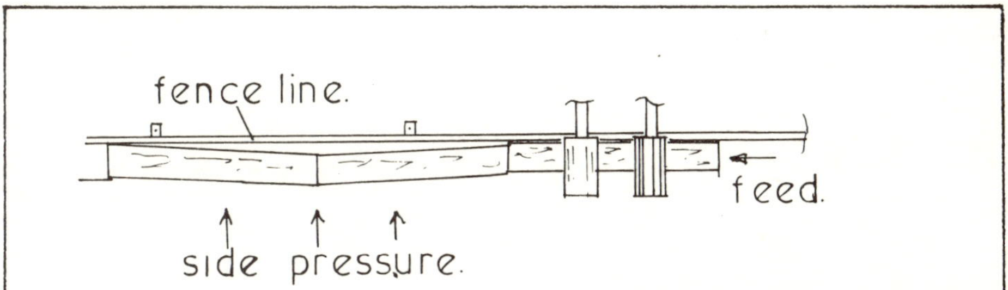

If the ends of short stock are not cut reasonably square, additional side pressure is required to force the work on to the fence. This is most noticeable on wide material.

entering the machine, it is not possible to add mouldings or other formations to the lower face at this stage with any degree of accuracy as the material has not been taken to width.

To carry out operations on the under face of the timber, a fifth head becomes necessary which is very often positioned at the outfeed end of the machine. Many four head machines are manufactured with a fifth head in mind, and have prepared faces ready to receive an additional cutter unit if required after installation.

This fifth head is also very useful for mounting circular saw blades to cut the planed material into a number of strips as it leaves the machine. This multiple method of working enables linear output to be greatly increased and is most advantageous when dealing with small sections. A machine producing small section work can be uneconomic, but if the full width capacity can be utilised by multiple working, so much the better.

An additional top head can serve a variety of purposes. The top head is the thicknessing head, and it can at times have to remove a considerable amount of waste. Joinery items, such as sills in window construction, can involve heavy cutting in the section formation. Material used for this particular item is also very often hardwood, and for cost reasons not always prime grade. If the cutting load can be distributed over two cutting heads a better product may be obtained, and a more balanced strain put on the machine. Feed speed too can be increased.

A study of the type of work involved in a particular unit can decide upon the selection of a machine regarding the positioning of the cutter heads. To order a moulding machine without giving consideration to its purpose, or perhaps accepting a machine because it was readily available, could be a mistake.

Slide heads on moulding machines are generally only two in number. One for straightening the timber on the fence side, and the other for taking the material to width. There is, however, an additional head which operates from the side, and it has become popular over recent years. This is termed a throating head, and its purpose is to form an anti-capillary groove on the vertical edge of the sill rebate.

To cut this groove without the use of this special head a very large projection could be necessary on the moulder, and in instances it may have to be done with an additional pass through another machine. The throating head can be set very close to the point of operation, so requiring very little projection of the cutter.

Two methods are in use to produce the

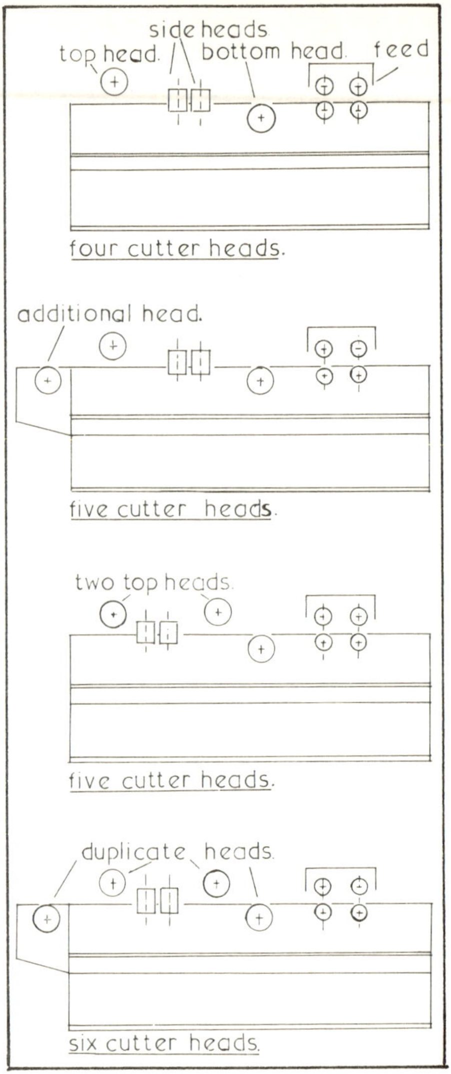

Line details showing the positioning of cutter heads on four, five, and six cutter planing and moulding machines.

necessary high speeds required on the cutter spindles. Separate motors for each cutter head is now the accepted standard in machine design. Some machines include a frequency changer which enables the cutter mounting heads to be fitted directly on to the motor shafts. This cuts out the use of driving belts and makes a very compact trouble free machine.

When belts are used, they are usually Vee belts

which are suitable for short drives. These have to be renewed from time to time, and should be fitted in complete sets. To renew say only one in a drive unit having a batch of four would put all the load on to the new belt which would result in slip and put excess strain on the belt.

The horizontal heads on a moulding machine may have outside supports to the mounting spindles, or be open-ended. Machines designed for woking wide material say over 150 mm are very often fitted with outside supports. These supports require to be removed when transferring the cutter heads to the servicing unit. This is however a very much simplified operation.

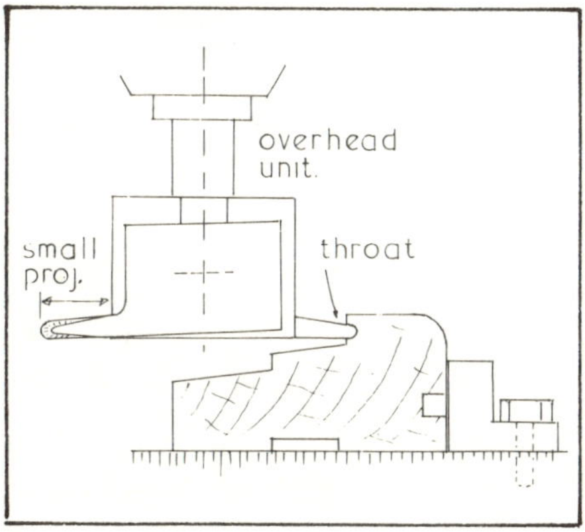

Purpose of an overhead throating unit fitted to a moulder. Note the small cutter projection required for this operation when using this unit compared to working from the outer side head.

Importance of working in the correct sequence of operations. Finger joints should be completed before the planing operation. Built up material. Fabrication should be done mainly in the rough, then machine to dimension finally.

If a machine is required for processing wide material continually, outside supports are well advised. Machines used only for narrow stock do not require outside supports to bearings which reduces machine cost and also setting up times.

A range of feed speeds is usually available on all moulding machines, and this is particularly useful if cutter rotation speeds are variable also. To use high feed speeds the following points should be observed.

1. The cutter unit should be in dynamic balance.
2. Cutters on the unit should be trimmed to identical cutting circles.
3. The higher speeds of cutter rotation should be used.

The most attention must be made to the faces of the timber which are to be visible in use. It may be necessary to trim the cutters on two heads only. It is preferable that trimmed cutters are used on the top heads, and outside head of the machine. This ensures that excessive heels will not force the timber away from the bed of the machine or the fence.

Solid profile cutters for moulded items fulfil the requirements of high speed feeding. They also simplify setting up procedures. The basic cost of this type of cutter head may soon be recovered if

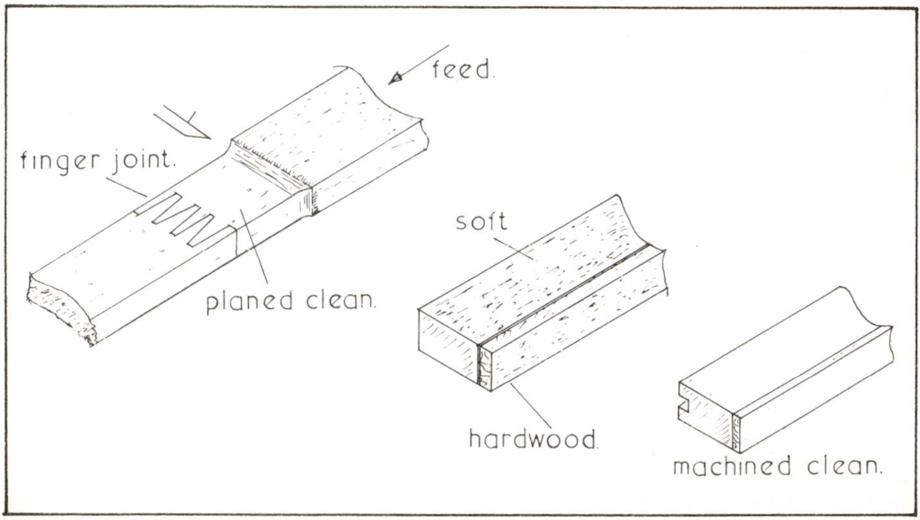

A heavy duty planing and moulding machine designed for continuous loading. The largest model of this Type 333 can accommodate timber up to 318 x 114 mm. Feed speed can be up to 61 metre/min. if required. (White, Paisley.)

there is sufficient requirement for its services.
In the smaller works unit, where a moulder may have only short runs, aids to speed setting up should always receive consideration.
Preparing material on the moulder has many advantages over separate planing and thicknessing operations. In addition to the square planing of the stock, grooving and moulding operations can be applied at the same pass through.
In the smaller works unit, it may be necessary to plane material in advance of requirement once the machine has been set. An advanced stock of prepared material can help with the fabrication of small orders, and it is very often the solution to dealing with these.
Suitable storage facilities must be made to accommodate advanced stock sections, or prepared material may deteriorate and become a loss.
Another aspect of the operation of a moulder is

Splitting saw details as applied to the outgoing head of a moulding machine. Advantages . . . Increased linear production. Better feeding of small section stock.

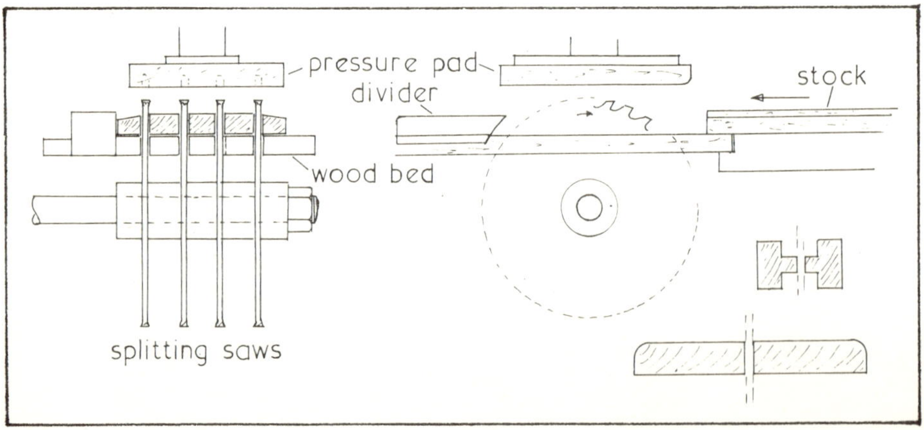

the method of offering the material to the machine.

In some establishments, large quantities of short material have to be processed. A system known as hopper feeding is used to keep the stock flowing through the machine. The material is stacked in the hopper unit at the infeed end of the machine, and it is automatically guided into the feed rollers. The feed from the hopper has to be such that the work is always backed up to maintain a constant flow, otherwise the quality of the work may not be up to the required standard.

This backing up action is very often provided within the hopper feed system, which in effect feeds the material at a slightly increased rate to that of the machine feed. A slipping action is involved also to maintain harmony in the process.

It is always advisable to have the ends of the stock being fed into moulding machines, squared off. Otherwise off square ends can introduce a force which is not directly in line with that of the direction of feed. This requires additional side pressure or the stock may be forced away from the fence.

In addition to hopper feeding for short material, automatic feeding tables are available for long timbers being processed. Equipment of this type becomes necessary when feed speeds of say 50 m per min. are being used. There would be no point in equipping a moulder for high rates of feed, and having a waiting period between the insertion of each piece due to the operator not being able to cope.

The design of the feed system used will depend upon the type of work involved. Furniture makers generally cut up the material into shorts before passing through the moulder. They have two reasons for this.

Hardwood requires grain selection, unlike most softwood jobs and short items very often can be straightened during the pass through the moulder, long lengths tend to spring back into curvature.

Builders requirements such as T and G boards for flooring or fascia work is most economically marketed in long lengths. Door makers, of quality standard, prefer to take the twist out of members before offering the stock to the moulder.

Pre-straightening units, which are in effect a surface planer, can be fitted at the intake of a moulder to improve the shape of the stock before it goes forward for processing.

Cutter heads which describe a large diameter cutting circle, and are equipped with a number of cutters, are capable of the highest quality of finish. Although by calculation, smaller diameter cutting circles with fewer cutting points and run-

A general purpose machine designed to meet the requirements of a large range of users in the various branches of industry. (Robinson, Rochdale.)

Setting the abrasive unit for cutter trimming (jointing) on the Wadkin 7 FB machine. The unit is traversed across the cutters with the block rotating.

Preparing to trim a moulding cutter profile. A purposely shaped abrasive stone is required. If profiles on the cutter sets vary excessively, further grinding may be found necessary.

ning at increased speed of rotation give a similar spacing of cutter marks, the finish may not be as good.

This can be due to the depth of the wavefield being related to the diameter of the cutting circle. Also it must be accepted that the cut is made on the up stroke of the motion, and the more gradual this takes place, due to large diameter the less severe any fracture of the timber surface. Examination of erratic grained timbers reveal these factors after planing.

Straight cutters can be trimmed during rotation, but moulding profiles are limited to the amount of trimming that can be done. Solid profile cutters with several cutting points, should produce good clean mouldings. The use of self centreing collets or cones must be considered when grinding and mounting in the machine if full efficiency is to be obtained.

In the preparation of moulding cutters for the square block, very often not enough consideration to honing is given after grinding.

It is not unusual to find only one type of slip stone available in the sharpening area. The type referred to is the one that is tapered in end section, and has two half rounded edges, or the remains of such.

Complete sets of honing stones are available including rounds of various diameters, triangulars, and small flats. Some consideration to the use of these aids can soon be reflected in the work produced. A quarter round member of a mould for instance should be a quarter of a given circle, not a lesser amount of a circle of larger diameter.

Moulding machines are used in many branches of the industry and their capabilities can be very versatile within limits. In carcase construction for furniture items (kitchen units are now classed as furniture) very often only the edge of the timber is exposed to view in the finished product. If offcuts of hardwood are available these can be quickly glued to rough softwood of, say, 50 mm by 25 mm dimension and put through the moulder after setting, probably adding grooves or rebates at the same time.

The increased time factor over using solid hardwood will be in the gluing operation but this can be electronically assisted in many factories. The hardwood may possibly be wasted otherwise, and the operation should show a marked gain with present rising timber costs.

Another scheme practised in some joinery production units where rebated and moulded glazing bars are involved. The bars are put through the machine, but planed and rebated only. The moulds are not formed at this first run through. A small amount is also left on the top face of the stock. The prepared planed and rebated section is then tenoned and scribed without any spelching being experienced due to its square state.

Finally, the bars are put through the moulder a second time with the cutters set to form the moulds and the pressure roll marks removed by

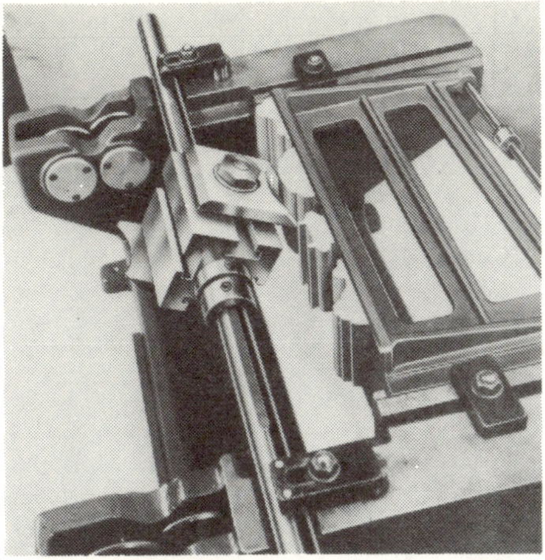

Placing cutters on a square block can be simplified by the use of a setting stand. Cutters can be positioned to sample mouldings.

dressing the top surface to dimension. Short members may be involved in this operation, and some additional pressure units may be required.

Establishments using finger jointing for waste elimination or to obtain exceptionally long members for laminated beam work, cut the finger formation in the unwrought timber and pass the cured member through the moulder finally. This saves time cleaning up the jointed portion, if the procedures were incorrectly planned, additional labour could be involved.

As referred to earlier in this article, the second bottom head on the moulder is often used for the purpose of mounting saws to divide the stock as it leaves the machine. There are problems involved in this method of working, and it has its limitations. Making one cut only is more trouble free than running a group of several saws, as the two parts can be guided and satisfactorily parted as they leave the machine.

Where a number of saws are involved, a considerable amount of heat is often generated around the unit which puts a general strain on the saws. The saws, only being small in diameter, require to run at high speed to produce the recognised rim speed of around 3000 m per min.

Saw gullets should be generous, and the teeth should have both front and top bevel to produce minimum resistance. This is a point which must be considered if tungsten carbide tipped saws are used. Very often these saws are supplied for saw bench work with very little tooth bevel to eliminate point weakness.

Additional push is required to operate these saws, although their lasting qualities are first class. Down pressure must be applied to prevent overriding of the timber as the teeth become blunt. Some timbers do not lend themselves to sawing by this method due to their ability to twist and nip on being parted. To quote some of the difficult ones from my experience, agba, utile and afromosia. More acceptable timbers are, softwood, obechi, ramin and limba.

Moisture content at the time of working can

This machine, of recent design, is available with four, five, or six cutter heads. Its unique method of frame fabrication gives a clean exterior outline. (Wadkin Model 7 FB.)

affect the suitability selection of a timber.
The method does produce a sawn face on the stock which may not always be acceptable for a purpose. Moulded work can at times be parted in the profile formation, a planed finish being produced. Shaped saddles very often have to be made to guide the stock as it leaves the cutter head.
Having set the moulding machine to what is considered correct, there are various schools of thought as to the procedure of getting the machine into operation. The sequence can on some machines be governed by the safety cut out arrangements in the electrical switchgear.
On some machines, unless the circuits are closed on all the cutter heads, the feed motor will not start. This is to prevent jamming should a head stop during operation.
Most machines are now fitted with what is termed an inching button. This enables fine control

A three cutter machine manufactured by Dominion of Halifax. The thicknessing cutter is driven with a 5.5 hp motor, and the two side heads have each 3 hp. Profile moulding cutters can be fitted to any of the three heads to carry out shaped work in addition to square planing.

A cutter setting and balancing stand. The block is being balanced on the "frictionless" supports. The blocks can also be set for cutter positioning using the pivoted table.

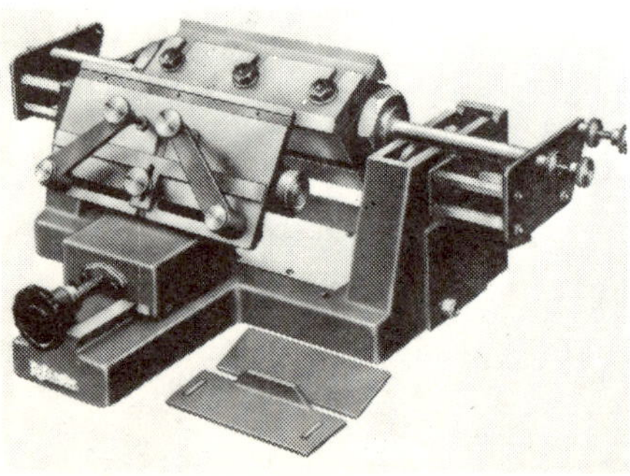

of the feed during the initial trial run. On machines where the heads can be started individually, and the inching button used, the result of each head can be tried in turn, careful check being made at each stage. If it is necessary to reduce the amount of cut slightly on a head, this may be done with the machine either in motion or stationary.
Should, however, an increase in cut be required on a head and the timber is in the machine, the adjustment must be made with the cutters rotating otherwise a jam will occur on an attempt to start up.
Trouble with feeding can be caused for a variety of reasons. Most moulding machines depend on push feed which is done entirely from the loading end. Machines are developing with what is termed through feed where a series of drive points are applied at intervals along the line of stock.
The principal feed rollers are serrated to increase frinction on the surface of the timber, but the application of pressure should always be kept to a minimum. Over pressure imprints the roller serrations into the timber which can cause permanent disfigurement. Pressure units holding the timber as it passes through the machine can retard the progress of flow if not sensibly applied.
Moulders using jointed cutters or front bevels, require more pressure than sharp hollow ground units. If heavy cutting can be done overhead, and on the outer-side unit, pressures can be kept to a minimum.
The lead in end of wooden pressure saddles should be bevelled or rounded to permit free entrance to the stock. Lubrication of the machine table and fence should not be overlooked, particularly when resinous timbers are being worked. Moving parts on pressure application units should also be lubricated.
Feeding trouble can have an effect on the work produced. It is not good policy to have cutter heads running in contact with the timber and the feed not operating. Heat is generated which will mark the stock, and although it may not destroy the cutter steel it will affect the fine cutting edge enough to lower the standard of work. If it becomes necessary to stop the feed while in cut, the inching reverse feed button should be pressed for as little as two seconds when the progression has ceased to take the cutting surface back from the cutter edge.
One multi-head machine not previously mentioned in this article is the three cutter. It is an economical form of multihead working, and on inspection it has other attractive points to offer.

Loading short material into a hopper feed. This ensures a constant flow eliminating halt marks on the work.

The Dominion model has a width capacity at its extreme of 305 mm (12in).

A fourcutter machine of the traditional type would be an extremely large piece of machinery to accommodate material of this dimension. Present day requirements in the builders' joinery field are for material mainly up to 200 mm in width, so a machine designed for 300 mm should happily accommodate a large range of standard work without having to operate at maximum capacity.

Advantages of portable power tools

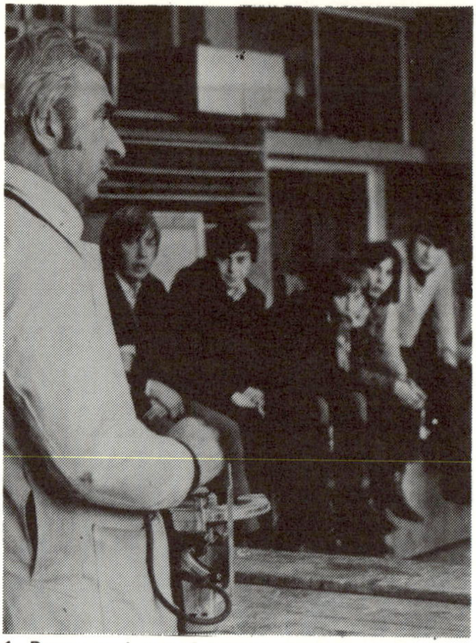

1. Power tool manufacturers are keen to give instruction in the use of their products. Above, Harold Derbyshire, Technical Lecturer of Stanley Tools, giving a portable power tool demonstration to students of the Department of Building, at Doncaster College of Technology.

Although a woodworking establishment may be equipped with a substantial range of machines, experience has shown that there is place for portable power tools within such a unit.

There are several reasons for this, the main one being the advancing efficiency of these portable tools, having developed beyond the novelty stage to a modern production aid.

A point, which must not be overlooked if immediate success is required, is the approach to their use. Some training may be required and the tool manufacturers fully realise this. They are most helpful in arranging demonstrations to show the capabilities of their products.

Some educational establishments also offer short courses on the use of portable power tools, and these can be particularly helpful to woodworkers with no experience of cutting by rotary action.

Points on safety are highlighted by demonstrators, not only regarding cutting, but also in the handling of power supply cables. Advice on the use of reduced voltage for site work is usually discussed. A few hours spent at a demonstration, or course, can be beneficial, and give an operator a new approach.

The operations which can be carried out by portable power tools in capable hands is extensive, but the following are a selection of examples where the portable tool may be more suitable than a full-sized woodworking machine.

Rip saw

The use of large sheets of panel boards is on the increase to meet the present-day demands of construction methods. Their cutting can at times, in a busy shop, be a problem unless a wide capacity circular saw bench is available.

A PORTABLE RIP SAW CAN MAKE A CUT ON ANY SIZE OF SHEET PROVIDING IT IS SUITABLY SUPPORTED.

If a guide lath is nailed or clamped to the panel

2. A portable circular saw cutting a large sheet of blockboard which could not be accommodated on a saw bench without removing the guard equipment. Note the guide lath which ensures a straight cut, and eliminates marking the full length of the board.

the under sole of the saw unit can be run against it. With the careful planning of supports, one man can carry out the operations.

It is not suggested that panels should be cut into small pieces using a portable saw, but large sheets can be broken down so as to be accommodated on a circular saw bench. Waney edged timber can also be first cut using a portable saw and a guide lath.

High speed router

The portable router can on some operations be used to advantage over a full-sized routing machine. This is in addition to the fact that the machine can be taken to the work when large units are involved.

Routing machines normally work overhead, on top of the work. This means that if the work lifts off the machine table momentarily, or the work is slightly in twist, an increased amount of timber is cut away in error.

This irregularity does not occur when using a portable router as the depth of the cut is governed by the bed plate of the tool resting on the work itself.

If the portable tool is lifted off the work during the cut, material is left on, and can be removed with another run through, no damage being done.

Worktops for tables and kitchen units that have been edged and surfaced with laminated plastic have to be edge trimmed as a final operation. Much cost is involved both in materials and labour to get the tops to this stage.

If the trimming is to be carried out on a spindle moulder it must be done working face side down if a small bevel is required on the laminated edge. There is a danger here of the work being scratched unless the machine table is in clean condition and kept so, which is almost impossible working plastics.

With a portable router, fitted with a small attachment, the trimming can be carried out working face side up. A laminated plastic trimming router is available which has been designed to meet this particular operation.

It has the advantage that it is lighter in weight than a general router, and the point of cut is more visible to the operator.

The sabre saw

This power tool is one no woodworking establishment should be without. For pierced work—which often occurs in the making of router jigs—it can be very useful. For one-off jobs in the machine shop, such as cutting a hole in a worktop to accommodate a sink bowl, the work can be carried out without interrupting a machine on the main production line.

A machine router would require a jig to

3. A portable router fitted with an attachment for edge trimming laminated plastic. For this operation a portable tool is often preferrable to taking the work to a machine.

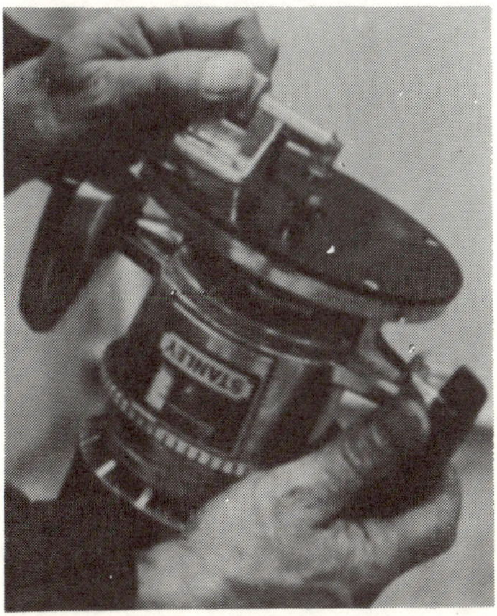

4. A Sabre Saw cutting pierced work for a jig assembly. This portable tool will fill the requirements of many woodworking departments that have only a limited call for a full sized jig saw machine.

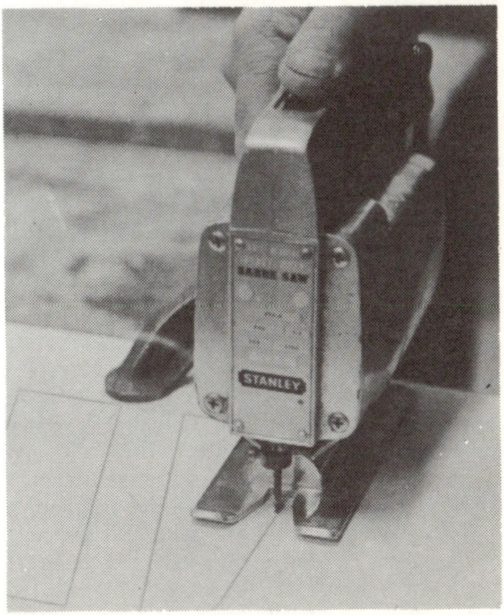

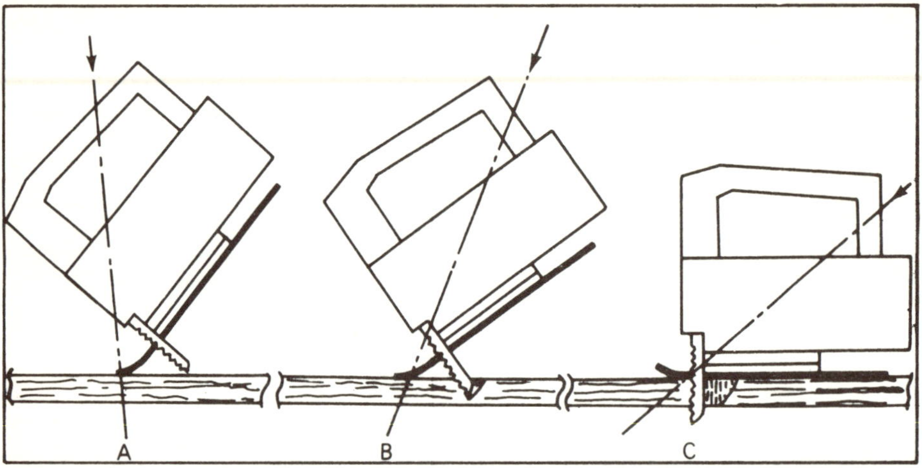

D1. A piercing cut can be commenced with a Sabre Saw without boring a hole. A. Shows the angle at which the tool should be positioned with the load on the front of the guide shoe. B. Having switched on the motor, the saw is led into the work. C. Full penetration of the work has been made, and the cut can now proceed.

carry out the operation, but not the sabre saw.

Many machine shops retain a full-sized jig saw to cope with only small amounts of pierced work. This may be carried out by a sabre saw, leaving valuable space for a more productive machine.

I think the sabre saw is a tool with a future as it has all the features of present-day demands. Reasonable cost and weight. No jigs required to operate.

It can be used for pierced or open work. It can cut out holes in many instances after work has been assembled. What other machine tool has these advantages? I can foresee further development of this tool and its method of cutting.

Sanders

Portable sanders can be divided into two groups regarding the finishing of wood. These are, belt sanders for heavy work, and the oscillating pad type, generally known as finishing sanders.

Portable belt sanders have a use in establishments where work is of such dimension that it cannot be accommodated on a sanding machine.

This type of work is on the increase with the development of adhesives, larger structures are being manufactured, such as built-up beams and arches, which demand a high standard of finish.

Finishing work on timber is an important operation. It can govern the marketing potential of a product.

Without mechanical assistance sanding can be time consuming and extremely hard work. Some skill is required in the use of a portable belt sander or its life can be shortened and the expected standard of work not obtained.

An untrained worker may consume more sander

5. Tracking the belt on a portable sander before attempting to use. The dust collecting bag, seen in the foreground, should always be attached during operation. A face mask should be worn under some conditions of working.

belts through incorrect tracking than actual wear on the timbers.

Finishing sanders are much more simple to use than belt sanders but they are confined to the finer type of work. These are principally used in workshops after the items have been assembled to give a final clean up and remove a minimum of timber.

They have proved very successful in these respects.

THEIR AIM IS ALSO TO REDUCE FATIGUE OF THE CRAFTSMAN, WHICH THEY DO.

Power Drills

The availability of a portable electric drill in a machine shop is a useful asset. It encourages the jig maker to build up his aids with screws rather than nails—and so produce a superior job.

Shabbily produced jigs frequently produce a poor standard of work. Electric screwdrivers are also an aid in jig building and can speed the work considerably.

Drills are available in a large range of sizes. Costs also vary depending on such things as the construction of the motor unit, and if any overload or selection of speed devices are fitted.

Added efficiency refinements increase the initial cost, but these are expected to increase reliability and produce a longer life tool.

A worker should not be burdened with a tool much larger than he actually requires for the job.

The only real way to beat rising costs is by increasing productivity. Operations which are at present being done by hand because they are not suitable for a machine may come within the scope of a portable power tool.

These operations often occur at a stage when some assembly work has taken place making it impracticable to put the unit on to a machine.

For a one off job to be carried out in a machine shop engaged on bath production a considerable interruption of the work flow may take place, involving loss. Portable power tools could carry out some of the operations involved, and so reduce the work loss.

If space or money is limited in a department, portable power tools could be of help.

Portable power tools should be suitably accommodated when not in use, such as in a cupboard, or boxed, if they are to be stored on a shelf. They should at all times be maintained in working order.

An operator endeavouring to use a tool which is not working correctly due to, maybe, only a minor fault, may be deterred from using this type of appliance in the future.

The maintenance of power tools includes cleaning and lubrication, to adjustable parts. The high speed bearings may, or may not require, lubrication by the user, some are sealed by the makers.

Saws require to be set and sharpened in keeping with the type of cutting to be undertaken.

Router cutters require to be rubbed up with a slip stone, and grinding will be required eventually. When grinding router cutters, back clearance, and the angle of approach must be maintained.

Tungsten carbide, solid or tipped cutters must be used when working laminated plastic. This also applies when plywood is being worked in quantity.

A study of the maintenance of portable power tools is well worthwhile for long term users. Although the tools referred to in this article are principally designed for working wood, they can also be used for working other materials. The tool manufacturers are always ready to advise or demonstrate on request.

Section 3 Processing Technique

Planing And Thickmessing

Method of cutting. Peripheral speed. Calculations. Pitch of cutter marks. Suitability of finish. Architects specifications. Planing chart.

Timber Planing On The Fourcutter.

Machine layout. Adjustments. Imperial and metric calculations. Setting scales. Use of various heads. Pressure unit. Multipoint cutter block.

Rebating And Grooving On The Fourcutter.

Cutter setting scale. Setting rebating cutters. Types of cutters. Balance. Tongue and groove. Clearance bevels. Robinson projection rule.

Producing Moulded Work On The Fourcutter.

The term "Moulder" Working abrasive timber. Geometrical development. Robinson Pro-set unit. Maintaining accuracy. Cutter setting stand.

Backfencing On The Spindle Moulder.

Advantages of the process. Moulding. Widthing. Setting fences. Pressure springs. Auto. feed.

Reverse Rotation On The Spindle Moulder.

Improved finish. Precautions to take. Double spindle machines. Economy of cutters. Power feed. Additional uses.

Methods Of Machining Bevels.

Purpose of use. Cutter profiles. Use of back stops. Geometrical functions. Bevelling with the saw. Planing saddle for thicknesser.

Time Saving In Setting Up. Frictionless Collars.

Setting cutters. Simplified machine setting. Preparation of jigs. Bandsawing shapes. Slotted collars. Safety points.

Simulated Adzed Finish. Reply to problem.

Spindle moulder. Cutter profile. Eccentric roller. Pitch of cuts. (Patent now granted on perfected attachment.)

Using The Straight Line Edger Saw.

Use of power feed. Two main types of machine. Saw speeds. Rate of feed. Riving knife? Advantages over push bench. Causes of throw back. Safety fingers.

Planing and Thickressing

Many woodworkers handling machine planed timber often pause to look at the finish on the surface. If it is in the extreme, in either direction, it usually brings forward comments of some kind as to how this may have occurred. By careful examination of the surface, it is possible to account for the state of the finish, and this can be quite interesting.

Theoretically it is considered not possible to produce a perfectly flat surface by feeding timber past a rotating cutter, but an acceptable finish can be obtained, to meet the various requirements of the trade, if the method of cutting is understood.

In cabinet work, and high-class joinery, it is generally accepted that external surfaces will require sanding before receiving the finishing lacquers. If a high standard of planing can be maintained, however, interiors of carcass work may not have to be sanded, and this can have constructional advantages. Sanding, which is often left as a final operation before assembly, can cause unsightly gaps and inaccuracies in the finished product (fig. 1).

In addition to the cutters of the machine being in good condition, they must have a good constant speed on the periphery (the circle described by the cutting edge), 1800m per minute being a good average for a modern production machine. To check the peripheral speed, without a special appliance, the speed of the motor must be noted, also the diameter of the pulley on the motor, and the machine.

$$\frac{\text{r.p.m. of motor} \times \text{pulley diam} \times \text{diam of cutting circle} \times 3.14}{\text{Diam of pulley on machine} \times 1000}$$

This will give the answer in metres per min. If metres per sec. is required divide by 60.

Example: —

$$\frac{\dfrac{1480 \times 300}{100} \times \dfrac{125 \times 3.14}{1000}}{1000}$$

Ans.= 1743m. per min.

Two points should be noted at this stage.

(a) It is not advisable to make a major increase in the peripheral speed of a machine without the advice of the manufacturers.

(b) The above solution is a theoretical one,

EFFICIENT CUTTING	DYNAMIC BALANCE	PITCH OF CUTTER MARKS AND CUTS PER INCH	BEARINGS	SAFETY	PRESSURE BARS	POWER
Setting Aids	Use of Cutter Balance	Number of Cutters	Ball Bearings	Factory Regs.	Set to Cutting Circle	Adequate Transmission
Cutter Jointing		Feed Speed	Lubrication	Use of Guards		Individual Motor, Belt Drives
Cutting Angles		Revs. per min.	Belt Tension			
Peripheral Speed						

Fig. 1. The gap indicated is caused by sanding after the joint has been made.

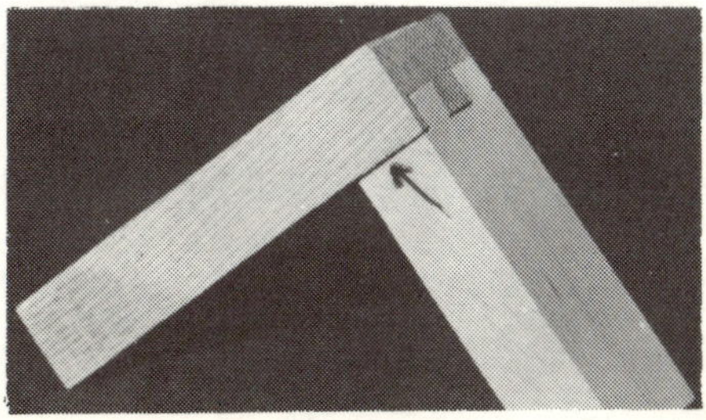

Fig. 2. Obechi photographed under a strong light to show cuts per inch. (Cutter mark pitch.)

and a certain amount of loss of revs. may take place due to belt slip and load during heavy cutting.

A cutter block revolving at 4,500 r.p.m. and having two cutters accurately set to a constant cutting circle strikes the wood being planed 9,000 times every minute. Now if the speed of the wood into the machine is 10m per min. the cutter mark pitch would be:

$$\frac{10 \times 1000}{2 \times 4500} = \frac{100}{90} = 1.1 \text{ mm pitch}$$

This is quite a good finish.

Fig. 2 shows a close-up photo of a piece of obeche taken under a strong light. The indicator tab on the top of the sample measures exactly one inch, and is divided into six equal parts. The cutter marks are approximately six to the inch, which is of course a low grade but easily visible.

The simple formula for the calculation of cuts per inch is as follows:

$$\frac{\text{Revs. per min. of block} \times \text{number of effective cutters.}}{\text{Feed speed in inches.}}$$

Take the following calculations:

$$\frac{4{,}000 \text{ r.p.m.} \times 4 \text{ cutters}}{50\text{ft. per min} \times 12} = \frac{80}{3}$$

$$= 26.6 \text{ cuts per inch.}$$

It must be noted that unless the cutters have been accurately set on the block, and also trued with a guided abrasive stone, a procedure known as cutter jointing, it is hardly likely that all cutters on the block will be registering efficiently on the timber.

Now, how many cuts to the inch do we require? This varies according to the type of work in hand. Packing case makers who prefer to plane their timber to give it precision for production, and enhance the appearance of their products, may get a satisfactory finish with 8 to 10 cuts per inch. This, too, may be suitable for fixing grounds, or temporary members. Joinery work generally should have 12 to 16 cuts per inch. Cabinet work and high-class joinery need 20 to 30 cuts per in. As stated previously, a certain amount of sanding may be dispensed with if a high standard of planing can be maintained on this type of work.

From these figures, it will be noted that, if full advantage is taken when beforehand planing is taking place, a considerable amount of time can be saved on a large batch of work by feeding the timber to give the finish most suitable for the finished product.

As technical knowledge advances, no doubt architects' specifications may contain permissible minimum cuts per inch required if parts are not to be sanded, instead of the familiar: "All machine marks to be removed." If technical advancement is to be made, and abridged by the academic, full knowledge of the factors involved in machine planing should be the aim of all concerned.

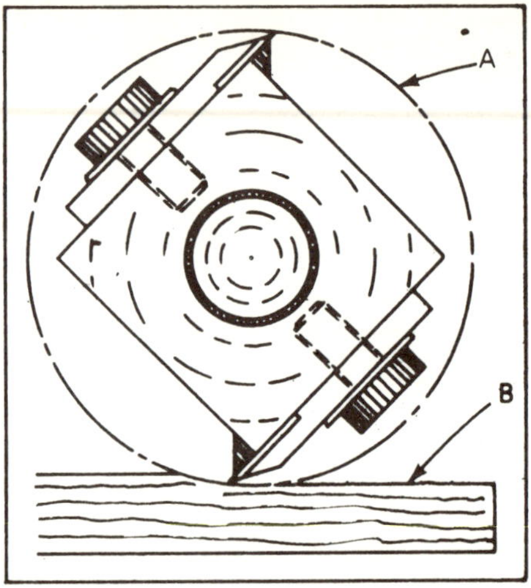

Fig. 3. A, cutting circle; B, cuts mm pitch.

If, even when the timber is firmly gripped during its progress through the machine by the feed rollers and pressure bars, uneven marks appear on the planed surface this could be due to wear in the bearings if the machine has done a considerable amount of service. This too, will be aggravated if the cutter block is not in complete dynamic balance, i.e., balance during rotation. The blocks themselves are balanced by the manufacturers, but it is up to the machinist in charge to attend to the balance of the cutters in use.

Cutter fixing bolts and other clamping devices should be carefully inspected each time the cutters are being inserted. Studs which are screwed into the block and receive a nut to complete the clamping operation have been known to work loose during cutter changing, with the result that the clamping nut reaches the end of the thread before pressure has been applied to the cutter. It is therefore necessary to ensure that the studs are screwed fully into the block.

The following chart gives a general picture of the points to note if efficient planning is to be achieved. It is self-explanatory if studied in conjunction with this article, and could be enlarged upon by the enthusiast.

Timber planing on the fourcutter

In the preparation of timber requiring square sections only, the setting time of a modern fourcutter need take very little longer than setting a thicknessing planer. The resultant output will be very much greater, since all of the four surfaces are worked at one pass through the machine, and it is possible to maintain a constant standard of finish.

This constant standard regarding surface finish and squareness, cannot always be obtained when large quantities of material are planed in a series of separate operations, probably involving different operators and machines. Prestraightening of timber on a surfacing machine before fourcutting is to advantage, if the time factor will permit, when the necessity arises.

It is of course necessary that the preliminary work has been done in the way of setting up on the fourcutter, so that the minimum of adjustments have to be made at the time of operation. These operational adjustments usually involve the releasing, and retightening of a few locking nuts.

It is desirable, in a machine design, that the number of spanners required for this operation is kept to a minimum. Double-ended spanners may have to be non-standard to meet this efficiency requirement, or the external sizes of the locking nuts may be designed with this refinement in mind.

In addition to the time factor in spanner manipulation, there is always the danger of a discarded tool finding its way into the revolving cutters when making these final adjustments if a number of tools are involved.

For square work, the setting of cutters in, or on, their mounting blocks is comparatively simple to that of moulded work. Where square blocks are used, either two or four cutters can be mounted on the block.

The reason for utilizing four cutters when two will do the work is to enable the timber to be fed through the machine at double the speed, and maintain the same quality of finish. This is a theoretical fact which can be proved by simple calculation, but a high standard of cutter set-

Layout of a fourcutter showing the sequence of the cutter heads. Not all machines have the heads positioned in this order, but the exceptions relate mainly to those which have more than the basic four cutting units.

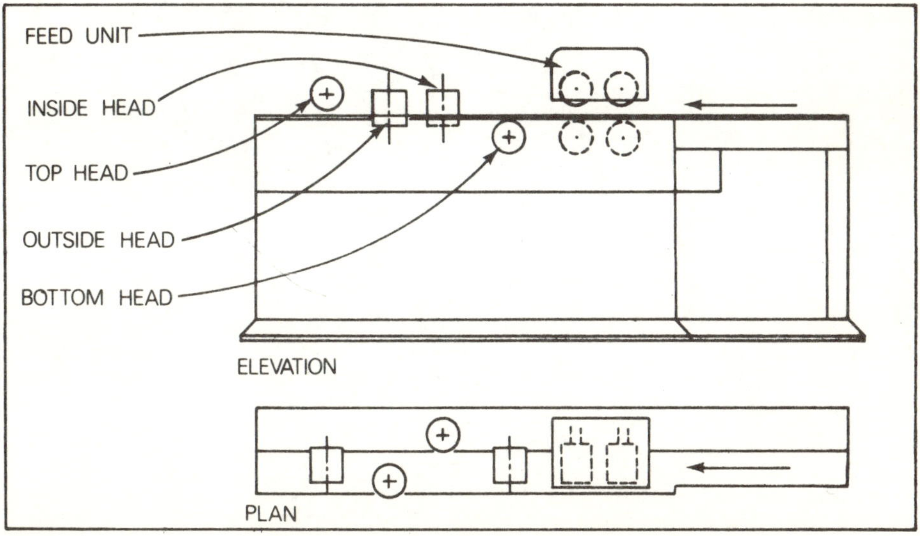

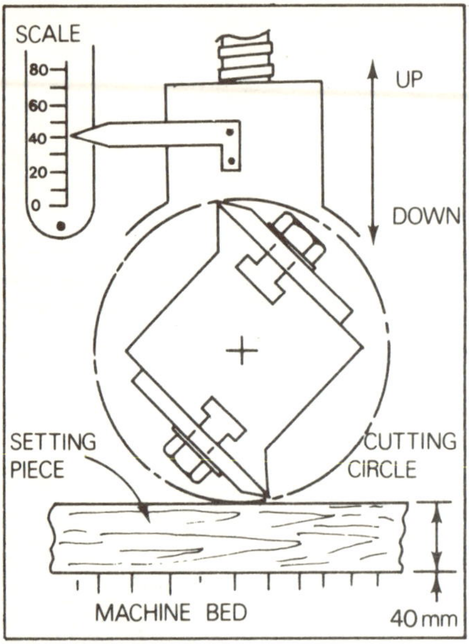

Detail of the top head of the fourcutter to illustrate how the machine can be set by either the scale, if provided, or by inserting a sample of prepared timber. It can also be noted here, that if the cutters were set giving increased projection on the block, the scale would read in error.

ting, and trimming, must be obtained if the theory is to be put fully into practice.

Examples, for machines where Imperial Measurement is in use:

$$\frac{\textbf{5250 R.P.M.} \times \textbf{2 Effective Cutters}}{\textbf{Feed 30ft. per min.} \times \textbf{12}}$$

$$= \frac{525}{18} \quad = \textbf{29 Cuts per inch.}$$

Now double the number of effective cutters, and double the feed speed through the machine . . .

$$\frac{5250 \times 4}{60 \times 12} =$$

$$\frac{5250 \times 4}{60 \times 12} = \frac{525}{18} = \textbf{29 Cuts per inch}$$

$$= \textbf{29 Cuts per inch.}$$

The same number of cuts per linear inch of material is obtained, but output has been doubled.

Example of a calculation using Metric Measurement:

Rotation is in revs. per second. Feed speed in millimetres per second. The cuts on the timber are measured in millimetres pitch

A typical fourcutter and moulding machine, common to many woodworking establishments over the last decade. The layout of these multi-head machines vary, and a great amount of written matter would be required to describe all the different types in detail.

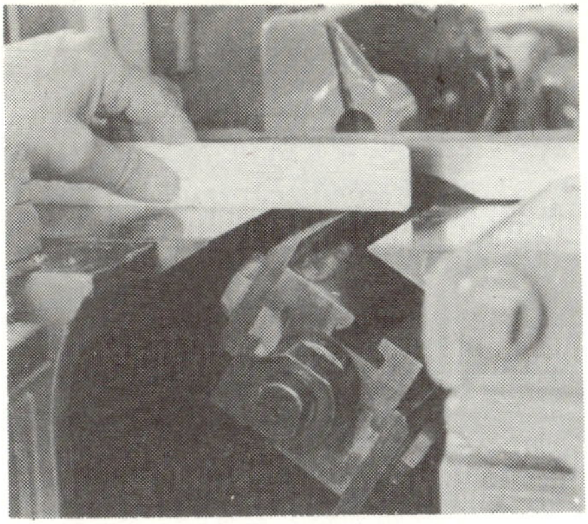

Setting the cutter block on the first head to line with the outfeed table. This table is fixed, but the cutter head can be raised and lowered as required. The infeed table can be adjusted to apply the amount of cut permissible.

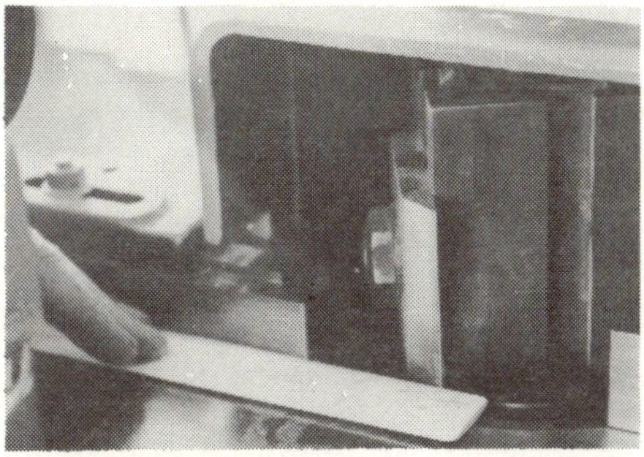

Setting the inside cutter head to line with the outfeed fence. The link fence precedes the cutter on this particular machine, and this can be adjusted to regulate the amount of edge cut. Some machines have the link fence on the outgoing section of the fence.

$$\frac{\text{Feed 160 mm per sec.}}{\text{90 Revs. per sec.} \times 2} = \frac{8}{9}$$

$= 0.88$ **mm Pitch of Cutter Marks**

In practice the calculated number of cuts per given measurement is not always obtained due to errors. This is understandable and many operators can point out why it is on their particular machine.

Circular cutter blocks are in use with more than four inserted cutters, in order to permit very high rates of feed speed. The success of these blocks depends very much on the skill of the machinists, and the efficiency of their servicing equipment.

Most fourcutters now have measurement scales on the outside head and the top head to assist

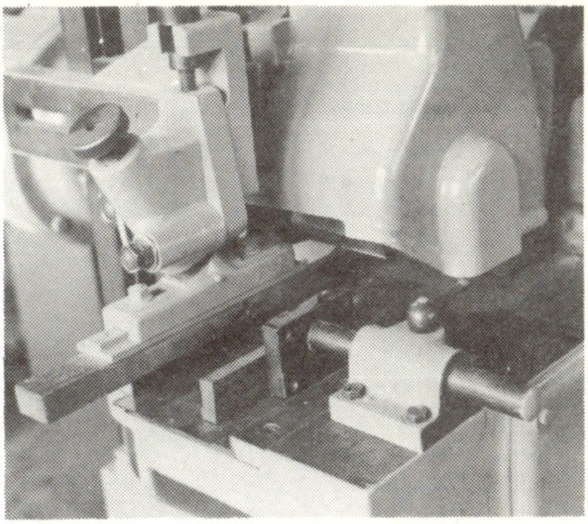

The output end of a fourcutter. The hood guards the top head which takes the material to thickness. The pressure pads grip the timber to prevent sag when the material is not adequately supported.

An illustration of a side pressure unit which is attached to the outside head of the machine. When the head is adjusted to a timber width, the pressure unit moves with it, so simplifying the operation.

with the quick setting to the required dimensions. These setting scales will only read correct if the cutters are mounted on the blocks to a given projection. This cutter projection. This cutter projection is usually stated by the manufacturers, but it can be determined by trial, or geometrically if desired.

One point is certain, that the cutting circle (the circle described by the cutters during rotation) must be greater than the extremity of the holding bolts. For this reason the cutting circle is usually termed the clearance circle.

The First Head

The setting of the first head on a fourcutter could be said to be similar to that of a surface planer. One difference is that the cutter block can be raised and lowered, and the outfeed table is fixed. The section of the table preceeding the cutter, which could be termed the infeed table, can be adjusted vertically to regulate the amount of cut.

The cutter edge should be set to line with the surface of the outfeed table, and the infeed table is lowered generally about 2 mm below this line. It is also convenient to set the feed rollers in the bed of the machine at this point. They should be very slightly above the surface of the table line.

The Side Heads and Fence

The fence on a fourcutter is built up in two or more sections. The first section of the fence terminates at the inside cutter head. This section of fence is adjustable to regulate the amount of cut on the inner edge of the timber.

The inside cutter head which is positioned vertical, should be adjusted to line with the outfeed portion of the fence. It is important that the infeed fence is parallel with the outfeed fence, although set back, or unsatisfactory working will be experienced.

Some machines are fitted with what is termed a link fence to ensure this working line is always maintained. The alternative to the link fence, is to line up with the aid of a long steel straight edge which can be obtained for this purpose.

The next cutter head on the machine takes the material to width, and is positioned on the outer side of the line of feed. Where a setting scale is not provided the head must be set by measuring the gap between the cutter and the fence. Some machinists insert a piece of timber of the finished size required against the fence and adjust the cutting unit to it.

The Top Head

This is the fourth head on the machine, which cuts on the upper surface of the material, and takes it to thickness. Here again, the thickness can be set with the scale on the machine, or by inserting a piece of timber of the required dimension. Once the timber has passed this head all four faces have been worked.

Pressure Units

Once the cutter heads and fences have been set the overhead and side pressures can be adjusted. These pressures are either spring operated, or by weights, sometimes a combination of the two.

The pressures units have usually a field of movement in excess of what is required in the variation of timber thickness, unless off-cuts are fed through the machine without widthing on the circular saw. When setting the pressures an uplift on load of 6 to 10 mm is suitable.

With a machine that has wear in the units, the higher figure will be required to take up the slack. High speed feeding may also require increased pressure to compensate the increased force set up.

The side pressure on a four-cutter can be incorporated with the outside head unit. That is to say that when the side head is adjusted to a timber width the side pressure goes with it. Once the pressure has been set in relation to the cutter, it can remain in this position for other widths of timber.

At the outfeed end of the machine it is customary to have an overhead and side pressure unit to firmly hold the work as it leaves the machine. Due to the fact that all the timber passing this point should be of constant dimension, only a small amount of spring action is necessary.

When working short material additional side and overhead pressures will be required. Each individual piece must be gripped at all times.

The pressure on the infeed roller unit should never be in excess. Timber can be permanently marked at this point due to over pressure. Failure to feed should be investigated within the machine.

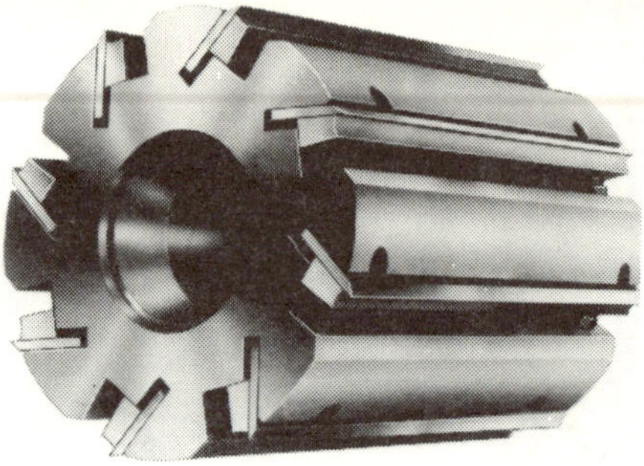

A circular cutter head with eight cutters as used on a fourcutter to permit a high rate of feed speed and still obtain an acceptable finish. Quieter running is also experienced with this circular unit over square blocks.

Rebating and grooving on the fourcutter

The first head on a four-cutter is designed for planing the underside of the timber only. The aperture in the machine table will not usually allow cutters to project beyond the cutting circle described by the planing cutters.

The use of this head for operations in addition to planing is an exception to the general rule.

A method of developing and applying a cutter projection scale for a square block as used on a fourcutter. The drawing must be prepared full size to suit the dimensions of the block and cutters. The projection of the cutter is divided into 5 mm units on the true measurement line.

Rebates can be cut by any of the other three heads of the four-head machine. A study of the work in hand can determine the most suitable approach.

In cutter planing, for either rebating or moulding, it is advisable to reduce the projection of the cutters beyond the block to a minimum. This puts less strain on the holding bolts, and ensures that cutters are not in danger of fouling other parts of the machine such as the pressure units or collecting hoods.

The workload should be divided over as many of the cutter heads as possible, bearing in mind the capacity of the motors on each individual head.

Many operators prefer to work rebates, or other formations, on the fence edge of the timber if these are to become involved in tenoning and scribing processes later.

Should any of the timber be under width, the unplaned part will be on the outside edge, and will not affect the accuracies of joint formation.

The advantage of cutting rebates on the outer edge of the timber, working with the side head, is that the additional force set up by the cutters in heavy work is supported by the fence. This eliminates the application of additional side pressure that would be required if a heavy cut was being made from the fence edge.

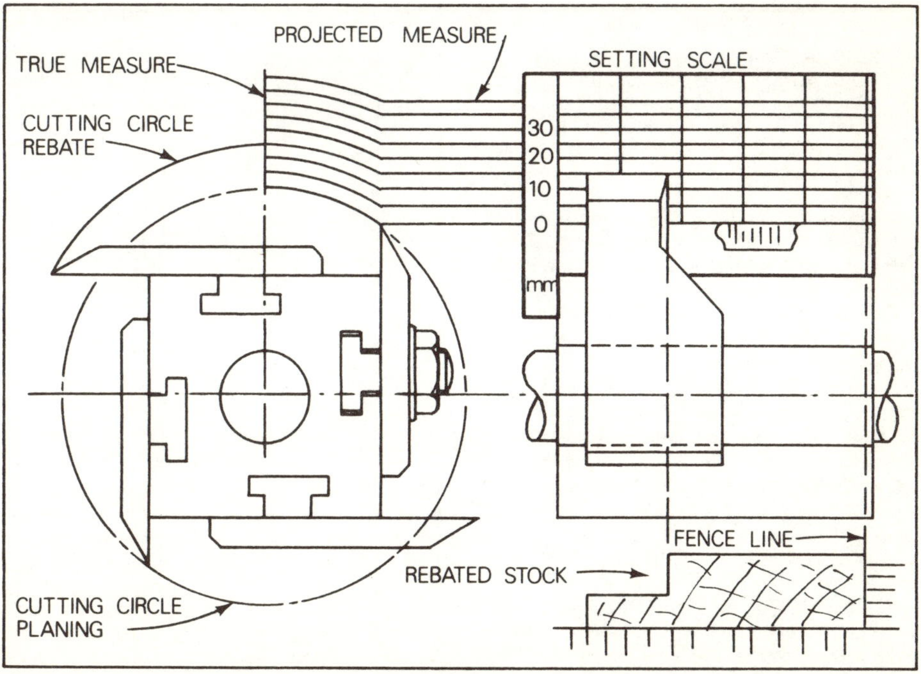

Pressures should, on multi-head machines, be as light as possible, as the feed depends entirely on the pushing action of the one feed unit on most machines.

Cutting rebates with the top head is ideal for many operations, as the work is well supported by the machine bed, and no increase in holding pressure is required beyond that for the planing operation.

When adding cutters to square blocks for rebating operations, the operator, or cutter setter, is confronted with the subject of balance. Not all are aware of just what is permissible.

Set ups vary considerably, and one can only make recommendations if all the precise requirements are not to be followed at all times.

For long runs, or repetitive lines, efficient balance during rotation should be aimed at. For shorter runs, static balance should at least be obtained, and some tolerance allowed during running balance.

For complete balance during rotation, the cutters must be matched both in shape and weight. They must then be fixed directly opposite each other on the block with identical projection. Holding boltage must be equal in size, and weight, for both cutters.

Any offset in the alignment of the pair of cutters would not show when mounted in, a cutter balancing stand, but there would be an error during high speed rotation. This situation is described as being in static balance, but not in dynamic, or running balance.

If it was planned to cut a rebate 44 mm wide using 25 mm cutters, a total of four cutters would be required. To stagger the cutters on opposing faces of the block using only two, would not be advisable.

On the other hand, if a groove 6 mm wide was required and only 5 mm cutters were available, two cutters would be permissible as the offset would be very small. In industry, technicalities have often to be overstrained to keep the work flowing, but the correct basic principles should always be kept in mind.

When rebating, in addition to the bevel on the cutting edge, it is essential that the adjoining edge which comes into contact with the side of the rebate should also be bevelled. This cuts down friction and prevents burn marks.

An angle of 5 to 10 deg. cut away is sufficient for this edge. Some operators prefer to grind the edge slightly away, leaving only the point to do the cutting.

Setting, rebating, or grooving cutters to the correct projection on the cutter block can be done with a projection scale. This scale can be developed geometrically for a given size of block.

Projection measuring scales are also obtainable from some machine manufacturers, in addition to more sophisticated appliances for cutter planning. To be able to set cutters to the correct requirement in the tool room is a worthwhile achievement.

Solid profile cutter heads are available in

A selection of tonguing, grooving, and rebating cutters as used on the fourcutter. These cutters are made from mild steel, and have a high speed steel working face. Tungsten carbide faced cutters are also available for working abrasive timbers.

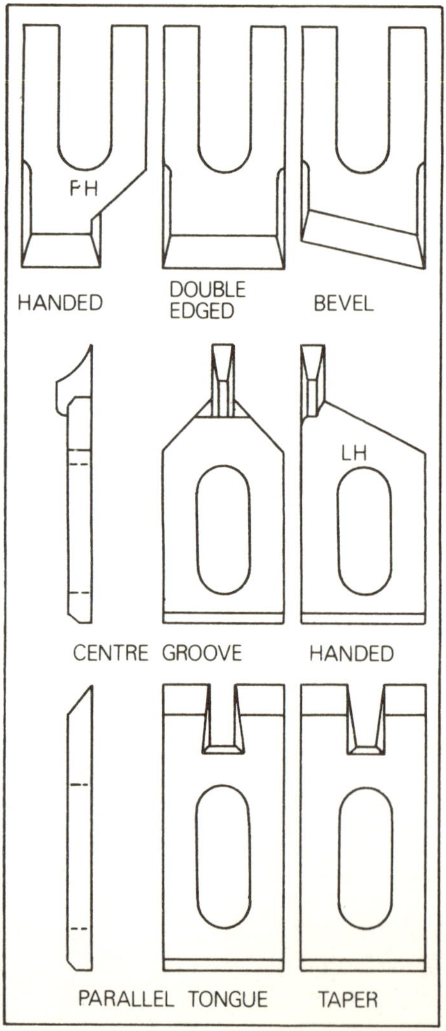

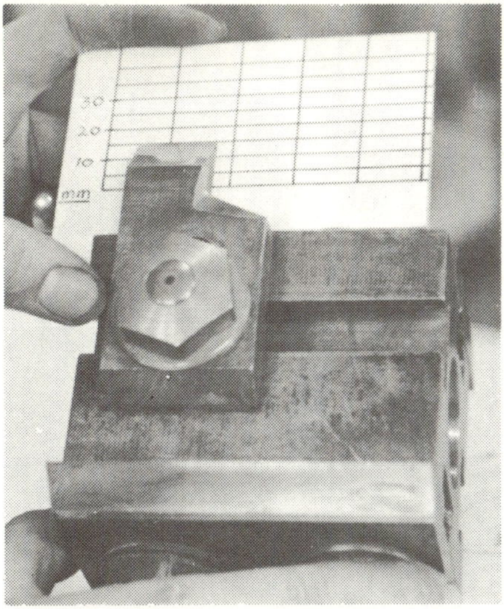

A cutter projection scale being applied to check a rebating cutter for the required distance beyond the planing line. The balancing cutter can also be set with the aid of the scale to the same positioning.

An example of rebated and bevelled stock leaving the machine.

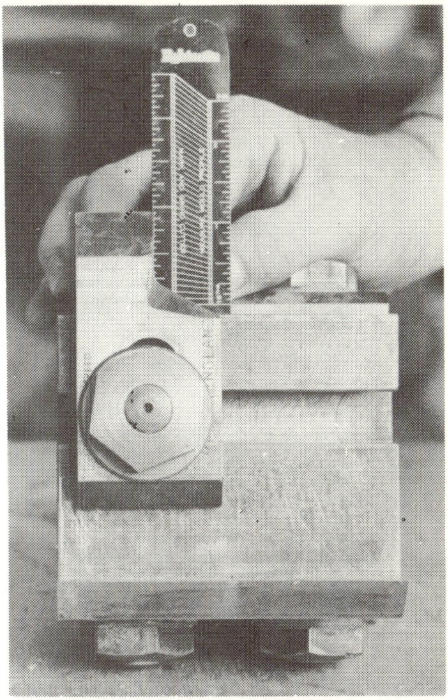

A Robinson Projection Rule being used to set a rebating cutter to the required projection. Other more advanced setting aids are also manufactured by this firm. (Robinson, Rochdale, Lancs.)

matched sets for use on the fourcutter for the forming of tongue and groove joints. If the groove is run on the fence side head, more support is given to the timber during feed, and any fall off in width will simply reduce the projection of the tongue without affecting the face of the board.

Tapered tongues are preferable from the point of view of cutter design, as three surfaces of the tool take part in the cutting, and clearance is always maintained. Assembly of the joints is also easier with this type of tongue.

It is also preferable for most types of work that the tongue is visibly out of centre on the edge of the board, to define a working face for assembly.

When a mould has to be formed using the top head, and a considerable amount of material has to be cut away, an easing can be done by rebating some of the waste away on a side head. By doing this, the load is reduced on the top head, and a better finish obtained on the mould. This method is particularly useful when working with abrasive or other difficult timbers.

As rebates cannot be machine sanded very conveniently some hardwoods benefit from the application of a small amount of front bevel on the cutters. This reduces the approach angle to a near scraping action, and prevents the tearing up of the grain.

Many four-head machines are designed in such a way that an additional bottom head can be added. This head is particularly useful for carrying out operations on the under side of the material.

Saws can also be mounted on the spindle for dividing work as it passes out of the machine. This fifth head can often do work that would otherwise have to be carried out on the spindle moulder after the fourcutting process.

The thickessing, and rebating operation being carried out on the top head of a forecutter. This head is located at the output end of the machine.

Producing moulded on the fourcutter

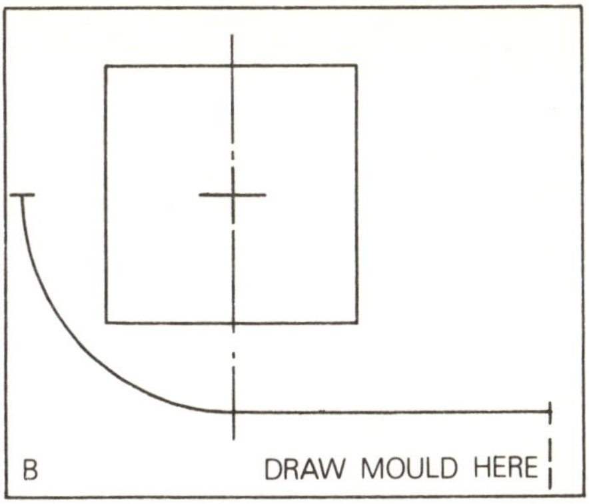

This information could be said to be standard for a given size of square block. It could therefore be printed out in quantity in advance. Only the minimum amount of plotting is then required on the shop floor.

Moulding on a fourcutter is very often combined with both planing and rebating, all at the one pass through the machine.

The production of moulded work on the fourcutter requires increased skill over that for square, and rebated work, as cutter preparation and setting become more complex. More than four cutter heads are also favoured on machines, hence we get the term "moulders" rather than fourcutter for this advanced type of work.

A higher standard of finish must also be aimed at, as cleaning up of sub-standard moulded work is much more of a problem than that of flat surfaces. Not all timbers are suitable for the manufacture of mouldings in quantity due to their erratic grain, unless one is prepared to spend a lot of time on selection.

The geometrical development of a cutter shape for a given moulding. The moulding is drawn in the position indicated in relation to the cutting unit. Arrows show the direction of progression in the plotting of the elongated shape of the cutter. Points two to six are followed through in a similar manner.

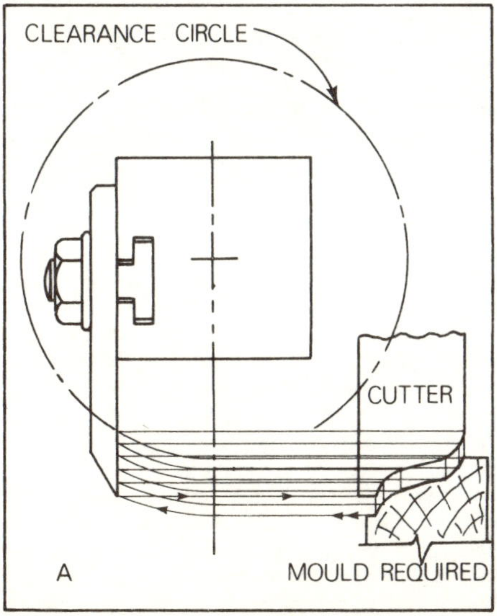

Some difficult timbers can be processed by working at low feed speeds, or with the application of a front bevel on the cutters, reducing the action to a scrape, rather than a cut. An unacceptable amount of wastage may also occur in the utilisation of the moulded section if the work is not up to standard, rather than spend productive time on hand sandpapering.

Most softwoods in use for building joinery mould well using high speed steel cutters, also such timbers as ramin, parana pine, Japanese oak, etc. Some timbers in the mahogany group can have erratic grain, and abura along with teak is noted for its abrasive action on machine cutters.

The production of moulded work on a fourcutter can be divided into a number of groups. The three main groups can be described as the following:

1. Moulding that is applied to square work using only one pair of cutters.
2. Moulding which require two or more pairs of cutters set in relation to one another.
3. Moulding in multiple, in which material is divided at the final stage, so increasing the linear quantity.

A single mould can be applied to timber passing through the machine for planing by either the side heads or the top head on a four head machine. The deciding factor on which head to use is the one on which the cutter will require the smallest projection. Two moulding cutters should always be prepared, ground identical in

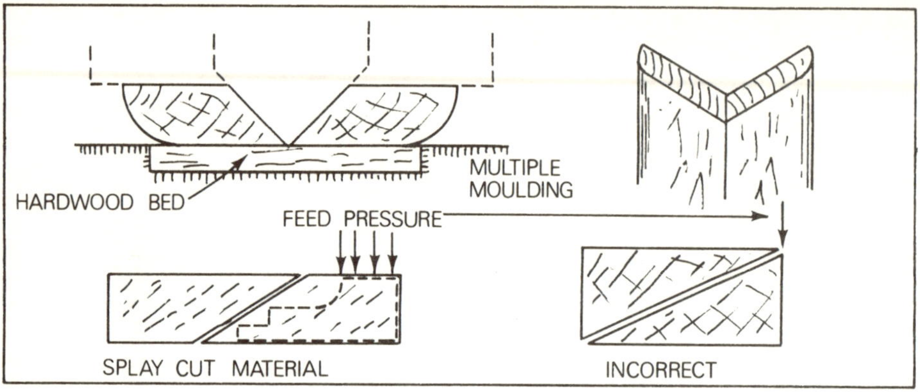

an aim to obtain running balance.

For intricate shapes some operators give a very slight projection to one cutter over the other when setting them on the block. This gives only a single cutter finish, but it does prevent an ill-ground cutter from destroying the mould formed by the leading cutter.

As it is seldom practicable to trim shaped cutters like straight ones during rotation, a single cutter finish must often be accepted. For this reason feed speeds for moulding have often to be reduced from those used for straight planing. The only alternative would be to increase the rotation speed of the cutters, but this would not be advisable if the cutter projections are not identical.

The operational life of a cutting edge must be related to the amount of material it has to cut away. If some of the waste material can be cut away before the stock passes through the four-cutter, longer runs and a better finish can be obtained.

When splay cutting is done to ease the cut it is important to leave about 25 mm of flat surface to enable the feed rollers to grip the work, unless a round-ended feed roll is fitted to the machine.

Where large quantities of moulding are being manufactured to supply a production unit, the stock should be bundled or batched in some way as it leaves the machine. The profile of the mould will change slightly due to wear and honing of the cutters.

This slight change can show an error when moulds are mitred during utilisation, if the batching system is ignored. Although a factory may be operating on continuous flow production, it is necessary at times to have batch production within the flow.

Moulding cutters should preferably be prepared in advance of requirement to reduce down time

Moulding in multiple can have several advantages including increased productivity. In the case of the corner fillets shown in the sketch, in hardwood, these would be matched for grain and colour as they leave the machine.

Consideration must be given to the application of feed roller pressure, when splay cutting is used in the preparation of timber for moulding.

A mechanical appliance for the development of cutter shapes. The Robinson Pro-Set. The elongated cutter profile can be projected direct from a sectional drawing of the required mould all in one operation avoiding accumulative errors.

of the moulding machine. When new profiles are required it may in many cases be necessary to develop the shapes of the cutters involved. How this is done will depend on what facilities are available. The aim is, of course, to ensure that when the set-up block is offered to the machine operator, it will need no further adjustment.

Many experienced fourcutter operators do manage to develop cutter shapes with the aid of a cutter projection scale. An accurate scale will record the elongation of projection, which is the leading factor, and from this an acceptable shape can on occasions be plotted. Success of this method depends on the experience of the operator, and the complexity of the mould.

Cutter profiles can be developed geometrically on the drawing board if working conditions are favourable. This process could, in fact, be speeded up and simplified now that photo printing and duplicating of drawings is reaching an advanced stage. Certain factors remain constant for a given machine, such as block sizes, and bolt clearance.

This part of the geometrical procedure could be printed off in bulk beforehand, leaving only the required shape of the mould to be drawn, and the cutter shape development completed.

Another method of developing cutter shapes is to use appliances designed by machine manufacturers for this purpose. These can be used successfully within the tool room, if not on the shop floor itself. An advantage of such as the Robinson Pro-Set is that the shape of the cutter required to produce a given section of moulding can be projected from a drawing all in the one operation. Where a number of operations are involved, errors can accumulate at the various stages of a procedure.

Where more than one set of cutters have to be used to form a moulded section, the cutters require to be set on blocks in relation to each other. A cutter setting stand is the ideal appliance to use for this purpose. Some setting stands also incorporate a balancing spindle, which checks the set-up block for static balance.

When mouldings of small sections have to be produced, it can be to advantage to pass the timber through the machine in multiple width and so manufacture a series of moulds at the one operation. The moulds are parted at the final head of the machine by saw teeth, or penetration of the shaping cutters.

Better feeding of the stock is experienced when working by this method, as narrow mould can break in the machine if worked singly. Productivity is also increased as more full use is being made of the machine. A fifth head is often added to a four-head machine mainly to carry out this parting operation which can be very advantageous.

A moulding cutter being set in relation to a rebating cutter on a square block. The block is mounted on a cutter setting stand, this simplifies the operation considerably.

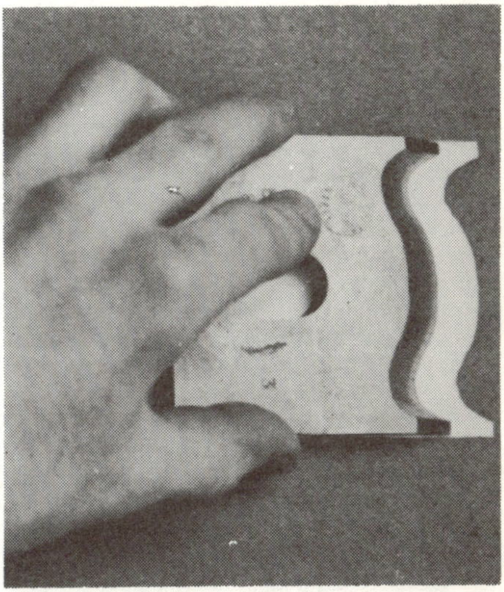

Comparing the profile of a cutter during the grinding operation, with a prepared template. The template can be referred to at any time when regrinding is required so maintaining the original shape.

A solid profile cutter head for shaping the moulded and rebated edge of window sash material. In addition to the time saving in setting up the fourcutter using this type of head, the mould profile is always maintained, and the multipoint finish permits high feed speeds.

Backfencing on the spindle moulder

On some operations on the spindle moulder, it is an advantage to use the fences to give support to the work rather than to utilise them to just act as a guide. With this method of working, known as backfencing, the work is passed through between the fence and the cutting unit. It has advantages over the traditional set-up, as less vibration is likely to occur within the stock being worked, and the thickness of the finished product is always constant. The backfencing set-up can be compared to a thicknessing machine on a smaller scale, the fence taking the place of the machine bed.

Work produced by this method can be of a high standard, but certain factors must be observed regarding safety which limits the operation to only certain types of work. It is not recommended for working short material, as the stock must be firmly gripped while it is passing through the machine. The danger points are at the commencement, and the termination of the cut, when holding pressures are generally reduced. The danger of a kickback is considerably increased when using the backfencing method if it is attempted by a careless operator. On the other hand it can be a very safe method indeed, if properly set up, as pressure springs and the fences act as guards. Pressure should be arranged as near to the point of cut as possible.

Moulding that has been made by backfencing mitres well, due to its constant dimension and profile. Architrave mouldings and moulded skirting boards have been successfully produced in this way from prepared square section. Glass beading can also be produced from offcuts in a minimum of time, the sections being moulded or bevelled in the dimensioning process at one pass through the machine. Narrow offcuts often accumulate in a factory, and backfencing can be an aid towards them being converted into usable sections.

Wide items, such as stair treads and risers, can be taken to accurate width by backfencing. The nosing mould can be formed during the widthing operation, this being a good saving in time. With this wide type of work, an automatic feed attachment can be used, making the set-up

Beading being made from square section material by the backfencing method. The material is fed between the fence and the cutter unit. The view is taken from the output end of the machine. A guard or waste collecting hood can be fitted for general safety.

Stair tread material being accurately taken to width and moulded in one operation by backfencing. Top pressure (not shown) can be applied with a spring unit or an auto-feed attachment.

The backfencing layout for working the thinner type of material. The through face board gives support to the stock being moulded. Spring pressures should be adequate, and applied close to the cutting unit.

highly productive. With the auto-feed, the rollers should be tracked to push the work hard up to the fence. It is alao advisable to keep the machine table slightly lubricated and free from resin deposits, to obtain smooth feeding.

Doors of all sizes may also be taken to width by backfencing providing one edge has first been

A cupboard door being taken to width using the back-fencing method. The machine table has been extended, and guide fence clamped in position. A more permanent bolted version could be constructed on these lines. A rebate or bevel could be applied to the door edge during the operation if required.

This backfencing set up is used when working wide material, and where the cut edge will bed to the output fence without tilting. An auto-feed unit can generally be used under this set up making it highly productive.

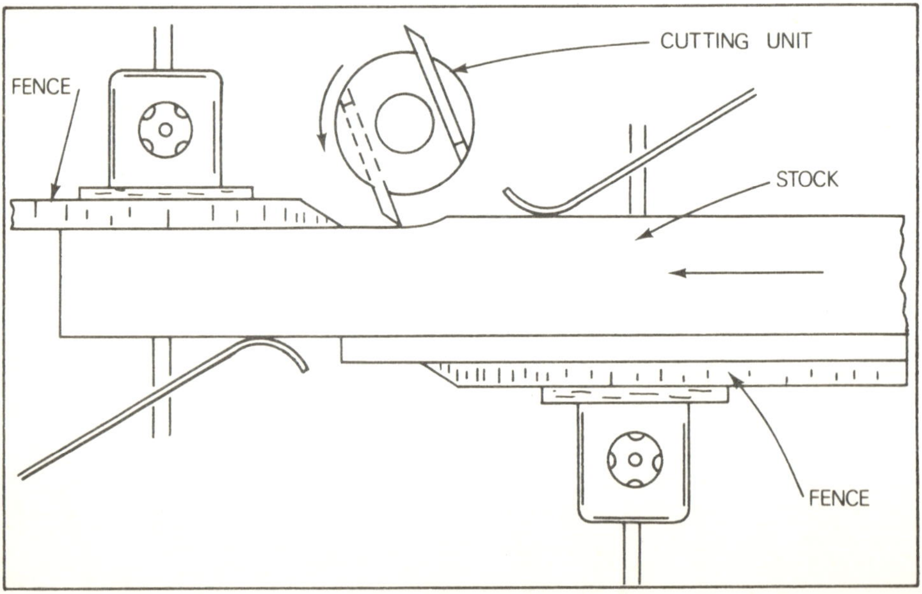

planed straight. The backfenced edge can be slightly bevelled for closing, or rebated to form a meeting. The slow method of handling doors with rebated meetings, would involve three separate operations instead of the one already described—namely (1) sawing to width, (2) planing the edge clean, (3) rebating. Errors could also occur during the processes.

For handling the wider type of item it may be necessary to extend the machine table. Extension arms may be either bolted to the machine or fixed with cramps for short runs. This is a case where it is to advantage to have accurately machined edges on the spindle moulder table.

As with most woodworking machine operations, it is not advisable to stand directly behind the line of feed of the material being worked. Large knots should be avoided if possible in timber selected for backfencing, as these can put a sudden strain on the edge of the cutters and reduce their efficiency. It is important that the cutters should be kept sharp, and carefully ground. Hollow grinding of the cutters is generally preferable, as heals are less likely to be formed than with straight ground. Feeding should take less effort with hollow ground cutters, and the danger of a kick-back will be reduced. When heals are formed on cutters, the timber is compressed during backfencing. This not only produces a poor finish but also retards the progress of feeding.

Preparation, and maintenance of the cutters for successful backfencing could be said to be more important than with the traditional method of working on the spindle moulder. Blunt cutters cannot force the work away from the fence, they simply set up an opposing force to the effort of feeding. It is regrettable that many workers walk on material that has to be passed through a machine. In this way grit finds its way into the cutting unit, and quickly destroys the edge.

When backfencing doors which have plywood faces to width, it will be necessary to use tungsten carbide tipped cutters when working in quantity. This type of cutter is generally more power consuming due to its design, but it should run for long periods without servicing. Failure to service when required will result in heat being generated, in particular if the work being processed is being power fed.

With the backfencing set up on the spindle moulder, it is not generally necessary for the operator to have his hands near the cutting unit, as pressure springs hold the work. When processing narrow material the fences provide the guard at the front of the machine, but the cutters are exposed at the back. These should be enclosed with a hood to prevent waste material flying when the machine is in operation. A push stick should always be at hand, as with all spindle moulder operations.

Reverse rotation on the spindle moulder

A second nut should be used on the spindle moulder when the machine is being run in the reverse direction. This particularly applies when the security of the cutters depends on the pressure from the nut, as in the case of slotted collars.

The majority of spindle moulders are used with one direction of rotation only, but it is an advantage to be able to run the machine in the reverse direction also.

With the older type of machines, which were driven by long flat belts, it was quite a simple operation to reverse the spindle rotation by removing the belt at the motor end and applying a twist in the opposite direction. With modern machines using short belt drives, or direct drive, incorporating a frequency changer, reverse rotation must be obtained with the aid of electrical switchgear. Where the motor and switchgear are suitably designed, the reverse action can be used as a brake in preferance to a manually-operated device.

When the spindle is being operated using reverse rotation, an additional nut should be used for locking purposes. Most manufacturers supply this locking nut with the machine, but many operators are not quite clear as to when it should be used. When slotted collars are being used,

A component being worked using right- and left-hand working. In this way a higher standard of work can be obtained, and hand finishing kept to a minimum. (Guards removed for clarity.)

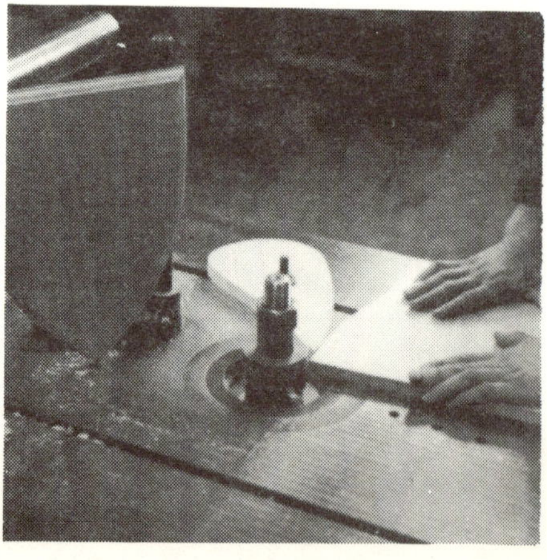

Stop rebating in pairs. Quantity work can be more speedily carried out by using both directions of rotation. Both hands of work can be run in, instead of taking the risk of dropping on. A good safety point.

the pressure from the nut is more important than with a square block, as it is this pressure that actually holds the cutters in position.

In establishments where reverse rotation is being used intermittently with normal rotation, it is advisable to have some form of indication as to in which direction the spindle is running. Lighting can have a stroboscopic effect on a cutter head, and actually make it appear to be rotating in the opposite direction. A person leading in on a ring fence could be in real trouble if he suddenly found that the cutter unit was travelling in the same direction as his work.

When shaped work is being rebated or moulded, it is always desirable to cut so as to smooth down the grain, rather than to tear it up. When components are being produced in quantity a double spindle machine can be particularly useful with the heads revolving in pairs. Components can be worked at the one handling, moulding down grain to give a first-class finish. Very little sanding is necessary working this way and many hours can be saved on repetition work, especially on hardwoods. Hand finishing may be eliminated with careful machine planning on some types of work.

Often when such items as door stiles are being stop rebated in pairs, it is possible to run in on one hand of stile, but it becomes necessary to drop in and run out on the other hand. The drop in operation will take much longer than the run in, and it also requires a more experienced operator to carry out the work. For quantity work reverse rotation can be used to advantage. One hand of stiles can be cut with normal

A double spindle moulding machine. This type of machine is particularly useful where both directions of rotation can be used to advantage. This applies to both straight or shaped work. A good feature to bear in mind when production planning.

Fuller utilisation can be made of expensive cutter heads by turning them over, and reversing rotation. The lower unused part of the cutter edge is then brought into use.

An operator using a spindle moulder with a controlled feed. The cutter head of this type of machine can be safely run in either direction. The cutters can be rotated in the same direction as the feed, this gives a high standard of finish.

rotation, and the other with reverse. Both can be run in, and the cutter unit can operate on the underside of the work for maximum safety. I think it would be true to quote that more accidents occur on the spindle moulder from dropping on than any other operation. Reverse rotation can play a part in safety planning.

It is standard practice to operate with the cutting unit on the underside of the work, if at all possible. With expensive equipment such as tungsten carbide rebating cutters all the wear takes place at one corner of the cutting face on normal rotation of the spindle. Good unused metal has to be removed from the other corner during servicing. Where reverse rotation is practised in a machine shop, the cutter head can be turned over for some operations and a greater life between services obtained.

It is not unusual to find spindle moulding cutters in the tool room which are not being used due to the fact that they are the wrong hand for the general run of work. These cutters could be used if reverse rotation was easily obtainable. Mistakes also occur in the ordering of prepared cutting units from the manufacturers regarding handing. Reverse rotation would make the cutters usable.

Fortunately the manufacturers of automatic feed units for spindle moulders have provided for both directions of feed. A right-handed operator can feel awkward feeding manually from the left-hand side of the machine. Working with an auto-feed considerably cuts down this awkwardness.

Reverse rotation can also be used to advantage on spindle shapers where the work is mounted on a jig which is fed past the cutting unit by a revolving sprocket engaging in a chain affixed to the jig. With this type of machine the cutter can be rotated in the same direction as the feed if desired. This very often improves the standard of finish. The work must be securely clamped to the jig to work in this manner.

Other uses of reverse rotation on the spindle moulder come under the use of special cutter heads as trenching, and slot dovetailing. Left-handed cutters are available and these can increase the versatility of the machine in particular when carrying out left- and right-handed operations.

To operate reverse rotation enthusiastically the machine must be fitted with a reversing switch. Having to remove covers and change over wires causes delays, and very often deters a busy machinist from making use of scientific development. To have a fully equipped machine is a point worth noting on a new installation, and a good marketing feature for the manufacturer.

Methods of machining bevels

A spindle moulder in the process of setting up for bevelling, using a Whitehill cutter head.

The bevel, or chamfer, is probably the most common form of moulding used in woodworking, and it also plays an important role in angular construction.

When bevels are produced by machine, their faces are sometimes found to be not perfectly flat. This not only makes their appearance less pleasing but, when the bevel is required to form a joint in constructional work, flat surfaces are essential.

The surface planer will produce excellent bevels on already planed stock, with the fence canted to guide the timber at the required angle. Stopped work, usually termed "stop chamfering", can also be carried out on this machine. A back stop should be used when "dropping on", and the bridge guard set to a minimum aperture. As both tables require to be lowered below the cutting circle, this operation needs more care than simple planing. The amount of kick-back expected when dropping on will be dependent on the amount of material being removed, and also the condition of the cutters. Blunt cutters on a machine are a greater danger than sharp ones.

When bevelling is done on the spindle moulder, or the four-cutter, the timber is laid flat, and the cutters ground to produce the angle required. Under these conditions certain geometrical functions are involved and, unless the machinist is aware of this fact, rounded faces, or hog-backed as they are termed, may result.

The geometrical development shows that in addition to the elongation always found in this procedure, the cutter edge requires a slight amount of curvature. Unless convex curvature is applied to the cutter when grinding, a perfectly flat bevel cannot be produced under this method of working.

The Whitehill pattern cutter block is very useful for machining bevels, as the cutters may be canted to produce the angle, but the curvature

A bevelling cutter being checked for a slight amount of curvature by holding it against a flat surface. The curvature required is only slight, but very necessary.

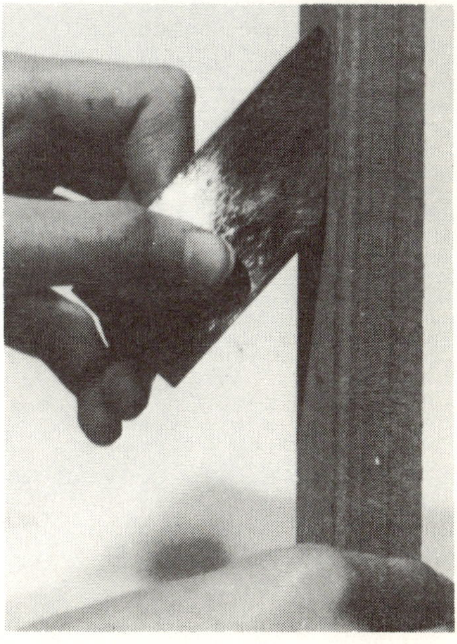

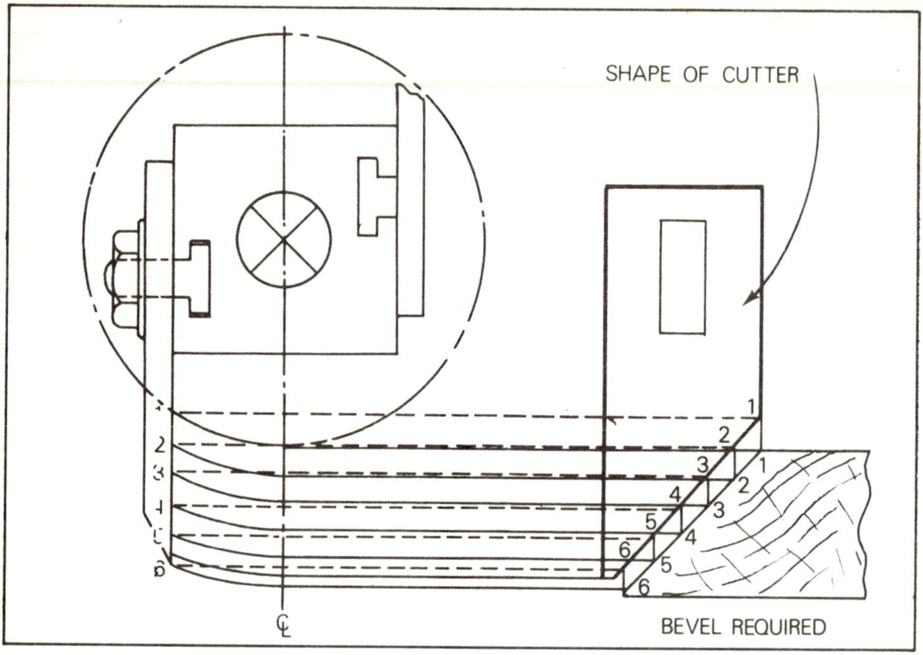

The geometric development for bevel cutters for the spindle moulder, or moulding machine. When cutter planing for the spindle moulder, cutting should be done on the underside of the work, if possible.

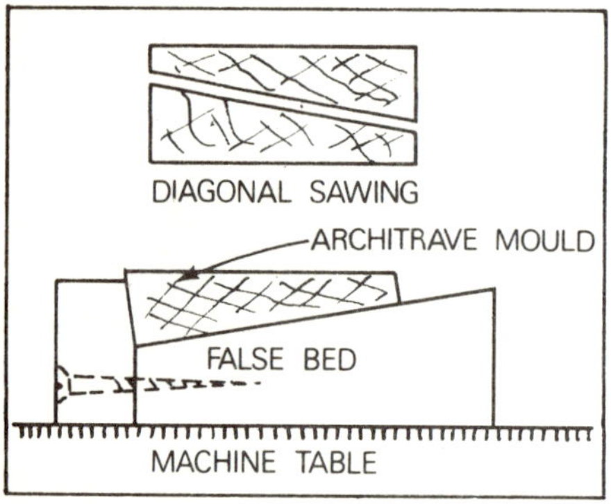

Diagonal sawing can often be an economical method of timber utilisation since only a small amount of material is wasted in processing. The sawn face can be planed on the thicknessing machine with the adaptation of a false bed secured to the under-table.

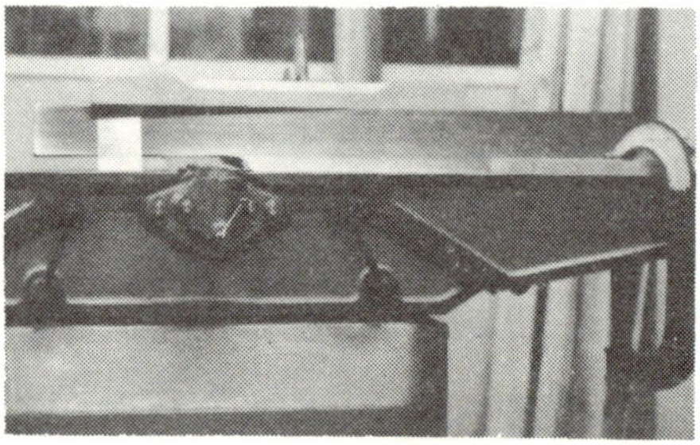

When "dropping on" for stop chamfering, a back stop should be clamped on the machine table to prevent a kick-back. The bridge guard should also be set before switching on the machine. This has been temporarily removed to illustrate the operation.

Precision bevelling is required for joints of this nature. Their faces must be perfectly flat for glue adhesion. Hog-backed surfaces would produce open joints.

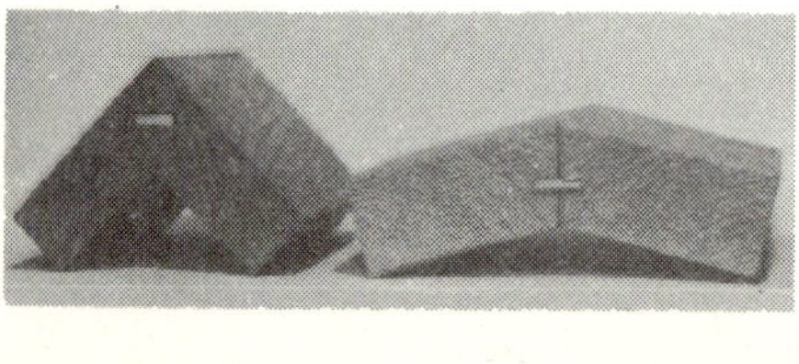

must, of course, be applied to the cutting edge.

Another method of producing bevels on long stock is by making use of the thickness planer. A false bed has to be made to give the required angle, and this must be either bolted or clamped to the under table of the machine. Hardwood should be used for constructing the bed-piece, or 18 mm ply is suitable for the wider type if well supported.

Narrow skirting boards or architraves can be

produced in this way from already planed stock. The bevelled surface produced is perfectly flat across the face, and the feed speed should be adjusted to give the finished surface required. The amount of material that can be removed at each pass through the machine is limited due to the pressure roller movement, but pre-sawing can help to speed procedure. Weather boarding can quickly be produced by diagonal sawing and planing in this way.

Bevelling on the circular saw to remove waste material before working a heavy moulding can provide safer working and a better finish. This method can also be useful when abrasive or curly grained timbers are to be moulded. A steady continuous feed should be made through the saw; stopping should be avoided during the cut if a clean bevel is required.

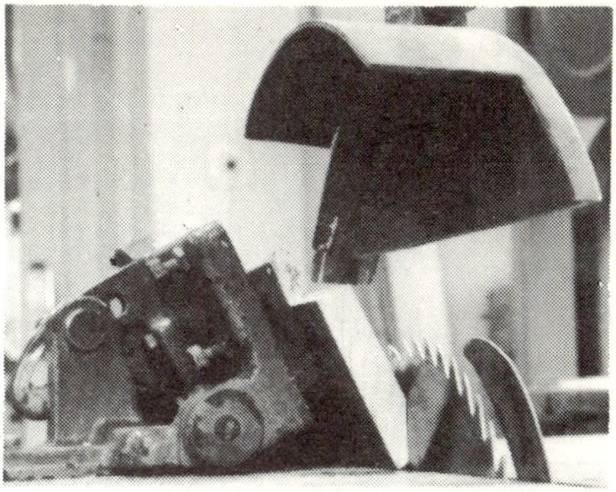

Bevelling on the circular saw is usually done to lighten the cut before moulding timbers of difficult texture. The saw blade should be lowered to a reasonable working height, and the overhead guard adjusted to its most effective position.

Time saving in setting up: frictionless collars

Setting up time on machines is classed by many as non-productive as no actual work is being turned out during that period. Success of the production time which follows the setting up, can depend very much on how well the non-productive period has been utilised.

A saving in non-productive time is always desirable, and any aids that can contribute towards this are a welcome asset.

Expenditure on some small items of equipment can in some cases help to reduce setting time, in addition to making an operation more progressive. When purchasing equipment of this type, it is essential that the goods supplied are exactly what is required or the whole gain of the project may be missed.

Shaping components for general joinery, have, in the past, been processed on the spindle moulder using a ring fence, and a square block. The setting up of this equipment can take a considerable amount of time due to the fact that checking and adjustments are involved, before everything is in correct alignment and securely bolted.

A safety type block and a ball bearing ring mounted in a cutter setting stand. The cutters in the block are in the process of being set to the same working diameter as the ring.

With the introduction of ball bearing collars and rings for the spindle moulder, setting time can be reduced considerably if their use is methodically planned. A less skilled operator can also set up using a ball bearing ring and a safety type circular cutter block.

For cleaning up square-edged shapes, the diameter of the cutting circle of the block should be identical with that of the guide ring. This can be obtained by setting the cutters in the block with the correct amount of projection. A 4¼in. (108 mm) diameter guide ring, is suitable for a 4in. (102 mm) diameter circular cutter block, the projection of the cutters making the cutting circle up to 4¼in. (108 mm). This relationship between the dimensions of the cutter block and the ring is an important point when planning to work by this method.

A guide template or former as they are often named, is secured to the workpiece to produce the required shape. Setting time of the machine by this method will take but a matter of minutes. If the shape of the cut is convex, it may not be necessary to remove the fences from the machine they will in fact act as a lead in, and a guard.

For concave shapes the fences will have to be removed, and provision made for leading the work into the cutters. Guards must also be provided.

The use of ball bearing guide rings with circular blocks is recommended for operators or students being trained on shaped work, as they are more pleasant to use than the ring fence and square block. Less vibration is experienced, and noise is reduced due to the small projection of the cutters which stir up only a small amount of the surrounding atmosphere. Ring fence working has, of course, much greater scope.

Before shaping on the spindle moulder it is in most cases advisable to cut away the unwanted material to within 3 mm of the finished line. This can be done on a band saw, enabling a light cut to be made safely in the spindle operation. Where components to be worked are small, they must be mounted in a jig, either singly or in batches.

When holding jigs are used it is usually convenient for the ball bearing ring to be placed on the underside of the cutter block, the bed of the jig acting as the former shape. When a plywood former only is used, the ring should be above the cutter block. The ring does act as a guard to

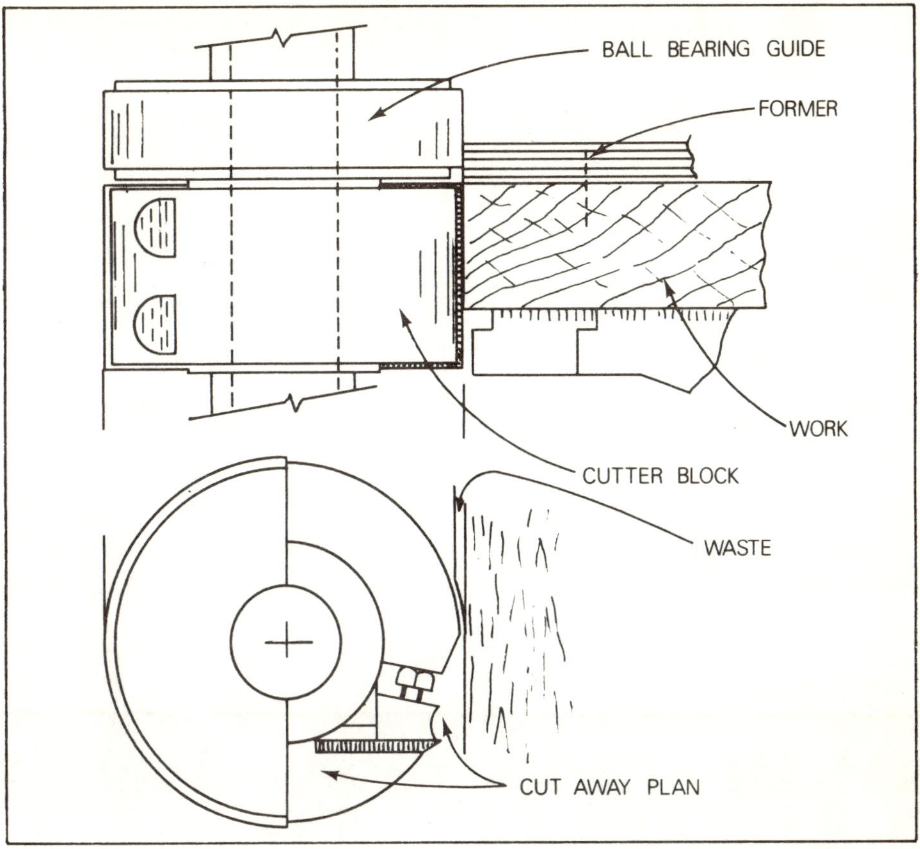

A ball bearing guide ring being used with a circular cutter block. The cutting circle of the block is identical to the diameter of the ring. The plywood former is prepared to the exact shape to which the work has to be processed.

some extent when positioned above the cutter, which is a point worth noting.

Jigs are less subject to wear on repetition work when ball bearing rings are used, as friction between the former edge and the ring is very small. This can eliminate the fitting of metal trims to the working edges of jigs in many instances. The making of these shaped metal trims can at times involve quite a lot of work using the available woodworkers equipment.

In addition to ball bearing ring units, slotted collars incorporating ball bearing rings are also available. This piece of equipment has many useful assets, but the cutters require to be set by the machine operator each time it is brought into use. Cutters can however be set projecting beyond the guide ring for forming a rebate or mould.

I usually find that if new standard cutters are used for this set up, the tail end of the cutters project out of the slots and would catch on the work.

It is therefore necessary to shorten cutters or use old ones that have lost length due to grinding. This point should be checked before offering the equipment for use.

Due to the fact that the slotted collars in general use are of a smaller diameter than circular blocks, work entailing a smaller radius of curvature can be carried out. It must be understood, of course, that the peripheral speed is reduced with the smaller diameter unit unless

Waste material is being cut away on a bandsaw machine. About 3 mm should be left on for the cutting operation on the spindle moulder.

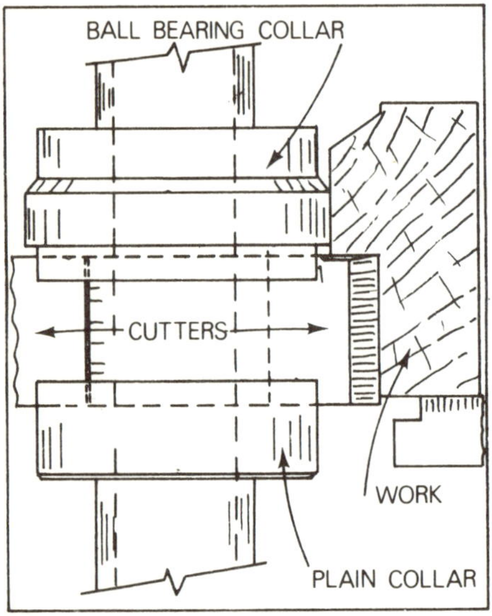

A slotted collar unit incorporating a ball bearing ring in the overhead section. When the work bears on the ring during the cutting process, the ring stops rotating, so cutting down friction to almost nil.

A circular block with the ball bearing ring positioned below the cutter. This applies when the work is held in a jig, the base of the jig acting as the shape former. Any clamps that are fitted must be positioned to enable guards to be used.

A circular block with the ball bearing ring mounted above. Note that plywood former projects beyond the work to give a lead in to the cutting operation. Guards must be applied before operating.

the revolutions of the spindle are increased.

Cutter heads of this type are usually designed for speeds of around 6,000 rpm. Much depends on how well the inserted cutters are matched and balanced at what speed the machine should be run, either at over or under the recommended figure.

When working with high speed rotation, as used in woodworking machinery, it is always advisable to follow the machine manufacturers' recommendations, but allowances must be made for deterioration in use.

For a general safety point of view, the ball bearing ring and circular block are more foolproof than the slotted collar assembly. The circular block can also be pre-set in the tool room. The slotted collar unit is more versatile but it has to be set up on the shop floor by the operator. The setting of cutters, on, or in, cutter heads should be confined to the tool room with its ideal conditions when ever possible.

Provision must always be made for leading in at the start of the cut when working on rings or collars. This can be done in a variety of ways:

1. Make use of the infeed fence.

2. By extending the former or jig beyond the workpiece.

3. By bolting a suitably shaped leading on piece to the table of the machine. This piece, due to its shape, is known to many as a "donkey's ear."

A slotted collar and ball bearing ring unit combined. The tail ends of the cutters must not project beyond the collars. For some operations, the machine fences can be positioned to act as a lead in for the work, and a guard.

Simulating adzed finish

Reply to a problem

PROBLEM

We are required to prepare softwood joists and beams with an adzed finish. As the quantity required almost precludes hand work, we would welcome any ideas of how this could be carried out by machinery.

G.W.O.

SOLUTION

The task of adzing a large number of beams entirely by hand can be a laborious job. If a machine is used, there is a possibility of the pattern repeating itself. This may, or may not be acceptable, depending on the final location of the beams. If, however, the major part can be accepted from a machine, leaving only a small amount to be completed by hand, I offer the following suggestion.

The spindle moulder will produce an undulating surface on timber similar to adzing, if an eccentric roller is fitted to the infeed fence.

This roller is a non-standard piece of equipment, and one that I have designed myself.

It is used in conjunction with an automatic feed attachment on the machine. Without the autofeed, it would probably still be possible but the work will be very fatiguing.

The eccentric roller is not power-driven. The passing timber rotates the roller due to friction, and the eccentric action guides the timber on and off the cutter unit. The surface of the roller is milled, like the face of a file, to provide the necessary grip as the timber is fed through.

The length of the apparent adze stroke produced is governed by the diameter of the roller. The one illustrated is 38 mm in diameter. Multiply this by 3.142 and this gives an adze stroke of 119 mm, one rotation of the roller. The larger the diameter of the roller the longer the stroke of the cut. The depth of the cut at its centre point is governed by the amount of eccentricity on the

The sketch shows the positioning of the parts concerned. The first feed roller should be directly in line with the bearing of the eccentric roller. As the timber goes forward from this position it revolves the roller, and is fed into the cut. The roller and mountings are made from steel, the face of the roller being crossmilled to provide grip. Having had successes with his experiments, Mr. Clayton has applied for a patent for the eccentric roller used. This has now been awarded.

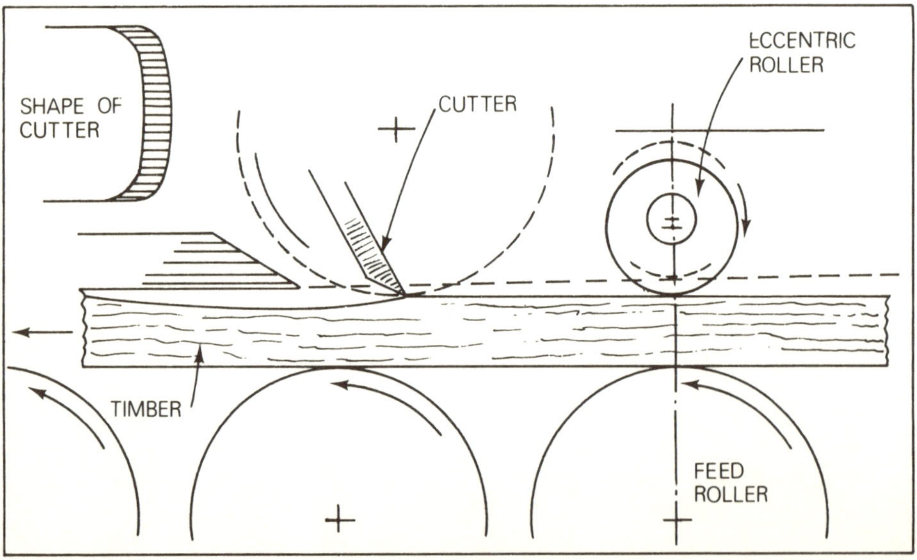

roller. The roller illustrated is a variable one, and can be set from nil to 4 mm eccentric. I would say from experience that 3 mm is generally the most suitable.

The shape of the cutters used should be slightly rounded, convex, to produce a slight hollow on the cut. Various types of cutter heads may be used according to the width of cut required. Circular block, square block, or slotted collars for narrow work.

A 153 mm circular block, and cutters, would process 306 mm wide material at two passes through the machine, and run very sweet. The centre meeting line may require a little handwork, this depends on the skill of the operator.

The surface of the timber being processed must be reasonably flat, although it does not have to be planed clean. The cutters give a smooth undulated finish over the entire surface. The cut should be as light as possible for both economy, and machine loading. The positioning of the roller and fence decides this.

If querist requires any further information, or assistance, I will be only too pleased to help. Please contact the Editor.

General view of the set-up on the spindle moulder with the auto-feed in the horizontal position. Example of work can be seen, produced with a 50 mm wide cutter.

View of the spindle moulder with the auto-feed moved out of working position to show the eccentric roller. Other types of cutter heads may be used, to suit the width of timber being worked.

Using the straight line edger saw

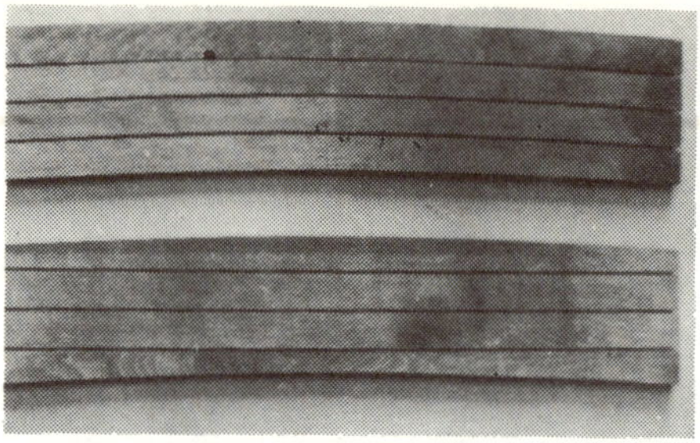

Showing difference between a board cut on a hand-fed saw bench and on a straight line edger, where curvature on board edge is not shown in the cut.

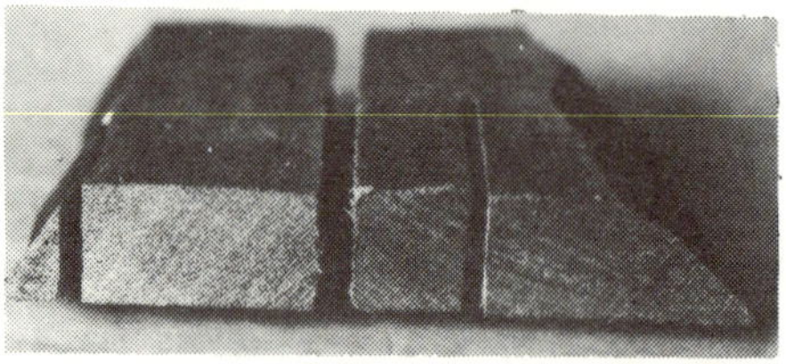

Waney offcuts (left) should be removed promptly by the taker off. Little or no danger of a throw-back when both sections (right) are wide enough to be gripped by the overhead pressure rollers.

Present-day production demands have created a demand for power-fed woodworking machines which will not only increase output, but will also in many cases produce a higher standard of work with less effort. The modern straight line edger saw could be classed as a machine in this category.

This machine was originally designed for trimming the edges of boards after they had been sawn from the log and was looked upon by many as a machine confined to saw-milling. The high performances of present-day machines of this type have found a place for them within the actual production line in the woodworking factory.

When a straight line edger is installed in a factory, the purchasing of timber with untrimmed edges, particularly hardwoods, can become an economical proposition. Providing long boards are crosscut into the shortest workable lengths before being edge-trimmed, waste can be kept to a minimum. Should these same boards be edge-trimmed in the full length before allocation to the project, much timber could be wasted.

Timber is fed through the straight line edger by means of a travelling chain track, working within the table, and is sometimes assisted by an overhead powered roller. Overhead pressure rollers also grip the timber firmly during its progress through the saw.

Two distinct types of machines are in use, depending on the location of the saw spindle. Some manufacturers arrange the saw underneath the table, similar to the normal saw bench, with a rise and fall incorporated. Others have the saw unit mounted above the bench, in which case this must be adjustable to accommodate the various diameters of saws. The feed chain on this type of machine has a line of renewable lead inserts in the centre to accommodate the extremity of the saw teeth. So when the saw is mounted below the table the chain is made up in two distinct sections, with the saw running between them.

The overhead pressure unit is raised and lowered by means of a hand-wheel situated at the front of the machine, reference being made to the setting scale. It should be noted that in both types of machines the raising and lowering arrangements for the saw spindle are independent of the pressure rollers. This is not always fully realised with the overhead machine.

The saw is driven direct from a motor revolving at approx. 2,900 r.p.m. This gives a rim speed on a 18in. (450 mm) diam. saw well in excess of 10,000ft. (3,000 m) per min. when not under load. Machines usually accommodate saws from 12 to 18in. (300 to 450 mm) in diameter.

Saws of a minimum diameter for the job should be used to reduce frictional resistance, and maintain the maximum of rigidity. The driving motor requires to be in the region of 15 horsepower to cut timber up to 5in. in thickness.

The saw blade should be of a strong gauge—around 12 B.W.G.—and the design of the teeth should be robust to stand up to continuous power feeding. Tungsten carbide tipped saws can be used for cutting abrasive timbers, or used for long periods without servicing on normal work. Fine toothed novelty-type saws can be used for cutting plywood, or other timber of light section.

The teed, which is driven by a motor independently of the saw spindle, is at the rate of 50 to 150ft. (15 to 50 m) per min. The slower speeds are intended for use when cutting shorts, to follow up one piece after the other. When the higher feed speeds are used, it may be necessary to have more than one person taking off and stacking at the back of the machine.

Although the machine has a fence to help position the timber on entry, it plays no part in guiding the timber during its progress through the machine. The timber is gripped between the chain and the overhead rollers, and fed in a straight line. Any curvature on the fence edge of

Modern straight line edger, with saw mounted below table.

An older model of machine than above, with saw mounted above the table.

the timber is not repeated in the saw cut, as it would be on the ordinary hand-feed saw bench.

This is particularly useful when preparing large quantities of timber for fourcutting. Narrow timber fed into a fourcutter bent usually comes out bent. A straight start is always advantageous.

With the introduction of a high-frequency glueing, where butt joints are very often acceptable if they are of a high standard, a modern straight line edger can meet this requirement. Also, edge lippings for chipboard and plywood can be cut very rapidly from the thicknessed board, a good method of off-cut utilisation.

To ensure perfectly ridge-free edges on the sawn stock, trimming attachments are available for dressing the edges of the saw teeth during rotation. This is an added refinement to certain models of this machine, which is not normally carried out on the circular saw. The fronts of the teeth can also be trimmed.

Two important points to note on the operation of the straight line edger are lubrication and sawdust extraction. The chain has a large amount of frictional surface, and although its speed is not fast compared with that of the saw spindle, its lubrication requires full attention in accordance with the manufacturers specification.

Straight line edger saws, being power fed, are not usually fitted with a riving knife. When both sections of the timber being sawn are of a wide dimension there is little or no danger of a throwback to a considerate user as they are firmly gripped by the feed arrangement.

When a narrow offcut is produced (say ¼in.in width) or a waney edge is sawn off, they could be left ungripped on the chain track. In these circumstances the offcut is in danger of being thrown back by the saw in the direction of the operator. To prevent these edgings being ejected, one or two lines of safety fingers are fitted at the infeed end of the machine. It is important that these safety fingers are maintained in good condition and kept in proper adjustment. The table below them should be kept free from chips of waste to ensure that the fingers drop fully after each sawing sequence.

On machines with overhead saws particular attention should be given to the condition of the lead inserts in the chain track. They should be replaced before they become excessively worn.

Other causes of timber being thrown back, or difficult feeding experiences, could be due to:
(a) Wear in the bearings of the overhead pressure rollers, which may enable the timber to be fed into the machine to a certain point where the force exerted by the saw may be greater than

the grip of the worn bearing, and so the feed action does not give satisfactory results; (b) Serrations on the chain track become worn smooth after long service and the gripping power is so reduced.

Due to the high rate of feed capable by these power-fed machines, ample working space should always be provided, particularly at the outfeed end, to prevent any danger of the taker-off being trapped.

Most straight line edgers of today are quite large machines and are, therefore, confined to the larger working units. But I have no doubt that the mini-edger will eventually appear to help the smaller man with its safe, effortless, precision sawing.

Straight line edger machine, with the saw blade positioned below the table.

Close-up view of the infeed end, showing the safety fingers.

Section 4 Scientific approach Electronics

Low Voltage Strip Heating

Use of adhesives. Economical cost. Comparison with R.F. methods. Use of transformer. Metal strip details. Jig construction. Setting times. Suitable moisture content. Advantageous facts. Edge Lipping.

Wood Machining For Radio Frequency Heating

Preparation of timber. Selection of operatives. Knowledge required. Use of butt joints. Planning edge lippings. Importance of moisture control. Wavefield in planing. Planning workflow. Saw produced lipping. Cutting panel boards. Brief efficiency guide.

Preservation Of Timber

Moisture in timber. Cause of decay. Damp proof courses. Timber in contact with brickwork. Dry rot. Sapwood in timber. Types of preservatives. Water borne. Organic solvants. Tar oils. In situ preservation treatment.

Moisture Content During Processing

Planning delays during production. Direction of shrinkage. Why shrinkage varies. Humidity control. Kilning and air drying. Using panel boards. Effect on mitres. Joint design. End cracking. Over Drying. Maching wet timber.

Working With Carbide Tipped Cutters

Abrasive timbers. Type of machine head. Cutter speed. Servicing. Diamond coated wheel.

Machining Difficult Timbers

Working plastics. Cutter bevels. Use of stellite. Tungsten carbide tips. Cutter maintainance. Limitation of shaping. Use of front bevel.

Cutter Grinding For The Spindle Moulder

Shaping cutters. Elongation allowances. Use of paper template. Protecting the eyes. Coolant. Left and right hand cutters. Amount of bevel required. Repeating cutter shape.

Working In The Tool Room

Servicing cutting units. Automatic machines. Location of tool room. Abrasive Wheel Regulations. Tool room equipment. Reference to publication "Circular Saws" by Plank and Stephenson. Abrasive wheels. Saw gulleting. Wide bandsaws.

A Look At New Developments

Improved safety. Saws for cutting sheet material. Trussed roof members. Automatic feed units. Wedge bed planer. Improved mortising machines. Automatic spindle shaper. Precision grinding and shaping. Jointing cutters. Grinding cutters "in situ".

Timber And The Cubic Metre

Change from Petrograd Standard to Cubic Metre. Simplified calcs. Metre run to cubic metre. Content of cubic metre, of given section.

Calculations and Planning Aids

Timber tables. Pulley speeds. Circular saws. Bandsaws. Cutter speeds. Pitch of cutter marks. Cutter balance. Strobo flash (photo). Moisture content. Logarithm tables. Line drawings of cutter blocks.

Low voltage strip heating

In woodworking establishments where efforts are being made to increase productivity, it is essential that output in the various departments should be kept in balance.
The woodworking machine, as a preparer of timber, has been accepted in all factories, and workshops, but not all have accepted the mechanical and scientific appliances available to carry out assembly operations.
Since the development of thermo-setting adhesives (adhesives in which the set can be accelerated with the application of heat) gluing operations can be speeded up considerably.
With the use of heat-producing appliances, glue lines can be set in a matter of minutes, instead of hours, so enabling the production of an article to proceed in a continuous flow.
The use of Radio Frequency heating, known as RF, is confined to the larger production units, due to the initial cost. Low Voltage Strip Heating, is, however, very economical to install, and operate. The main component is a heavy duty transformer, and the average cost being around £30.
Its uses are limited only to the ingenuity of the user. Many operations being carried out with RF heating in the larger establishments can be done by the small man with strip heating, the actual curing time taking a little longer.
LV strip heating may be used for the simple lipping of panel boards and many other operations with the aid of built-up jigs. If a compressed air supply is available for the operation of cramping heads, efficiency can be increased considerably.
The heavy-duty transformer required reduces the mains voltage of 240 volts, to a very safe working voltage between 10 and 1.66 volts. This makes the method workable by all groups of operatives, and electrical insulation provides no problems in the construction of jigs.
The metal strip that consumes the electrical energy and provides the heat, is usually about 50 mm in width and 24 gauge in thickness. It should be of mild steel, or iron, galvanised or tin plated to prevent staining of the work. It may, if desired, by mounted on asbestos, in some instances, to direct the heat to the work rather

Fig. 1. A quick and efficient example of low voltage strip heating in operation. Two blockboard panels in process of being lipped with hardwood. The heating strip is sandwiched between the two panels. A sheet of hardboard or similar, laid across the cramps will prevent the heat being transferred downwards. Lipping 4 mm in thickness can be sufficiently set for removal from the cramps in about 5 min.

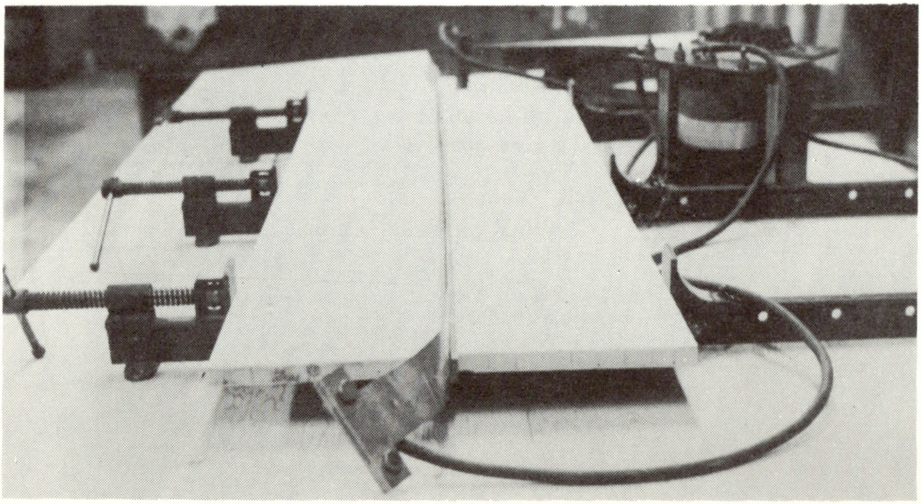

Fig. 2. An arrangement for edge lipping panels with the work in a near vertical position. The set-up can be a permanent one in a workshop, as it takes only a minimum of floor space. The heating strip rests on a firm shelf which is surfaced with asbestos. With a strip three or four metres in length, several components may be in the course of processing at the same time.

than into the jig. The temperature of the strip during operation should be as high as possible without scorching the timber.

Items being processed should be clamped under pressure to prevent any foaming of the adhesive. This is a very important factor; the higher the pressure, the more successful the joint.

Edge lippings should be as thin as practicable for the purpose required, no tongues or grooves being necessary. Preheating of the components before placing in position will speed the setting time. A 4 mm hardwood lipping strip, preheated, will be sufficiently set for removal after 3 minutes. Working temperature is normally about 100 deg. C. Laminated plastic edging strips can be applied without any difficulty. They cannot be applied to tops which have been fabricated using impact adhesive. Edging strips should in these instances be applied before the surface facing.

The temperature of the metal strip can be adjusted by either selecting a different tapping on the output side of the transformer, or fitting a regulator to vary the voltage on the input side.

With the transformer illustrated, under operation 1.66 volts heats 1.5 metres of strip to 105 deg. C.

Fig. 3. A jig designed for board jointing using butt joints, or others. Boards up to one metre in length can be accommodated, and unlimited in width. Pressure to the glue line is applied with sash cramps but overhead pressure to give surface alignment to the joint is by compressed air. Heat is applied from both above and below, and under this concentration 22 mm thick boards can be set in 5 min. one joint line at a time. (Jig constructed in The Building Department of Doncaster College of Technology. Transformer is by Pye Thermal Bonders Ltd., Cambridge).

Fig. 4. Novelty jig designed for the fabricating of small boxes of various types, in two, three minute cycles.

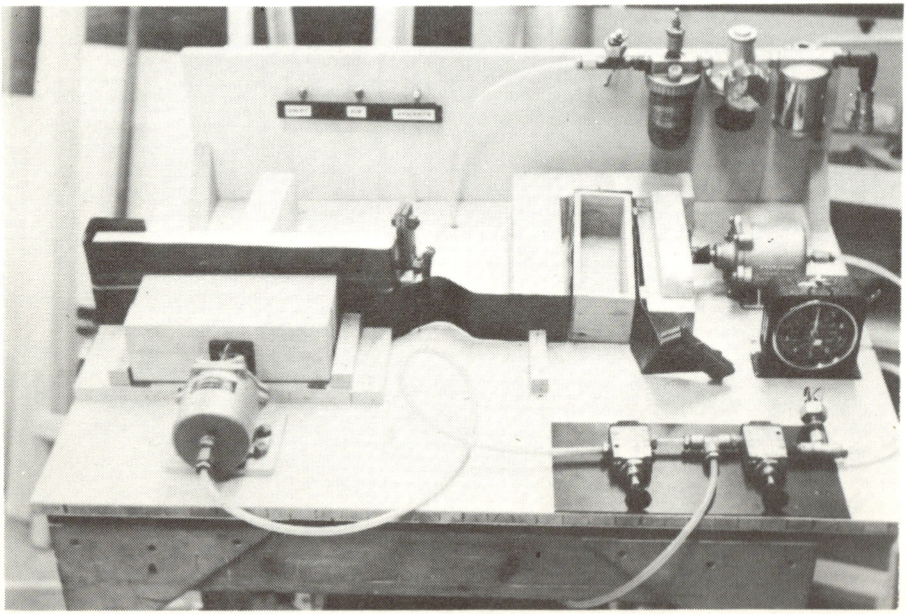

3.33 volts heats 3 metres of strip to a similar temperature of 105 deg. C. It must be understood that the electrical conductivity of different metals vary. Width and gauge of the heating strip also affect its performance.

Synthetic resin adhesives, urea formaldehyde, and others which set on the application of heat are suitable for processing with LV strip heating. The particular grade of the adhesive is not generally important, as in RF heating where the electrical conductivity of the glue line sometimes has to assist the set.

The moisture content of the timber being processed should preferably not exceed 15 per cent. if reliable results are expected. Sudden localised heat, applied to moisture-laden timber can have disastrous results, and the chemistry of the adhesive has to be considered.

Some of the points in favour of Low Voltage Strip Heating are:

1 Speeds output. Often increases quality also, as it eliminates the use of nails or pins.
2 Safe to use electrically, by all grades of operatives.
3 Economical in cost, both on installation and operation.
4 Work can either be taken to the source of heat, or the heat taken to the work.
5 Jigs are simple to construct. No complicated electronics involved.

The lap joints on the side components are coated with adhesive and placed in the first position of the jig along with the ends. Under heat and pressure they will set in three minutes. The bottom to the box is then applied in the second position of the jig in a similar time. With both positions occupied, boxes are produced at the rate of one very three minutes.

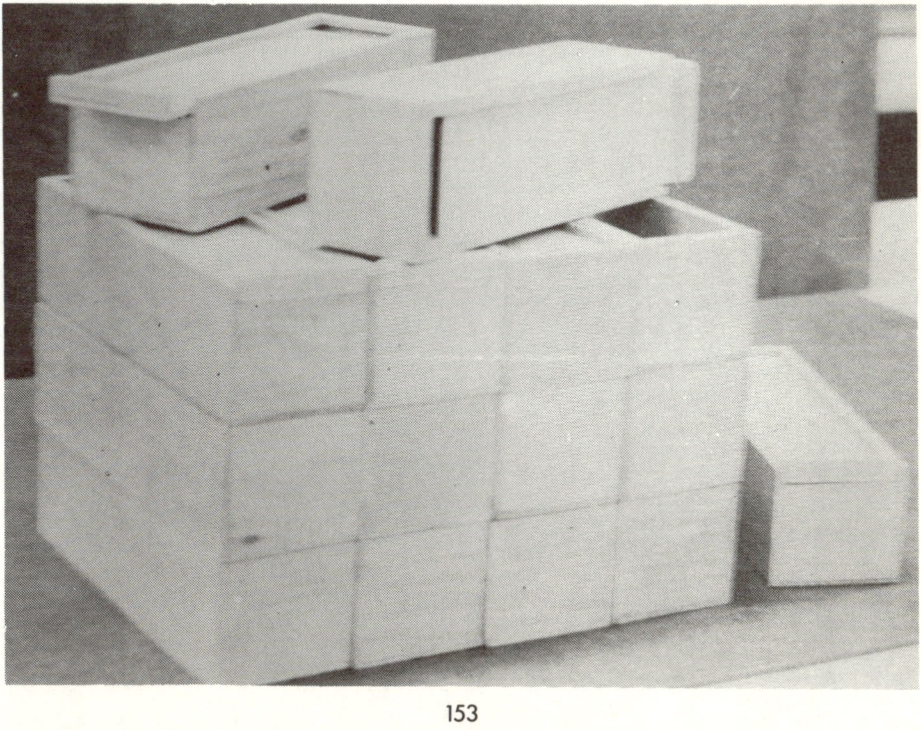

Wood machining for R.F. heating

Quite a lot of information has been put forward in the general use of RF heating, from the point of view of the equipment manufacturer, during the last decade. Information has in fact now reached a stage, where it is fully realised that unless components for assembly are machined to a reasonably high standard, both quantity, and quality of the output from RF can be below that expected for the capital outlay.

Success in RF heating depends on the reliability, and application of three major functions. Electronics, adhesives, and the preparation of components for assembly, namely, wood machining. It is with the preparation of timber, and wood machining, this article is concerned, and refers mainly to board jointing, and the application of lipping to panel boards, and with others in mind.

Who Does What

In a busy factory, it is not usually a highly skilled cabinet maker that is withdrawn from the assembly line, to carry out RF operations of the simpler continuous process type. His services are too much in demand in his own section. Instead the person trained to be the RF operator, may be classed as more of a process worker. His or her role in the production unit is just as important as one of a more versatile nature, and skill. The process worker cannot, however, be expected to rectify faults in the machined parts with hand tools. It is the duty of the person in charge of the machine section, to ensure that work is up to the required standard, before it goes forward for RF processing.

Knowledge of Timber

It is in the interest of departmental management, to have some understanding of timber technology. This can contribute considerably in the success of RF heating. An understanding of how various timbers behave under different conditions can be very useful. This information can be obtained either from technical study, years of practical experience, or trial and error. The latter method can be the most expensive. Scientific aids should be made use of in a progressive factory. An understanding of moisture content in timber is most essential. Apart from the fact that timber over 15 per cent moisture content takes longer to cure in the RF unit, its behaviour during machining and immediately after can create faults.

Planned Flow of Production

As butt joints are preferred for RF work, timber must be reasonably out of twist, edges square to the face, to obtain results with the minimum of effort. It must be remembered that timber is continually on the move, adjusting itself to the humidity conditions it is exposed to. For this reason it is good policy to pass boards through the RF jointing process as soon as possible after preparation before any movement can take place. It is folly for large quantities of board jointing to be prepared, and left standing for long periods before jointing. The amount of build up of work permissable can vary depending on the moisture content of the timber, and the surrounding conditions. Excessive heat, for instance, blowing from a fan in a factory heating system, can create havoc on a stack of prepared boards, in a very short time.

The Butt Joint

Where butt joints are used, and in theory, they are the most suitable for RF work, overhead

Checking surface alignment on test samples prepared for butt jointing. Edges must be absolutely square to the face and completely free from ridges.

pressure is required to give alignment. For this reason boards should be out of twist, and also planed reasonably smooth to allow free movement, bringing surface friction to a minimum. A system of rollers on overhead pressures would reduce friction.

Quality of Planed Edges

The preparations of straight, square, planed edges for board jointing, is usually carried out on a power-fed machine. The sessentials are, that the edges shall be straight, square to the face, and have a finish free from ridges, caused by snipped or blunted cutters.

Any one of the above factors, not in keeping with the requirements can cause a butt joint to fail. Personal experience has shown, that on some timbers where planing efficiency could not be maintained it could be advantageous to use a form of T and G joint. Efficiency would be lost in the aspect of glue pressure, but the final result can be more acceptable than a doubtful butt joint.

Another point to consider on the preparation of edges for board jointing is the wavefield, or cutter marks per inch. Machine planed work is produced by rotating cutters, and this produces a series of waves. To ignore this fact entirely, would not be technically correct. Craftsmen of the past often used to shoot machine prepared edges by hand, to reduce the thickness of the line the dark animal glue made. Modern machines can produce joints that do not require a follow-up of hand work.

Looking at Wavefield

Edges fed into a machine, at too great a speed for the cutting unit, will produce a widely spaced wave field. This can result in a thick glue line, and possible foaming in the joint. A suggested figure of at least 20 cuts per 20 mm should be aimed at. This figure is usually well exceeded.

This shows an enlarged view of the wavefield, on the glue line of a butt joint. Twenty cuts per 20 mm plus is recommended.

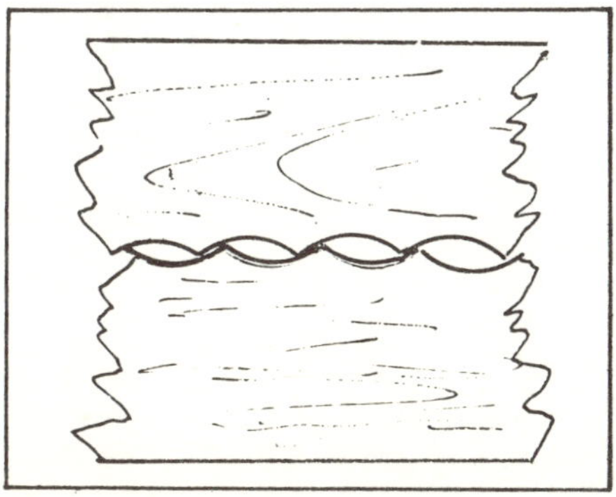

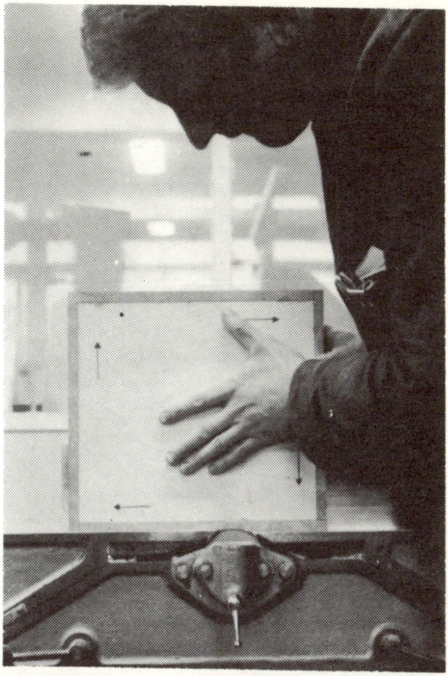

A specimen panel is being trimmed on a surface planer. As the edge lippings have been arranged to follow around the panel, there is no danger of splintering at the end of the cut. (For clarity, the bridge guard has been removed).

Cutter heads on power-fed edge jointing machines are usually of a large diameter, and have quite a number of cutters mounted on each. If a constant rate of feed is to be maintained, then an accurate setting of cutters must be maintained also. Cutter marks are determined by the feed speed, the number of effective cutters, and the revolutions of the cutter block.

$$\frac{1000 \times \text{Feed Speed (m/min)}}{\text{Number of Effective Cutters} \times \text{R.P.M.}}$$

Example

$$\frac{1000 \times 12}{6 \times 3000} = 0.66 \text{ mm Cutter mark pitch.}$$

The same set up but with only two cutters effective.

$$\frac{1000 \times 12}{2 \times 3000} = 2.00 \text{ mm Cutter mark pitch.}$$

This would not produce a very good butt joint.

Widthing of Prepared Panels

Where board jointing is being done in large quantities, using random width material, it is ad-

Two methods of planing edge lippings: (A) The sandwich system, where the edge lippings are enclosed between the sides. (B) The follow round method, which has several advantages over "A" although the finished appearance may not always be acceptable. Arrows indicate the direction of feed into the profiling cutters.

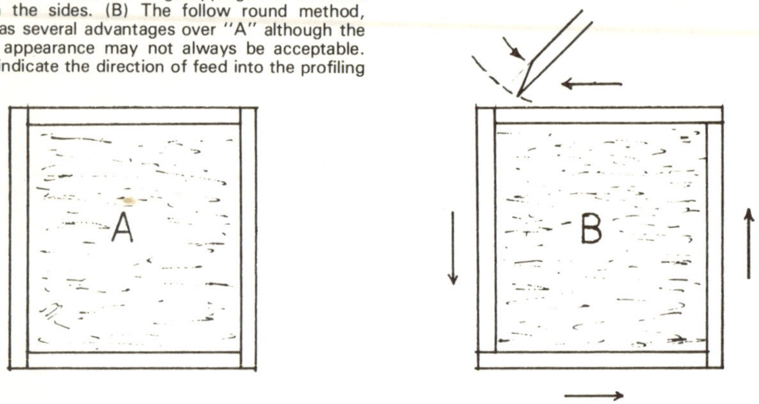

visable to produce panels of approximately the same width for the convenience of cramping. An extra operation carried out by machine aid, can save much time at the RF unit. The amount of piston movement on compressed air cramping heads is understandably limited, and time can be taken up by inserting packing pieces of varying widths in order to obtain pressure. Parallelism of the individual board edges, will also improve the resultant joint, although this may not always be adhered to, but it may cause undue slip in the cramping operation, if ignored in the extreme.

Aid to Adhesive Control

From the point of view of the wood machinist, the less adhesive that is extruded from the joint, the better, for the benefit of future operations. Excess use of adhesive should be avoided to give the minimum of squeeze-out. Squeeze-out can be arrested to a certain extent, when jointing the thicker type of timber, by machining small grooves in the glueing edges, near the extremity. These will accommodate the excessive adhesive, similar to an anti-capillary groove in an opening sash window frame, acting on the incoming moisture. Grooves of this type can be applied to the timber in the same pass through the machine for the jointing operation with suitably equipped cutter heads.

Edge Lipping

In the preparation of edge lippings, the moisture content of the timber used is again of major importance. If the lippings are to be over-veneered in a heated press, after application to panel boards, the moisture content would preferably be most suitable around 10 per cent, to ensure the minimum of shrinkage during pressing.

Rectangular four-cut section is ideal for edge lippings, and it is advisable to make the lipping 0.5 mm over size to allow the lipping to be levelled to the panel board. As all the over-size in the lipping is pushed to one face of the panel board in the RF process, excessive over-size should be avoided. This can eliminate trimming with cutters later, and a finish obtained by sanding only.

If lippings are produced straight from the circular saw using planed-to-thickness material, care should be taken to keep the saw dimension constant. The straight line edger, or a multyrip saw can be used for this purpose. If it is possible to trim the edges of the saw teeth in addition to the front of the teeth during rotation, ridge-free sawing may be obtained. Some manufacturers of the straight line edger saws, do provide an attachment for this purpose.

Application of Edge Lipping

Lipping applied to one edge only of a panel, provides little difficulty. It is advisable, however, to cut both panel and lipping over-length, and trim completed unit after application.

Where all four edges of panels have to be lipped, accuracy at all stages must be observed by the machinist. The three main points to consider are:

1. The lipping must be constant in dimension, and square.
2. The panel board must be cut to constant dimension and square.
3. The accurate length of lippings.

Good quality panel boards can usually be relied upon to be square on delivery at the factory. These are, more often than not, cut in both directions on a circular saw, using only the ripping fence as a guide, and no other squaring aid. If this method is used, both uncut sheets and the cut panels must be constantly under check. Blunt, or improperly tensioned, saws can cause elongated snaking in the saw cut; this must be avoided.

The fence should also be checked for parallelism with the line of saw. Tungsten carbide tipped saws should be used for cutting chipboard or multiply in quantity. To be certain of squareness, ripping and squaring should be defined as two operations, and carried out on the appropriate machines.

Lipping on Four Edges

Where Lippings are required on all four edges of panels, and the final product has to be moulded, or trimmed by revolving cutters, the arrangement of the lippings can be planned to advantage. The method, best described as the follow round system, each lipping is cut with one projecting end. It has two advantages over the sandwich system. There is less chance of a reduction of pressure in the joint, due to one lipping holding another off. Lippings can, in fact, be cut very slightly short, to advantage. Also, provided the lipped component is fed into the revolving cutters in the correct follow round sequence, no spelching will occur, and a good rate of feed speed can be maintained. Where the layout off the lipping in this manner may be objectionable, in the finished product, the thickness of the lipping should be kept to a minimum.

Looking at Safety

Very often, heavy cuts have to be made on edge lippings by the spindle moulder operator, it is not unusual for perhaps fifty per cent of the material to be cut away to form the required profile. Lippings can, and have, parted from the panel board during the moulding operation. There departure speed would be in keeping with the peripheral speed of the cutter head, say 2000 m per minute or 33 m every second. For this reason no chances should be taken in the preparation of edge lipped work for profiling. Correct machining techniques are important, not just from a production point of view, but for safety also.

WOOD MACHINING EFFICIENCY GUIDE FOR RF HEATING

Board Jointing

Check moisture content.
Material planed out of twist.
Straight square edges, free from ridges.
Wave field 20 cuts per 20 mm plus.
Provision for minimum adhesive extrusion, if required.
Production control. To suit day to day capacity of RF unit.

Edge Lipping

Check moisture content 10 per cent for hot press work.
Uniformity of lipping for sectional dimension.
Lippings square to correct lengths.
Follow round method, if acceptable.
Squareness of panel boards, and constant dimension.
Advance preparation not objected to.

Checking moisture content with an electrically-operated meter. This is an important factor in successful R.F. heating.

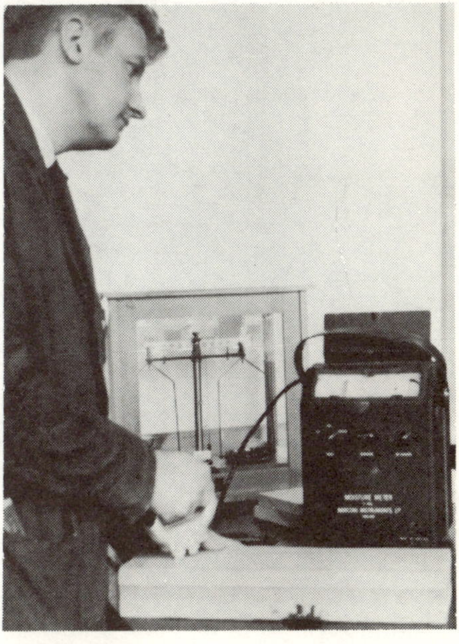

Preservation of timber

Timber is a direct product of nature, and its life span as a serviceable material can be governed by the way in which it is used constructionally, or what precautions are taken regarding attack by its enemies.

Unfortunately, timber is hydrophilic, it has a great attraction for water. Unless the amount of moisture in contact with timber is controlled, or the absorption properties reduced, its constructive life span can be in danger. The average moisture content of timber in habited rooms in a domestic building is about 12 per cent., possibly even lower in centrally heated areas.

Timber is not in danger of rot or fungal attack unless the moisture content exceeds 20 per cent. How wet is 20 per cent. plus? To persons using timber daily, 20 per cent. and over is most definitely wet as a material for working or living in close contact with. Moisture can be felt on the timber, in particular on a newly cut surface, and can be seen if compressed with the end of a steel rule.

The moisture will also create rust stains on woodworking machine tables. A joist weighing 27 kg at 12½ per cent. moisture content would weigh approx. 29 kg at 20 per cent. This additional weight would be noticeable to the experienced user.

However, when the figure 20 per cent. is

Water-borne pressure and vacuum treatment plant at Bawtry Timber Co. Doncaster. The processed stack of t and g boards have just been withdrawn from the pressure chamber. The chemical storage tanks can be seen in the background, behind the purpose built control and recording building. Left, Mr. Brian McQueen, director Bawtry Timber Co. and Mr. David Brunton, technical representative of Rentokil Ltd. The processing unit has an adjoining area for the orderly stacking of incoming timber items. This no doubt helps with efficiency of batch planning.

A lift of constructional timber being positioned for pressure treatment with the aid of a fork-lift truck. Note the timber is tight stacked, skidding of individual layers not being necessary.

referred to in relation to a structural member of a building it only requires a very small area of, say, a joist or rafter to have excess moisture to start fungal decay which can then spread to other parts. The use of timber preservatives in particular in locations where there is a danger of excess moisture can well be applied.

The constructional use of timber adjoining foundations in buildings are governed by strict regulations regarding their insulation from ground moisture. Although these regulations may be fully observed at the time of construction, changes in the situation may occur due to either manual effort or failure in the materials adjoining the timber.

The damp-proof course in a building may be at 150 mm above external ground level on a newly completed building, but very often the ground level is raised over the years by the formation of concrete paths, or other garden features.

Timber is more subject to rot when it is used for constructional purposes along with other types of materials. Exposed softwood readily absorbs moisture, and gives it up again quickly. An untreated window frame in contact with a brick wall will be kept at a high rate of moisture content much longer than it would be in an all-timber building.

The contact area, therefore, between timber and brick should be kept as small as practicable. Under present day economic constructional methods, many window and door frames are built directly into the outer skin of a brick cavity wall instead of being positioned in a reveal behind. This method usually includes projecting timber cills. The use of preservative treatment under these conditions cannot be over-stressed.

When economy is being practised on a building project, to disregard timber preservation could be in error as it can in many instances assist constructional procedure.

In the scientific use of timber, sectional dimensions are being reduced more and more. Old type buildings can, and do, in many instances, stand up to an amount of fungal and insect attack without undue weakening of the timber structure. Modern construction requires the safeguard of preservation treatment, and it is understandable that it can be found written in to many specifications.

It would not be unreasonable where rustproofed timber connecting plates are used for framing roof truss units to assume that the timber would be protected from moisture also.

In the factory production of building units, such as cladding panels, and window frames, the persons concerned with the actual making of the products may never have had experience of the hazards of a building site. The request for preservative treatment may in some instances come from the builder. He may have to educate the supplier as to his requirements.

Ground floor joists and adjoining timbers are probably the most common source of attack by Dry Rot (merulius lacrymans). The accepted causes of this infection is moisture in excess of 20 per cent. on untreated timber, and lack of ventilation. Another contributing factor can be timber containing large amounts of sapwood. Sapwood is the outer or immature part of the tree. Preservative treatment applied under pressure can penetrate sapwood, and so make it a much more repellent material. Observation has shown that over the years faster methods of growth are being used for timber. This gives a wider spacing of the growth rings which can be more subject to fungal attack if not treated.

Examination of constructional layouts can determine the degree of necessity for preservative treatment of the timber involved. (A) Shows a method of construction at a window opening which is being used extensively in this basic form in many parts of the country. Surface contact between wood and brick is at its maximum keeping moisture present for long periods. (B) A method which is more favourable from a weathering point of view. This method is still prominently used in Scotland. It was used extensively in the north of England by local building unit until national groups moved in from the south. It is evident that preservative treatment is more necessary with versions of type A than B.

Several types of preservatives are used in the treatment of timber. Specialists will advise on the most suitable process for the purpose required, which is very often described by a trade name. The suitability of a treatment is governed by such factors as whether it is concerned with rough constructional material, or machined joinery components.

Interior or exterior use must be considered in the choice of chemicals, as leaching, a washing out action can take place if exposed to weather in some cases. Water repellents are also added to preservatives to provide durability.

These are economical in cost, and consist of chemicals dissolved in water. The chemicals mainly used are copper-chrome-arsenate. These chemicals are not subject to leaching, and so are suitable for both interior or exterior work. Other types of chemicals are available from some manufacturers which are for inside use only.

The preservative is inserted into the timber by a system of vacuum and pressure. Its use in building is for structural members such as floor joists and roofing members. It is not normally used for prepared joinery items as the moisture content is raised considerably during treatment. Specialists have quoted a cost of about £12 for treating the structural timber of a three-bedroomed house.

These consist of chemicals dissolved in spirits and can be used in a variety of ways to treat

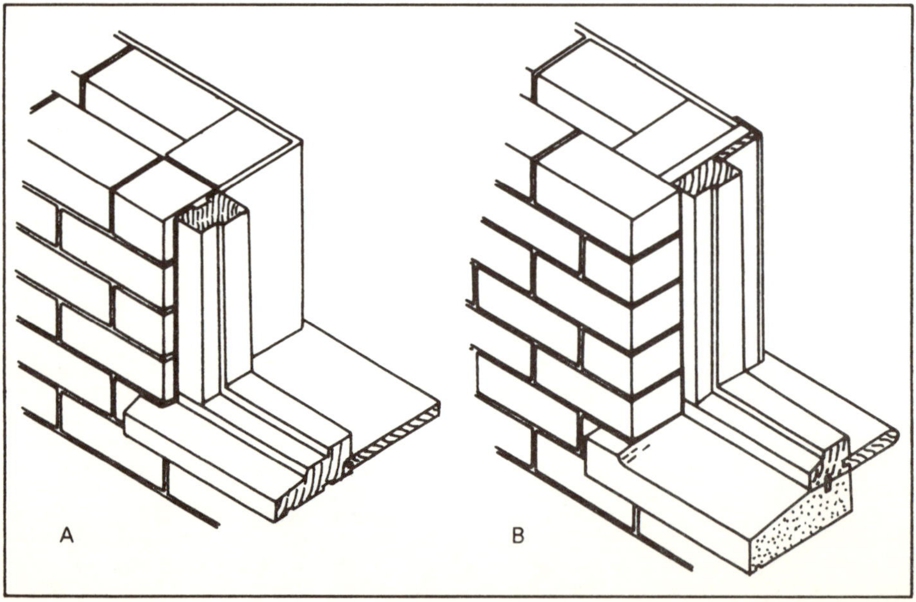

Assembled frames being grouped for immersion treatment.

joinery components or completed items. The moisture content of the timber is not affected, and there is no corrosion to metal fittings. Only a very short time is required after treatment before other decorative finishes can be applied.

Application of the preservative can either be by special plant, or immersion in a tank for periods of one to three minutes. The plant multi-vac treatment gives complete penetration of the sapwood. Various types of this preservative are available, each having their own characteristics.

Due to the spirit content the liquid is inflammable and care must be taken if used in a confined space.

These substances can be defined as tar, and creosote. They are used mainly for work remote from habitable buildings. They have a purpose in the preservation field of an industrial nature.

The following are some of the interesting points taken from one of several data sheets of Rentokil Laboratories Ltd. I have chosen this information as it should be of interest to the greatest number of readers. Data sheet No. 3b.

Joinery Preservative.

Description: Organic solvent based for preservation of fungal decay in timber.

Uses: Specifically for use in preservation of interior and exterior joinery timbers which are to be subsequently overpainted, varnished or treated with Rentokil Water Repellent Finishes. (Data Sheet 4b). Complies with Requirements of The National House-Builders' Registration Council.

Availability: Packed in 5 gal. and 40 gal. drums or delivered in bulk. Not for sale to the general public.

Application: By complete immersion only for 1-3 minutes, according to specification.

Specification: Condition of timber before treatment:

(a) The timber shall be free from all signs of attack by wood destroying fungi, sap-stain fungi and insects.

(b) The surfaces of the timber shall be free from dirt, grease, ice, paint and other foreign matter.

(c) The moisture content of the timber shall not exceed 22 per cent.

(d) All timber shall be cut and machined before treatment.

Treatment: The timber shall be completely immersed so that all surfaces are covered for a minimum period of one minute. Treatment can be carried out in component or assembled form, though component is preferable.

If any fabrication such as boring or removal of horns is carried out after treatment, any exposed surfaces shall be liberally brushed with Rentokil Joinery Preservative, normally available from the firm carrying out treatment, or from Rentokil Laboratories Ltd.

Timber after treatment. The timber shall be open stacked in a dry, well ventilated space.

Gluing: Allow 24 hours minimum between treatment and gluing.

Knotting: Allow 24 hours minimum between treatment and knotting, which should be applied before painting.

Overpainting: Allow 24 hours minimum between treatment and use of proprietary paint, varnish or Rentokil Finish Systems.

Flash-point: Over 100 deg. F.

Restoration. With older buildings being restored to use, which is becoming a present trend, timbers have often to receive preservative treatment in situ. Suitable chemicals and spray treatment is preferable to brushing. A spray gives better penetration to surface cracks, open joints, and difficult corners. Specialists carrying out this type of work normally provide a report as to the standard to which the work has been done.

Assistant with material in this article was given by Rentokil Laboratories Ltd., East Grinstead; Mr. David Brunton, Tech. Rep.; and Mr. Brian McQueen, Bawtry Timber Co., Doncaster. Photographs: Rentokil and John R. Clayton, and Cuprinol Ltd.

Moisture content during processing

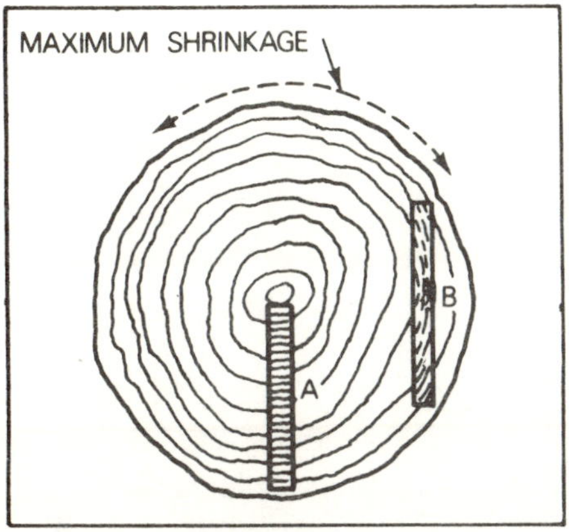

Sketch A: A board of timber cut from the log at position (A) will be less affected in width by a change of moisture content than a board cut at position (B). For this reason we get variation in the amount of shrinkage in a batch of material.

In the large scale production of timber products, it is essential to have some knowledge of the types of materials being used. Due regard must be paid to the problems that can be created due to the changing values in moisture content during the manufacturing stages.

Changes in moisture content very often do take place during the various processes in machining, particularly if the work is not continuously progressive.

Halts during the sequence of machining operations can be either planned ones, to allow the timber to reach a more stable percentage of moisture content, or delays due to other factors not previously anticipated.

Unplanned delays of some duration can create, in some instances, machining difficulties in the later stages of processing.

There is little doubt that work which passes through the machining stages progressively without delays is the most economic.

Wastage is reduced if the work fits snugly into prepared jigs, and less deterioration of the material generally takes place.

Although a batch of timber may be kiln dried to a predetermined moisture content in board form, when cut into a number of components each will adjust itself if given time to do so. Variations of shrinkage occur due to the fact that the components are all from different parts of the tree. The structure of every piece is in some way different.

Timber will adjust itself to the humidity of the atmosphere to which it is exposed. Temperature conditions in the machine shop must be in keeping with the type of work being produced, to keep the moisture content as stable as possible.

Some manufacturers of building joinery cut kilning of timber to a minimum by storing timber in skid in open sheds for a period, and planning delays during the machining stages.

Providing the delays take place according to plan, this method can work well, but it has its limitations as storage space is required within the machining unit.

Delays are usually planned prior to fourcutting, after the timber has been rough-cut to size, or in such items as drawer material, this may be fourcut over-width and dimensioned at the time of requirement.

With hardwood production, kiln drying is essential for large scale production, as the loss of moisture is very slow compared with that of softwood under natural seasoning conditions.

When working with man-made forms of timber, such as plywood, blockboard, and chipboard, the effect of moisture changes is considerably restricted. Care must be taken in the design of products which combine both fabricated sheet materials and solid timber.

Edging strips applied to panel boards must be from dry material, or discrepancies may occur when shrinkage takes place.

Mitred mouldings, which shrink in width due to loss of moisture after assembly, show a gap at the inner edge of the joint due to the geometrical change in the angle.

Quantities of moulding that are machine mitred and left standing for a period of time, may well be found to be in error at the time of assembly. It is preferable that mouldings should not be mitred until the time of requirement, in particular if the moisture content is in error.

Where the intersection of mouldings or moulded

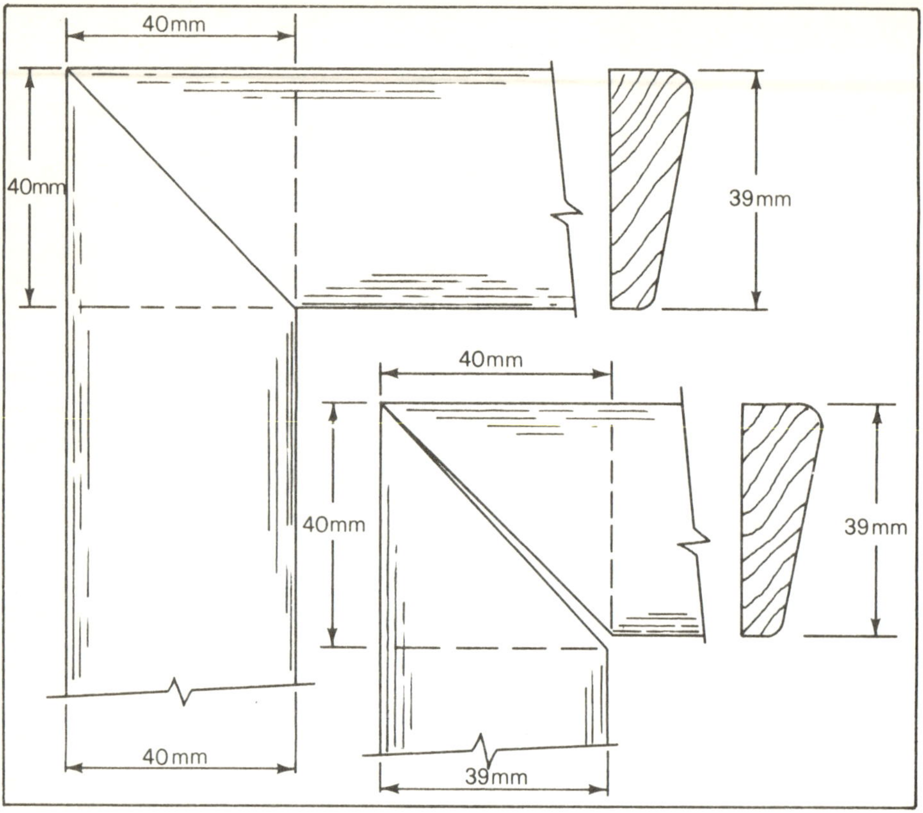

material can be scribed over, rather than mitred, in fabrication design, inaccuracies due to shrinkage of the timber can be prevented.

Joinery designed for exterior use where moisture content variations are bound to occur benefit from the through scribed joint which the present-day machine produces.

The scribing operations can in most cases be carried out at the same pass through the tenoning machine along with the joint formation, whereas mitring would, in fact, be an additional operation.

Although the use of solid timber for wide panels has been very much reduced with the introduction of panel boards, instances do occur when solid material is still used. Wastage due to end cracking will take place if these items such as for table tops, or shelves, are left for long periods solidly stacked in a heated workshop.

This is due to the atmosphere reducing the moisture content at the ends of the stacks only.

If the wide panels had been suitably fixed to their

Sketch B: Shows how the angle of a mitre changes if shrinkage takes place after the joint has been cut. It is not always advisable to mitre cut large quantities of mouldings in advance of requirement.

1. Variation of dimensions in a batch of components caused by delay in the production flow, can account for inaccuracies during machining operations. Recesses for metal fittings are frequently cut on an overhead routing machine. Depth of the cut will vary if the width of the hinging stiles in the above photo are not constant.

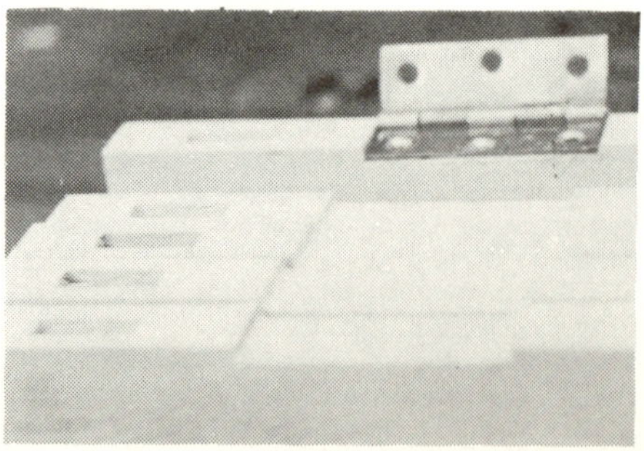

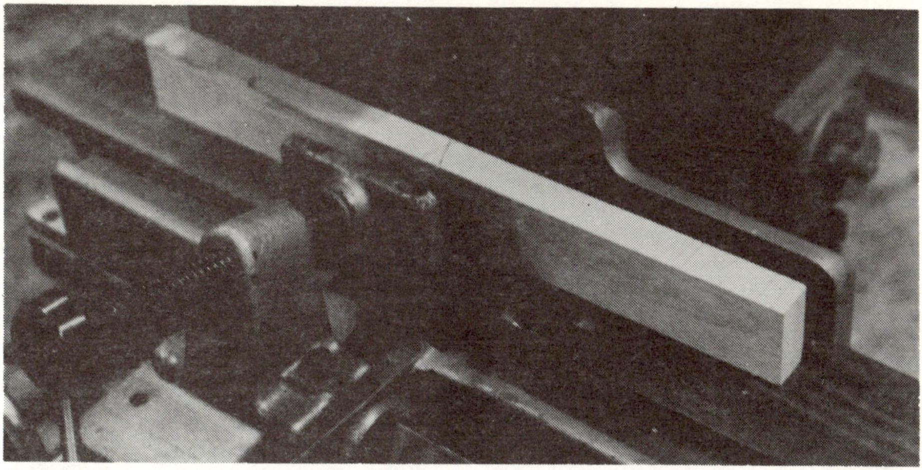

2. Working faces must always be recognisable either by marking, or moulded edge, to enable this face to be in contact with the fence when machining. To assume that a mortise, for instance, is in the centre of a stile, and that the recognition of a working face is unnecessary is incorrect, when considering that variations of timber thicknesses could have occurred.

3. Through scribing to joints, in particular for external joinery products, to maintain efficiency under fluctuating moisture conditions. Production machines are produced with this method of construction in mind.

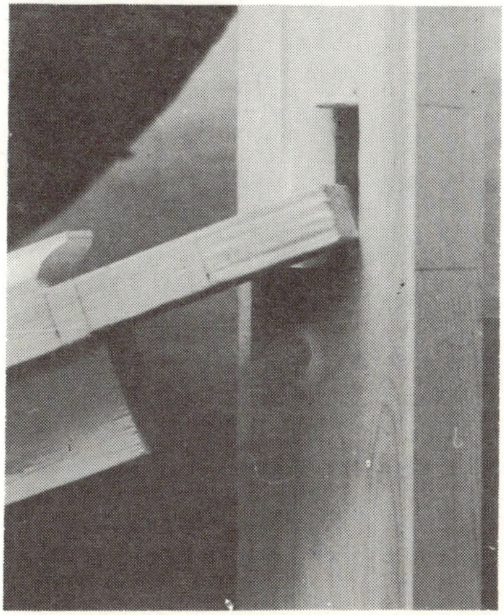

respective units, with regard made to shrinkage, less wastage would be likely to occur. Plan for the completed units to be waiting for the wide panels, not the wide panels waiting for the units. The constructional design of a product must very often be governed with the effect of moisture content changes in mind. The main consideration to the manufacturer is that the goods should be of acceptable quality when they leave the factory.

It is also preferable that the design is such that moisture changes during the product's use will not be unduly harmful to the article.

Timber can in some circumstances be over dried in the manufacturing process. An example is in the case of an external door which is framed and filled in with T and G boards. The boarding must not be over-dried, and tightly forced into the rebated section.

If this is done much damage may be caused to the door when it is fixed due to the swelling of the boards, the amount depending on what sealing treatment it has received.

Finished goods have often to be warehoused until time of dispatch. Deterioration can take place here due to moisture content changes if the fact is ignored in the basic design of a product.

Drawer sides, for instance, should not be planed to be in contact with a cabinet side across their full width. Any swelling of the drawer sides would wedge the drawer completely. Narrow guides should always be planed between the drawer and the carcase end.

Stock control is important, which may well govern the quantities involved where batch production is in operation in a machine department. When timber is converted from the log to a

marketable material it is in theory possible to cut it in such a way as to reduce shrinkage in the width direction of the board. However, due to economical reasons this is more often than not ignored.
An exception to this is the case of certain hardwoods such as oak which has to be cut with the saw radiating to the centre of the log to produce figure.
This method of conversion is known as quartering.
Timber cut in this way is more expensive due to the waste factor and handling, but it is the most desirable from the movement due to moisture content changes point of view.
One North Yorkshire manufacturer of national repute works only in naturally air dried oak. This must surely only be possible, with wide items at least, made from quartered material.
The efficiency of timber utilisation can be increased with scientific application as this successful home and church furnisher has proved.
Woodworking machines in general use are manufactured for processing timber which is reasonable free from moisture. The machined faces, and adjustment threads must be periodically lubricated with a light grade of oil in particular when machining timber containing a visible content of moisture.
Fortunately, cutter faces, which are made from hardened steel, are not subject to attack by moisture in the same way as the machine frame.
It is desirable, however, that cutters working on the wetter batches of timber should be hollow-ground, and as free from heals as possible. Heals on the cutters will compress the soft nature of the wet timber at the time of cutting, and an uneven surface will appear as the timber dries out.
Where machines are fed with friction rollers it is often found necessary to increase the pressure on the rollers to obtain drive if the timber is wet.
The surface of the timber may be damaged in this way, and actual faults may be visible in a finished product that have been caused in the early machining stages.
Waste extraction systems which operate by conveying material in a flow of air can become clogged when an excessive amount of moisture is included. This is due to the increased weight of the waste material and the increased frictional resistance of the particles.
It is not possible to put laboratory conditions within a large production unit at all stages, a supervisor on the shop floor can only endeavour to make the most of what facilities are available.

4. Home grown oak in the process of natural air seasoning. This can take a long period of time compared to that of kilning. The amount of vegetation growing around the stack rather suggests this. One year per 25 mm of timber thickness is often quoted as a time guide. Note that the thinner boards are positioned at the top of the stack for first removal.

Working with tungsten carbide tipped cutters

Machine cutters tipped with tungsten carbide were originally in demand for machining abrasive timbers such as teak and abura, and so were confined to only a small section of the woodworking industry.

Where large quantities of these types of timber have to be machined, carbide-tipped cutters are indispensable if production is to be kept up to present-day expectations.

Abrasive timber users, however, now probably form the smallest category of users of carbide-tipped cutters, due to the introduction of laminated plastics, synthetic-resin adhesives, and the economically priced man-made material chipboard.

When large quantities of multi-ply have to be machined on the spindle moulder or high-speed router, the glue lines between the laminæ soon leave their mark on the cutters if they are of the standard high-speed-steel type. Small quantities may, of course, be worked with high-speed-steel cutters provided sharpening is done frequently, and this usually includes grinding also.

In the case of machining laminated plastics prefabricated with timber, carbide-tipped cutters become really a must. Only a few feet of the more durable plastic-surfaced materials may be worked before deterioration of high-speed-steel cutters is very much in evidence.

As plastics are coming more and more into use, it is inevitable that workers in wood will have to be fully conversant with all the technicalities involved.

For trimming the edges of 18 mm plywood worktops surfaced with laminated plastic, from experience I would suggest the spindle moulder using a 5in. (125 mm) diameter Whitehill pattern block, r.p.m. 6,000, using 1¼in. (30 mm) carbide-tipped cutters. The reasons for suggesting this type of cutter head are economy in cutter cost, versatility, and efficient cutting speed.

If so desired only one of the two cutters mounted in the head may be carbide-tipped for economy reasons, provided it is given slightly more projection.

The cutters can also be tilted in the head if a bevel is required. This is very convenient, as carbide-tipped cutters cannot be ground to a different profile with the usual woodworkers' grindstones.

Provided a small amount of bevel on the top and bottom edges has been requested when ordering the 1¼in. (30 mm) cutters, they will also be very useful for rebating plywood or chipboard.

Grooving the edges of chipboard in quantity for tongueing in cover lippings requires either a ¼in. (6 mm) thick carbide-tipped saw for the spindle moulder or a pair of strong grooving cutters for either the square block or slotted collars.

It is essential that these cutters should be strongly constructed, as any vibration set up within the cutter may cause fragmentation of the carbide tip.

Using carbide-tipped cutters on the high-speed router should be done with due respect to the additional cost of these tools. They should not be overloaded by taking too heavy a cut. Feed should be continuous, no stopping while in contact. Overheating can be caused if these operating points are ignored combined with the high speed of rotation and the nature of the material being worked. Overheating will definitely shorten the life of the cutters, but provided care is taken they give excellent service.

Most cutter manufacturers will service carbide-tipped cutters if this cannot be done within the plant.

As long as cutters are carefully used they can be kept sharp with a diamond wheel. This is a circular disc which has a coating of diamond dust around the outer extremity of one face. It is usually about ¼in. (6 mm) in width only. Grinding, or lapping as it is termed, is done as with a cup wheel on the side of the wheel, not around the outer periphery. Hollow grinding is not desirable. A Norton D150 wheel is suitable for this purpose.

The grinding appliance used should be of a high-precision standard; clamping and traverse arrangement for the cutter should be rigid.

When sharpening router cutters all lapping should be done in the inside of the wings, and the original amount of hook must be maintained. This is much the same as with high-speed-steel router cutters, except that the amount removed will not be as great.

With spindle moulder cutters the method is not

the conventional one. Sharpening with the diamond wheel is done on the face of the cutters and is confined to the carbide-tipped section. By this method any profile of cutter can be sharpened with the cup-styled diamond wheel.

Most large woodworking concerns have readily equipped themselves with a full range of tungsten carbide equipment, but I have endeavoured to show in this brief text that even the small user can join in this necessary development without excessive outlay.

Machining difficult materials

With the introduction of plastics, and the increased use of plywood and chipboard, problems can arise for the woodworking machinist regarding the durability of cutting tools. Some special treatment to cutting tools is also required for machining some timbers which are of an abrasive nature.

Where standard high-speed steel cutters, ground to the conventional angles, are not suitable for the job in hand due to the failure of the cutting edge, various methods may be adopted to remedy this.

Some timbers, such as the African mahoganies, tend to tear badly even when planed or moulded at a low feed speed. This tearing of the grain can be lessened considerably by application of a slight amount of bevel on the front face of the cutters. This additional bevel alters the angle at which the rotating cutter meets the timber, so giving it more of a scraping action rather than a chipping one.

When applying this front bevel to the cutter, care should be taken not to grind beyond the hard steel facing, on the built-up type of cutters. This method also strengthens the cutting edge considerably, and abrasive types of timbers such as abura may be machined in this way.

When the above method can be adopted, no additional cutters are required, and experience has shown that it does suit in many instances, and gives pleasing results.

When abrasive timbers have to be worked in quantity the use of stellite may prove advantageous. Stellite is obtainable in rod form, and is applied to the cutting tool with the use of oxy-acetylene welding equipment. Stellite is available in various grades; it is used for many purposes including the coating of shovels on large excavators.

The face of cutters, or saw teeth, require to be recessed to take the stellite, and experience is required in the use of the welding torch. The flame must be suitably adjusted or the properties of the stellite may be destroyed. It is a comparatively simple operation for an experienced welder. Deposits of stellite are made in excess of

A tungsten carbide tipped cutter mounted for lapping on the front face with a diamond dust-coated wheel.

A high-speed router cutter mounted for lapping.

requirement, and the tip may then be taken to shape on the normal grindstone. Stellite cannot be dressed to shape with a hand file, this indicates a much harder tooth, in the case of a saw.

For cutters, if the stellite is correctly applied, it will be found more durable than high-speed steel. Due to the fact that it can be worked on the normal grindstones it is more versatile than the more expensive tipping methods. It is ideal for runs of specials.

For working many of the present-day materials on woodworking machines in even moderate quantities, tungsten carbide tipped cutters and saws are a "must."

Tungsten carbide tipped tools are, of course, a more expensive approach than the other methods described for working difficult materials. Their cost, however, need not be prohibitive as I will later indicate. It is advisable, however, to confine their use to operations that cannot be carried out suitably by other means. Many operators do in fact prefer high-speed steel cutters on softwoods.

A tungsten carbide tipped circular saw in constant use under power feed may run for several weeks without removing from the bench for attention. This saves a great amount of time in saw changing, and maintenance.

Maintenance of tipped tools, however, requires special equipment, although this may be done in a modified form with only a small amount of precision grinding.

Cutter shapes must also be ordered to the exact profile required for alteration is not possible as in the case of high-speed steel. Carbide tips have to be manufactured with their final shape in mind, allowing only a small amount for dressing.

Provided tipping tools are given careful use, and regular attention, they can be sharpened on a diamond wheel mounted on a precision grinder. This process is known as lapping, and only a very small amount of metal is removed. Lapping is done on the front face of the cutter, not on the back bevel as with normal cutters.

For machining the edges of laminated plastics, bonded to plywood, tungsten carbide tipped cutters are the only solution. Cutters perform excellently on the spindle moulder using a 5 in. (125mm) diameter Whitehill pattern cutter block, at 6,000 r.p.m. A pair of cutters is desirable, but only one need be tipped from the point of view of economy.

Manufacturers of tungsten carbide tipped tools do accept their products for servicing, and quick return. Also, as these tools are now being used in other trades, in addition to woodworking, servicing can often be obtained locally.

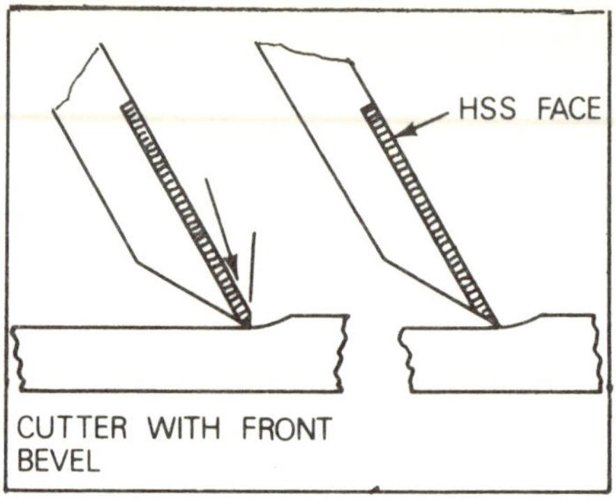

A small amount of bevel applied to the front of standard planing cutter (left). Sketch on right shows cutter before application of front bevel.

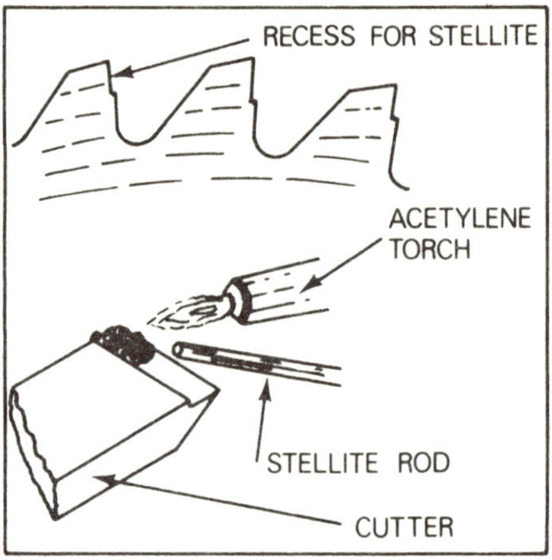

Circular saw teeth recessed ready to receive stellite. The cutter is shown receiving deposit of stellite with the aid of an oxy-acetylene torch.

Tungsten carbide tips are cast to approximate final shape. Cutter blanks are recessed to receive tips for brazing, as shown in the sketches.

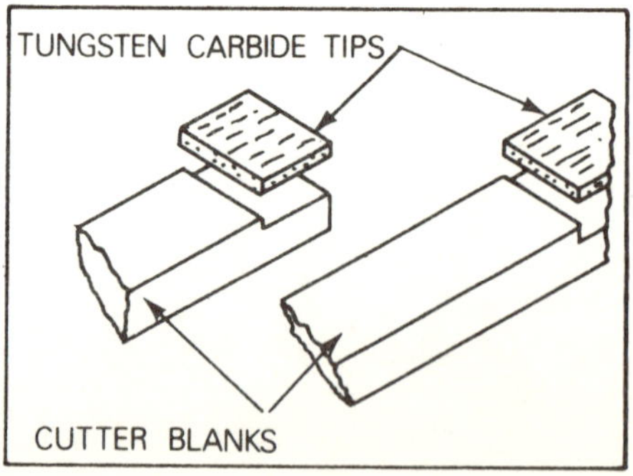

Cutter grinding for the spindle moulder

Fig. 1. Grinder with rest set in horizontal position for first operation in grinding.

Fig. 2. Grinder with rest set at an angle for bevelling operation.

Many operators of woodworking machinery are quite efficient at their work, but have little opportunity to take part in the preparation and maintenance of cutters. In the larger woodworking units, cutter grinding is often confined to the toolroom, and as specialisation is becoming more and more the order of the day, it is regrettable that fewer machinists are likely to become proficient in all branches of their craft.

Most cutters today, as far as profile is concerned, are simple compared with the requirements of the past. Large elaborate mouldings have virtually disappeared.

To prepare cutters for the everyday requirements of joinery or cabinet work, a definite line of procedure should be recognised if success is to be accomplished.

Assuming a cutter requirement for the spindle moulder has to be taken from a full-sized drawing, the shape of the moulding required can be traced with carbon paper on to a piece of stiff paper. The approximate profile of the cutter can then be readily seen. Before attempting to cut out a grinding pattern from the trace, a slight amount of elongation must be allowed for. This can, of course, be developed geometrically, but less this is carried out with the greatest of accuracy at all stages, it may be safer to assume that the elongation could be between 0.5 mm and 1.5 mm for the smaller sizes of cutters.

After selecting the necessary piece of steel for a cutter, the shape required can be marked on to it by drawing along the edge of the paper pattern with a sharp pencil.

For the beginner it is advisable for the shape to be ground on the steel before any back bevelling is attempted. The rest on the grinder should be set in an horizontal position and used during grinding.

At this point it is worth mentioning that the operator should wear protective goggles, as steel chips or grit may fly towards the eyes at any unexpected moment. Also, the feeling of security helps the operator with his concentration.

If a concave shape is required on the cutter, the radius of curvature on the edge of the grindstone should be slightly less than that of the cutter to allow for comfortable working. The operator should not hestitate in changing grinding wheels, or making use of a stone dresser as required. A grinding unit with two stone mountings is very convenient, and a great time saver.

A generous container of cold clean water should be at hand to immerse the cutter periodically. The aim should be to keep the cutter cool, rather than cool it down after excessive heating.

Fig. 3. A simple appliance to help with the repetition of cutter shapes.

After the cutter has been ground to the shape of the paper templet, the next step is to grind the necessary bevels on the back. The purpose of the back bevel is to provide a sharpness angle on the cutter, and give clearance to the cutting circle. Unless both these conditions are observed successful cutting will not be accomplished.

Consideration, too, must be given as to which side of the cutter is to be bevelled. It is advisable to operate cutters on the underside of the work on the spindle moulder when possible. Should the rotation of the spindle moulder be reversible, either side of the cutter could be bevelled, but not all machines are fitted with this refinement, and left-hand working is not always appreciated.

To commence bevelling, the rest on the grinding appliance should be set at the maximum amount of bevel required, and the cutter held firmly to it at all times. It will be found that the amount of bevel can be varied by working either on the centre front of the stone or towards the edges without raising the cutter from the rest.

The maximum amount of bevel is required parallel to the central line of rotation. The amount can be reduced as the profile of the cutting edge gradually changes to a line at right angles to the centre line of rotation. When the top or bottom edges of the cutter are running in the cut, a small amount of bevel is beneficial at these points.

For a beginner to attempt to grind freehand without a rest is suicide, and will only result in shabby work, and discouragement. Unbalanced pairs of cutters are also liable to be produced.

Having successfully ground one cutter to the desired shape, it is generally necessary to prepare another identical cutter to increase efficiency during use. Fig. 3 shows a simple appliance made from a piece of Formica secured to a strip of hardwood, to assist in the accuracy of repetition.

After completing both the cutters they should be checked on a balance to ensure equal weight, and any correction required made accordingly. Although this may not be considered necessary with the smaller sizes of cutters, it is part of the correct procedure and most essential with large cutters operating at high speeds.

Fig. 4. As a safety precaution goggles should be worn during grinding operations. They also assist in the operator's concentration.

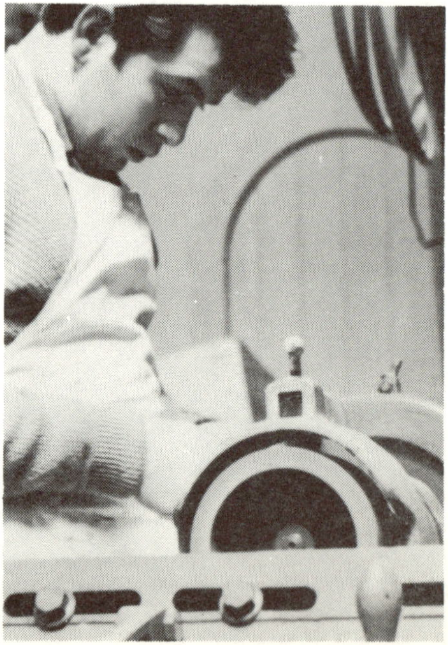

Working in the tool room

Close-up view of a high speed router cutter positioned for grinding, using a cup-type abrasive wheel.

The servicing of cutting units in a woodworking establishment is very necessary to keep a flow of production. The range of equipment required is governed by the type of plant in regular operation.

In a small works unit, toolroom work may be limited to a skilled machinist putting in a few hours of overtime to maintain the machines in condition without stopping procedures during the main working day. This manner of keeping machines in condition is often preferable if no separate toolroom is available, and sharpening operations have to be carried out within the machining area.

Where the number of machines merits an organised toolroom, this is very often built up over a period of years to meet the requirements of the plant as it develops. In this way it is not unusual to find much used servicing equipment at the circular saw sharpening area, and the newer equipment, for the more sophisticated machines.

With ever increasing labour costs, and toolroom working being not directly on output production, the call for automatic machines in this area is bound to increase. In a well organised toolroom, one operator, and perhaps a junior can have several automatic machines working at the same time. It need hardly be said that a toolroom must be in competent hands, by a person who is familiar with the equipment and the economics of his job.

The case of brazing and sharpening a narrow band saw blade is one that is frequently debated. Unless efficient equipment is available it can, in fact, be cheaper to throw the broken blade away and buy a new one. This is based on labour cost. If the servicing can be carried out within a group procedure using automatic equipment, it could be worthwhile.

Positioning of toolrooms or sharpening areas are

A grinder that takes up a very small amount of space, designed for the preparation and servicing of cutters. The tool rest is easily adjustable. Long planer blades, as used in circular blocks, can be successfully ground with the use of the attachment.

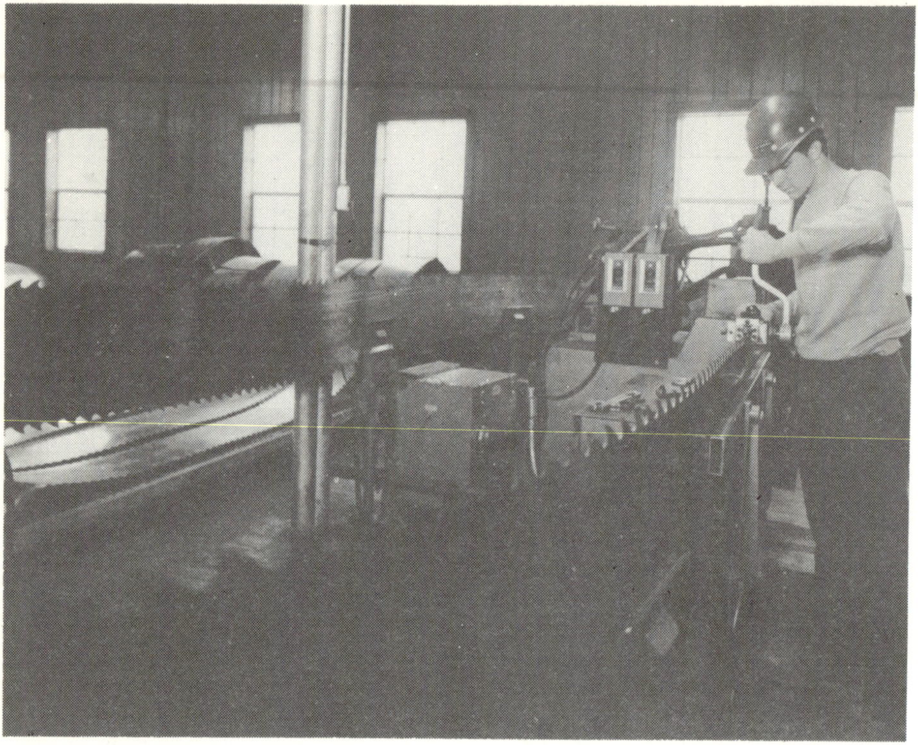

Setting teeth on a wide double-edged bandsaw blade. The operator is Mr. Joe Carrol. The metal dust collecting unit can be seen in the photograph which collects waste from the sharpening operation.

preferable away from excess noise and factory dust. In some establishments they are found adjoining the machine shop, perhaps divided off by open wired screens. While this arrangement gives close contact for quick co-operation, and supervisory aspects between the two departments, it is not ideal. Others favour double glazing in more advanced contact when a completely enclosed toolroom area is constructed. More efficient conditions can be experienced in this way regarding sound insulation, heating, and dust-free atmosphere, where precision operations are being continually carried out.

A recent addition to the regulations regarding machinery in industry is the request that any person whose job of work entails the mounting of abrasive grinding wheels should have attended an approved course on the subject. The regulations are published under the reference (SI 1970 No. 535) The Abrasive Wheel Regulations. Some of the factors referred to in the regulations I quote below in brief form which may encourage interested readers to pursue further:

1 The mounting of abrasive wheels.
2 Hazards arising during use, and precautions necessary.
3 Methods of marking abrasive wheels as to type and speed.
4 Methods of storing, handling, and transporting.
5 Inspection, testing, and checking for damage.
6 The functions of all components used such as flanges and washers.
7 Methods of dressing abrasive wheels.
8 The adjustment of work rests.
9 The requirements of the regulations generally.

As all these factors relate very closely to industrial usage, I have no doubt that persons involved will enjoy the recommended instruction as I did on attending such a course recently.

It is necessary to know the spindle speeds of the various machines where abrasive wheels are to be mounted, and compare this with the information given on the wheel it is proposed to use.

In most toolrooms or servicing areas in the

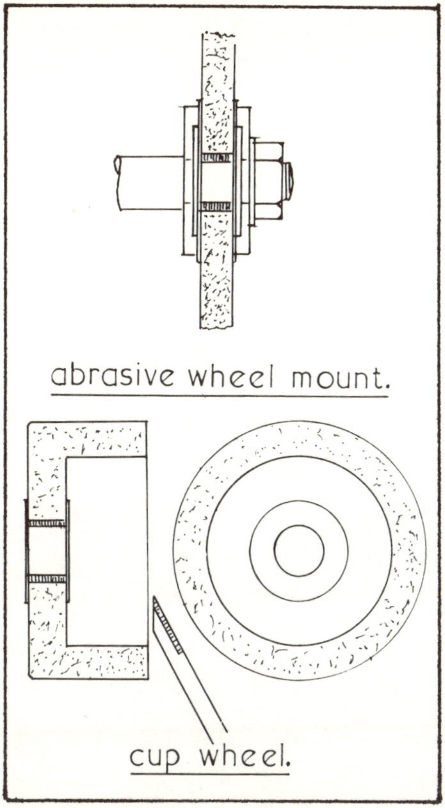

Abrasive wheels must be mounted between collars which have a recessed inner face. Paper pads should also be present on both sides of the abrasive wheel.

Two methods in use for the spring setting of circular saw teeth. The hand setting tool, and a setting stand which applies the set with a hammer blow or by lever action. Setting pliers are also available which are suitable for many types of teeth.

woodworking industry the circular saw blade is very much in evidence. One needs to visit the new saw blade manufacturing factory of Micor at Sheffield to realise that a large amount of equipment is necessary to produce high standard blades. To keep the saws in condition during servicing within the woodworking factory toolroom, some mechanised equipment is necessary to make the job economical and reduce manual skill to an acceptable level. To produce rigidity in a saw blade during use, the plate during manufacture is subject to rolling under controlled pressure. This process at Micor is followed by skilled manual hammering.

The hammering operation is one that may have to be repeated in a toolroom after the saw has had a prolonged period of use. The hammering operation is one that requires experience and also an understanding of what the eventual aim is to achieve. A recent publication by authors Eric Stephenson and David Plank entitled *Circular Saws*, explains fully the servicing of circular saws, including a chapter on hammering and tensioning, explained in a way that is easy to understand. Written material of this kind has not been obtainable in the past, the subject of saw doctoring being rather a closed shop. Availability of a clean faced anvil and suitable hammers enables tensioning procedure to be followed.

Due to sharpening, the projection of circular saw teeth become less, so reducing the area of the gullet. The purpose of the gullet is to house the cut waste until it can be ejected when the portion of the saw leaves the timber. In saw manufacturing the gullets are stamped out during tooth formation, but in service it is usual to maintain the gullets by grinding. This should be a periodical gradual process, a little and often. Heavy grinding can destroy the temper of heat treated material.

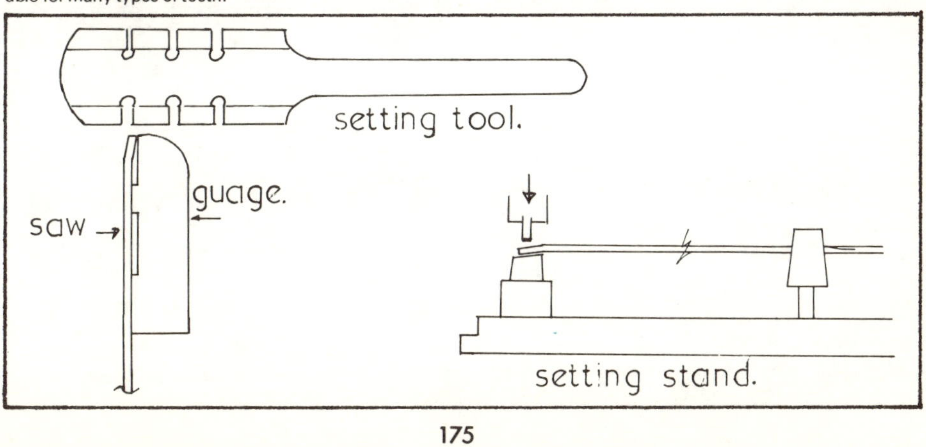

Gulleting machines fall into various categories. They can be very much a hand plus skill operation, or a machine fully automatic which will both gullet and sharpen circular saws. On considering the purchase of a machine for maintaining saw teeth it is advisable to make quite sure what its capabilities are. A simple type of machine can in some circumstances be more suitable than a highly sophisticated one. I have experienced machines which have been beyond the ability of a flow of operators to use them. Designers should bear in mind that instruction handbooks frequently get mislaid, or are delivered to the front office along with the account and never reach the works. Instruction tags on machines of foreign manufacture are usually in their own native tongue. There are, however, helpful exceptions.

Automatic machines which are designed for gulleting only, produce teeth with edges square to the face of the plate. Saws can usually be sharpened with this type of machine up to a stage, but front and top bevels have to be applied by hand filling. Without any bevel on the teeth, work is hard to feed into the machine when sawing, and is not generally satisfactory. A fully automatic machine will sharpen saws, complete with front and top bevel to the teeth. More than one pass may be required on some machines to obtain requirement.

Saw teeth should be set before final sharpening so that any bevels that are applied remain unaltered.

In the use of sharpening and gulleting machines, the push arm which feeds the tooth to the abrasive stone should be in operation on the tooth immediately before the cut. In this way the

A saw doctor at work at the Micor saw factory in Sheffield, the world famous steel city. The saw is being methodically hammered to produce tension within the plate.

Saw doctor checking saw blade to determine "tight" and "loose" areas.

Large circular saw blade being refitted with tungsten carbide tips.

teeth are kept even in size. Positioning the push arm several teeth away can reproduce inaccuracies in tooth formation. Some machines are equipped with indexing wheels which enable teeth to be recut if a change of purpose is required. When this refinement is available the number of teeth should be kept in mind when ordering any new saws. An indexing arrangement on circular saw servicing equipment is a very useful asset.

As previously mentioned in this article, narrow bandsaw servicing equipment requires to be automated and as efficient as possible if it is to be an economical proposition. Many bandsaw users do have their blades serviced outside the works unit due to the economic factor. Two methods are in general use for jointing blades. These are electric brazing and butt welding.

In electric brazing, cleanliness is very important, both in the appliance contacts and the blade being processed. Failure of the brazing metal to liquefy under heat is usually due to unclean surfaces. The metals used in foil form are either silver solder or brass. A suitable flux must also be used which protects the cleaned surfaces from oxidisation and enables the hot metal to flow. Prepared jigs for filing should always be readily available, and in clean condition.

Bandsaw blades which are subject to sharpening and setting by automatic means should be maintained with an even number of teeth. Failure to do this may mean that when setting, complications will occur that can result in broken teeth due to undue levering. It is also recommended that the set should be reduced at the point of jointing to avoid bumping due to excess bulk.

In the butt welding method higher temperatures

Saw sharpening and gulleting machine.

are used which fuse the two ends of the blade together. A slight compression motion takes place at the time of fusion which forms a small bulge of metal which requires to be levelled off after cooling.

The grinding operations of cutters can be divided into a number of groups. To be able to carry out all the groups within a works unit a considerable amount of equipment is required. Machines are available, however, termed universal grinders, that can carry out a large number of operations with the use of attachments. The groups in mind regarding cutter

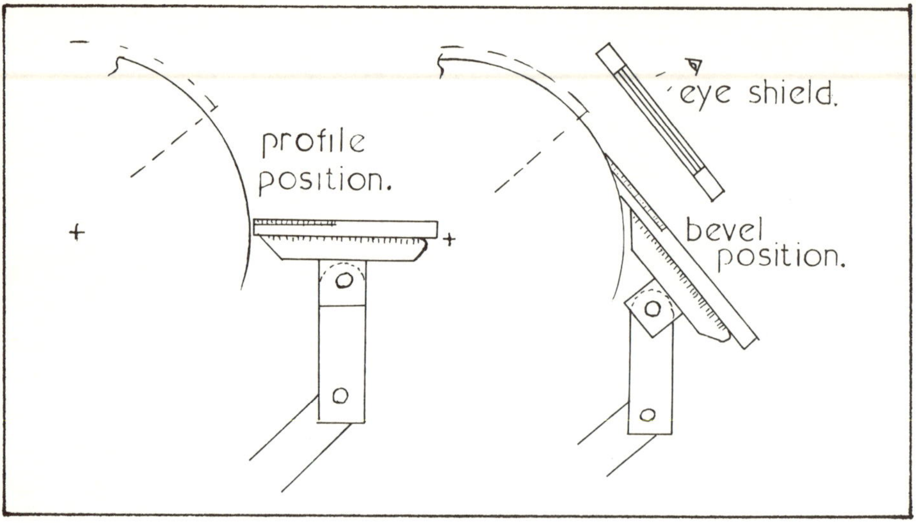

servicing are: freehand grinding, namely the forming of profiles on spindle moulder blanks, etc.; long knife grinding for planing machines; solid profile cutters for moulding work; small solid cutters for routing, dovetailing, and spindle moulder trenching, etc.

The increasing use of tungsten carbide tipped cutters also calls for high precision equipment for servicing at frequent intervals rather than let edges get into a very bad state. A light treatment process known as lapping can be carried out with an abrasive wheel which has a diamond impregnated surface.

The ability to shape cutters from blanks for the spindle moulder or moulding machine can only be gained by experience. Although the type of grinder required for this purpose may be

Requirements of a grinder for preparing cutters. The horizontal rest position is required for the formation of cutter profiles. For bevelling the rest must be tilted but only a small clearance gap maintained.

Brief wide bandsaw details. A. Section of untreated saw blade. B. Inner surface of blade is stretched between pressure rollers. C. Amount of stretch or tension is compared with a metal gauge. Wheel surfaces on which the blade runs may be flat or crowned.

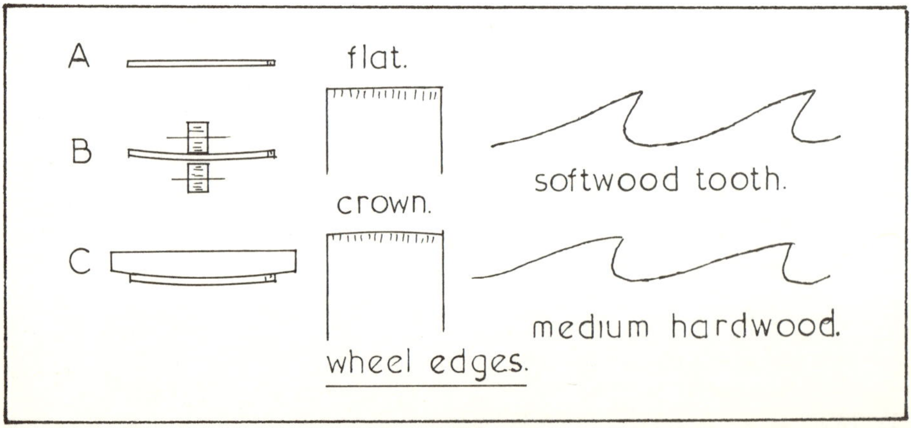

basically simple, several points should be considered in its selection. It is essential that it is equipped with a tool rest which can be positioned either level or inclined and still maintain only a small clearance gap between the rest and the abrasive wheel. These first points rule out many grinders which are not designed with machine woodworking cutter preparation in mind. A machine which carries two abrasive wheels is always advantageous. A flat edged wheel is usually kept in one mounting position, and shaped edge wheels used in the other. Wheel changing is then kept to a minimum.

Operators of abrasive wheels require eye protection at all times during use. Some machines are, or can be fitted with see-through screens as a safeguard against particles coming into contact with the operator. Protective goggles should always be available where grinding operations are to be carried out. Abrasive wheels must be suitably guarded, only the section in use being exposed.

General outline of gulleting and sharpening procedure of circular saw teeth by an automatic machine. Gulleting machines produce square faced teeth only. Front bevels to teeth are produced by more advanced machines. Top bevels have in some instances to be produced by a secondary run.

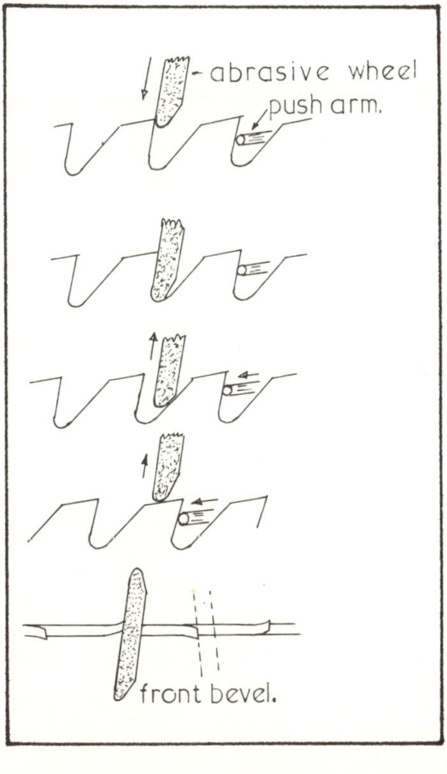

The basic procedure for preparing a shaped cutter from a blank is first to determine and record the profile required. This can be marked on the face of the cutter with a sharp pencil. Care must be taken at this point that the cutter is being prepared the correct hand. It is preferable that the profile is ground with the machine rest in the horizontal position first. The cutter should be kept cool by frequent immersion in clean water. Providing fingers are not rubbed across the cutter face the pencil markings will remain. Cutting and clearance bevels are applied with the rest suitably adjusted. Cutting edges should always be honed with a lubricated slip stone before use.

Long knife grinding requires a specialised machine to permit suitable mounting for the cutter to be methodically fed past the abrasive unit. Cup-type abrasive wheels are often favoured for this operation as they are capable of producing a straight or variable amount of hollow ground bevel. They also maintain the same size of working periphery. The propulsion of the carriage in which the cutter is mounted may be either mechanically propelled or hand operated.

A toolroom operator requires to plan his work according to which machines are automatically operated and which require hand motivation. He can then give the most efficient output with the least effort. The skill in the use of the long knife grinder comes mainly in the mounting of the blade. Care must be taken that other blades that make up the cutting unit are positioned in such a way as to produce the same overall dimension to obtain balance during rotation. Knife positioning and machine setting marks should be noted. The cutting surface of the abrasive unit should be dressed before starting the set in preference to in the middle of the operation. Abrasive cuts should be light and the traverse should be kept in motion during contact.

Solid profile cutters for the spindle moulder or moulding machine should preferably be ground on a machine which has indexing facilities. This refers to the positioning of the cutter faces around the periphery of the block. If the positioning of these faces are altered unevenly the block will become out of balance. Also, due to clearance diminish which these blocks must have, the lower faces will cease to play a part in the cutting. The mounting of solid profile blocks on an indexed grinder compares the toolroom machine with that of the one it was manufactured on. Discrepancies may have to be evened out over a series of sharpenings. Blocks of this type should always be serviced on the same machine.

Cutters for high speed rotation, such as routers and dovetailers are usually services with abrasive wheels of small diameter. High spindle speeds are required for the smaller wheels to produce a suitable peripheral speed. This is taken into account with grinders designed for this purpose, and universal grinding machines usually require an attachment to obtain the increase in revolutions. Attachments are also available to service high speed router cutters on the machine itself, using the lower of its working speeds.

In addition to toolrooms for servicing machines which produce goods from prepared timber, another type of set-up is that relating to a timber conversion mill. Here, servicing is confined to saws and the engineering aspects that keep the plant in operation. In countries which grow timber in profusion, the persons in charge of saw maintenance have a very important job, which is well recognised. No doubt there is a limited number of such posts in this country where much of the know-how did originate relating to the treatment of tool steels. We use the term, Saw Doctor for the saw technician, in the USA Head Filler is often quoted, which may, or may not be, just about the same classification.

For heavy duty conversion of timber from the log, the wide bandsaw is principally used. For the smaller type of log, gang reciprocating saws may be preferred. The servicing of wide bandsaws requires a considerable amount of working area and specialised equipment relating to the width of blades, and their made up length.

For jointing saw blades a lap grinder is required to prepare the surfaces for scarfing. A special clamp is used to hold the prepared joint in position while heated tongs are applied to melt the brazing metal. Although the procedure is similar to that of jointing narrow bandsaw blades, it is on a much larger scale which calls for more equipment.

Wide bandsaws in the course of servicing require to be checked for projecting lumps caused through local overheating, and these must be hammered out on an anvil. The anvil is usually positioned near the end of the levelling plate, an important unit in the equipment. Tensioning of wide bandsaw blades is done mainly with a roller unit. The purpose of tension is to ensure that the outer edges are strained tight during use. Linear stretching of the inner area of the saw will provide for this and also allow for expansion on the heated cutting edge. A saw without tension treatment would wander on the cutting edge, and could be difficult to control on the pulleys.

Tension in a saw can be measured on the levelling plate with the aid of curvature gauges. The gauges require to be matched to the pulley faces on the machine. Some faces are flat, others slightly convex.

Friction clearance to the saw blades can either be by spring setting or swaging. Swage setting is popular with this type of saw which consists of spreading the tooth point and side dressing with the aid of two special tools. Each tooth cuts the

Servicing wide bandsaw in a tool room in the USA

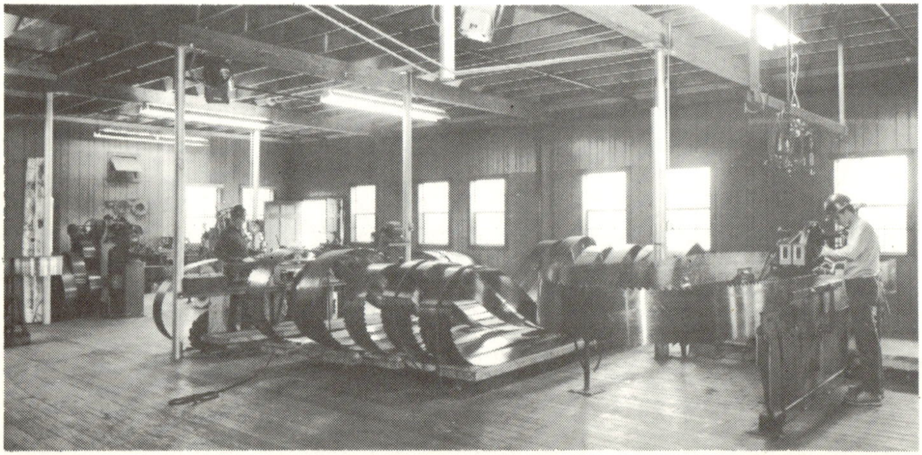

full width of the kerf which is an advantage over spring setting.

Tooth sharpening and gulleting is done by grinding, very often all in the one operation. Gullets need to be kept free from ridges which encourage cracks in the blade. Sharpening machines designed for this purpose usually provide for several shapes of teeth, a subject much discussed in this field. For tooth work the saw blade is positioned on edge, while for tensioning it is laid flat. This requires quite a large service area along with storage. Organisation and tidiness are important in maintaining safety standards.

(The book, *Circular Saws,* by Eric Stephenson and David Plank, is available from Thomas Robinson and Son Ltd., Railway Works, Rochdale. 152 pages, price £1.62 including postage).

A look at new developments

When we look at developments related to the machine processing of timber, this can involve improvements to existing machines and also the introduction of new equipment to meet present day requirements.

Due to the change in constructional methods, and the introduction of new materials, changes are bound to occur in processing to maintain the standard of efficiency expected from mechanisation.

Make-do modifications are very often carried out by machinists on the shop floor in the first instances, but once a requirement has become established it is not long before go-ahead machine manufacturers satisfy the demand by modification or additions to their range.

A typical example of this is the wide cutting capacity that has become required to cope with the cutting of panel boards. On the older type of machines that were designed mainly for ripping solid timber, the width cutting capacity was restricted either by the limit of fence adjustment or the guard support. Make-do arrangements on circular saw benches can increase the accident potential as well as infringe the regulations regarding operation.

Early saw benches were provided with rising tables to control the amount of blade projecting for such operations as cutting out rebates and grooving. In some instances an open space would be created between the table and the bench frame which exposed the saw blade. Present day machines which are designed for carrying out a range of operations are provided with a saw spindle which can be raised and lowered. This ensures that the non-operative part of the saw is fully enclosed within the bench at all times.

In domestic buildings the factory production of framed roof truss units has called for the use of crosscutting machines for preparing members. A machine has been specially designed for this

View of drive mechanism of modern moulding machine equipped with through feed.

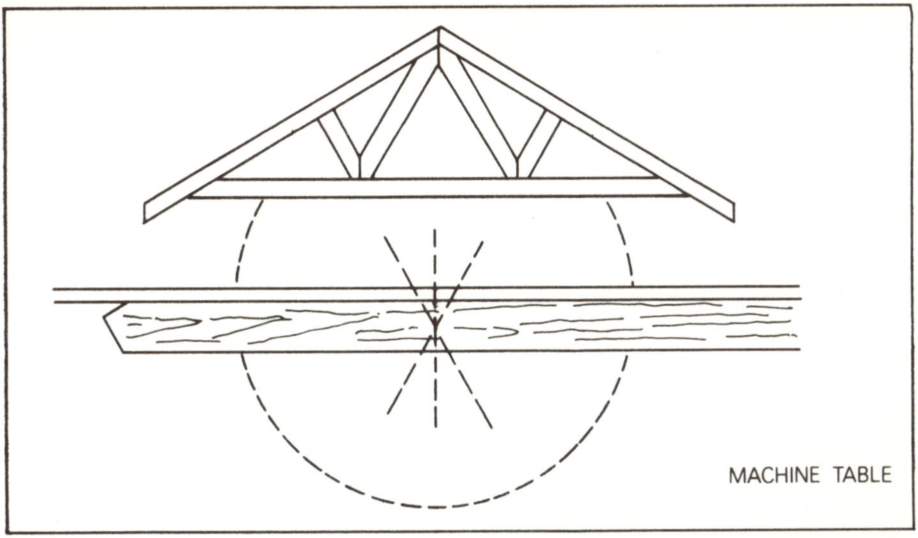

Framed roof truss members can be cut on a specially designed model of crosscut circular saw. (See photo of Robinson machine).

purpose which is very versatile in use. The saw blade when not cutting is located below the bench and its action stroke is pneumatically operated. The design of the machine permits a wide range of angles to be cut in an economical manner with a minimum of effort to the operator.

In workshops where space is limited, saws have now been designed which will cut panel boards standing on edge. With this type of machine it is usual for the panel to remain stationary, and the circular saw is traversed across it. Position stops on the machine enable repetition work to be carried out.

A high standard of accuracy can be obtained with this layout of machine, often better than feeding material along a guide fence on a push bench where there is always a danger of a snake line cut if the fence line does not run parallel with that of the saw. Cutting methods similar to those which this machine uses can be found in large establishments where panel boards are manufactured, for accurate dimensioning of the products on completion.

It is at times regrettable to see timber used in prominent places in a building which has an inferior surface finish regarding machine woodworking. This can often be prevented at little extra cost with the use of simplified modern aids, or, if more consideration is given to design planning, in relation to plant available. If timber is to be used straight from the planing machine without a sanding operation, a high standard of cutter pitch finish must be obtained, and the cutter edges need to be kept sharp. If machine sanding is possible a slight increase in the cutter mark spacing could be permitted.

This means feed speed through the machine could be increased. Timber wall cladding is much used in hotel foyers and banking establishments. If machining marks are visible an artificial effect is created which hides the natural features of the timber grain. Where facilities are only available for machine sanding flat surfaces on cladding material, the section profile should be

Trenching head fitted into a circular saw bench.

Specially designed circular saw cross-cut for angle cutting roof truss members. The saw unit and table can be readily set to stops to produce the required angle of cut. (Thomas Robinson, Rochdale.)

planned with this in mind, so that the greater part of the exposed surface can have some treatment. If a shaped profile sanding machine is available the design can be of a more complicated nature.

The spacing of cutter marks can be reduced by increasing the number of effective cutters on the block, or reducing the feed speed of the timber. Most multi-head planing machines now have attachments for trimming the cutters to a common rotation circle. New developments have simplified this operation, along with setting aids, which brings the process within the capability of the average user.

Portable attachments are also available which can sharpen cutters without having to remove them from their mounting blocks except for increasing the projection. A unit of this type could be particularly useful in the smaller establishment where servicing equipment is often very limited. It could save cutters having to be sent out for the grinding operation which can cause delays.

On thicknessing machines it is customary for the table or bed, as it is often called, to be raised and lowered by screw action. Support is given to the table by the screw thread, and steadiness is provided by adjustable guides. Any slackness in the guides will cause the table to rock during the planing operation, and this can be very

Automatic feed unit fitted to a spindle moulder in small production unit to dress doors to width.

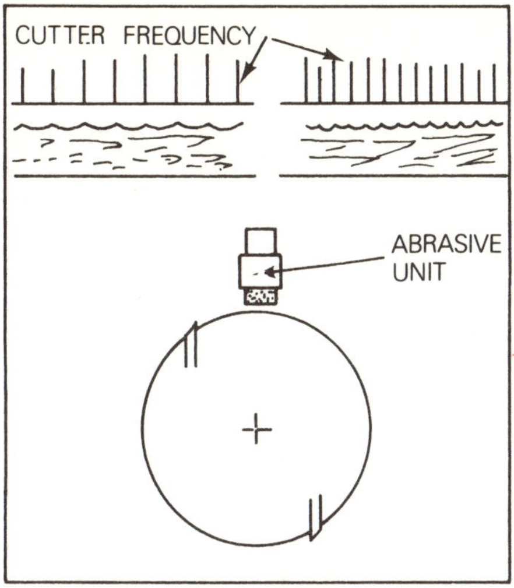

Sketch shows theoretical effect on planed finish to timber when both cutters on a block are trimmed to a common cutting circle. Left, only one cutter cutting. Right, both cutters operational.

An advanced form of spindle moulder for carrying out shaping operations with the aid of power fed higs. (White, Paisley.)

noticeable at times on machines which have had long service. As more wear occurs in some sections of the guide contact surface than others, due to the frequency of use, perfect adjustment cannot always be made to the slide pads. The effects of table rock are mostly noticeable at the commencement and finish of the planed stock, but it can in fact produce an inferior surface throughout the full length. A recent introduction to provide a more rigid bed table is a system known as the wedge bed.

This method has been used previously on very large machines but probably not on those in everyday use. The raising and lowering action of the thicknessing table can be likened to a pair of folding wedges. It is fully supported and no rock is at all possible during use. Also due to the large contact surface it should not be readily subjected to wear. This system is particularly suitable for heavy loading, such as the thicknessing of wide panels, and other forms of heavy duty planing. It has always been an accepted fact by many, that work processed on a wedge bed machine is very often superior to that of screw thread support type.

There is little doubt that improvements to both mortising and tenoning machines have still kept this method of material framing in use, even in the highly sophisticated production units. In the past the hand craftsman was reluctant to use such items as metal adaptors for securing members, but today's economics usually make the

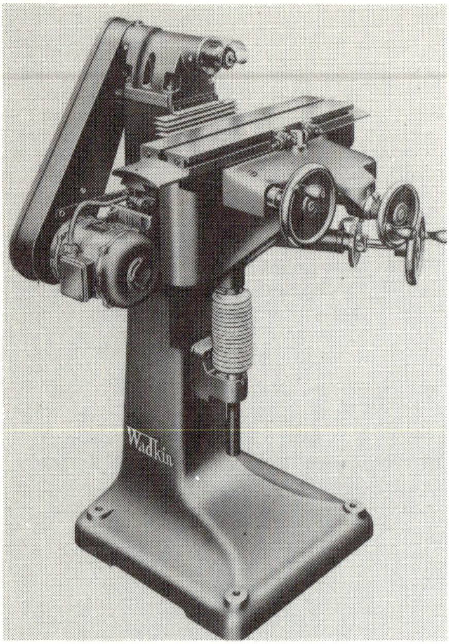

Machine designed for grinding cutters of small diameter such as for dovetailing and the highspeed router.

Whitehill pattern cutter head fitted to a spindle moulder.

decision. Machines for joining timber will only continue to be used while they can compete.

A simple study of machine mortising shows that there are are three governing factors upon which improvements in performance can, and have, been made. These are: 1. The locating of the timber; 2. The cramping of the timber; 3. The operation of the cutting head. If all these three factors can be improved upon in an installation from purely hand skill application, a marked degree of efficiency should be obtained.

Locating stops on mortising machines are an important feature as they determine the accurate positioning of the cut. Their action is usually combined with the table traverse to fix the length of the mortise cut. All the locating equipment requires to be of a high engineering standard, and capable of adjustment within the range required.

The cramping of the timber in the machine has advanced from screw action to pneumatic, and in some cases hydraulic operation. Many mortise machines already in use have been converted to pneumatic cramping by suitably mounting a compressed air operated cylinder. A ribbed rubber sole fitted to the cramping shoe helps to provide grip to the timber and can be a helpful addition if air pressure is limited. Hydraulic pressure units work from a source built up within the machine, and are oil operated. The same pressure source operates the stroke movement of the cutter head. Machines are also in use which use compressed air for both the head movement and cramping operations.

The installation of a compressed air supply in a production shop has many uses. In addition to being used on cramping heads it can also be applied for the use of operating portable power tools. Air operated tools have a less security or loss factor than electrically driven ones. This is due to the fact that they are seldom begged or borrowed for use outside the factory, as a compressed air supply is necessary to use them.

Probably the most popular automatic shaping machine used in building joinery over recent years is the White model MP, the design of which is based on that of a spindle moulder. It is used in conjunction with former jigs which are usually constructed within the works unit. This machine could be said to come within the category of being designed to meet the requirements of automatic shaping or dimensioning of the larger type of component. It is, however, also used on small items relating to furniture production. Framed units such as sashes can be dimensioned and edge profiled on this type of machine at the one pass-through.

Automatic feed units attached particularly to spindle moulders have reached a stage of development which makes them a reliable and profitable investment. Not only do they increase output, but they make some operations possible that would otherwise not be. Converting a machine to power feed which these attachments do, ensures a constant quality of finish to the work. The output will be either all good, or perhaps unfortunately all bad. If the latter applies some attention is evidently required to the cutting unit. Items that have become twisted or bent due to waiting periods between processing operations, can be more successfully worked on a machine with automatic feed than by hand operation. The waste factor is often reduced by its use.

The increased use of tungsten carbide tipped cutting tools has been a welcome development to those working new materials. When laminated plastics were first introduced to machine woodworking these types of cutters were little known. Their use had been confined mainly to establishments working with abrasive types of timber such as teak and abura. The pattern now has changed and it is almost impossible to operate a woodworking machine shop without the availability of tungsten carbide tipped cutters.

For servicing tungsten carbide tipped cutters, special equipment has been designed to give the high precision standards required. These tools for instance cannot be ground free hand, but must be mounted for application to the sharpening unit. Grinding wheels used within the works unit for servicing, are usually of the diamond dust impregnated type which require care in use regarding their high cost and fragile nature. J.K.O. Cutters Ltd., of High Wycombe have designed much equipment in this particular field, both in the cutting tools and servicing equipment.

Most plywood is now bonded with synthetic resin adhesive of various types, and requires tungsten tipped cutters to work it in quantity. Plywood cladding panels used for external infill in building, often require dimensioning and rebating in the factory unit, and material such as this is bonded with a high grade of moisture resistant adhesive which is not workable with high speed steel cutters. This also applies to sheet material used in formwork, if it has to be bevelled, rebated etc. by machine, tungsten tip-

Advanced model of high speed router cutting apertures on large panel boards. The guide pin and former is located overhead. (Wadkin Ltd., Leicester.)

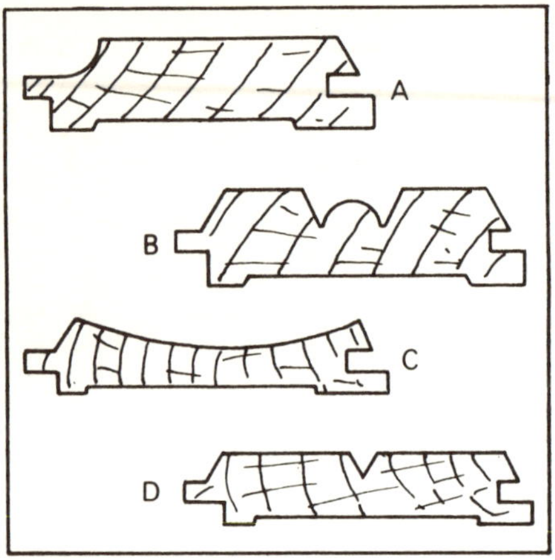

A study of wall cladding sections from the point of view of producing a machine sanded finish. A B and D could have the main portion of the exposed surface sanded on standard machines. Section C would require a special profile sanding operation. An alternative would be to select material and give it exceptional care when feeding through the moulding machine.

Portable cutter grinding device for sharpening cutters on the block. Under this system, if cutter blocks are accurate, further trimming of the cutters to a common circle should not be required. Approximate sketch based on attachment produced by Wuidart Engineering Ltd., Shefford, Bedfordshire.

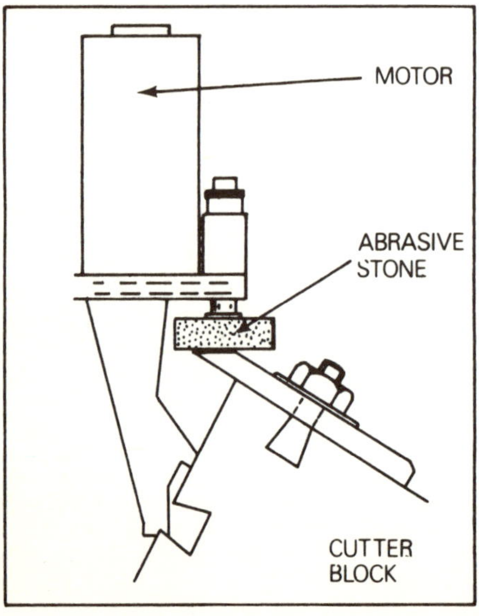

ped cutters require to be used, even for a small amount.

Most of the panel boards, plywood, chipboard, blockboard etc., are difficult to work by hand processes due to the nature of their construction. To work them by machine successfully, particularly in quantity, tungsten carbide tipped cutters are necessary. They form an economical type of construction from a labour point of view as quick results can be obtained using suitable equipment. The joint formation method of these materials is limited mainly to trenching, rebating, and say grooving.

Other jointing possibilities may be claimed by marketers and probably can be successfully applied under some circumstances. When these panel boards are used, such types as veneered blockboard, or chipboard, have a very high standard of finish on the face. Care must be taken that any adjoining solid timber must be sanded to the same quality of finish or the whole grading of the work will be reduced. Grooved in, panels, also should be tight up to the face of the groove, no gap being visible or rattle detectable when tapped.

Aids to the determination of moisture content in timber being used in machine woodworking are a necessity in most production units. This point has become more important during recent years due to advancement of living standards in domestic buildings where all the house is very often now heated instead of only the main living area. The accepted method of checking moisture content within the production unit is by the use of an electronic aid which can be obtained in portable form. Results are quickly obtained in this way with a minimum of interference to the production flow. If a section is cut from the timber in an instance where the internal moisture content is in doubt a satisfactory reading can be obtained.

The weight method of determining moisture content is very useful for checking timber that outside the range of a moisture meter. Kiln operators no doubt favour this method as they have to deal with a very large range of moisture, and handle timber in a condition quite unsuitable for admittance to a machine shop. The nature of the job in hand will decide the standard of accuracy required in the moisture readings, and the conditions within the working area may well have an effect on maintaining a given figure.

Working methods have gradually changed over recent years due to the use of thermo-setting adhesives. If heat is to be applied to timber in order to accelerate the set of the adhesive, loss of moisture will occur if the heat period is

Up to date cramping systems (hydraulic) and carriage movement controls designed for maximum efficiency on a mortising machine. (Brookman, Leicester.)

prolonged. The moisture content of timber used in this way must not be excessive, or localized drying out may occur around the source of heat which will distort or fracture the fibres.

Although constructional methods have in many instances become more simplified, a greater application of scientific knowledge is advisably required for satisfactory working. The use of suitable adhesives is important for the job in hand. It is necessary for the machinist who is preparing timber to know the circumstances under which the gluing operations will be carried out.

Under some conditions, assembly must take place as soon as possible after the machining operation. Build-ups of un-assembled components must not be allowed to accumulate under these circumstances. Radio Frequency gluing methods which have seen considerable introduction over recent years can be affected in this way on some types of operations. The method has the advantage that heat is only applied for a very short period of time. Figures of 60 sec. or 90 sec. being quite common.

All woodworking establishments have their own particular methods of work progress which is very often decided by the mechanised plant available. The introduction of additional machines can change procedures. Some operators may be reluctant to make changes and an educational period may be experienced within the unit before full advantage of the capital outlay can be fully realized.

Unfortunately we seem to be living in an age when standards have at times to be reduced to meet market figures. Additional mechanisation, more machines, is the only way to endeavour to maintain standards.

Joinery and furniture production have in recent years become more closely linked, and construction methods do vary in these two fields of woodworking. To combine the two some points must be disregarded or costs will not be comparative between the methods of approach. One important fact that manufacturers of joinery have in mind is that of factors relating to weathering. This does not apply to the furniture maker. Also the builders joiner has to consider load bearing, and the meeting up of his work to other trades.

It is for these reasons and probably others that

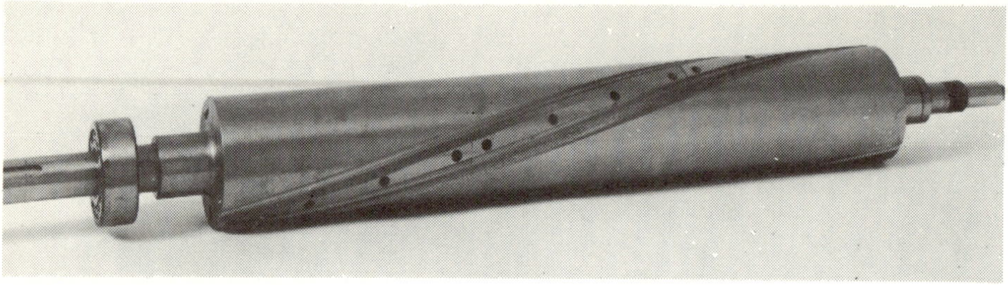

when the builders joiner becomes involved with furniture items such as kitchen units or built in robes he may involve an unnecessary amount of material and joint formations that has been customary in his craft. The principal requirement of the furniture maker is decor. It must look right as seen by the eye. Standards can acceptably drop, and do, on locations that the eye cannot readily see. This approach to construction is accepted as it meets a price bracket, more skill may be involved in the study of what to leave out than what is put in.

The Helical Cutter Block.
Cutter block for a planing machine designed with noise reduction in view. Two knives perform an 180 degrees helix in the length of the block, and are made from 0.56mm thick bandsaw steel.
Publication with courtesy of Princes Risborough Laboratory, Building Research Establishment.

A builder joiner may work for a long time before he realizes that, if he is merging into a different section of the industry he must make changes and adjust his plant to meet requirements.

Timber and the cubic metre

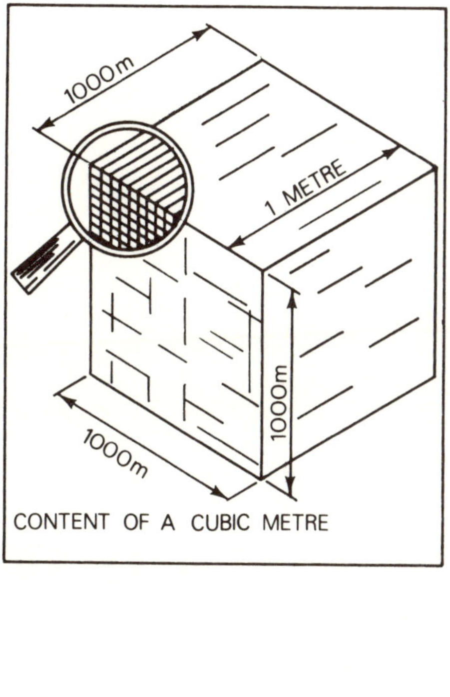

CONTENT OF A CUBIC METRE

In timber utilisation, there have been three main methods of measurement in general use after it has been converted from the log to a marketable material.

1 Linear, or running feet, as it is often called, in which case the sectional dimensions of the timber must be stated.
2 The cubic foot. The unit mostly used in the marketing of hardwoods.
3 The Petrograd Standard, consisting of 165 cubic feet of timber.

With the introduction of the metric system of measurement, the above terms will be phased out. How will the metric terms affect our way of thinking, and will they be adaptable to our present methods of calculation? An experienced supervisor in a production shop, can very often quickly assess the number of cubic feet of hardwood he will require for a job, just as a key man of a flooring gang on a housing scheme can quote his requirements in standards, probably without even setting his measuring rule out.

The linear term will stay with us under metrication, but it will be running metres, and the sectional dimensions will be in millimetres.

The cubic foot is to be replaced by the cubic metre. This is in fact a very much larger unit. One cubic metre (m^3) is equal to 35.315 cubic feet. Timber priced at £2 per cu. ft. will work out at approx. £70.60 per m^3.

As the cubic metre bears no relation to the Petrograd Standard the latter will no longer be used. During the change-over period it can be noted that $4\frac{3}{4}$ m^3 is approximately equal to 1 Std. There is a suggestion in the trade that a new standard may evolve, consisting of 5 cubic metres (5 m^3).

When carrying out timber calculations on the shop floor it has always been useful to remember that in one standard of time there is 23 760 running feet of 1in. by 1in. If this figure is divided by the sectional dimensions of the timber involved, the number of running feet in a standard can be quickly arrived at.

Example. Calculate the number of running feet in 1 Std. of 2in. × 6in.

$$\frac{23\,760}{2 \times 6} = 1\,980 \text{ running feet.}$$

If 1 980 is divided by the rate of feed into a processing machine, say a circular saw or fourcutter, the machining time per Std. can be arrived at.

$$\frac{1\,980}{\text{Feed speed 33ft. per min.}}$$

$$= 60 \text{ minutes running time.}$$

The above methods of calculation can be applied to the cubic metre once the user understands the factors involved.

1 Square metre (m^2) 1 000 mm × 1 000 mm = 1 000 000 square mm (mm^2)

1 Cubic metre (m^3) = 1 000 mm × 1 000 mm × 1 000 mm = 1 000 000 000 cubic mm (mm^3)

So instead of dividing 23 760, as in the case of the Petrograd Std., we divide 1 000 000 (one million) by the sectional dimensions in millimetres to arrive at the number of running metres in one cubic metre of a given section.
Example. How many running metres of 100 × 25 mm in one cubic metre?

$$\frac{1\ 000\ 000}{100 \times 25} = 400 \text{ metres}$$

It may also be necessary to calculate the number of cubic metres in a given metre run of timber of a given section. This can be determined as follows:

$$\frac{\text{Metres Run} \times 1\ 000 \times \text{Sectional Dimensions}}{1\ 000\ 000\ 000}$$

As 1 000 occurs constantly on both the top and bottom line, this can be eliminated to read

$$\frac{\text{Metres Run} \times \text{Sectional Dimensions}}{1\ 000\ 000 \text{ (A million)}}$$

Example. Calculate the number of cubic metres in 800 running metres of —50 mm × 25 mm.

$$\frac{800 \times 150 \times 25}{1\ 000\ 000} = \frac{8 \times 15 \times 25}{1\ 000}$$
$$= 3 \text{ cubic metres } (3 \text{ m}^3)$$

It will be noted that the figure of one million is used in both computations, running metres to cubic metres, and cubic metres to running metres. Simple figures have been used to give a quick clear example of the methods used.
Short-cuts will evolve as time goes by for the sizes of timber used by different sections of industry, both for quantities and cost.

With the introduction of decimal currency there will most certainly be a big swing towards metrication in timber trading, as costing will be simplified if the two are run together.

Calculations and Planning Aids

Some calculations have been applied in various parts of this book when dealing with the particular machine involved. Several examples have however been grouped together in this section along with helpful tables.

lineal metres per m^3

mm	16	19	22	25	32	38	44
13	4807·692	4048·583	3496·503	3076·923	2403·846	2024·291	1748·252
16	3906·250	3289·474	2840·909	2500·000	1953·125	1644·737	1420·455
19	3289·474	2770·083	2392·344	2105·263	1644·737	1385·042	1196·172
22	2840·909	2392·344	2066·116	1818·182	1420·455	1196·172	1033·058
25	2500·000	2105·263	1818·182	1600·000	1250·000	1052·632	909·092
32	1953·125	1644·737	1420·455	1250·000	976·563	822·368	710·227
38	1644·737	1385·042	1196·172	1052·632	822·368	692·521	598·086
44	1420·455	1196·172	1033·058	909·092	710·227	598·086	516·529
50	1250·000	1052·632	909·091	800·000	625·000	526·316	454·545
63	992·063	835·422	721·501	634·921	496·032	417·711	360·750
75	833·333	701·754	606·061	533·333	416·667	350·877	303·030
100	625·000	526·316	454·545	400·000	312·500	263·158	227·273

lineal metres per m^3

mm	50	63	75	100	115	125	138
13	1538·462	1221·001	1025·641	769·231	668·896	615·385	557·414
16	1250·000	992·063	833·333	625·000	543·478	500·000	452·899
19	1052·632	835·422	701·754	526·316	457·666	421·053	381·388
22	909·091	721·501	606·061	454·545	395·257	363·636	329·381
25	800·000	634·921	533·333	400·000	347·826	320·000	289·855
32	625·000	496·032	416·667	312·500	271·739	250·000	226·449
38	526·316	417·711	350·877	263·158	228·833	210·526	190·694
44	454·545	360·750	303·030	227·273	197·628	181·818	164·690
50	400·000	317·460	266·667	200·000	173·913	160·000	144·928
63	317·460	251·953	211·640	158·730	138·026	126·984	115·022
75	266·667	211·640	177·778	133·333	115·942	106·667	96·618
100	200·000	158·730	133·333	100·000	86·957	80·000	72·464

mm	150	175	200	225	250	275	300
13	512·821	439·560	384·615	341·880	307·692	279·720	256·410
16	416·667	357·143	312·500	277·778	250·000	227·273	208·333
19	350·877	300·752	263·158	233·918	210·526	191·388	175·439
22	303·030	259·740	227·273	202·020	181·818	165·289	151·515
25	266·667	228·571	200·000	177·778	160·000	145·455	133·333
32	208·333	178·571	156·250	138·889	125·000	113·636	104·167
38	175·439	150·376	131·579	116·959	105·263	95·694	87·719
44	151·515	129·870	113·636	101·010	90·909	82·645	75·758
50	133·333	114·286	100·000	88·889	80·000	72·727	66·667
63	105·820	90·703	79·365	70·547	63·492	57·720	52·910
75	88·889	76·190	66·667	59·259	53·333	48·485	44·444
100	66·667	57·143	50·000	44·444	40·000	36·364	33·333

Many calculations relating to woodworking machines involve the circle. Once the simple formula relating to its use are understood calculations become a straightforward procedure. The working methods I have shown in the following examples are the ones I consider the most easy to remember.
The circumference of a circle may be given a variety of names such as periphery, cutting circle, or rim as in the case of a circular saw. π is usually taken as 3.142. Four figure logarithm tables can be useful, also slide rules, and electric calculators for the more fortunate.

Basic calculations

The Circular Saw

To calculate the distance around the rim having measured its diameter.

π x diam.
Example for a saw 600 mm diam.
3.142 x 600 = 1884.9 mm

If the r.p.m. of the saw spindle was 1480 calculate the rim speed in metres per min.

$$\frac{1884.9 \times 1480}{1000} = 2789.6 \text{ m/min. Or } 46.49 \text{ m/s}$$

The above two examples could be set down in one equation if the rim speed was required for a given diam of saw at a known r.p.m.

$$\frac{3.142 \times 600 \times 1480}{1000} = \underline{2789.6 \text{ m/min}}$$

To calculate the tooth pitch for a given number of teeth on the same saw as above. 600 mm diam.

$$\frac{3.142 \times \text{diam}}{\text{number of teeth.}} \quad \text{Example} \ldots \frac{3.142 \times 600}{66} = \underline{28.56 \text{ mm pitch.}}$$

To calculate the spindle speed required for a circular saw of a given diam to produce a rim speed of 300 metres per min.

$$\frac{\text{Spindle speed} \times 500 \text{ mm (saw diam)} \times 3.142}{1000} = 3000$$

Spindle speed x 1.571 = 3000

$$\frac{3000}{1.571} = \underline{1909.6 \text{ r.p.m.}}$$

Bandsaw

To calculate the length of a bandsaw blade given the wheel diameter, and the maximum distance between the wheel centres.
Wheel diam. x 3.142 + distance between centres x 2–50 mm

Example . . . 600 mm x 3.142 = 1885 + 1150 + 1150 = 4185 – 50 = 4135 mm

Ans. *4135 mm after allowing for strain.*
To calculate the tooth speed of a bandsaw blade. This can be taken as the peripheral speed of the wheel that drives it. Assume that the machine is belt driven from an electric motor.

$$\frac{\text{Motor r.p.m.} \times \text{pulley diam}}{\text{Pulley on machine}} \times \frac{\text{wheel diam.} \times 3.142}{1000}$$

$$\frac{750 \times 200 \times 700 \times 3.142}{200 \times 1000} = 1649 \text{m/min or } 27.48 \text{m/sec.}$$

No allowance has been made for any belt slip.

Pulley Speeds

A simple rule to remember regarding pulley speeds and belt transmission is, "To multiply by the driver, and divide by the driven."
Example . . . A shaft rotating at 1480 r.p.m. is fitted with a 150 mm diam. pulley. It drives a machine carrying a 100 mm pulley. Calculate the speed of the machine shaft.

$$\frac{1480 \times 150 \text{ (driver)}}{100 \text{ (driven)}} = \underline{2220 \text{ r.p.m.}}$$

Where other factors are the unknown this equation can still be kept in mind and the unknown substituted by a letter.

Example . . . Calculate the diameter of a motor pulley which rotates at 1480 r.p.m. if the machine pulley is 100 mm diam. and the r.p.m. is to be 3330.

$$\frac{1480 \times P}{100} = 3330$$

$$14.8 \times P = 3330$$

$$P = \frac{3330}{14.8}$$

Pulley diam. = $\underline{225.0 \text{ mm}}$

Cutter mark pitch of rotating blocks

Formula . . . $\frac{\text{Feed speed in metres per min.} \times 1000}{\text{Number of effective cutters} \times \text{r.p.m.}}$

= Cutter mark Pitch.

Example . . . $\frac{15 \times 1000}{2 \times 4500} = \underline{1.66 \text{ mm pitch}}$

Some technicians like the number of cuts per 25 mm as this is similar to cuts per inch.

Formula . . . $\frac{\text{Number of effective cutters} \times \text{r.p.m.} \times 25}{\text{Feed speed metres per min} \times 1000}$

Example . . . $\frac{2 \times 4500 \times 25}{15 \times 1000} = \underline{15 \text{ cuts per 25 mm}}$

Calculate the r.p.m. of a cutter block required to produce a 1 mm cutter mark pitch if there are to be 4 cutters operative and the feed speed is 18 m per min.

$\frac{18 \times 1000}{\text{r.p.m.} \times 4} = 1 \text{ mm}$

$\frac{4500}{\text{r.p.m.}} = 1 \text{ mm}$

r.p.m. = $\underline{4500}$

For 1.3 pitch.
2 cutters.
18 m/min.

$\frac{18 \times 1000}{\text{r.p.m.} \times 2} = 1.3$

$\frac{9000}{\text{r.p.m.}} = 1.3$ $\qquad \frac{9000}{1.3} = \underline{6923 \text{ r.p.m.}}$

Moisture Content Calculations

Calculation involved in the weight method.

$\frac{\text{Weight of sample from batch, usually termed wet sample} - \text{Oven dry sample} \times 100}{\text{Oven dry sample}}$

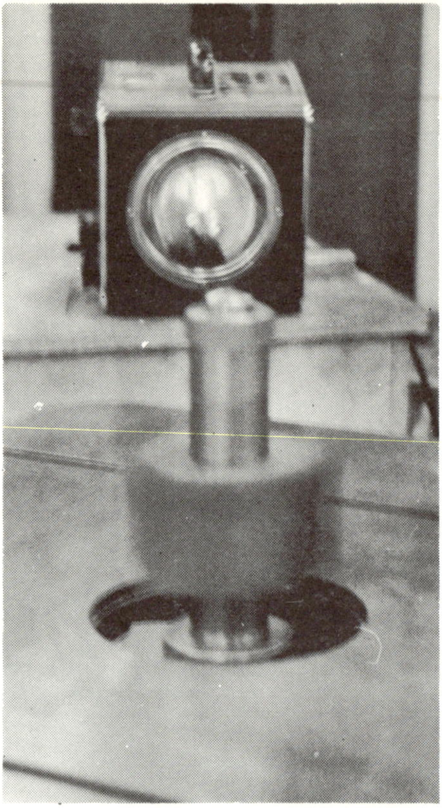

A stroboflash unit being used to check the number of revolutions per minute of a cutter head. The frequency of the flashing beam can be varied until it is in sympathy with the r.p.m. A reading is then taken from the scale on the unit.

Example . . . $\frac{45\text{g} - 40\text{g} \times 100}{40\text{g} \times 1}$

$\frac{5 \times 100}{40}$

$\underline{12.5\% \text{ moisture content}}$

The alternative method of determining moisture content is with the use of an electrically operated meter. The range covered by meters is usually between about 8% and 25%.

Calculations on the balance of cutters

Force = Mass x Acceleration.

$$\text{Centripetal Acceleration} = \omega^2 r = \frac{V^2 r}{r^2} = \frac{V^2}{r}$$

$$\therefore \text{Centrifugal Force} = \frac{Mv^2}{r}$$

$$\text{Velocity of rotating Mass} = V = 2\pi rN \text{ m/min.}$$
$$= \frac{2\pi rN}{60} \text{ m/sec.}$$

$$\therefore \text{Centrifugal Force} = \frac{M}{r}\left(\frac{2\pi rN}{60}\right)^2$$
$$= \frac{4\pi^2 MRN^2}{60^2}$$
$$= \underline{0.01097\ MRN^2}$$

M = mass (kg)
N = revs per min
R = radius of gyration (m)

In calculations the constant can be used as 0.01 to simplify working, but 0.011 will give a more accurate answer.

Examples of calculations to determine the effect of ill balance in a rotating cutter block.
Using the formula 0.011 MRN^2

Ill balance 9 grams.
Radius of gyration 65 mm
R.P.M. 4800

$$\frac{0.011 \times 9 \times 65 \times 4800 \times 4800}{1000 \times 1000} = \underline{148.26 \text{ newtons}}$$

Ill balance 12.5 grams.
Radius of gyration 47 mm
R.P.M. 5525

$$\frac{0.011 \times 12.5 \times 47 \times 5525 \times 5525}{1000 \times 1000} = \underline{197.27 \text{ newtons}}$$

Aids for students

A series of large sized line drawings of cutter blocks and mounting heads as used on the spindle moulder and moulding machine. Students can make direct reference to these when problem solving, and produce work of a high accuracy standard.

Solid Profile. Multipoint finish. Used on all forms of moulding machines. Quiet at high speeds. Quick to set up.

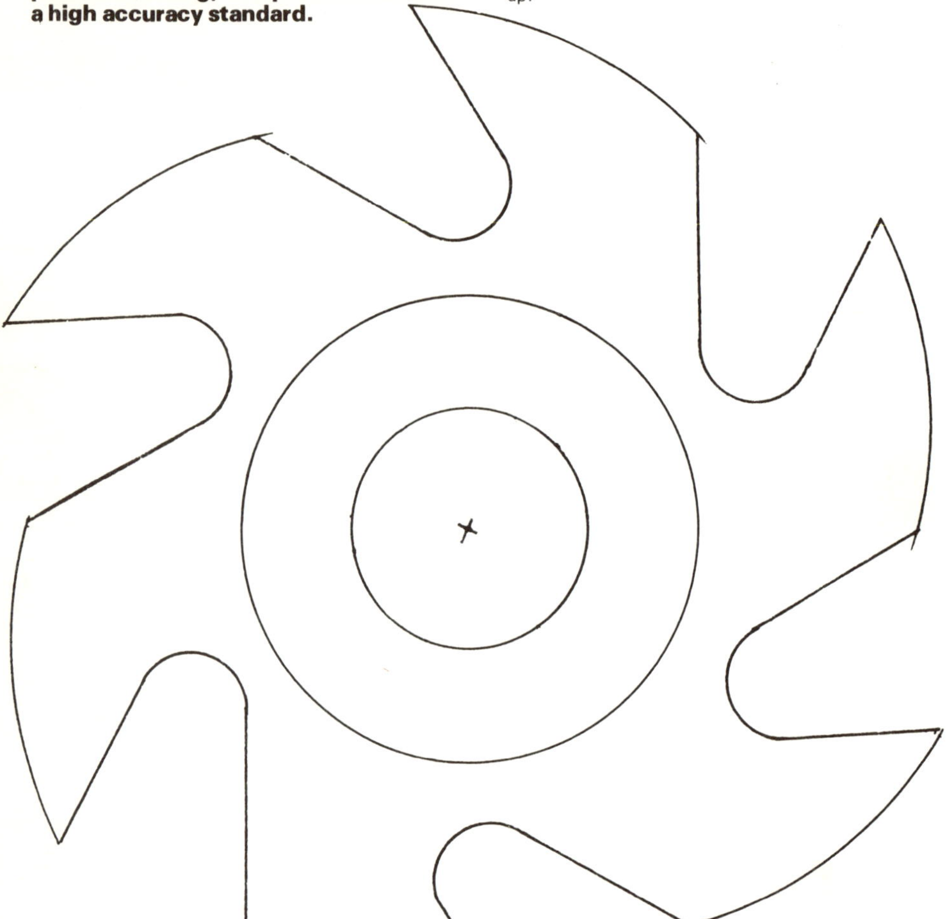

SOLID PROFILE.

MILLED TO PATTERN

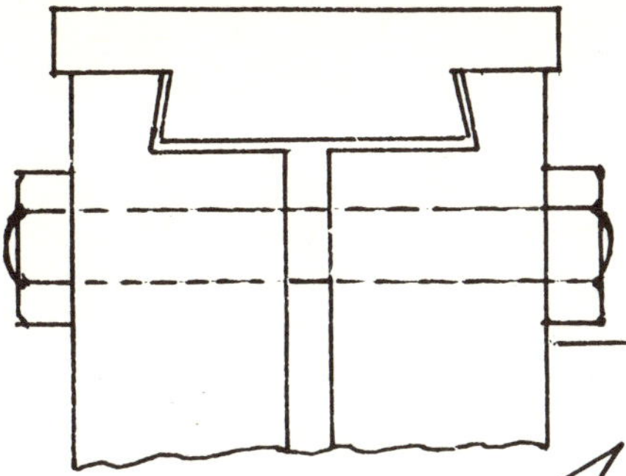

Milled To Pattern. An unlimited number of cutter profiles can be mounted on this type of head. Its multipoint finish and large diameter produces good results in the lower speeds of revolution range

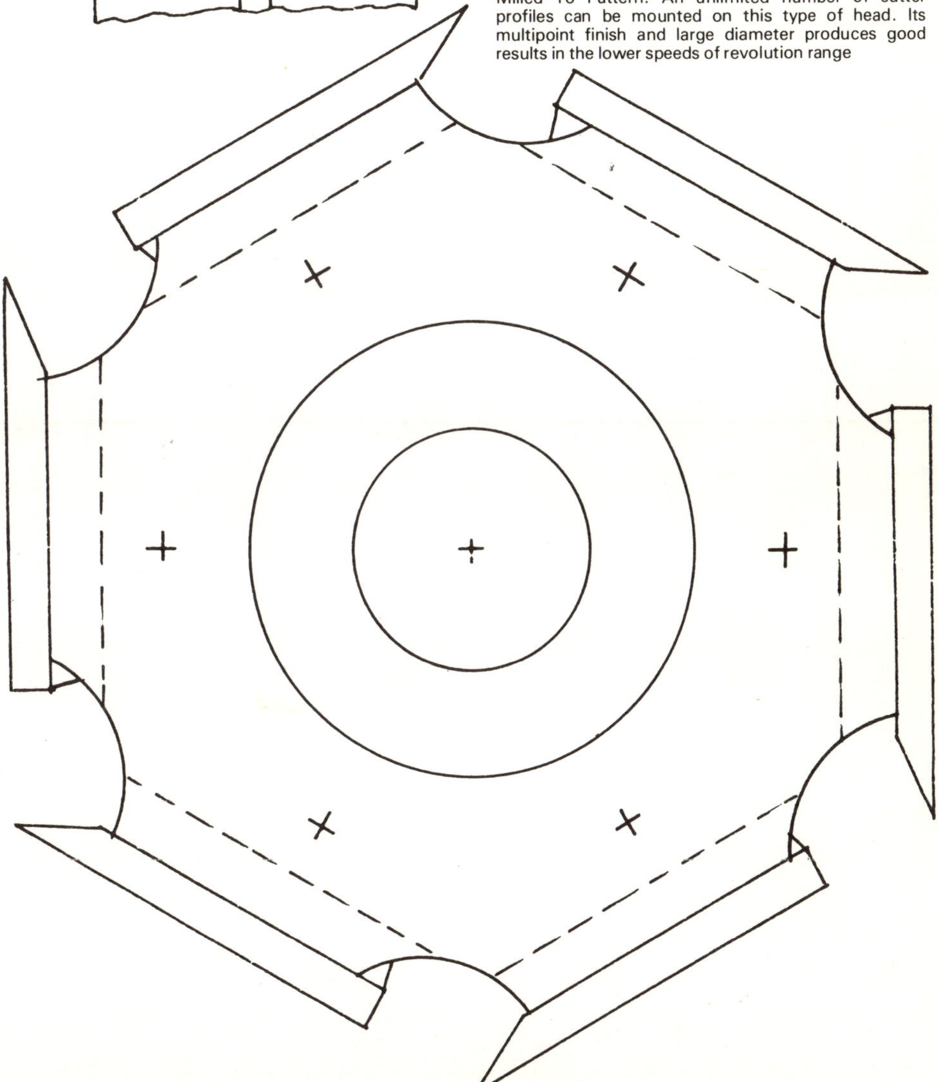

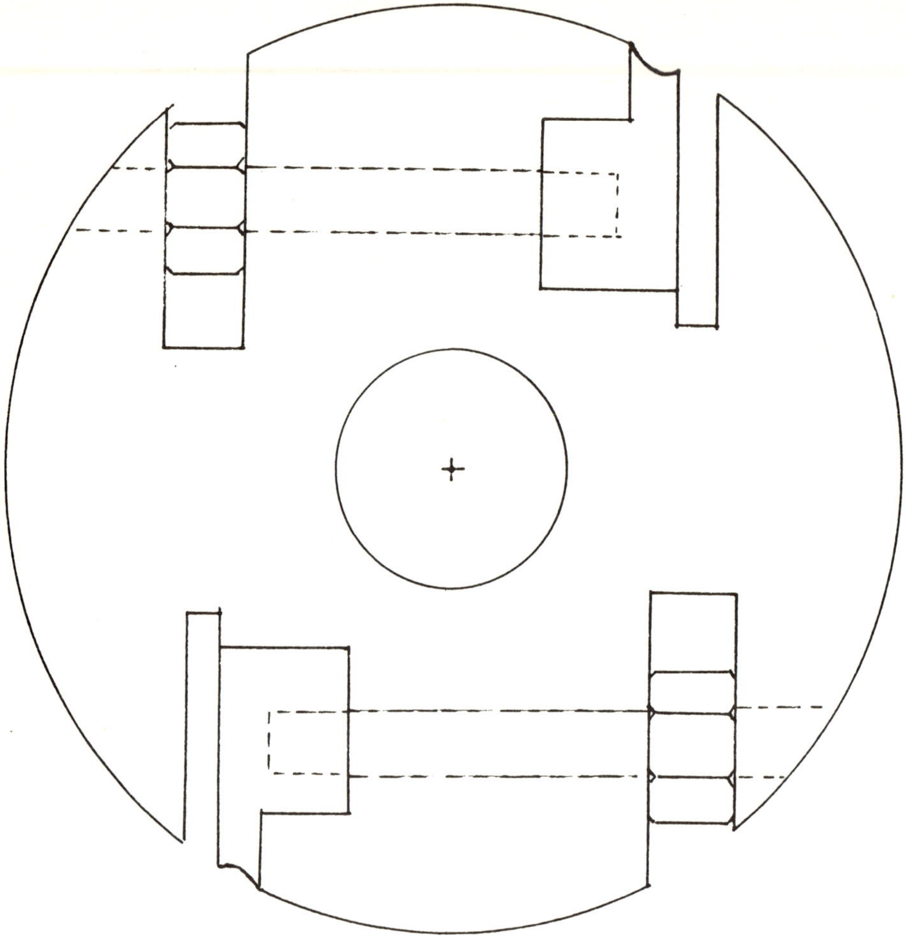

Whitehill Block. Economical on cutter steel. Cutters may be tilted in the block. Quiet in use. Available in a range of diameters and thicknesses.

WHITEHILL BLOCK

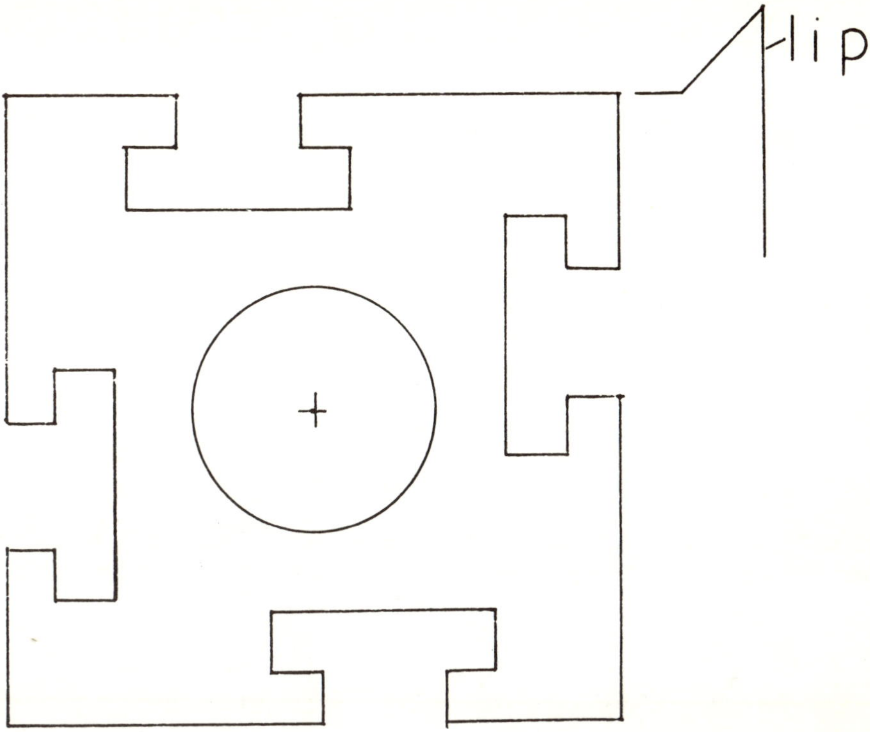

Square Block. tee slots. Used extensively on moulding machines. Several pairs of cutters may be mounted on the block at the one set up. The lip refinement gives additional support to the cutters.

SQUARE BLOCK tee slots.

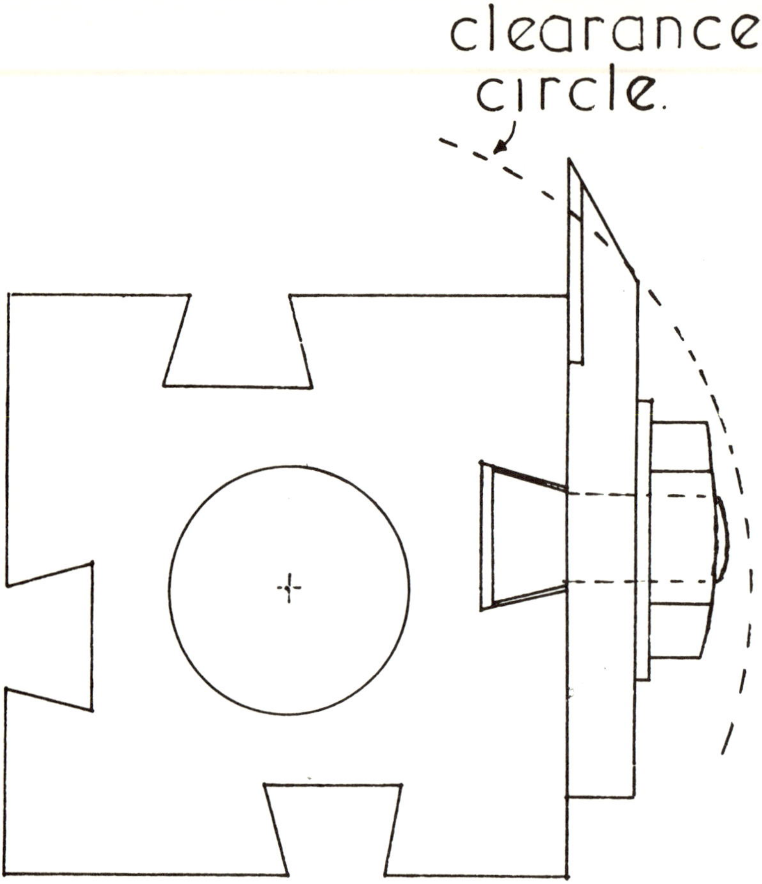

Square Block. dovt. slot. Now confined mainly to the smaller sizes of square blocks. Very often found on scribing heads on tenoning machines, and similar locations.

SQUARE BLOCK dovt. slots.

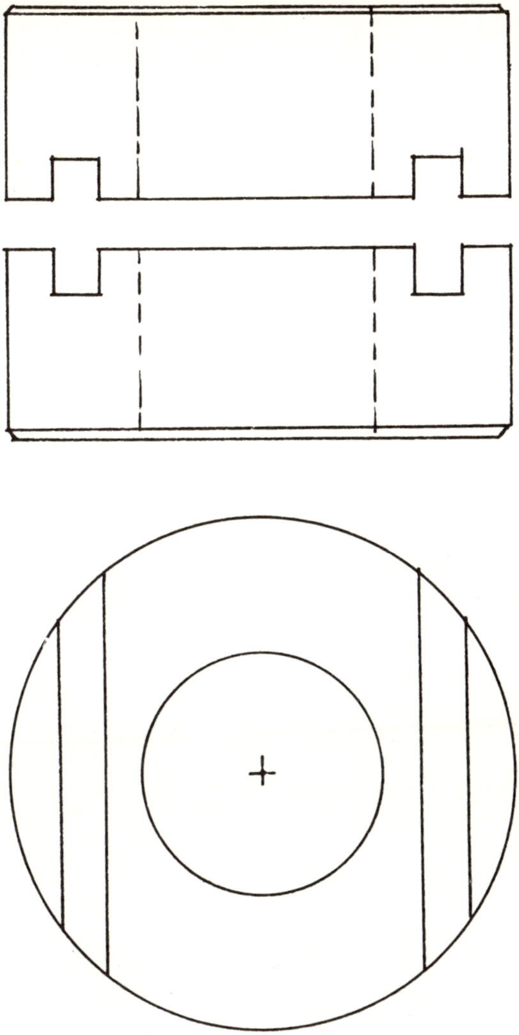

Slotted Collars. As used on the spindle moulder. More refined types are also available to cope with cutters of slightly differing widths, and those equipped with a frictionless ring.

SLOTTED COLLARS.

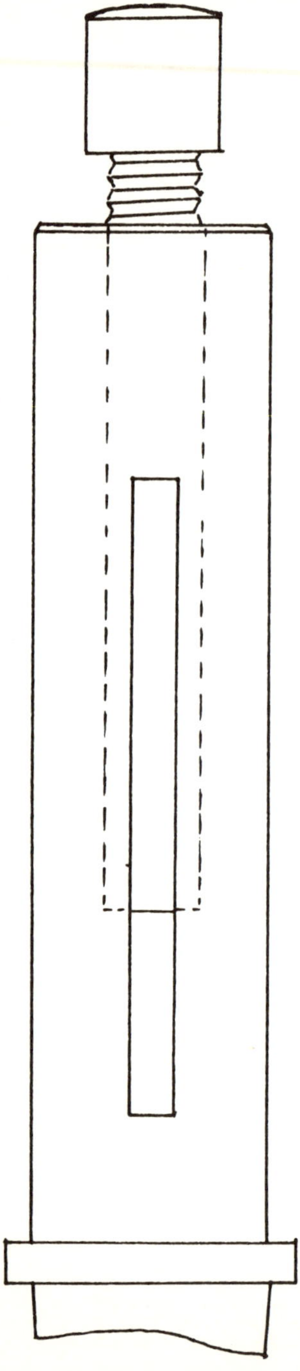

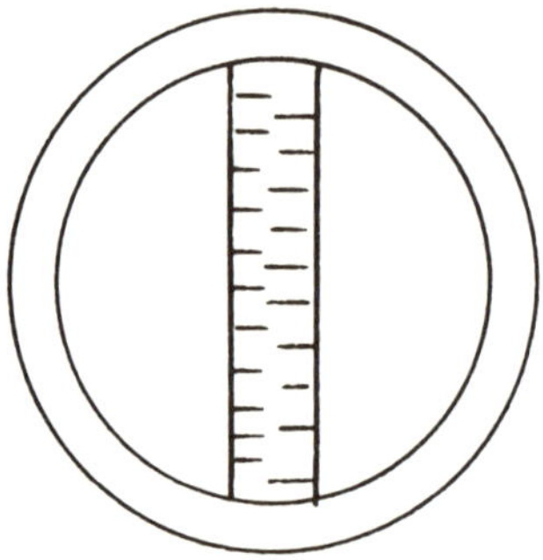

French Head. Spindle moulder cutter head. Used mainly by cabinet manufacturers, and has been replaced considerably by the highspeed router. Cuts with scraping action.

FRENCH HEAD

TRENCHING

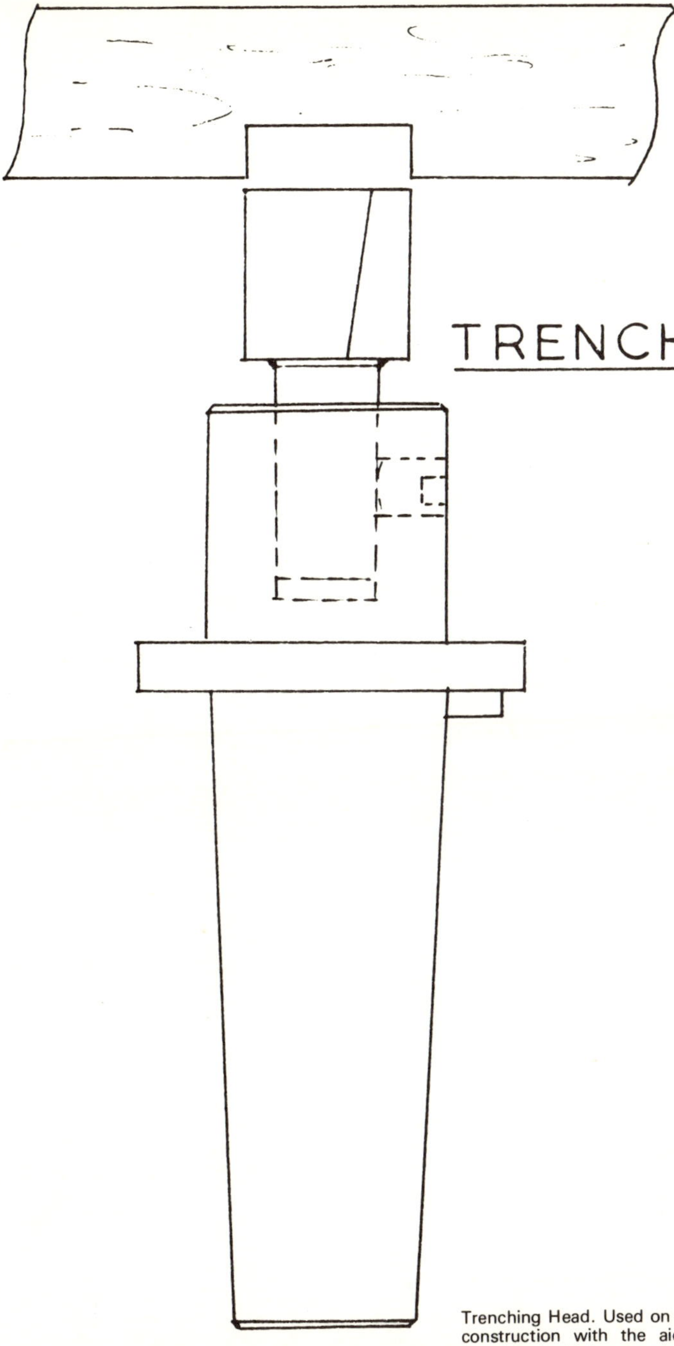

Trenching Head. Used on the spindle moulder in stair construction with the aid of a guide attachment. Requires the higher speeds of rotation on the machine.

DOVETAILING

Dovetailing Head. Used with an attachment on the spindle moulder. Various sizes of dovetails can be produced with the range of cutters available and guide combs on the attachments.

LOGARITHMS

	0	1	2	3	4	5	6	7	8	9	1	2	3	4	5	6	7	8	9
10	·0000	0043	0086	0128	0170	0212	0253	0294	0334	0374	4	8	12	17	21	25	29	33	37
11	·0414	0453	0492	0531	0569	0607	0645	0682	0719	0755	4	8	11	15	19	23	26	30	34
12	·0792	0828	0864	0899	0934	0969	1004	1038	1072	1106	3	7	10	14	17	21	24	28	31
13	·1139	1173	1206	1239	1271	1303	1335	1367	1399	1430	3	6	10	13	16	19	23	26	29
14	·1461	1492	1523	1553	1584	1614	1644	1673	1703	1732	3	6	9	12	15	18	21	24	27
15	·1761	1790	1818	1847	1875	1903	1931	1959	1987	2014	3	6	8	11	14	17	20	22	25
16	·2041	2068	2095	2122	2148	2175	2201	2227	2253	2279	3	5	8	11	13	16	18	21	24
17	·2304	2330	2355	2380	2405	2430	2455	2480	2504	2529	2	5	7	10	12	15	17	20	22
18	·2553	2577	2601	2625	2648	2672	2695	2718	2742	2765	2	5	7	9	12	14	16	19	21
19	·2788	2810	2833	2856	2878	2900	2923	2945	2967	2989	2	4	7	9	11	13	16	18	20
20	·3010	3032	3054	3075	3096	3118	3139	3160	3181	3201	2	4	6	8	11	13	15	17	19
21	·3222	3243	3263	3284	3304	3324	3345	3365	3385	3404	2	4	6	8	10	12	14	16	18
22	·3424	3444	3464	3483	3502	3522	3541	3560	3579	3598	2	4	6	8	10	12	14	15	17
23	·3617	3636	3655	3674	3692	3711	3729	3747	3766	3784	2	4	6	7	9	11	13	15	17
24	·3802	3820	3838	3856	3874	3892	3909	3927	3945	3962	2	4	5	7	9	11	12	14	16
25	·3979	3997	4014	4031	4048	4065	4082	4099	4116	4133	2	3	5	7	9	10	12	14	15
26	·4150	4166	4183	4200	4216	4232	4249	4265	4281	4298	2	3	5	7	8	10	11	13	15
27	·4314	4330	4346	4362	4378	4393	4409	4425	4440	4456	2	3	5	6	8	9	11	13	14
28	·4472	4487	4502	4518	4533	4548	4564	4579	4594	4609	2	3	5	6	8	9	11	12	14
29	·4624	4639	4654	4669	4683	4698	4713	4728	4742	4757	1	3	4	6	7	9	10	12	13
30	·4771	4786	4800	4814	4829	4843	4857	4871	4886	4900	1	3	4	6	7	9	10	11	13
31	·4914	4928	4942	4955	4969	4983	4997	5011	5024	5038	1	3	4	6	7	8	10	11	12
32	·5051	5065	5079	5092	5105	5119	5132	5145	5159	5172	1	3	4	5	7	8	9	11	12
33	·5185	5198	5211	5224	5237	5250	5263	5276	5289	5302	1	3	4	5	6	8	9	10	12
34	·5315	5328	5340	5353	5366	5378	5391	5403	5416	5428	1	3	4	5	6	8	9	10	11
35	·5441	5453	5465	5478	5490	5502	5514	5527	5539	5551	1	2	4	5	6	7	9	10	11
36	·5563	5575	5587	5599	5611	5623	5635	5647	5658	5670	1	2	4	5	6	7	8	10	11
37	·5682	5694	5705	5717	5729	5740	5752	5763	5775	5786	1	2	3	5	6	7	8	9	10
38	·5798	5809	5821	5832	5843	5855	5866	5877	5888	5899	1	2	3	5	6	7	8	9	10
39	·5911	5922	5933	5944	5955	5966	5977	5988	5999	6010	1	2	3	4	5	7	8	9	10
40	·6021	6031	6042	6053	6064	6075	6085	6096	6107	6117	1	2	3	4	5	6	8	9	10
41	·6128	6138	6149	6160	6170	6180	6191	6201	6212	6222	1	2	3	4	5	6	7	8	9
42	·6232	6243	6253	6263	6274	6284	6294	6304	6314	6325	1	2	3	4	5	6	7	8	9
43	·6335	6345	6355	6365	6375	6385	6395	6405	6415	6425	1	2	3	4	5	6	7	8	9
44	·6435	6444	6454	6464	6474	6484	6493	6503	6513	6522	1	2	3	4	5	6	7	8	9
45	·6532	6542	6551	6561	6571	6580	6590	6599	6609	6618	1	2	3	4	5	6	7	8	9
46	·6628	6637	6646	6656	6665	6675	6684	6693	6702	6712	1	2	3	4	5	6	7	7	8
47	·6721	6730	6739	6749	6758	6767	6776	6785	6794	6803	1	2	3	4	5	5	6	7	8
48	·6812	6821	6830	6839	6848	6857	6866	6875	6884	6893	1	2	3	4	4	5	6	7	8
49	·6902	6911	6920	6928	6937	6946	6955	6964	6972	6981	1	2	3	4	4	5	6	7	8
50	·6990	6998	7007	7016	7024	7033	7042	7050	7059	7067	1	2	3	3	4	5	6	7	8
51	·7076	7084	7093	7101	7110	7118	7126	7135	7143	7152	1	2	3	3	4	5	6	7	8
52	·7160	7168	7177	7185	7193	7202	7210	7218	7226	7235	1	2	2	3	4	5	6	7	7
53	·7243	7251	7259	7267	7275	7284	7292	7300	7308	7316	1	2	2	3	4	5	6	6	7
54	·7324	7332	7340	7348	7356	7364	7372	7380	7388	7396	1	2	2	3	4	5	6	6	7
55	·7404	7412	7419	7427	7435	7443	7451	7459	7466	7474	1	2	2	3	4	5	5	6	7
56	·7482	7490	7497	7505	7513	7520	7528	7536	7543	7551	1	2	2	3	4	5	5	6	7
57	·7559	7566	7574	7582	7589	7597	7604	7612	7619	7627	1	2	2	3	4	5	5	6	7

LOGARITHMS

	0	1	2	3	4	5	6	7	8	9	1	2	3	4	5	6	7	8	9
58	·7634	7642	7649	7657	7664	7672	7679	7686	7694	7701	1	1	2	3	4	4	5	6	7
59	·7709	7716	7723	7731	7738	7745	7752	7760	7767	7774	1	1	2	3	4	4	5	6	7
60	·7782	7789	7796	7803	7810	7818	7825	7832	7839	7846	1	1	2	3	4	4	5	6	6
61	·7853	7860	7868	7875	7882	7889	7896	7903	7910	7917	1	1	2	3	4	4	5	6	6
62	·7924	7931	7938	7945	7952	7959	7966	7973	7980	7987	1	1	2	3	3	4	5	6	6
63	·7993	8000	8007	8014	8021	8028	8035	8041	8048	8055	1	1	2	3	3	4	5	5	6
64	·8062	8069	8075	8082	8089	8096	8102	8109	8116	8122	1	1	2	3	3	4	5	5	6
65	·8129	8136	8142	8149	8156	8162	8169	8176	8182	8189	1	1	2	3	3	4	5	5	6
66	·8195	8202	8209	8215	8222	8228	8235	8241	8248	8254	1	1	2	3	3	4	5	5	6
67	·8261	8267	8274	8280	8287	8293	8299	8306	8312	8319	1	1	2	3	3	4	5	5	6
68	·8325	8331	8338	8344	8351	8357	8363	8370	8376	8382	1	1	2	3	3	4	4	5	6
69	·8388	8395	8401	8407	8414	8420	8426	8432	8439	8445	1	1	2	2	3	4	4	5	6
70	·8451	8457	8463	8470	8476	8482	8488	8494	8500	8506	1	1	2	2	3	4	4	5	6
71	·8513	8519	8525	8531	8537	8543	8549	8555	8561	8567	1	1	2	2	3	4	4	5	5
72	·8573	8579	8585	8591	8597	8603	8609	8615	8621	8627	1	1	2	2	3	4	4	5	5
73	·8633	8639	8645	8651	8657	8663	8669	8675	8681	8686	1	1	2	2	3	4	4	5	5
74	·8692	8698	8704	8710	8716	8722	8727	8733	8739	8745	1	1	2	2	3	4	4	5	5
75	·8751	8756	8762	8768	8774	8779	8785	8791	8797	8802	1	1	2	2	3	3	4	5	5
76	·8808	8814	8820	8825	8831	8837	8842	8848	8854	8859	1	1	2	2	3	3	4	5	5
77	·8865	8871	8876	8882	8887	8893	8899	8904	8910	8915	1	1	2	2	3	3	4	4	5
78	·8921	8927	8932	8938	8943	8949	8954	8960	8965	8971	1	1	2	2	3	3	4	4	5
79	·8976	8982	8987	8993	8998	9004	9009	9015	9020	9025	1	1	2	2	3	3	4	4	5
80	·9031	9036	9042	9047	9053	9058	9063	9069	9074	9079	1	1	2	2	3	3	4	4	5
81	·9085	9090	9096	9101	9106	9112	9117	9122	9128	9133	1	1	2	2	3	3	4	4	5
82	·9138	9143	9149	9154	9159	9165	9170	9175	9180	9186	1	1	2	2	3	3	4	4	5
83	·9191	9196	9201	9206	9212	9217	9222	9227	9232	9238	1	1	2	2	3	3	4	4	5
84	·9243	9248	9253	9258	9263	9269	9274	9279	9284	9289	1	1	2	2	3	3	4	4	5
85	·9294	9299	9304	9309	9315	9320	9325	9330	9335	9340	1	1	2	2	3	3	4	4	5
86	·9345	9350	9355	9360	9365	9370	9375	9380	9385	9390	1	1	2	2	3	3	4	4	5
87	·9395	9400	9405	9410	9415	9420	9425	9430	9435	9440	0	1	1	2	2	3	3	4	4
88	·9445	9450	9455	9460	9465	9469	9474	9479	9484	9489	0	1	1	2	2	3	3	4	4
89	·9494	9499	9504	9509	9513	9518	9523	9528	9533	9538	0	1	1	2	2	3	3	4	4
90	·9542	9547	9552	9557	9562	9566	9571	9576	9581	9586	0	1	1	2	2	3	3	4	4
91	·9590	9595	9600	9605	9609	9614	9619	9624	9628	9633	0	1	1	2	2	3	3	4	4
92	·9638	9643	9647	9652	9657	9661	9666	9671	9675	9680	0	1	1	2	2	3	3	4	4
93	·9685	9689	9694	9699	9703	9708	9713	9717	9722	9727	0	1	1	2	2	3	3	4	4
94	·9731	9736	9741	9745	9750	9754	9759	9763	9768	9773	0	1	1	2	2	3	3	4	4
95	·9777	9782	9786	9791	9795	9800	9805	9809	9814	9818	0	1	1	2	2	3	3	4	4
96	·9823	9827	9832	9836	9841	9845	9850	9854	9859	9863	0	1	1	2	2	3	3	4	4
97	·9868	9872	9877	9881	9886	9890	9894	9899	9903	9908	0	1	1	2	2	3	3	4	4
98	·9912	9917	9921	9926	9930	9934	9939	9943	9948	9952	0	1	1	2	2	3	3	4	4
99	·9956	9961	9965	9969	9974	9978	9983	9987	9991	9996	0	1	1	2	2	3	3	3	4

ANTI-LOGARITHMS

	0	1	2	3	4	5	6	7	8	9	1	2	3	4	5	6	7	8	9
·00	1000	1002	1005	1007	1009	1012	1014	1016	1019	1021	0	0	1	1	1	1	2	2	2
·01	1023	1026	1028	1030	1033	1035	1038	1040	1042	1045	0	0	1	1	1	1	2	2	2
·02	1047	1050	1052	1054	1057	1059	1062	1064	1067	1069	0	0	1	1	1	1	2	2	2
·03	1072	1074	1076	1079	1081	1084	1086	1089	1091	1094	0	0	1	1	1	1	2	2	2
·04	1096	1099	1102	1104	1107	1109	1112	1114	1117	1119	0	1	1	1	1	2	2	2	2
·05	1122	1125	1127	1130	1132	1135	1138	1140	1143	1146	0	1	1	1	1	2	2	2	2
·06	1148	1151	1153	1156	1159	1161	1164	1167	1169	1172	0	1	1	1	1	2	2	2	2
·07	1175	1178	1180	1183	1186	1189	1191	1194	1197	1199	0	1	1	1	1	2	2	2	2
·08	1202	1205	1208	1211	1213	1216	1219	1222	1225	1227	0	1	1	1	1	2	2	2	3
·09	1230	1233	1236	1239	1242	1245	1247	1250	1253	1256	0	1	1	1	1	2	2	2	3
·10	1259	1262	1265	1268	1271	1274	1276	1279	1282	1285	0	1	1	1	1	2	2	2	3
·11	1288	1291	1294	1297	1300	1303	1306	1309	1312	1315	0	1	1	1	2	2	2	2	3
·12	1318	1321	1324	1327	1330	1334	1337	1340	1343	1346	0	1	1	1	2	2	2	2	3
·13	1349	1352	1355	1358	1361	1365	1368	1371	1374	1377	0	1	1	1	2	2	2	3	3
·14	1380	1384	1387	1390	1393	1396	1400	1403	1406	1409	0	1	1	1	2	2	2	3	3
·15	1413	1416	1419	1422	1426	1429	1432	1435	1439	1442	0	1	1	1	2	2	2	3	3
·16	1445	1449	1452	1455	1459	1462	1466	1469	1472	1476	0	1	1	1	2	2	2	3	3
·17	1479	1483	1486	1489	1493	1496	1500	1503	1507	1510	0	1	1	1	2	2	2	3	3
·18	1514	1517	1521	1524	1528	1531	1535	1538	1542	1545	0	1	1	1	2	2	2	3	3
·19	1549	1552	1556	1560	1563	1567	1570	1574	1578	1581	0	1	1	1	2	2	3	3	3
·20	1585	1589	1592	1596	1600	1603	1607	1611	1614	1618	0	1	1	1	2	2	3	3	3
·21	1622	1626	1629	1633	1637	1641	1644	1648	1652	1656	0	1	1	2	2	2	3	3	3
·22	1660	1663	1667	1671	1675	1679	1683	1687	1690	1694	0	1	1	2	2	2	3	3	3
·23	1698	1702	1706	1710	1714	1718	1722	1726	1730	1734	0	1	1	2	2	2	3	3	4
·24	1738	1742	1746	1750	1754	1758	1762	1766	1770	1774	0	1	1	2	2	2	3	3	4
·25	1778	1782	1786	1791	1795	1799	1803	1807	1811	1816	0	1	1	2	2	2	3	3	4
·26	1820	1824	1828	1832	1837	1841	1845	1849	1854	1858	0	1	1	2	2	3	3	3	4
·27	1862	1866	1871	1875	1879	1884	1888	1892	1897	1901	0	1	1	2	2	3	3	3	4
·28	1905	1910	1914	1919	1923	1928	1932	1936	1941	1945	0	1	1	2	2	3	3	4	4
·29	1950	1954	1959	1963	1968	1972	1977	1982	1986	1991	0	1	1	2	2	3	3	4	4
·30	1995	2000	2004	2009	2014	2018	2023	2028	2032	2037	0	1	1	2	2	3	3	4	4
·31	2042	2046	2051	2056	2061	2065	2070	2075	2080	2084	0	1	1	2	2	3	3	4	4
·32	2089	2094	2099	2104	2109	2113	2118	2123	2128	2133	0	1	1	2	2	3	3	4	4
·33	2138	2143	2148	2153	2158	2163	2168	2173	2178	2183	0	1	1	2	2	3	3	4	4
·34	2188	2193	2198	2203	2208	2213	2218	2223	2228	2234	1	1	2	2	3	3	4	4	5
·35	2239	2244	2249	2254	2259	2265	2270	2275	2280	2286	1	1	2	2	3	3	4	4	5
·36	2291	2296	2301	2307	2312	2317	2323	2328	2333	2339	1	1	2	2	3	3	4	4	5
·37	2344	2350	2355	2360	2366	2371	2377	2382	2388	2393	1	1	2	2	3	3	4	4	5
·38	2399	2404	2410	2415	2421	2427	2432	2438	2443	2449	1	1	2	2	3	3	4	4	5
·39	2455	2460	2466	2472	2477	2483	2489	2495	2500	2506	1	1	2	2	3	3	4	5	5
·40	2512	2518	2523	2529	2535	2541	2547	2553	2559	2564	1	1	2	2	3	4	4	5	5
·41	2570	2576	2582	2588	2594	2600	2606	2612	2618	2624	1	1	2	2	3	4	4	5	5
·42	2630	2636	2642	2649	2655	2661	2667	2673	2679	2685	1	1	2	2	3	4	4	5	6
·43	2692	2698	2704	2710	2716	2723	2729	2735	2742	2748	1	1	2	3	3	4	4	5	6
·44	2754	2761	2767	2773	2780	2786	2793	2799	2805	2812	1	1	2	3	3	4	4	5	6
·45	2818	2825	2831	2838	2844	2851	2858	2864	2871	2877	1	1	2	3	3	4	5	5	6
·46	2884	2891	2897	2904	2911	2917	2924	2931	2938	2944	1	1	2	3	3	4	5	5	6
·47	2951	2958	2965	2972	2979	2985	2992	2999	3006	3013	1	1	2	3	3	4	5	5	6
·48	3020	3027	3034	3041	3048	3055	3062	3069	3076	3083	1	1	2	3	4	4	5	6	6
·49	3090	3097	3105	3112	3119	3126	3133	3141	3148	3155	1	1	2	3	4	4	5	6	6

ANTI-LOGARITHMS

	0	1	2	3	4	5	6	7	8	9	1	2	3	4	5	6	7	8	9
·50	3162	3170	3177	3184	3192	3199	3206	3214	3221	3228	1	1	2	3	4	4	5	6	7
·51	3236	3243	3251	3258	3266	3273	3281	3289	3296	3304	1	2	2	3	4	5	5	6	7
·52	3311	3319	3327	3334	3342	3350	3357	3365	3373	3381	1	2	2	3	4	5	5	6	7
·53	3388	3396	3404	3412	3420	3428	3436	3443	3451	3459	1	2	2	3	4	5	6	6	7
·54	3467	3475	3483	3491	3499	3508	3516	3524	3532	3540	1	2	2	3	4	5	6	6	7
·55	3548	3556	3565	3573	3581	3589	3597	3606	3614	3622	1	2	2	3	4	5	6	7	7
·56	3631	3639	3648	3656	3664	3673	3681	3690	3698	3707	1	2	3	3	4	5	6	7	8
·57	3715	3724	3733	3741	3750	3758	3767	3776	3784	3793	1	2	3	3	4	5	6	7	8
·58	3802	3811	3819	3828	3837	3846	3855	3864	3873	3882	1	2	3	4	4	5	6	7	8
·59	3890	3899	3908	3917	3926	3936	3945	3954	3963	3972	1	2	3	4	5	5	6	7	8
·60	3981	3990	3999	4009	4018	4027	4036	4046	4055	4064	1	2	3	4	5	6	6	7	8
·61	4074	4083	4093	4102	4111	4121	4130	4140	4150	4159	1	2	3	4	5	6	7	8	9
·62	4169	4178	4188	4198	4207	4217	4227	4236	4246	4256	1	2	3	4	5	6	7	8	9
·63	4266	4276	4285	4295	4305	4315	4325	4335	4345	4355	1	2	3	4	5	6	7	8	9
·64	4365	4375	4385	4395	4406	4416	4426	4436	4446	4457	1	2	3	4	5	6	7	8	9
·65	4467	4477	4487	4498	4508	4519	4529	4539	4550	4560	1	2	3	4	5	6	7	8	9
·66	4571	4581	4592	4603	4613	4624	4634	4645	4656	4667	1	2	3	4	5	6	7	9	10
·67	4677	4688	4699	4710	4721	4732	4742	4753	4764	4775	1	2	3	4	5	7	8	9	10
·68	4786	4797	4808	4819	4831	4842	4853	4864	4875	4887	1	2	3	4	6	7	8	9	10
·69	4898	4909	4920	4932	4943	4955	4966	4977	4989	5000	1	2	3	5	6	7	8	9	10
·70	5012	5023	5035	5047	5058	5070	5082	5093	5105	5117	1	2	4	5	6	7	8	9	11
·71	5129	5140	5152	5164	5176	5188	5200	5212	5224	5236	1	2	4	5	6	7	8	10	11
·72	5248	5260	5272	5284	5297	5309	5321	5333	5346	5358	1	2	4	5	6	7	9	10	11
·73	5370	5383	5395	5408	5420	5433	5445	5458	5470	5483	1	3	4	5	6	8	9	10	11
·74	5495	5508	5521	5534	5546	5559	5572	5585	5598	5610	1	3	4	5	6	8	9	10	12
·75	5623	5636	5649	5662	5675	5689	5702	5715	5728	5741	1	3	4	5	7	8	9	10	12
·76	5754	5768	5781	5794	5808	5821	5834	5848	5861	5875	1	3	4	5	7	8	9	11	12
·77	5888	5902	5916	5929	5943	5957	5970	5984	5998	6012	1	3	4	5	7	8	10	11	12
·78	6026	6039	6053	6067	6081	6095	6109	6124	6138	6152	1	3	4	6	7	8	10	11	13
·79	6166	6180	6194	6209	6223	6237	6252	6266	6281	6295	1	3	4	6	7	9	10	11	13
·80	6310	6324	6339	6353	6368	6383	6397	6412	6427	6442	1	3	4	6	7	9	10	12	13
·81	6457	6471	6486	6501	6516	6531	6546	6561	6577	6592	2	3	5	6	8	9	11	12	14
·82	6607	6622	6637	6653	6668	6683	6699	6714	6730	6745	2	3	5	6	8	9	11	12	14
·83	6761	6776	6792	6808	6823	6839	6855	6871	6887	6902	2	3	5	6	8	9	11	13	14
·84	6918	6934	6950	6966	6982	6998	7015	7031	7047	7063	2	3	5	6	8	10	11	13	15
·85	7079	7096	7112	7129	7145	7161	7178	7194	7211	7228	2	3	5	7	8	10	12	13	15
·86	7244	7261	7278	7295	7311	7328	7345	7362	7379	7396	2	3	5	7	8	10	12	13	15
·87	7413	7430	7447	7464	7482	7499	7516	7534	7551	7568	2	3	5	7	9	10	12	14	16
·88	7586	7603	7621	7638	7656	7674	7691	7709	7727	7745	2	4	5	7	9	11	12	14	16
·89	7762	7780	7798	7816	7834	7852	7870	7889	7907	7925	2	4	5	7	9	11	13	14	16
·90	7943	7962	7980	7998	8017	8035	8054	8072	8091	8110	2	4	6	7	9	11	13	15	17
·91	8128	8147	8166	8185	8204	8222	8241	8260	8279	8299	2	4	6	8	9	11	13	15	17
·92	8318	8337	8356	8375	8395	8414	8433	8453	8472	8492	2	4	6	8	10	12	14	15	17
·93	8511	8531	8551	8570	8590	8610	8630	8650	8670	8690	2	4	6	8	10	12	14	16	18
·94	8710	8730	8750	8770	8790	8810	8831	8851	8872	8892	2	4	6	8	10	12	14	16	18
·95	8913	8933	8954	8974	8995	9016	9036	9057	9078	9099	2	4	6	8	10	12	15	17	19
·96	9120	9141	9162	9183	9204	9226	9247	9268	9290	9311	2	4	6	8	11	13	15	17	19
·97	9333	9354	9376	9397	9419	9441	9462	9484	9506	9528	2	4	7	9	11	13	15	17	20
·98	9550	9572	9594	9616	9638	9661	9683	9705	9727	9750	2	4	7	9	11	13	16	18	20
·99	9772	9795	9817	9840	9863	9886	9908	9931	9954	9977	2	5	7	9	11	14	16	18	20

Section 5 Safety aspects

Cut Out Accidents on the Circular Saw

Reference to The Woodworking Machinery Regulations. Common danger areas. Safety scheme in the U.S.A. Safety in Training. Guard adjustment. Inspection of saw plates.

Safety and the Young Operator

Change of environment. Trust in superiors. Instruction in safety. Training in machine operation. Safety publicity. Use of push stick. Prevention of boredom. Progression of trainee. Guard adjustment. Importance of taker off. Working small components. Heat and light. Dressed for the job.

The Use of Jigs and Work Holders

Who makes jigs. When are jigs required. Jig design. Weight of jigs. Jigs for the circular saw, spindle moulder, high-speed router. The band saw. Jig storage.

Safety on the Spindle Moulder

Machine speeds. Versatility of machine. Knowledge required by operator. Methods of working. Siting of machine. Shaped work. Shaw guard. Push stick. Pressure springs. Easing the cut. Dropping on. Use of auto feed. Tabulation of standard operations.

Planning for Safety

Selection of operatives. Movement of operatives. Training systems. Heating and ventilation. Noise. Housekeeping and waste. Layout of machines. Choice of machines. Type of materials worked. Automatic feeds. Sectional feed rollers. Planning by prototype. Design of jigs. Lighting. Productivity payments.

Safety on the Planing Machine

Bridge guard. Cutter block. Short material. Sectional feed rollers. Automation.

Comments on the Woodworking Machines' Regulations 1974

Introduction. Basic alterations. The regulations.

Cut out the accidents on the circular saw

Too much attention cannot be focused on safety in the use of woodworking machinery, especially to new entrants to the industry, occasional users, and machine operators who are continually on one particular machine or operation and are suddenly switched to a different type of machine work.

There can be little doubt that operators kept continually on one particular task become dulled to the requirements of the other plant around them, and safety may well be lacking in some cases. It must be said, on the other hand, that these operators often become super-efficient at their particular job and are an asset to their employer.

The Woodworking Machinery Regulations cover in a few words a large amount of ground regarding safety—providing operators are prepared to interpret them in relation to their own particular requirements. I feel it is the duty of persons in charge to enlarge upon these important regulations and pass them on to operators. This is and has, of course, been done in various ways, such as by the technical colleges and machine manufacturers in poster form, but there is still much scope for SAFETY publicity to be displayed in an original manner.

Fig. 1 shows a circular saw bench in use with several mistakes being made as regards safety.

1. The riving knife is more than 12 mm from the back of the saw teeth.
2. The guard should be lowered to the line of the seat of the gullet of the teeth or below.
3. The front guard should be adjusted to within 6 mm of the timber being cut.
4. A cutting list on the bench distracts the eye of the operator.
5. Spanners left on the bench may find their way into the revolving blade.
6. The stop switch and isolator is not easily accessible due to timber being stacked against the bench.
7. String or ragged clothing should not be in evidence. . . .

It should be pointed out that if any one of the above mistakes is being made during operation the operator is endangering himself. Next time you are in the vicinity of a circular saw in use look and see if any of these mistakes are apparent; make no delay in pointing them out to the operator.

Fig. 2 shows a much better set up on the same machine, where a supervisor can see the operator is working with due regard to safety.

One method on a large plant in the U.S.A. recently in the pursuance of safety was for workers to spend five minutes daily in groups to discuss safety. They claim that the reward for this was less absenteeism due to the lower accident rate, plus reduced anxiety that unpleasant happenings can bring.

I doubt if such a plan can be applied in this

Fig. 1: WRONG

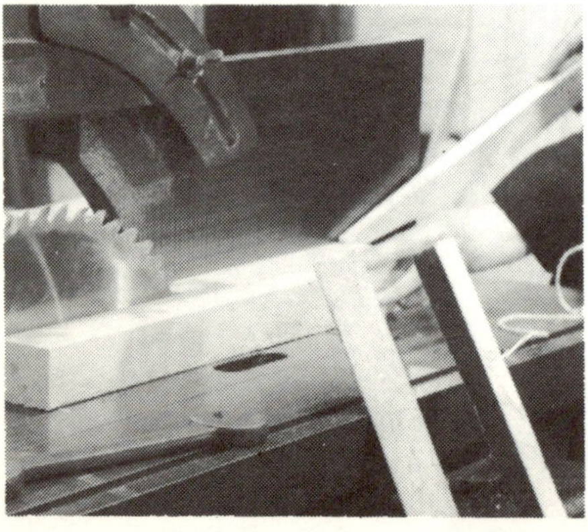

Fig. 2: RIGHT

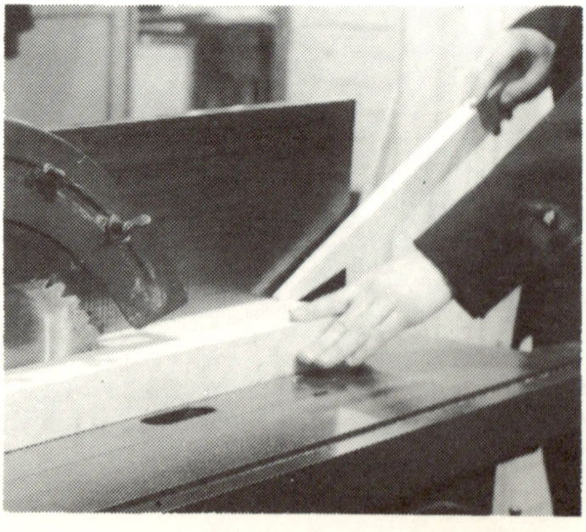

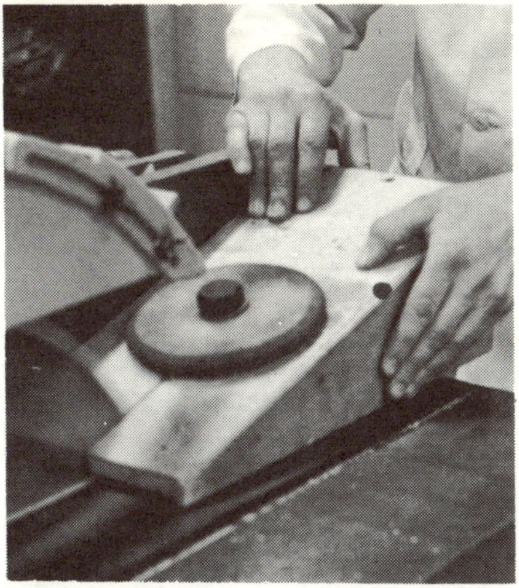

Stoning down the teeth on a circular saw using an abrasive wheel mounted on a jig. The operation carried out in this manner can be safely controlled.

country due to so many other more popular topics being available for momentary discussion, but safety could be put on the agenda at all works meetings at the various levels.

Examiners' bodies, too, throughout the country could stress more on safety in the preparation of their syllabuses which would automatically make students pursue the requirements of accident prevention more fully.

However, although all the usual precautions can be taken on machines, unexpected situations do arise, and may well take an operator unaware. Some timbers tend to nip or bind during ripping, the cause being erratic grain or case hardening due to faults in kilning, setting up stresses within the board. For this reason all timber being cut, in particular hardwood, should be fed with due care until it has got into contact with the riving knife. For timbers subject to this annoying habit of binding, a little extra set on the saw is helpful giving a wider kerf. Wedges, too, should be at hand to be driven into the cut beyond the riving knife to reduce undue stress on both operator and machine.

When a board is nipped during the first few inches of engagement with the saw, some idea of the rapidity of the throwback can be arrived at if given thought, and it is considerable. The rim speed of a circular saw, working efficiently, is in the region of 10,000ft. per min. which is approx. 3,000 metres. To put this into visual reality—if the saw was a wheel being driven along the road its speed would be approximately 120 miles per hour. Therefore, if the timber is gripped and thrown from the outer extremity of the revolving saw, this is the speed at which they will part company.

Adjustment to guards should not be done when the machine is in motion; although elevating handles may not be in the proximity of the saw blade, it must be remembered that if a metal guard is wound down on to the revolving teeth, a shower of metallic chips may be fired at some unfortunate person.

Finally, never work with a blunt saw, also inspect saws regularly for cracks, and should any be found, have them treated by a competent person, or abandon the blade altogether.

Safety and the young operator

STOP. A push stick should always be used when ripping on a circular saw, although the gap between the saw blade and the guide fence is wide enough to allow the hand to pass through. The white line on the bench indicates the position of the cutting edge of the saw, and no hand should pass beyond during the actual ripping operation.

The subject of safety relating to woodworking machinery can be broken down into a number of categories. This can be a much more efficient approach than trying to deal with the subject as a whole.

Age group is a category which is worthy of note, and it could well be a very good starting point for anyone making a detailed study of the subject.

Although accidents unfortunately occur in all age groups of machine operators, in the case of the younger person it is very regrettable. It is important that the new entrant to industry should be told about the dangers involved in the use of the particular machines which he is to be concerned with. One does hear of accidents occurring over the years that suggests that this is not always done in an effective manner.

It must be remembered that the change from school to the industrial production unit involves an entirely different environment. During his school years his activities have been planned within an acceptable ring of safety, and occasions have been few when he has been requested to carry out duties outside that ring.

Advice tags can be attached to machines where young people are in the course of training. The example here shows a bridge guard on a surface planing machine.

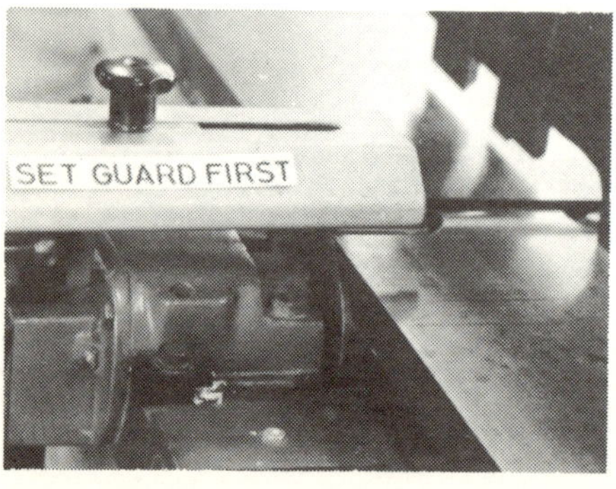

When a young person enters a machine shop he expects to be trained in the use of the equipment his predecessors have developed over the years. **He puts his trust in those around him.**

In addition to being taught the advancing technology of what the machines can do he has every right to be instructed in the aspects of safety relating to the machines.

Few woodworking machine manufacturers attach any advice tags on their machines such as, "Adjust guard and riving knife before use". "Do not attempt to feed material shorter than 400 mm through this thicknessing machine." "Adjust the bridge guard before starting the machine". I have seen a tag on a bandsaw saying, "Take the strain off the saw blade when **not** in use."

In spite of these permanently built-in safety instructions not being present, there is nothing to prevent a person responsible for safety to add them to the machines which are likely to be used by persons in training.

To my mind these would be much more effective than having posters on the wall about occurrences far remote from the machines in question.

Young persons, understandably, copy the habits of their elders, and it is important that they are in the charge of a suitable person from the start. If they see that an experienced operator is following a certain instruction quoted on the machine, they will be reluctant not to do likewise.

By nature a developing mind likes to experiment: this is pobably one reason why advancement is made over the generations. This experimentation must, however, be kept under observation and controlled. I think that anyone who has worked in a machine shop for a number of years must have seen an apprentice tickling the teeth of a rotating circular saw with a lath while his superior's back has been turned.

There can be two suggested reasons for him doing this unnecessary act.

He wants to see if the saw really cuts, or he is just plain bored. Boredom can be the cause of accidents in all age groups, and efforts should be made to prevent, or relieve it.

In the larger woodworking establishments, both trained operators and apprentices are often kept on the same machining operation for long periods of time. This is done for the convenience of management in many cases, and it does also produce a specialist. It also enables employment to be offered to the less versatile type of person, those who would not otherwise be employable.

This type of person may prefer to be static as he very often accepts his limitations.

The more enthusiastic apprentice should be moved around the various machines, not only just to prevent boredom, but also to progress his training.

A plan of progress, however, that has been suitable for one young person, may not be suitable for another. Young people do not all develop at the same rate, and to transfer an operative to work of a more advanced, or hazardous nature, before he is ready for it, could put him in the accident potential category.

It is not unusual for an apprentice to ask to be moved to carry out an operation on another machine that has attracted his interest. What are the safety points a supervisor should consider? The following is a brief suggestion of how a decision should be made . . .

1. **Does the operator's past record show that he will be capable of safely carrying out the anticipated machine process?**
2. **Will it be possible to have him adequately supervised during the initial stages?**

If the answer to both of the above questions is "No", then he should not be moved.

If short pieces of timber must be worked, two push sticks can be used to advantage. This method is known as "knife and forking".

If the answer to number one is "Yes", and to number two "No", a certain amount of risk may be involved regarding his safety. This needs consideration according to the nature of the work involved. To move a trainee for production flow purposes without giving consideration to safety is indeed an error.

In the use of machines, safety is a combined operation between the individual and the environment in which he is situated. This is by no means on a fifty-fifty basis neither is it consistently proportional.

In the case where a cutter head has been insufficiently guarded, the responsibility of operational safety lies very much with the operator and not the machine. A few adjustments to the guards could probably swing the situation in the environmental direction and put less responsibility on the operator.

This should be the aim for young persons in training.

A study of these facts can reveal that it is not the particular machine that regulates safety, but the environment, which is very often governed by the setting up of the machine.

Most new entrants to the industry spend a period of time at the output end of machines taking off the processed timber. There are varying degrees of danger involved in this job of work.

The back of a revolving circular saw is regarded as more lethal than the front, since any garment or limb caught in it will be pulled into the machine. The regulations regarding this machine should be followed in detail, particularly when a young person is assisting.

On a double ended tenoning machine with a

These two illustrations are part of an environmental study of a machining operation—stop chamfering door rails on the spindle moulder. (Above) safety has been taken care of mainly by the planning of the set up of the machine. Cutting is being done on the underside of the timber. A through face board has been fitted. Stops have been attached to prevent kick-back and location. The overhead pressure would be applied, and a push stick could be used. (Below) it is doubtful if any experienced machinist would make all the mistakes shown in this illustration at the one time. Safety here would depend very much on the operator, as opposed to the machine in the previous illustration. Cutting is being done on top of the work. Pencil lines are used to give location instead of stops. No through face board or overhead pressure. A push stick would only be of limited use as both hands would be required to hold the work. Operating time would be longer and work could be less accurate.

continuous bed feed, the scribing cutter heads are very often in the vicinity of the taker off. These cutters should be adequately covered with hoods, and their presence should be explained to anyone working at the output end of the machine.

Straight line edger circular saws are not always fitted with riving knives as they are mechanically fed machines. Very narrow offcuts which fail to get pressure can be thrown back in the direction of the operator unless they are promptly removed by the taker off. Responsibility for safety can at times depend on the secondary person on a machine.

Many young operators seem to be prone to working short material. They seem to have the idea that a short piece of timber is safer to work than a long length. This is quite incorrect of course.

When small components are to be manufactured, material should be prepared in safe workable lengths, and only cut into short pieces for the final machining operations. It is in fact a good plan not to leave short ends of material in the vicinity of circular saws and surface planing machines.

It can be pretty nerve racking to come across a youth in the middle of planing a piece of wood 50 mm in length when the opening between the two tables is 75 mm.

Young persons in training tend to omit the use of a push stick on the circular saw when cutting material to such a width that it permits them to pass their right hand between the rotating saw blade and the guide fence.

Hands should not pass beyond the cutting point of the saw at any time during the actual ripping operation. It is in fact quite unnecessary. It is particularly dangerous to work in the above manner when cutting plastic surfaced material as the hand can slip.

Guards should be set to a fine degree when young persons are in the course of training.

Adjustment to the guards while the cutting unit is rotating should not be encouraged.

As an apprentice goes through the process of training it is customary for him to have machines set for him to operate by an experienced person. Later he will do his own setting up but this should be checked before use. His efforts will depend very much on the way he has been instructed, and also the interest shown by those looking upon his own efforts.

An adequately heated workshop is a point worth noting where young people are employed on machines. Heating could be considered more important than bright lighting to the young, but

this statement could well be reversed for the more mature with toughened skins, and failing sight. Timber requires to be firmly gripped for many machining operations.
Anyone who has experienced working a high-speed machine fitted with an extractor fan in an unheated workshop on a frosty morning will appreciate my recommendations.
Fortunately heating problems apply to only certain times of the year but one cold day can be a long existence to an unprepared worker of the younger age group.
Young people should be encouraged to dress suitably for the type of work in which they are engaged. This is an industrial aspect which has rather gone astray with what could be described as the changeover from clothes to gear. Some do apply the rage sensibly, but others at times need guidance within the industrial unit, regarding their personal approach to safety.

The use of jigs and work holders

1. This table leg tapering jig for use on the circular saw has been fitted with an extension handle. This is an aid to quicker and safer working, as the operator has no need to pause, to pick up the traditional push-stick, to complete the cut.

Appliances for holding timber components during machining processes are used in many branches of woodworking, and they contribute considerably to the range of operations made possible with the standard type of machine.

These working aids are quite often made by the operator himself, at the point of requirement, a minimum of time having to be spent on the project. In the larger establishment, where production planning can be applied to a greater degree, jigs are very often designed and constructed beforehand to prevent delays in the production line. This advance preparation has many advantages; a suitable craftsman can be selected to do the job, and the jig may be fully tested before being handed over to the production line. One point often overlooked is to ensure that machined stock is dimensioned accurately to fit snugly in the prepared jig. It is, in some factories, quite a common occurrence, for several batches to come along successfully dimensioned, then a batch slightly in error. Communication between departments regarding production procedures is an important factor.

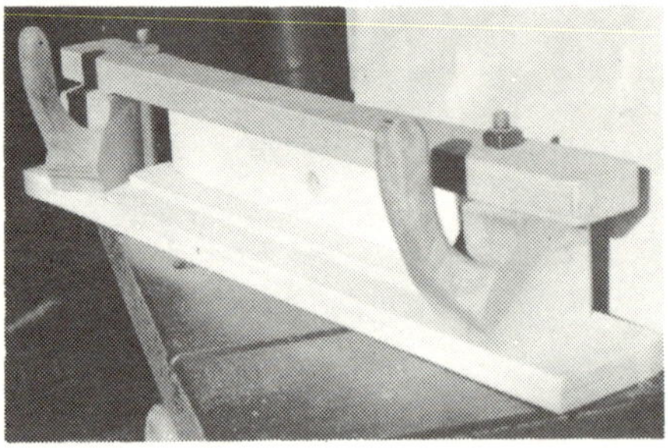

2. A shaping jig for use on the spindle moulder. Note the handles incorporated in the design which enables the operator to work with his hands, rather than just with his finger tips.

3. A router jig for small components. The jig is designed to enable the guard to be used, and comfortable hand grips are fitted at a most suitable angle to reduce fatigue to the operator.

When are jigs and work holders required

1. To assist in the machining of small components.
2. To enable the machine to process more than one component at the same time.
3. To eliminate marking out all pieces to be worked.
4. To prevent spelching of end grain.
5. For machining parts to a predetermined shape.

Holders, and jigs in most cases, also contribute towards safe working.

Design of jigs:

Safety. Jigs should always be designed with the safety of the operator in mind. Their design should be such that the statutory guards can still

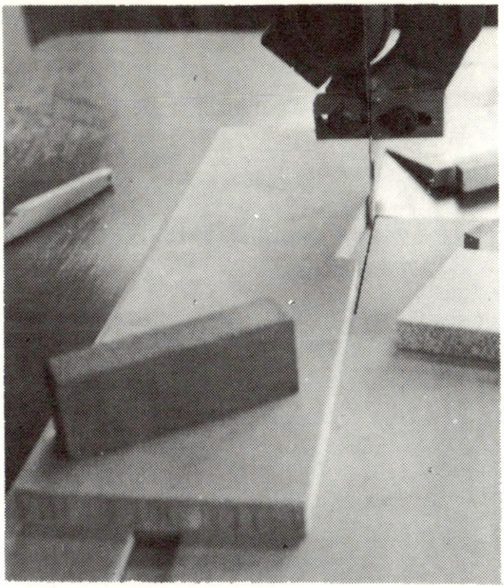

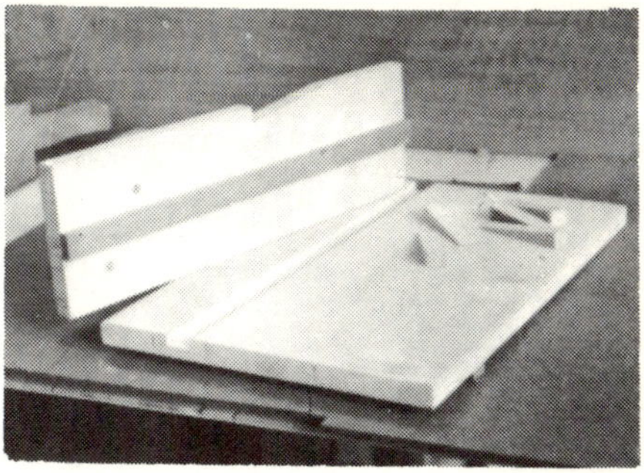

4a. Several types of jigs can be applied to band-sawing machines. Left is a jig for cutting wedges. The base board terminates level with the back of the saw blade, this allows the cut wedge to fall away. (4b) Parts of the jig removed from the machine.

be utilised in a reasonable manner. It is preferred that the jig should be held in the palm of the hands, rather than with the finger tips. Handles or grip blocks should be fitted whenever possible.

Jigs of the larger type should be skeletonised to cut down weight. The smaller type of jig can be more pleasant to use if it is built up from stout material to absorb the kick from the cutting unit. Screws should be used in preference to nails, permanent holding pieces should also be glued to prevent movement due to vibration. Points of the jig that are subjected to wear should be faced with a touch material—in some cases metal may be used.

If it is possible to design the jig to carry out more than one operation while the timber is located, much time may be saved in handling. Loading and unloading can often take longer than the cutting operation itself.

Work should be held firmly in the jig by some form of clamping device. Some operations require only wooden turn-buttons, but where metal devices are used they should be positioned well clear of the cutting point.

The Circular Saw:

An operation often carried out on the circular saw is the tapering cut on table legs. The jig should be designed so that the foot of the leg meets the saw first, enabling the saw to make a full bite. If the cut is taken from the top end, side strain will be put on the saw, in particular if it is not very sharp, and a snaking cut could result.

If an extension handle is fitted to the jig, safer and quicker working will be achieved. Some jig makers terminate the jig unit immediately at the end of the leg; this means a push stick must be used to complete the cut for safe working. An extension handle will eliminate the use of a push stick.

The Spindle Moulder:

Shaped work using a ring fence can in most cases be carried out confidently providing jigs are properly designed for the work. Beginners should not be misled by unreliable illustrations made by persons who have probably never attempted the job. An operator should be happy with the set up; therefore, the less experienced should spend more time on the preparation of his jig than a fully experienced person. The possibility of a shaped component breaking up during working must always be borne in mind. Several light cuts may, in some instances, be preferable to one heavy cut. It is generally safer with the work mounted on a jig, than without.

The High Speed Router:

Probably more jigs are used on the router than on any other machine as it lends itself to repetition work.

Jigs designed for working on the guide pin should allow for at least $\frac{3}{8}$in. (9.52 mm) projection of pin above the table.

Trenching slots should be stopped at the outgoing end of the jig to prevent the jig passing beyond the cutter. Danger can and has been experienced in bringing the jig back into the

guide slot when this point has been ignored. The Perspex guard should be effectively positioned, even on jig work.
Where a jig is not designed by the operator himself, it has proved good policy to confer with the machinist who will be using the jig on some aspects of its construction. Not all operators are ready to accept other people's developments, and this period of consultation can help in the success of an operation of the more difficult type.
It has often been noted that a shabby jig will produce shabby work; a good job can often be determined at the jigging-up stage.
Where a standard type of jig is in successful operation it is still good policy to be on the look-out for even further improvement to be made. Quick loading and unloading is essential, also waste disposal from the jig. The use of dowels, wood or metal, instead of blocks of wood for component location on the jig board, offers less resistance to wood waste.
Storage of jigs always seems to be a problem and finding them, another. Jigs should be listed and numbered as an aid to location. A colour code can also be useful, relating to different products of the department.

Safety on a spindle moulder

Many improvements have been made to the spindle moulder during the past two decades, such as individual motorisation, forward and reverse rotation, increased speeds and variation in speeds with a minimum of adjustments. The latter makes it possible to have the correct speed on the periphery—the circle described by the cutters during rotation—when different cutter heads are used.

The spindle moulder is a very versatile machine—hence its popularity in the woodworking industry—but it could be said that it is due to this same versatility that accident prevention on this machine becomes more of a problem.

I will try to clarify my statement. Let us assume that a spindle moulder is installed in a production line simply to rebate the meeting edges of assembled cupboard doors. The safest type of cutter head—which, I suggest, would be the solid profile type—would be used. If the machine is to be hand-fed, an electronic device could be fitted to prevent the operation of the machine until the principal guard is in correct adjustment. A mechanised feed attachment would make the operation safer and less fatiguing, so increasing output.

Many accidents occur when only a small amount of work has to be done on a certain operation and the operator is reluctant to take full safety measures in his setting of the machine.

It should also be remembered that an experienced operator may not realise that he is not using the safest method of working with this particular machine even though fully competent on another type of machine in the plant.

It is always advisable, from a safety point of view, to work with the cutters on the underside of the timber. The timber itself then acts as a guard during its progress through the machine, and it is only when the machine is empty that the cutters are exposed, making the fitting of other guards necessary (see fig. 2).

The working gap in the fences should at all times be set to a minimum. For this reason, no major adjustment should be made in any direction when the machine is in motion.

The use of a through board—a piece of sound timber about 9 mm thick—when securely fixed to the fences increases the safety factor considerably, and is a necessity when short work is being moulded. It is also ideal when training an operative, as most of the rotating head is hidden

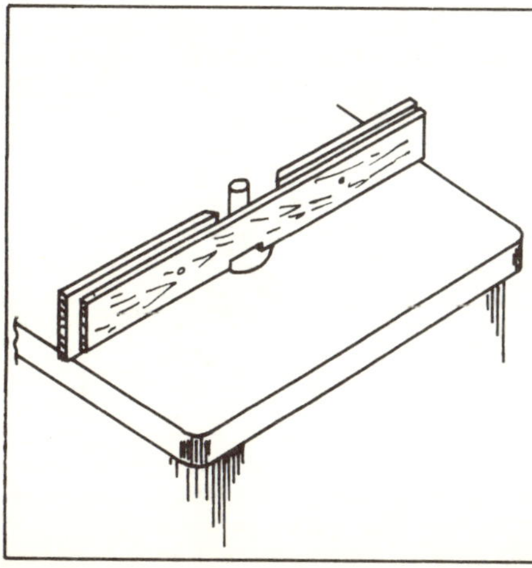

Fig. 1. A through board fitted across the fences of a spindle moulder.

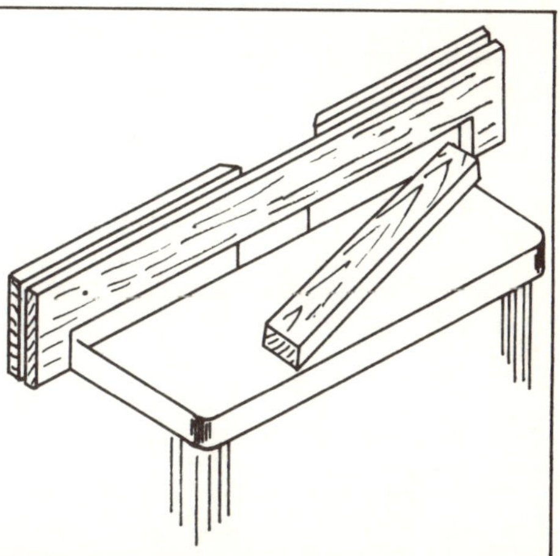

Fig. 3. A stop arrangement for "dropping on."

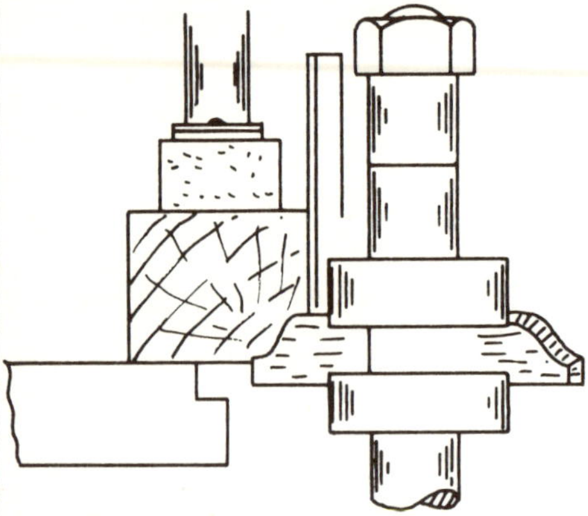

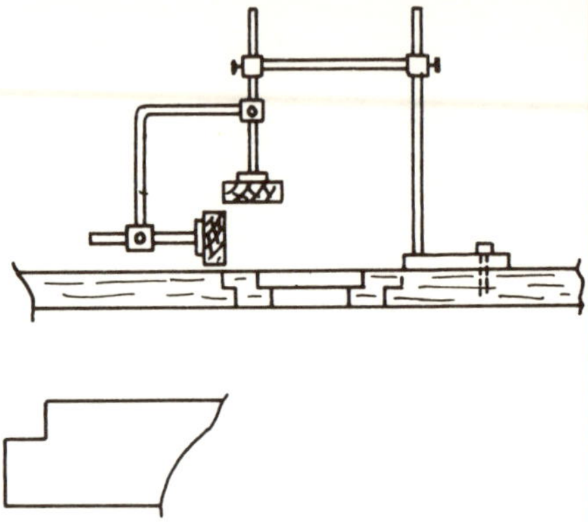

Fig. 2. A set-up, with the cutters operating on the underside of the timber which protects the operator from the cutters.

Fig. 4. A typical Shaw guard mounted on a spindle table. Adjustments can be made in any direction.

behind the board, so giving him more confidence in his work (see fig. 1).

Alertness and concentration when using a machine are most important. An operator's method of approach will be affected if his mind is occupied in other directions—this is a cause of many industrial accidents.

Siting of the machine can also play a part in accident prevention. A spindle moulder should not be placed near a doorway if this can be avoided. The movement of personnel and goods, and the slamming of doors does not assist concentration.

When shaped work is being moulded, it is advisable to do it at a time when there is not too much noise from surrounding machinery. The operator depends on sound and touch in the progression of his work, and if he cannot hear his own machine he is dependent on touch alone.

The Shaw guard has always been looked upon as a good aid to safety on the spindle moulder and rightly so, as it not only keeps the operator's fingers away from the cutters but also holds the work for him. The holding shoes should be set with just the correct amount of pressure for the job in hand, and a little lubrication on all frictional surfaces will give efficient progression, free from jerks (see fig. 4).

An alternative to the Shaw guard is the use of vertical and horizontal pressure springs. A Perspex or slotted metal visor guard can normally be used in conjunction with these. The advantage that the use of springs has over the Shaw guard is that the springs have four points of pressure adjustment when all are in use, the Shaw guard only two. They should be adjusted to apply pressure close to the opening in the fences; but not too close, or this may cause the work to be dipped into the cutters when commencing to cut.

A wooden push-stick should always be at hand on a spindle moulder, and if it is being used near the cutters it should be made from a firm softwood rather than a dense hardwood or metal to minimise the kick-back in the event of contact with the cutters.

Small work should be mounted in a holding jig, and if the work entails only a straight cut a through board can also be used.

When a heavy cut has to be made, or a cut which removes the major part of a section of timber, it is advisable to either saw away a portion of the waste first or mould in a series of cuts. On shaped work the series-of-cuts method is a good approach for the beginner on this type of work, the number of cuts being decreased as the worker gains experience. Here again, cutting should be done on the underside of the timber, if possible.

When "dropping on"—that is, commencing a cut other than at the beginning of a member—it is always advisable to fit a back stop to take the kick as the cutter meets the timber. If the cut is a heavy one, it is better done in stages (see fig. 3).

One attachment to the spindle moulder which has gained popularity during the past decade is the automatic feed. In addition to its increased production potential it has been a good step towards safer working. It enables an operator to work with his hands rather than just his fingers, which should be the aim of all machinists. Many operations can be carried out on the spindle moulder with this attachment, in perfect safety, which would not otherwise be recommended or would be very fatiguing (see fig. 5).

One method of improving safety in a machine-shop, where a number of operations are repeated from time to time, is to record and tabulate the operations. The machinist, whether he is the regular one or otherwise, can then look up the operation on his table, which should tell him which cutter head to use, the machine speed required, which guard must be fitted and whether a through board or holding jig is necessary.

Should an accident occur under these circumstances, the first thing to check would be the charted recommendations to see if they had been followed. Initially, a scheme of this kind is simply a matter of organisation. Then comes its application, followed by results.

To what better use could organisation be put than to safety?

Fig. 5. A spindle moulder fitted with an automatic feed attachment. *(Photo by J.K.O. Cutters Ltd., High Wycombe.)*

Planning for safety

Although most woodworking establishments recognise the statutory regulations regarding safety in the operation of woodworking machines, accidents still occur. This makes one realise that safety does not just mean providing a guard for a machine, and leaving it at that. Many other factors contribute towards safety, some of them in fact may be said to be quite remote from the machine itself.

1. Fire extinguishers for emergency use on electrical equipment, should be of a type that contains a non-conducting agent. This can be either carbon dioxide, as seen above, or liquids such as chlorobromomethane, or carbon tetrachloride. The liquid type can have a toxic effect if used in an unventilated area.

In a large factory an operator is often employed continually on one machine. He usually has some experience on taking up his post, but he should, however, be kept under observation for a period of time. If he is a suitable operative he will most likely become a safe and efficient worker after a very short period.

In the case of a smaller establishment an operator may have to move around various types of machines, as day-to-day routine requires. The danger factor here is much higher, and care must be taken in the selection of operatives for jobs of this type. A loger period of observation of the operator's capabilities may be necessary. A check on the amount of previous experience is advisable, also technical qualifications, and the size and type of establishment where experience has been gained.

In a busy factory where the work for one machine depends upon the output from another, absenteeism can affect the flow of work. It is not unusual for a worker to be moved from one machine to another at short notice. Unless thought is given in the selection of a suitable operative, a danger point may well arise. Advance notification regarding absence from work is always advisable, from the point of view of safety. Also, supervisors should be familiar with the capabilities of each of his operatives.

It is essential that a young entrant to machine woodworking should receive some training, apart from his daily work. This can be either at a technical college, or at a training school within the factory. This gives him the opportunity to learn safe procedure, in his own time, rather than simply copying the methods of others.

We, as human beings, are only comfortable between a very small range of temperatures. When we have to work outside this range, we begin to lose operational efficiency. In some types of work this is not important, as long as conditions are not in the extreme. In machine woodworking, however, extreme cold can be a hazard where individual pieces are being worked. Waste extraction fans draw heated air as well as waste timber, from the machine area, and heating systems require to be designed to cope with this.

The sound woodworking machines make, unless overstrained or out of balance, is not objectionable. In many aspects, they can be likened to a form of music. What is objectionable to an operator is a sudden burst of noise, from, say, a slamming door, or hand operations being carried out in the near vicinity. This can upset concentration, which is at times very important. It is preferable that the machines should be divided

Fire risk. Wood waste should not be allowed to accumulate on switch gear.

3. An automatic feed attachment fitted to a spindle moulder. This is a modern aid to safer working. It can be used for all through moulding work, including some curved operations.

from work benches. Also, that heavy load machines should be well away from fine dimension ones.

General tidiness is important from a safety point of view. A period should be set aside weekly, or even daily to make working conditions comfortable. Fire risk is increased considerably in an untidy factory, and where dust is allowed to accumulate on electrical switchgear. Fire-fighters called during the night, expect to find clear gangways. Particular attention should be paid to machine areas. Ready access to fire extinguishers should at all times be available.

Where mechanically-fed machines are used, ample working space is of great importance at the output end. Takers-off have been trapped due to lack of clearance space.

Layout of machines, both order, and spacing is governed by the type of work generally carried out. A department designed for small components would be unsafe if switched to long work without replanning. The worst position for a spindle moulder to be used on shaped work, would probably be on the corner of a clearway. Out-coming stock from machines should not cross doorways.

Woodworking machines are very versatile and a machinist is often tempted, or compelled, to carry out an operation on a machine that was not designed for that purpose. Before carrying out such experiments, the safety factor should be carefully considered. Consultation should be made if in doubt, starting at bench level, and taken higher if so desired. Much more could be written on this aspect illustrating the dangers of many operations that could be involved.

A machinist who has worked entirely on softwoods, and suddenly takes a job using hardwoods and plastics, needs to take a certain amount of care. Kilndried hardwoods in particular tend to nip and bind when being hand-fed through a circular saw. The use of a push-stick is important, and a few wedges at hand can be very useful. Plastics require protective eye shields, and sometimes gloves also.

In the larger production units more and more machines are being fed mechanically as automation advances. This is a good step towards safety, as operators are working at a much greater distance from the cutting point, than they would be if fed by hand. For the smaller works automatic feed attachments for standard machines are now available, and not only do they increase safety, but production also. Their use should be encouraged, and their capabilities more publicised.

Many machines have incorporated ideas to

improve the safety factor. The sectional feed roller and pressure bar on some thicknessing machines can be taken as an example. This makes a much firmer grip on the timber being planed, so making the risk of a kick-back less likely. Safety planning should be considered in the selection of woodworking machines.

When planning for large-scale production, a prototype of an article to be manufactured should be constructed in advance. This not only helps speedy production, but also the selection of machines to be used to carry out operations. Safety can be in mind and planned in advance along with production methods. Short components can be machined in multiple, and safe working jigs prepared in advance.

Jigs, and work-holders, although probably classed as being two different pieces of equipment, can be regarded as much the same thing from a point of view of safety.

Care should be taken in their design and construction, a shabby jig usually produces shabby work. Their design should be such that guards on the machine are still able to be used. A badly-designed jig cannot be accepted as an excuse to break statutory regulations. It is good policy to have the operator responsible for using the jig to have some say in its design or construction if possible. He will work with it more happily under these circumstances. Not all machinists are co-operative to other people's ideas.

Methods of artificial lighting have improved considerably over the years, and it is not unusual to find both artificial and natural in use at the same time. Many machines have reduced voltage spot lamps fitted, and low voltage should be adhered to if the lighting unit is in danger of being fouled by the rotating parts of the machine. Where lighting is poor in a factory; general unrest will result, and a slowing down of production. Regulations say natural lighting should be provided if at all possible, but this, in any case, is limited only to certain months of the year. A.C. current which is normally used for lighting can have a stroboscopic effect on rotating objects, and make them appear to be stationary. It is a safety point to bear in mind when working with artificial lighting.

Most operatives in addition to agreed wages, are paid by results also. Methods of assessing these earnings in machine departments can either be by a collective process, or the individual. I quote these systems, as I consider the collective or group method to be the better from a safety point of view. With individual working, an operator tries to get rid of the work as quickly as possible, irrespective of quality and often safety also. With the collective method a sense of co-operation throughout is more in evidence. Poor quality work, requiring a second run through, affects the whole group. High standards of working are often accompanied by good standards of safety.

4. Additional lighting in close proximity to the point of operation can help the concentration of the machinist. These lights should be of reduced voltage to eliminate danger. Usually 25 volts obtained with the use of a mains transformer.

Grouped isolation switches and control point. A useful arrangement in a training establishment.

Safety on the planing machine

Modern planing machines are capable of working to very fine limits and, providing they are well maintained, they should give safe and efficient service. Statutory regulations require that all present-day surface planers which are fed by hand must be fitted with a circular, safety-type, cutter block. While this refinement will not prevent the user from accidentally putting his hand into the rotating cutters it may reduce the severity of the accident. A cutter block of this type can only remove a small amount per revolution. This cannot be said of the square block, as was in use on earlier machines.

An adjustable bridge guard is also required on a surface planer and this may be one of several types. The simplest is a piece of arched sheet metal mounted in an adjustable holder, as shown in fig. 1a. It should be long enough to bridge the entire length of the cutter block when required to do so. Its rigidity and design should be such that it will at no time come into contact with the rotating cutters. The guard should be easily adjustable and it is better to make adjustments before starting the machine. Only minor adjustments should be made with the machine running. These conditions also apply to the telescopic bridge guard (fig. 1b). The advantage of this type of guard is, of course, space saving, as it does not project far outside the machine when not in full-extent use. Other forms of bridge guards incorporating a link design are in use on machines mainly of Continental manufacture.

One strong reason why even fully experienced machinists should make efficient use of the bridge guard is that juniors or other trainees tend to copy their working procedure. It is much better to inherit a good habit than a bad one.

A section of the cutter that is not always guarded on older models of planing machines (and often on the combined planer and thicknesser) is the section between the back of the fence and the driving pulley. This can expose a considerable amount of cutting surface and is just the place a bi-standing junior may interest himself in. If the machine is positioned by a wall the need for protection at this point is not so great as if it is in a position of access from all sides. However, all parts of the cutter not in use should be adequately protected.

The surfacing of short material, say under 400 mm long, is a point which needs some consideration. The holding jig illustrated in fig. 2 makes this a safer proposition. Even with the jig in use only a fine cut should be attempted at one time. In the event of the wood tilting into the cutter while using the jig I doubt if the operator's

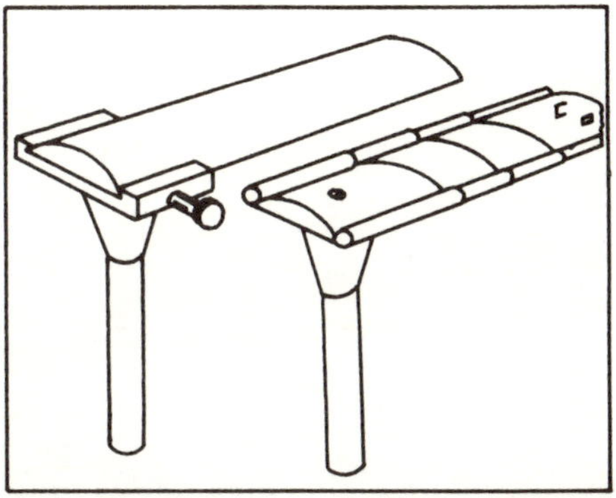

Adjustable and telescopic bridge guards, which must be fitted over surface planer cutters before the machines are used.

A jig for feeding short pieces of material into a planer.

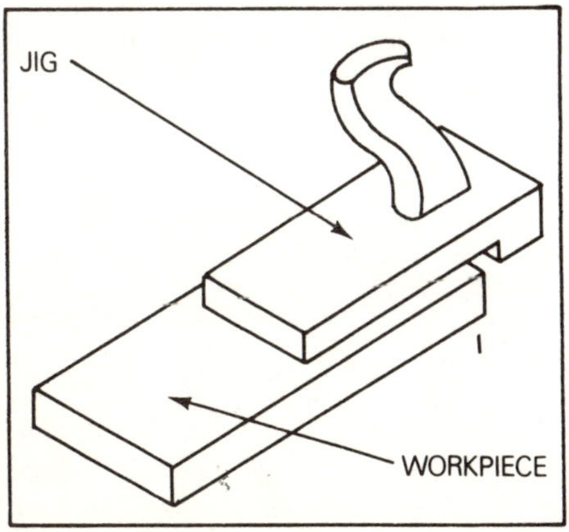

hand would ever reach the cutters, but he may get a kick that would draw his undivided attention if he was working carelessly!

When "dropping on," either for jobs like stop-chamfering or other decorative work, a back-stop should always be used to prevent the work from being thrown back when it comes into contact with the cutters. The degree of kick expected will, of course, be determined mainly by the amount of timber to be removed. This should receive consideration.

On the thicknessing machine the planing of short material needs careful attention to prevent kick-back. If the shorts are of sufficient length to be bridged by both feed rollers, theoretically the operation may be considered workable; but in practice this is not always the case. Short material in particular should always have a flat-faced side to lay on to the bed of the machine. If this is not so it is liable to spin around in the machine; then it may be struck by the revolving cutter-block and thrown out.

A method designed to prevent "shorts" from spinning off line in the machine is to fix two guide pieces on the table bed, a little wider apart than the width of the material to be planed. These guide pieces can either be bolted to the table or fixed with clamps.

Two other points worthy of mention with a view to accident prevention are:

(1) When inserting timber into an automatically fed machine it is not advisable to stand directly behind the line of feed. In the event of a throw-back, for any reason, the line of feed is the most dangerous zone.

(2) Never bend down and look directly into a thicknessing machine when planing timber. If you must look in, look from a corner or from behind. Better still, first stop the machine.

One modern aid to safer thicknessing is the introduction of the sectional feed roller and pressure bar. More than one piece of timber may be fed into the machine at one time with perfect safety, even if the timbers are of varying thicknesses. This means increased productivity and finish—in addition to increased safety. As the roller is broken up into a number of sections, individually sprung, the whole surface of timber in the machine receives pressure and feed instead of maybe only one corner of the thickest piece, as with the standard, solid feed-roller.

With increasing use of automation, accidents on woodworking machinery may tend to be caused by timber being ejected from automatically fed machines, while risks of trapping fingers and hands should decrease. This refers, of course, to the larger woodworking units. Automation should, however, reduce the accident rate providing safety is catered for in the design for advancement of the work. The sectional feed-roller, as illustrated, is an example of modern development to meet the requirements of the future.

Note bridge guard set over cutter. (Bursgreen Machine)

Bevelling operation on surface planer.

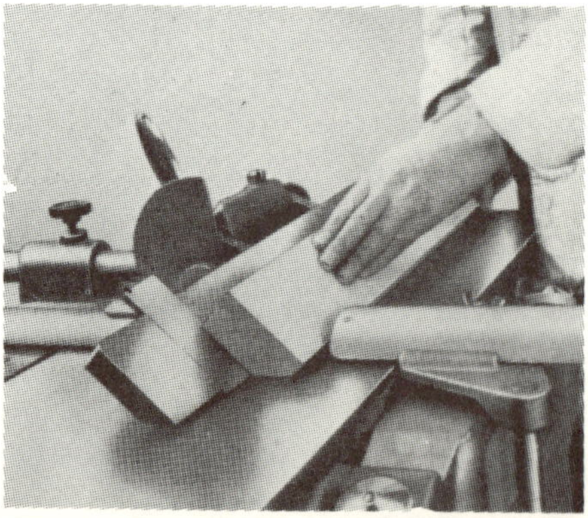

Comments on the Woodworking Machinery Regulations 1974

All persons involved in the use of woodworking machines should make themselves familiary with the current Regulation.

The Regulations are issued by the Home Office, and they have recently been revised, the changes becoming operational from November 1974. For existing machines a period of time has been allowed for some of the modifications to be made.

Many woodworking establishments will be affected by the introduction of the 1974 Regulations, and a few points are listed below in which they will probably be involved.

1 The amount of bench surface required on the circular saw, between the back of the blade and the taker off's position.
2 Sequence of operation of switch gear on a multi rotation speed machine.
3 Waste collection systems.
4 Limitation of operations on the surface planer.
5 Reference to noise.
6 Conditions relating to the sale or hiring of woodworking machines.
7 Training of operatives.

This list of points is not a complete one regarding changes to the Regulations from those in force prior to the Draft Regulations published in 1971 and 72. A study of the 1974 Regulations which follow these notes will reveal this.

The Woodworking Machinery Regulations are enforced by Law, and have to be complied with, usually to the satisfaction of the local Inspectorate. Experience has shown that situations do arise when an establishment is in doubt as to whether a new addition to the plant conforms to the Regulations. In cases of this type, it is customary to call in the Factory Inspector, who will make his recommendations.

Some safety-conscious establishments do operate accident prevention standards to a greater degree than those enforced by the Regulations. This makes the point quite clear that it can be beneficial to, add on, to accommodate such practices as the training of operatives, or carrying out work in, say, difficult environmental conditions. More information is given on previous pages.

1974 No. 903

FACTORIES

The Woodworking Machines Regulations 1974

Made - - - -	23*rd May* 1974
Laid before Parliament	10*th June* 1974
Coming into Operation— *All Regulations except Regulation* 41 -	24*th November* 1974
Regulation 41 - -	24*th May* 1976

Arrangement of Regulations

The Secretary of State:—

(*a*) in exercise of powers conferred by sections 17(3), 76 and 180(6) and (7) of the Factories Act 1961**(a)** and now vested in him **(b)** and of all other powers enabling him in that behalf; and

(*b*) after publishing, pursuant to Schedule 4 to the said Act of 1961, notice of the proposal to make the Regulations and after the holding of an inquiry under that Schedule into objections made to the draft,

hereby makes the following Regulations of which all with the exception of Regulation 15 are special Regulations:—

(a) 1961 c. 34. **(b)** S.I. 1968/729 (1968 II, p. 2108).

PART I

APPLICATION, INTERPRETATION AND EXEMPTIONS

Citation, commencement, revocation and amendment

1.—(1) These Regulations may be cited as the Woodworking Machines Regulations 1974 and shall come into operation on 24th November 1974 with the exception of Regulation 41 which shall come into operation on 24th May 1976.

(2) The Regulations specified in columns 1 and 2 of Schedule 2 to these Regulations are hereby revoked to the extent respectively specified in relation thereto in column 3 of that Schedule.

(3) Regulation 67(2) of the Shipbuilding and Ship-repairing Regulations 1960**(a)** and Regulation 42 of the Construction (General Provisions) Regulations 1961**(b)** shall not apply to the parts of woodworking machines required by these Regulations to be guarded or to have other safeguards.

Interpretation

2.—(1) The Interpretation Act 1889**(c)** shall apply to the interpretation of these Regulations as it applies to the interpretation of an Act of Parliament, and as if these Regulations and the Regulations hereby revoked were Acts of Parliament.

(2) In these Regulations, unless the context otherwise requires, the following expressions have the meanings hereby assigned to them respectively, that is to say:—

"approved" means approved for the time being for the purposes of these Regulations by certificate of the Chief Inspector;

"circular sawing machine" means a sawing machine comprising a saw bench (including a bench in the form of a roller table and a bench incorporating a travelling table) with a spindle situated below the machine table to which a circular saw blade can be fitted for the purpose of dividing material into separate parts, but does not include a multiple rip sawing machine, a straight line edging machine or any sawing machine in the operation of which the blade is moved towards the material which is being cut;

"cutters" include saw blades, chain cutters, knives, boring tools, detachable cutters and solid cutters;

"factory" includes any place to which these Regulations apply;

"machine table" includes, in relation to a circular sawing machine, any frame which supports the material being cut;

"narrow band sawing machine" means a sawing machine designed to be fitted with a blade not exceeding 50 millimetres in width in the form of a continuous band or strip the cutting portion of which runs in a vertical direction, but does not include a log band sawing machine or a band re-sawing machine;

"planing machine" means a machine for surfacing or for thicknessing or a combined machine for both those operations but does not include a multi-cutter moulding machine having two or more cutter spindles;

(a) S.I. 1960/1932 (1960 II, p. 1427). **(b)** S.I. 1961/1580 (1961 II, p. 3207).
(c) 1889 c. 63.

"principal Act" means the Factories Act 1961 as amended by or under any other Act;

"sawmill" means premises which are used solely or mainly for the purpose of sawing logs (including square logs) into planks or boards;

"squared stock" means material having a rectangular (including square) cross section of which the dimensions remain substantially constant throughout the length of the material;

"surfacing" means the planing or smoothing of the surface of material by passing it over cutters and includes chamfering and bevelling, but does not include moulding, tenoning, rebating or recessing;

"vertical spindle moulding machine" includes a high-speed routing machine; and

"woodworking machine" means any machine (including a portable machine) of a kind specified in Schedule 1 to these Regulations for use on all or any one or more of the following, that is to say, wood, cork and fibre board and material composed partly of any of those materials.

Application and operation of Regulations

3.—(1) These Regulations, other than Regulation 15 (which relates to the sale or hire of machinery), shall apply to any of the following, in which any woodworking machine is used, that is to say, to factories and to any premises, places, processes, operations and works to which the provisions of Part IV of the principal Act with respect to special regulations for safety and health are applied by any of the following provisions of that Act, namely, section 123 (which relates to electrical stations), section 124 (which relates to institutions), section 125 (which relates to certain dock premises and certain warehouses), section 126 (which relates to ships) and section 127 (which relates to building operations and works of engineering construction).

(2) In relation to the parts of woodworking machines required by these Regulations to be guarded or to have other safeguards, the provisions of these Regulations as respects guarding and the provision of other safeguards are in substitution for the provisions of section 14(1) of the principal Act and accordingly the provisions of that subsection shall not apply in relation to any such parts.

(3) The provisions of Regulation 12 are in substitution for section 3(1) of the principal Act and accordingly the provisions of that subsection shall not apply in relation to any room to which that Regulation applies.

(4) Except as provided in paragraphs (2) and (3) of this Regulation, the provisions of these Regulations shall be in addition to and not in substitution for the provisions of the principal Act.

Exemptions

4. The Chief Inspector may (subject to such conditions, if any, as may be specified therein) by certificate in writing (which he may in his discretion revoke at any time) exempt from all or any of the requirements of these Regulations—

(*a*) any particular woodworking machine or any type of woodworking machine; or

(*b*) any operation or process or any class or description of operations or processes; or

(c) any factory or any part of any factory or any class or description of factories or parts thereof,

if he is satisfied that the requirements in respect of which the exemption is granted are not necessary for the protection of persons employed. Where such exemption is granted, a legible copy of the certificate, showing the conditions (if any) subject to which it has been granted, shall be kept posted in any factory in which the exemption applies in a position where it may be conveniently read by the persons employed.

PART II

ALL WOODWORKING MACHINES—GENERAL

Provision and construction of guards

5.—(1) Without prejudice to the other provisions of these Regulations, the cutters of every woodworking machine shall be enclosed by a guard or guards to the greatest extent that is practicable having regard to the work being done thereat, unless the cutters are in such position as to be as safe to every person employed as they would be if so enclosed.

(2) All guards provided in pursuance of the foregoing paragraph of this Regulation shall be of substantial construction.

Adjustment of machines and guards

6. No person shall, while the cutters are in motion—

(*a*) make any adjustment to any guard on a woodworking machine unless means are provided whereby such an adjustment can be made without danger; or

(*b*) make any adjustment to any part of a woodworking machine, except where the adjustment can be made without danger.

Use and maintenance of guards, etc.

7.—(1) At all times while the cutters are in motion, the guards and devices required by these Regulations and all such safeguards as are mentioned in Regulation 8 shall be kept constantly in position and properly secured and adjusted except when, and to the extent to which, because of the nature of the work being done, the use of any such guard, device, or safeguard is rendered impracticable:

Provided that the said exception shall not apply to the use of any guard required by Regulations 18(1), 21(1) or (2), 22(1), 23, 28, 30 or 31.

(2) The said guards, devices, and safeguards, and all such appliances as are mentioned in Regulation 14(1)(*b*) shall be properly maintained.

Exception from obligations to provide guards, etc.

8. Regulations 5, 16, 21, 22, 26, 28, 30, 31 and 36 shall not apply to any machine in respect of which other safeguards are provided which render the machine as safe as it would be if the provisions of those Regulations were complied with.

Machine controls

9. Every woodworking machine shall be provided with an efficient device or efficient devices for starting and stopping the machine and the control or controls of the device or devices shall be in such a position and of such design and construction as to be readily and conveniently operated by the person operating the machine.

Working space

10. There shall be provided around every woodworking machine sufficient clear and unobstructed space to enable, in so far as is thereby practicable, the work being done at the machine to be done without risk of injury to persons employed.

Floors

11. The floor or surface of the ground around every woodworking machine shall be maintained in good and level condition and, as far as reasonably practicable, free from chips and other loose material and shall not be allowed to become slippery.

Temperature

12.—(1) Subject to the following provisions of this Regulation, effective provision shall be made for securing and maintaining a reasonable temperature in every room or other place (not in the open air) in which a woodworking machine is being worked.

(2) In that part of any room or other place (not in the open air) in which a woodworking machine is being worked, a temperature of less than 13 degrees Celsius shall not be deemed at any time to be a reasonable temperature except where and in so far as the necessities of the business carried on make it impracticable to maintain a temperature of at least 13 degrees Celsius.

(3) Where it is impracticable for the aforesaid reasons to maintain a temperature of at least 13 degrees Celsius in any such part of a room or place as aforesaid, there shall be provided in the said part, to the extent that is reasonably practicable, effective means of warming persons working there.

(4) There shall not be used in any such room or place as aforesaid any heating appliance other than an appliance in which the heating element or flame is so enclosed within the body of the appliance that there is no likelihood of the accidental ignition of any material in that room or place by reason of contact with or proximity to the heating element or any flame, except where the heating appliance is so positioned or protected that there is no such likelihood.

(5) Paragraphs (2) and (3) of this Regulation shall in their application to parts of factories which are used as sawmills have effect as if for the references to 13 degrees Celsius there were substituted references to 10 degrees Celsius.

(6) No method of heating shall be employed which results in the escape into the air of any such room or place as aforesaid of any fume of such a character and to such extent as to be likely to be injurious or offensive to persons employed therein.

Training

13.—(1) No person shall be employed on any kind of work at a woodworking machine unless—

(*a*) he has been sufficiently trained at machines of a class to which that machine belongs in the kind of work on which he is to be employed; and

(*b*) he has been sufficiently instructed in accordance with paragraph (2) of this Regulation,

except where he works under the adequate supervision of a person who has a thorough knowledge and experience of the working of the machine and of the matters specified in paragraph (2) of this Regulation.

(2) Every person, while being trained to work at a woodworking machine, shall be fully and carefully instructed as to the dangers arising in connection with such machine, the precautions to be observed, the requirements of these Regulations which apply and, in the case of a person being trained to operate a woodworking machine, the method of using the guards, devices and appliances required by these Regulations.

(3) Without prejudice to the foregoing provisions of this Regulation, a person who has not attained the age of 18 years shall not operate any circular sawing machine, any sawing machine fitted with a circular blade, any planing machine for surfacing which is not mechanically fed, or any vertical spindle moulding machine, unless he has successfully completed an approved course of training in the operation of such a machine. Save that where required to do so as part of such a course of training, he may operate such a machine under the adequate supervision of a person who has a thorough knowledge and experience of the working of the machine and of the matters specified in paragraph (2) of this Regulation.

Duties of persons employed

14.—(1) Every person employed shall, while he is operating a woodworking machine—

(*a*) use and keep in proper adjustment the guards and devices provided in accordance with these Regulations and all such safeguards as are mentioned in Regulation 8; and

(*b*) use the spikes, push-sticks, push-blocks, jigs, holders and back stops provided in accordance with these Regulations,

except (in cases other than those specified in the proviso to Regulation 7(1)) when, because of the nature of the work being done, the use of the said guards, devices or other safeguards, or of the appliances mentioned in sub-paragraph (*b*) of this paragraph, is rendered impracticable.

(2) It shall be the duty of every person, being a person employed by the occupier of a factory and trained in accordance with Regulation 13, who discovers any defect in any woodworking machine in that factory or in any guard, device or appliance provided in accordance with these Regulations or in any such safeguard as is mentioned in Regulation 8 (being a defect which may affect the safe working of a woodworking machine) or who discovers that the floor or surface of the ground around any woodworking machine in that factory is not in good and level condition or is slippery, to report the matter without delay to the occupier, manager or other appropriate person.

Sale or hire of machinery

15. The provisions of section 17(2) of the principal Act (which prohibits the sale or letting on hire of certain machines which do not comply with the requirements of that section) shall extend to any woodworking machine which is for use in a factory and which is not provided with such guards or devices as are necessary, and is not so designed and constructed as, to enable any requirement of the following Regulations to be complied with, that is to say, Regulations 9, 16, 17(3), 21, 22, 24, 25, 26, 27, 28, 30, 31 and 39 in so far as the requirement applies to that woodworking machine.

PART III

CIRCULAR SAWING MACHINES

Guarding of circular sawing machines

16.—(1) That part of the saw blade of every circular sawing machine which is below the machine table shall be guarded to the greatest extent that is practicable.

(2) There shall be provided for every circular sawing machine a riving knife which shall be securely fixed by means of a suitable device situated below the machine table, be behind and in a direct line with the saw blade, have a smooth surface, be strong, rigid and easily adjustable and fulfil the following conditions:—

(*a*) the edge of the knife nearer the saw blade shall form an arc of a circle having a radius not exceeding the radius of the largest saw blade with which the saw bench is designed to be used;

(*b*) the knife shall be capable of being so adjusted and shall be kept so adjusted that it is as close as practicable to the saw blade, having regard to the nature of the work being done, and so that at the level of the machine table the distance between the edge of the knife nearer to the saw blade and the teeth of the saw blade does not exceed 12 millimetres;

(*c*) for a saw blade of a diameter of less than 600 millimetres, the knife shall extend upwards from the machine table, to a height above the machine table which is not more than 25 millimetres below the highest point of the saw blade, and for a saw blade of a diameter of 600 millimetres or over, the knife shall extend upwards from the machine table to a height of at least 225 millimetres above the machine table; and

(*d*) in the case of a parallel plate saw blade the knife shall be thicker than the plate of the saw blade.

(3) Without prejudice to the requirements of Regulation 18(1), that part of the saw blade of every circular sawing machine which is above the machine table shall be guarded with a strong and easily adjustable guard, which shall be capable of being so adjusted and shall be kept so adjusted that it extends from the top of the riving knife to a point above the upper surface of the material being cut which is as close as practicable to that surface or, where squared stock is being fed to the saw blade by hand, to a point which is not more than 12 millimetres above the upper surface of the material being cut.

(4) The guard referred to in the last foregoing paragraph shall have a flange of adequate depth on each side of the saw blade and the said guard shall be kept so adjusted that the said flanges extend beyond the roots of the teeth of the saw blade. Where the guard is fitted with an adjustable front extension piece, that extension piece shall have along the whole of its length a flange of adequate depth on the side remote from the fence and the said extension piece shall be kept so adjusted that the flange extends beyond the roots of the teeth of the saw blade:

Provided that in the case of circular sawing machines manufactured before the date of the coming into operation of this Regulation, the requirements of this paragraph shall not apply until two years after the said date and in the case of such machines, until the expiration of the said period, the said guard shall have along the whole of its length a flange of adequate depth on the side remote from the fence and shall be kept so adjusted that the said flange extends beyond the roots of the teeth of the saw blade.

Sizes of circular saw blades

17.—(1) In the case of a circular sawing machine the spindle of which is not capable of being operated at more than one working speed, no saw blade shall be used thereat for dividing material into separate parts which has a diameter of less than six-tenths of the diameter of the largest saw blade with which the saw bench is designed to be used.

(2) In the case of a circular sawing machine which has arrangements for the spindle to operate at more than one working speed, no saw blade shall be used thereat for dividing material into separate parts which has a diameter of less than six-tenths of the diameter of the largest saw blade which can properly be used at the fastest working speed of the spindle at that saw bench.

(3) There shall be securely affixed to every circular sawing machine a notice specifying the diameter of the smallest saw blade which may be used in the machine in compliance with paragraph (1) or (2) (as the case may be) of this Regulation.

Limitations on the use of circular sawing machines for certain purposes

18.—(1) No circular sawing machine shall be used for cutting any rebate, tenon, mould or groove, unless that part of the saw blade or other cutter which is above the machine table is effectively guarded.

(2) No circular sawing machine shall be used for a ripping operation (other than any such operation involved in cutting a rebate, tenon, mould or groove) unless the teeth of the saw blade project throughout the operation through the upper surface of the material being cut.

(3) No circular sawing machine shall be used for cross-cutting logs or branches unless the material being cut is firmly held by a gripping device securely fixed to a travelling table.

Provision of push-sticks

19.—(1) A suitable push-stick shall be provided and kept available for use at every circular sawing machine which is fed by hand.

(2) Except where the distance between a circular saw blade and its fence is so great or the method of feeding material to the saw blade is such that the use of a push-stick can safely be dispensed with, the push-stick so provided shall be used—

(*a*) to exert feeding pressure on the material between the saw blade and the fence throughout any cut of 300 millimetres or less in length;

(*b*) to exert feeding pressure on the material between the saw blade and the fence during the last 300 millimetres of any cut of more than 300 millimetres in length; and

(*c*) to remove from between the saw blade and the fence pieces of material which have been cut.

Removal of material cut by circular sawing machines

20.—(1) Except as provided in paragraph (3) of this Regulation, where any person (other than the operator) is employed at a circular sawing machine in removing while the saw blade is in motion material which has been cut, that person shall not for that purpose stand elsewhere than at the delivery end of the machine.

(2) Except as provided in paragraph (3) of this Regulation, where any person (other than the operator) is employed at a circular sawing machine in removing while the saw blade is in motion material which has been cut, the machine table shall be constructed or shall be extended over its whole width (by the provision of rollers or otherwise) so that the distance between the delivery end of the table or of any such extension thereof and the up-running part of the saw blade is not less than 1200 millimetres. Provided that this requirement shall not apply to moveable machines which cannot accommodate a blade having a diameter of more than 450 millimetres.

(3) The requirements of paragraphs (1) and (2) of this Regulation shall not apply to a circular sawing machine having a saw bench in the form of a roller table or a saw bench incorporating a travelling table which (in either case) is in motion during the cutting operation.

PART IV

MULTIPLE RIP SAWING MACHINES AND STRAIGHT LINE EDGING MACHINES

Multiple rip sawing machines and straight line edging machines

21.—(1) Every multiple rip sawing machine and straight line edging machine shall be provided on the operator's side of the in-feed pressure rollers with a suitable device which shall be of such design and so constructed as to contain so far as practicable any material accidentally ejected by the machine and every such device shall extend for not less than the full width of the said pressure rollers.

(2) Every multiple rip sawing machine and straight line edging machine on which the saw spindle is mounted above the machine table shall, in addition to the device required to be provided under paragraph (1) of this Regulation, be fitted on the side remote from the fence with a suitable guard, which shall extend from the edge of the said device along a line parallel to the blade of the saw at least 300 millimetres towards the axis of the saw and shall be of such a design and so constructed as to contain as far as practicable any material accidentally ejected from the machine.

(3) In the case of multiple rip sawing machines and straight line edging machines manufactured before the date of the coming into operation of this Regulation, the requirements of this Regulation shall not apply until two years after the said date.

Part V

Narrow Band Sawing Machines

Narrow band sawing machines

22.—(1) The saw wheels of every narrow band sawing machine and the whole of the blade of every such machine, except that part of the blade which runs downwards between the top wheel and the machine table, shall be enclosed by a guard or guards of substantial construction.

(2) That part of the blade of every such machine as aforesaid which is above the friction disc or rollers and below the top wheel shall be guarded by a frontal plate which is as close as is practicable to the saw blade and has at least one flange at right angles to the plate and extending behind the saw blade.

(3) The friction disc or rollers of every such machine as aforesaid shall be kept so adjusted that they are as close to the surface of the machine table as is practicable having regard to the nature of the work being done.

Part VI

Planing Machines

Limitation on the use of planing machines

23. No planing machine shall be used for cutting any rebate, recess, tenon or mould unless the cutter is effectively guarded.

Cutter blocks for planing machines for surfacing

24. Every planing machine for surfacing which is not mechanically fed shall be fitted with a cylindrical cutter block.

Table gap

25.—(1) Every planing machine for surfacing which is not mechanically fed shall be so designed and constructed as to be capable of adjustment so that the clearance between the cutters and the front edge of the delivery table does not exceed 6 millimetres (measured radially from the centre of the cutter block) and the gap between the feed table and the delivery table is as small as practicable having regard to the operation being performed, and no such planing machine which is not so adjusted shall be used for surfacing.

(2) In the case of planing machines manufactured before the date of the coming into operation of this Regulation, the requirements of the foregoing paragraph of this Regulation shall not apply until twelve months after the said date.

Provision of bridge guards

26.—(1) Every planing machine for surfacing which is not mechanically fed shall be provided with a bridge guard which shall be strong and rigid, have a length not less than the full length of the cutter block and a width not less than the diameter of the cutter block and be so constructed as to be capable of easy adjustment both in a vertical and horizontal direction.

(2) Every bridge guard provided in pursuance of paragraph (1) of this Regulation shall be mounted on the machine in a position which is approximately central over the axis of the cutter block and shall be so constructed as to prevent its being accidentally displaced from that position.

(3) In the case of planing machines manufactured before the date of the coming into operation of this Regulation, the requirements of this Regulation shall not apply until twelve months after the said date, and until the expiration of the said period such machines for surfacing shall be provided with a bridge guard capable of covering the full length and breadth of the cutting slot in the bench and so constructed as to be easily adjusted both in a vertical and horizontal direction.

Adjustment of bridge guards

27.—(1) While a planing machine which is not mechanically fed is being used for surfacing, the bridge guard provided in pursuance of Regulation 26 shall be so adjusted as to enable, so far as is thereby practicable, the work being done at the machine to be done without risk of injury to persons employed.

(2) Except as provided in paragraph (4) of this Regulation and in Regulation 29, when a wider surface of squared stock is being planed or smoothed, the bridge guard so provided shall be adjusted so that the distance between the end of the guard and the fence does not exceed 10 millimetres and the underside of the guard is not more than 10 millimetres above the upper surface of the material.

(3) Except as provided in paragraph (4) of this Regulation, when a narrower surface of squared stock is being planed or smoothed, the bridge guard so provided shall be adjusted so that the end of the guard is at a point not more than 10 millimetres from the surface of the said material which is remote from the fence and the underside of the guard is not more than 10 millimetres above the surface of the feed table.

(4) When the planing or smoothing both of a wider and of a narrower surface of squared stock is being carried out, one operation immediately following the other, the bridge guard so provided shall be adjusted so that when a wider surface is being planed or smoothed the underside of the guard is not more than 10 millimetres above the upper surface of the material and, when a narrower surface is being planed or smoothed, the end of the guard is at a point not more than 10 millimetres from the surface of the said material which is remote from the fence.

(5) Except as provided in paragraph (6) of this Regulation, when the planing of squared stock of square cross section is being carried out, the bridge guard so provided shall be adjusted in a manner which complies with the requirements either of paragraph (2) or of paragraph (3) of this Regulation.

(6) When the planing of two adjoining surfaces of squared stock of square cross section is being carried out, one operation immediately following the other, the bridge guard so provided shall be adjusted so that neither the height of the underside of the guard above the feed table nor the distance between the end of the guard and the fence exceeds the width of the material by more than 10 millimetres.

(7) When the smoothing of squared stock of square cross section is being carried out, the bridge guard so provided shall be adjusted in a manner which complies with the requirements either of paragraph (2) or of paragraph (3) or of paragraph (6) of this Regulation.

Cutter block guards

28.—(1) In addition to being provided with a bridge guard as required by Regulation 26, every planing machine for surfacing which is not mechanically fed shall be provided with a strong, effective and easily adjustable guard for that part of the cutter block which is on the side of the fence remote from the bridge guard.

(2) In the case of planing machines manufactured before the date of the coming into operation of this Regulation, the requirements of the foregoing paragraph of this Regulation shall not apply until twelve months after the said date.

Provision and use of push-blocks

29. When a wider surface of squared stock is being planed or smoothed and by reason of the shortness of the material the work cannot be done with the bridge guard adjusted as required by Regulation 27(2), a suitable push-block having suitable handholds which afford the operator a firm grip shall be provided and used.

Combined machines used for thicknessing

30. That part of the cutter block of a combined machine which is exposed in the table gap shall, when the said machine is used for thicknessing, be effectively guarded.

Protection against ejected material

31.—(1) Every planing machine used for thicknessing shall be provided on the operator's side of the feed roller with sectional feed rollers, or other suitable devices which shall be of such a design and so constructed as to restrain so far as practicable any workpiece ejected by the machine.

(2) Paragraph (1) of this Regulation shall not apply to any machine manufactured before the date of coming into operation of this Regulation; provided that—

(*a*) not more than one work piece at a time shall be fed to any such machine, and

(*b*) there shall be securely affixed to every such machine a notice specifying that only single pieces shall be fed.

PART VII

VERTICAL SPINDLE MOULDING MACHINES

Construction, maintenance and mounting of cutters etc.

32. Every detachable cutter for any vertical spindle moulding machine shall be of the correct thickness for the cutter block or spindle on which it is to be mounted and shall be so mounted as to prevent it, so far as practicable, from becoming accidentally detached therefrom.

Provision of false fences

33. Where straight fences are being used for the purposes of the work being done at a vertical spindle moulding machine, the gap between the fences shall be reduced as far as practicable by a false fence or otherwise.

Provision of jigs or holders

34. Where by reason of the nature of the work being done at a vertical spindle moulding machine it is impracticable to provide in pursuance of Regulation 5 a guard enclosing the cutters of the said machine to such an extent that they are effectively guarded, but it is practicable to provide, in addition to the guard required to be provided by Regulation 5, a jig or holder of such a design and so constructed as to hold firmly the material being machined and having suitable handholds which afford the operator a firm grip, the machine shall not be used unless such a jig or holder is provided.

Design and construction of guards for protection against ejected parts

35. Every guard provided in pursuance of Regulation 5 for the cutters of any vertical spindle moulding machine shall be of such a design and so constructed as to contain, so far as reasonably practicable, any part of the cutters or their fixing appliances or any part thereof in the event of their ejection.

Provision and use of back stops

36. Where the work being done at a vertical spindle moulding machine is work in which the cutting of the material being machined commences otherwise than at the end of a surface of the said material and it is impracticable to provide a jig or holder in pursuance of Regulation 34, the trailing end of the said material shall if practicable be supported by a suitable back stop where this would prevent the said material being thrown back when the cutters first make contact with it.

Limitation on the use of vertical spindle moulding machines

37. No work shall be done on a vertical spindle moulding machine being work in which the cutting of the material being machined commences otherwise than at the end of a surface of the said material and during the progress of the cutting the material is moved in the same direction as the movement of the cutters, unless a jig or holder provided in pursuance of Regulation 34 is being used.

Provision of spikes or push-sticks

38. Where the nature of the work being performed at a vertical spindle moulding machine is such that the use of a suitable spike or push-stick would enable the work to be carried on without unnecessary risk, such a spike or push-stick shall be provided and kept available for use.

Machines driven by two speed motors

39.—(1) Where the motor driving a vertical spindle moulding machine (other than a high-speed routing machine) is designed to operate at two working speeds the device controlling the speed of the motor shall be so arranged that the motor cannot run at the higher of those speeds, without first running at the lower of those speeds.

(2) In the case of machines manufactured before the coming into operation of this Regulation, the requirements of the foregoing paragraph of this Regulation shall not apply until twelve months after the said date.

PART VIII

EXTRACTION EQUIPMENT AND MAINTENANCE

Cleaning of saw blades

40. The blade of a sawing machine shall not be cleaned by hand while the blade is in motion.

Extraction of chips and other particles

41. Effective exhaust appliances shall be provided and maintained at every planing machine used for thicknessing other than a combined machine for surfacing and thicknessing, every vertical spindle moulding machine, every multi-cutter moulding machine, every tenoning machine and every automatic lathe, for collecting from a position as close to the cutters as practicable and to the extent that is practicable, the chips and other particles of material removed by the action of the cutters and for discharging them into a suitable receptacle or place:

Provided that this Regulation shall not apply to any high-speed routing machine which incorporates means for blowing away from the cutters the chips or particles as they are removed or to either of the following which is not used for more than six hours in any week, that is to say, any vertical spindle moulding machine and any tenoning machine.

Maintenance and fixing

42.—(1) Every woodworking machine and every part thereof, including cutters and cutter blocks, shall be of good construction, sound material and properly maintained.

(2) Every woodworking machine, other than a machine which is held in the hand, shall be securely fixed to a foundation, floor, or to a substantial part of the structure of the premises, save that where this is impracticable, other arrangements shall be made to ensure its stability.

PART IX

LIGHTING

Lighting

43. In addition to the requirements of subsections (1) and (4) of section 5 of the principal Act and the Factories (Standards of Lighting) Regulations 1941**(a)**, the following provisions shall have effect in respect of any work done with any woodworking machine:—

(*a*) the lighting, whether natural or artifical, for every woodworking machine shall be sufficient and suitable for the purpose for which the machine is used;

(*b*) the means of artificial lighting for every woodworking machine shall be so placed or shaded as to prevent glare and so that direct rays of light do not impinge on the eyes of the operator while he is operating such machine.

(a) S. R. & O. 1941/94 (Rev. VII, p. III: 1941 I, p. 280).

Part X

Noise

Noise

44. where any factory, or any part thereof, is mainly used for work carried out on woodworking machines, the following provisions shall apply to that factory or part, as the case may be:—

(*a*) where on any day any person employed is likely to be exposed continuously for 8 hours to a sound level of 90dB(A) or is likely to be subject to an equivalent or greater exposure to sound—

(i) such measures as are reasonably practicable shall be taken to reduce noise to the greatest extent which is reasonably practicable; and

(ii) suitable ear protectors shall be provided and made readily available for the use of every such person;

(*b*) all ear protectors provided in pursuance of the foregoing paragraph shall be maintained, and shall be used by the person for whom they are provided in any of the circumstances specified in paragraph (*a*) of this Regulation;

(*c*) for the purposes of paragraph (*a*) of this Regulation, the level of exposure which is equivalent to or greater than continuous exposure for 8 hours to a sound level of 90 dB(A) shall be determined by an approved method.

Signed by order of the Secretary of State.

Harold Walker,
Joint Parliamentary Under Secretary of State,
Department of Employment.

23rd May 1974.

SCHEDULE 1

Regulation 2(2)

Machines which are woodworking machines for the purposes of these Regulations

1. Any sawing machine designed to be fitted with one or more circular blades.
2. Grooving machines.
3. Any sawing machine designed to be fitted with a blade in the form of a continuous band or strip.
4. Chain sawing machines.
5. Mortising machines.
6. Planing machines.
7. Vertical spindle moulding machines (including high-speed routing machines).
8. Multi-cutter moulding machines having two or more cutter spindles.
9. Tenoning machines.
10. Trenching machines.
11. Automatic and semi-automatic lathes.
12. Boring machines.

SCHEDULE 2

Column 1 Regulations revoked	Column 2 References	Column 3 Extent of Revocation
1. The Woodworking Machinery Regulations 1922.	S.R. & O. 1922/1196 (Rev. VII, p. 458: 1922, p. 273).	The whole Regulations.
2. The Woodworking Machinery (Amendment) Regulations 1927.	S.R. & O. 1927/207 (Rev. VII, p. 462: 1927, p. 440).	The whole Regulations.
3. The Woodworking (Amendment of Scope) Special Regulations 1945.	S.R. & O. 1945/1227 (Rev. VII, p. 462: 1945 I, p. 380).	The whole Regulations.
4. The Railway Running Sheds (No. 2) Regulations 1961.	S.I. 1961/1768 (1961 III, p. 3410).	In the Schedule, the items numbered 2, 5 and 9.

EXPLANATORY NOTE

(This Note is not part of the Regulations.)

These Regulations impose requirements as to guards and certain other safety devices for woodworking machines used in factories and certain other places to which the Factories Act 1961 applies.

The Regulations also impose requirements as to working space, condition of floors, noise, lighting and temperature in those factories and places and as to the training of persons operating woodworking machines.

The Regulations prohibit the sale or letting on hire for use in factories and other places to which the Regulations apply of woodworking machines which do not comply with specified provisions of the Regulations as to guards and other safety devices.

As respects guards and other safeguards for woodworking machines, the provisions of the Regulations are in substitution for the provisions of section 14(1) of the Factories Act 1961 and as respects the temperature of rooms, they are in substitution for the similar provisions of section 3(1) of the said Act.

Regulation 67(2) of the Shipbuilding and Ship-repairing Regulations 1960 and Regulation 42 of the Construction (General Provisions) Regulations 1961 (which require the secure fencing of dangerous parts of machinery) are amended so that they no longer apply to the parts of woodworking machines required by these Regulations to be guarded or to have other safeguards.

The Regulations supersede the Woodworking Machinery Special Regulations 1922 to 1945 which are revoked.

Section 6 Construction topics

Georgian Bow Window. Reply to problem

Planning details. Opening saches. Material sections. Glass sizes. Stormproof sashes. Material list. Cost 1972.

Getting the Most Out of Chipboard

Product design. Use of solid timber. Material content. Density. Tungsten carbide tipped saws. Tongues and grooves. Fixing bearers.

Louvres. Their Design and Construction

Decorative features. Angle of slats. Trenching methods. Dado heads. "Louvre lath" system.

Drawer Design and Construction

Fourcutting sections. Moisture content. Drawer front design. Guide methods. Application of adhesives. Time-saving methods.

Dovetailing with the Spindle Moulder

Pitch of cutters. Depth of pin. Types of drawer fronts. Spindle speed. Eliminating splintering.

Multi-Spindle Dovetailing

Life of cutters. Cutter sharpening. Planning cutter sets. Machine loading. Work holding methods. Curved work. Cupboard construction.

Ladderback Chair in Pine

Component plan. Cutting list. Upholstery details. Lathe work. Joint design. Order of assembly.

Dressing Stool

Setting out. Construction details. Upholstery details. Cutting list.

Chain Link Fruit Bowl

Geometrical setting out. Laminating material. Method of gluing. Turning in lathe. Cutting list.

Constructing Honours Board. Reply to problem

Period design. Dentil mouldings. Contemporary design. Mould sections.

Aid to Woodworking:

Need for skilled assistant. Machine preparation. No failures. Metric measurement. Advantages.

How to Plan a Woodwork Room

Age groups. Types of benches. Tool storage and control. Tool quantities. Use of power tools. Introduction of machines.

Georgian bow window

Reply to a Problem

PROBLEM

I have to install a Georgian type bow window. Unfortunately, I have been unable to obtain any details of construction.

I would be pleased if you will let me have any information that is available, or advice on the construction and installation of a window 7ft. 10in. wide by 4ft. 6in. high.

L.F.P.

SOLUTION

Having recently constructed a bow window 8ft. by 5ft., and installed it in a home extension, I can offer querist the benefit of my personal experience.

In my case, and this probably applies to querist also, the window is the only one in the room, and, therefore, has to be provided with opening sashes to conform with the Building Regulations. The opening sections must total not less than 1/20th of the floor area. If other windows are available to provide the necessary ventilation in the room, as in the case of a through lounge for instance, the construction of the bow window could take a different form from the one described here—being more of an assembly of glazing bars within a frame.

It is advisable to draw out full-size a horizontal and vertical section through the proposed window to enable the various measurements, joint locations, and bevels to be obtained. The

A. Sections show how the window is built up in a series of similar frames. Only the outer edge of the head and sill has curvature.

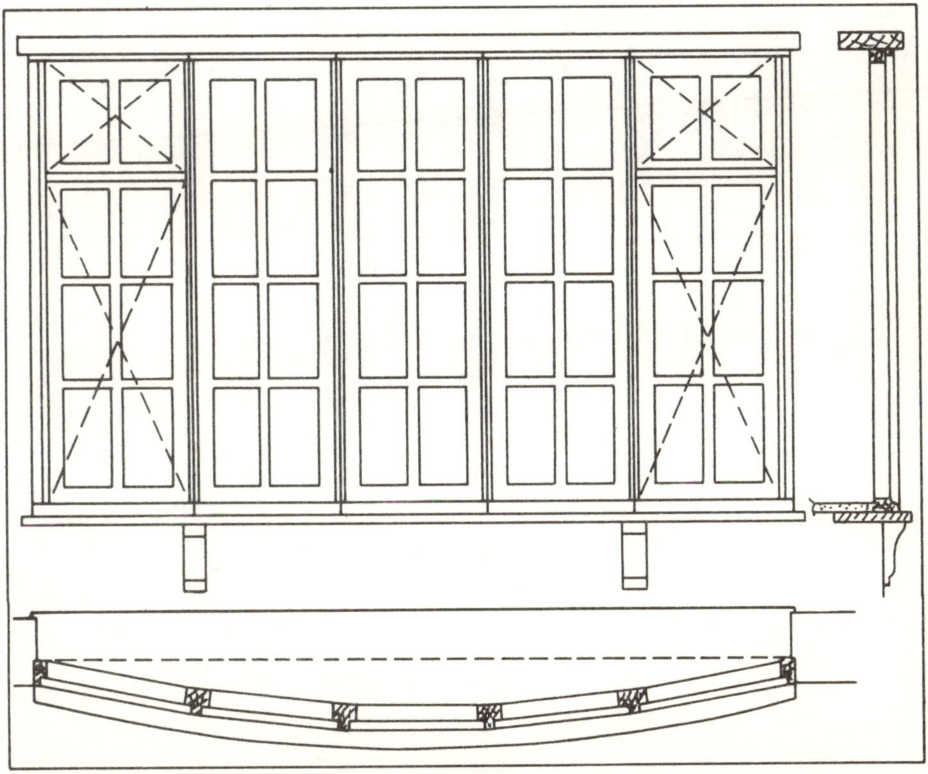

1. Recently constructed window measuring 8ft. by 5ft. constructed by the method described in this answer.

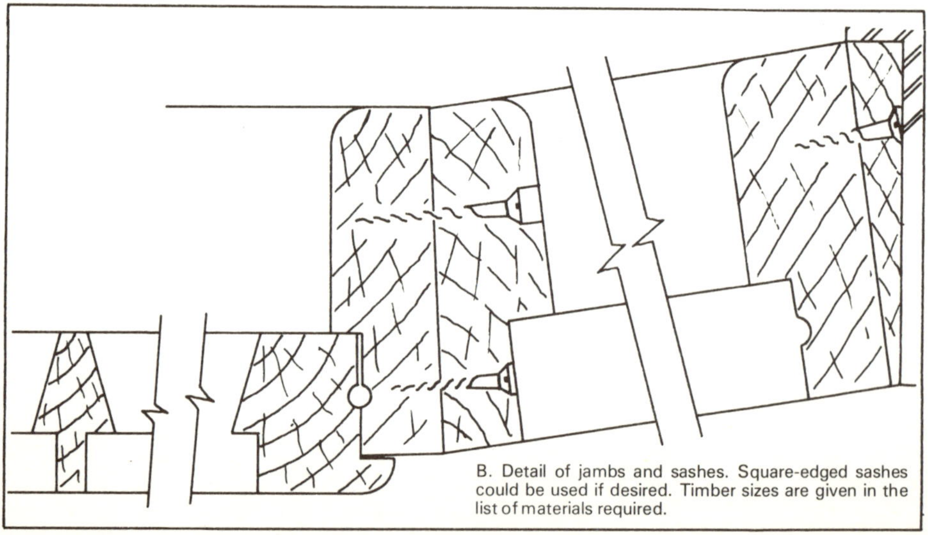

B. Detail of jambs and sashes. Square-edged sashes could be used if desired. Timber sizes are given in the list of materials required.

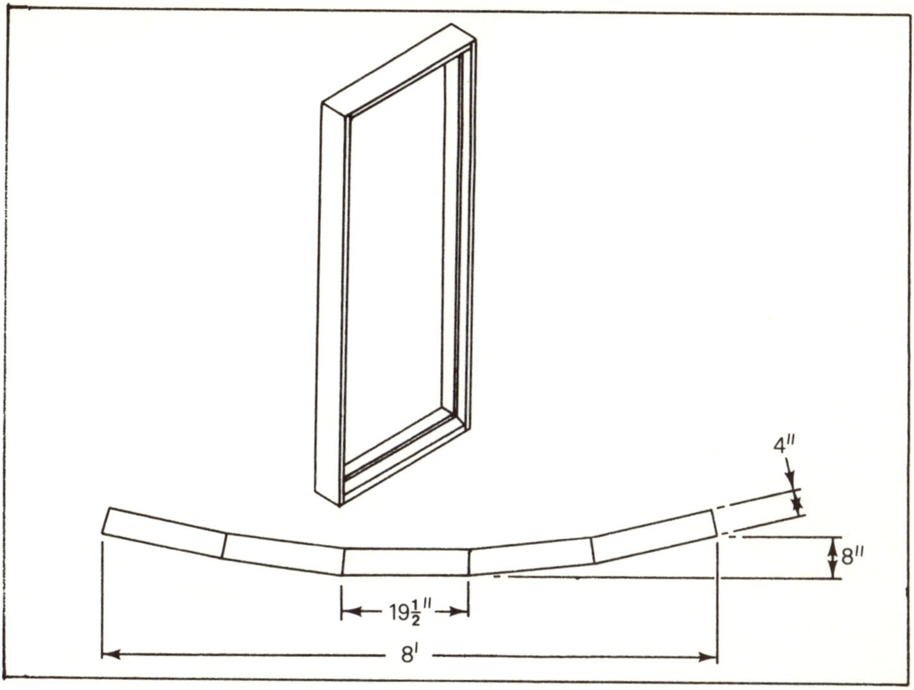

projection of the bowed curve in the case of my 8ft. window was 8in., so this could be reduced for a 7ft. 10in. unit.

In Georgian window design the relation between the height of the glass panes and the width can be important if the full period effect is to be obtained. From my experience of making an 8ft. by 5ft. window I can say that 7ft. 10in. by 4ft. 6in. will give a better pane size using the same form of construction.

For the convenience of a one-off job I would recommend that the window should be built up in five frame units plus a through sill and head. The outer edges only are shaped to give the bow on head and sill.

Transomes are added to the frames which require opening sashes, the other frames have fixed sashes the full height of the frames. The bow effect is obtained by applying about ½ in. of bevel to the vertical edges of the five frames. Rebates for sashes are formed before assembly of the frames, but the inner edge can be moulded after assembly with a portable router if desired.

Stormproof type sashes admit more light than square edged, due to the increase in overlap of timber. Synthetic resin adhesive should be used for bonding the various members and frames to-

C. To simplify setting out, plywood patterns can be made to fit the required opening. The edge bevel of the frames can also be determined.

D. This information may be of interest to querist, if he wishes to apply it. It shows the method used to determine the proportion of width to height of a Georgian window pane. This could also be calculated:

$$\frac{\text{width of glass}}{\cos 45\ \text{deg.}} = \text{height of glass.}$$

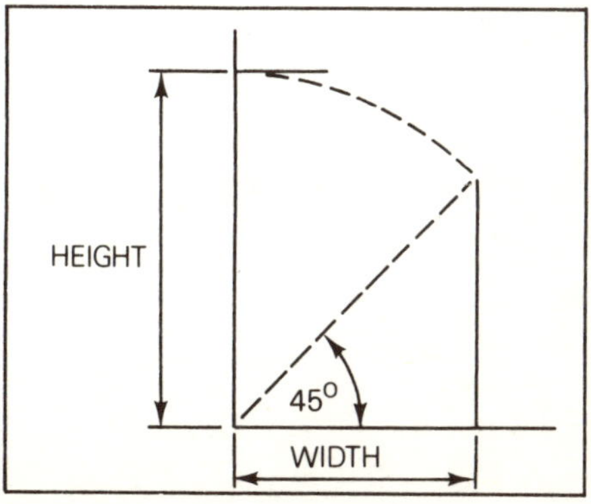

gether. Pressure should be applied with G cramps in addition to screwing.

The usual grooves should be provided to carry the window bottom and linings if required. I used Contiplast for the window bottom as the width amounted to about 16in. at the widest part.

It is important that the horizontal glazing bars line through in the completed window, care must be taken in the marking out, considering that some frames include transomes and others have not.

This method of construction is useful where space is limited, and final assembly can actually be carried out in the site area under dry conditions. The method also is suitable for complete machine production of the components in repetitive style. An approximate list of timber is given below for a window 8ft. by 5ft. sawn sizes.

10 Jambs 4ft. 9in. by 4in. by 1½in.
10 Head/Sill 1ft. 8in. by 4in. by 1½in.
2 Trans. 1ft. 8in. by 4in. by 2in.
1 Main Sill 8ft. by 9in. by 1½in.
1 Main Head 8ft. by 9in. by 3in.
80ft. 2in. by 2in. sash material.
4ft. 3 in. by 2in. sash material.
45ft. 1¼in. by 2in. glazing bar.
1 No. 8ft. by 1ft. by 6in.
Contiplast window bottom.

Costs as I found them several months ago were:
Timber (sawn) about £14.
Contiplast £3.50.
Glass £4 (40 panes).
Lead flashing £7.

Getting the most out of chipboard

Cutting chipboard with a tungsten carbide tipped saw. The overhead pressure spring, has been adapted to fit on the guard, this holds the board firmly at the point of cut. The spring can help to avoid spelching on veneered chipboard and it also enables a much faster rate of feed to be used when cutting plain board without the danger of overriding the saw.

Design of a product to be produced in quantity, is often governed by the environment in which the article is to be used, and also the material to be utilised in its construction.

Items produced for private use can generally be of a lighter construction than those used publicly. Free-standing units require different treatment of construction than those which are fixtures. A lightly constructed cupboard unit fixed in a recess may give good service for many years, but the same unit utilised as a movable item could have only a very short life.

Similar rules also apply to the materials used. Man-made chipboard can be used entirely for many forms of construction, but the scope of its uses can be extended considerably, if it is combined with a small amount of solid timber. Carefully planned construction can utilise all the advantages of chipboard as a consistent engineered material, and the solid timber used can be made a feature in the design.

A strip of gummed paper or masking tape placed along the line of cut should produce a clean finish if other methods have failed. This method can take up a considerable amount of time, and is mainly used in fine cabinet work on exotic veneers.

It is not uncommon for establishments producing items in quantity to have goods returned damaged. This can be due to gross carelessness after despatch, or points overlooked in the initial design. Free-standing cupboards in communal use, such as in schools, frequently suffer damage at base level, external corners, or from the ill-use of doors. These are the points at which it is advantageous to combine a small amount of timber when working in chipboard. The machining operations involved are very simple ones, and often stock sections can be made on the moulding machine which keeps costs to a minimum.

To work chipboard successfully its composition should be understood. The basic material used in its manufacture, are prepared wood chips, and synthetic resin adhesive. These are bonded together under pressure and heat, along with small quantities of other additives, according to the requirements of the completed board. To work the completed board in quantity it is necessary to use tungsten carbide tipped tools in the machine. These cost more than the traditional high speed steel, but with careful use their output life should recover the additional expense.

Different densities of chipboard are produced,

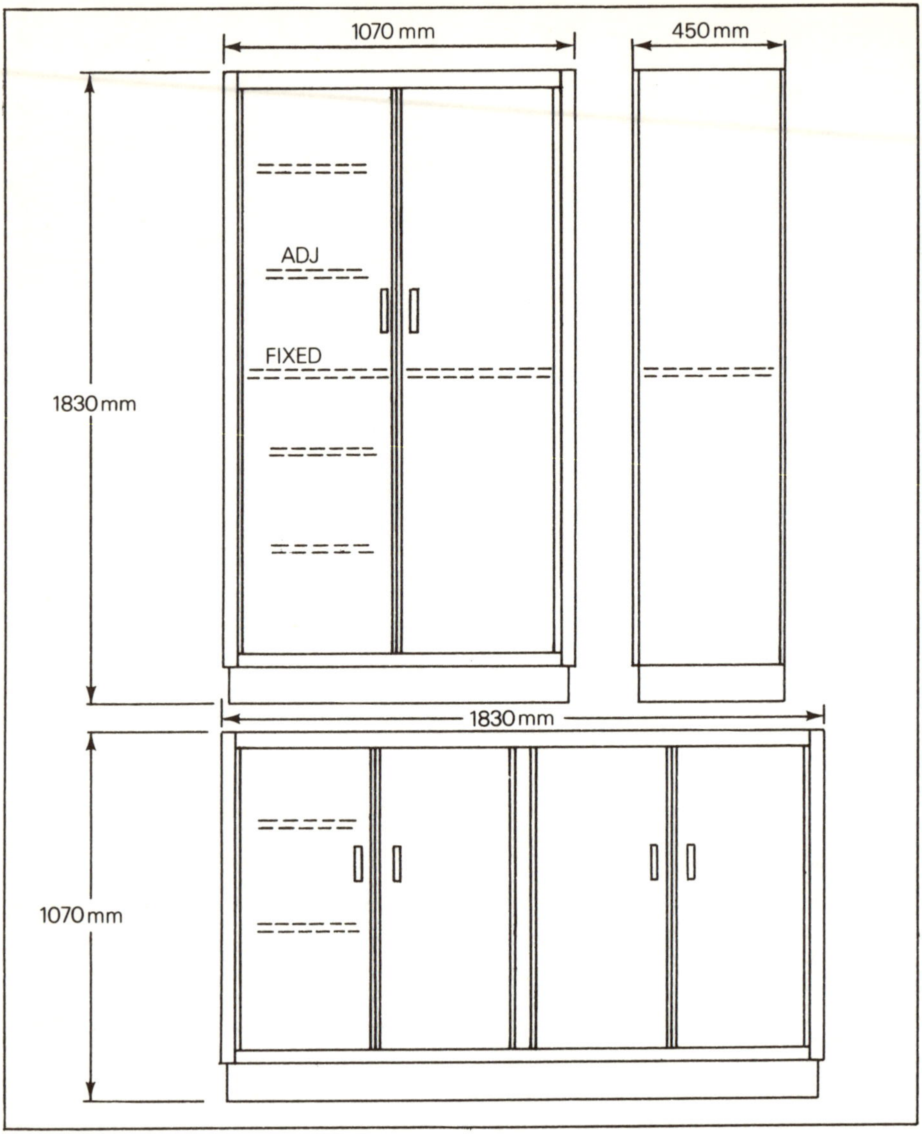

Outline design for storage cupboards, measuring 1830 mm by 1070 mm by 450 mm in depth. A choice of two designs is given, both having the same amount of storage capacity. Veneered chipboard is the main visible material used, supported with hardwood at the points where experience has shown the greatest wear takes place.

which also varies the weight of the material. Where veneering can be carried out within the production unit, the heavier board can be utilised for cupboard sides, and a lighter weight for doors. This prevents the unit from overbalancing when large doors are opened with the cupboard unloaded. Chipboard will keep straight after veneering in a hot press, which is one of its advantages over some materials. The effect of moisture, gain or loss, is uniform throughout the board.

Edge lipping can be applied to chipboard, either by tongue and grooving, or butt jointing under pressure using low voltage strip heating, or radio

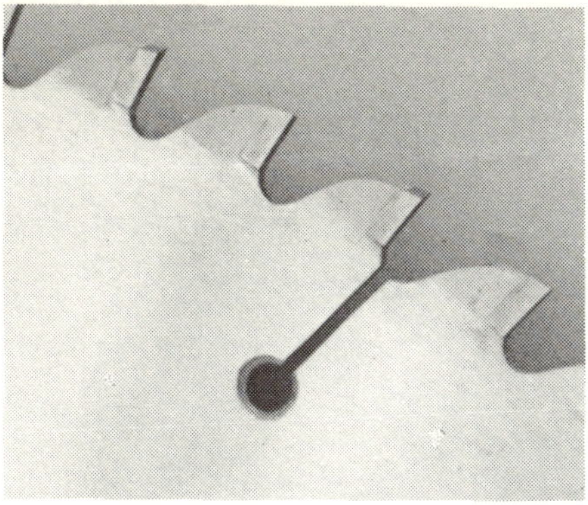

Close view of a tungsten carbide tipped saw. Each tooth is individually tipped, and requires to be handled with the utmost care when not in the machine. The saw should not be stood on the teeth. The slot in the saw blade, one of four, is a refinement in the design to improve efficiency, and to relieve any undue stress during operation. (Saw supplied by Wadkin Ltd., Leicester).

frequency methods. The edge lipping, if over-veneered, should be as light in section as practicable, to permit the minimum amount of shrinkage in the heated press.

To give a clean cut on the circular saw to veneered chipboard, the following points can be of help.

The saw should be set at a low position in the bench. Its height should be such that it will cut through the board, plus about 6mm. This permits the saw teeth to leave the cut gradually instead of with a chopping action.

The throat in the saw bench should be a neat fit up to the saw tip. This point of the machine should be given a service before the cutting of veneered work is commenced.

Spelching of the veneer can also be caused by the board vibrating up and down during cutting. If a holding-down spring can be arranged from the overhead guard, this can improve results. This method works well when cutting thin veneered plywoods also.

I have known saw operators stick a strip of gummed paper down the line of cut; this does prevent spelching, but it also takes a considerable amount of time to remove afterwards, and should be used as a last resort only.

For forming tongues and grooves on chipboard, tungsten carbide tipped cutters must be used, and a good rate of feed maintained. Cutters have a longer life if the material being processed is kept moving, so preventing a build up of heat in a confined area. The machine, too, should be adequately powered to maintain the necessary revolutions under load. Tungsten carbide tipped cutters have a blunter sharpness angle than high speed steel, and so take more power, which may, or may not be noticeable on these small operations.

Wooden trim for applying to chipboard can be prepared on the four cutter or moulding machine. Standardisation of sections should be arranged within the works unit, making the sections as interchangeable as possible. Beech trim gives good service for school work, as it is durable, and it keeps straight during processing. From my experience, if a choice can be made of either grooving chipboard or forming a tongue, I would always choose to groove. A groove leaves twice as much of the chipboard intact, and it also cuts away the centre of the board which is very often made up of a larger type of chip. In this way a more balanced form of construction is achieved.

Where load-carrying bearers are fixed to chipboard these should be bonded with adhesive in addition to any metal fixings used. If the bonding can be done under pressure, in a heated press, using synthetic resin adhesive, a quick and efficient operation will result.

In machine production, construction details often have to be decided at shop-floor level. Specifications or drawings frequently only give outline details of the job required. Materials used should not be exploited beyond their limitation. Success of a product can depend on having made the most efficient use of a material costwise. If an economically priced material like chipboard is to be used, labour costs preparing the necessary hardwood trim to go with it must be

A horizontal section through the cupboard showing the hardwood edgings tongued to the chipboard. It will be noted that the edgings are all similar in dimension to keep machining procedure as economical as possible.

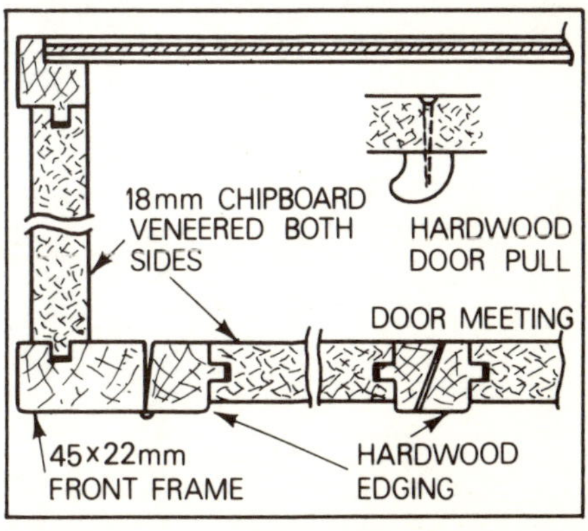

kept to a minimum. Bulk production of trim on a multihead moulding machine (fourcutter, etc.) is the answer, making the sections as interchangeable as possible. In this way, store cupboards have been successfully produced using veneered chipboard as the basic visible material, supported at the points of stress with hardwood timber.

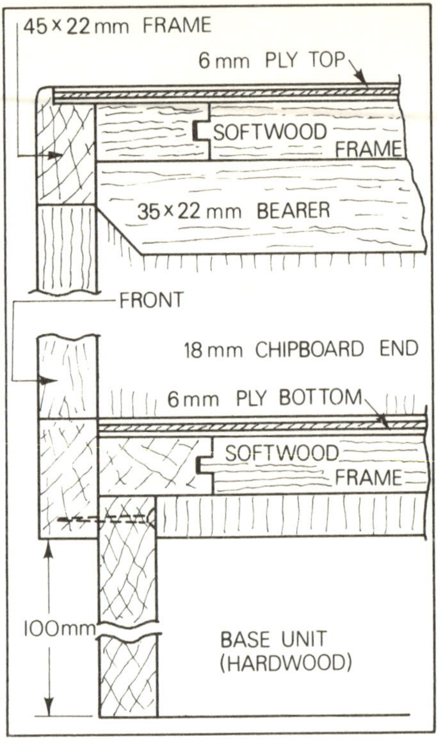

A vertical section through the cupboard showing the hardwood front frame, and the softwood internal framing. The base unit is a box frame, dovetailed at the corners for maximum strength.

Louvres - their design and construction

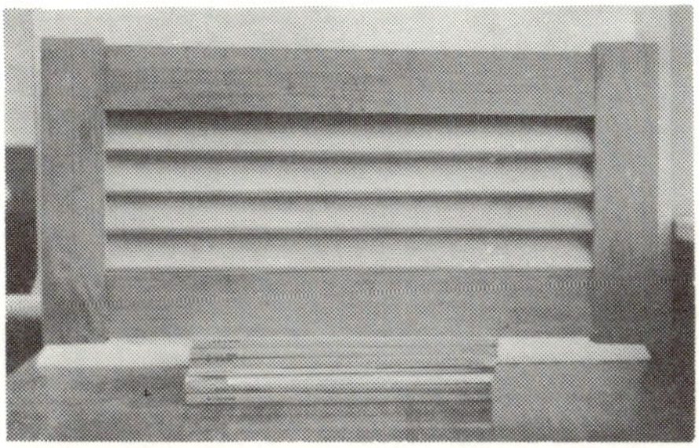

Louvres pitched at 60 deg. show more of the face of the timber than the edge. There is no necessity for the louvre slats to project beyond the face when they are simply being used as a decorative feature.

Louvres pitched at 45 deg. and projecting beyond the face of the stiles. The mortise and tenon method of construction has been used here. No nails or pins are required by this method, making it suitable for furniture finish.

In the past louvres have been used only as a means of ventilation, and their design has been aimed at efficiency in this respect, rather than appearance. When used externally it is the general practice to let the louvre slats project beyond the face of the framing into which they are housed, for weathering purposes. For louvres designed for internal use, either for the passage of air or as a decorative feature, there is generally no necessity for the slats to project beyond the face. An exception to this, however, is if the framing housing the slats is, say, under 22 mm in thickness, some projection may be necessary to allow the slats to give an acceptable amount of lap.

From a decorative point of view, the steeper the angle of the slats the more the surface grain becomes visible. Slats set at a low angle, 45 degrees or less, show very little of their face, and lots of edge. Slats set at 60 deg. to the horizontal tend to be more decorative, especially if it is desired to show the natural grain of the timber. Lap is also made more possible with the thinner type of framing generally required in this type of work. The 45 deg. angle of pitch may be considered more suitable for external use, as less timber is directly exposed to the elements.

The louvre slats may be framed to the supporting stiles in a variety of ways. This depends on the purpose for which they are to be used, and also very often the mechanical aids available to do the job. Probably the quickest way, to produce a one-off job at least, is to trench the stiles on a pull-out cross-cut saw, using an adjustable dado head. These cutter heads can be adjusted to suit different thicknesses of slats within a given range. Once the spacing of the cuts has been decided, very little marking out is necessary, as setting marks or stops can be arranged on the fence, to align with the cut that has just been produced.

This dado head method is particularly suitable for external louvres, including the construction of louvre fencing, often used as a wind break. It must be noted that stiles must be trenched in pairs as they will not turn over, and become right and left hand.

Louvre stiles may also be mortised with a hollow

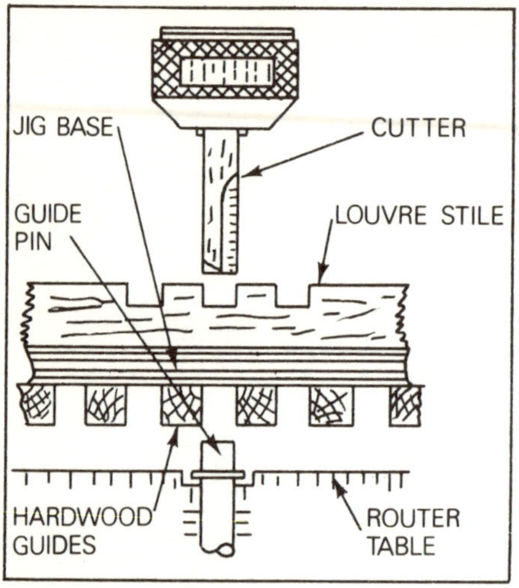

Sketch shows the relative positioning of the cutter, jig, and guide pin, on a high speed router being used on a trenching operation. The size of the cutter must be selected to suit the louvre slats. The guide pin should be a precise fit in the slots of the jig or oversized cuts may occur.

A travelling head cross-cut saw, fitted with an adjustable dado head will quickly trench stiles to carry louvre slats. This method can be used for all thicknesses of material, providing a through cut is not objected to.

The Louvre Lath system. A quick method to use for constructing or converting doors to louvre style. It is designed so that the two sections of material can be prepared on a four-cutter, and the stile section trenched on a high speed router.

square chisel and auger. The chisel is set in the mortise machine to the pitch angle of the slats, and usually only one, or two insertions of the tocl is necessary. The slats may then be tenoned a handful at a time, by machine, no angular work being necessary. Slats can either be projecting or otherwise by this method.

Louvre units used in furniture, and decorative screens, preferably have the slats inset on the stiles, either just on the face side or on the back also. If the above mortise and tenon method is not used, the slats must be trenched in on a high-speed routing machine. This leaves a rounded end on the cut, and the slats can be moulded, preferably during the four-cutting process, to fit the cut. For the trenching of the stiles a jig may be used to work in conjunction with the guide pin on the router, or if the router is equipped with a sliding table, a different arrangement can be made. A high-quality job can be produced by the router method, if the material is carefully selected, and machined to the correct dimensions and profiles.

An alternative furniture method, or one that can be used for converting panelled doors to louvre style, is what I call "the louvre-lath system". A quantity of stile material, stile lath, is prepared in about 2 metre lengths, and 34 mm by 9 mm in section. This is then stop trenched on the router to a depth of 6 mm. The set up for this can be very simply arranged, it is much more easy to trench this light section, than to trench heavy door stiles. The slats can be produced on a four-cutter, and the materials cut to suit the opening required. This method has great possibilities, once the material has been machined it can be utilised both by the craftsman and the do-it-yourself enthusiast.

Since the introduction of louvres as a means of decor, several firms are specialising in their manufacture. Some do in fact advertise in the Building Trade Journal. Products by the specialist, which I have seen in this line, have been of a high standard no doubt achieved by careful selection of material and precision machine work.

Simple set up for trenching stiles for the Louvre Lath system. This high speed router is equipped with a traversing table. Very little marking out of stiles is necessary once the operation has been planned.

Drawer design and production

1. A detail view of a tier of drawers with stepped fronts. The overhanging part of the drawer fronts conceal the supporting rails in the cascase framing, and so give a complete frontage of the drawer front material. This could be a laminated plastic or decorative veneer.

2. Inset runners in drawer sides should be a sliding fit at the machining stage or additional work may be involved later on. Drawer sides of this design will tighten up on the runners if shrinkage takes place due to the timber being used with too high a moisture content.

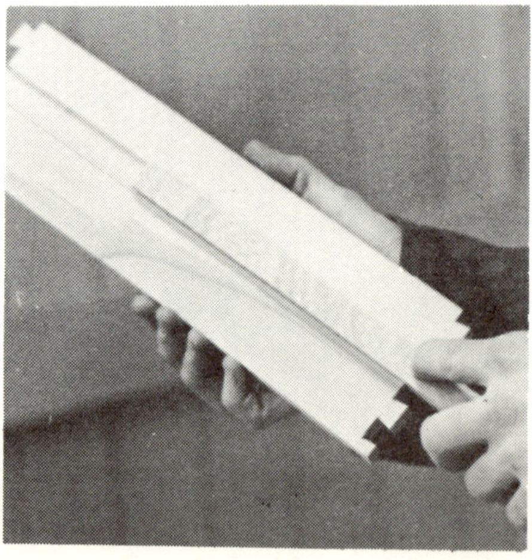

In the design of joinery, or cabinet work, there are a variety of types of drawers that can be progressively manufactured by machine. Each individual type has its own features which make it the most suitable for a particular purpose.

The arrangement of the design can be varied to introduce such features as compactness, economy in production, and time saving in fitting into the carcase unit.

When planning to use drawers, in particular for quantity production, it is important that the most suitable type for the project is selected. Where work is being carried out to a specification, the type of drawer to be used may be strictly defined. The customer can at times, of course, be advised by the manufacturer.

Once the dimensions and type of drawer to be used have been determined, the sections for the various members, namely, fronts, sides, and backs, can be planned.

For large-scale production, section preparation will be carried out at one pass through a four-cutter, or moulder, as multihead machines are called. Machining timber in the length is more progressive than handling a large number of short pieces. Lengths of two to three metres can be stacked conveniently for transporting.

Moisture content of the timber is an all-important factor in successful drawer production. Over-dried timber will swell if completed goods are stored in a damp warehouse or building site. Over-wet material may shrink in the completed article, and cause inaccuracies in some types of drawers.

There is a relationship between the type of drawer being manufactured, and the acceptable moisture content of the timber. Blockboard, or better still, laminboard, is quite often used for drawer fronts as it is not so subject to movement as solid timber. It is also suitable for veneered work.

The core of these built boards should run the

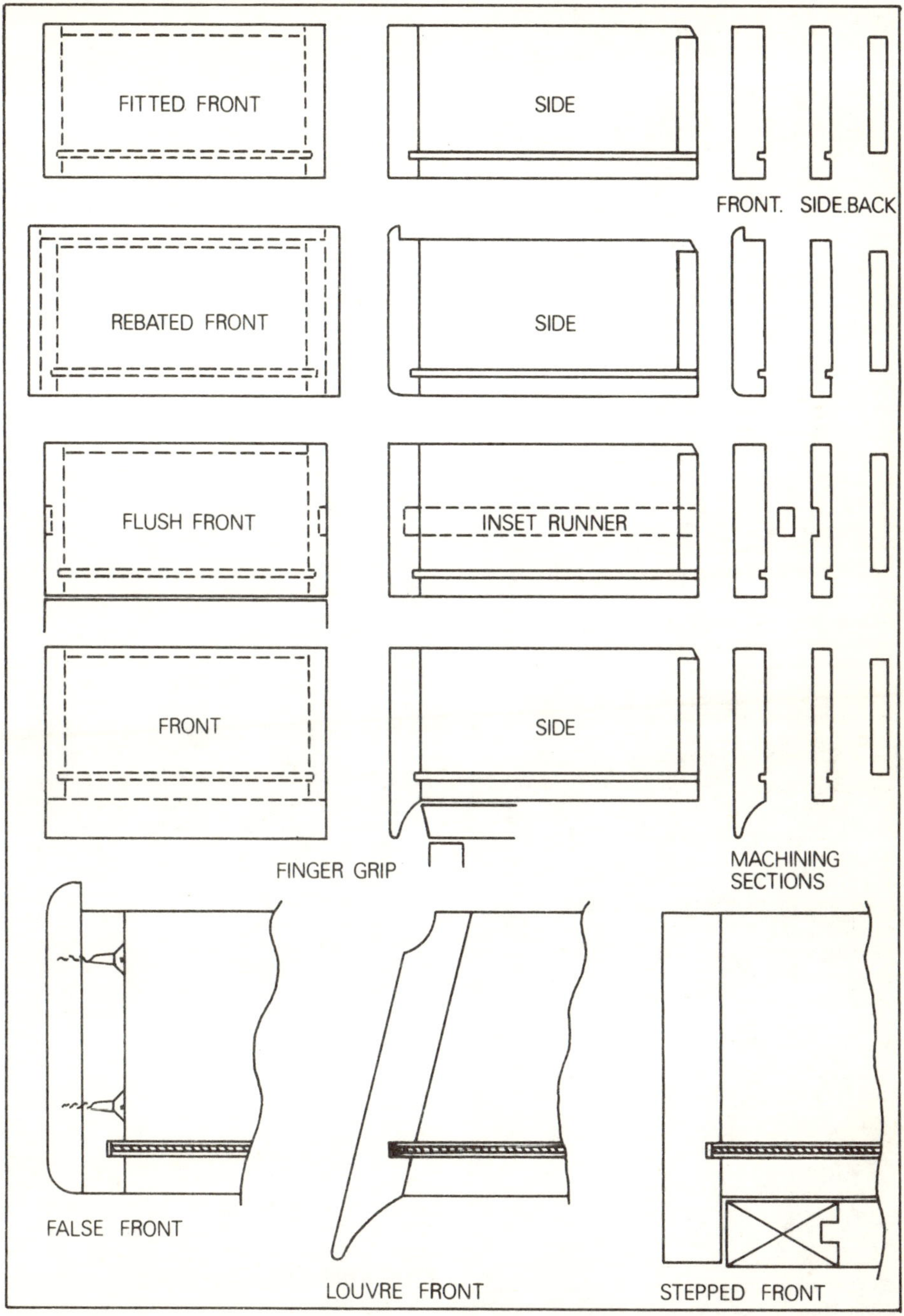

A guide to the planning of material sections for various types of drawers suitable for machine production.

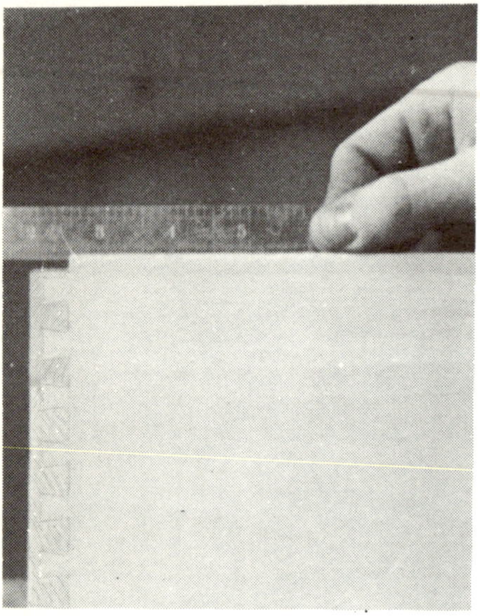

3. Drawer backs should be positioned slightly down from the sides to reduce fitting time, and make hand planing less complicated. Some operators dovetail the members flush and reduce the backs on a surface planer before assembly.

4. Using an applicator for applying adhesive to a dovetail joint which has been made from a reject drawer side. This can help to speed the assembly operation when no other specialised appliance is available.

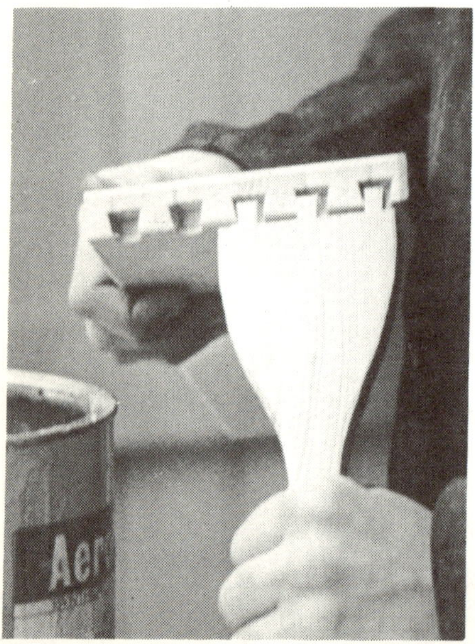

length of the drawer front, to provide end grain for the dovetail pockets.

Drawers with fitted front require a high standard of accuracy in their manufacture. This also applies to the units into which they have to be fitted. Many operators cut the back member of this type of drawer 1 mm shorter than the front, to reduce planing time in fitting.

The back member should also be set down from the sides to make planing of the sides easier, should this be required. The accuracy standard of a drawer production line can usually be assessed by the amount of shaving around the operators fitting drawers into carcases. Bonus can be gained, or lost at this point, due to machining standards.

Drawers with rebated fronts should require very little fitting time as ample clearance can be allowed in their manufacture. This can be a considerable saving if a large quantity is involved. This type of drawer is suitable for use under damp conditions, such as in kitchens or outbuildings, as clearance can be made without being visible.

Flush front drawers which can have inset runners require no front dividing rails or other guide members. The saving here is in the carcase construction, fewer members being required. Where blockboard ends are used for carcase construction, and runners can be trenched into this, or glued and screwed. Finger grip fronts include the handle in the design of the drawer front. This design can be attractive, and saves the cost of handles and fitting time.

Stepped drawer fronts are used where an unbroken panel is required in a tier of drawers, either for a veneered effect, or in painted work. They also enable the carcase front rails to be of a less costly material than the main structure as they are concealed behind the drawer fronts.

False fronts are used as an economy in the use of hardwoods. Also stock drawers can be fitted up at short notice with the fronts of the material required. This enables flexibility to take place by stocking a selection of drawer fronts instead of complete drawers.

Louvre fronts involve additional labours in machining but this can be kept to a minimum by careful planning before putting the material through the moulder. The fitting of this type of drawer can generally be less precise than that of a flush-fitting drawer, as the upper edge of the front is usually hidden. Finger grips are often included in the design of louvre fronts, and inset runners also.

Inset runners which engage in grooves in the drawer sides give very smooth running providing everything is in alignment, and out of twist. It must be understood, however, that the bearing surface is much less than in drawers running in the traditional manner. For this reason the harder types of wood should be used for both the runners and the drawer sides.

For fitted drawers which may have to be planed by hand at the running-in stage the sides should not be of a material which is difficult to work. Clear softwood, meranti, or obechi are suitable timbers for easy working. Beech, parana pine, and such, can be time-consuming in quantity work, in particular if the machining work is not up to standard. Drawers designed for heavy work may have to be the exception where strong material is necessary.

Modern dovetailing machines used in drawer construction have become so simple to operate that it is now the planning of the type of drawers that requires the attention.

Standard joinery producers have good scope ahead with the use of drawers to enhance their designs to bring them into competition with furniture.

Dovetailing with the spindle moulder

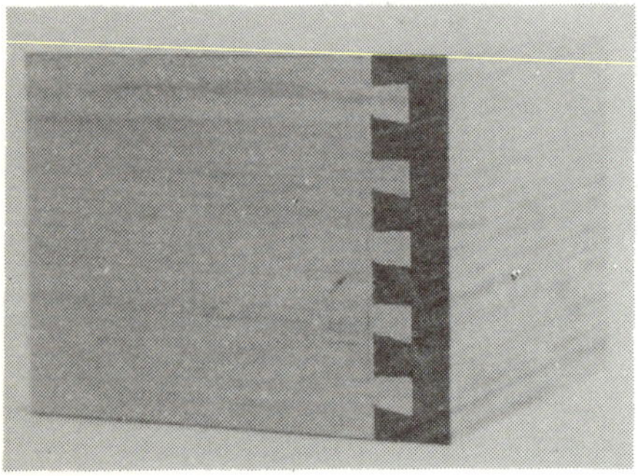

1. Front detail of a machine produced dovetailed joint on a flush fitting drawer. The positioning of the dovetail pins on the drawer side should be such so as to enclose the groove which carries the drawer bottom.

2. Rebated type of drawer front. Dovetail pockets commence at rebate distance from the end of the drawer front. This must be noted in the setting up of the machine, or the depth of the pockets will be found to be inadequate.

3. Close up view of a dovetailing attachment being used on a spindle moulder. A pair of drawer sides for the louvre fronted type of drawer are in position for the dovetailing operation.

Not all woodwork producing units require the full-time services of a machine that is designed solely for the cutting of dovetail joints. Nevertheless, some work requiring dovetails may arise from time to time, and the production unit is faced with a series of options on the matter. In some cases it may be possible to alter the constructional design of a product, and so enable another type of joint to be used. A second solution would be to send the work out to another establishment. This may cause some delay and additional cost. A third alternative would be to make use of a dovetailing attachment on the spindle moulder.

The dovetailing attachment will produce excellent work, and the time taken should not be excessive, providing all the necessary parts for the machine are readily available. It need hardly be said that the output will be nothing like that of a multicutter dovetailing machine, and its width capacity is limited to material of around 12 inches (300 mm). This makes the attachment suitable for the majority of drawer construction work, as it can cope with the various types in present-day demand.

Several sizes of dovetail cutters may be used, and the distance from centre to centre, of the dovetail pins, is described as the pitch. In imperial sizes $\frac{3}{4}$in. and 1in. pitch are the ones in general use. Metric sizes will probably be about 19 mm and 25 mm when they eventually become available. It is necessary to change the guide comb when a different size of cutter is to be

4. Front detail of the joint of a louvre type drawer. The ends of the drawer sides must be cut to the required angle before dovetailing. These must be worked in pairs.

5. General view of dovetails. This pattern is common to all machine dovetails produced with rotating cutters. The depth of the pockets is automatically determined to suit the pins once the indicator scale has been set on the dovetailing attachment.

used. This is quite a simple operation requiring the removal of about three screws.

To obtain maximum strength of dovetail pins, the timber thickness indicators on the attachment should be set at the appropriate measurement (thickness of drawer side) before components are clamped. These indicators are

6. Dovetail pins should be produced as strong as possible. If the indicator scale is set at too low a figure, weak pins will be manufactured.

located at each end of the attachment, and they should be set identical with each other.

Adjustable stops are provided to locate the components for dovetailing, and a certain amount of skill is required for quick accurate setting. Stops should be set for left- and right-hand working, to enable face marked edges to be adjacent to the stops at all times. Although it is possible to process both members of a joint in one operation, not all machinists work in this manner.

Some prefer to pocket all drawer fronts and backs first, then dovetail pin the sides later as a separate operation. This method saves handling too great a variety of components which tend to confuse. An assistant can be of help to speed the clamping, and unclamping of components. If an assistant is available, this may well decide the method of working.

When setting up, a test joint should be made to check for alignment, and tightness. If the joint is slack, this can usually be corrected by raising the cutter slightly. Should this be ineffective, the guide collar fitted to some cutters may be overworn causing the cut to be oversized. The collar should be renewed.

Drawers with rebated fronts can be dovetailed with the spindle moulder attachment, but the fronts must, in this case, be dovetailed independent of the sides. It will be necessary to increase the set on the timber thickness indicators by the amount of the rebate, for the processing of the fronts only. This enables the cutter to travel the increased distance required, which is actually drawer side thickness plus rebate. An alternative to moving the thickness

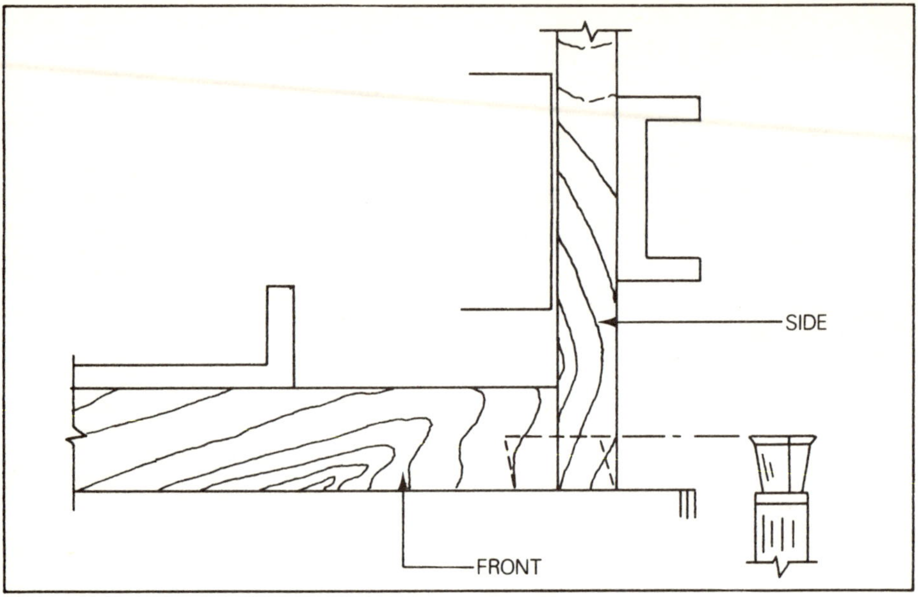

Sketch A shows the relative positions of a drawer front of the flush fitting type, and a drawer side, clamped in the dovetailing attachment.

Sketch B. One method of dovetailing rebated drawer fronts is to insert a cut away stop piece to allow the front to be positioned the rebate amount forward. The drawer sides must be dovetailed as a separate operation.

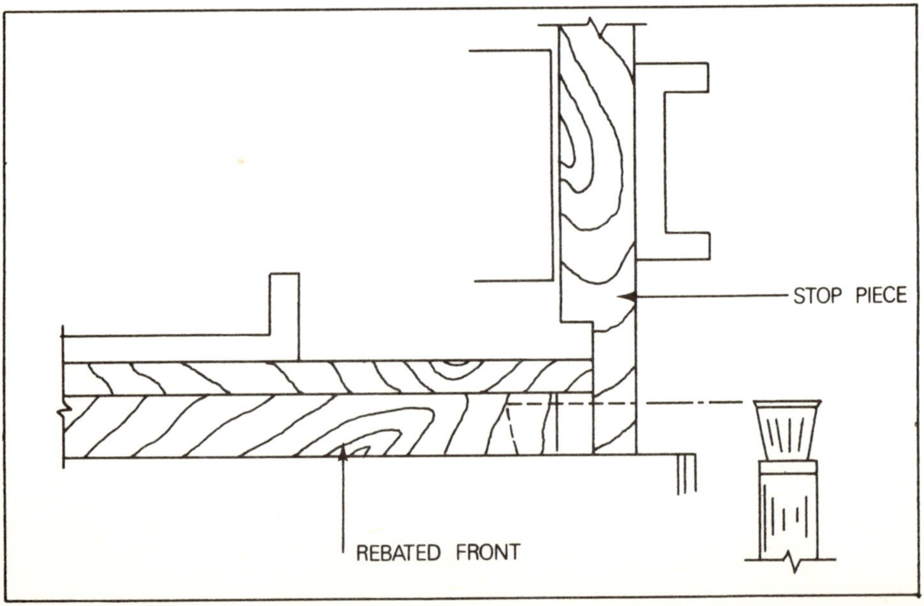

indicators, is to rebate the vertical stop-piece, allowing the drawer front to be positioned rebate distance forward. This saves disturbing the set on the attachment.
Louvre fronted drawers, which are gaining popularity at the present time, can be dovetailed without any difficulty. The drawer sides require to be cut to the angle of the slope of the front, then dovetailed in pairs in the normal way.
Where a variety of spindle speeds are available on a machine, the highest possible should be used. This is due to the small diameter of the dovetailing cutters, compared to slotted collars or Whitehill cutter blocks, for which this machine is mainly designed.
Some timbers tend to splinter at the commencement of the cut. This can be reduced by inserting a hardwood packing piece adjacent to where the split is taking place. Spurr-headed cutters are also available, which are designed to give clean cutting at the lower speeds. They also permit faster feed-in speeds on automatic machines.
If drawer fronts, and backs are to be machine sanded internally, this should be done before dovetailing, or inferior joint will result. The drawer sides may be sanded at any stage.
From a work-study point of view, stacking tables or trollies should be positioned at each side of the operator. He should not have to hunt around for each piece to put in the machine. Stacking on the machine itself, hinders the work, and can in many machine operations be a source of danger. This dovetailing operation on the spindle moulder, if done in quantity, can be fatiguing. An operator may prefer to work seated on a stool of suitable height during the cutting operation. The machine output can be measured on this operation, and the productivity factor noted for future reference.

Multi-spindle dovetailing

1. Louvre type front.

2. Rebated front.

3. Fitted front.

With the introduction of multi-spindle dovetailers the operation of dovetailing has been speeded up considerably. Setting up time is reduced also with this type of machine which is very much to advantage when dealing with short batches of work.

As the joint forming operation is spread over a number of cutters, instead of only one, in the case of a single spindle machine, less frequent servicing is required. Also due to the fact that the cutters on a multi-spindle machine are only in contact with the timber for a very short period of time per sequence, overheating of the cutting edge is unlikely.

This is a point which requires consideration on woodworking machines where small diameter cutters are rotating at high speeds.

Overheating can be caused by too long a duration in cut. Once the cutting edge is destroyed, frictional heat increases, and clouds of blue smoke are sometimes in evidence.

The short duration in cut on the multi-spindle dovetailer must surely account for the long life of the cutters.

It is important that when sharpening the cutters that the angle of approach, or hook, as it is often called, is maintained. The cutters must also have back clearance to ensure that the working edge has the greatest projection.

If these points are ignored, an additional load will be put on the spindle bearings, and inferior work may also be produced.

Drive

due to the fact that dovetail cutters are of small diameter, high rotation speeds are necessary to give an acceptable speed on the cutting edge.

It must, however, be recognised that the finish required on the machined parts is a gluing surface, not necessarily a planed one. For this reason, acceptable results can be obtained at

4. A dovetailing machine cutter mounted for sharpening using a cup type abrasive wheel.

6. A close up view of the cutters of a 15 spindle machine. The cutters on this machine (Brookman) all have the same direction of rotation.

5. A multi-spindle dovetailer of the smaller type capable of processing material up to 400 mm in width. As a general rule drawers in domestic use seldom exceed this width, which makes this machine an attractive proposition for a large number of establishments.

speeds considerably lower than that of a high speed router.

Higher speeds will permit a greater rate of feed and can be particularly advantageous on automated machines.

The method of obtaining high speed rotation to the spindles of these machines using standard electric drive is being achieved by two methods.

Both have points in their favour from an operational point of view, but the method described first below is the more advanced in engineering design which is gaining its popularity.

One method is to have the cutter spindles driven through a spiral gear system, which converts the horizontal rotation to vertical. The gear ratio is such that the required step up in revolutions is obtained all in the one transfer.

This calls for a very high standard in gear design which these machines have.

Due to the fact that all the spindles are driven individually from a common gear shaft they all rotate in the same direction. This is very convenient from a servicing point of view and cutter stocking.

It can also simplify setting up in some procedures. The entire gear system is encased in an oil bath, which, in addition to reducing wear, accounts for the silent operation of the machine.

Another method of obtaining drive to the spindles is to have adjoining spindles linked by helical gears. Under this system spindles rotate in opposite directions. In this design of machine left and right handed cutters are required.

This can involve complications in cutter servicing, bearing in mind that all the cutters must be ground to exactly the same dimension.

The helical gear train from spindle to spindle does not produce any increase in motor speed, so additional gearing arrangements are also required to obtain this.

Very little splintering or spelching of timber is experienced on modern dovetailers, but this can be further reduced by planing an ingoing cut at both ends of the work on machines that have dual rotation. On the other hand, a less considerate operator may produce outgoing cuts at both ends of the work.

Cutters should be kept in sets, and ground identical with a cup type grinding wheel. The cutters must be mounted, not held free hand, or variations are inevitable.

Provision is made on dovetailing machines to make allowance for the reduction in cutter dimension due to grinding.

This also provides for tight and loose fitting of the joint.

Some operators keep a set, or part set of cutters for working abrasive materials such as chipboard or plywood where the glue line can be offensive. This method prevents a full set of, say, 25 cutters being ground at more frequent intervals, when perhaps only a part set of, say, 10 cutters is required.

The planning of cutter sets is well worth while in multi-spindle dovetailing. The development of multi-spindle dovetailing machines has influenced the design of timber products during the last decade.

Under slower methods of dovetailing it was less time-consuming to produce units of the storage class with doors than with drawers.

Drawers can now be probably machined more economically than doors due to the advancement of the machine. To produce a mortise and tenon joint two separate machines are required.

A dovetail joint requires only one machine and operator to form the components.

For this reason, when designing prototypes for large scale production, if members can be dovetail jointed it may well be more economical than other methods.

The output capacity of a dovetailing machine is governed by the mechanised aids for clamping the work, and whether or not the feeding cycle is automated or hand operated.

It can be to advantage to have an assistant to help loading and unloading of the machine.

Fully mechanised machines are less fatiguing to operate and so contribute to efficiency.

Output can be recorded on this type of machine operation for cost purposes, which is to advantage to all when payment by results schemes are in operation.

It is desirable that the machine should be loaded to capacity at each cutting sequence when on production runs to give maximum output, and

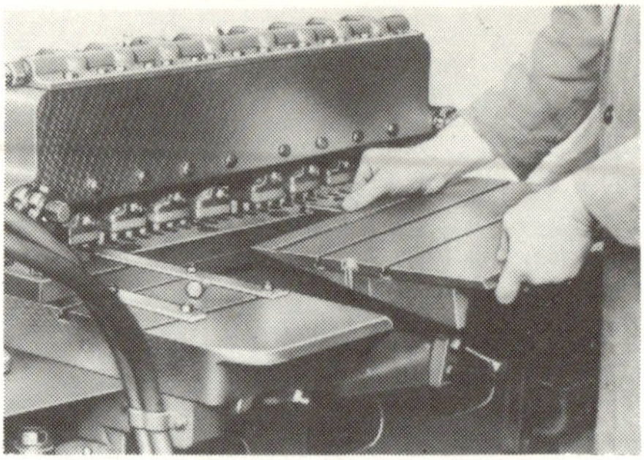

7. A machine fitted with a removable bed. This enables work to be dovetailed which has projections or curvature as in the case of shaped drawer fronts.

8. A dovetailing machine loaded for left and right hand working. This is important in particular if the material is likely to have variation in width.

9. A machine fitted with pneumatic cramp operation. The table movement is hand operated. Machines are also available from this manufacturer which are fully automatic.

distribute load over as much of the machine as possible.

Jig frames can be constructed from hardwood to give component location within the clamps if so desired.

When designing components for dovetailing the pitch of the cutters (distance from centre to centre) of the machine to be used should be kept in mind to give a balanced joint. It will be found that a machine with, say, 25.4 mm (1in.) pitch will give the best results with timber sizes in multiples of this figure.

Half pins at the edge of the work should be avoided if possible. Grooves for the location of drawer bottoms should also be planned to line with the centre of the dovetail pockets so as not to be visible in the completed job.

Face edge working is always recommended, in case of variation in timber sizes, so right and left hand setting of the machine is required for most operations.

Assembly of dovetailed work, in particular wide items, should be done as early as possible after machining. The practice of "trying up" before final assembly should not be encouraged as damage to the joint can be done in this way.

Some operators cut the dovetail pockets a small amount over in depth to allow for adhesive. Providing the joint is a grip fit this method is acceptable and can be to advantage in the case of fitted drawers where hand planing is involved if the drawer is oversize.

A. Shows a method of forming a framing joint using a mortise and tenon.

B. Shows the same timber section which has been turned on edge to make machine dovetailing possible. The dovetailing operation could, in many instances, be less time-consuming, and would also distribute the work-load over a greater proportion of the plant. The dovetailing machine forms the complete joint in one cutting operation, not so the mortise and tenon.

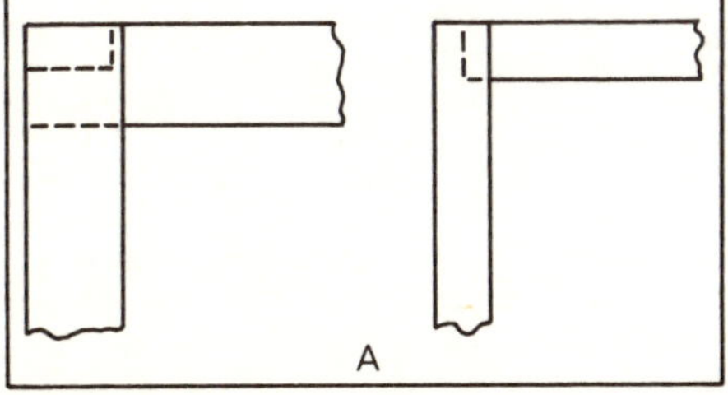

A

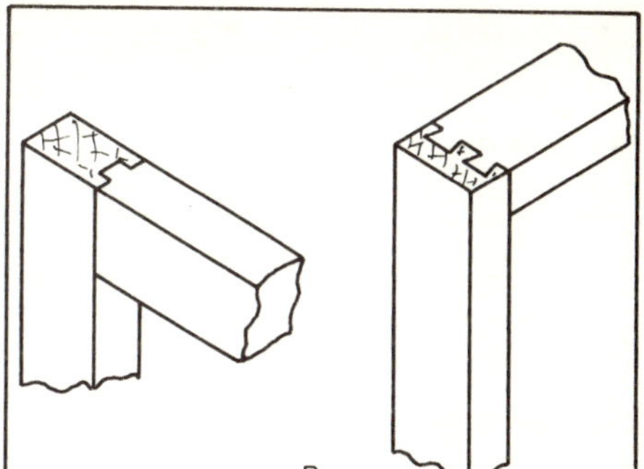

B

C. Outline of a method of cupboard or wardrobe construction using dovetailed frames and panel boards. Box type units can be constructed in a minimum of operative time in this manner. A dovetailing machine and a dimension saw are the principal machines required. A large selection of prepared panel boards are now available.

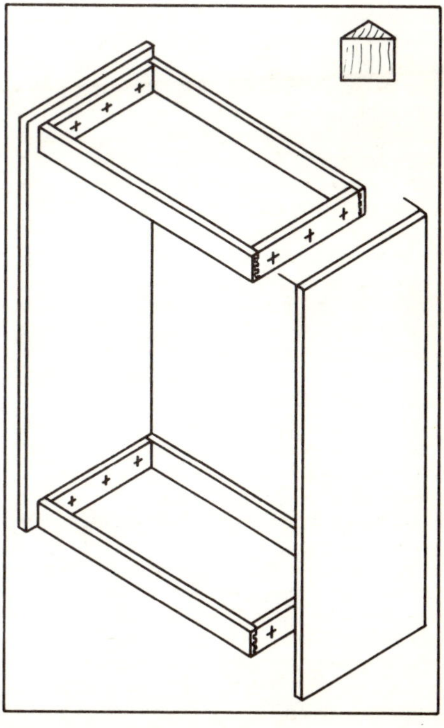

A ladderback chair in pine

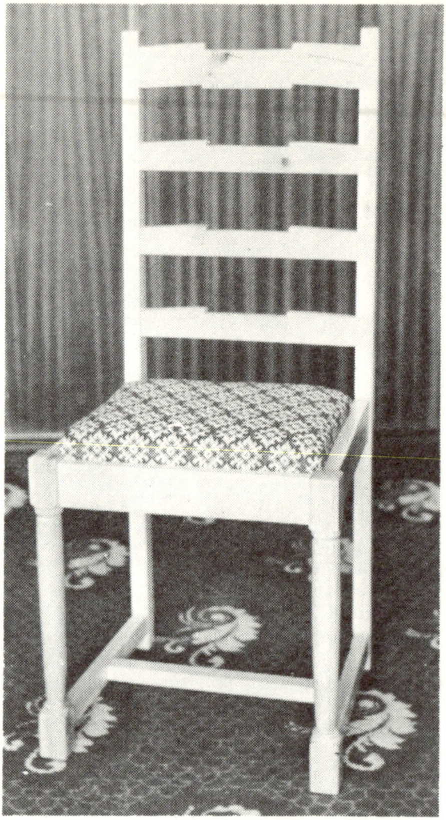

Fig. 1. The completed chair. The seat covering material is in bright red, green, and cream tapestry, which gives a contrast with the natural wood.

This is a simple design in softwood, planned for economy in cost, and to give a touch of a bygone age. Natural pine furniture is finding a place within the home, and this design of chair can be made in sets, or as a one-off for use in the hall or the bedroom.

Chairs for domestic use can be satisfactorily constructed in softwood, providing certain points are observed. When designing, the sections of the components should be slightly increased over those for hardwood. This is mainly to reduce the weakening of the timber at the points of joint formation. Care should be taken in the balanced design of the joints, not too much material should be cut away by a mortice, yet the tenon must be strong enough to carry the load. It is also advisable to keep the work under pressure in cramps until the adhesive has fully set. Corner brackets should be diagonally grained, and should be in hardwood; they should be fitted, well glued, and screwed with gauge 10 screws. The plywood seat unit is also screwed in through the corner brackets to increase the diagonal rigidity. Metal domes should be fitted to the legs to permit sliding without jarring. If all these points are observed there is every chance of success.

Material for the back legs must be free from cracks or weakening knots, and some careful selection of material for these parts is important. Some knots in other members can enhance the appearance. Remember that extra length on the front leg material will be required for mounting in the lathe. A 9 mm or ⅜in. chisel is suitable for all the mortice work for either hand or machine.

The cutting list gives linear dimensions for a chair with parallel sides, but if a diminish is required towards the back some members will have to be shortened. A full-sized setting out would also be required to obtain the necessary angles. A diminish of about 25 mm at each side is suitable, but a beginner could make the chair with parallel sides for which a setting out is not fully essential.

The turned legs should be made first if there is any doubt whether the drawing can be followed accurately on this operation. The long tapered section of the leg should be made slightly bowed to add to the appearance, and it is actually easier to produce in this manner. Care must be taken to keep the legs clean after turning, and they should be wrapped to prevent discoloration if they are not to be used immediately.

The ends of the chair should be glued up first, and allowed to set, as the front rail is dowelled into the leg. The dowel extend into the tenons of the side rails, so pegging the joint. The dowels must be in hardwood, 9 mm or ⅜in. dia.

As with all natural finished woodwork, the final

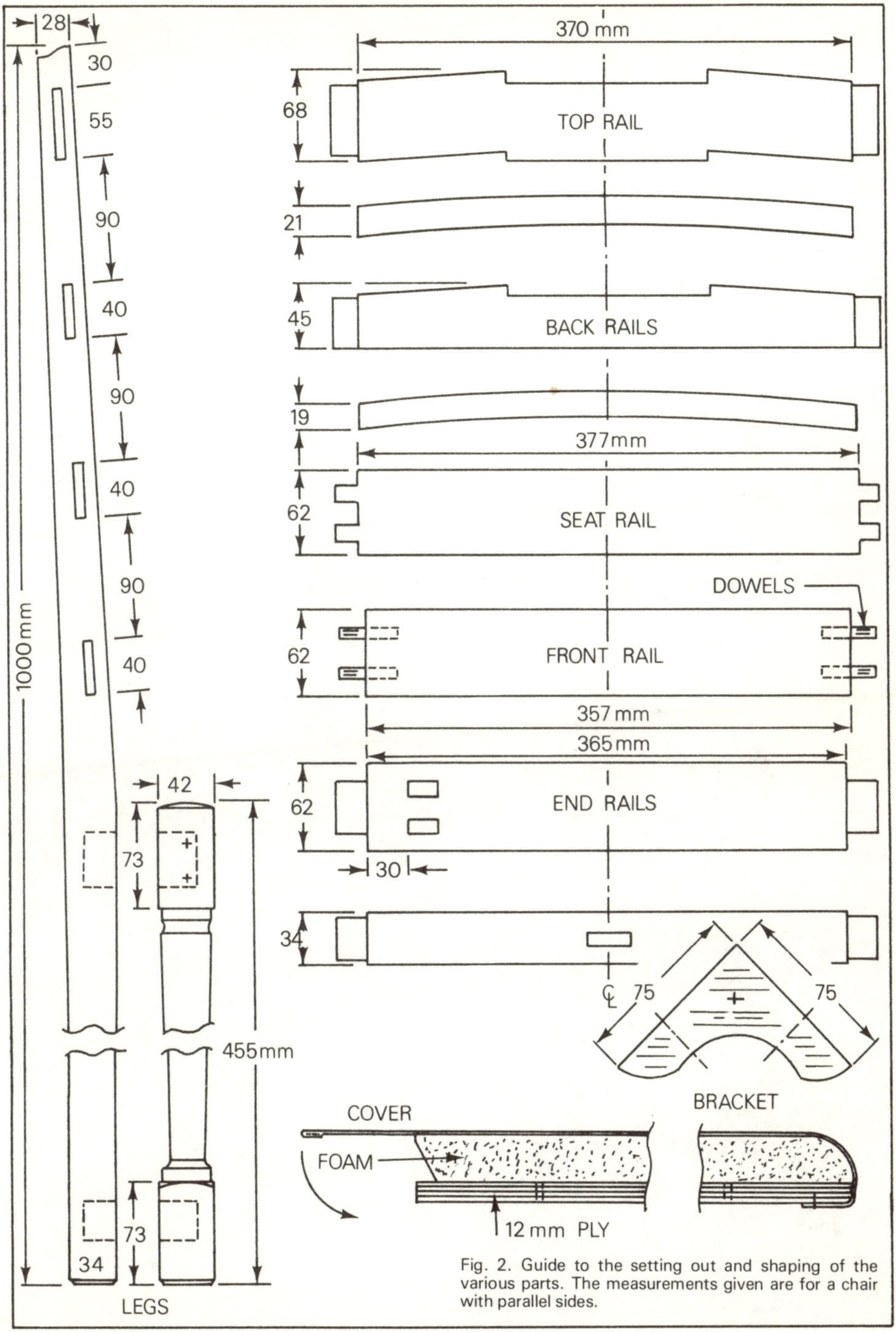

Fig. 2. Guide to the setting out and shaping of the various parts. The measurements given are for a chair with parallel sides.

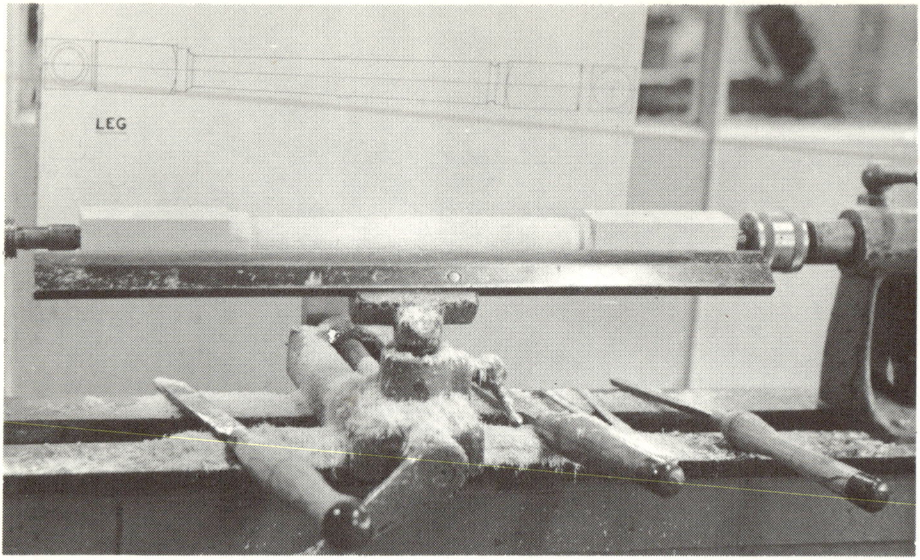

Fig. 3. One of the front legs in the course of turning in the lathe. A full sized working drawing is positioned behind for quick reference. Only about three lathe tools are required, and calipers to check the diameters.

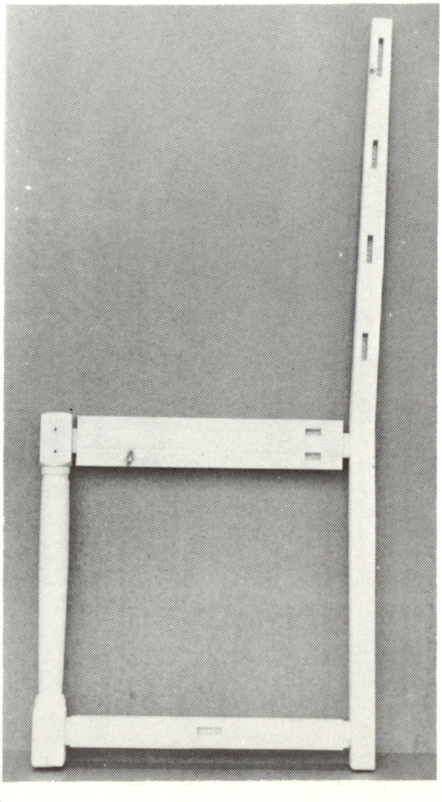

Fig. 4. View showing the hardwood corner brackets glued, and screwed 12 mm below the railedge. The brackets are bored for the fixing of the upholstered unit.

Parts List

No. req'd.	*Description*	*Long mm*	*Wide mm*	*Thick mm*	
2	Back legs	1,000	65	29	Softwood
2	Front legs	455	42	42	
1	Top back rail . .	414	68	32	
3	Back rails	414	45	29	
1	Seat rail	412	62	22	
1	Front rail	357	62	22	
2	End rails	415	62	22	
2	End rails	415	34	22	
1	Centre span rail . .	412	34	22	
1	Bracket material . .	300	50	25	Hardwood
1	Seat board	370	320	12	Plywood
1	Chip foam	370	320		
1	Cover	500	450		Tapestry

Finished sizes in millimetres.

cleaning up is important. The sealing can be clear (white) french polish, or polyurethane varnish. This should be applied as soon as possible after the cleaning up operation to preserve the natural colour as much as possible.

Upholstery

This can be approached in a variety of ways according to the ability of the enthusiast. The most simple method is to build up on a 12 mm ply board with 25 mm chip foam. If the foam is undercut at the edges a clean round will result when the material is pulled taut. The completed seat unit must be secured with screws when the polishing operation has been completed.

A compact dressing stool

Designed for use where space is limited providing a seat, storage compartment, and incidental shelf. This useful item of furniture gives the maker a chance to try his hand at a number of crafts namely, woodworking, painting, polishing, and upholstery all in reasonably simple form.

The supporting ends are made from 18 mm blockboard from which circles of 300 mm in diameter are cut in the indicated position. If the cut-outs are done by hand tools it is recommended that the circles should be marked out on both sides of the blockboard by deeply scoring with the point of a beam compass. This will reduce splintering during the cutting operation and make later repair work unnecessary. The edges of the holes should be spokeshaved level and reasonably smooth, then faced with veneer. Self adhesive strip veneer is now available, or impact adhesive can be used on plain veneer for this purpose.

The vertical edges of the supporting ends should be faced over, also the top edges. This strips of hardwood are preferred for this as they can be rounded slightly at the corners to give a more pleasing touch to the unit. These, too, can be secured with impact adhesive or other types under pressure.

The box unit which supports the seat has a paint finish so can be made from any close-grained timber, Parana pine being very suitable. The corners are lap dovetailed either by hand or mechanical means, and the mahogany type ply bottom should preferably be grooved in. Six holes are bored and countersunk in each end for No. 8 gauge screws. The joints should be well

Parts List

No. req'd.	*Description*	*Long mm*	*Wide mm*	*Thick mm*	*Material*
2	Ends	435	400	18	Birch blockboard
2	Box fronts	450	62	22	Parana pine
2	Box ends	290	62	22	Parana pine
2	Box linings . .	430	50	9	Mahogany
4	Box linings . .	260	50	9	Mahogany
1	Bottom	270	60	4	Mahogany plywood
9	Tray rails	486	22	12	Mahogany
1	Seat board	450	400	12	Plywood

Also required: 1 piece 25 mm thick foam 450 mm by 400 mm; 2 metres piping cord; approximately 0.75 metre 50 in cover; 1 pair 50 mm brass hinges and screws; 18-1¼in. by 6 brass screws; 12-1½in. by 8 steel ditto.

All timber sizes are net and allowances must be made for waste, etc.

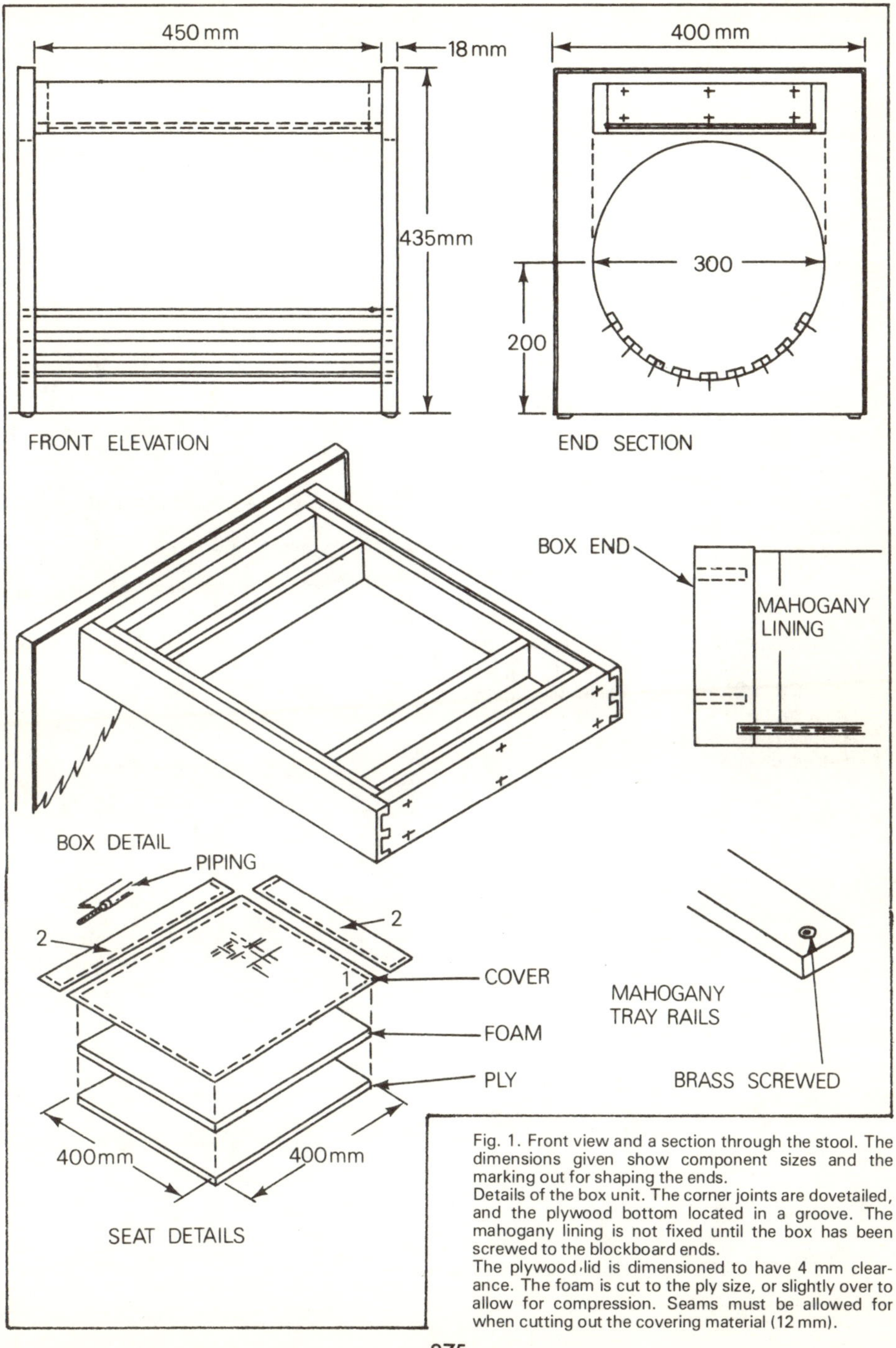

Fig. 1. Front view and a section through the stool. The dimensions given show component sizes and the marking out for shaping the ends.
Details of the box unit. The corner joints are dovetailed, and the plywood bottom located in a groove. The mahogany lining is not fixed until the box has been screwed to the blockboard ends.
The plywood lid is dimensioned to have 4 mm clearance. The foam is cut to the ply size, or slightly over to allow for compression. Seams must be allowed for when cutting out the covering material (12 mm).

glued and cramped on assembly.

Having completed the main ends and dove-tailed box they can be glued and screwed together and painted before attaching any of the polished or upholstery work. The painting process will require undercoating several times and rubbing down, or alternatively a cellulose finish may be preferred. Remember you cannot mix the two processes.

When the paintwork is completed the polished mahogany lining is fitted to the box unit, and this will conceal the construction screws in the ends. The under-tray slats are fixed with brass or chrome plated screws countersunk level.

The upholstered lid which forms a seat is built up on 12 mm ply which is dimensioned about 4 mm less than the 450 mm space between the two ends. This is to allow for the thickness of the covering material. The foam, 25 mm in thickness is cut to the same dimensions as the plywood. The ply corners should be radiused but not the foam as this extra bulk is required to give a firm corner.

When cutting out the covering material, 12 mm should be allowed for seams, after assessing how much the material will stretch in the tacking operation. Piping is made by covering piping cord with material, and tightly machine-stitching. The strip of material should be 37 mm in width and 1,800 mm long. The inside of the lid requires to be lined to obtain a satisfactory finish, this can be of the covering material, or quilting which is readily obtainable.

Fig. 2. The inside of the box unit showing the mahogany lining. The lining is built up with glue and panel pins and pushed in as a unit.

Chain-link fruit bowl

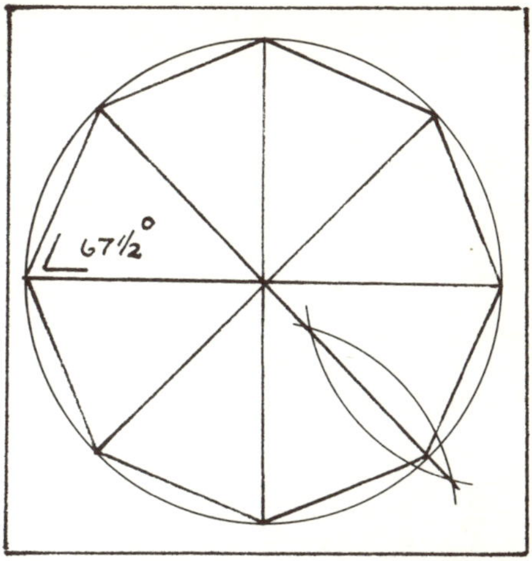

Fig. 2. The geometrical setting out required. This should be drawn full size. A circle of 9in. diam. (230 mm) gives a finished bowl of about 8in. (204 mm). Although an octagon is shown here, any regular polygon could be used.

Fig. 1. Illustration of completed fruit bowl in use.

Fig. 3. The prepared timber sections, in contrasting hardwoods. Cascamite powdered resin adhesive was used to bond the components, and this must be done under pressure.

The construction of a fruit bowl of this type requires the introduction of geometrical skill in addition to the ability to use the wood turning lathe.

Two contrasting colours of hardwood should be used and sycamore combined with either mahogany or walnut gives pleasing results. If the preparation of material can be machine-assisted, so much the better, as this will speed the work considerably. It is also advisable to prepare material for more than one bowl while the

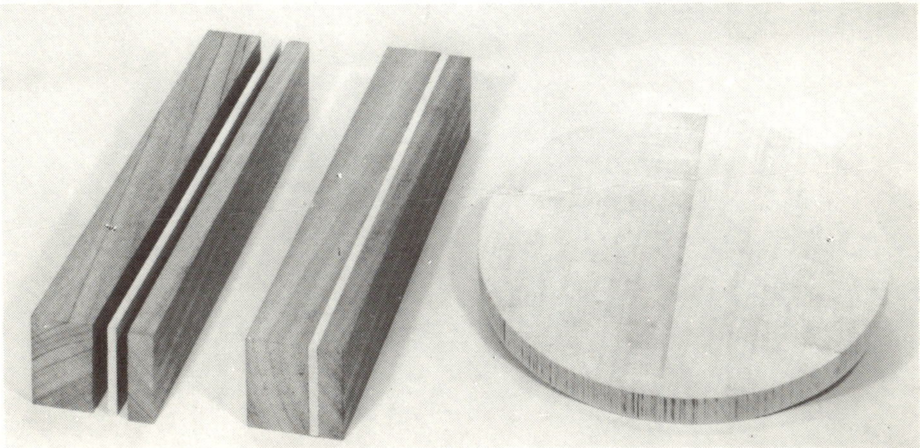

Fig. 4. It is advisable to prepare a test set of parts using softwood for the benefit of setting up the saw to the correct angle. A plywood template prepared from the drawing can be very helpful, and this can be saved for future use.

Fig. 5. The glued sections are here being cut to the required angle and length. The saw used is of the hollow ground type requiring no set on the fine teeth. This gives an almost planed finish to the cut. Note also the backing piece to prevent spelching.

machines are set, as the quantity of timber required is very small.

It is necessary to set out an octagon the full size required to determine the size of the segments, and the all important angle can be taken from the drawing. All segments must be of equal length, and cut at an angle of 67.5 degrees. These points are important to give neat intersections of the chain links in the completed bowl. Accurate centring of the built up bowl on the face plate of the lathe is also important in this respect.

Materials required for an 8in. (200 mm) diameter bowl

1 piece 33in. by 2¼in. (850 mm by 57 mm by 32 mm) walnut.
1 piece 33in. by 2¼in. by ⅜in. (850 mm by 57 mm by 9 mm) walnut.
1 piece 33in. by 2¼in. by $\frac{3}{16}$in (850 mm by 57 mm by 4 mm) sycamore.
1 piece 9in. by 9in. by ¾in. (230 mm by 230 mm by 19 mm) sycamore.

The above are planed sizes.

Fig. 6. A set of parts successfully prepared for glueing. If one length of material is used the grain marking will follow around the completed bowl if so desired, providing the parts are placed in the order of cutting.

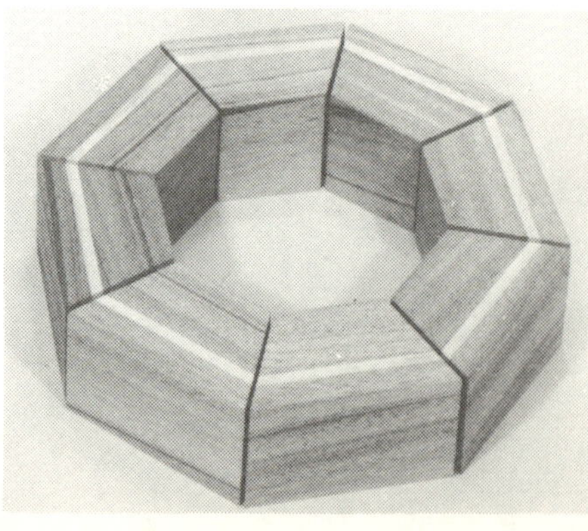

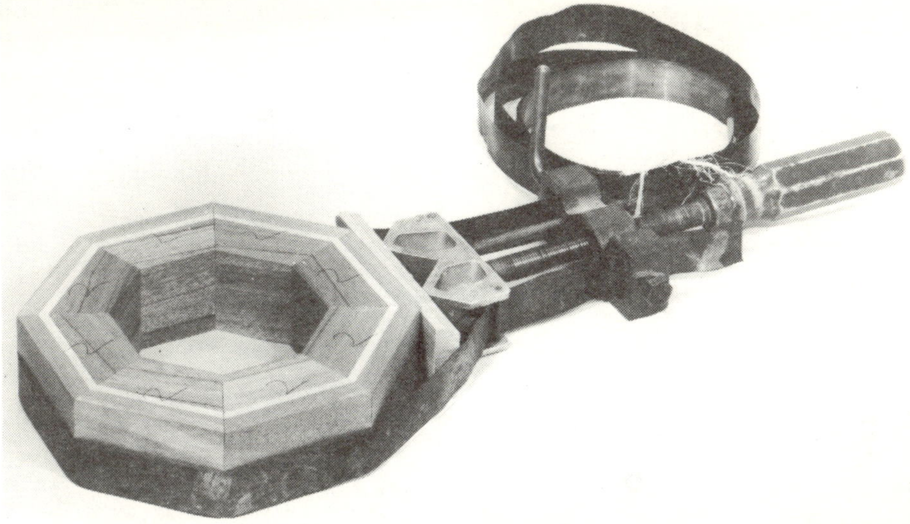

Fig. 7. The segments are firmly gripped in a metal strap cramp for bonding together. Most operations using resin adhesives require lots of pressure to give good results. The surfaces should be adequately coated with adhesive, and the excess cleaned off at once.

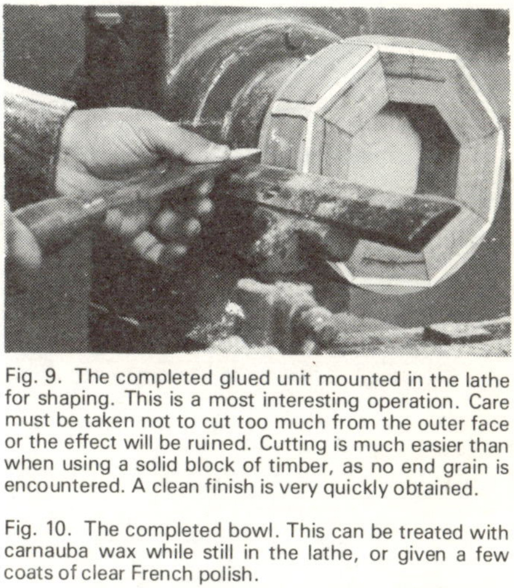

Fig. 9. The completed glued unit mounted in the lathe for shaping. This is a most interesting operation. Care must be taken not to cut too much from the outer face or the effect will be ruined. Cutting is much easier than when using a solid block of timber, as no end grain is encountered. A clean finish is very quickly obtained.

Fig. 8. The second stage of glueing. If a screw-down press is not available, a number of small G cramps can be used. Packing pieces should be used to prevent pressure damage to the work.

Fig. 10. The completed bowl. This can be treated with carnauba wax while still in the lathe, or given a few coats of clear French polish.

Constructing honours board

Reply to problem

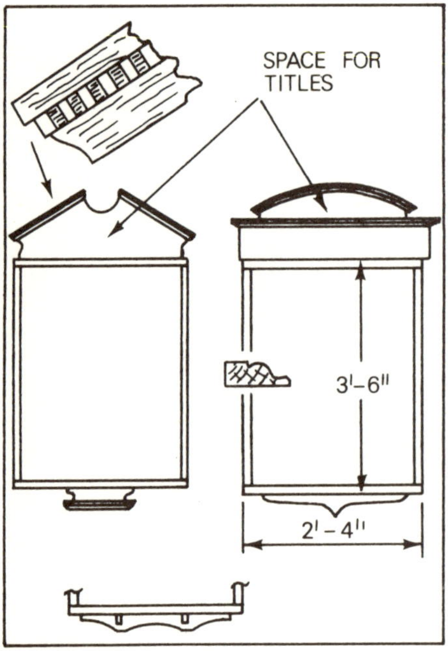

PROBLEM

I have been asked to make two boards of honour for my college, to record annually the names of members who have held office. I would appreciate suggestions, alternative designs, or improvements to those shown in my sketches.
Since the college was founded about 40 years ago I feel the design should be in keeping, perhaps along classical lines but not too funereal.
The timber will be oak and the signwriting in gold leaf. W.K.S.

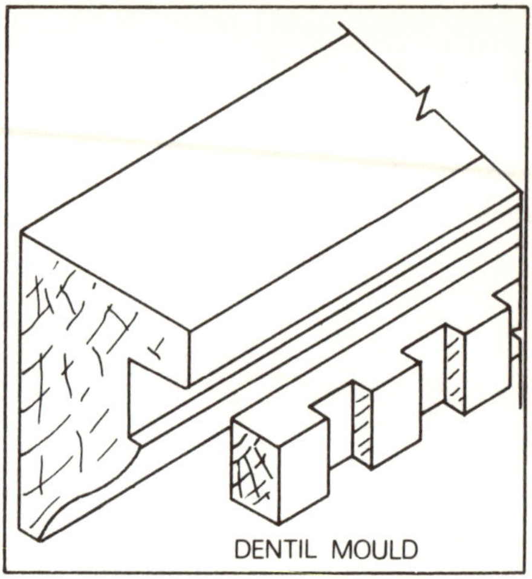

Dentil mouldings can be made in two sections for ease of manufacture. Fixing screws can also be located behind the insert piece.

SOLUTION

Querist seems to be quite definite on the type of honours boards he is going to make. I would say that his designs date back more than the 40 years age of the school, although his school may have been fitted out in this style.
What he should ask himself is: "Will my efforts of carrying out this work in period style be appreciated?" If so, by all means have a go, otherwise it will be much easier to make do with a more simple design as used in our present age.
The most suitable material for the main backboard will be 18 mm veneered blockboard, whatever his design. This is preferred to using solid timber for wide panels, as schools are subject to severe central heating, which can cause movement. The matching of grain and figure on the main board is important, also the evenness of colour, in particular if it is to be finished natural. If these points are ignored the finished article may look inferior. It is, in fact, a good plan to stand the panels in their intended fixing location during preparation to see how the light affects the grain. Turning the panels, end-for-end can make a difference with oak-veneered surfaces.
It will be advisable to mount the blockboard on a softwood back frame made up of 75 mm by 25 mm material. This will help to maintain a flat surface and ensure a close fit to the wall. All the edges of the blockboard must be concealed with oak strips or veneer, this also applies to the

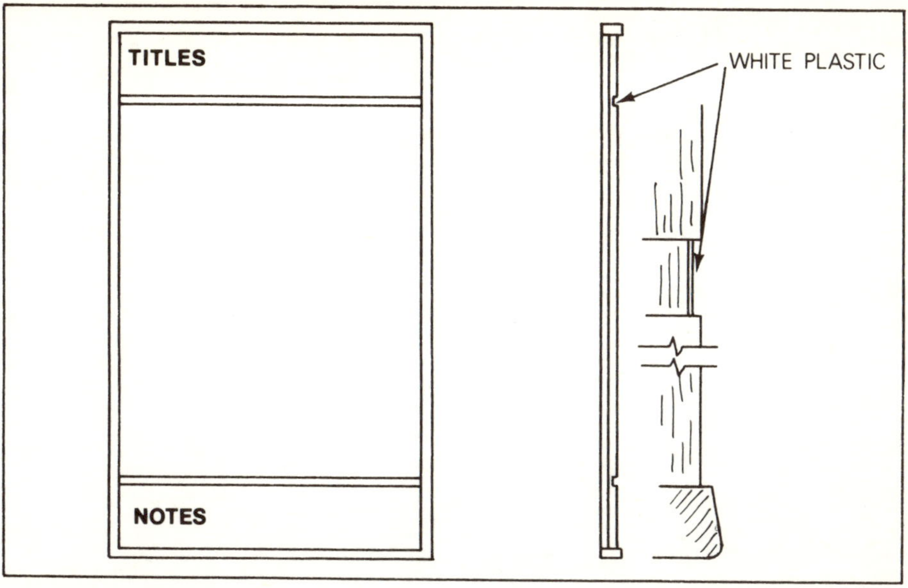

A simple design for an honours board incorporating the use of a modern material, white plastic. The moulded edge capin would be tongued to the front panel, and a softwood frame screwed from behind.

Suggestions for mouldings around the edge of the boards. The sections of the corner pateras blocks could be matched to that of the mouldings if desired.

backing frame. No metal pins or screws should be visible on the face in this kind of work, this can be achieved with careful planning.

If the dentil mould is used, this can be made in two parts. The main body of the mould is grooved to take the dentil section. This is glued into the groove after the mould has been fixed. Quite a lot of time could be spent on these raking and curved moulds if they are to be geometrically correct in all their aspects. Only a small amount is required, however, and this could be made either by hand tools or machine.

The curved pediment mould would entail a fair

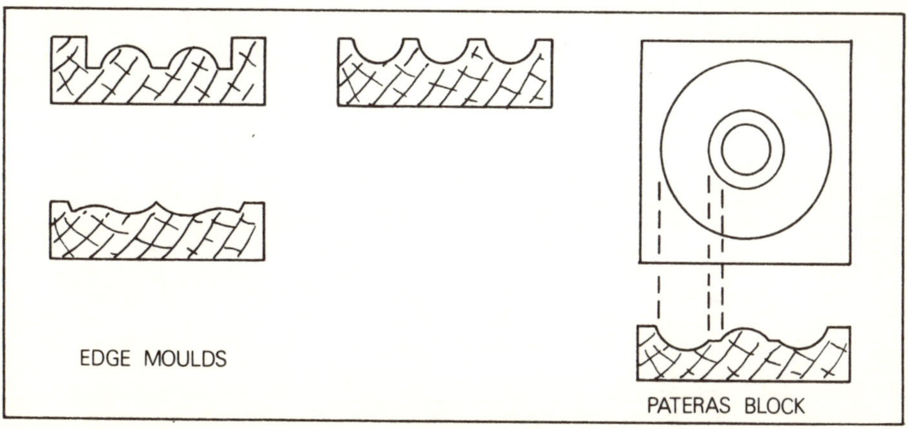

amount of work, unless a spindle moulder is available. This shaped top section could be left off altogether in that design, if a more simple project is required. The flat mould around the edge of the boards should be a more balanced design than the one shown in his sketch. I have included several suggestions for this moulding, and the corner pateras. The pateras section could be similar to the mould section, this would provide scope for matched lathe work.

I think the overall dimensions of the boards are correct inasmuch that the two can be cut from one sheet of 8ft. by 4ft. blockboard including the built-up work. This point should be kept in mind if any major change is made to the project.

My sketch shows the outline of a present-day design incorporating a small amount of white plastic. The younger people of the school may appreciate this type of design, but I have no wish to change querist's enthusiasm for the finer arts. With simple designs a high standard must be aimed at with such points as the selection of timber, close fitting joints, and the final clean up. Should any further advice, or help with the preparation of the mouldings be required by machine, please contact me through the Editor.

Aid to woodworking

With the training of immigrants in hand, the increased school-leaving age in view and the introduction of metric coming over the hill, new systems of teaching are bound to develop from necessity. The familiar statement about this year's lesson preparation being of no use for next year will probably be more true now than ever before.

The construction industry, for instance, is already in advanced years of a gradual change to the metric system. The deciding factor for a junior, or even an adult, gaining a particular job in employment in the near future may depend upon whether or not he is capable of working in metric. Training in the use of the metric system cannot commence too soon, in particular for those preparing to enter a craft.

The increased school-leaving age will give a further compulsory year of study. It will provide opportunity to bridge the gap between school and the wage-earning world. The bright student will be "rarin' to go" but what of the backward and not-so-bright?

The following scheme has been devised for, and tested on, groups of the not-so-bright, also groups of varying abilities, and others. It relates to instruction in woodwork, and could be described as the assisted handwork system. Its aim is to give confidence and results.

To operate the scheme it is necessary to have access to a range of medium weight woodworking machines. Most schools have some already, but the installation of two or three more may help to operate the scheme fully. The Wadkin Bursgreen range is ideal for this purpose, being compact and simple to install.

The machines are not intended for operation by young people; the selection of a workshop assistant of a suitable type should be made to carry out the simple operations required. Success of the scheme depends very much on the preparation work.

The correct approach would be to make a prototype of a selected design of model. Present-day design of stools, chairs, and coffee tables lend themselves well to machine production. When a

A view of a section of a class of immigrant students.

design is completed, batch production of components can begin. Not all operations, however, will be carried out by machine. A certain amount of work will be left to be done by the student before assembly can commence. The basic idea is to bring the project within his capability, not to do the job for him in its entirety.

The amount of work done by machine preparation can be governed by three factors. (a) The complexity of the model. (b) The ability of the students. (c) The number of class hours available for completion.

Backward individuals can be catered for by requisitioning of more operations to be carried out by machine on a certain number of components.

With assisted handwork, in theory at least, there should be no failures. There should also be less waste of materials, and in establishments where the sale of completed models is encouraged incoming finance may help in the purchase of equipment.

This system is also useful in teaching where communication between teacher and student does not conform to normal standards. This occurs in the case of the partially handicapped, such as the deaf, and also with immigrants.

I quote these two groups as I have had some personal experience of them—happy experience, and I think the assisted handwork system, which I used, contributed towards it. It is much easier to convey instructions with the aid of a model that is taking shape than a pile of the raw material. Enthusiasm, too, is much more quickly stimulated in the project, and the problem is not usually getting the students to start work, but getting them to stop!

Preparation

Metric measurement was used with both groups, in preparatory drawings and in the actual work. Transferring to millimetres from drawings to timber provided good inauguration.

Success for the scheme depends very much on the ability to get the preparation work done. Many instructors are capable of doing this themselves if time permits. The use of woodworking machinery, for the enthusiast, is a fascinating experience. The scheme is suggested for use in the additional year at school, when students will be looking for something different—assisted handwork.

Looking ahead, this method of working could also be successfully used for classes in woodworking for girls or women. I cannot claim experience of this type of class (women brandishing saws have not, fortunately, come within my line of duty). I have, however, been able to observe their abilities in furniture production in industry. It is upon this experience that I could easily visualize their adaptability to this type of assisted creative work.

Another view in the workshop, showing a student at work on a piece of furniture.

The term assisted handwork, used in this text, relates only to woodworking. Probably instructors in other crafts may consider it could be applied to their subject. It very likely could, as it is mechanical aids that have made this possible. Most goods today are the product of a machine at some stage; but this is why we very often have to buy what we are offered, rather than what we want.

Advanced knowledge of industrial production methods can help in the planning of assisted handwork. It is in this field that I would recommend research. Many textbooks provide excellent designs for craft work, but advanced methods of production are not usually explained.

Try taking a look at industrial production methods for your next year's lesson preparation. The knowledge gained could be of help to young people preparing to take up employment.

How to plan a woodwork room

Efficient operation of a woodwork room in a school or college can often be influenced by the initial planning. The fact has always to be borne in mind that it is customary for such a room to be used by a number of groups of students, probably of varying ages and abilities. If the two latter can be approximately defined, it will at least help with decision to some extent.

The selection of the type of work-benches to be installed can be governed by the floor area, in relation to the number of students to be accommodated at one time. Individual benches, per student, take up more floor space than benches designed to accommodate two or more students. There will also be a differential in cost. Experience has shown that a student or a factory worker, in command of his own bench, has a certain prestige which may well reflect in his work.

Benches with cupboard space below for the storage of models are often selected where other storage accommodation is not available. This can be quite a sensible plan, but it also has disadvantages. Tools often get misplaced under this type of enclosed bench, and the job of waste removal from the floor can be cumbersome to those responsible. The ideal type of bench would be one with only a limited amount of underfill, to allow visibility, and housekeeping.

If tools are to last, they must be of a high standard of quality in relation to durability. Some manufacturers offer more than one grade of tools. The cheaper grade are intended for occasional use only. In the selection of a tool or piece of equipment consideration should be given on how check, and control, can be made on the ancillary parts relating to it. It is very often the

Non-Vocational students in an adult education centre

Trade student

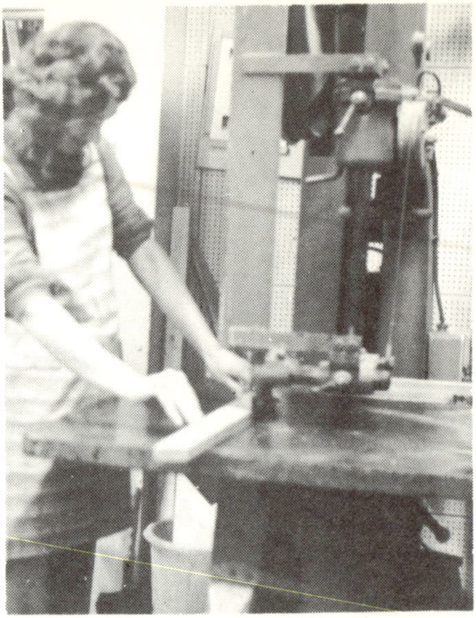

Creative study activities.

small parts belonging to a tool that become mislaid, so making the tool unserviceable.

Spare parts, or a complete tool of many items, should be kept at hand, as a bad image can be created if tools are offered for use that are not in working order.

Tools and equipment in the woodwork room can be classified into groups for documentation purposes.

1 Measuring and marking equipment.
2 Saws.
3 Planes.
4 Edge tools.
5 Shaping equipment.
6 Boring and drilling.
7 Screwing and nailing.
8 General equipment.

No one student needs all items of equipment at one time, but some tools are in more demand than others. Helpful information, based on experience, can be obtained from tool makers regarding the quantity of each tool required for a given group of students. Ref. Stanley Tool Co., Sheffield. This can be helpful to the less experienced planner.

Knowledge of the tools in general use can help the instructor in charge in his methods of tool check and control. Instead of having one large storage unit for all tools, he can withdraw those which he considers the general tools in everyday use, and allocate them in locked up kit form to each bench.

Furniture restoration

A kit of this type could consist of the following:

Tenon saw.	Try square.
Dovt. saw.	Bevel.
Coping saw.	Rule.
Hammer.	Smooth plane.
Set of chisels.	Jack plane.
Pincers.	Screwdrivers.
Marking gauge.	Bradawl.
Mortise gauge.	Nail punch.

Not all establishments favour this system, since it means a fair amount of preparation—and also key work—but it has its advantages. If only 10 students are present in a room equipped for 20, then 10 tool cupboards can remain locked. The value of each kit could be as much as £20, which means tools to the value of £200 are safely locked up. Also students must use the tools from the allocated cupboard, and respect them.

Cupboards housing equipment should be at "walk around" height, for easy checking, not under a bench where an instructor has to descend to his hands and knees to view.

In classes for the more mature students, the use of power operated hand tools should be encouraged. For this reason, power supply points should be installed at frequent intervals to keep trailing electrical cables to a minimum. These tools should be demonstrated before being handed over to students, and their danger points clearly indicated. Insulation on wiring, mainly near the point of entry to the tool, should be inspected frequently.

Woodworking machinery within the hand work room should be limited to say, a turning lathe, and a tool grinding appliance. Machines for preparation work can add unlimited interest to woodworking, but they should be preferably accommodated in an adjoining room. Hand operations such as hammering distract a machine operator, and noise and dust from machines can be unpleasant to a hand worker.

Woodworking machines for this type of work should be of the medium weight type. These machines should be operated by a suitably trained person (they can in fact turn a woodwork room into a mini-production unit).

For an expenditure of around £1,500 a selection of machines may be purchased, which will give service for many years at very little annual cost.

Suggested machines could be:

Circular saw. (Dimension type.)
Bandsaw.
Combined planer and thicknesser.
Mortising machine. (Square chisel.)

Conditions should be made as comfortable as possible where human beings are spending a section of their life.

Section 7 Machining for building requirements

Door Design and Construction

Setting out rods. Timber selection. Joint formations. Core filling. Provision for furniture. Economical doors. Dowel methods. Raised panels. Edge lippings. Double margin doors. Wardrobe doors. Heated press. Surfacing stiles. Final trimming.

Manufacturing Kitchen Units

Need for fitted units. Construction methods. Sub-assembly system. Working laminated plastics. Edge trimming. L.V. Strip heating. Tungsten carbide tipped cutters. Carcase dimensions. Fourcutting timber sections.

Window Construction

Comparison of methods. Types of machines required. Rebating and moulding. Jigs for shaped work. Corner lock joints. Use of cutter blocks. Advanced methods. Rebating on surface planer. Solid profile cutters. Preservation treatment.

Internal Trim to Buildings

Use of standard sections. T. and G. boards. Door casings. Storey frames. Linings. Backfencing. Allowance for plaster. Building blocks. Widthing joints. Trim for windows. Cutter preparation. Circular architraves.

Wardrobes and Cupboards

Stock sizes available. Advantage of fitted furniture. Front frame construction. Carcase construction. Choice of materials. Laminboard, plywood, chipboard, etc. Cutting sheet material. Plinth units. Sectional construction. Interior drawers and trays. Doors, sliding and hinged. Cylinder cupboards. Removable ends. Tank supports.

External Trim to Buildings

Preparation of timber. Moisture content. Effect of prolonged wetting. Scientific aspects. Weathering bevels to sections. Quality of planed finish. Design of cladding material. Fourcutting methods. Use of swage saw. Splay sawing. Ranch type fencing. Fascia boards. Gate construction. Setting out tips.

Shopfitting

Planning to suit labour requirements. Prevention of waste. Machining long material. Use of wide timber. Preparation of fixing grounds. Construction of display units. Shop front construction. Preparing timber to receive glass. Fret saw machines. Wood letters.

Aids for Site Carpenters

Increasing productivity on site. Knowledge of requirements. Geometrical aspects. Roofing by machine. Use of jigs and templates. Fitting doors and furniture. Power tools. Compressed air units. Use of prepared plugs, pellets, screw blocks.

Stairs For Today

Planning machine layout. The Building Regulations and stairs. Determining tread and riser dimensions. Explanation of the terms 'Tread and Rise'. Stock sections of material used. Trenching machines. Other trenching methods. Modern requirements. Open tread stairs. Continuous handrails. Combination of wood and metal construction.

Door Design and Construction

Typical glazed screen with door. Setting out becomes necessary in the planning to ensure that the glazing bars line through. Also, as the door is not located in a central position the question of handling will be involved. The setting out rods should be prepared full size.

Doors used in building have to conform to several basic standards to enable them to utilise fittings which are readily available. Even with the most economic form of flush door provision must be made for the secure fixing of the latch and handle furniture.

This usually consists of a block of timber within the core adjoining the closing edge of the door. The positioning of the securing block is very often indicated on the door edge if a mortise has not already been cut to receive the latch.

Mortising done within the factory unit can save a considerable amount of hand time on the site, and if any consideration to hinge recessing can also be given this is a valuable asset.

Although flush doors have been popular for several decades, no acceptable surface mounting latch has evolved, of a decorative nature, and at a cost to compete with a mortised-in unit. The surface mounting rim latch era virtually en-

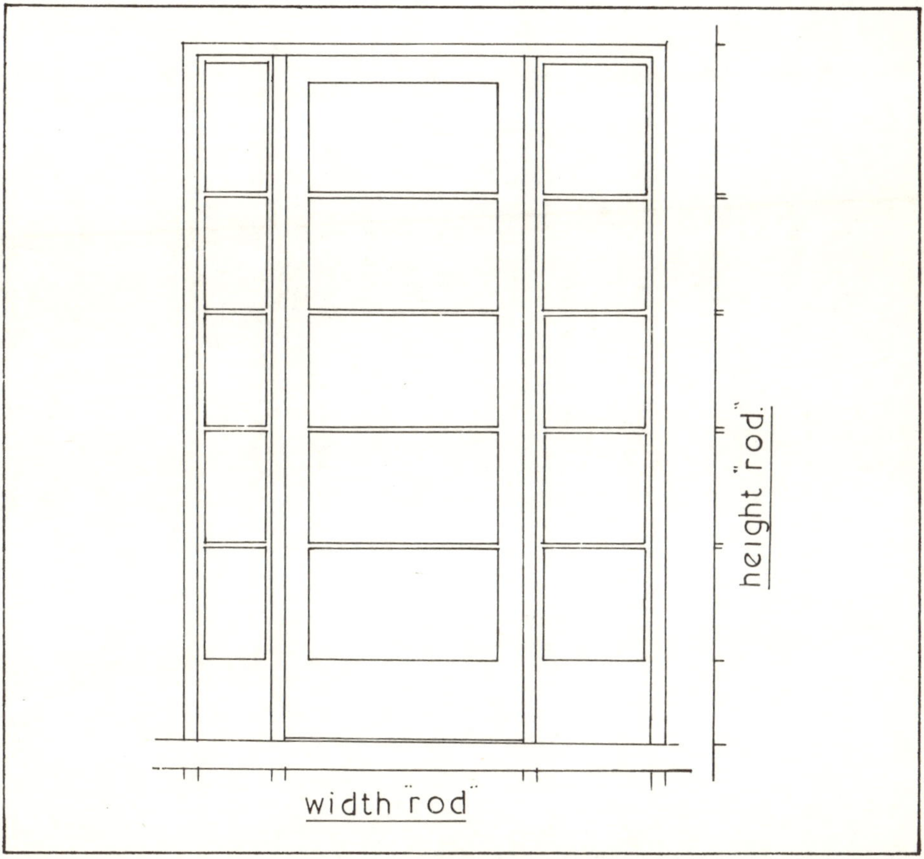

much scope for enthusiastic designers to create present-day forms of doors used in the past. It is now possible to fabricate a series of false stiles and rails on the surface of a flush door to give a period type effect, using a suitable adhesive.

Panelled doors are also being produced by high pressure moulding methods. These developing types of construction eliminate cracks due to joint failures as found in many of the traditional types of framed doors.

A feature of a framed and panelled door is the admiration of the craftsmanship which it displays. Methods which merely give an imitation of the real thing are not favoured by all but may have to be accepted mainly for economic reasons.

Modern machining techniques lend themselves well to framed door construction, and are capable of producing work of a constant high standard. Efficiency standards depend upon the selection and preparation of the material, joint design, and provision for movement where such items as wide panels are subject to humidity variations.

In the construction of framed doors it is desirable ded with the introduction of flush doors.

For external doors provision must also be made for the fitting of a letter box plate. Probably the least acceptable position is in the bottom rail of a framed door unless the width of the rail exceeds, say, 250 mm.

Plates fixed near the step level are subject to additional weathering in the way of rain splashing upwards as well as down, so are better located well up the door surface.

Entrance units do at times incorporate the letter plate independent of the door itself which is an excellent idea as incoming mail can be conveniently dropped on to a side table positioned adjacent to the door, and not on the floor.

Flush doors provide little scope for the designer, and features are limited mainly to the surface finish.

Doors faced with decorative veneers are preferred by many to painted surfaces, particularly for interior use. If the natural beauty of the timber remains visible, this can often suggest a basis to a furnishing scheme within the room.

Period type panelled doors are returning to favour for exterior use, and this should provide

Consideration must be given to the selection of timber when the grain is to provide a feature in the completed door. Double thickness timber deepcut gives perfect matching to a pair of stiles. Panels are preferably cut from same board for grain to follow through.

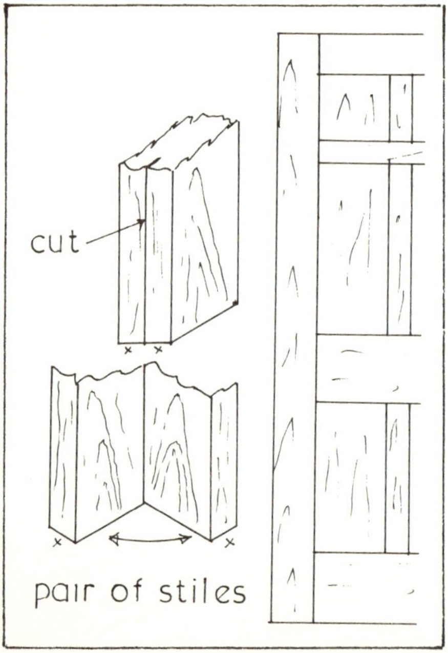

Economical door construction for wardrobes, etc. The polished panel board provides furniture finish. Skeleton core from ex 50 x 25 assembled in jig with metal stables. Backing skin from plywood or hardboard. Panels applied under pressure.

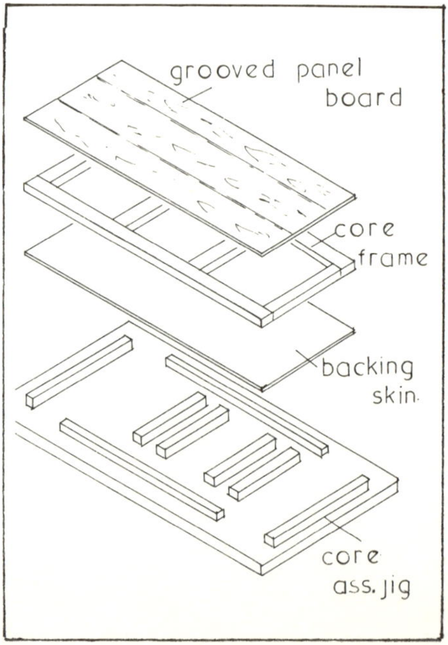

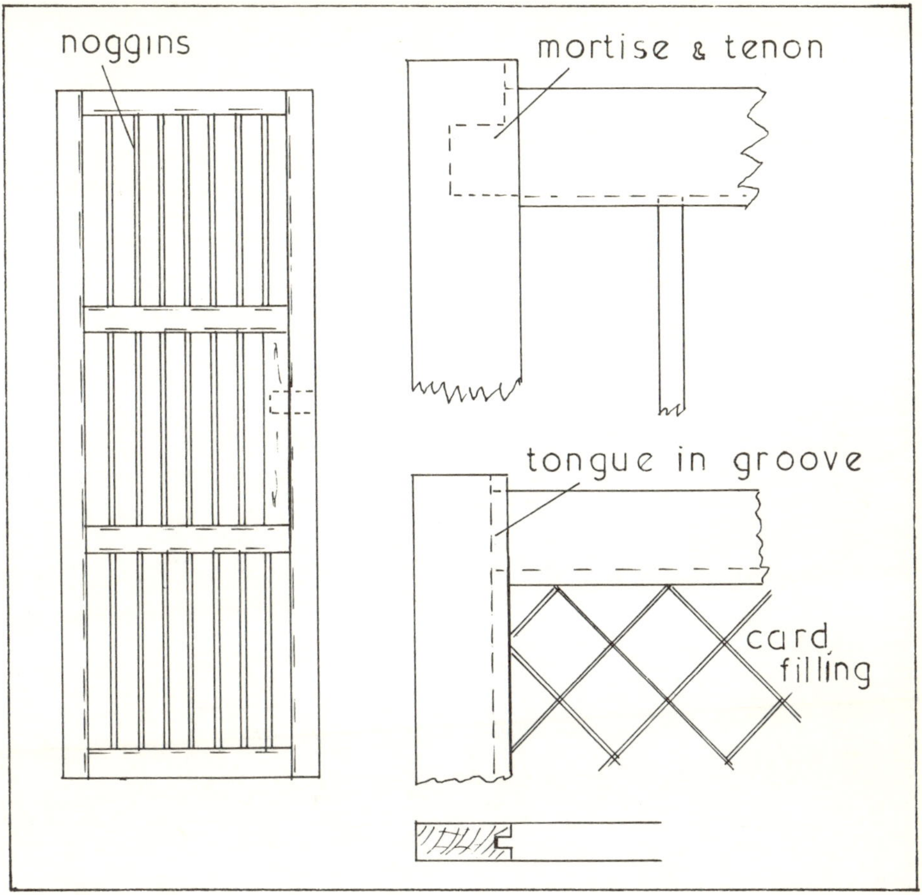

Joint construction of flush door is related to the efficiency of the pressing of the surface panels. Example: (a) The use of impact adhesive and weights. Framing joints should be mortised and tenoned. (b) Using a heated press and synthetic resin adhesive. Tongue in groove method would be satisfactory.

that the timber has a moisture content not exceeding 15 per cent.

In a heated building it will decrease further than this after a period but if over-dry material is used initially, swelling may occur causing additional work in easing.

The material should be surface planed and edged before being passed through a thicknessing machine. Planing should not commence until the material has been dried to an acceptable moisture content or the surfacing and straightening operation could be just a waste of time.

Where such material as 200 mm x 20 mm is sawn down the centre to make door stiles 100 x 50, a waiting period even if only overnight to let the timber adjust itself for movement before planing can be beneficial.

Material selection and preparation regarding moisture applies to both the small producer and the larger manufacturer. The small man generally selects the higher grade of material from his stock when making doors, but when buying in for large production it is essential that the consignment is of the constant required standard.

Kiln drying is often resorted to as this then ensures that movement will be limited during processing. The higher grade type of timber is usually free from twist when in the rough and lends itself to mechanically fed straightening

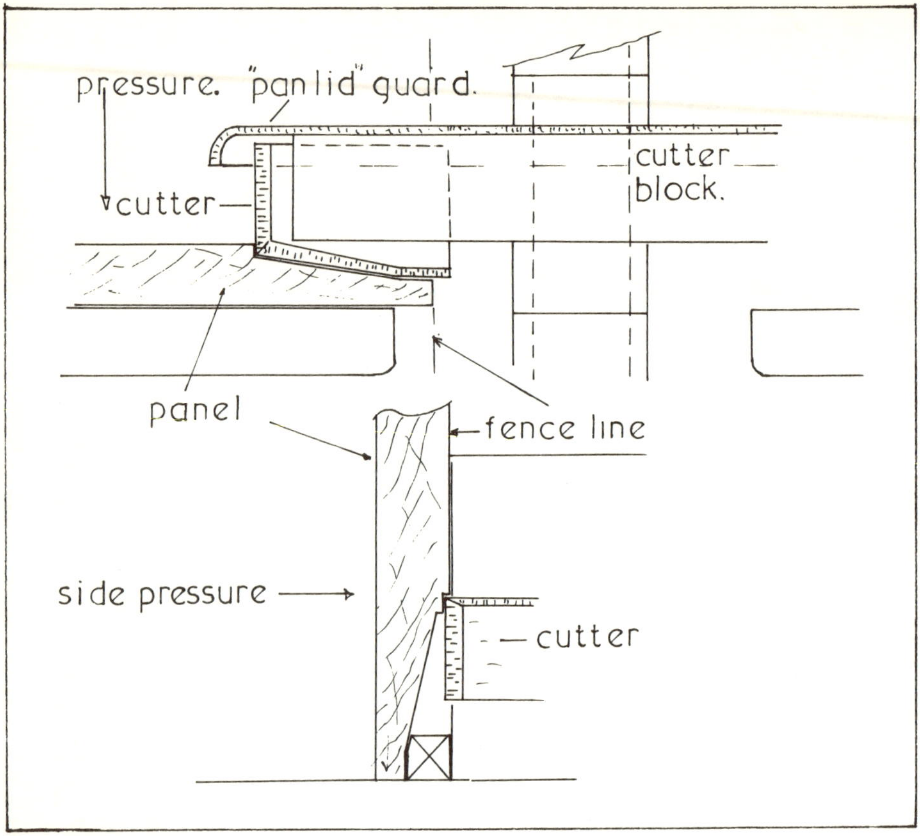

Working raised and fielded panels on the spindle moulder with the cutter on top. This maintains constant thickness of the tongue. Note the provision of a lid guard for the operators's safety. Additional fillets can be formed with the panel standing on edge to reduce cutter production.

Complicated mould profiles as found on period type doors lend themselves to dowel jointing more than mortising and tenoning if hand operations are to be eliminated.

planers such as fitted to the infeed of a four-cutter.

After the planing and thicknessing operation,.it is customary to cut members to a constant length when working in quantity production.

In the case of tenoned members, the dimensioning is carried out with the cut off saws during the pass through the double-ended tenoning machine.

The importance of setting out, or preparation of

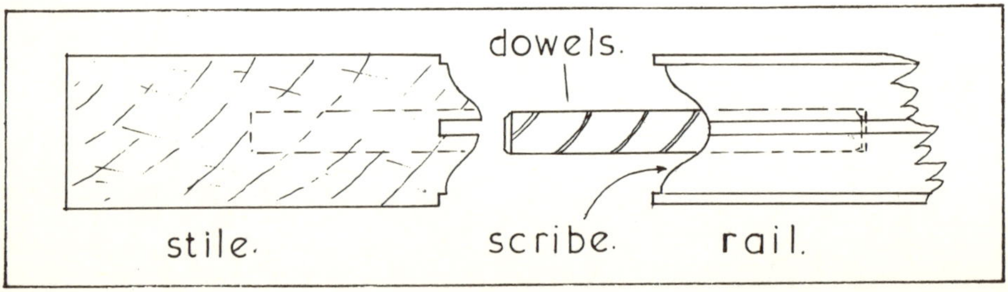

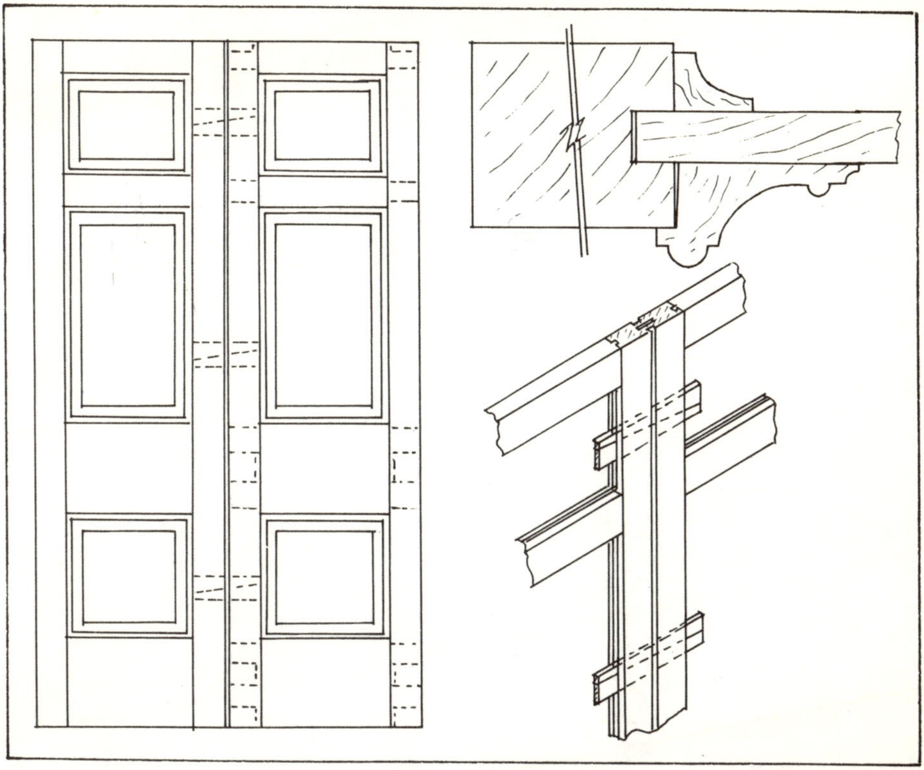

Double margin door: typical design of a door of this pattern often found on public buildings or superior types of residence. Consideration must be given to the order of assembly to ensure that all the mortise and tenon joints can be wedged.

the rod as it is termed by some, cannot be over-emphasised in the planning stage of a newly introduced item.

It is useful in door construction where two or more doors are required to fill an opening, and rail dimensions have to be determined considering meeting rebates, etc.

A graphical solution, which a setting out sheet provides, is more assuring than a mathematical one in many circumstances. When a number of glazing bars are involved the positioning of these can be carefully planned on the rod and transferred to the work at the time of requirement.

Information taken from the rod can also be very helpful in the preparation of cutting lists, keeping waste to a minimum.

In marking out door material for mortising and tenoning, the stiles must be face marked in pairs. Where the door is to have a natural finish consideration must be given regarding the matching of the grain pattern, and also colour.

This point does not apply to painted work only to items which are to have what is termed "furniture finish".

In quantity working not all the rebates, grooves and moulds may be applied during the four-cutting operation, as it may be necessary for some of the cuts to be stopped. Design of a product should take into consideration this as it adds cost.

Standards of design are accepted on these lines although at times they are not quite correct. Garage doors for instance in which the lower section is filled in with match boarding and the upper part glazed, are frequently found with the putty on the outside.

This is done so that a through rebate carries the boarding below and the glass in the upper portion of the stile. The face side of an external door is on the outside, and although the putty may be acceptable from a weathering point of view it does not produce a face side finish.

Unlike a door, the face side of a window is on the inside of the building, except in the case of,

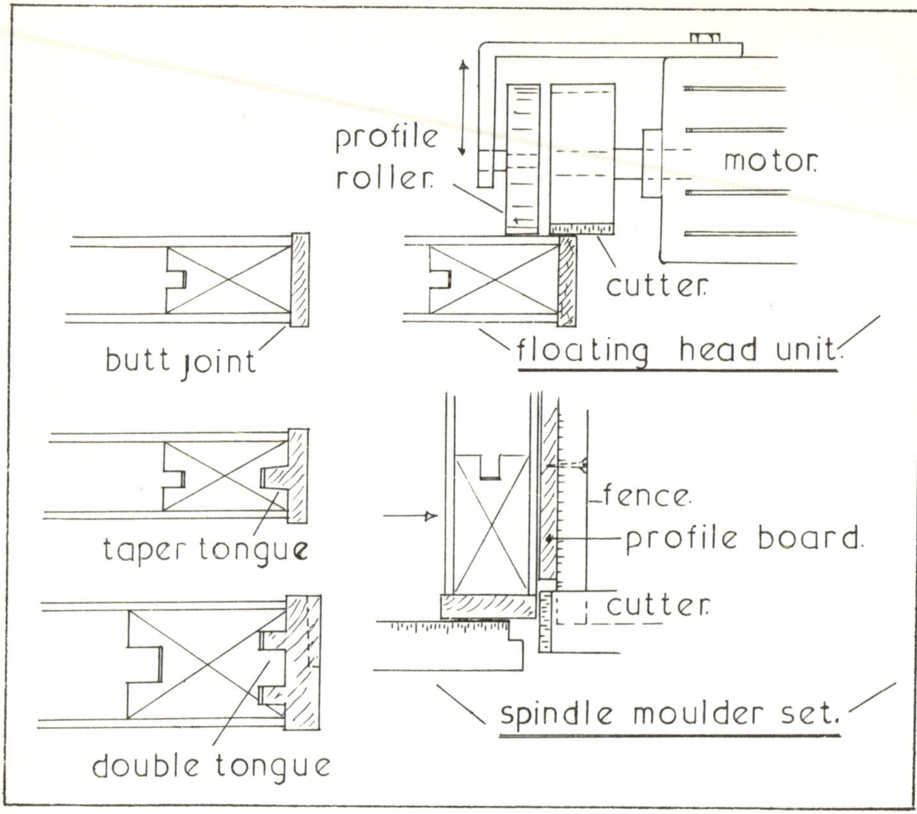

Methods of attaching edge lippings to doors. Butt jointing most suitable for electronic methods. R. F. and L. V. strip heating. Double tongues may be necessary on heavy duty doors with rebated meetings.

say, a shop window where the viewing customer should have the privilege.

Where rebates or moulds have to be stopped these have to be formed on the spindle moulder, in pairs when they relate to the stile members. This can mean running in on one hand of the stile, and dropping on to the cutting unit and running out on the other.

The dropping on can be dangerous to the unexperienced, and supporting stops should be fitted to the machine to prevent kickback.

Figures show that more accidents occur on the spindle moulder through the dropping on operation than any other, and particular care should be taken if a wobble saw is involved. Dropping on can be eliminated altogether with the use of reverse rotation, and still keep the cutter operating on the underside of the work.

This point should always be considered when quantity working, or installing switch gear to a new machine.

Working raised and fielded panels can involve a large amount of cutter projection when operating the spindle moulder, and the methods of working require some consideration. To ensure that the thickness of the panel remains constant for fitting into the grooves of the door framing some operators prefer the cutting to be done overhead instead of the underneath more safe procedure.

Additional attention must be made to the guarding of the cutting unit, and it is important that ample down pressure is applied to prevent the work from lifting off the machine table or the increased risk factor will not be merited.

With hardwood in particular, which requires a high finish, it can be to advantage to make the

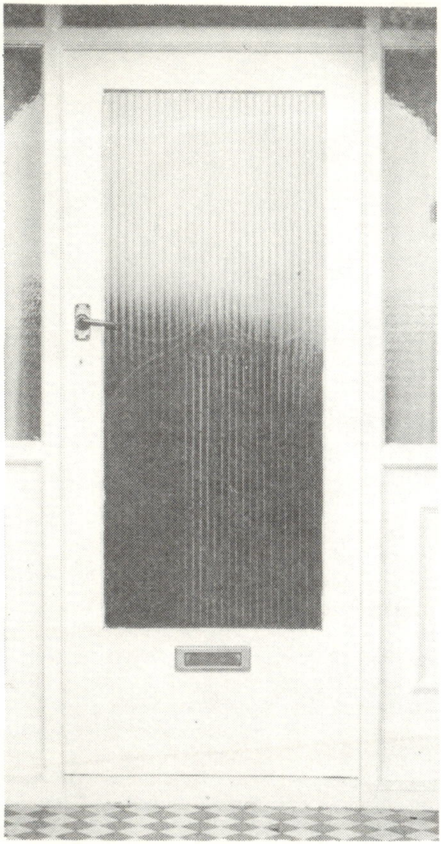

Bottom rails on external doors should be of a generous width if they are to accommodate a letter plate.

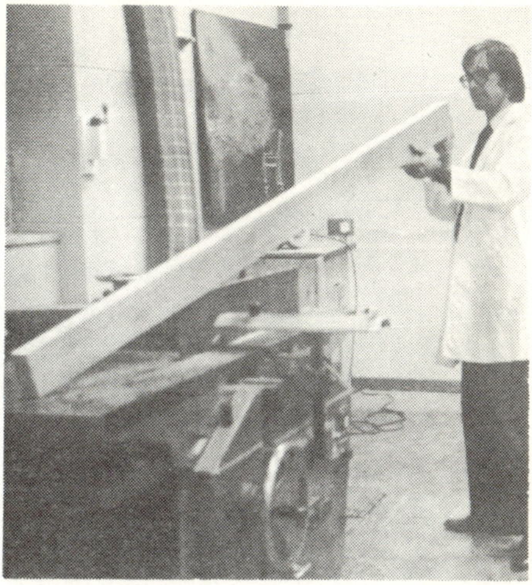

Door stiles should be surface planed, preferably hollow face down, before passing through a thicknessing machine.

Example of economic construction of wardrobe or cupboard doors providing instant furniture finish. Grooved wall board pressed on to skeleton frames.

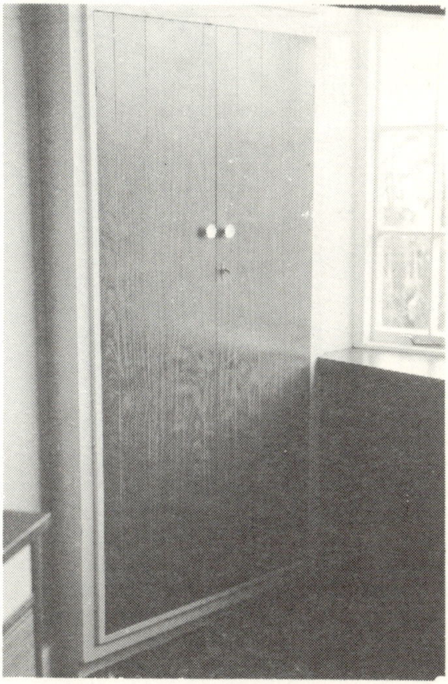

cut in two stages—a heavy cut first, followed by a fine finishing cut with rehoned cutters.

The additional time taken machining will be saved several times over in the hand cleaning operation to follow.

In many instances the operator will have to mould the ends of narrow panels, so it is necessary that a through face board is fitted across the fences of the machine to provide support.

For the mortise and tenoning operations it is important that the working face is always positioned against the fence when mortising, and down to the bed of the machine when tenoning.

Providing these rules are followed any discrepancy in the thicknesses of the timber will

A heated multi-daylight press suitable for the manufacture of flush doors. Other uses include veneering and the application of laminated plastics. (Interwood London).

Machine designed specially for dressing of edge lippings on flush doors. Also suitable for trimming plastic laminate edgings to work tops, etc. (JKO Cutters Ltd. High Wycombe.)

be directed to the opposite face of the work. Efficient thicknessing is important when the tenoning operations also include scribing, in particular if a double scribe is involved.

When marking out rails for tenoning, gauge marks should be applied to the end of the rail in addition to the edges of the tenon. This helps with the setting of the cutter head.

The cutter set at its maximum sweep can be conveniently positioned to the guage mark on the end of the rail. The shoulder cutters on the cutter head determine the effective length of rail which governs the overall width of the door.

Long and short shoulders may be involved and this should be defined at the time of marking out. Long shoulders are required when a rebate occurs on a door stile if a scribed portion is involved on the rail to intersect with a mould on the stile.

In framed section design it is customary to make rebate depth the same as the penetration of the mould when both are involved. This simplifies setting procedures when tenoning and makes mistakes less likely.

Cases do occur when shoulders have differing lengths of protection from that of the line of the stile but these are not the general rule.

Interior doors have been successfully produced using dowel joints instead of mortise and tenon. Dowelling in some circumstances does give more scope for the scribing of intricate mould

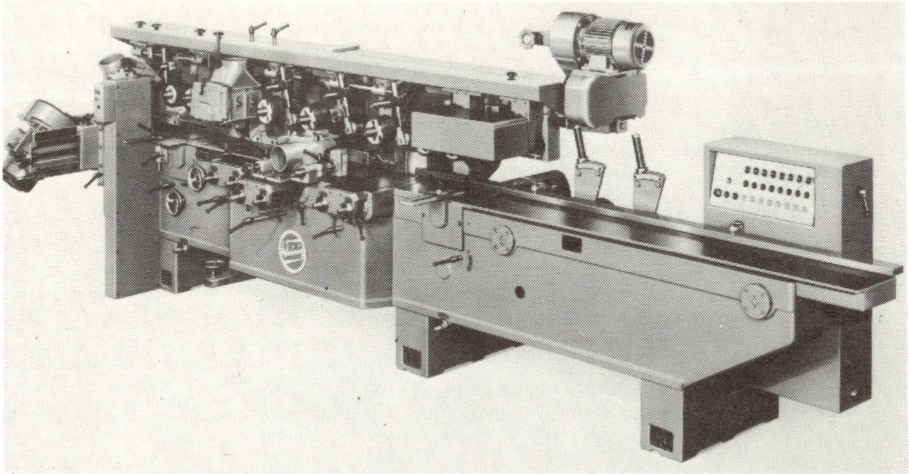

sections as there is no tenon in the way of the cut.

It is advantageous where the door panels are of less thickness than that of a tenon, if one was used. It is customary for the rail ends to be bored for dowels before they are scribed. This ensures accurate insertion of the drill bit.

The construction of flush doors, where sheet material is mounted on a core, can vary according to the method employed in the fixing of the sheets to the supporting material.

If the panels are securely bonded with adhesive under pressure, the joints involved in the framing of the core need only be of a simplified nature.

This usually comprises a tongue on the ends of the cross rails located into grooves in the upright members. If due to the non-availability of a press, the panels can only be lightly glued, then a secure mortise and tenon joint must be formed at the intersections of framing members.

Machining accuracy is important when preparing core material for flush doors, so that the built up cores can go straight to the panel press without any surface levelling.

The door cores on quantity production work are usually built up in jigs to speed up operations, and bring the work within the capabilities of a worker who has only had a limited amount of training.

As the skin panels which are used on flush doors are usually only up to about 4 mm in thickness, it is necessary to provide support at least every 75 mm of vertical height of the door. In the small joinery unit it is customary to insert a series of members of light section, often termed noggings.

Door production specialists favour the use of

Surfacing table fitted to the infeed of a fourcutter moulding machine. Its purpose is to prepare a flat surface on such items as door stiles prior to the fourcutting operation.

Edge lipping levelling attachment fitted to a double ended tenoning machine. (White, Paisley.)

honeycomb cardboard filling methods which keep the door down to a minimum of weight and give the necessary support to the panels.

Methods are also in use involving curled wood shavings, or inserted plywood offcut strips.

When applying panels to cores using a heated press to speed the process, several factors must be kept in mind. The moisture content of the core material must not be excessive, or some distortion may occur which may result in an inferior product.

If a lower grade softwood is used, it may be more subject to effective movement than a clear straight grained timber unless the moisture content is reduced to 12 per cent or below before pressing.

Some manufacturers use straight grained hardwoods of light timber section for flush door cores, such as ramin or obechi, or what the market has available in the price range at the time of requirement.

The cost factor is balanced with the reduction in timber content if a keen control is kept on wastage. Linear jointing of core framing by finger jointing reduces waste to a minimum and no delays need be experienced if R F heating is used for curing the joints.

In a heated press the air within the door core is in an expanded state at the time of pressing. When the door cools on leaving the press a vacuum effect is experienced within the core which pulls the skin panels tight to the interior supports

If these supports are insufficient a wave effect will be seen or felt on the door surface.

The vacuum effect is to advantage on a door with a well balanced core, but if it is desired to prevent the inner pull, slots or bore holes must be provided to allow the air to circulate with the outside atmosphere.

Experience of working temperatures on heated presses, and the use of thermo-setting adhesives is essential for efficient results. Material spoiled in the pressing operation cannot generally be used for some other work, and goes entirely to waste.

Preheating of components is practised by some operators engaged on thermo-setting work to cut down the cycle time within the processing unit. To bring skin panels straight to a hot press

Double-ended power fed machine for dressing of edge lippings on flush doors and cabinet work. Tungsten carbide tipped cutters are generally used on machines of this type to cope with glue lines and laminated plastics. (JKO Cutters.)

from a cold damp store is not to be recommended, as trouble may result from a combination of factors.

Radio frequency methods of setting adhesive lines is favoured in many establishments for applying edge lippings to flush doors.

The advantages of this method can be particularly beneficial when quantity work is involved.

Only butt joints are required between the lipping and the door.

This simplifies the manufacture of the lipping and also saves high grade material. No grooving operation is required in the door edge. Pressure is applied to the glue line throughout the complete setting operation giving a first class joint to accurately prepared work.

Smaller working units may have to use the traditional methods of the past but the introduction of impact adhesives can be helpful under some circumstances if correctly applied.

Flush doors, after pressing require to be taken to dimension and any surface of the edge lip which is protruding levelled off. The levelling off can be done on the spindle moulder suitably set, or with a more sophisticated unit known as the floating head.

This unit can be a small machine designed for this purpose or an attachment to a double ended tenoning machine. The advantage of the floating head over the use of say the spindle moulder, is that the cutter projection is guided with a roller which runs in close proximity of the point of operation.

The trim can be set to a very fine degree without any danger of fouling a surface veneer or a hardboard glaze, at any slight projecting area.

The overall dimensioning of doors is a point well worth giving consideration to when large quantities are involved with view to saving fitting time on the site.

When door mounting frames and casings come from the one source and doors from another, the door maker may play safe and supply his goods slightly over size.

Should the openings in the frames be under size this could result in perhaps as much as 6 mm to be planed off the edge of a door, which is both hard work by hand methods and time consuming on the site.

The sanding operation of framed and panelled doors by machine methods needs careful consideration in particular with hardwoods which may be furniture grade finish.

Doors passed through three drum sanders, and speed sanders pay no heed as to the direction of the grain of the various members.

If the sanders are worked efficiently in the way that they are designed for, various grades of paper, ending up with a fine grit, results may be acceptable for the major part of the belt life. If further attention is necessary, and overhead sanding operation may be required to remove score marks from the cross rails on the doors.

It should be possible to take doors straight from a mechanically fed multi-belt sander, or three drum, straight to paint finishing, but it must be remembered that the sanding papers cannot be at their best at all times.

There may be high points on the grit of a brand new belt, and deposits of gum may develop on a belt that has had considerable use. The skill of sanding lies very much with the machine operator.

It is customary to leave lugs on door stiles to protect against damage during transit.

Manufacturing Kitchen Units

In new domestic buildings, kitchen units complete with worktops are becoming an accepted part of the structure rather than an added extra. Prior to the fitted kitchen era as we know it today, the builder's work was very often limited to a floor to ceiling store cupboard and in some instances factory preparation was simply a front frame complete with doors. Shelving arrangements and in some cases a return end, were left to the ingenuity of the fixer which involved a considerable amount of site work. This work was often carried out under cold damp conditions.

A piece of joinery which occupants have to live in close contact with, hygienically, as in the case of kitchen equipment, is better added on near completion of the building. To enable as little disturbance as possible to be made to the wall finishes complete cupboard units are desirable. Wooden ground laths or fixing plugs can be pre-planned if required although modern fixing aids assisted with the use of tungsten carbide tipped drills make advanced preparatory work almost unnecessary.

The construction of kitchen units, being an item which has developed fairly rapidly, involves the use of new types of materials. The units have in fact provided scope for the introduction of plastics and have to some extent been used as trial grounds for the testing of durability before extending uses to more demanding purposes.

Working these modern materials with machines that were initially designed for woodworking can provide difficulties unless the

Free standing kitchen furniture cupboard storage units

correct type of cutters and mounting heads are used. Establishments working laminated plastics in large quantities probably have a full range of tungsten carbide tipped equipment, but many of the smaller work units may have to improvise and get the most out of the facilities available.

In working plastics fabricated to timber, some thought must be given to planning the work to suit the equipment available. If this is not done machine work may come to a sudden stop and hand operations may have to be resorted to. An example of this is in the fixing of plastic lippings to worktops, and trimming flush on the spindle moulder. If say the two shortest edgings are fixed first, then trimmed, followed by the other two, the set up is a very simple one. But if all the edges are applied before the trimming operation the brakes will be suddenly applied while methods are sought of a more complicated nature.

Also cases do arrive where it is desirous to apply laminated plastic in sheet form in a heated press, and to fix the edge lipping with a contact adhesive. The lipping will have to be applied after the pressing operation as the heat could destroy the contact adhesive. Contact adhesive is frequently used for lipping work which is other than straight as fix can be obtained without the need to construct pressure jigs in many instances.

For applying plastic edge lipping of sound

Cabinet end made from 6 mm plywood. The trenched back stiles and top and bottom rails are pressed on. The mortised front stiles are added after. Grooved on. Glue blocks rubbed into the corner with hot animal glue.

Components should be designed for interchangeability.

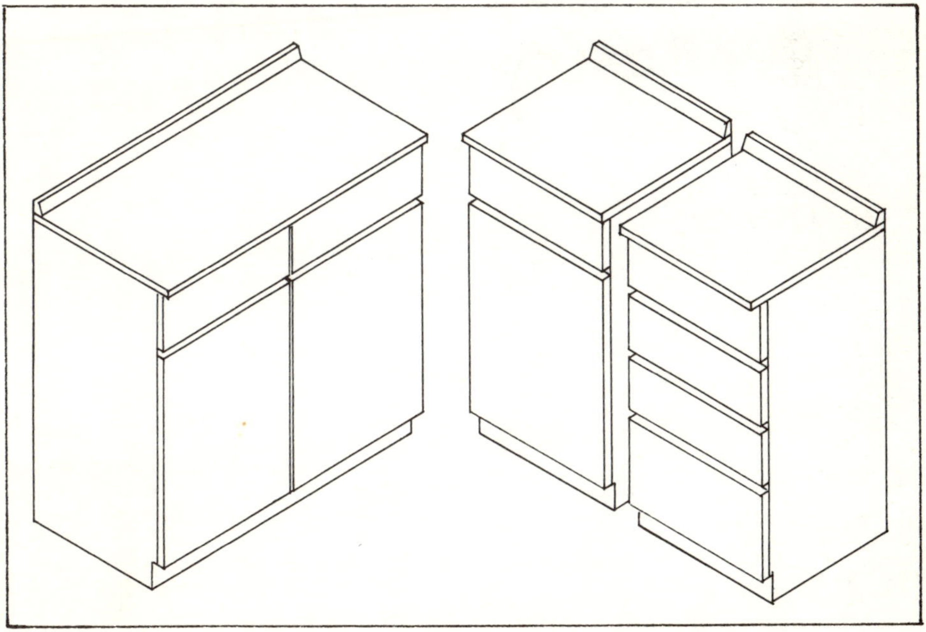

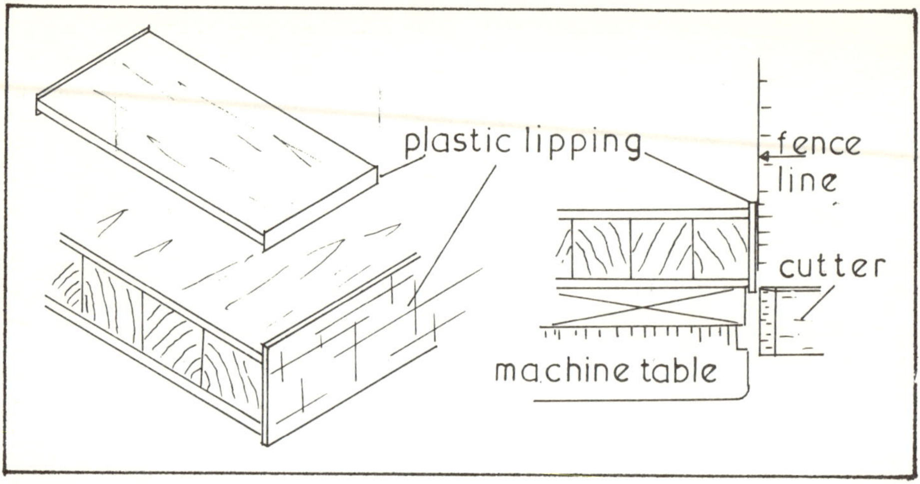

Trimming plastic edge lipping can be done on the spindle moulder working horizontally as shown, or with the work vertical. Trimming should commence after lipping the two opposing edges. If all four lippings are applied before trimming a more complicated set up is required.

Serviceable wall unit with rebated and moulded doors. Designed for machine production.

quality, the most efficient method considering many aspects is the use of low voltage strip heating. The equipment is economical in cost, and due to the heat conductivity factor of laminated plastic material the glue line can be set within three minutes using a suitable adhesive. An operator can very often be kept fully occupied on an LV strip unit, preparing, applying and removing. Trimming facilities should be located near to the LV unit which can help the flow of work and keep the operator fully occupied. Items edge lipped under this method can go forward to a heated press for further processing if required. The lippings are always applied under pressure which gives a reliable bond.

For trimming the edges of laminated plastic tungsten carbide tipped cutters must be used. High speed steel cutters as used for wood will become blunt after only a very small amount of cutting. The sharpness angle of tungsten carbide cutters is not prepared as acute as that of high speed steel to give longer lasting properties. Large diameter cutter blocks will give better cutting when they can be applied, rather than small ones that very often have to be used in high speed routers due to the nature of the work.

If a choice can be made on an operation between router working and a spindle moulder type machine, the spindle will usually give the most satisfactory lasting results. Machines are available specially designed for trimming plastic edging, and the cutter heads used have a working diameter of about 100 mm.

In the construction of the carcass for kitchen units there are various methods of approach:

(a) Solid material may be used such as parana

Sub assembled frames

Carcass built up in the traditional joinery manner using a large amount of machine produced joints. Runners and bearers are added after, not sub-assembled frames.

pine, faced chipboard, blockboard, etc.
(b) An entire carcass can be framed using ex 50 x 25 mm section material, the ends being covered with a thin facing ply skin.
(c) A more scientific approach where bearers are pressed on to a ply skin to form ends and a series of sub-assembled frames provide shelves and drawer runners.
The method used is very often decided by the quantity to be manufactured. The solid framing method may be preferred for specials or one offs as it can be prepared with the minimum number of joints. Material cost will be higher than in the other two methods.
Carcasses built from ex 50 x 25 mm section give good scope for the involvement of standard woodworking machines, joint formation being at its maximum by this method. It is very much a joinery method, sound construction, any plywood used being simply a covering material.
The third method which has evolved from furniture production relies on the plywood panels to give rigidity to the unit. It is particularly suitable for the application of sub-assembly methods which enable components to be built up into frames for storage on batch production work.
Standardization within the factory is important when producing a line of goods so that parts can be interchanged between the various items. This applies to door and drawer dimensions in addition to framing components. This limits the number of jigs required and machine settings which leads to the maximum amount of actual production time. Due to the large range of laminated plastics it usually becomes necessary to limit the number of colours available as standard. Whether additional colours can be made available as specials, at additional cost, is a point for consideration.
It is customary to design drawers in such a way as to reduce fitting time to a minimum. This adapts itself well to kitchen cabinet work, as drawers require to be slack-fitting to meet the varying conditions of humidity in their environment. Drawers can be prepared with rebated fronts, or false overhanging fronts which permit a small amount of clearance to go unnoticed. No trimming should be required at the fitting point for drawers made to high machining standards for these types.
Types of drawers are now being manufactured with plastic material for sides and backs, and in some cases fronts also. Under this system cabinets need to be designed to meet the drawer dimensions available. If the cost of the system is more economic than the traditional wood drawer, its use could well develop in this section

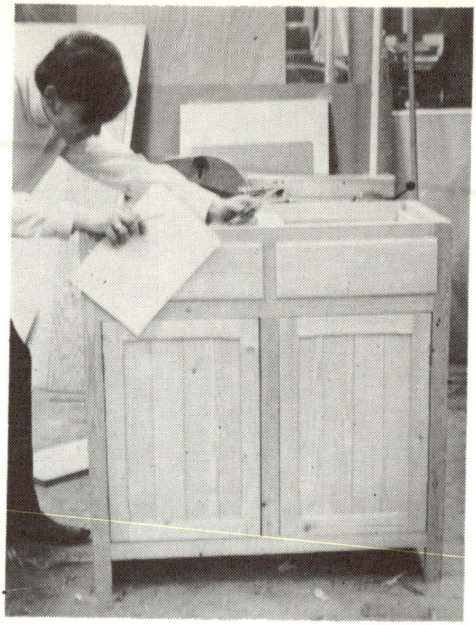

Solid timber construction using joinery methods as a feature of the design.

Dimensioning kitchen cabinet doors on a White (Paisley) automatic shaper. The rebated and moulded edge profile is formed at the same pass.

of the industry. The plastic lining to the drawer is of an hygienic nature which is acceptable to food storage. Construction at the moment is not by the traditional dovetailing but this could well be introduced as a means of widening its scope and satisfying some sections of the industry.

Manufacturers in the woodworking industry do require to make changes from time to time in order to survive or get ahead of their competitors. New developments which come along require investigation as to their suitability for a particular line product.

Doors used on kitchen furniture can be found under at least four classifications. (1) Fitted, in which the doors are hung within the frame. (2) Rebated, which gives a dustproof effect and reduces fitting time. (3) Surface hung, in which the doors usually span the full width of the cabinet. (4) Sliding. This type of door is particularly useful where space in the kitchen is limited. The fitted type of doors are not usually favoured for kitchen work due to humidity variations. Doors with rebated and usually moulded fronts satisfy the purpose in many ways and are used extensively on cabinets that have a paint finish.

In quantity work the completed door assemblies are dimensioned on a jig which produces the rebated and moulded edge profile at the one pass. Chipboard is often used as a door core material when the doors are surface hung. If the chipboard can be edged with wood lippings, more secure fixing can be obtained for hinges and other fittings. Surface hung doors are favoured when the front of the unit is to be plastic faced. With the addition of false fronts to the drawers the entire frontage can be plastic faced which eliminates a finishing process within the works unit.

Sliding doors manufactured to the quality of hinged doors and equipped with suitable running track can be very attractive. Unfortunately many sliding doors do not meet this specification and are not capable of displaying a very high standard. Doors made from plywood or glass working directly into wood grooves is a set up in its lowest form. Extruded channel sections are now available in plastics and aluminium which can improve the action of the lighter type of sliding door at slight extra cost.

The various types of doors require the appropriate fittings, and the availability of these, particularly to the smaller works unit, can at times be the deciding factor as to which method to use. Fitted doors present no problem as either surface mounting or butt hinges may be used. Rebated doors require hinges to seat in the rebate, and very often rebates have to be prepared to suit the hinges available. Lift off type hinges are supplied left and right hand.

Surface hung doors usually are hung on hinges of the pivot type acting on the outer corner of the door. This is to enable cabinets to be butted together and allow the doors to open without binding. Recessing the door edges to accommodate pivot hinges can at times produce machining difficulties when equipment is limited.

Handles to both doors and drawers very often incorporated within the wood machining operation as projecting handles are not favoured in kitchen furniture. Most kitchens are small in spite of what we see in glossy magazines and projecting items can be a hazard.

Large-scale producers of kitchen units may

Basic requirements of a low voltage strip heating set up. Plated iron strip, transformer and cables. (Pye Thermal Bonders, Cambridge.)

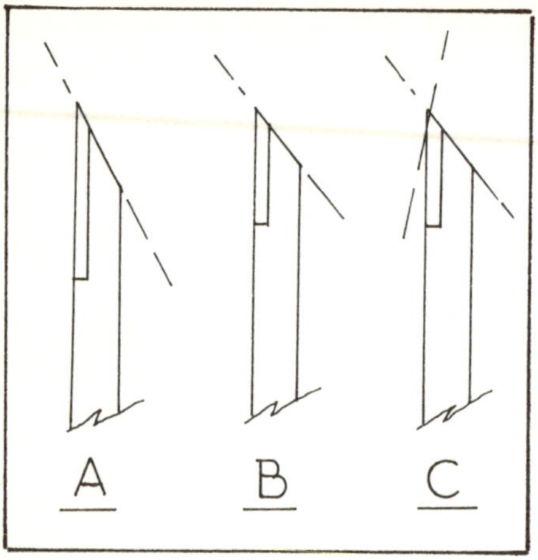

(A) High speed steel cutters have a sharpness angle of about 30 deg. when working softwood. (B) Tungsten carbide cutters as used on plastics have a less acute angle. (C) The application of a front bevel can improve the lasting properties of the edge if chipping is being experienced.

either be working to dimension standards recommended nationally or their own in close proximity. Several factors are important regarding dimensions of cabinets. Consideration must be given to the dimensions of sink tops which are available. The standard depths are 457 mm (18in.) and 533 mm (21in.). Base units are usually made to the lower figure and making out pieces added when the greater depth is required. The length of sink tops, which are very numerous, act as a guide as to the length of cabinets to produce. A cabinet produced as a base for a sink can form the foundation of a work top unit also and the necessary machining carried at the same set with slight modifications.

The height required for kitchen worktops can vary to meet up with other appliances. The demand from my experiences is from 840 mm up to 915 mm. The higher figure is usually requested when such items as washing machines are to be accommodated underneath the worktop. Height adjustments can be conveniently made to cabinets if they are designed with removable base plinths. Being able to supply cabinets over a range of heights can be a marketing feature, but it requires to be planned in the initial stages.

In some kitchen schemes base units are used in the form of a room divider or island unit. In this form both sides of the cabinets must have a face finish. The cabinets are usually constructed from standard base units with the addition of various refinements. In domestic dwellings with through planning, open shelves can be mounted on the top of base units to create a kitchen area.

Although in modern planning, kitchen furniture items are in the main fixtures to tie in with the plumbing and other services, there is a demand for removable furniture also. This is created by such as the rising executive type of householder who moves house every few years to fill a higher post in another area. Freestanding kitchen units for the accommodation of food-preparing requirements can be in the form of reproduction design dressers. These can be conveniently produced say on a secondary line in a joinery unit. Matching tables and seating units can add further scope to the line.

Veneering processes need not be required in this branch of furniture making which makes it suitable for an add on to joinery production without specialized additional plant. The timber used in these items is mainly pine or oak. Elm is also being used. Working in solid timber, not built-up boards such as blockboard, requires attention to be paid to the moisture content of the material.

In constructional design provision must also be made for humidity changes if buckling or cracks are to be prevented. When selecting material for natural pine finish such items as knots and grain become a feature. Grain patterns require to be matched, and any blue stains usually found in the sap wood should not be included. Bleaching processes are being used which brings the surface to a more constant shade if this is desired. When working in oak some items may be preferred in veneered form; ready prepared panel boards of many types are readily available.

Kitchen furniture lends itself well to batch production. Although many of the components involved are common to the various units produced continuous flow production could be wasteful. Machined components standing for a period of time can deteriorate unless special care is taken in material selection, preparation and storage. Batch production does also permit modifications to be made in constructional design with a minimum of wastage and to accommodate timber size fluctuations. Batches of say 200 cabinets provide enough components to merit pallet stacking which is very suitable due to their convenient length. Rough crosscutting is preferably done prior to fourcutting on framing items; this enables material in process to be passed along by mechanized transfer systems if so desired.

These transfer systems between machines

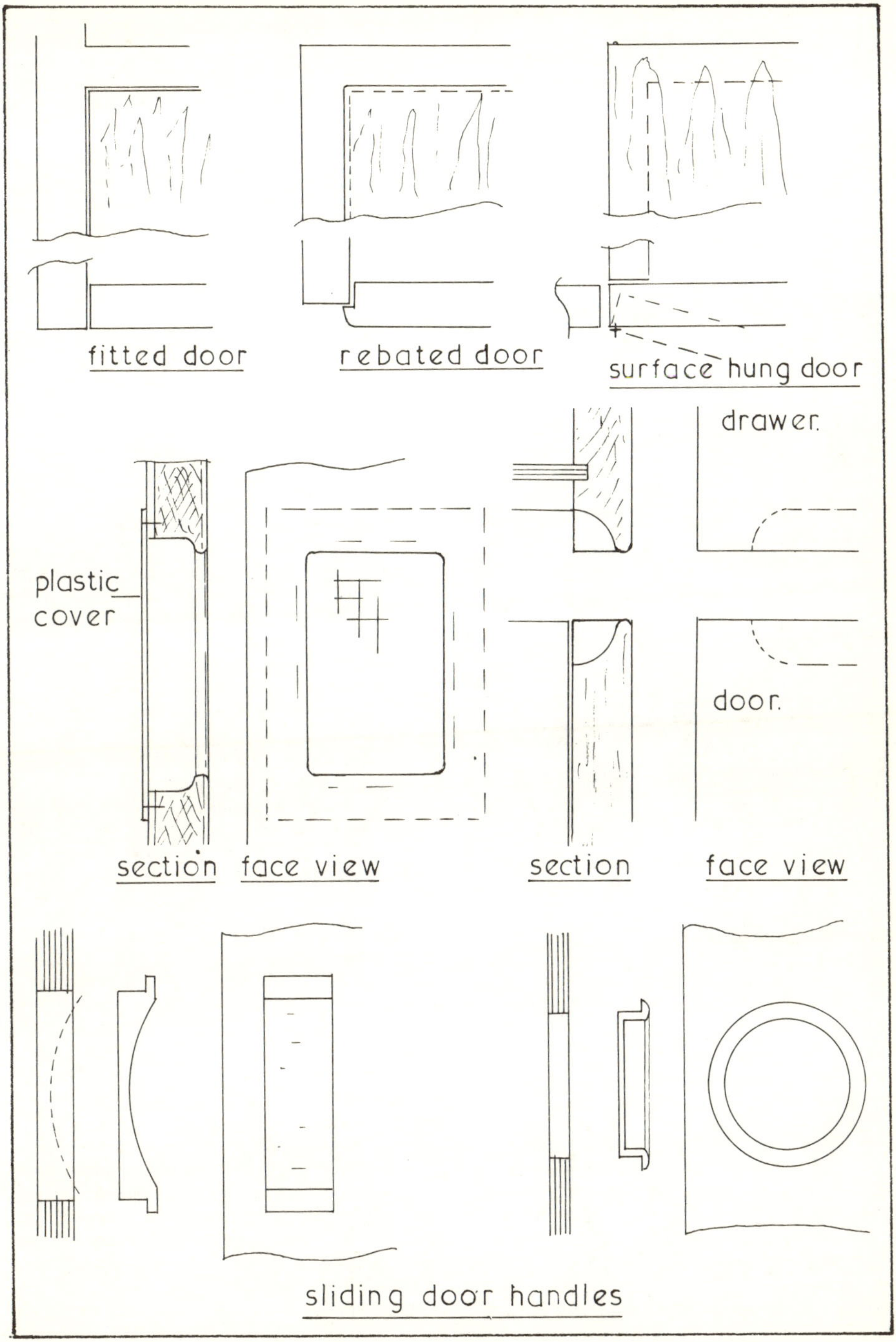
fitted door
rebated door
surface hung door
drawer.
plastic cover
section
face view
section
door.
face view
sliding door handles

reduce labour costs and quickly recover their initial cost. Numbers required of components can be counted out at the early stages eliminating annoying deficiencies or excess wastage. Fourcutting the shorter type of item as used in this work can benefit from the use of hopper feed. This relieves the operator for periods and gives a continuous flow to the stock which should always be the aim when feeding timber to produce a high grade finish.

All profile formulations such as grooves and rebates can be carried out during the fourcutting operation as details usually run through in this type of work. Stopped formations may occur in sink cabinets to provide access for the bowl or other plumbing fitments. These cutouts are usually a routing operation and handing has to be considered depending whether the bowl is to the right or left of the drainer section. Drawer material having more surface width than the framing material is most suitably fourcut in about 2 m lengths which are convenient for stacking. Modern design of fourcutter with through feed should feed drawer material in short precut lengths more efficiently than the traditional push feed.

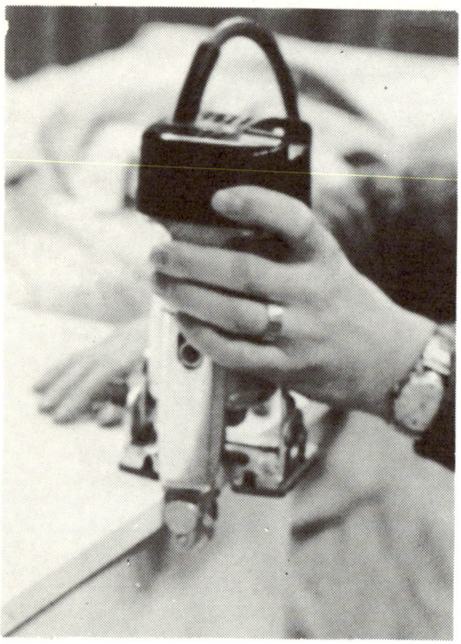

Trimming laminated plastic with specialised tool

Trenching of vertical members to carry shelves and drawer runner assemblies are usually processed on the high speed router with the aid of jigs. In large production units the double end tenoner may be used if it is equipped with an overhead beam and trenching head.

Components machined with sub-assembly in mind are usually taken straight from the machining area to the first assembly process. This prevents deterioration or loss due to careless stacking and pilfering. Assembly of the components with the use of pneumatic equipment can speed the operation considerably from hand worked cramps. A minimum of skill is also required to operate an assembly jig in which the components are positioned. Pneumatic jigs should not only be limited to the sub-assembly operation, but they can also be designed for assisting with the final assembly making bench work unnecessary. By working in this manner the accuracy standards for dimensions and squareness will be constant, not varying from one bench assembler to another as the case could be. Prepared drawers and doors will then be accepted by the carcass with the minimum of hand labour.

Hinge for flush-finish door

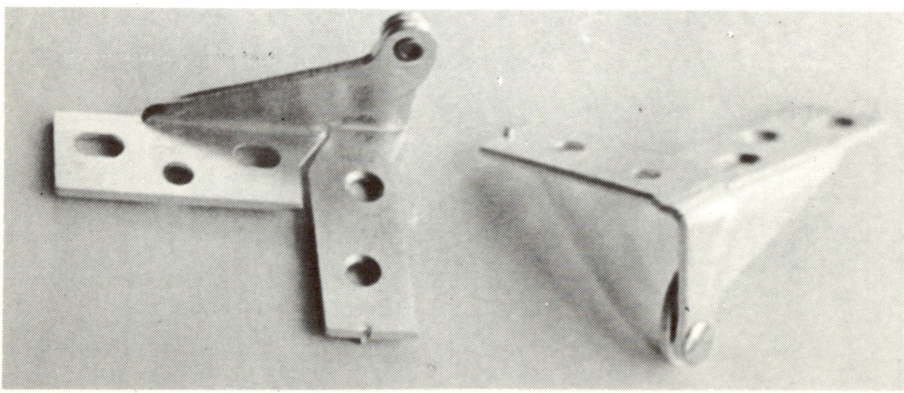

Window Construction

In the processing of window material sections, most of the operations could be called standard except when curvature is involved, and this usually requires the introduction of jigs. The range of machines required are preferably of the heavy duty type but the medium range of machines can be successfully used if consideration is given to working procedures.

Rebates to carry opening frames can be in the region of 50 mm x 12 mm under some types of construction. A heavy duty machine will make the cut quite easily at the one pass through and probably apply a mould or bevel at the same time.

On a lighter machine it may be advisable to cut some of the rebate section away with a saw, or to rebate with cutters in two stages. The method used should at all times be progressive.

To overload a machine and have to wait for the power unit to cool down is not satisfactory.

Particular care must be taken when rebates do not run through on a member, and require to be stopped. Running in on the spindle moulder is always preferable to dropping on and running out. When left and right hand items are required, reverse rotation can provide running in on both hands of the item.

Safety standards can be increased by correct utilisation of the machine. Extra time taken in setting up can often be recovered in the long term, if not on the particular job in hand, by more progressive working generally, and the elimination of accidents.

Many small joinery units are involved in the manufacture of window frames to meet special requirements. Equipment for machining can be

Comparison sketches of head and sill details of the two principal types of window construction in general use.

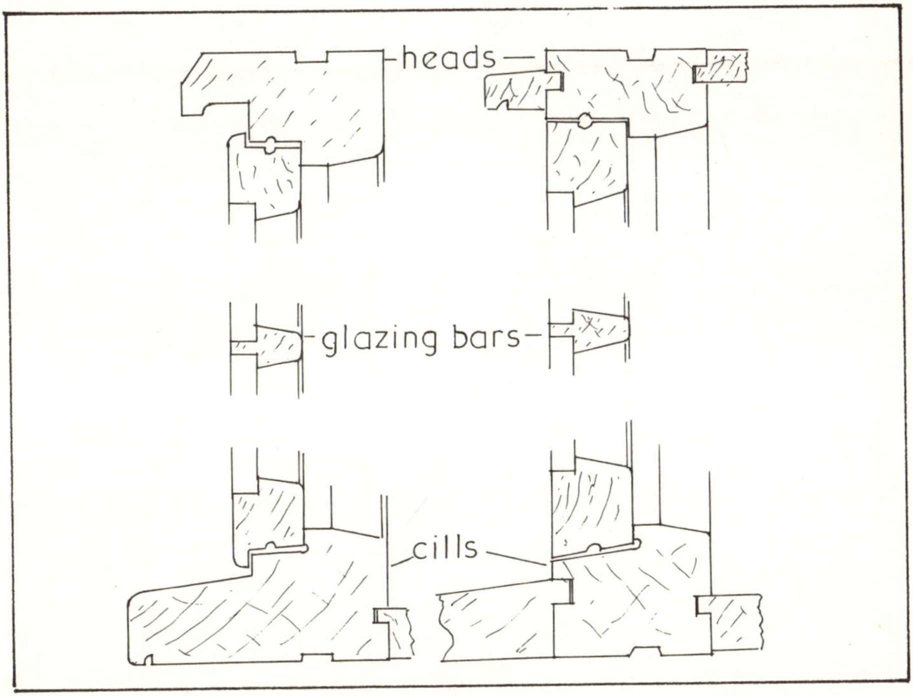

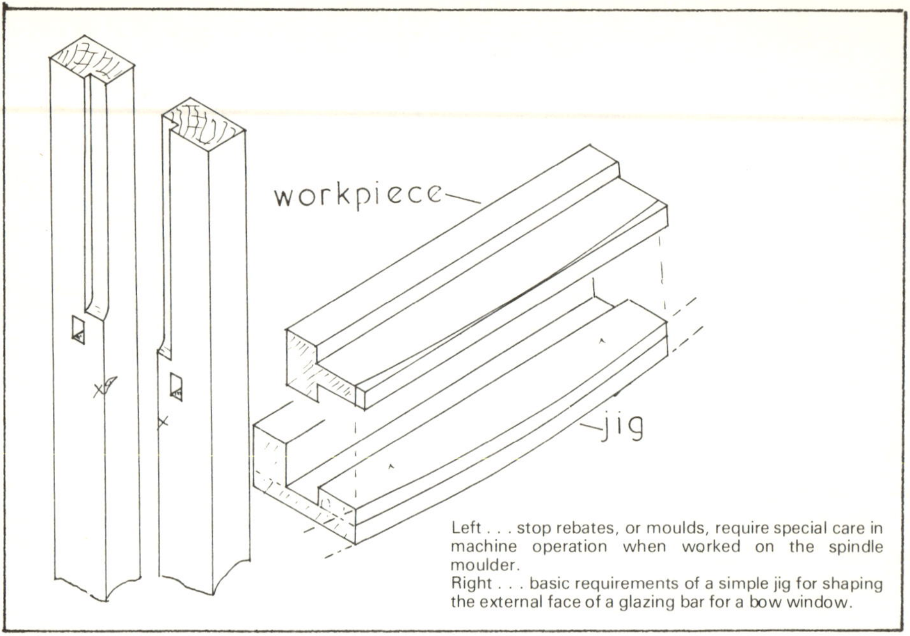

Left . . . stop rebates, or moulds, require special care in machine operation when worked on the spindle moulder.
Right . . . basic requirements of a simple jig for shaping the external face of a glazing bar for a bow window.

limited in some circumstances, and this may at times be a contributing factor to the noticeable accident rate relating to such items as window manufacture in the smaller unit.

Timber used in the construction of windows is subjected to severe changes in humidity, and this requires to be taken into account in their design and construction.

Left . . . a rounded corner gives a continuous flow of paint coverage ensuring a complete seal.
Right . . . an example of one of the possible layouts of a combed joint to sash material. The mould detail is not ideal for scribing but it is a present-day requirement. The alternative suggested is more simplified.

It is desirable that the sectional area of members should not be in excess of requirement to give the necessary joint formations, and rigidity.

The greater the sectional area of timber involved the more movement experienced due to humidity changes. Loss of moisture can cause the timber to crack if the structure is not designed with this in mind, and an increase may be the reason for opening sashes to become wedged.

Examination of window frames in old stately homes shows that many of the members involved are of slender construction compared with the heavy architraves and other interior

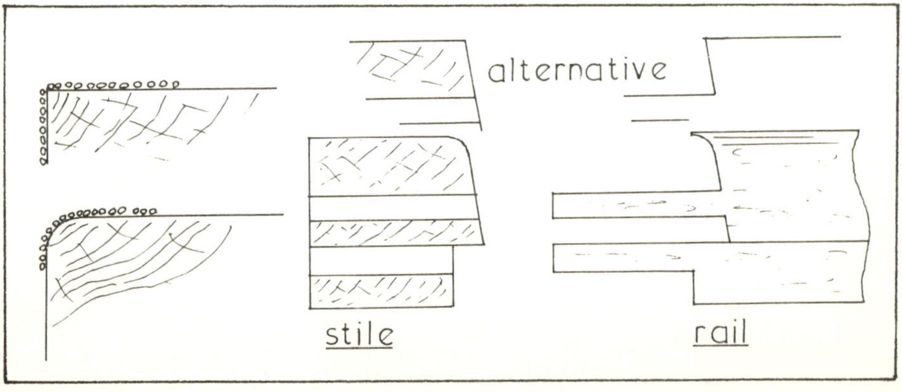

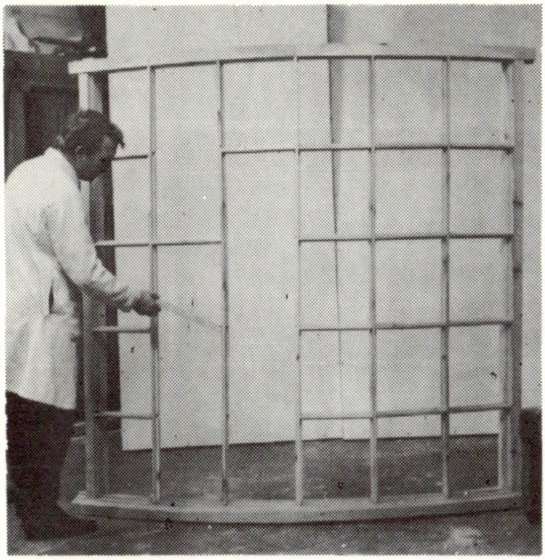

Fitting horizontal glazing bars into a bow window. Curvature of the members in this particular unit is confined to the head and sill only.

Cutters are obtainable for shaping rebated and moulded sash stock either as a single or built up form. Single cutters are not suitable for continuous use as serving difficulty will be experienced.

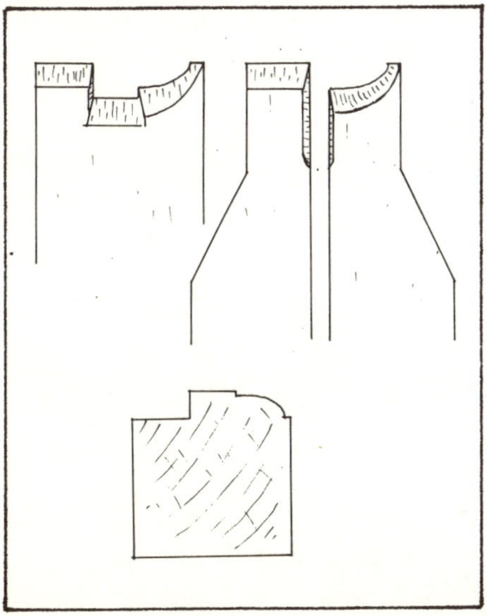

items. The slim line of the glazing bars is particularly noticeable.

In the larger production unit, window sections are usually prepared at the one pass through the moulding machine (fourcutter). Where no multihead machine is available the material has to be surface planed face and edge, followed by thicknessing. Moulds rebates and other profiling operations have to be carried out on the spindle moulder. This latter method although more time consuming has some advantages over fourcutter preparation.

Face sides can be more efficiently selected, and defects cut out during the rebating operations. Spelching can be eliminated in the tenoning and scribing operations by planning the machine sequences. Mortising may be done before or after the profiling, as desired, to obtain continuous machine loading.

Cutter blocks. Square cutter blocks are often favoured on the spindle moulder for the preparation of timber sections involved in window construction. This is due to the fact that a series of sets of cutters may be mounted on a square block to add more than one profile detail at a pass through the machine.

Cutter positioning is preferably done on a cutter setting stand in the tool room area, where cutters can be set to a drawing or a previous sample of the section required.

Balance is important on the cutter heads and pairs of cutters must be used.

Where two or more pairs of cutters are to be used they require to be set in relation to one another. The setting stand, or a prepared setting template can be a help in this respect.

Heavy cutting is very often involved in the fourcutting of sill sections, and some easing of the cut may be necessary in the form of play sawing before offering the item for moulding. Where a moulder has more than one top cutting head, the load should be divided to give more even strain to the machine.

On moulders with, say, six cutter heads, solid profile cutters could be used throughout if large quantities of work is involved. This type of head has several advantages over the square block when cost will permit its use. Setting up time is very much reduced.

Multipoint finish is obtinable which permits a high rate of feed speed. Section profile is constant from one batch to another. Solid profile heads run much quieter than square blocks. Their servicing can be fully mechanised with a minimum of equipment if desired.

Square cutter blocks are versatile, being adaptable for a variety of operations, and cutters can, if necessary, be prepared within the works unit, or altered to suit requirements.

For processing window sections on the spindle moulder an automatic feed unit can be particularly useful. Due to the heavy cutting involved in some of the work, hand feeding can be fatiguing as a considerable amount of pressure is required to grip the timber and keep it positioned against the fence.

Output can also be considerably increased with the use of a feed unit when a multihead moulding machine is not available.

The failure of window frames in service usually occurs in the vicinity of joint formations. Sills are most subject to rot due to their location, and for this reason hardwood is often used to balance the life of the unit. Changes of joint formations have occurred with the introduction of machine methods which should increase their lasting properties. Through scribes to moulded rail shoulders which machine working provides are superior to the stopped variety as produced by the hand worker.

Any flow of moisture entering a through scribe can pass without being trapped. Sash material can be comb jointed instead of the traditional mortise and tenon. This method permits outside rebates to be formed to produce what is generally termed stormproof windows.

Moritse and tenon joints are not very efficient with this type of sash as a large amount of the material is cut away. An important point to remember when cutting material to working lengths, is to avoid knots in joint formations. If this point is ignored a joint may fail at the assembly stage beofre the item has given any service.

For the main structure of window frames, mortise and tenon joints are used. Advanced processing methods are experimenting with mitred external members, and forming die pressed toothing on the contact surfaces.

The surfaces are then coated with adhesive and pressed together. R. F. heating can set the joint in about 30 seconds. By this method no end grain need be exposed to attract moisture.

Chain mortising is very often used instead of the hollow square chisel on window construction to reduce machining time, and due to the fact that most of the mortises go through. The chain can be fed completely through the timber from one face.

When glazing bars of narrow section are involved, it is necessary to mortise with the square chisel due to the limited width of the cut.

On some mortising machines which are fitted with both chain and chisel, provision is made to align the chisel cut with that of the chain. Under this system both types of mortising can be carried out at the one handling on such items as door stiles involved with glazing.

This adjustment can be a useful refinement as very often the picking up and returning to the

Grinding head for mounting solid profile cutters. Note the indexing arrangement for positioning the cutter faces. (J.K.O. Cutters Ltd., High Wycombe).

Rebating of stock can be carried out on the surface planer if the machine is of suitable design. Current Factory Regulations say that "No planing machine shall be used for cutting any rebate, recess, tenon or mould unless the cutter is efficiently guarded." Photo. Wadkin Leicester.

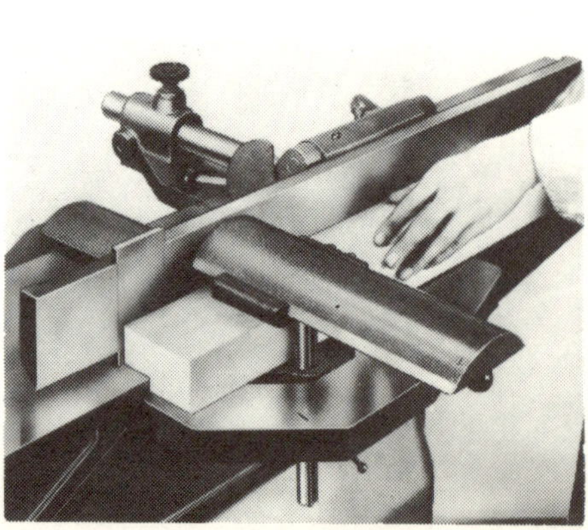

Comb jointing sash material on a tenoning machine. The rail item is being processed using the tenoning heads, bottom scriber head, and combing saw fitted to the top scribing head.

stack of a member can take as long as the actual cutting operation.

In the design of window section members it is not possible to diverge to any great extent from traditional patterns. External formations must be such as to repel the weather and maintain durability. Surface coatings such as paint do not readily adhere to sharp external corners. If the sharp corner is removed and preferably a quarter round formed the surface pull will permit the coating to continue unbroken from one face to another.

Grooves and cut aways are formed in rebates and on the edges of sashes to prevent the admission of water by capillary action. They also provide a temporary storage point and aid dispersal when any water that enters is subjected to wind pressure. The grooves can usually be worked at no additional cost along with the rebating operation in the case of the window frame, and in the external dimensioning and profiling of the sashes.

The sill member of a window usually involves operations that do not occur on other items which makes additional setting up of cutting units necessary. Jambs heads, mullions and transomes, all have the majority of labours in common. Rebates on the sills require to be on the bevel to convey moisture.

For small quantities cutters can usually be tilted on the square block to give the required angle if no prepared cutters are available. Sills must also be grooved to accommodate the interior window board, and if wooden linings are required to the jambs and head these members will have to be grooved also. Projecting sills which extend beyond the face of the building require to have a groove cut on the underside usually termed a drip or throat to disperse the water at that point.

In the smaller works unit, windows with hinged openers are very often manufactured square edged, not rebated. When sashes can be fitted individually this method may be satisfactory for the location in which they are to be located, usually a known one.

A large production unit manufacturing for stock, is not in favour of fitting each individual sash, so the rebated and moulded method known as stormproof serves their requirement well. Slack

fitting of the sashes is favoured under this system as it fully eliminates capillary action by keeping the surfaces apart within the frame.

Time controlled immersion type preservation unit. Assembled sashes are positioned for processing on the right, and on the left individual window framing components are accommodated. This installation is one of many offered by Cuprinol Ltd., Frome, Somerset.

The stormproof type window has proved itself since its introduction to use, following the change from vertical sliding sashes to hinged.

Sliding sash windows have excellent properties regarding the exclusion of driving rain. Their use now is mainly limited to renovations and some period types of domestic buildings. Most of the sliding sash windows in use today have been made in the local joinery works. Modern joinery production lines can produce this type of window by batch production using standard equipment should the demand arise.

Material section for the manufacture of this type of window can be rapidly produced on a moulding machine. Also due to the requirement of an amount of narrow items in the form of beads, careful planning can reduce waste to a minimum.

Sliding sash windows balanced by weights require to be fitted into a reveal, usually behind the outer skin of the wall. This is because the weights have to be accommodated in a box section that has a projection of about 50 mm. Spring-loaded spiral units have been developed over recent years which can in some circumstances eliminate weights and make way for a more compact construction of the window unit.

Methods are also being called for at the present time for converting sliding sash windows to hinged openers. The aim of this type of conversion is to eliminate structural disturbance as much as possible within occupied accommodation. The amount of the existing window frame to be removed may well depend upon its condition regarding decay. The general aim is to remove only the sashes, staff bead and parting beads, and the new unit is fitted between the pulley stiles.

Although window sizes will vary considerably even within the same building due to the source from where they were made, mentioned previously, it should be possible to produce standard sections of material to meet the requirements of most of the conversions.

Window frames that have curvature on plan, such as the now popular bow windows, are usually planned in such a way that the glass for economy reasons is quite flat, and the curvature is limited to the timber in the frame. Full sized section setting out is required before windows of this type can be produced.

Jigs will also be required if quantity work is to be involved. If the shape can be confined to a true sweep of the radius of a circle the amount of jig work can be kept to a minimum. The curvature on the horizontal glazing bars if each individual

Completed window frames in the process of immersion. The unit is designed to suit the location. (Photo. Cuprinol Ltd.)

one is to have any, is usually confined to the exterior edge only.

The amount of curvature may only be small, but the use of a simple shaping jig to achieve this can enhance the finished appearance of the window. A more antique effect can be created in a bow window by providing a small amount of curvature to the vertical glazing bars.

A slight barrel effect is created which gives the impression that the window is carrying a load, or under strain due to age.

In the construction of the traditional type of bay windows the present tendency is to build these up from standard frames. This method is very accommodating within the works unit as it reduces the number of lines being produced. It also helps with storage and provides the builder with more ready availability. Standard units produced, modified to suit requirements, assembled within the factory can produce a satisfactory item.

Bay windows designed as such and made to a particular requirement can be a costly item which funds may not always permit. The customer must ensure that he is getting the extra value in the way of refinement or the exercise can be done without material gain.

It is important that supporting walls for bay windows are constructed to dimensions to suit the frames available. This is usually accomplished by working to a template which should be on hand at the early stages of the building operation.

Current practice, particularly in domestic buildings, is to make the structue to meet the standard joinery available. Failure to do this will increase costs.

The preservation of timber involved in the manufacture of window frames can be taken as a continuation of the industrial processing. It is an operation that at times, to meet specifications, cannot be ignored. Houses built under the protection of such organisations as the House Builders' Registration Council, and many local authorities, specify the application of preservative treatment to acceptable standards.

In the case of window frames, treatment can be carried out either in the individual component form after all the joints and profile formations have been completed, or in the assembled window. It is desirable for full efficiency that no further cutting into the material should take place after the preservative treatment has been completed. Penetration of the preservative is usually claimed to involve the entire sapwood if any is present, and some distance into the fully mature timber.

The method of applying the coating or part impregnation can be done in two ways.

The component form method usually involves the stack of parts to be put in an enclosed cylinder.

A vacuum is created, drawing all the air out of the surface cells of the wood. The preservative is then allowed to enter the chamber to take the place of the air. After the removal of the preservative a second vacuum is created to exclude the excess preservative, so reducing the amount of liquid required to a minimum.

Completed window frames are often treated by

The number of cutters that can be accommodated on a square block is limited to two of the faces, ad identical balancing cutters must be fixed to the other faces.

immersion in an open form of tank. Frames are either suspended or lowered in on a platform to reduce handling to a minimum.

The time spent within the tank is usually noted and controlled to suit individual specifications. The types of preservatives used are usually spirit based as it is desirable that they should not have an effect on the moisture content of the timber.

Drying out after processing is in the region of 24 hours according to the surrounding temperature and air flow.

Although the majority of windows used in a building today are the product of a high mechanised establishment, there is without a doubt a place in the manufacturing field for the smaller unit. Batch production specialists do not favour supplying items outside their particular range as they tend to reduce efficiency flow.

The action of specialist units passing orders on to the smaller man is not unknown.

Window frames, unlike, say, furniture manufacture, with its many complications, can be produced with the minimum of mechanical aids, and in an economic working space. The basic number of machines required can be counted on one hand.

Some large joinery producing units have been founded on a bread and butter line consisting of window frames. The waste factor regarding material is confined to linear dimension if boards of suitable section are utilised.

There is an opportunity on all members for defects to be cut away in the rebating or other profile forming operations. As timber costs increase there may well be efforts to cut down the amount of timber involved in window sections. This will require the increased use of combed joints, invooving not only the sashes but the main frame also.

Sill members will probably be tilted, as they are in some countries, to obtain the necessary weathering without having to increase the sectional dimensions with that of the rest of the frame.

This slenderising can have advantages, as suggested at the beginning of this article, but the inclusion of the other scientific aspect, preservation treatment, should not be overlooked.

Internal Trim to Buildings

The requirements of prepared timber sections in linear form can be standardised to some extent, particularly for use in domestic building. Patterns do vary from one part of the country to another, standards having been set up locally by a large producer in the area at some time.

The smaller producer is often compelled to adopt the leading patterns in order to match up and so continues to use them.

If cutters have to be made to prepare a moulded section then they may as well be used for further runs.

Trim such as architrave mouldings for door and window openings have reduced considerably in sectional dimension from those found in buildings fitted out in the early part of this century. The change may not have occurred due to cost alone, but also to meet the introduction of simple lines involving little elaboration.

This simplification has reduced the application of skill required by the wood machinist, who no doubt must have had some difficulty at times to cope. Cutting lists may well have contained items requiring 200 x 32 (8 x 1¼) for skirting boards, and 175 x 50 (7 x 2) for architraves in the principal rooms of a dwelling.

The amount of material cut away in the moulding formations was considerable as examination of those still in existence shows. Some items of trim are utilised by fixers for a variety of purposes other than that for which they are intended. One typical example is floor boarding, which is often used by joiners on the site to make ledged and braced doors.

This liberty extends to within the joiner's shop at times, whether or not it is the correct procedure. In the making of T and G boards its multipurpose uses is not always kept in mind. Boards intended for flooring only, can have the upper portion of the T and G joint a little proud of that on the lower edge to ensure a close joint on the visible face.

If a number of boards of this type are put in clamps, face side up, they are likely to fly up in the air when pressure is applied, very often to the surprise of the worker.

Boards made in this way are quicker to lay when flooring, but they require some adjustment to the joint design if they are to be glued up into panels for, say, cupboard shelves. Skirting boards of the wider types have been used for apron linings to stair wells, also as boxing material to pipe runs. The much reduced width of present day skirting used on domestic work must limit its alternative uses.

Occasions arise when items have to be matched up for extensions or repair work, and skill is required on the part of the machinst to produce

The purpose of an architrave mould is to bridge the gap between the door casing and the brickwork. Plinth blocks solve intersection complications. Grooved floor bead simplifies the fixing of skirting boards.

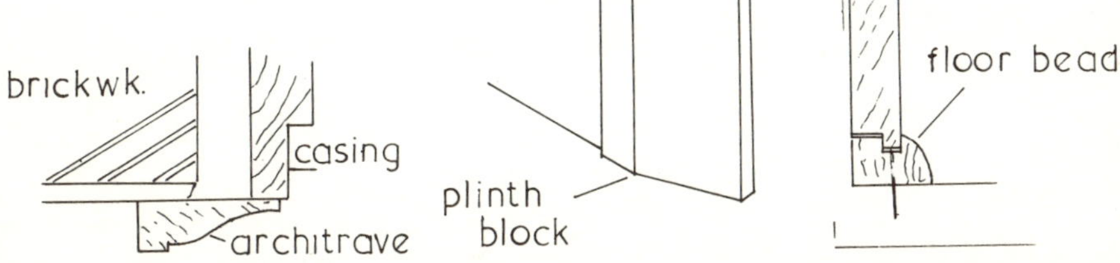

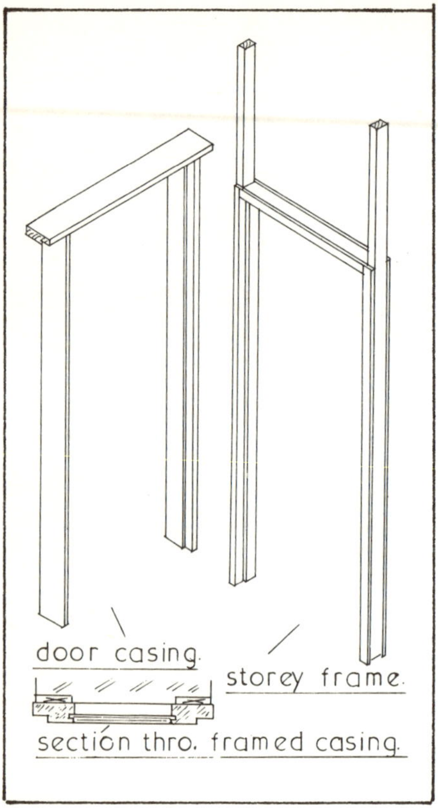

Door casings are used for lining openings in brickwork or timber framed partitioning. Storey frames are for use with lightweight building blocks. Thick masonry walls require framed panel casings.

Boarding designed for rapid floor laying has a gap on the unseen face of the joint. It is unsuitable for cramping up into panels without adjustment to the joint.

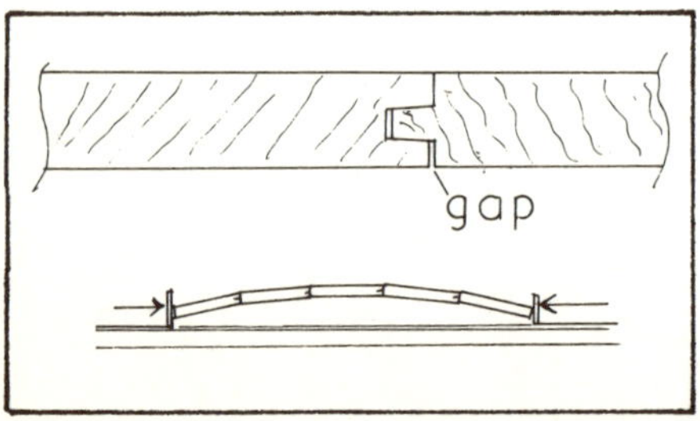

section profiles in an acceptable amount of time. **When mouldings have to be formed on the thinner type of timber on the spindle moulder, particularly on quantity work, the backfencing set up will produce the most efficient work.** This is due to the fact that the timber is supported directly opposite the point of cut, which reduces vibration, the operation being similar to a fourcutter set up using the thicknessing head.

Cutters must be kept sharp for backfencing, they should be preferably hollow ground, and free from heels. Timber should be moulded in long lengths for safety, as shorts have a tendency to kick back, mainly at the commencement of feed.

Moulded architraves and skirting boards should be fed at a speed through the spindle moulder or multihead machine to give an estimated 25 cuts per 25 mm of run.

It is preferable, too, that the feed speed should be constant. A selection of feed speeds on a length of timber, as obtained by hand feeding, very often can determine the professionalism of an operator.

The aim is usually to reduce sanding to a minimum with the production of linear quantity work, and this can only be achieved by regulating feed speeds through the machine and keeping the cutters in condition.

A fixing aid to skirting boards which is machine produced is the grooved and moulded floor lath. The under edge of the skirting requires to be rebated to form a tongue to fit the groove.

The use of this floor lath method on the site eliminates having to scribe the skirting to fit any undulations in the floor surface.

It also copes with settlement that takes place due to shrinkage in the floor joist during the drying out period after completion. Skirting boards should never be side nailed into the floor through the face, and this lath fixing method makes it entirely unnecessary.

Interior door frames in domestic work are of two main types. These are termed as door casings and storey frames.

Door casings are used as trim to openings in brickwork or timber framed partitions. In the case of brickwork they are fixed to wooden plugs driven into the joints then cut to provide a plumb surface.

Allowance in the casing width material must be made to accommodate the plaster finish to the brickwork—12 mm to each face is usually considered sufficient in practice although more is at times recommended.

Moulding machine with assisted feed unit making T. and G. floor boards.

Unless the casings are accurately machined the fixer may have difficulty in obtaining the standard of work required to hang the door on completion. The head member of the casing must always be checked for level before fixing and the bottom end of the upright members scribed to the floor if necessary.

Casings are usually rebated to a depth of about 12 mm by door thickness plus 3 mm. The additional 3 mm is important to allow for clearance and paint thicknesses. Deeper rebates than 12 mm are also required when fire check doors become involved.

volved.

Storey height frames are used for door openings when the adjoining wall is to be built of lightweight blocks which would not carry wooden fixing plugs. The frames are designed in such a way that they assist the precise construction of the wall and for this reason they are fixed before building commences.

The storey frames are made the complete height

Internal trim for window openings.

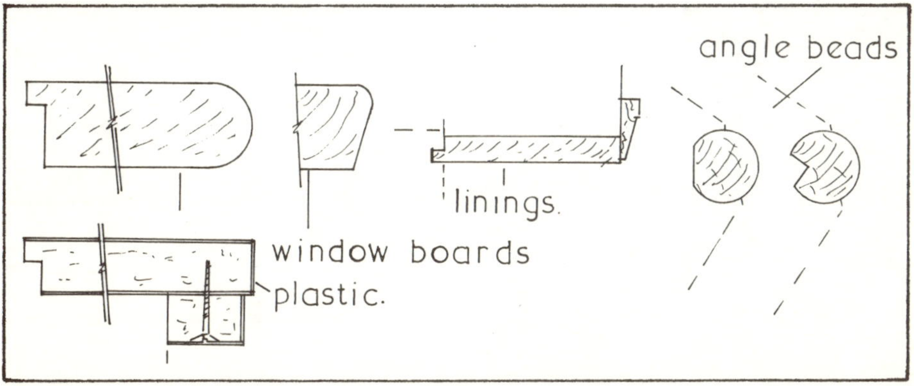

Mechanised unit for applying preservative treatment to timber to meet specifications for building requirements.

Preparing cutters on a balancing stand for the production of architrave moudling.

of the room, plus about 150 mm which allows for fixing to the joints above. The inner faces of the jambs and head are rebated as in door casings, and the outer surface is recessed to accommodate the building blocks.

A range of thicknesses of building blocks are available, starting at about 50 mm, so the width of the storey frame material finished requires to be block thickness plus, say 25 mm.

Preparation of the foot of the jambs for fixing to the floor, can either be a stubb tenon, easily produced on a machine, or a 12 mm dia. hole, bored for a hardwood or metal dowel.

In the manufacture of storey frames the portion of the jambs above the head line which projects beyond the wall face, must be cut away to allow a clear line for the plaster.

It is essential that the machined parts should be straight and out of twist, for as mentioned earlier they form an aid in the building of the wall. Some selection of the timber used for this purpose is recommended. Frames of this type are often delivered to the site unassembled in an effort to keep the material straight by careful stacking.

Door casings or linings, as they are often

Four examples of widthing joints. Butt, T. and G., loose tongue, and reversible joint.

Rebated casing material leaving a fourcutter moulding machine.

termed, to thick masonry walls as found when renovating old buildings, have to be of a considerable width.

For this reason they are preferably built up in panel form. Their design can either be in reproduction style with mouldings, or flush inset panels. The rebated section which carries the door is frequently repeated on the other edge of the casing to give a balanced appearance.

This does help from a production point of view as all the external members of the panel frame are of the same section. Infill panels would in plywood or other built up board in today's form of construction, although solid timber was used in the past.

Fixing of wide casings is usually to prepared rough ground laths due to the uneven state of the masonry type of wall. This method also enables anchorage to be obtained in the most secretive locations of the finished panel.

In the design of architrave mouldings for fixing to door casings two points must be kept in mind. To enable the door to open well beyond 90 degrees an architrave mould must have the greater part of it cut away at the edge adjoining the opening.

The outer edge of the mould requires to have sufficient thickness to carry the end section of the adjoining skirting board.

If there are to be intersection difficulties at this point either to material thicknesses or complicated moulds, plinth blocks require to be fitted to the foot of the architrave moulds.

Interior trim to window openings can consist of a window board (window bottom) wood linings and architraves. Wood linings, correctly tongued to the window jambs and head provide a superior finish to that of plaster.

Linings fixed at 90 degrees to the window frame provide no complications either in their manufacture or fixing. Splayed linings to the upright members only, is sometimes favoured. Plywood of a suitable grade can be used for linings, 12 mm in thickness. For the window board solid timber is still very often used, but plastic faced sheet materials are also favoured.

Solid material can be easily worked on the site to meet any variations in requirements which frequently occur. Machining operations in the manufacture of window boards is confined to planing and thicknessing, moulding and rebating.

Wide boards may have to be jointed, and there are a variety of methods which suit the purpose. Adhesives used for the gluing operation in this location should be of a moisture resisting type as

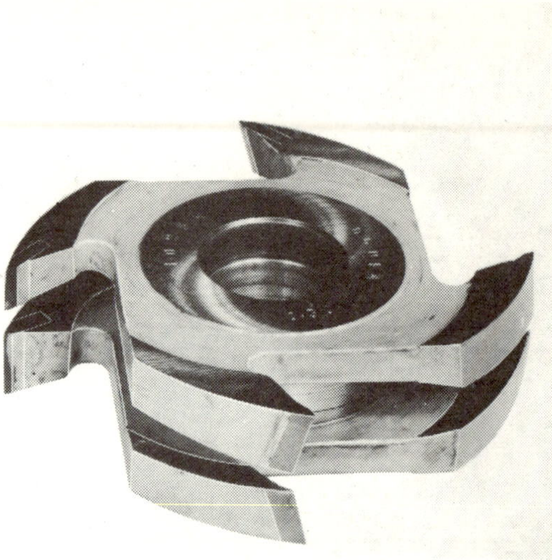

Tungsten carbide tipped tongue forming cutter which is suitable for working plywood, plastics, chipboard, etc. (J. K. O. Cutters, High Wycombe.)

condensation may be present from time to time.
Widthing joint methods used in timber preparation can include the following . . . Butt joint, tongue and groove, loose tongue, or reversible type tongue and groove joint. Butt joints are favoured for radio frequency methods as it gives pressure under cramping to the whole area of the joint.

Tongue and groove jointing is suitable for many purposes, but it can require two set-ups on the machine which can be time consuming for small quantities.

Loose tongue methods give the maximum amount of timber width, the tongue being a separate item. This method is often used to obtain a given dimension with a limited amount of material. The reversible joint is usually produced with the aid of a solid profile type cutter head.

It is highly progressive as both members of the joint are put through the machine at the same set. One point is very important, however. All the timber must be exactly the same thickness. One of the rules of machine woodworking is broken in the way the timber is positioned in the machine in producing this joint.

Both sides of the timber are regarded as working faces, hence the importance of identical thicknessing.

Other items that the machinist has to prepare for the fixer on the site include requirements for the interior of cupboards. Shelving is required in a variety of widths and is usually prepared from 25 mm nominal thickness of timber.

This is an item that can be made up from the lower grade type of timber generally spoken of as whitewood. (Not redwood). Timber of this classification is not used for exterior purposes, due to its poor weathering ability, but its clean appearance in spite of a fair share of knots, making it very suitable for shelving.

Supporting rails for shelves are produced in linear form with either a chamfered or beaded edge. Ex 75 x 25 mm material produces a section that can have multi-purpose uses on the building site. Manhole frames for trimming the access hole into the false roof space, can be constructed from such material.

Angle bead, as used on external corners as a means of obtaining a finish to plaster work has been replaced to some extent by metal trim. Wood bead has its advantages in use being very convenient for carrying screw hooks or nails, particularly on chimney breasts where household oddments are accumulated. Wood bead is made from ex 25 x 25 mm softwood, circular in end section, and has either a flat portion or a right angle notch grooves to assist fixing.

It is an item that can be made up from accumulated offcuts in a joinery unit that is attached to a building concern.

It may not be, in fact, an economical venture to buy boards of clear grade timber and produce the mould in multiple on the fourcutter unless the demand was there for a very large quantity.

Mouldings: The use of moulding as a form of decor is limited in present-day design, but the machine worker has at times requests for a section of mould to be produced.

Quantities of moulding of the smaller sections are usually produced on the moulding machine in multiple form. That is, a piece of timber several times the width of the required mould is fed into the machine and with suitably prepared cutters a number of strips of moulding are made at the one pass.

Better feeding of the machine is experienced when working in this manner as the feed roller has more surface on which to drive, and less breakages are likely on fine beadings.

When working on the spindle moulder with planed material, moulding is very often "stuck" as it is termed, on the edge of a wide board and then cut off with a fine tooth saw. This is a convenient method of working for small quantities and has several safety factors in its favour.

Mouldings of larger sections are prepared singly and some consideration must be given to the sequence of working and their design. It may be necessary for the timber to make more than one pass through the spindle moulder in order to obtain the required profile.

Which cut is made first will be decided by how the stock is going to support itself after some of the material has been cut away. It may be necessary for a supporting saddle to be made and fixed to either the bed or the fence of the machine.

Cutters have in the main to be ground by what is known as freehand, for moulded work which involves a considerable amount of experience to obtain success. The grinding appliance should be fitted with an adjustable tool rest which will help considerably with the operation.

Many grinding appliances found in woodworking establishments are unsuitable for cutter making as required in machine woodworking. Geometrical factors must be kept in mind when shaping cutters in order to produce mouldings of pleasing design.

The fact that a cutter is not positioned at right angles to the fence line on the spindle moulder when making the maximum cut means that the cutter profile must be an elongated version of the mould shape.

This means that additional projection must be allowed for in shaping, although the height dimension remains as the mould.

Experienced machinists on moulding profiles which they are familiar with can very often estimate the amount of elongation required. The more complicated cutter profiles require to be geometrically developed with either a specialized aid, or on the drawing board.

Cutters should not be used straight from the grindstone; they require to be honed with a slip stone lubricated with light oil, or a mixture of oil and paraffin.

Failure to carry out the honing operation will produce work with a surface consisting of a series of ridges. The use of a selection of honing slips of various shapes can improve the quality of the work for the enthusiastic operator, and can be well worthwhile.

Correctness of shape of some mouldings produced can be checked for accuracy. Four pieces of quadrant mould positioned together should produce a true circle. Four scotia mould sections, a true form of ellipse when the cut faces are positioned inwards.

Intricate forms of moulding, such as architraves for use with semi-circular headed door frames require advanced skill in their manufacture.

Due to the fact that the requirement is only for small quantities usually, jigs involved must be kept to a minimum. To produce a moulding in semi-circular form the shape has either to be built up by laminating, or made in sections and jointed.

Shaping in the square section can be done with the aid of a jig, or former nailed to the work, on either the high speed router or the spindle moulder.

The mould profile on the face of the timber could involve a considerable amount of cutter projection if worked flat on the spindle moulder.

Cutting can be done in stages with the work positioned face to the fence if a suitable saddle is prepared and fixed to the machine. It is necessary that the initial shaping jig, or former is a true radius of a circle or the moulding operation, working on a saddle may not be fully successful.

Cutting should be light, preferably done in a series of stages to prevent undue pressure on the work.

A through face board should be fixed across the fences of the machine, as this not only acts as a guard, but prevents chips from being injected into the cut.

Wardrobes and Cupboards

The stock range of floor to ceiling storage type cupboards is limited, and therefore some consideration should be made in the planning of a building as to the sizes available.
In present day construction methods such items as windows and doors have reached a point of standardisation in as much that a builder knows he can get a repeat of dimension from his supplier at the time of requirement.
Batch production reduces cost, and the more

Wardrobe unit on a production line. Designed for quantity production for use in a student accommodation block at a university.

Hanging robe with store cupboard above fitted into recess. It basically consists of a front frame only in softwood, painted, and fitted with polished veneered doors. Shelves are supported on bearers fixed to walls.

timber items that can be included in a building from the line without involving specials the more economic will be the final result.
In a new building, cupboards fitted prior to the sale to the customer can have several advantages. In addition to the attractive features which such items as fitted wardrobes in bedrooms offer, they are in a sense articles of furniture required by the occupier, and it is paid for at an all-in cost of the house, on mortgage or otherwise.
Tax privilege can sometimes be gained in this way also as housing is usually considered more essential than luxury furniture.
There are two distinct methods of approach in the construction of cupboard accommodation, both of which can be assisted by supplies from the production line. Cupboards can be supplied in the form of front frames with doors only, or complete carcase units.
Very often cupboards are positioned in recesses

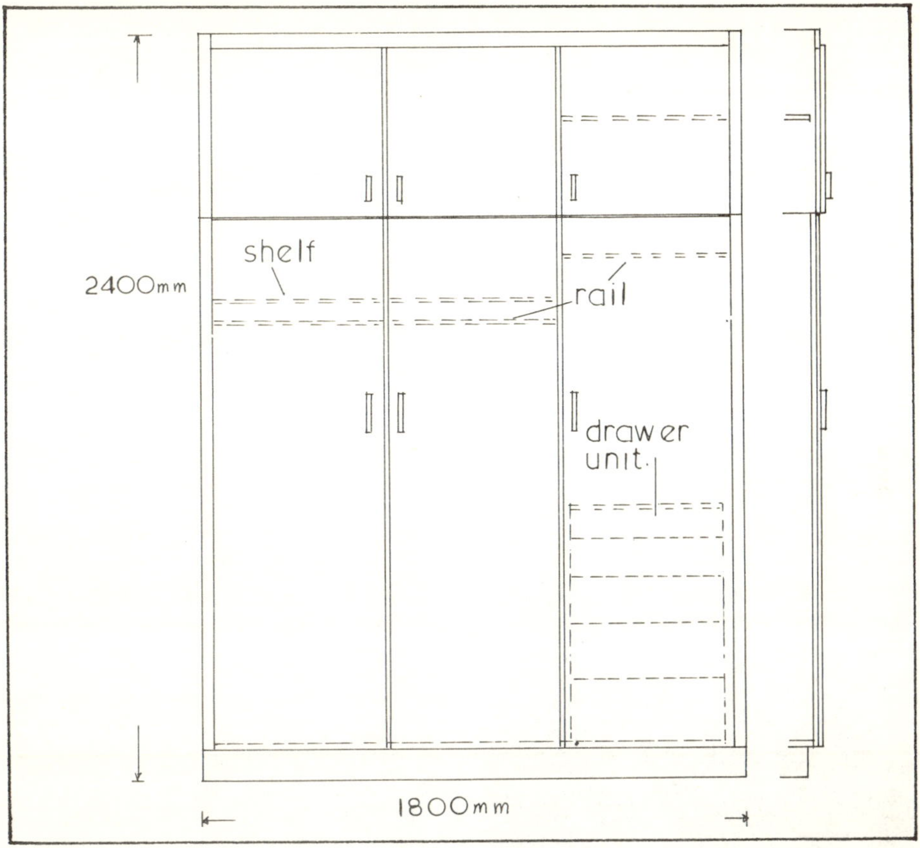

General outline of a storage unit designed for making up in either two or three separate carcases mounted on a plinth unit. Provision is made for long and short hanging, shelf and drawer accommodation, and long-term storage above.

adjoining chimney breasts, and the front frame method becomes a very tempting proposition under these circumstances.

There are, however, disadvantages in creating such as hanging wardrobes in this way, as the depth is limited to that of the recess. A substantial robe should be in the region of 500 mm in depth to hang clothes comfortably.

One scheme which has developed favour, probably due to the fact that fewer chimney recesses are being created, is to fit a series of carcase units across the end of a room. This gives a clean finish which also simplifies carpet fitting and decorating.

In the planning of floor to ceiling box type units it must be kept in mind that it is not possible to erect a structure of this type in one assembled carcase in a completed room. A front frame can be erected, but the diagonal measurement of a box unit would not permit it.

The method usually adopted to overcome this is to manufacture the cabinets in two height sections. The lower very often is the hanging robe, and a store cupboard positioned above. Mounting the cupboards on loose base plinths can assist with the height problem if one full carcase is required to meet a specific frontage plan.

Construction methods of front frame systems provide no difficulties for machine production, but complete carcase units involve the use of wide material which can be difficult to accommodate on some machines.

Chipboard with various types of surface finishes is frequently used due to its competitive cost with other sheet material. Tungsten carbide

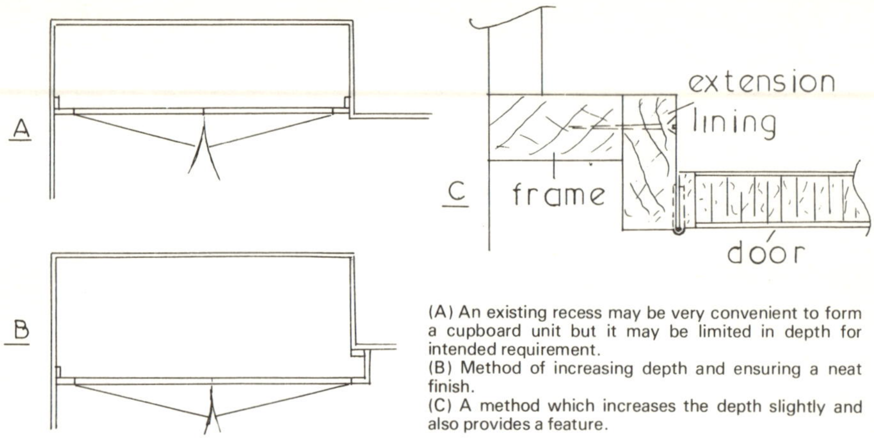

(A) An existing recess may be very convenient to form a cupboard unit but it may be limited in depth for intended requirement.
(B) Method of increasing depth and ensuring a neat finish.
(C) A method which increases the depth slightly and also provides a feature.

Cutting large dimension blockboard using a portable saw. Note the guide lath which ensures a straight cut.

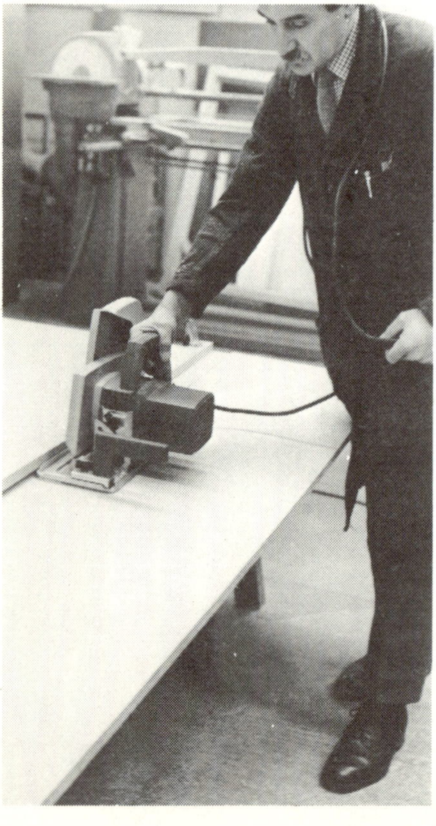

tipped cutters are required when working this material in quantity. It is an ideal material for use in large panel form, particularly in vertical location. It is generally not subject to twisting with temperature variations which may be experienced with other types of panel board.

As chipboard is manufactured under hotpress conditions it lends itself well to further hotpressing for applying bearers or surface veneers.

Solid timber edge lippings incorporated as a feature can give welcome support to external edges not only in use but during storage in stock rooms, and in transit.

Solid edge lippings are preferably tongued on to the chipboard, the tongues being formed on the solid timber and the chipboard grooved.

In this way, the centre portion of the chipboard is cut away, which is usually less dense, leaving the more durable section intact.

When selecting fittings, handles, locks, etc., for fitting to chipboard, consideration should be given to their ability to permit secure anchorage. This is particularly important if the units are to be subjected to public use where durability standards need to be substantially increased over those required in private locations. Handles on doors and drawers should be through screwed from inside.

Locks should be of the surface mounting type to eliminate the cutting away of the chipboard near to the fixing screws. Shoot bolts should be of generous length to permit adequate fixing screws, which should be of the double grip type which have a deep cut thread the full length of the shank. Wood edge lippings to doors can help

Large width capacity saw bench cutting sheet material. The machine has been designed with this purpose in mind. Wadkin. Model BGP.

considerably with the firm anchorage of fittings on cupboards which are to be subjected to heavy wear.

An alternative method to construct carcases from either chipboard or blockboard is to produce frames from ex 50 x 25 mm material and face these with sheet material. This can prove an economical form of construction when a number of box units are placed together to fill a space.

Inner skins can be of hardboard, and some frames can be left in skeleton form where they meet up with a covered end. Ready polished and decoratively grooved wall board can be used to advantage in visible locations, and this material can be obtained in room height dimensions in a range of cost grades.

Construction methods can vary very much depending on the plant available. Establishments that are equipped with a heated press usually find that it becomes involved on operations of most of their lines of production.

This also applies to electronic methods of curing adhesives such as low voltage strip heating and radio frequency methods. The latter system eliminates the use of tongues on edge lippings and exploits the use of modern adhesives developments to the full.

Knowledge of the application of the various types of adhesives and setting methods can give an establishment an advantage over its less informed competitors. Some advantages are: lower waste factor, reduction in timber content, and continuous work flow.

When built up panel material is used such as

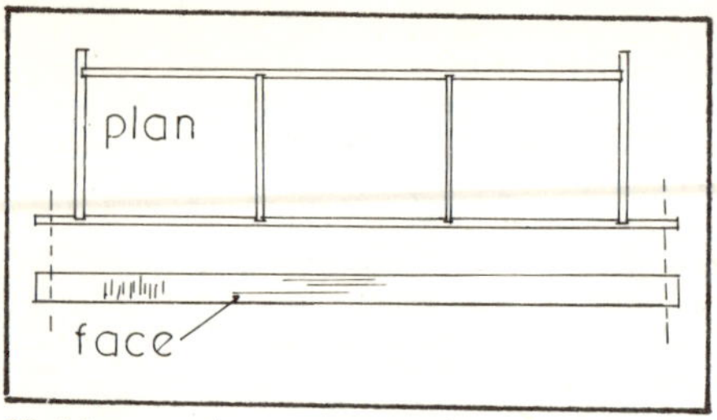

Plinth bases can be constructed using a trenching head on a pull-out cross-cut saw, or on a high speed router. The front member is made with additional length to allow for fitting on site. The face can be cross veneered or plastic covered.

Constructional methods for carcases using various materials.

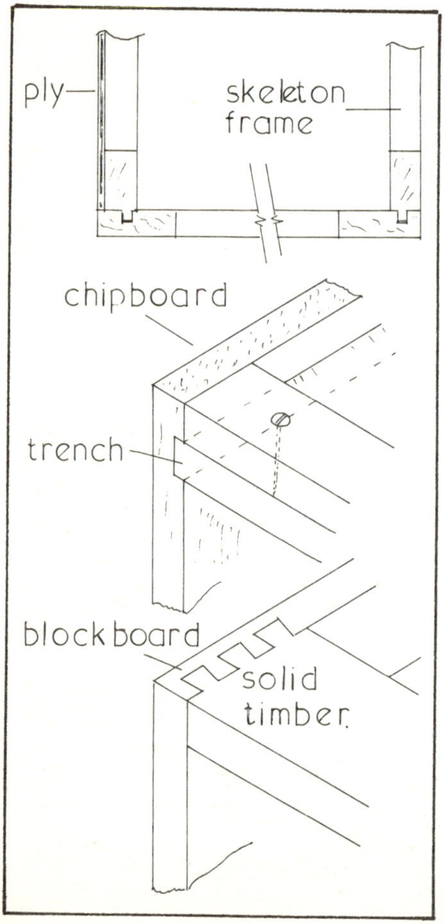

blockboard or laminboard, the doors should preferably be made from the latter. This is due to the more intricate structure of the core which is designed to resist twisting of the panel.

If the surface is to be veneered, the direction of the grain on the panelboard must be at right angles to that of the veneer to prevent cracking.

Both sides of the panel must be veneered to balance the force set up or the door will no longer be flat. The core of the laminations should preferably run vertical for maximum rigidity and give efficient holding power to the hinging screws when edge lippings are not involved. Light gauge screws, as used for hinges, have little holding power into end grain of timber.

The types of material available at the time of requirement may not always permit all of the ideals to be met, but they should be kept in mind when purchasing and planning the cutting of the material.

The cutting of large sheets of panel board can create difficulties in a workshop where space is limited. When positioning machines on installation the working space which large sheets require must be considered.

In established machine shops some reluctance is at times experienced when suggestions are made regarding the re-deployment of machines to meet changing requirements. One machine which can help with panel board cutting within a confined space is the model which operates with the material standing on edge. Although a machine of this type may at first appear to have a limited variety of uses, it can be used for many forms of square cutting, and angular work also, suitably jigged.

It is not good practice to remove the guard from a circular saw bench in order to increase the width cutting capacity to meet a requirement. It is also an infringement of the safety regulations. Where a dimension cannot be obtained on the saw bench available, a cut can at times be made with the aid of a portable rip saw.

A guide lath fixed to the material will ensure a straight accurate cut.

Another point to consider when cutting panel boards is the quality of the finished edge regarding ragging of the grain. Various precautions can be taken to increase the efficiency of the cut. The most shoddy type of work is usually produced when an operator takes over a circular saw to do a one-off job without making any adjustments to the machine.

The mouth or slot through which the saw passes should be as close to the saw as possible. This

Corner combing attachment fitted to the spindle moulder. This method can be used for jointing trays for cupboard units, or drawers which are fitted with false fronts.

can be achieved by running in a part sheet of plywood and securing when other methods are not possible. The saw teeth should only project above the table the panel thickness plus about a further 6 mm.

This reduces the chopping action of the saw tooth to a minimum and permits a greater number of points to operate in the cut.

Progression of the material through the cut should be continuous, not in a series of jerks as can be seen, and heard, from time to time.

Overhead pressure springs which prevent board flap, a common contributive factor to bad cutting, will increase the efficiency if they can be applied.

A tungsten carbide tipped saw will cut continuously for several weeks without attention on the most difficult abrasive types of panel boards in general use.

An operator who is continuously engaged in this field of work, takes a pride in the efficiency of his cutting standards regarding accuracy of dimensions and clean finish. Squareness of panels is also important, particularly when jig working is to be involved in later stages. The one-off worker should keep the specialists methods in mind and apply as time allows.

Wardrobes and cupboards that are to be fixtures do not require the same amount of rigidity as those which are freestanding. Sometimes back panels to cupboards which are to be fixtures are left off. To get the maximum rigidity from a back panel it should be well glued and screwed on to the carcase.

Back panels located in a groove do not have as good a stiffening effect. A rigid front frame system helps considerably with the fitting and successful operation of doors.

Often doors are now hung on the face of the front frame rather than within it. This reduces fitting time, and in the case of the larger type of door as on wardrobes no binding is experienced should the door drop a little during use. Quite often wardrobes are fitted with shelves and nests of trays.

The aim should be to construct these interior fitments as a framed unit which will involve only a small amount of time fixing within the main structure. Rigidity will also be obtained by working in this manner rather than screwing a multitude of bits and pieces within the carcase.

Curing the glue line on door edge lippings using low voltage strip heating. Pye Thermal Bonders equipment.

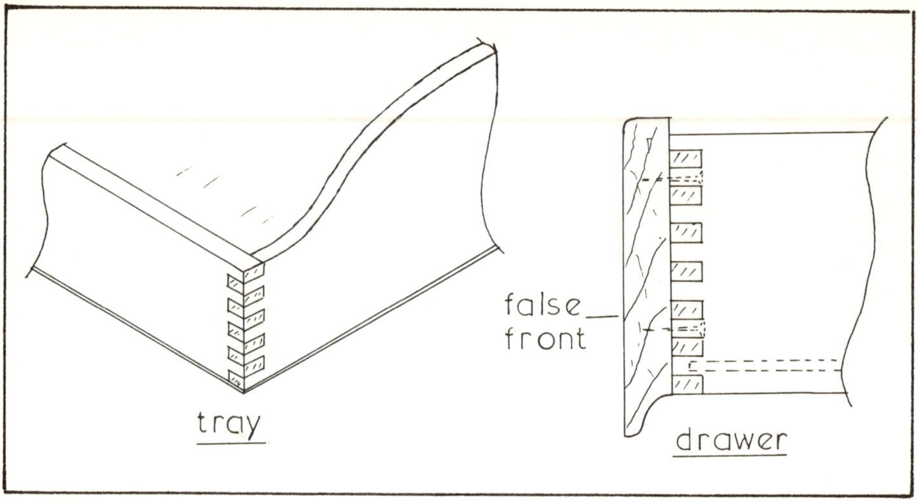

Interior trays should be of light construction, box combing to the corner joints usually being preferred to dovetailing. With cupboards painted on the outside, interior fitments can be in such timber as meranti or similar type of the lower grade hardwoods.
A combination of polish and paint finish is accepted in our present age. It is not unusual to fit polished hardwood-faced doors to painted cabinets.
In the planning of floor to ceiling cupboards it may be necessary for the setter-out to pay a site visit to measure up the project. If the units are to be enclosed within existing walls at either end, accurate width measurements require to be taken, at both the floor and ceiling levels.
It is quite good policy to make a framed plinth unit, say 100 mm in height, and take it along if possible and fit it in to the location.
In an established home the carpet can be cut at the plinth fitting stage which prevents hold-ups when the actual carcases arrive. Having got the base plan under control the height can receive consideration.
In the height planning, measurements must be taken of any cornice moulds or other projections that may prevent doors from opening in the completed unit.
Ideally the cornice mould if intersected should be returned along the front of the cupboards, but this may not always be possible or practical. The positioning of hinged doors must be considered in relation to the amount of room available to allow them to open. Circumstances have occurred where an opened door has come into contact with a heating source.

Trays and drawers for wardrobe interiors can be comb jointed in preference to dovetailing if desired. This method can be more suitable for the light sections used for this purpose.

Hinged doors should preferably be limited to a maximum width of 600 mm. Sliding doors benefit from lots of width from the point of view of balanced working.
In spite of wardrobe doors being over-tall in relation to their width, they operate without effort using present day fittings designed for this purpose. The doors are suspended from above, usually on nylon wheels running in a metal track. Guide shoes only are fitted to the lower edge of the door.
To endeavour to slide doors of wardrobe dimensions in the base groove would not be satisfactory. Sliding door fittings are obtainable in packs including all the necessary parts.
The number of doors concerned and opening width is catered for. If any difficulty is encountered in obtaining secure fixing to chipboard or the end grain of timber it can be to advantage to screw a batten of sound timber to the top edge or the door first.
Sliding doors also require a substantial hanging rail with a width of at least 70 mm to carry two lines of doors. Sliding doors do take up a little more of the cupboard depth than hinged doors, as two thicknesses of door have to be allowed for, plus a clearance space of say 6 mm.
The increased amount required to take sliding doors over hinged must be kept in mind when producing in quantity and interior fitments such as trays and shelves are being made as a

standard to fit both types of door arrangement.

It is quite common to fix a hat storage shelf in a wardrobe about 225 mm from the top. For hinged doors the shelf is brought very close to the inner face of the door. The reason for this is to accommodate a finger catch linking with the first closing door.

The shelf positioning has to change when sliding doors are involved.

Cylinder cupboards as used to house domestic water heating systems need to be approached with the advancement of living standards in mind. The installation of central heating can involve the use of sections of the plumbing system used for water heating in some circumstances.

Cupboards should be constructed of such a size that room to manoeuvre is provided for. Cupboard ends that for several decades were match boarded, can now be covered with decorative wallboard. Suitably mounted, it can be fixed with brass screws in cups for easy removal when plumbing services require attention.

Front frames with doors are still very much favoured for this cupboard as it gives the plumber the maximum amount of freedom to do his work.

Also, adequate support has to be provided when the water storage tank has to be accommodated in the cupboard in addition to the cylinder.

Support is usually given by the back wall to one end of a bearer and by a timber upright fixed behind the front frame stile. Standard sizes of front frames are available to suit tank dimensions. The size of the frames should be checked before constructing tank platforms or specials may become involved.

Cylinder cupboard frames require additional support members if a water storage tank is to be accommodated in the upper section. A framed loose end, easily removable, can be to advantage for servicing and adding to the enclosed installations.

External Trim to Buildings

The life span of timber used externally can be very much governed by the way in which it is prepared initially. Timber utilised with a high moisture content which will repel surface coatings and cause failure in joint formation is doomed from the start. For some types of work, pressure application of preservative is recommended with the moisture content of the timber in excess of 20 per cent. This is because the cells in the timber are at the most suitable state to accept the preservative. Further drying should take place after this process before any attempt at framing is made or the application of surface coatings.

Softwood timber which is principally used in building work, takes up moisture rapidly if left unprotected in exposed locations. It will also dispel the moisture quickly when conditions are favourable. Deterioration starts when the timber is kept in a high state of moisture content for long periods.

This can be caused by lack of ventilation, or with being in close contact with another material which is more reluctant to part with the moisture than the timber.

A typical example of this is when windows are built into the external skin of a cavity wall, which has of recent years become very common practice. After a period of damp conditions, the frame, if not suitably protected, may contain an unacceptable amount of moisture. A favourable change of weather conditions would dry out excess moisture quickly, but the members adjoining brickwork or other dense construction material may be kept in a damp state for a much longer period of time.

Although the methods which we use in building are decided by what we can afford to pay, they are at times scientifically primitive from the point of view of timber usage.

The design of timber sections for exterior use should always keep in mind the necessity for shedding moisture. Grooves in a horizontal

Timber infill units and built up fascia boards form a prominent feature of a new clubhouse building.

tongue and groove assembly, should face downwards to prevent moisture being trapped whenever possible. Expansion must be allowed for when wide material is used or bowing may be experienced.

Joints made with the utilisation of the material itself can in many circumstances be more satisfactory than the introduction of metal fittings. Joint failures due to working timber initially at too high a rate of moisture content, or incorrect design, can result in the admittance of moisture and shorten the life of the unit. Nails well punched in below the surface and filled in appear to survive outdoor conditions when the timber is maintained, but their use in more exposed positions such as fencing requires special consideration.

It is uncommon to find fencing staves which have had good preservative treatment, dropping off due to the nails rusting through after a considerable period of service.

Types of nails are available which should give extended life to structures of this type, to an accepted number of years to satisfy the customer. Some timbers, such as English oak, can assist in the decay of iron-based fittings. Stain marks on the timber detect that chemical action is taking place.

Timbers which are to be painted or coated with the now popular types of polyurethane varnish, can benefit from care at the machining stage. Failure to provide a satisfactory surface to which to apply a protective coating can affect the durability of the timber in use. Most coatings are at their best applied at an even thickness.

Rest seat designed to last, using timber.

A swage type saw blade operating in a circular saw bench. This blade is tapered on the fence side of the plate only and is designed for cutting thin strips, as used in woven fencing, etc., with the minimum of kerf waste.

When rough patches occur on the timber, or the wavefield of the rotary cutting action is very pronounced, uneven thickness of the surface coating will result. Rubbing down, which under these circumstances has to be done between coats, can expose the high points of the timber. The final coat may well be the only covering to some parts of the surface. If no rubbing down is attempted an inferior finish is produced. Fortunately, on some work, such items as fascia boards are located at a good distance from the casual observer, but a keen eye will very often be able to detect the quality of finish that has been obtained by the wood machinist.

Decorative boardings as used for built up fascia work are at times also used for surface cladding. Its uses in these fields are increasing to stimulate design. The timbers used for external work are mainly cedar and various grades of softwood. Some sections are designed in such a way that encourages secret nailing, a point worth considering when planning a production run. Also in the machining of sections the back face is very often recessed, the centre portion being cut away.

This is done for two main reasons. It permits the board to bed firmly on the edges instead of maybe rocking on a high point in the centre. It also gives the principal rigidity to the face of the

Ranch type fencing in a rural setting.

Vertical louvre fence designed to give through vision from the approach side and screening from the opposite direction.

Typical products of the joinery mill. The finish displayed on the building is very often that which is prepared by the machinist on these items as conditions are not always favourable to do "cleaning up" on the site.

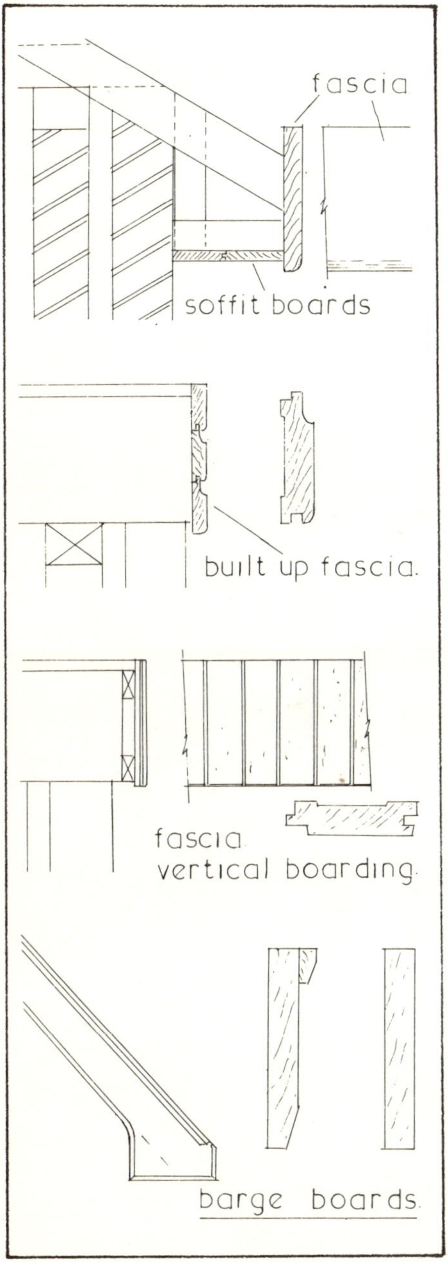

section which will not be unduly affected by any pull on the back.

It is desirable that all timber should be protective coated before being fixed externally. For this reason such items as tongues which fit in grooves should not be formed over-tight if they are to be used for external formations. Wedge type tongues can very often be the most suitable if their application permits.

When preparing tongue and grooved parts of boarding on the moulding machine, it is customary to run the stock with the groove to the fence side. Under this method of working any timber which is under width slightly will result in a loss of a little of the tongue which is acceptable up to a point. A rough edge on the grooved portion would not be acceptable at all.

Since the development of synthetic resin adhesives it has been possible to produce plywood which will stand up to exterior use.

This has enabled this type of material to be used for such items as fascia boards, soffits, and infill panels.

For working this material by machine, tungsten carbide tipped cutters are required due to the abrasive nature of the glue lines. If material of this type is used in large sheet form, it is preferable that provision should be made in the constructional planning to allow for expansion which has been found to occur with some grades of material.

Early treatment of the surface will reduce movement, and such refinements as cover fillets, and over deep grooves will help to cope with expansion should it occur. The practice of slot screwing instead of simply boring has been used on the production line to ensure a trouble-free item.

Care must also be taken in this multiple panel field when other types of materials are bonded to it, such as laminated plastic or metallised sheeting. The different rates of expansion experienced in hot pressing may produce panels anything but flat. A balancer material may have to be applied to the back face, usually of a less costly material. Another solution is to press the panels cold, but this will slow down output and may not be acceptable in some establishments.

Timber weather boards have a variety of uses and are manufactured in a number of manners and designs. For economy they are sometimes used straight from the saw or with one face planed only. Moulded and rebated weather boards can be manufactured from the rough timber at one pass through the moulding machine. Ex 100 mm x 25 mm gives a substantial weather board, but quite often due to economy reasons a thinner material is used.

If a batch of material contains boards for putting through the moulder which are likely to be under thickness, it is preferable to work with the finished face down to the bed of the machine.

This will leave any unplaned patches on the back of the board which is not visible in use. A second bottom head on the machine can be beneficial for working this method as moulding cutters are not generally used on the surfacing head of the machine.

The unplaned type of weather boards which are very often produced in rural areas are used for such items as fencing and light animal enclosures. The aim in manufacture should be to provide a constant finish to the surfaces by maintaining continuous feeding to the saw.

Power feed can help with this if it is available.

The sawn finish is favoured for agricultural uses due to the fact that it readily absorbs preservatives, more so than a smooth planed surface. Splay sawing, the term given to their method of manufacture, can be done on either a circular saw or a band resaw. A band resaw will create a saw kerf probably only half the width of that of a circular saw, generally speaking, which means a greater amount of material will go into the product rather than to waste.

For reducing saw kerf waste on the circular saw when producing thin material, say less than 15 mm, a swage saw blade can be used to advantage. This type of blade is of stout gauge in the centre of the plate, tapering on one face only, the fence side, to a very light gauge at the outer rim. The amount of set on the teeth should understandably be very slight to reduce waste to a minimum, but the bevelled side should have a little more set than the flat side for ideal working. Saw blades of this type usually have felt packings in the bench, and these may require adjustment if the blade is lowered to suit the thickness of material being cut, which is one of the factors which should be considered to reduce friction.

A swage saw blade will only cut thin slices off a slab of timber, as the cut piece has to spring away to permit passage. It will not cut, say, a board of 150 x 75 mm down the centre. An attempt at this would result in binding and a throw back, much to the detriment of the blade, and maybe the operator also.

Band resaws, an enlarged version of the narrow bandsaw to briefly describe, are capable of rip-

In the construction of gates joints should be through mortise and tenoned and pegged. Horizontal members weathered. Note extension to stile below bottom rail. Wide gates should have tie or brace member.

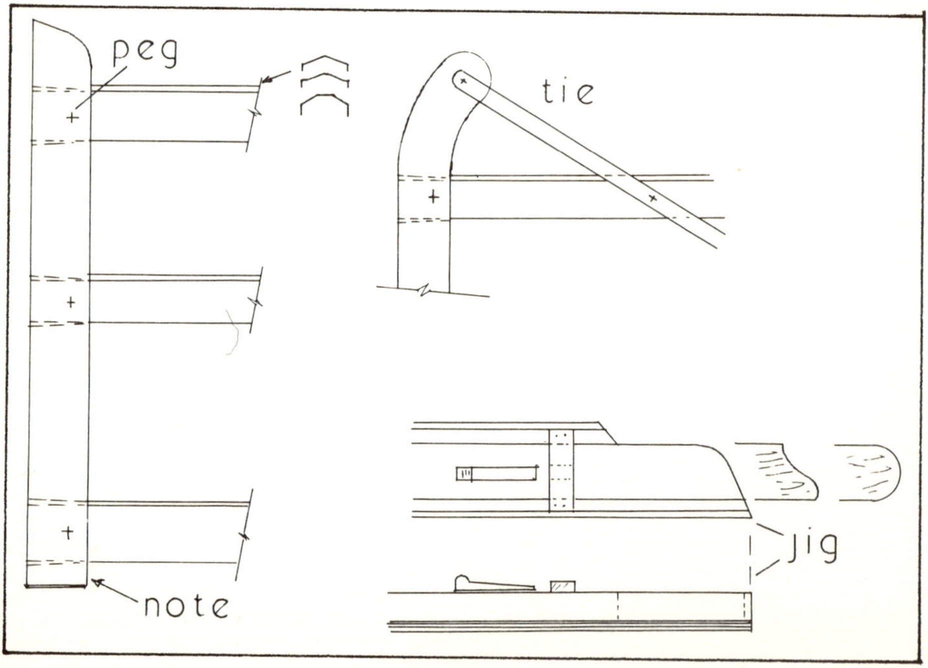

ping timber with only a very small amount of waste in the saw kerf. This can be maintained continuously with little effort and as power feeding is usually fitted to this type of machine as standard, it is a much more productive approach than that of swage sawing on the circular saw bench.

Ranch type timber fencing very often now takes the place of boundary walls as a more contemporary and economical form of meeting a requirement. This may in some instances be a form of short-term economy but it does permit available funds to be distributed initially, until such a time when updating of facilities becomes possible.

Ranch fencing battens bolted to concrete posts should provide many years of service, but all-timber erections are quite common and should

Wide bandsaw machine, suitable for converting round logs, or resawing slab material. This type of machine is an advancement on the circular saw for estate work, and of course many other purposes. (Photo: Stenner, Tiverton, Devon).

be favourable providing the material is suitably treated.

Various type of this pattern of dividing unit are developing. A recent one to my notice is where planks are fixed alternately up the height on one face of the post and then the other. This makes a vertical channel with openings through which climbing plants can be trained to grow as an added feature.

Another type of timber fencing involves the use of a louvre design. The louvre slats, however, are mounted vertically instead of the usual horizontal.

This type of fence can be constructed as a wind break, and can to some extent control the direction of air flow. It can also give privacy looking from one direction, and visibility from the other. This type of fencing can be quickly constructed from planed stock using a trenching head in a pull-out crosscut saw.

In the construction of timber gates several points should be noted to ensure that the article will give service for an acceptable period of time. Horizontal members should be weathered to shed moisture. The stiles should preferably project lower than the under edge of the bottom rail to maintain strength. This is the location which is very often the first to fail in service. Mortise and tenon joints should be pegged in addition to being through and wedged.

Like other exterior items protective coatings should be applied before the timber picks up moisture.

Paint is quite often applied to gates during the assembly process, although it is not a very attractive operation to the workers involved if it is in a wet state.

Softwood timber gates can have a service life comparative to hardwoods, providing material selection, construction, and some care in use is taken into consideration. Hardwoods fail very often due to a low quality of timber being used. Also, paint does not generally adhere to hardwoods as satisfactorily as to the softer material. Their additional weight can make them self-destructive if not suitably braced.

Gates lend themselves well to machine production, and only a small amount of the plant need be involved. They are an item that can be manufactured from standing offcuts in the larger production unit when machining capacity requires to be utilised.

Height members are usually constant in a design, width members vary in length to suit a variety of openings.

Pierced work or shaping to infill components can be jigged for processing on the high speed

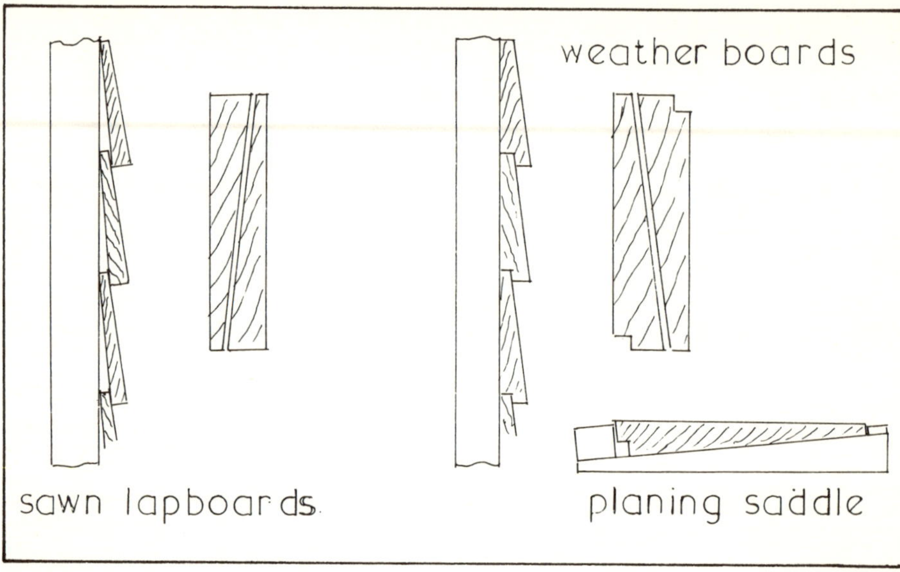

Typical examples of agricultural type lap boards, and weather boards.

router. Routing is preferable to jig sawing or bandsawing as a planed finish is obtained straight from the machine which may need little or no further attention.

Through mortising to the principal members is most speedily carried out using the chain attachment in the machine. The stiles should be cut to a constant length before mortising so that they may be set to stops eliminating marking out to a minimum.

The rails should be cut to the nett finished length during the tenoning process, this saves an operation after the assembly stage. Shaping the tops of the stiles can be done to a variety of patterns with the use of a jig on the spindle moulder. Infill components which are thinner than the main framing should be sanded before assembly.

Shopfitting

In spite of the introduction of many new materials used in shopfitting threre still remains a call for the woodworker and the application of his craft. Sometimes he is required to play a major role in the introduction of alternative materials to work, and so instead of his skills declining, as many people think, they are actually extending into other fields.

Unit construction of items is aimed at whenever possible to enable work to be carried out within the factory with the use of mechanical aids.

Timber used as a feature along with other materials to form an attractive shop front.

Sketch of a typical shop front. Various types of material can be used but timber is nearly always involved for some of the principal items.

Shopfitting is to some extent a specialized section of the buidling industry and it is not unusual for the component parts of an installation to be manufactured in one part of the country and transported to another a considerable journey away. Organisation is required under these circumstances which affects everyone in the establishment at some time or other. Situations do arise when the machinist is asked for component parts to make up a delivery load, and he finds that the timber is still in the rough state in the yard or in the process of kiln drying.

There is much less likelihood of items being forgotten or left behind if as much of the work as possible can be framed into units in the factory.

Wastage of material can also be reduced to a minimum in this way as it is confined to only one source instead of two. Also due to the specialised nature of the work, staff are required in many instances to be resident away from home.

This is generally not an attractive feature, which has to be kept to a minimum.

In the initial fitting out of shop premises, completion dates can play an important part as it may be desired to catch a particular trading season of the year.

Unit construction of fitments can enable the

work to be prepared in advance, leaving only fixing to take place on the site. Items such as cover moulds and facings must be provided for in keeping with the adjoining work, this being an aspect which at times is neglected and make-do strips of, say, hardboard are substituted That is the situation perhaps at its worst, but it can be seen.

Items required in shop fitting in which the woodworker may become involved include the following: External window framing. Entrance door and frame. Sign area and fascia. Pilasters. Blind box. Window display area. Window backs. Serving counters. Display units and stands. Stock accommodation cupboards.

Work can also involve the lining of walls with sheet material and suspended ceilings. Stairs and handrail work may be called for in the fitting out of the larger unit.

Much of the work involved, particularly the fixtures, have to be individually constructed to suit the particular job in hand.

Showcase items may be obtained from specialist producers under some circumstances, but they are very often manufactured by shopfitting establishments as part of their production flow.

This enables capital investment to be used to the full rather than having top grade plant standing unused.

Batch production of free-standing items, such as display cases can be introduced if space permits, and very often a showroom area is provided for in this branch of the industry.

The amount of standardisation that is possible in shopfitting work could be said to be limited to working procedures within the unit involved. Repeat designs will occur, but measurements will mostly likely be different.

Stock sections of material can help, although they may have to be limited to softwood items such as fixing grounds, for cost reasons. A considerable amount of hardwood and sheet material is involved in shopfitting, and waste can add to cost very quickly if it is not carefully considered.

For some items, relating to the site dimensions, waste may be unavoidable, but in the planning of interior fitments which are to be repeated in quantity, the sizes of the sheet material concerned should be determined before setting out the work. In an establishment which is producing a number of lines, offcuts can at times be directed to another product, but it is not good policy to produce waste in the hope that a suitable job will turn up for it.

In shopfitting work it will be found that the length of timber items are frequently longer than, say, the 3 m used in domestic building work. Provision must be made for this in the planning of machine shops with this type of work in mind.

It is not unusual to find trap doors in walls positioned on the outfeed line of, say, spindle moulders in the more compact shop, to allow the occasional extra long member to pass

General points relating to shop front construction. Glazing sections must be designed for the rebate line to follow through. Metal angle plates and handrail bolts add to the rigidity of corner joints. Metal faced timber mouldings are extensively used.

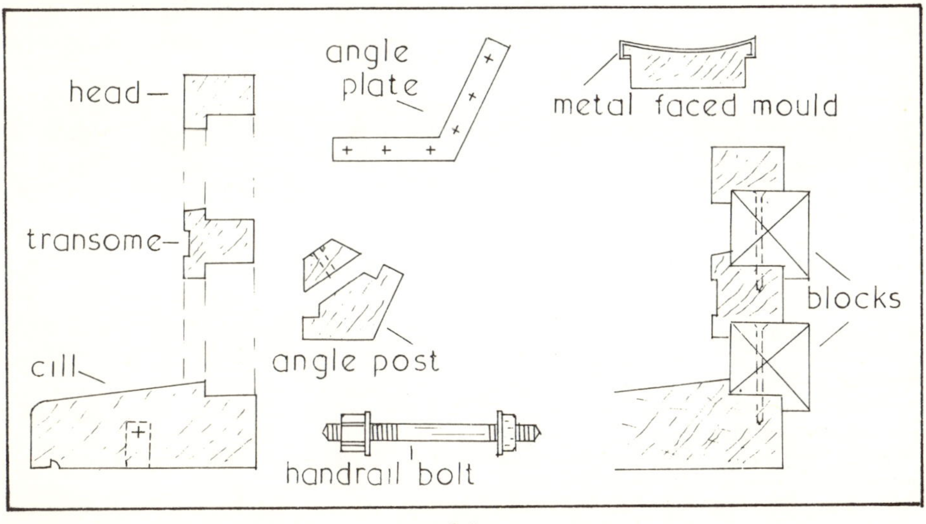

through. Also, at the infeed end a movable support unit can be very helpful to assist the operator in holding the work at the required height.

The tendency in machine design today seems to be to reduce the size of work tables, and this calls for additional support both at the infeed and outfeed of machines.

Factory regulations which are being formulated at the present time are making recommendations in this direction to make it impossible for the taker-off on a circular saw bench to be able to reach the teeth of the blade.

With small machine tables, the rule of never to stack items of timber or leave spanners on the working surface is becoming more important, for not only are they likely to come into contact

Fine beading is prepared on the spindle moulder using a wide strip of material, then cut off on the dimension saw. Glass beads should be designed to show a fillet or have a slight overhang.

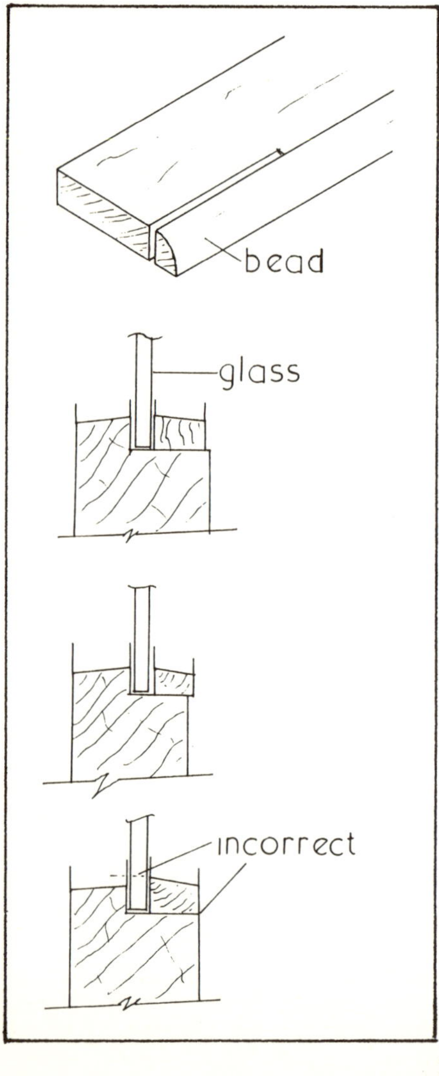

Wide boards for counter tops can create a problem in planing from the rough timber. A wide board cut into strips and the alternate faces/reversed on reassembly can have advantages. It is not good policy to cut a wide board down the centre and re-joint.

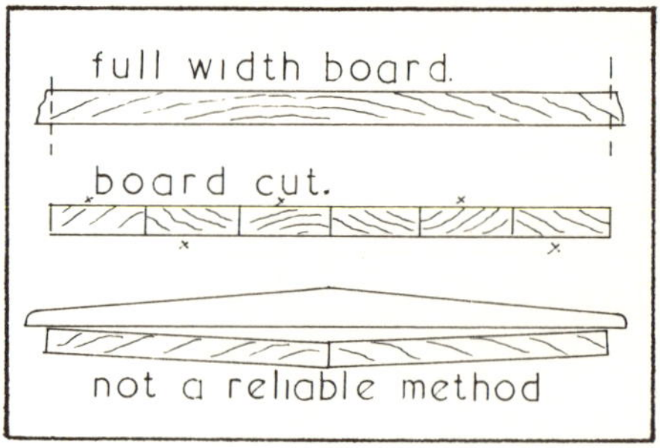

Preparing clean rebates for glass on the spindle moulder. One saw cut only can help. Two saw cuts are used for difficult timber, followed by a light cutter finish. A face board fitted across the fences of the machine will reduce splintering to some extent. The work must be pressed firmly to the face board.

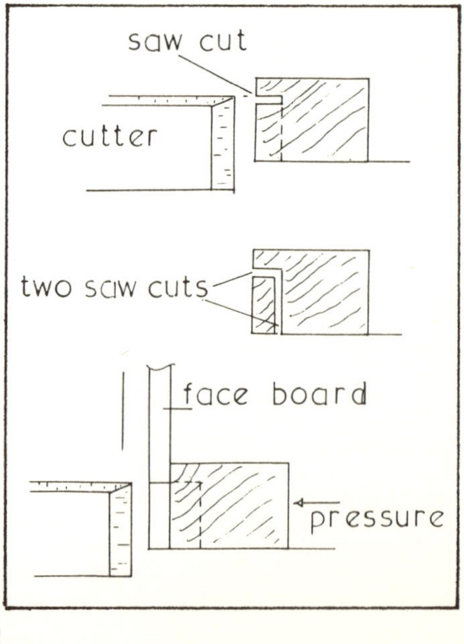

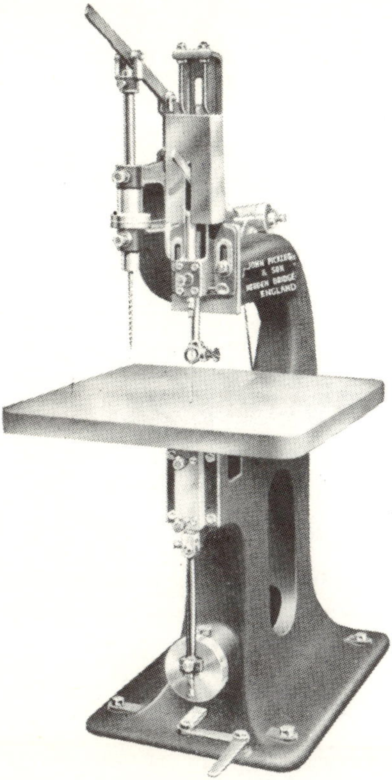

(A)

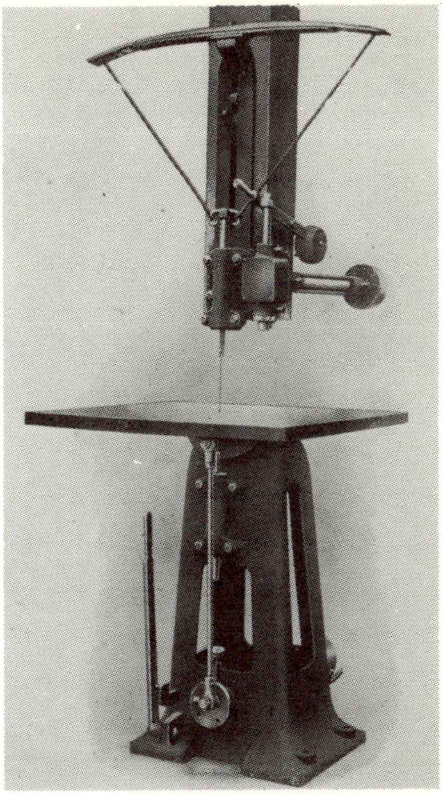

(B)

Fretsawing machines which are found in use where pierced work is involved, such as the manufacture of wood letters. (a) Swan-neck type which has a limitation according to the depth of the throat. (b) Machine in two sections. The upper portion is fixed to an overhead beam.

with the rotating cutter system, but also a hand can be in danger when placing or removing articles.

When feeding long timber into machines which are power fed, adequate space must always be made to prevent the taker-off being trapped. It is good policy when feeding long items into a machine to let each one be lifted clear after processing before the next member is fed in.

If this is not done the end on push can create a danger point that the operator may not be aware of.

The surface finish on long timber is very often better than of that produced on shorts due to the fact that imperfections usually occur at the commencement and end of a cut. It is, however, more difficult to straighten long material in the planing operation and remove twist. The twist or wynd as it is sometimes termed, should be removed for most types of work although continuous bend can at times be accepted as it will straighten out on fixing or framing in.

Modern fourcutting machines are fitted with straightening tables at the infeed to assist with the straightening of long items of timber.

To assist with the fixing of storage and display units to walls it is customary to face the surfaces with lining frames. The walls are sometimes rendered before the fixing of the frames but quite often the frames are fixed direct to the brickwork.

This method is known as "dry lining". Frames require a less number of fixing points than strip working and a continuous flat surface is more readily obtained by this means.

They provide an excellent base for fixing sheet wall material. The timber for the wall frames, although not visible on completion of the work,

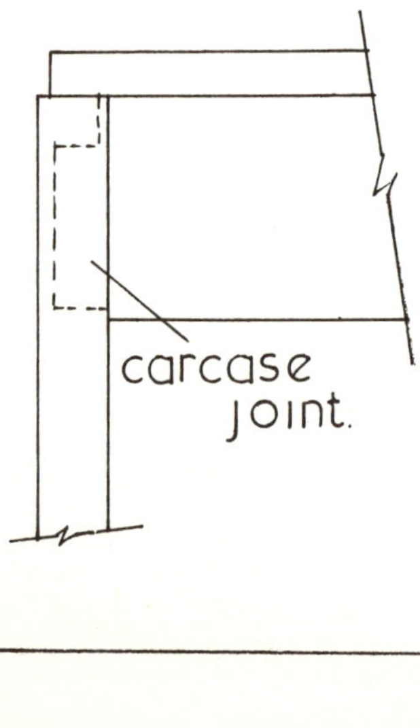

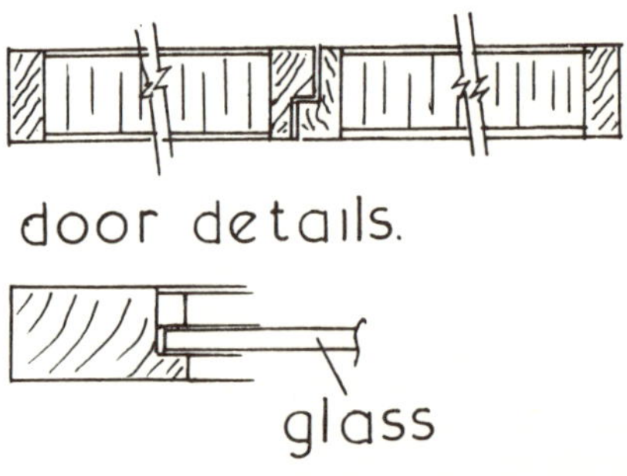

Basic design for display case with storage space below. Approx. size, 2000 mm x 900 mm x 300 mm. The ends shelves and solid doors are made from 18 mm laminboard, preferably veneered. The front rails are in solid timber, the top one being cut out for the insertion of an item card. The base is 25 mm square tube section.

(a) Mortise machine being used to prepare material to receive a handrail bolt nut.

is usually planed on the fourcutter.
A suitable section can be as small as ex-50 mm x 25 mm. A high rate of feed is permissible on the machine for this type of work, the visible cutter mark pitch on the surface being no detriment.

Counter units

For many years counter tops were principally made from mahogany due to its many favourable characteristics for this purpose. Although other materials in the synthetic field have replaced mahogany for counter tops some useful information can be compiled from a study of the preparation of wide boards.
Planing material from the rough could be an embarrassment to the machine operator as widths required were frequently in excess of 200 mm. The writer has personally seen, in the 1930-40 period, wide mahogany tops being planed from the rough by hand.
Since then, portable surface planing machines have been brought into use which can be an aid to processing material too wide for the standard type of machine. At the particular age in time quoted, it would have been unthinkable to cut the board and rejoint it as any defect shown up by the high polished finish applied would have meant immediate rejection by the customer.

Today, with the application of scientific aspects and improved gluing techniques, the approach has changed.
Wide material is usually cut into strips, say 150 mm wide, preferably on a straight line edger saw. The material is then planed and prepared for jointing. At the jointing stage we have to consider whether we want a panel that will keep flat or if consideration must be given to the decorative grain features.
For the panel to have the minimum pull regarding curl, the boards must be glued alternatively one face up then one face down from their original position before being cut. Some care must also be taken which needs a good eye to judge, or what is known in the trade as a football jersey effect may be created in the finished product—a number of different coloured stripes which change when viewed from different angles.
It is not good policy to cut a wide board down the centre to be able to plane the surfaces then glue together. Failure is common with this method of procedure for various reasons. The amount of pull on the completed joint could be very strong with humidity changes. It can easily be fractured, say during transport due to leverage.
Any "out of squareness" in the preparation of the joint would result in a much magnified effect when the edges were glued together. Each section of the board may curl individually causing the joint to fail.
In theory the greater number of strips a wide board is cut into and rejointed the more likely it is to be a success.

(b) Boring for the bolt shank.

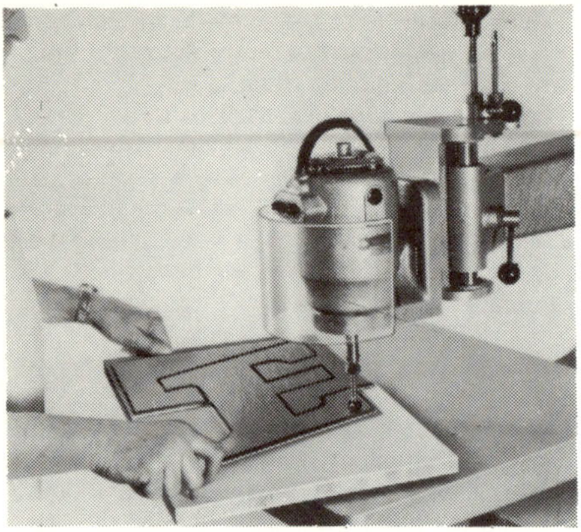

(a) Cutting out wood letters with a high-speed router.

(b) The underside of the router jig showing the former which operates against the guide pin in the machine table. (Trend-Elu).

Plastic-faced panel boards have very much replaced solid mahogany tops although they do not have the same warm feeling to the touch.

When facing large sheets with plastics, a backing plastic must be applied as a balancer to keep the surface flat.

Although in the main panels are usually from 25 mm material, it is customary to build this up at exposed edges to double this amount or even more. Under this method of working, edge coverings must be applied after the main surfaces have been covered.

Low voltage strip heating using synthetic resin adhesives may in many instances give a more lasting bond than contact adhesives for this purpose.

In shopfitting work, the woodworker has on many items to consider the use of glass. This is in the main fixed into rebates in the timber and particular care requires to be taken in their formation on slender material.

Hardwoods have frequently either erratic or sloping grain which will tear in the rebating operation if consideration is not given to the method of approach. On timbers of this type it is advisable to make a fine saw cut to prevent rub with the edge of the rebating cutter, or even make two cuts at right angles to remove the waste material altogether.

A small amount may be left in under the latter method in order to machine to a planed finish if so required.

Some machinists working on small quantities, score the rebate line with a marking gauge, this will help to prevent splintering in some instances.

Others fit an improvised scratch arrangement on the spindle moulder when working with an automatic feed unit. Some selection of the quality of the material is required for slender items, and more than the average amount of waste may have to be allowed for to produce work of an acceptable standard.

The preparation of fine beading for securing glass is also a point worthy of mention. It is important that the dimensions of the bead are exactly the same as the depth of the rebate in that direction.

If it is oversized, a line will be visible through the glass, and this may well be coated with bedding mastic. Undersized beads will give the reverse so giving an unattractive feature from the other side. As glass has thickness some of the inner edges of the fixing bead or mastic can be seen when viewed from some angles so it is important that the work is clean in all aspects and it is usual to stain the wood edges and apply colour to the mastic.

When fixing mirrors in timber framing it is customary to stain the rebates matt black to prevent reflection from the edge of the glass.

Any splintering on the corner of the bead adjoining the mirror may well show double, particular care must be taken with this type of work.

When fixing beads with panel pins the pins should be positioned as far away from internal corners as possible, and still give firm anchorage.

This enables the bead to be removed when carrying out repairs without damaging. If a pin was inserted, say 25 mm from an interior corner it would be very difficult to remove, particularly in hardwood, without chopping the bead away.

Sliding a hammer across the face of the glass is

the safest method of driving in fixing pins, but some form of scratch prevention shield is advised even if it is only stout paper.

Hammer heads are made from hardened steels and they can wear into a condition that is capable of scratching the surface of glass with a minimum of effort.

Shop windows are usually glazed from the inside to give a face finish. on the outside of the framing. The securing of the fixing beads or moulds is usually done with raised head screws.

These can be bored in advance to reduce work on the site, allowance being made for final trimming. Fixing of the principal glazing members prepared within the factory lies in the hands of the craftsman on the site and every endeavour should be made in the planning to give him some flexibility.

Preparatory work may be very much in the hands of the woodworking machinist and his close associates.

A combination of wood, metal, and plastics can well be involved. Experience tends to relate that if the glass comes along slightly in error adjustments are expected to be made to the frames for the job to progress. This introduction of a flexibility feature may result in a job being completed today that would otherwise may have to be sent back to the production unit and be held up for a week.

The use of handrail bolts, for instance, for angular joints will allow a member to be removed without damage if it is fitted with this in mind to meet a doubtful location. These bolts can be fitted quickly and accurately in the machine shop, no hand operations need be involved other than that of assembly.

Should dowels also be required in addition to the handrail bolt, cluster type boring head units are available to speed this operation.

Cutting out letters from wood can be done with the use of a high-speed router, or the fret saw, a machine also termed the jigsaw. Jigsaws of the heavy duty types can be found in use of two distinct types.

One is the swan-necked model which has a limitation as to the width of work it can accommodate, usually about 600 mm from the saw blade to the machine frame. This enables a large amount of work to be catered for with some manipulation. The second type is a machine which is fitted up in two parts. The base section provides the drive and the worktable.

The overhead section is suspended from the roof members or an overhead beam in the workshop

This arrangement allows for large items to be worked and its limitation is governed to the space within the workshop.

Machines of this type are still in use in boat building establishments and vehicle body works more so than in joinery. With the increased use of large sheets of panel boards in many branches of the woodworking industry a new phase of use could develop for this type of machine.

The reciprocating drive to the saw blade is obtained with a crank arrangement generally referred to as the Pitman Link. Some machines have a selection of saw speeds which is very often obtained with the use of an arrangement of stepped pulleys. The maximum speed of the drive shaft is usually limited to within 1,500 rpm. Tension is kept on the saw by spring arrangements, either leaf springs which are sometimes constructed of hardwood, or a system of coil springs. One other feature that can be very useful is that the worktable can usually be canted.

This enhances the scope of design with such items as wood letters without any additional effort except the setting up of the machine. For one-off jobs the jigsaw may be preferred to the high-speed router which requires a jig to be made before a letter can be produced.

The jigsaw can help considerably in the making of jigs for the router and this is the purpose for which they are principally used today. A router will produce a planed finish to the edge it has cut which may need little or no further cleaning up.

Sawn edges, however fine, always require some hand finishing.

The ideal method of working when machines are available is to cut out letters of, say, 9 mm plywood with the jigsaw using a fine blade. This narrow edge can be cleaned up with little effort and the letter used as the former component on a jig for the high-speed router.

Letters can then be cut from, say, ex-25 mm mahogany or other reliable material.

Portable jigsaws, a recent development, are particularly useful for pierced work which includes the making of wood letters. They also have the advantage that they can be used on the site.

It is important that the work should be clamped to a bench or other firm base when using this tool or the life of the blade will suddenly terminate.

Aids for site carpenters

The production factor of the craftsman working on the building site may be influenced by what aids that can be offered to him in the way of mechanisation. Many operations on timber items can be applied within the factory before they reach the site, and this is one line of approach to study to achieve the maximum output for a given labour force.

Portable power tools can prove favourable on, say, extension or alteration work where their safe keeping can be controlled.

How much can the site worker be assisted by mechanised aids? Conditions vary, but this article suggests some methods of approach which may be applied in part or in full.

They do require to be handled by a responsible type of person both from the point of view of obtaining efficient use, and regarding their general cure.

Extension and alteration work is probably a field where portable power tools are an attractive proposition.

Where timber items are produced within the factory for use on the site the system can fail to some extent if the supplier is not fully conversant with exactly what is required.

One must always remember that there are operatives producing joinery items in large factory units that have little or no site experience.

It need hardly be said that somewhere in the production unit there must be a technician who has the necessary knowledge of what is required both in the manufacturing process, and the limitations of acceptability on the building site.

The production operatives are specialists in their particular field of work within the factory, and it is not unknown for their efforts to receive words of praise on the site.

However, when errors do occur they do not always have to be large ones to cause inconvenience. Window linings or casing material is, for instance, only visible on one face after fixing. The material should be prepared from the rough timber with this in mind, and passed through the fourcutter in such a manner that any unplaned patches due to thickness variations will end up

on the non-visible face when fixed on the site.
The introduction of factory prepared trussed rafter units to reduce operations on the site is in the main confined to roofs with gables.

Roofs with hipped ends involve additional geometrical involvements in the timber framing.

With the application of basic geometry many of the members can be cut to the required length and bevel within the factory. The success of the off-site method can depend to some extent on the general accuracy of the building at roof level.
The theory of the preparation of roofing timbers can vary in practice due to a combination of factors which may arise. In a hipped roof, say, on the traditional pair of semi-detached houses, the common rafters are usually cut to a calculated length and a group of selected straight ones are used to support the ridge in the early stages of erection.
The preparation of these rafters could be said to be a constant factor which is always welcomed in machine production. The length of the four hip rafters should in theory also be constant but unfortunately in practice they are often found to differ.

A lightweight metal jig used as an aid to fix door casings to enable doors to be fitted with the minimum of adjustment. Door jigged to size in factory, and recessed for hinges and furniture.

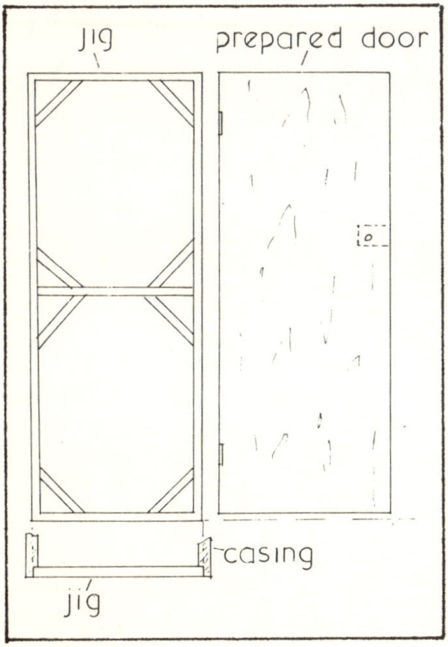

This can be due to at least two factors. The wall plates may be out of level at some point, or the building is not a true rectangle.
When taking measurements for the lengths of the wall plates it is always advisable to take a diagonal measurement also. This will give a more complete picture of the standard of accuracy involved.
Too many variables in individual component members can upset procedures, and also call for the services of a higher experienced type of operative in the machine preparation.
If pre-cut roofing members or stock size trusses are to be used, this should be understood by all concerned with the building from its early stages of construction.
Jack rafters, which form part of a hipped roof require to be cut to a bevel which involves both the edge and the face of the member. This cut can conveniently be made on a pull out cross-cut circular saw which is on most models designed to accommodate compound angles.
The machine manufacturers go to a considerable amount of planning in this type of machine to enable the cut to be made in roofing work, but its potential is probably not being used by builders as much as it could be.

The length of the jack rafters diminish proportionally to their spacing, so stops may be fitted on the machine at regular intervals when this has been worked out.

It is customary to use common rafter length material for making the jack rafters so that no waste is produced. The offcut from the longest jack rafter, automatically produces the shortest jack rafter of the opposite hand, all at the one cut, and so on.
Soffit boarding as fitted to the eaves of a roof is supported on right-angled timber brackets. The brackets consist of a horizontal member and a hanger.
With the aid of a circular saw, material which would otherwise probably be scrap can be converted for use in this kind of location without buying further material.
Circumstances very often control as to how far machining aids can be applied to roofing work, but when we consider that the carpenter has to use a great amount of energy in the preparation of the timbers if no mechanical aids are available.
In addition to this he has to get his various members to their fixing location very often a considerable height above ground, then carry out heavy nailing processes manually.
If some machine preparation can be introduced it will lessen the demand for heavy manual effort

on the site.
The hanging of doors on the building site can be time consuming if no special effort is made to plan the operation when quantity work is involved.
In the machine shop doors can be taken to overall dimension both in width and height to a fine degree of accuracy.
Recessing can also be carried out for hinges and furniture by mechanical aids.
The efficiency continuity will break down unless the precision is extended also to the fixing of the door frames and casings on the site. In the factory, jigs are used for repetition production, and in some instances they can be used on the site, if operatives are educated to do so.
Fitting and hanging a door on the site by traditional methods can take in excess of one hour in reasonable circumstances without the furniture being considered.
A door casing fitted into position with a skeleton-type jig can probably be fitted up with a door that has been factory dimensioned and recessed in less than half the time, and probably end up a much cleaner job.
In a pair of semi-detached dwellings, some 20 interior doors may be involved. Some effort between the site and the production unit could bring substantial rewards.
If the door casings can be consistent in dimension and squareness this will also apply to architrave moulds which can also be prepared in advance.
A small amount of additional length should be advisably left on the upright members to permit scribing to the floor should it be necessary.
It is always essential that a door casing head should be fixed level, irrespective of any error in the floor line.
Ready hung door systems are marketed by some joinery manufacturers in various forms, and should save a considerable amount of time on the site if correctly applied.
On the site wood plugs are always in demand for driving into the seams in brickwork for fixing joinery requirements. These can be cut on a circular saw or a bandsaw but it is advisable to use some form of saddle or the operation can be dangerous due to the small material involved.
Plugs cut with the axe on the site are favoured by many fixers due to the fact that they can be

Marking templates for repetition operations on the site. Used for marking hinge locations and other metal fittings.

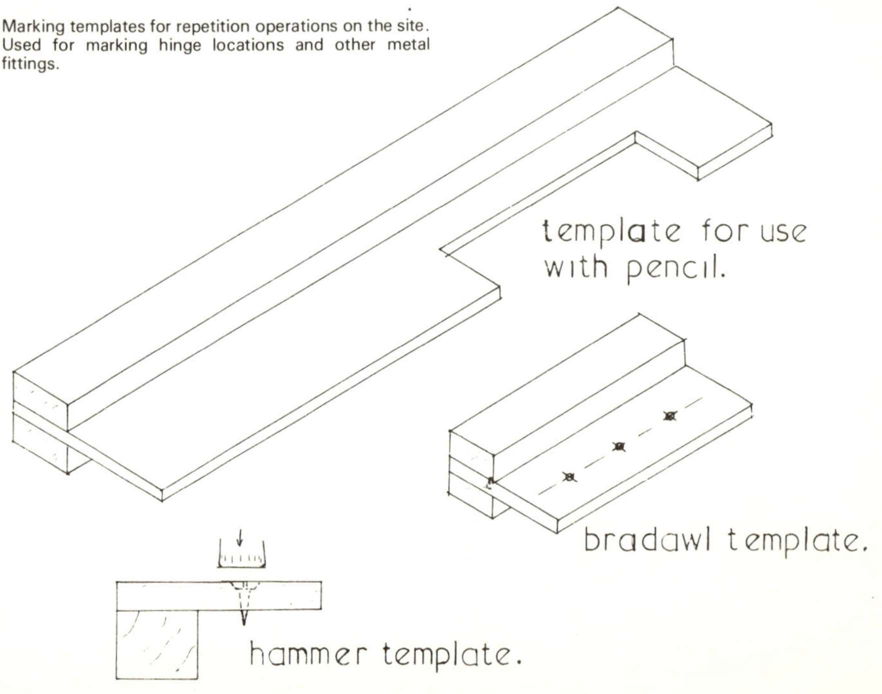

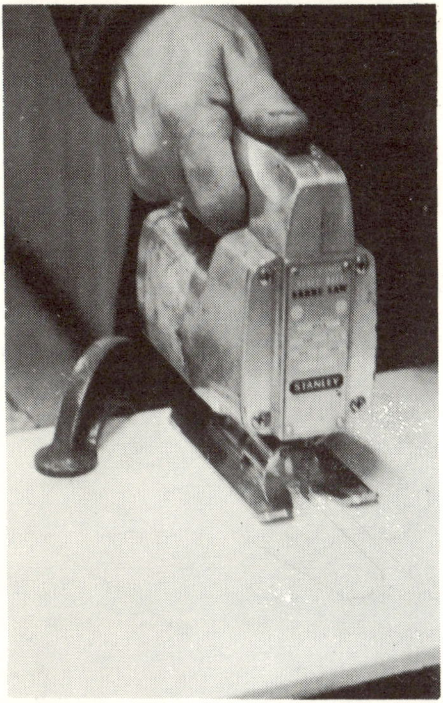

Portable jigsaw. A large variety of blades are available for this type of power tool (Stanley Tools).

Portable electric power planer, the Tarplaner.

cut to twist as they are driven into the joint.

It is not unusual to see an experienced fixer giving axe treatment to a factory produced plug to obtain this twist, and this may well be accompanied by a few words of criticism from him.

This twist detail on the plug cannot be produced by simple machine methods, but it is advisable when making plugs to vary them in thickness as seams are not all the same through a building.

Wooden grain pellets for plugging holes in timber which have been counter bored to conceal screw heads, can be made with a special cutter for this purpose with either a portable electric drill or a high-speed router.

The advantage of using grain pellets over, say, a piece of dowelling, is that the grain pattern and direction can be matched. Even on paint finished work they should be used as end grain has different absorbancy to that of surface grain which can be detrimental to the finished work.

When pellets are made at the time of requirement the same batch of timber can be used as what the work has been constructed from, so getting the exact match for grain and colour.

Another small item which can be very useful at some stages on the site when fitting up is the ready bored screw block.

These consist of blocks of timber about 70 mm in length by 22 mm square. They are bored twice on two faces and countersunk, usually for a number ten screw.

They are used in locations where they are not fully visible and can be very useful for assembling blockboard into box formation on the site. When adding on to kitchen units of wardrobes they aid progression considerably and once a craftsman has got into the habit of using them he likes to have some at hand.

They can, of course, be glued in addition to screwing if so desired. The blocks can be made very quickly under workshop conditions, but their preparation on the site can be laborious to the extent that a less attractive method may be used to do the job.

Although the use of jigs on the site is limited, marking templates are quite often used. Typical ones are those used for marking out the recessing for door hinges when they have not been provided for in the factory.

They can also be made for the marking out for the fitting of given types of door furniture. A template located on the edge of a door can give the position of the centre of the bore hole required for a night latch without the use of a measuring rule. Not only do templates speed the operation, but once proved they prevent errors also.

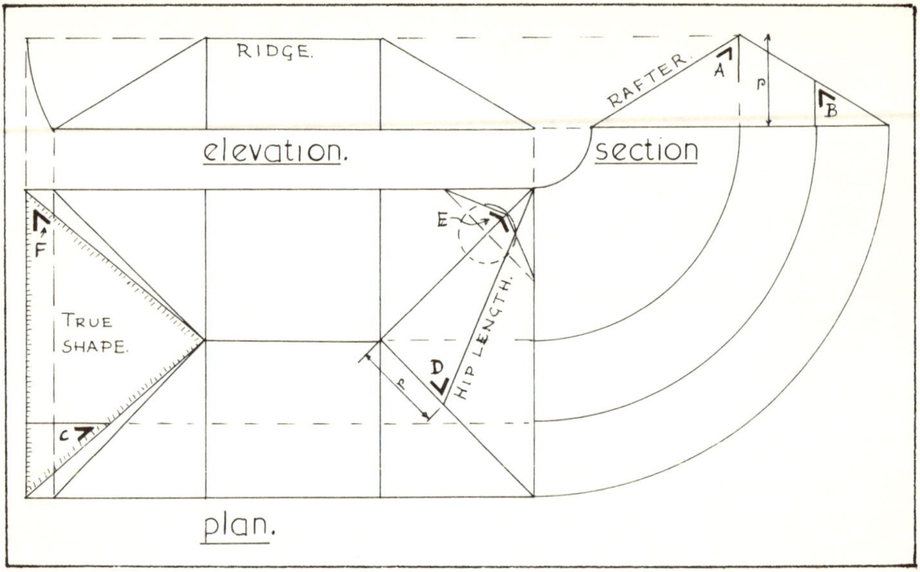

Basic geometrical details relating to a hip roof which could apply to the machine operator. A. Common rafter plumb cut. B. Jack rafter plumb cut. C. Jack rafter edge cut. D. Hip rafter plumb cut. E. Backing bevel to hip rafter. F. Bevel for roof covering material. Seat cuts can usually be accepted as at right angles to plumb cuts on a member.

Probably one of the most trying types of job for its size is the fitting of small ball type catches on cupboard doors when they are in difficult locations.

A marking template indicating the correct location of the screw holes by inserting a bradawl will ensure success at the first attempt with a minimum of effort.

Moulds for concrete work can be produced to a higher standard of detail with the aid of woodworking machines than those produced entirely by hand methods on site. The lack of design of many concrete cast products is due to the fact that the potential of machines has not been put to use in the making of the moulds.

Wooden pellets for concealing screw heads, made with cutter fitted to portable power drill or a high-speed router.

In addition to the actual profile formations that woodworking machines can produce in this field of work, the construction of the mould boxing or formwork can be of an efficient and accurate standard that will permit repetition of use with the minimum of deterioration.

Where a quantity of identical members are required for such items as those involved in formwork to stanchions and beams, these provide ideal scope for machine preparation.

With new timber no difficulty will be experienced, but when reclaimed material is involved some considerations will have to be followed. Nails require to be removed, and the timber should receive a good wire brush treatment if it is not to be in direct contact with the surface finish to the concrete.

The circular saw is the most suitable machine to use on reclaimed timber as tungsten carbide tipped saws can be used.

They will give satisfactory service on material which is abrasive and will cut through an occasional nail without undue damage.

Rough usage will, of course, mean more frequent

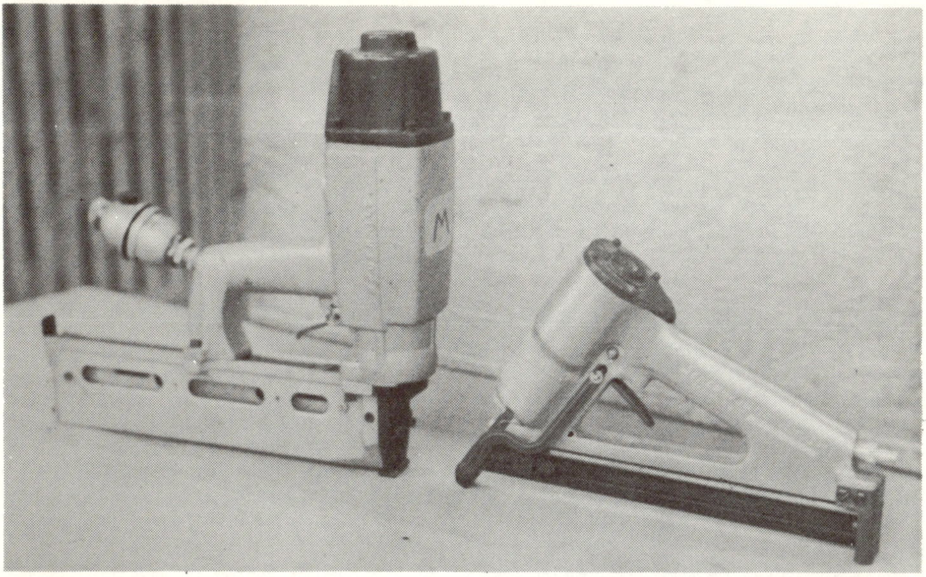

Compressed air operated nailing guns. They can save much time and effort on repetition nailing.

servicing and this will most probably mean returning the blade to the manufacturers as these saws cannot be sharpened with a file as in the case of untipped blades.

When using tungsten carbide tipped blades the work should preferably be positioned against a fence.

If not the tips are liable to be subjected to side leverage if the timber is not fed in a straight line through the saw. This applies particularly to crosscutting operations where tips can be levered off due to freehand cutting.

Operations which could be carried out by machine. (1) Plumb and seat cut and birdsmouth to rafters. Halving and bevels to wall plates. (2) Cuts to jack rafters. (3) Hip, plumb cut, backing and foot detail. (4) Bevels and mitres to purlins. (5) Apex boards to accommodate hip rafter.

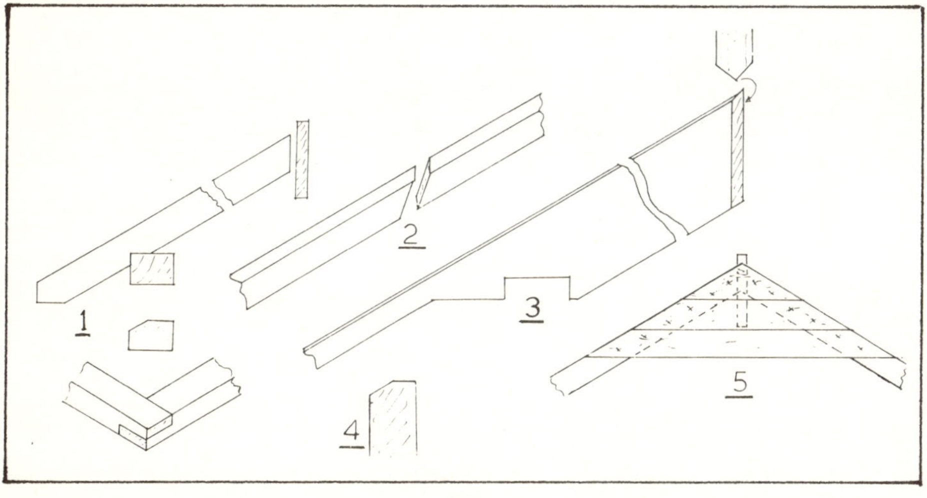

Compressed tools

Compressed air-driven tools can be used to advantage on locations where electrical power is not available. The compressor unit can be driven with an internal combustion engine such as petrol operated or diesel fuel.

Compressed air can be transmitted to almost any location with a high safety factor either with a system of permanent pipes or temporary ones.

It is also clean in use. The portable power tools that are available for operation by compressed air are in the main more compact than electrically operated ones.

Their power may at times be limited but this is determined by the size of the generator and the efficiency of the transmission.

Air tools are seldom borrowed by operatives for personal use, as a pneumatic source is necessary for them to operate.

Compressed air, generally termed pneumatics is now used extensively in woodworking factories, not only to operate the tools but also to automate the handling of work.

On the building site it has potential for tool operation, in particular where electrical power is not available.

The woodworking tools principally used with pneumatic power are, drills, screwdrivers, sanders, nailers, and cramping devices.

In operations such as floor laying where a considerable amount of repetition nailing is involved, pneumatic application is the answer not only to speed the work, but to conserve the energy of the worker also.

In the use of these tools skill in their operation is required just as in the case of electrically operated tools. Safety aspects change with the different types of energy source.

Insulation is important in the electrical field along with voltage control to suit the working location. Compressed air can be a source of danger in some environments if handled carelessly.

Dust, and in particular metal chips, such as drilling waste can be blown into a person's eyes by the blow down happy type of individual that seems to get fascinated with the use of an open-ended air pipe.

Compressor units capable of maintaining a pressure of up to 80 lb/sq. in. are suitable for most woodworking tool requirements. The storage capacity of the compressor unit depends on how many appliances are likely to be in use at any one time.

In woodworking factories the air system is also often used for the spray application of paint and other wood finishes. This could have a place in site work also.

Success with power-operated tools on the site probably comes with the method in which they are introduced.

A mobile unit, or control point may be the answer. Failure to organize in some way could result in the project being short-lived and expensive. A survey of the repetitive type of jobs

Compressed air operated drills. Note the compactness of power-operated tools of this type.

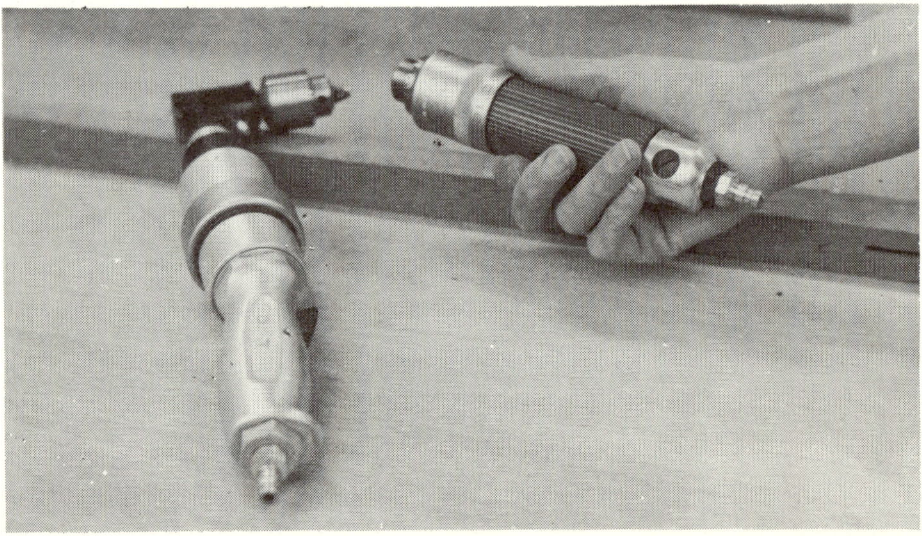

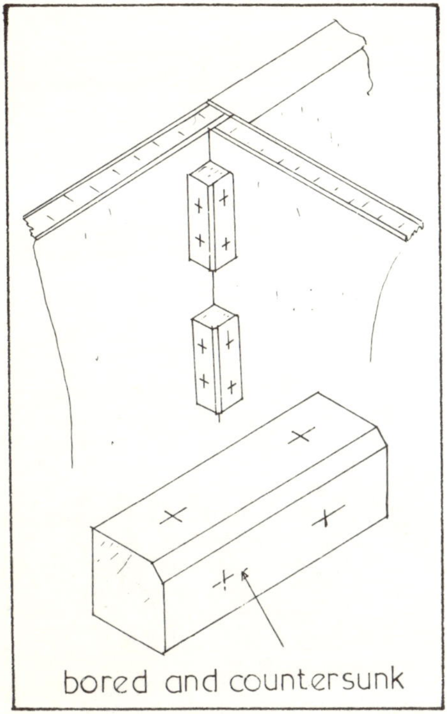

Two-way bored screw blocks, factory produced to aid fitting up operations on the site.

Transformer for reducing mains voltage to 110 volts which must be used for portable power tools used on exposed site locations.

which are being carried out by unmechanized methods could give a lead as to what may be required.

Working methods have a tendency to become static, not all operatives welcome changes in procedure, unless they can vialize immediate financial results in their favour.

Mechanisation approach to wood trades in domestic building

Floor joists	Crosscutting and joint formations. Factory processes for quantity work.
Roofing	Trussed rafter units. Bevels to framed roof members. Factory cut.
Floor laying	Pneumatic nailing devices.
Door casings	Fix to jigs.
Doors	Jigged to size in factory. Recessed for fittings.
Templates	Used for repetition marking out on site.
Fixing aids	Two-way screw blocks. Grain pellets. Wood plugs.
Mouldings	Pre-cut architraves.
Formwork moulds	Aided with factory equipment.

Electrically operated power tools on site. (Reduced voltage.)

Pneumatic operated power tools.

Organisation of power control point. (Mobile or fixed.)

Mechanisation as a means of reducing timber waste by re-use.

Stairs for Today

Modern stair unit constructed of metal and timber.

The manufacture of stairs by machine production is an operation in which the mechanical processing of timber can be put to good advantage. Wide timber is involved which works planing machines to acceptable capacity, and there are a number of items of like dimension in the way of treads and risers which makes setting up worth while.

Stair strings, the members which carry the treads and risers, can be the longest items of timber worked in a machine shop which is preparing material for domestic buildings. In the planning of a machine area, these particular members should be kept in mind to ensure adequate linear capacity.

The Building Regulations lay down quite a large amount of detailed instruction which requires to be followed on stair design. These regulations can be followed, with the aid of drawings in the recent publication by John Stephenson, "Building Regulations in Detail", which is obtainable from the "Building Trades Journal". The regulations differ for the locations of the stairs, namely, those in private use, or those termed to be in common use. Much of the information can act as a guide to the planning of a staircase, and it is probably a section of the Building Regulations that is well worth making a study of for those engaged in the woodworking industry, and to some extent remote from the building site.

Very often in the smaller type of domestic building, space is limited for the stair unit, but if the dimensions laid down within the regulations can be applied, then an acceptable flight of srairs can be produced. The angle of pitch at which the stairs are to the floor line is determined by the ratio of the rise to the width of the tread surface, less the projecting nosing. If the effective tread surface is the same as that of the rise, then the stair pitch would be 45 degrees, which is

Specimen of finish to a stair foot. The box step is a present-day version of the bullnose step.

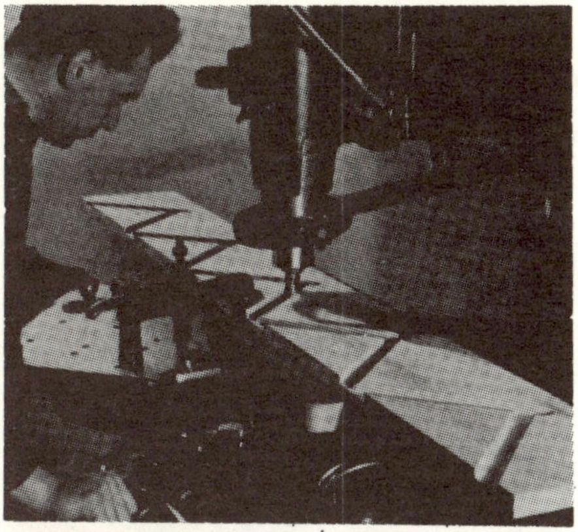

Trenching a stair string member on a Wadkin recessing machine which is fitted with positioning stops.

Treads and risers being fitted into the stair string.

outside the permitted 42 degrees for a private building.
In addition to making reference to statutory regulations as to the suitability of tread and rise dimensions, other formula has been used for guidance over the years. One approach is to accept that the average forward progression of a person per stride is said by be about 575 mm. It is, however, considered that twice the amount of progressive efficiency is involved in the rise motion. From this we say that tread width plus twice the rise should equal around 575 mm. Suitable figures for this could be 225 mm + 175 mm + 175 mm = 575 mm.
Regulations say that for private stairs the treads should be not less than 220 mm going (the term "going" is not generally accepted to include the overhanging nosing) and the rise not in excess of 220 mm. Other regulations apply to open tread flights, tapered treads, winders, and fire prevention measures.
To plan a flight of stairs it is necessary to know the height between the two floor levels concerned, the amount of going available, and the overall width. Whatever the type of unit that is to be made, the terms rise and going, are always with us, and once this has been successfully applied to a simple straight flight more complicated work becomes more easily understandable. From measurements the planning of a straight flight can be done mathematically only, or with a combination of graphics and maths. Much can be said for planning with the aid of a sinple scale drawing although experienced workers in this field very often prepare strings from purely mathematical calculation. The length of the stair strings can be conveniently scaled off a drawing, cutting down waste to a minimum.
The term "going" is the distance from the face of one riser to the face of the next. The "rise" is the vertical distance from the surface of one tread to the surface of the next. Additions must be made to the width of material required for the treads and risers to include nosings tongues and overlaps.
Some timber suppliers carry a stock of prepared tread, riser, and string sections. This is prepared in such a way that it can be cut to the required widths and not upset the intersection arrangements of the joint formations. The tread material is usually bullnosed on the front edge and grooved on the underface adjoining the nosing. The back edge is offered square and can be taken to the width required. The riser material is rebated on one edge to form a tongue to locate in the groove of the tread. The other edge of the riser is left square. By stocking tread material of say ex 275 mm x 32 mm and 275 mm x 25 mm and riser material ex 200 mm x 25 mm and 200 mm x 19 mm many requirements can be met from the rack. Of recent years 12 mm plywood has been used for stair risers, and it is an item for which narrow accumulated offcuts can be used. To cut new full sheets may or may not be economical. We can consider the exact waste factor when working with sheet materials, and also for stair risers only one face is visable after fixing which permits an economical grade of material to be used.
Tread material in domestic building is ideally made from ex 32 mm thickness of stock. Due to the cost factor this has been reduced by many manufacturers to ex 25 mm. If such timbers as

parana pine are used it will have the stability of a thicker grade of joinery softwood and be quite suitable for the purpose. Treads made from too light a thickness of material may be subjected to creaking early in use if not particularly well glue blocked behind at the intersection of treads and risers. Much can be said for the use of hot animal glue for rubbing in blue blocks. Some of the modern cold application types of adhesives are not affective unless they are applied under pressure, and this does not occur in the insertion of the blocks.

For producing stair section material in quantity, the larger types of moulding machines are required. Extended types of thicknessing machines known as "three cutters" can be useful for this type of work. The material used must be to some extent selected, and dried to an acceptable moisture content before planing. For stockpiling 15% would be suitable, if it was more than this, deterioration may take place. If it was over dried it may well pick up moisture in the store shed. Cracks and loose knots make the timber unsuitable for this purpose, and some examination is necessary when feeding into the planing unit to ensure that any permanent defects will not end up on the exposed faces.

The trenching of stair strings to carry the treads and risers can be carried out in a variety of ways. The most efficient method is, of course, to use a machine specifically designed for this purpose. Stair trenching machines are available which either cut only one string at a pass or a pair of strings. The principal on which they work is a former pin guided in a metal template which controls the pattern produced by the cutter, or pair of cutters in the dual machine. Once the machine has been set to produce the required cut for the treads and risers, no further marking out is necessary. The shape of the cut to accommodate the nosing profile can be varied to some extent by fitting additional plates to the guide template.

Stair trenching can also be progressively carried out on the spindle moulder using an attachment. A special cutter head is required in which to insert a trenching cutter. The speed of rotation should preferably be the maximum available on the machine. The guide pin which engages in the template is supported on a robust arm which must be positioned concentric with the cutter. The template is clamped to the stair string having been set to the required pitch to give the tread and rise measurements. The template is designed in such a manner that it will produce both the left and right hand strings so forming a pair, one at a time. It is as well to note, that stair

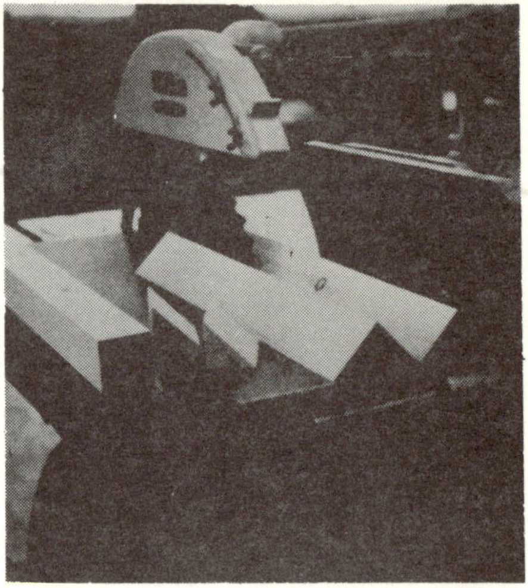

Saddle fitted to a circular saw bench for diagonal cutting glue block material. Guard would be lowered when operating.

Experimental spiral stair unit constructed within an open cylinder.

Pickles Ransome double head trenching machine.

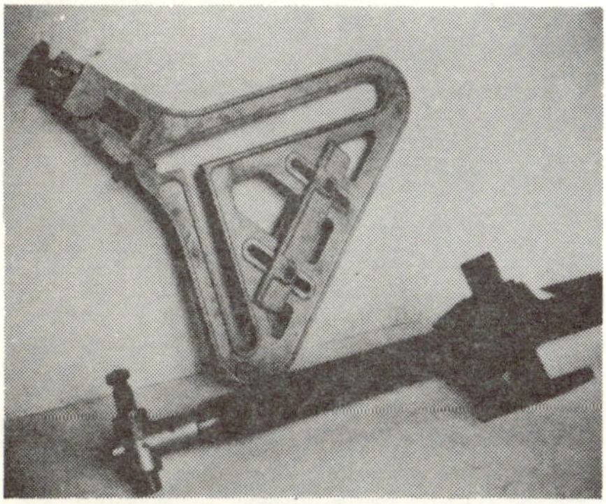

Attachments for stair trenching on the spindle moulder.

Cutting stair treads to width by backfencing on the spindle moulder. The nosing mould is also being applied. Guards would be fitted before operating.

strings must be cut in pairs regarding the trenching operation, they will not turn around and become a pair, as some unfortunate people have found out the hard way!

Highspeed routers, recessing machines and able routers can all be adapted to stair trenching, with either standard attachments, or jigs produced on the shop floor. The method used is dependent on the amount of stair work generally carried out within the works unit. The jigs or templates must be designed to produce pairs, as previously pointed out. In the case of the highspeed router, if one hand of string has been cut, this actual member can be used as a former to cut the opposite hand, working on the guide pin. This can be very acceptable for one off jobs. Allowance for wedges must be made in the trench cut in the designing of jigs both for the tread and riser member. The sequence of operating when cutting the trenching in the strings can effect the quality of the completed work. The aim should be to provide the best finish on the portion of the cut that is to be visible on the assembled unit. It is usually preferable to make this part of the cut first while the grain is well supported, then finish on the interior edges. It is always necessary to make more than one pass through the cut, as the trenches are tapered to accommodate the wedging.

Treads generally have a moulded nosing and are grooved on the underside to take the riser. In domestic grade work the back edge of the tread is left square as this simplifies assembly, and reduces the number of joint formations involved. The back edge should, however, be planed to give a well fitting joint with the riser. For this reason, backfencing on the spindle moulder is a very useful operation for the final width trim as it gives a planed finish and provides a high standard of accuracy. Risers can also be taken to dimension in this manner although a sawn edge could be accepted due to its location.

Scotia moulds have been used to a great extent at the intersection of the tread and riser but the tendency is to omit this member in present day practice. The mould in most cases served no purpose as it was very often pinned in dry and had only decorative value. Most stairs are now completely carpeted and the scotia mould has limited use unless securely glued and tongued to support the nosing.

Treads and risers which intersect with newel posts must be trenched and recessed in. One rule which is applied at this point, is that the face line of the riser should always be in the centre of the newel. Trenching and recessing on the newels can be most conveniently carried out on

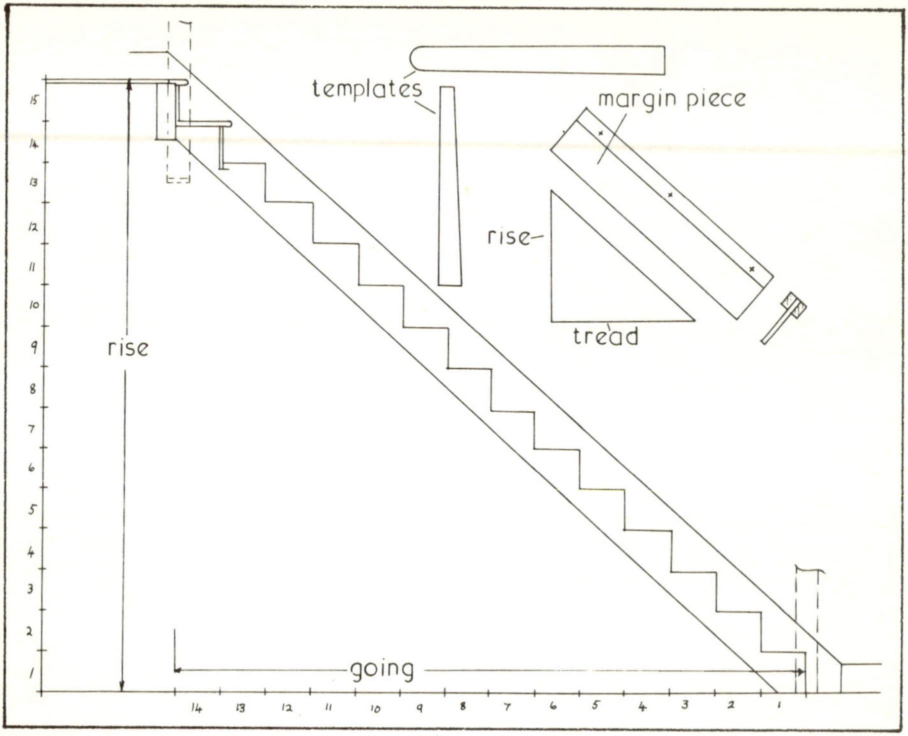

Basic planning for stair construction. Hand production methods require a considerable amount of marking out with the use of templates etc. In repetition machining marking out is considerably reduced.

Continuous handrails procedure in present day construction methods. Systems of supporting treads on beam string member.

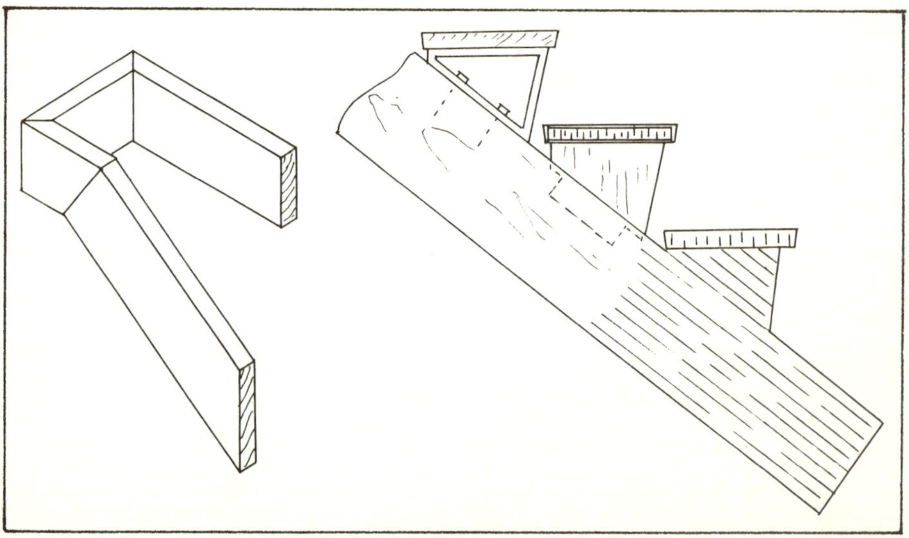

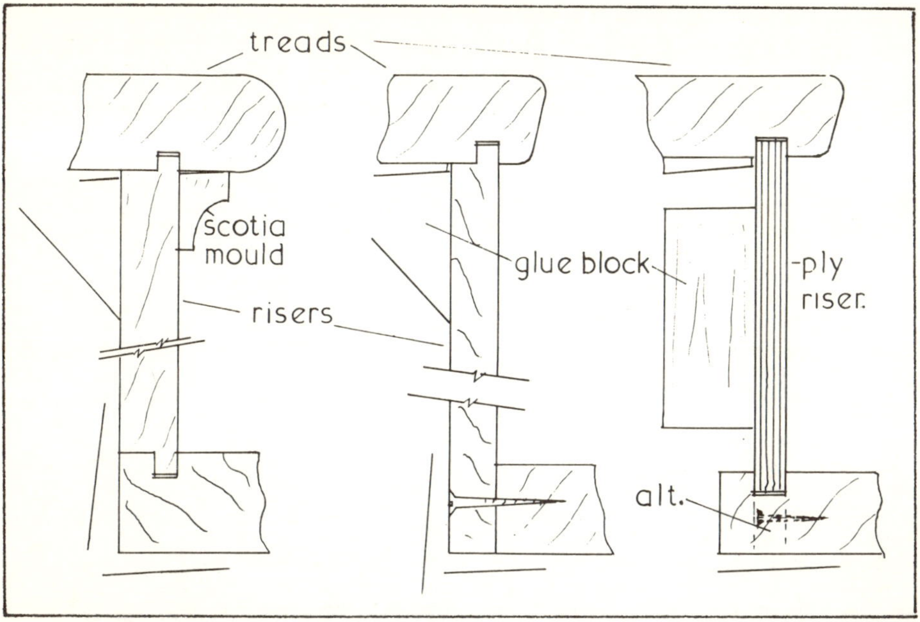

Various construction methods used at the intersection of treads and risers.

the highspeed router. For quantity work the operation can be done with the aid of a jig, this will speed the work considerably and maintain a standard of accuracy. Mortising will also be necessary on the newel posts to carry the stair strings and handrails.

Over the last decade there has been a considerable change in stair design. This has been partly as an endeavour to combat the rising costs in labour and materials, and also in an effort to use timber in a more decorative manner. In domestic building the feature which can be created with stairs is rather limited due to lack of space. Stairs fixed against a well or worse still, between two walls do not display their full decorative ability, and simply serve as an item of necessity. With the trend towards more open planning in interior design stairs can contribute more, and so increase the scope of the designer. Stairs constructed with an open space in place of a riser member immediately cut out the requirement of any spandril framing, as a sealed section underneath the flight in these circumstances would be incorrect. The floorspace could be occupied by a freestanding storage unit as demands require. Under the open tread method of construction, the treads can be either trenched into the supporting strings, or supported on them. The necessary seating for the treads can be formed in a variety of ways and some methods require a new method of approach to stair construction from the point of view of machining. Instead of string being trenched they may require to be mortised to accommodate what we may call pitch blocks to carry the treads. This operation should provide no difficulty for standard machines which can be fitted with a locating stop to position in a mortise after it has been cut. This method would be much better than fitting a very long stop bar to the machine, and also reduce the amount of setting out.

The cubic content of timber required for the open tread type of staircase can be more than the traditional type of stairs due to the increased thickness of the material required. Also the quality standards of the material may have to be increased as very often a natural finish is required on the completed work instead of painting. Due to the general design of the modern type of staircase, members can be built up by laminating material, and treads in particular could be produced from accumulated waste with the use of electronic equipment. To use solid timber as cut from the log, say ex 250 mm x 50 mm is not good scientifically as it can be subject to movement with humidity changes. If the treads are trenched into the strings, fully enclosed or projecting, as in industrial type stairs, movement of the timber may be resisted regarding cupping, but if the treads are supported on the strings some curvature may result which will be very visible.

Staircase construction as we have known it in the past has been based on the product of the hand worker, and machines have been designed to copy their working method. Under the new move forward in stair design they can be planned to suit the processes of more standard machines. Few jobbing joiners have stair trenching machines in their workshops but they do have those for mortising and tenoning which can be used under new construction methods. This should encourage development in this field and it may not be very long before stair components will be available in kit form to meet modernization requirements.

A combination of metal and timber is also being used to construct stairs. The string member, either of metal or timber, becomes more of a supporting beam to which metal brackets are fitted to carry the timber treads. Under this system of working, stairs can be constructed with the minimum of equipment making a packet supply arrangement quite possible.

Production of handrail sections have always been an item for the moulding machine or spindle moulder to display their capabilities. Elaborate mouldings are not in demand in our present age and the requirement is for the plainer type of handrail. The continuous type of handrail which was a feature of geometrical ingenuity has been replaced by straight members mitred at carefully planned intersections. Handrails of this type are often to be found very much as a feature in department stores and hotels where polished hardwood is used of a much more generous section than is actually required to guide a person in transit. Some planning is necessary to prepare and construct a system of handrailing of this type to make possible continuity using a standard section of material. An angular change in plan for instance, cannot be made at the same point as an angular change in elevation. It has to be carried out in two stages preferably clear of each other. Timber is still favoured for handrails in many locations even where the stairs have to be of a more non-combustible material to understandably comply with fire regulations.

Jig for positioning stock in the cutting of stair wedges on the circular saw or bandsaw.

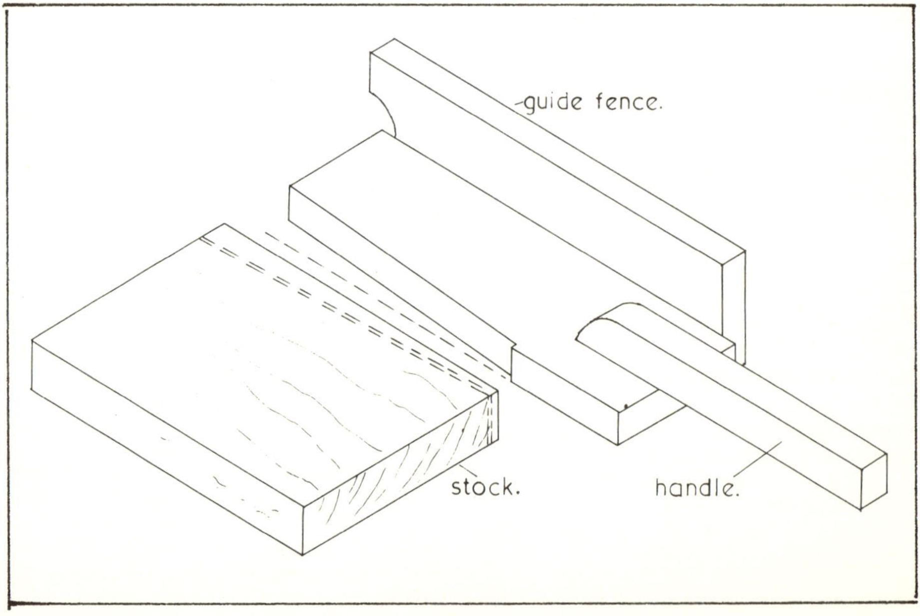

List of manufacturers and suppliers of woodworking machinery and ancillary equipment in the United Kingdom

Abis & Co. (Birmingham) Ltd., Dennis Rd., Sparkbrook, Birmingham, B12 8BB. 021-449 3781/6.

Airmetal Ltd., 12 Salisbury Rd., Leicester, LE1 7QU. Leicester (0533) 29717.

Air Plants Ltd., Batten St., Aylestone Park, Leicester, LE2 7PB. Leicester (0533) 833581.

Aldridge Belting Ltd., 49 Loverock Rd., Reading, RG3 1HB. Reading (0734) 582379.

Algin Air Ltd., 59-65 Goldney Rd., London, W9 2AS. 01-286 0285.

Andersons (Denton Holme) Ltd., Denton Holme Sawmills, Carlisle, Cumberland, CA2 5EQ. Carlisle (0228) 26242.

H. E. Appleby & Co. Ltd., Anne Rd., Smethwick, Warley, Worcs. 021-558 1521.

Arpal (Engineers) Ltd., Abford House, 15 Wilton Road, London, SW1. 01-828 6946.

Atkin & Sons (Birmingham) Ltd., 110 Bradford St., Birmingham 12. 021-772 1840.

Atkinson & Co. (Saws) Ltd., Bower St., Sheffield, S3 8RU. Sheffield (0742) 24748.

Aublet, Homer & Co. Ltd., 103 Worship St., London, EC2. 01-247 0934.

Baron Bros. Ltd., Circle Hse., Lady Lane, Leeds 2. Leeds (0532) 35081.

J. F. Behrens (GB) Ltd., Swinemoor Industrial Estate, Beverley, East Yorks. Beverley (0482) 886175.

Paul Bessire, 118 Holborn, London, EC1. 01-405 1351.

Black & Decker Ltd., Cannon Lane, Maidenhead, Berks. 062-882 2130.

W. J. Blackmur Ltd., 18 River Rd., Barking, Essex. 01-594 5591.

P. Blood & Co. Ltd., Arch St., Rugeley, Staffs. Rugeley (088 94) 2414.

Borst Bros. Ltd., Taylor's Rd., Stotfield, Hitchin, Herts. Hitchin (0462) 730277.

Bosch Ltd., Rhodes Way, Radlett Way, Watford, Herts. Watford (92) 44233.

Bostitch Division of Textron Ltd., Edenbridge, Kent. Edenbridge (073 271) 3041.

Boulton & Paul (Joinery) Ltd., Riverside Works, Norwich, Norfolk, NOR 72A. Norwich (0603) 60133.

Bradshaw Fan & Ventilating Co. Ltd., 190 London Rd., Hazel Grove, Stockport, Cheshire, SK7 4DQ. 061-483 3908.

Branson Baker Ltd., Dawley Trading Estate, Stallings Lane, Kingswinford, Staffs. Kingswinford (038 44) 3237.

Bristol Saw Mills & Transport Co. Ltd., South Liberty Lane, Bedminster, Bristol 3. Bristol (0272) 664231.

R. S. Brookman Ltd., Parkside Works, Rothley, Leicester, LE7 7NS. Rothley (053 724) 2323.

Henry Brown & Sons Timber Ltd., PO Box 9, Dunstable Rd., Luton, Beds. Luton (0582) 30841.

Buchanan & Wilson Ltd., 501 High Rd., Ilford, Essex. 01-478 5756.

Buck & Hickman Ltd., Whitechapel Rd., London, E1. 01-247 7676.

Burgess Products Co. Ltd., Leicester Rd., Sapcote, Leicester, LE9 6JW. Sapcote 292.

D. Burkle & Son Ltd., 174/8 Elthorne Rd., Upper Holloway, London, N19 4BE. 01-272 4061/4.

Bursgreen (Colne) Ltd., Lodge Holme, Trawden, Colne, Lancs. 028-24 5310.

Calder Woodworking Machinery, Station Rd., Sowerby Bridge, Yorks, HX6 3LA. Halifax (0422) 31861.

Canavon Partners Ltd., Portway & West Town Rd., Avonmouth, Bristol. Avonmouth (027 52) 2180.

J. Carr & Riley, Herries Rd. South, Sheffield, S6 1QN. Sheffield (0742) 343695.

Central Woodworking Machinery Co. Ltd., Moll Springs, Netherton, Huddersfield, Yorks.

Chain Saw Products Ltd., 33 Broughton St., Manchester, M8 8LZ. 061-834 9385.

Chesterman & Co. Ltd., 17/20 Shillibeer Place, York St., London, W1. 01-262 2296.

Christensen Diamond Products (UK) Ltd., Ashford Rd., Ashford Common, Ashford, Middlesex. Ashford (69) 58671.

W. H. Clay Ltd., 15/27 Rockingham St., Sheffield, S1 3NW. Sheffield (0742) 25262.

Clipper Manufacturing Co., Thurmaston Boulevard, Barkby Rd., Leicester, LE4 7JB. Leicester (0533) 767847/8; 768422/3.

Colchester Lathe (Distributors) Ltd., Hythe, Colchester, Essex. Colchester (0206) 5161.

A. E. Coles (Bridgwater) Ltd., Hamp Green Rise, Bridgwater, Somerset. Bridgwater (0278) 2580.

William Cook & Sons Ltd., 24 Elliot St., Cranstonhill, Glasgow, C3. 041-221 1733.

James Cooke (Bootle) Ltd., St. John's Rd., Liverpool 20. 051-922 2272.

A. Cooksley Ltd., Riverside Works, The Causeway, Staines, Middlesex, TW18 3AG. Staines 57244.

Cooper & Sons (Sheffield) Ltd., St. Mary's Gate, Sheffield, S2 4QB. Sheffield (0742) 20347/8.

Coronet Tool Co. Ltd., Alfreton Rd., Derby. Derby (0332) 47508.

Crosby & Co. Ltd., Craven Hse., West St., Farnham, Surrey. Farnham (025 13) 23123.

Croydon Screw Co. Ltd., 1127a London Rd., Norbury, London, SW16. 01-764 9559.

Cuprinol Ltd., Adderwell, Frome, Somerset. Frome (0373) 3017; 3521/2; 3261/2.

A. L. Dalton Ltd., Canal St., Nottingham, NG1 7HX. Nottingham (0602) 53917/8.

Danarm Ltd., Slad Rd., Stroud, Glos., GL5 1RF. Stroud (045 36) 2451.

Danckaerts Woodworking Machinery Ltd., 2/6 East Road, City Road, London, N1 6AG. 01-253 7155.

Davis & Timmins Ltd., Lichfield Rd., Trading Estate, Tamworth, Staffs. Tamworth (0827) 3351.

Dexter & Co. (High Wycombe) Ltd., Queen's Rd., High Wycombe, Bucks. High Wycombe (0494) 25861.

J. Dixon (Joinery) Ltd., Greenfield Lane, Balby, Doncaster, Yorks, DN4 0PS. Doncaster (0302) 852881.

Dominion Machinery Co. Ltd., Hipperholme, Nr. Halifax, HX3 8JG. Halifax (0422) 22258/9.

Dufaylite Developments Ltd., Cromwell Rd., St. Neots, Hunts., PE19 1QW. Huntingdon (0480) 73391.

Duncan Robert (Timber) Ltd., Green Lane Sawmills, Felling, Gateshead, NE10 0JS. Gateshead (0632) 693097.

Dust Control Equipment Ltd., Thurmaston, Leicester, LE4 8HP. Syston (053 723) 3333.

Dustraction Ltd., PO Box 75, Mandervell Rd., Oadby, Leicester, LE2 5ND. 0537-22 3212.

Eadon Moses & Son Ltd., Club Mill Rd., Sheffield 6. Sheffield (0742) 348131.

Allen Edgar Engineering Ltd., PO Box 42, Shepcote Lane, Sheffield, S9 1QW. Sheffield (0742) 49054.

Elliott-Lucas Ltd., Churchbridge Works, Cannock, Staffs., WS11 3JR. 0922 414414.

Elsworth Ltd., Herries Road South, Sheffield, S6 1QN. Sheffield (0742) 348183.

Elvicta Handtools Ltd., Crickhowell, Breconshire. Crickhowell (087 381) 287.

Emmerich (Berton) Ltd., Kingsworth Industrial Estate, Notton Rd., Ashford, Kent. Ashford (0233) 22684.

Essanbee Products Ltd., 16 Hanbury St., London, E1 6QP. 01-247 4311/7; 8721/3.

Evans Bellhouse Ltd., Newton Heath Sawmills, Manchester, M10 6EU. 061-681 2231; 2635.

Evode Ltd., Common Rd., Stafford, ST16 3EH. Stafford (0785) 3191.

J. Arthur Farrington & Son Ltd., Hamil Rd., Burslem, Stoke-on-Trent, Staffs. Stoke-on-Trent (0782) 87114.

W. A. Fell Ltd., Bridge Iron Works, Windermere, Westmorland, LA23 1HR. Windermere 2461.

Firthbourn Ltd., 124 Portland Rd., London SE25 4PN. 01-654 1552; 7811.

Harry Fisher & Co. Ltd., Kingfisher Works, Rockingham St., Sheffield, S1 3PF. Sheffield (0742) 21650.

Frost Associates, Ponsharden, Falmouth, Cornwall. Falmouth (0326) 311955.

Furniglas Ltd., 136 Great North Rd., Hatfield, Herts. Hatfield (45) 65358.

George Galloway & Co. Ltd., 5 Timberbush, Leith, Edinburgh. 031-554 251.

E. Garlick & Son, 2 Orange St., Sheffield 1. Sheffield (0742) 25412.

Germac Machinery Sales, 4 Kingshill Court, Manor Rd., Barnet, London, EN5 2LB. 01-440 7762.

Peter Gickel Ltd., 466 Cranbrook Rd., Ilford, Essex. 01-554 8238.

G.K.N. Screws & Fasteners Ltd., Heath Street Division, PO Box 61, Heath St., Smethwick, Warley, Worcs. 021-558 1441.

Th. Goldschmidt Ltd., York Hse., Station Rd., Harrow, Middlesex, HA1 1LH. 01-863 7766.

Gomex Tools Ltd., Orchard Rd., Finedon, Wellingborough, Northants. Finedon (093 362) 492.

Granville Tin Plate Co. Ltd., Rabone Lane, Smethwick, Warley, Worcs. 021-558 0801/2.

Hallmacrome Ltd., PO Box 39, 39 Macrome Rd., Wolverhampton, Staffs. Wolverhampton (0902) 752001.

Hibberd Bros. Ltd., Dorset Works, 66 Meadow Rd., South Lambeth, London, SW8. 01-735 1461.

E. A. Higginson & Co. Ltd., Bunns Lane Works, Mill Hill, London, NW7. 01-959 2808.

Hollis (Hull) Ltd., Craven Hall, Hull, Yorks. Hull (0482) 20791/20807.

Charles Homes (Halesowen) Ltd., Old Hawne Lane, Halesowen, Worcs. 021-550 1101.

Horsley, Smith & Sherry Ltd., Rippleway Wharf, River Rd., Barking, Essex. 01-594 7111.

C. F. Howden Ltd., 588/640 Garscube Rd., Glasgow, G20 7BJ. 041-332 2163/4.

Hughes & Hudson, 16 Burgess St., Leith, Edinburgh, EH6. 031-554 1507.

Hyett Adams Ltd., Stonehouse, Glos. Stonehouse (045 382) 2496.

George Ibberson Ltd., 123 Trafalgar St., Sheffield, S3 4GN. Sheffield (0742) 25117.

Interwood Ltd., 326 Old St., London, EC1V 9DN. 01-739 9866.

Jakeway Timber Co., Woodland Works, Cwmbran, Mon., NP4 2YP. Cwmbran (063 33) 2551.

J K O Cutters Ltd., Hughenden Avenue, High Wycombe, Bucks. Hygh Wycombe (0494) 21051.

Kine Engineering Co. Ltd., Multico Works, Salfords, Redhill, Surrey. 0293-4 2444.

Kunz Engineering Ltd., Levenbank Works, Balloch, Alexandria, Scotland, G83 8QA. Alexandria 2212/3.

Gordon Laird Ltd., Dunford Hse., City Rd., Newcastle-upon-Tyne, NE99 1SC. Newcastle-upon-Tyne (0632) 26121.

Lohmann & Co. Ltd., The Mill Trading Estate, Acton Lane, London, NW10 7NP. 01-965 8981.

Magnet Joinery Sales Ltd., Royd Ings Avenue, Keighley, Yorks, BD21 4BY. Keighley (053 52) 7311.

Makita Electric (UK) Ltd., Unit 2, Monaco Works, Station Rd., Kings Langley, Herts. Kings Langley (40) 67142; 63276.

William Mallinson & Sons Ltd., 130 Hackney Rd., London, E2 7QR. 01-739 7654.

Manor Joinery Works Ltd., Barking-By-Pass, Barking, Essex. 01-594 3052.

W. Marsden & Co. Ltd., Leads Rd., Hull, Yorks. Hull (0482) 76242.

Alexander Marshall & Schleicher, Phoenix Works, Birchfield Rd., Redditch, Worcs. Redditch (073 92) 64422.

F. W. McConnel Ltd., Temeside Works, Ludlow, SY8 1JL. Ludlow (0584) 3131.

Measuring & Process Control Ltd., Phoenix House, Manor Way, New Rd., Rainham, Essex. Rainham 53311.

Merry & Co. (Manchester) Ltd., Keymer St., Manchester, M11 3HA. 061-273 4505.

Micor Saw Services, 51/53 City Rd., London, EC1Y 1AY. 01-253 8677.

Midland Plant (Leicester) Ltd., Oakland Rd., Welford Rd., Leicester, LE2 6AN. Leicester (0533) 56433.

Modern Machinery (London) Ltd., 12a Arthur Court, Queensway, London, W2 5HW. 01-229 7195; 4966.

Moldow Ltd., 46 High St., Solihull, Warwicks., B91 3TB. Solihull 2892; 2718.

C. D. Moniger Ltd., St. Anna Works, Overbury Rd., London, N15. 01-800 5435.

F. K. Moore & Son Ltd., Haine Road Industrial Estate, Ramsgate, Kent. Thanet (0843) 53440.

W. Moore & Son, 41 Geoffrey St., Preston, Lancs., PR1 5JU. Preston (0772) 55007.

William Moss & Sons Ltd., Queens Rd., Loughborough, Leicestershire. Loughborough (050 93) 61551.

G. T. Mountfield Ltd., East St., Maidenhead, Berks. Maidenhead (0628) 30543.

Muirhead & Sons Ltd., PO Box 9, Grangemouth Sawmills, Grangemouth, Stirlingshire, FK3 8XF. Grangemouth (032 44) 3294.

Multico Co. Ltd., Salfords Industrial Estate, Redhill, Surrey, RHL 5ER. 02934 2444.

Nash Fisher Ltd., Novers Lane, Bristol, BS4 1QU. Bristol (0272) 661021/3.

National Adhesives and Resins Ltd., Slough, Bucks., SL1 4DF. Slough (75) 29191.

R. A. Naylor Ltd., PO Box 34, Chester Rd., Warrington, Lancs. Warrington (0925) 32632.

James Neil (Sheffield) Ltd., Napier St., Sheffield, S11 8HB. Sheffield (0742) 26761.

G. Ney (UK) Ltd., Wessex Rd., Bourne End, Bucks., SL8 5D7. Bourne End (062 85) 25885.

Thomas Niven Ltd., Murrell Hill Sawmills, Carlisle, CA2 5NS. Carlisle (0228) 26277.

Norris Woodworkers Ltd., Glynne St., Farnworth, Bolton, Lancs., BL4 7DL. Bolton (0204) 73363.

North London Saw Works Ltd., Station Approach, Waltham Cross, Herts. Waltham Cross (97) 26181.

Orton Saws Ltd., Middle St., Beeston, Notts. Beeston 254043.

A. & F. Parkes & Co. (London) Ltd., Hambro Hse., Vintners Place, Upper Thames St., London, EC4V 3HD. 01-236 3625.

Parkinson Cowan GWB, PO Box 4, Dudley, Worcs. Dudley (0384) 55455.

George Parnall & Sons Ltd., Lodge Causeway, Fishponds, Bristol. Bristol (0272) 654261.

W. K. & C. Peace Ltd., Eagle Works, Sheffield Rd., Tinsley, Sheffield 9. Sheffield (0742) 41235.

Pellcrest Ltd., Dover Works, Dover St., Maidstone, Kent. Maidstone (0622) 26708.

John Pickles & Son (Engineers) Ltd., Mytholme Works, Hebden Bridge, Yorks. Hebden Bridge (042 284) 2113.

Pye Thermal Bonders Ltd., 26 James St., Cambridge. Cambridge (0223) 57590.

Rex Hacksaw & Tool Manufacturing Co. Ltd., Albion Way, Exhibition Grounds, Wembley, Middlesex. 01-902 6186.

John Reynolds & Sons (Birmingham) Ltd., Crown Works, Old Meeting Street, West Bromwich, Staffs. 021-553 2754.

Reynolds & Wilson Ltd., Lion Hse., Red Lion St., Richmond, Surrey. 01-940 7667.

John Riddiough & Co. Ltd., Valley Sawmills, Barrowford Rd., Colne, Lancs. Colne 411.

E. T. & Lee Roberts, Don Works, Northumberland Park, London, N17. 01-808 2486.

Thomas Robinson & Son Ltd., Railway Works, Rochdale, Lancs., OL16 5NB. Rochdale (0706) 47811.

Harold G. Ruddick & Co., New Lane, Havant, Hants., PO9 2NF. Havant (070 12) 6128.

Rye Machinery Sales (High Wycombe) Ltd., Bridge St., High Wycombe, Bucks., HP11 2EW. High Wycombe (0494) 28931.

Sacme Ltd., Dover Works, Dover St., Maidstone, Kent. Maidstone (0622) 26708.

Sadolins (UK) Ltd., Shire Hill Industrial Estate, Saffron Walden, Essex. Saffron Walden (0799) 3490.

Sanderson Bros. & Newbold Ltd., PO Box 6, Attercliffe Steel Works, Newhall Rd., Sheffield, S9 2SD. Sheffield (0742) 49994.

Savecrest Ltd., Lloyds Bank Chambers, Manor St., Bridlington, Yorks. Bridlington (0262) 5169.

J. H. & I. Sankey, 31 Church St., Warrington, Lancs., WA1 2SX. Warrington (0925) 35868.

J. Scadding & Son Ltd., Eugene St., Pennywell Rd., Bristol, BS5 0TW. Bristol (0272) 556032.

Sharp Bros. & Knight Ltd., Wellington Rd., Burton-on-Trent, Staffs., DE14 2AJ. Burton-on-Trent (0283) 64851/6.

Simplatroll Ltd., Caxton Rd., Bedford, MK41 0HT. Bedford (0234) 52191.

Skil (GB) Ltd., 2b Thames Avenue, Windsor, Berks. Windsor (95) 69525.

Slack, Sellars & Co. Ltd., Mowbray St., Sheffield, S3 8EZ. Sheffield (0742) 79242.

B. Smith & Son (Sawmill Engineers) Ltd., Wellington St., Bingley, Yorks. Bingley (097 66) 3145.

J. J. Smith & Co. Ltd., Marlborough Works, Waddicar Lane, Melling, Nr. Liverpool, L41 1DX. 051-546 9421.

Snowden, Cooper & Sons Ltd., King Edward St., Grimsby, Lincs., DN31 3LR. Grimsby (0472) 2633.

Sonneborn & Rieck Ltd., Jaxa Works, 91/95 Peregrine Rd., Hainault, Ilford, Essex. 01-500 0251.

Robert Sorby & Sons Ltd., Woodseats, Sheffield, S8 0SR. Sheffield (0742) 54251.

Southmead Timber and Joinery Works Ltd., Kelston Rd., Southmead, Bristol BS10 5EP. Bristol (0272) 626746.

South West Joinery Co. Ltd., Pembroke St., Gloucester, GL1 4EQ. Gloucester (0452) 36181.

Spencer & Halstead Ltd., Bridge Works, Ossett, Yorks, WF5 9AW. Ossett (092 43) 5121.

Spear & Jackson (Industrial) Ltd., Aetna Works, Saville St., Sheffield, S4 7UR. Sheffield (0742) 20202.

Spear & Jackson (Tools) Ltd., Hand Tool Division, St. Paul's Rd., Wednesbury, Staffs., WS10 9RA. 021-556 1255.

Stanley-Bridges Ltd., Nelson Way, Cramlington, Northumberland.

Starrett & Co. Ltd., The L. S. Jedburgh, Roxburghshire, TD8 6LR. Jedburgh 2285.

Startrite Machine Tool Co. Ltd., 69/71 Newington Causeway, London, SE1. 01-407 7356.

Stenner of Tiverton Ltd., Lowman Works, Tiverton, Devon, EX16 4JX. Tiverton (088 42) 3691.

Steinemann Beadon Ltd., Suite 35, Hodford Hse., 17/27 High St., Hounslow, Middlesex. 01-572 0901.

Sundstrand Sanders, Division of Shipston Engineering Co. Ltd., Shipston-on-Stour, Warwicks. Shipston-on-Stour (0608) 61676.

Taylor Bros. (Saws) Ltd., Adelaide Works, Mowbray St., Sheffield, S3 8RV. Sheffield (0742) 79242.

G. Taylor & Co. Ltd., 22 Bonchurch St., Leicester. Leicester (0533) 21287.

J. B. Thorne & Son Ltd., 2 Station Rd., Syston, Leicester, LE7 8NU. Syston (053 723) 3931.

H. Todd & Son Ltd., Browhead Works, Eastern Avenue, Burnley, Lancs. Burnley (0282) 3066.

Tor Equipment Co. Ltd., Lambretta House, Purley Way, Croydon, Surrey. 01-686 2499.

Trend Elu Machinery Ltd., Stirling Corner, Barnet By-Pass, Borehamwood, WD6 2AG. 01-953 0711.

Trojan Ltd., Kingsley Hse., 12 Trojan Way, Croydon, Surrey, CR0 4XL. 01-681 3111.

Turnell & Odell, Broad Green, Wellingborough, Northants. 093 33 2061.

Cecil W. Tyzack Ltd., 79/81 Kingsland Rd., London, E2. 01-739 7126.

W. Tyzack, Sons & Turner Ltd., Little London Works, Sheffield, S8 0UE. Sheffield (0742) 51066/70.

Wadkin Ltd., Green Lane Works, Leicester, LE5 4PF. Leicester (0533) 769111.

P. M. Walker & Co. (Halifax) Ltd., PO Box 22, Hollybank Works, Greetland, Halifax, Yorks., HX4 8HB. Halifax (0422) 3427/9; 3684.

R. H. Walker Ltd., Falcon Works, Cotton Mill Row, Sheffield, S3 8RV. Sheffield (0742) 24748.

The Walpamur Co. Ltd., Wood Finishes Division, Wellington Works, Woodley, Cheshire, SK6 1RN. 061-430 2292.

Watbeare Overseas Ltd., Cantrell Works, Ivybridge, Devon. Ivybridge (075 54) 365.

J. C. Waterman & Sons Ltd., 78/82 Silwood St., London, SE16. 01-237 2248.

Webb Condensor Co. Ltd., Jubilee Hse., Denmark St., Maidenhead, Berks. Maidenhead (0628) 25121.

Western Machinery & Equipment Co. Ltd., Redlake Trading Estate, Ivybridge, Devon. Ivybridge (075 54) 2375.

Thomas White & Sons Ltd., Laighpark, Paisley, Scotland, PA3 4DA. 041-889 3137.

William Bros. of Sheffield, Green Lane, Sheffield, S3 8SF. Sheffield (0742) 77365.

Williams (Hounslow) Ltd., Hibernia Rd., Hounslow, Middlesex. 01-570 7766.

Wilson Bros. (Leeds) Ltd., 46 Victoria Rd., Holbeck, Leeds, LS11 5AG. Leeds (0532) 40516.

Womersley & Broadbent Ltd., Denholme Gate Rd., Hipperholme, Halifax, Yorks. Halifax (0422) 22405.

J. E. Woodall & Co. Ltd., Coronation Works, Lodgefield Rd., Gorsty Hill, Halesowen, Rowley Regis, Warley, Worcs. 021-559 1927.

Wood Handrail Co. Ltd., 167 Culford Rd., London, N1 4DT. 01-808 4488.

Woodworking Methods & Machinery Ltd., 44 Prestbury Rd., Cheltenham, GL52 2DA. Cheltenham (0242) 55105.

Wuidart Grinding Machine Co., Clifton Rd., Shefford, Beds.

List of trade associations, professional bodies and societies, research organisations etc., associated with the woodworking industry in the United Kingdom

Advisory Service for the Building Industry, 18 Mansfield St., London, W1M 9FG. 01-580 6244.

Association of British Plywood & Veneer Manufacturers, Epwroth Hse., 25 City Rd., London, EC1. 01-628 5801.

Association of British Wood Wool Manufacturers, 21 Tothill St., London, SW1. 01-930 6711.

Association of Shopfront Section Manufacturers, Lenning Hse., Mason's Avenue, Croydon, Surrey, CR9 3LL. 01-686 1047.

British Furniture Manufacturers Association, 17 Berners St., London, W1P 4DY. 01-580 5115.

British Lock Manufacturers Association, National Westminster Bank Chambers, 52/54 Lichfield St., Wolverhampton, WV1 1DJ. 0902-20638; 26791.

British Wood Preserving Association, 62 Oxford St., London, W1. 01-580 3185.

British Wood Pulp Association, Epworth Hse., 25 City Rd., London, EC1. 01-628 5801.

British Woodwork Manufacturers Association, 26 Store St., London, WC1E 7BT. 01-636 9075/6.

Building & Allied Trades Credit Enquiry Bureau, Zodiac Hse., 163 London Rd., Croydon, Surrey, CR9 2RP. 01-686 5644.

Building Board Manufacturers Association of Great Britain Ltd., Plough Place, Fetter Lane, London, EC4A 1AL. 01-583 0686.

Building & Civil Engineering Holidays Scheme Management Ltd., Manor Royal, Crawley, Sussex. 0293-26911.

Building Research Station (Department of the Environment), Bucknalls Lane, Garston, Watford, Herts., WD2 7JR. Garston 74040.

City & Guilds of London Institute, 76 Portland Place, London, W1N 4AA. 01-580 3050.

Chipboard Promotion Association Ltd., 7a Church St., Esher, Surrey. Esher 66468/9.

Construction Industry Training Board, Radnor Hse., 1272 London Rd., London, SW16 4EL. 01-764 5060.

Council of Forest Industries of British Columbia, Templar Hse., 81 High Holborn, London, WC1V 6LS.

Creosote Producers Association Ltd., Plantation Hse., Mincing Lane, London, EC3. 01-626 3494.

Door & Shutter Association, Glen Hse., Stag Place, London, SW1E 5AT. 01-834 8769.

Felt Roofing Contractors Advisory Board, Victoria Hse., Southampton Row, London, WC1B 4EA. 01-405 0670.

Fibre Building Board Agents Association Ltd., Epworth Hse., 25 City Rd., London, EC1 1AR. 01-628 5801.

Fibre Building Board Development Organisation Ltd., 6/7 Buckingham St., London, WC2N 6BZ. 01-839 1122/4.

Fibre Building Board Federation, Audley Hse., 9 Margaret St., London, W1N 7LF. 01-637 7031.

Finnish Plywood Development Association, Broadmead Hse., 21 Panton St., London, SW1Y 4DR. 01-930 3282.

Fire Protection Association, Aldermary Hse., Queen St., London, EC4. 01-248 5222.

Forestry Commission, 25 Saville Row, London, W1X 2AY. 01-734 0221.

Guild of Architectural Ironmongers, 52/54 High Holborn, London, WC1V 6SP. 01-242 7772.

Gypsum Products Development Association, Ferguson Hse., 15/17 Marylebone Rd., London, NW1 5JE.

Hardboard Advisory Service, 6/7 Buckingham St., London, WC2N 6BZ. 01-839 1122.

Hardwood Agents & Brokers Association, Epworth Hse., 25 City Rd., London, EC1Y 1AR. 01-628 5801.

Hardwood Flooring Manufacturers Association, Clareville Hse., Oxendon St., London, SW1. 01-839 3381.

Home Timber Merchants Association of England & Wales, Blackburn Hse., 1 Warwick St., Leamington Spa, Warwicks. 0926 29905.

Incorporated British Institute of Certified Carpenters, Alderman Hse., 37 Soho Sq., London, W1. 01-437 6588.

Institute of Machine Woodworking Technology, 107b Liverpool Rd., Formby, Lancs. Formby 77130.

Institute of Wood Science, 62 Oxford St., London, W1. 01-580 3185.

Insulating Board Advisory Service, 6/7 Buckingham St., London, WC2N 6B2. 01-839 1122.

Laminated Plastics Fabricators Association, 14/16 Bruton Place, London, W1X 7AA. 01-499 8268.

Machine Tools Trades Association, 25 Buckingham Gate, London, SW1. 01-834 7542.

Men of the Trees Society, Crawley Down, Crawley, Sussex. Copthorne 2536.

Metrication Board, 22 Kingsway, London, WC2B 6LE. 01-242 6828.

National Association of Shopfitters, Lenning Hse., Mason's Avenue, Croydon, Surrey, CR9 3LL. 01-686 1047.

National Physical Laboratory, Teddington, Middx., TW11 0LW. 01-977 3222 Ext. 3136.

Saw Manufacturers Association, Light Trades Hse., Melbourne Avenue, Sheffield, S10 2QJ. 0742 63084.

School Furniture Manufacturers Association Ltd., Bucklersbury Hse., Bucklersbury, London, EC4. 01-248 4499.

Scottish Timber Merchants & Sawmillers Association, 216 West George St., Glasgow, G2 2PF. 041-248 5181.

Society of Church Craftsmen, RWS Galleries, 26 Conduit St., London, W1R 2TA. 01-629 8300.

Society of Designer Craftsmen, 6 Queen Sq., London, WC1.

Softwood Agents & Brokers Association, Epworth Hse., 25 City Rd., London, EC1Y 1AR. 01-628 5801.

Timber Building Manufacturers Association of Great Britain Ltd., 4 High St., Epsom, Surrey. Epsom 24481.

Timber Research & Development Association, Hughenden Valley, High Wycombe, Bucks. Naphill 3091.

Timber Trade Federation of the United Kingdom, Clareville Hse., Whitcomb St., London, WC2. 01-839 1891.

Wood Chipboard Manufacturers Group, 47 Piccadilly, London, W1V 0DN. 01-734 2041.

Wood Wool Slab Manufacturers Association, Audley Hse., 9 Margaret St., London, W1N 7LF. 01-637 7031.

The Worshipful Company of Carpenters, Carpenters Hall, 1 Throgmorton Avenue, London, EC2N 2JJ. 01-588 7001/2.

Index